# TEXTS AND VIOLENCE IN THE
# ROMAN WORLD

From the bites and scratches of lovers and the threat of flogging that hangs over the comic slave, to murder, rape, dismemberment, and crucifixion, violence is everywhere in Latin literature. The contributors to this volume explore the manifold ways in which violence is constructed and represented in Latin poetry and prose from Plautus to Prudentius, examining the interrelations between violence, language, power, and gender, and the narrative, rhetorical, and ideological functions of such depictions across the generic spectrum. How does violence contribute to the pleasure of the text? Do depictions of violence always reinforce status-hierarchies, or can they provoke a reassessment of normative value-systems? Is the reader necessarily complicit with authorial constructions of violence? These are pressing questions both for ancient literature and for film and other modern media, and this volume will be of interest to scholars and students of cultural studies as well as of the ancient world.

MONICA R. GALE is Professor in Classics at Trinity College Dublin. Her publications include *Myth and Poetry in Lucretius* (Cambridge, 1994), *Virgil on the Nature of Things: The* Georgics, *Lucretius and the Didactic Tradition* (Cambridge, 2000), and a commentary on Lucretius Book 5 (2009).

J. H. D. SCOURFIELD is Professor of Classics at Maynooth University and a Vice-President of the Classical Association. His publications include *Consoling Heliodorus: A Commentary on Jerome,* Letter *60* (1993).

# TEXTS AND VIOLENCE IN THE ROMAN WORLD

EDITED BY

## MONICA R. GALE

*Trinity College Dublin*

## J. H. D. SCOURFIELD

*Maynooth University*

CAMBRIDGE
UNIVERSITY PRESS

# CAMBRIDGE
## UNIVERSITY PRESS

University Printing House, Cambridge CB2 8BS, United Kingdom

One Liberty Plaza, 20th Floor, New York, NY 10006, USA

477 Williamstown Road, Port Melbourne, VIC 3207, Australia

314–321, 3rd Floor, Plot 3, Splendor Forum, Jasola District Centre, New Delhi – 110025, India

79 Anson Road, #06–04/06, Singapore 079906

Cambridge University Press is part of the University of Cambridge.

It furthers the University's mission by disseminating knowledge in the pursuit of education, learning, and research at the highest international levels of excellence.

www.cambridge.org
Information on this title: www.cambridge.org/9781107027145
DOI: 10.1017/9781139225304

First published 2018

Printed in the United Kingdom by Clays, St Ives plc

*A catalogue record for this publication is available from the British Library.*

ISBN 978-1-107-02714-5 Hardback

*To the memory of Shilpa Raval*

# Contents

# Notes on Contributors

WILLIAM FITZGERALD is Professor of Latin Language and Literature at King's College London, having taught previously at the University of California and Cambridge University. He has published books and articles on Latin literature and comparative literature, most recently *How to Read a Latin Poem if You Can't Read Latin Yet* (2013) and *Variety: The Life of a Roman Concept* (2016).

MONICA R. GALE is Professor in Classics at Trinity College Dublin. She is the author of *Myth and Poetry in Lucretius* (Cambridge, 1994), *Virgil on the Nature of Things: The* Georgics, *Lucretius and the Didactic Tradition* (Cambridge, 2000), and other books and articles on late-Republican and Augustan poetry. She is currently working on a commentary on the complete poems of Catullus for the Cambridge Greek and Latin Classics series.

BRUCE J. GIBSON is Professor of Latin at the University of Liverpool. His publications include *Statius: Silvae 5* (commentary, with text and translation; 2006), *Polybius and His World: Essays in Memory of Frank Walbank* (co-edited with Thomas Harrison; 2013), and *Pliny the Younger in Late Antiquity* (co-edited with Roger Rees; 2013), as well as articles and book chapters on a wide range of Latin texts in prose and verse. He is currently writing a commentary on Pliny's *Panegyricus*.

JOHN HENDERSON was once Professor of Classics at Cambridge and is Life Fellow of King's College. He has ranged all round classical studies, singling out imperial Latin authors for particular textual violence.

DUNCAN F. KENNEDY is Emeritus Professor of Latin Literature and the Theory of Criticism at the University of Bristol. He is the author of *The Arts of Love: Five Studies in the Discourse of Roman Love Elegy* (Cambridge, 1993), *Rethinking Reality: Lucretius and the Textualization of Nature* (2002), and *Antiquity and the Meanings of Time: A Philosophy of Ancient and Modern Literature* (2013), as well as numerous articles that explore interpretative approaches to Greek and Latin literature.

DAVID KONSTAN is Professor of Classics at New York University and Professor Emeritus of Classics and Comparative Literature at Brown University. Among his many publications are *Roman Comedy* (1983), *Greek Comedy and Ideology* (1995), *The Emotions of the Ancient Greeks: Studies in Aristotle and Classical Literature* (2006), and *Beauty: The Fortunes of an Ancient Greek Idea* (2014). He is a past President of the American Philological Association (now the Society for Classical Studies), a Fellow of the American Academy of Arts and Sciences, and an Honorary Fellow of the Australian Academy of the Humanities.

PAUL ALLEN MILLER is Vice Provost and Carolina Distinguished Professor at the University of South Carolina. He is a former editor of *Transactions of the American Philological Association*, and the author of many books, including *Lyric Texts and Lyric Consciousness: The Birth of a Genre from Archaic Greece to Augustan Rome* (1994), *Subjecting Verses: Latin Love Elegy and the Emergence of the Real* (2004), *Postmodern Spiritual Practices* (2007), and most recently *Diotima at the Barricades: French Feminists Read Plato* (2016). He has edited fourteen volumes and published numerous articles on Latin, Greek, French, and English literature and philosophy.

CAROLE E. NEWLANDS is College Professor of Distinction in the Arts and Sciences at the University of Colorado Boulder. Her main publications include *Playing with Time: Ovid and the* Fasti (1995), *Statius' Silvae and the Poetics of Empire* (Cambridge, 2002), *Statius: Silvae, Book II* (Cambridge, 2011), *Statius, Poet between Rome and Naples* (2012), *A Handbook to the Reception of Ovid* (co-edited with John F. Miller; 2014), and *Ovid* (2015). She is currently at work on a book concerning the reception of classical literature in Scotland.

DONNCHA O'ROURKE is Lecturer in Classics at the University of Edinburgh. His doctoral career at Trinity College Dublin was followed by a British Academy Postdoctoral Fellowship, held at the University of Oxford. He is the author of articles on various aspects of Augustan poetry, especially elegy, and of a forthcoming monograph on the reception of Virgil in Propertius 4. His current research focuses on the reception of Lucretius in the elegiac genre.

SHILPA RAVAL achieved her bachelor's degree at Drew University in 1991 and her Ph.D. at Brown University in 1998. She was Assistant Professor of Classics at the University of Missouri-Columbia from 1998 to 2000 and Assistant Professor in the Department of Classics at Yale University from 2000 until her untimely death in 2004 at the age of thirty-four. She was the author of "'A Lover's Discourse": Byblis in *Metamorphoses 9*' (2001) and 'Cross-Dressing and "Gender Trouble" in the Ovidian Corpus' (2002).

J. H. D. (DAVID) SCOURFIELD is Professor of Classics at Maynooth University (National University of Ireland Maynooth). His publications include *Consoling Heliodorus: A Commentary on Jerome, Letter 60* (1993), *Texts and Culture in Late Antiquity: Inheritance, Authority, and Change* (ed., 2007), and articles and book chapters on the Greek novel, ancient consolatory writing, and twentieth-century classical reception. He is currently working on a comprehensive study of the ancient consolatory letter, and a monograph on E. M. Forster and Classics.

EFROSSINI (EFI) SPENTZOU is Reader in Latin Literature and Classical Reception at Royal Holloway University of London. She is the author of *Readers and Writers in Ovid's* Heroides: *Transgressions of Genre and Gender* (2003), *Reflections of Romanity: Discourses of Subjectivity in Imperial Rome* (with Richard Alston; 2011), and *The Roman Poetry of Love: Elegy and Politics in a Time of Revolution* (2013), and co-editor (with Don Fowler) of *Cultivating the Muse: Struggles for Power and Inspiration in Classical Literature* (2002). She is currently co-editing with William Fitzgerald a volume on the production of space in Latin literature.

# *Preface*

This volume began with a casual domestic conversation. Wondering one morning whether, as specialists in classical Latin poetry and late Antiquity respectively, we could find a suitable topic for a collaboration, we found ourselves drawn to violence – or more specifically, its representations in Latin literature. The initial outcome was a panel presented at the Classical Association Centenary Conference held at the University of Warwick in 2003. Encouraged by the lively discussion that the papers inspired, we then decided to embark upon a fuller and more systematic exploration of representations of violence in Latin texts from the mid-Republic to the late Empire and across a wide spread of literary genres. It seemed to us that, whereas violence (of various kinds) as a social and political phenomenon in the Roman (as in the Greek) world and depictions of violence (of various kinds) in particular ancient texts had come under scholarly scrutiny in recent years, an investigation specifically dedicated to its literary representations might help to identify and crystallize some central issues in a way beneficial to literary scholars and cultural historians alike. In framing the project, and in engaging with our contributors as they sent us successive versions of their chapters, we were also mindful of the significance of violence and its representations in the contemporary world, and the often heated debates around violent films, computer games, and other cultural phenomena. Of great relevance to our topic too is the relationship between violent acts and violent rhetoric, a theme brought starkly into focus by two shocking events which occurred during the preparation of this volume: the attempted assassination of US Congresswoman Gabrielle Giffords (and the associated killing of six people) in Tucson, Arizona in January 2011, and the murder of British MP Jo Cox in the run-up to the Brexit referendum of June 2016. Both acts of violence were widely linked in the media to the strident and inflammatory style of rhetoric that had become prevalent in the British and American political arenas, in Gabrielle Giffords' case specifically utilizing the imagery of the gun. We hope, then, that the book will have something to say to readers outside as well as within the community of classical scholars and students.

These aspirations for the volume should not, however, be taken to imply a claim of comprehensiveness. Every reader will be able to think of further texts or genres which would merit discussion under the rubric of violence; we ourselves would like to have included chapters on (for example) Horace's *Epodes* or the epigrams of Martial, but as anyone who has edited a collective volume will be aware, the best intentions cannot always be realized. An absence of a different kind concerns us much more closely. Shilpa Raval, a rising star at Yale University, had begun to work with David Konstan on what is now Chapter 1 when she died unexpectedly, and tragically young. Neither of us ever met Shilpa, though one of us had had the privilege and pleasure of sharing with her by email a mutual enthusiasm for a modern 'text' full of representations of violence in both serious and less serious mode: Joss Whedon's *Buffy the Vampire Slayer*. Although she did not live to see the work through to completion, she is appropriately credited as co-author of Chapter 1, and the whole volume is dedicated to her memory.

It will have become apparent that (for a variety of reasons) this book has been a long time in the making. We would like to thank Michael Sharp of Cambridge University Press and all our contributors for their patience and forbearance, and trust that they, and all our readers, will find it worth the wait.

MRG/JHDS

# Abbreviations

In general, abbreviations for ancient authors and texts follow the conventions of the fourth edition of *The Oxford Classical Dictionary* (ed. S. Hornblower, A. Spawforth, and E. Eidinow; Oxford, 2012); the exceptions should cause no difficulties. Journal titles are abbreviated according to the system of *L'Année philologique*. The following common abbreviations are also employed:

| | |
|---|---|
| *ANRW* | H. Temporini and W. Haase (eds.), *Aufstieg und Niedergang der römischen Welt: Geschichte und Kultur Roms im Spiegel der neueren Forschung* (Berlin and New York, 1972– ). |
| LSJ | H. G. Liddell and R. Scott (eds.), *A Greek-English Lexicon*, 9th edn., revised by H. S. Jones (Oxford, 1940), with a supplement by E. A. Barber (1968). |
| *OED* | *Oxford English Dictionary*. |
| *OLD* | P. G. W. Glare (ed.), *Oxford Latin Dictionary* (Oxford, 1968–82). |
| PG | J.-P. Migne (ed.), Patrologia Graeca (Paris, 1857–66). |
| *RE* | A. F. von Pauly, G. Wissowa, *et al.* (eds.), *Paulys Real-Encyclopädie der classischen Altertumswissenschaft* (24 vols., 19 vols., and supplement (15 vols.); Stuttgart, 1893–1980). |

# Introduction
## Reading Roman Violence

*Monica R. Gale and J. H. D. Scourfield* [*]

## I   Violence and Rome

Roman history begins with an act of violence. Even before its walls are completed, the newly founded city is already stained by the blood of Romulus' twin brother Remus. The story is suggestive. In the imaginary of Roman writers, the killing of Remus came to afford a paradigm for other conflicts, civil war above all; and yet there were also other, less negative, ways of construing Romulus' foundational act of murder.[1] For us, the story might, in the first place, seem emblematic of a culture in which violence was widely prevalent; but the availability to the Romans themselves of a positive evaluation of the fratricide reminds us too that this was a culture in which (within certain limits) violence could be claimed as a good.[2]

---

[*] We should like to thank Catharine Edwards, Duncan Kennedy, and the Cambridge University Press readers for their valuable comments on an earlier draft of this introduction. Translations from Greek and Latin texts are our own.

[1] For the murder of Remus as paradigmatic of civil conflict, see esp. Hor. *Epod.* 7.17–20, Luc. 1.93–5; also Virg. *G.* 2.533 with R. F. Thomas 1988: 262 *ad loc.*, who notes that the apparently innocent phrase *Remus et frater* picks up the earlier references to fraternal strife at 2.496, 510; and *Aen.* 1.292–3, where, conversely, the apparent reconciliation of Remus and Romulus/Quirinus seems to mark the end of civil discord. A more positive construction is placed on the killing by, e.g., Livy 1.7.2, Ov. *Fast.* 4.837–48, the latter attributing the murder not to Romulus but to his subordinate Celer (warning to potential invaders); Prop. 3.9.50, Flor. 1.1.8 (foundation sacrifice). See further Jal 1963: 407–10; Wiseman 1995, esp. 9–17; Bannon 1997: 158–73; also Dench 2005: 20–5, on the similarly polyvalent character of another violent episode associated with the kingship of Romulus, the rape of the Sabine women.

[2] We should note at the outset that the definition and terminology of violence are themselves problematic. As we point out in Section III below (pp. 20–1), and as Gibson argues in more detail in Chapter 9, both the English word and its nearest Latin equivalent, *violentia*, regularly carry a negative charge, which is matched by a tendency to place *approved* acts of 'force' or 'coercion' under other rubrics. The attentive reader will observe that we ourselves have found it impossible to avoid aligning with such ideologically determined usages altogether, particularly in discussing issues of legality.

I

In its historical realities and its representations alike, the body that was Rome could indeed be said to be deeply marked by sanguinary reds and the blue-black of bruises. Our concern in this volume lies specifically with literary representations of violence in the Roman world; and yet these cannot be wholly disentangled either from other forms of representation, such as myth, or from the material and social contexts within which such representations were formulated. The relationship between violence in the text and violence in the world at large is in fact one of the book's central themes, and one of our aspirations is that it should contribute to an enhanced understanding of the place of violence in Roman culture as a whole, as well as sharpening our awareness of some of the problematics of violence and its representations in our own culture.

The book offers a series of explorations of literary violence across a period of six centuries and a wide range of texts and genres. The nature of the violence depicted varies considerably from text to text, and the approaches taken by our contributors naturally show similar variation. But through the series of chapters, united by their common focus, several major thematic strands emerge. In this Introduction, we seek first (Section I) to give an impression of 'real-world' Roman violence, with due regard to its political, social, and cultural contexts and the attitudes which direct, inform, or police it. Following this, we give (Section II) an overview of representations of violence in classical (especially Roman) myth and literature, taking a broad generic approach to the latter, and attempting to identify, in a provisional way, general tendencies in the character of the representations and their modern interpretation. Against this dual background, we then consider (Section III) the central theme of violence and power, in which issues of language are also implicated, proceeding in Section IV to what can be seen in part as a specific instantiation of this, the relationship between violence and gender. In the final part of the Introduction (Section V) we examine at somewhat greater length a question that we take to be fundamental to any ethically serious consideration of the representation of violence in written (as in other) texts, namely, the potential impact of such representations on the individual reader and on society at large. Our discussion thus draws together and seeks to offer a critical analysis of some of the main threads running through the various chapters which follow, elaborating on individual contributions as it does so; in keeping with our vision of the book as (we hope) more than the sum of its parts, we have not provided a sequential summary of the chapters in the manner characteristic of collaborative volumes.

'Rome', wrote Keith Hopkins, famously, 'was a warrior state';[3] and the embedding of violence in Roman culture is attested in the first place by the militarism which informed Roman society and ideology.[4] Many of the original readers of the texts considered in this volume will have had first-hand experience of armed conflict. Under the Republic, seasonal campaigning was the norm; for members of the elite, military service was a traditional preliminary to the holding of public office.[5] Under the Empire, *pax Romana* was, paradoxically, a precarious condition, founded upon and sustained by the threat of retaliatory violence by Roman forces: revolts and border wars were frequent, and the notion that peace was something to be imposed, when necessary, on recalcitrant barbarians appears to have been widely accepted.[6] From an ideological perspective, it seems significant that *virtus*, or 'manly virtue', is a concept particularly at home in the military sphere, while *gloria*, or prestige, is traditionally acquired primarily through military achievement: the capacity to inflict and endure violence on the field of battle is an essential (if sometimes theoretical) component in Roman notions of masculinity and authority in the political arena.

At the same time, less positively evaluated forms of violence were all too familiar for long periods of Roman history. The first century BC was dominated by a series of bloody and brutal civil wars, from the Social War to the Battle of Actium, and civil conflict is scarcely less prominent a feature of the Imperial period: notoriously, only a minority of Roman emperors died of natural causes. Writing in AD 396, Jerome catalogues at some length the often violent deaths of recent rulers, together with other upheavals which, he claims, have characterized contemporary history (*Ep.* 60.15–16): his deceased *laudandus*, Nepotianus, was fortunate to have been freed from the necessity of witnessing such horrors. Strikingly,

---

[3] Hopkins 1983: 1.

[4] On Roman militarism see further O'Rourke, Chapter 4 below, esp. pp. 125–6.

[5] For military service as a standard step in a political career, and on imperialist ideology under the Republic, see Harris 1979, esp. 10–41. The normative status of warfare in the Republican world-view is also underlined by the tradition, referred to in the *Res gestae* (13), that the ritual act of closing the gates of the Temple of Janus – signifying the attainment of a state of peace throughout the empire – had been performed only twice in the entire history of Rome before the birth of Augustus.

[6] On the ideology of *pax Romana* see Woolf 1993, with consideration of revolts and other forms of violence in the provinces during the Imperial period at 185–9. Mattern 1999: 81–122 argues that the threat of retaliatory violence was central to imperial policy under the Principate; see also 162–202 on the importance of military victory and conquest in enhancing both the image of Rome and the prestige of the individual, especially the emperor. The notion that peace must, if necessary, be imposed upon the conquered is most famously articulated by Virgil's Anchises (*Aen.* 6.851–3), whose *parcere subiectis et debellare superbos* ('spare the conquered and crush the proud', 853) might fairly be described as a distillation of Roman imperialist ideology; cf., e.g., Cic. *Off.* 1.35; Aug. *RG* 3.1–2, 26–7; Suet. *Aug.* 21; Plin. *Pan.* 16–17.

the same topos could be plausibly employed with reference to periods as diverse as the early first century BC (Cic. *De or.* 3.8, on the death of L. Licinius Crassus) and the reign of Domitian (Tac. *Agr.* 44.4–45.3).[7] All these passages convey a powerful sense, albeit in rhetorically loaded contexts, of a world in which violence regularly served as a political instrument, whether of the ruling power, in quelling or punishing opposition, or of those who aspired to rule. In this connection we might think, too, of the episodes of rioting and other forms of popular violence that erupted periodically throughout Antiquity, from the mobs incited or organized by P. Clodius Pulcher and others during the power-struggles of the late Republic to the circumcellions of North Africa in the fourth and early fifth centuries AD.[8] Not all such outbreaks, of course, were motivated by political (or religious) considerations: Tacitus, for example, in his brief but memorable account of a riot that broke out at a gladiatorial show in Pompeii in AD 59 (*Ann.* 14.17), offers a snapshot of something akin to modern football hooliganism. The historian records that this incident was sparked off by exchanges of insults between the Pompeians and the inhabitants of the neighbouring town of Nuceria: in this instance, then, the motivating factor appears to have been rivalry between local communities.[9]

There was also a more obviously 'Wild West' aspect, fostered by the lack of systematic policing even in the major cities, and by huge economic inequalities.[10] For travellers, the risk of physical attack or robbery with

---

[7] Cicero writes that Crassus was spared the horrors of the Social War and the bloody power-struggles that followed; Tacitus similarly observes that Agricola was fortunate in not living to witness Domitian's purge of senatorial opponents in the final years of his reign. On the topos, see further Scourfield 1993: 196.

[8] On mob and gang violence in the late Republic, see Nippel 1995: 47–57, 70–84, Lintott 1999: 67–88; for the Imperial period, Africa 1971; on circumcellions, Shaw 2011: 630–720, 828–39; on violence in late Antiquity in general, Drake 2006.

[9] Tacitus reports numerous injuries and casualties, especially among the Nucerians (*ergo deportati sunt in urbem multi e Nucerinis trunco per vulnera corpore, ac plerique liberorum aut parentum mortis deflebant*, 'in consequence, many of the Nucerians were carried to the city, their bodies mutilated by wounds, and many lamented the deaths of children or parents'). Fagan 2011a: 93–6 draws attention to the limitations of the analogy with modern sports-related violence, noting that this is the only instance on record of rioting amongst arena crowds; the incident should be understood rather in terms of social tensions, apparently inflamed in some way by the show. On local rivalries and associated violence, see also Fagan 2011b: 488–9.

[10] On the lack of systematic policing under the Republic in particular, see Nippel 1995, esp. 16–26, 85–112. More recently, Fuhrmann 2012 has argued at length for a greater degree of institutionalization in policing under the Empire than is commonly allowed; he notes, however, that 'policing in the Roman Empire' – which was largely carried out by soldiers – 'was often focused on preserving the interests of the state and cooperative elites' (234) rather than on protecting ordinary people, and it should at all events be borne in mind that the familiar institution of an

violence was particularly acute. Banditry and piracy were endemic to the Roman world.[11] The younger Pliny responds without surprise to a correspondent's report of the recent disappearance of a distinguished *eques* who had journeyed as far as Ocriculum on the Via Flaminia and then simply vanished; a similar fate, says Pliny, befell his own fellow-townsman Metilius Crispus, who, after setting out for Rome, was never heard of again, and is presumed dead (*Ep.* 6.25). Juvenal suggests, through his creation Umbricius (3.278–308), that the streets of Rome itself are unsafe by night, at least for those who cannot afford an escort: the perils of urban life include not only robbery, but the unprovoked violence of the drunken bully, who will not let his victim escape without a beating. Though we will naturally suspect some satiric exaggeration here, references elsewhere to random assaults on the street or, more generally, to the dangers of travelling the city on foot, especially after dark, testify to a widespread perception of interpersonal violence as rife within the urban centre as well as without.[12] While such perceptions cannot be taken as accurate pointers to the actual incidence of muggings or other kinds of violent crime, they plainly have a basis in historical reality.[13] References in literary texts (including outright fictions) thus converge with other forms of evidence[14]

---

independent and specialized police force is a modern phenomenon, emerging in the eighteenth and nineteenth centuries (cf. Nippel 1995: ix, 1–2, 115–19; also Fagan 2011b: 486–7, with helpful comparative comment on Rome and early modern Europe). On links between poverty and crime, see Grünewald 2004: 25–31, Morley 2006: 33 ('the poor are by far the most likely to become victims of crime as well as its perpetrators'); cf. also D. Braund 1993: 206, who notes that fugitive slaves, as well as discharged soldiers and sailors, might resort to piracy or brigandage.

[11] Shaw 1984: 8–12 (= 2004: 331–5) notes that deaths at the hands of bandits were sufficiently common to have given rise to a formulaic expression found on tombstones, *interfectus a latronibus* ('killed by bandits'), while Roman legal texts list attacks by bandits as common causes of death (along with old age and sickness), and as 'natural disasters' for which no legal action may be taken. See further Grünewald 2004: 14–32, and on the persistent problems of piracy, de Souza 1999, esp. 97–224.

[12] Such assaults by elite youths, individually or in gangs, constitute something of a topos: see, e.g., Cic. *Cael.* 20 (Caelius alleged to have assaulted married women returning from a dinner-party); Tac. *Ann.* 13.25, Suet. *Ner.* 26 (similar behaviour, as well as assaults on male citizens and robbery, attributed to the emperor Nero); Apul. *Met.* 2.18 (Photis warns Lucius to come back early from dinner, to avoid falling foul of a gang of 'most noble' youths that has been terrorizing the neighbourhood). For the dangers of nocturnal travel more generally see, e.g., Prop. 3.16.1–6; Tib. 1.2.25–8; Petron. *Sat.* 82.2–4; Plin. *NH* 8.144; Juv. 10.19–22.

[13] Ancient perceptions regarding the ubiquity of such acts of violence may usefully be thought of as a *tertium quid*, mediating between historical realities and the representation and manipulation of those realities in the literary texts; cf. Fagan 2011b: 469–70: 'ancient anecdotes and fiction can act as mirrors that reflect social attitudes, assumptions, and realities, even if the immediate context is highly dubious or even fantastical' (see also 490, where Fagan argues that the level of interpersonal violence in Roman society cannot be gauged with any degree of certainty). Cf. also pp. 18–19 below, with n. 80.

[14] See n. 11 above.

to reveal a society in which the individual was at considerable (if unquanti-fiable) risk of a direct encounter with physical violence.

Still more germane to the concerns of this book than such instances of criminal assault is the institutionalization of various forms of violence in Roman culture. We have already mentioned the centrality of military values to Roman masculine (and national) identity: the institutionalized violence of warfare offers a privileged arena for the Roman male to demonstrate both his personal superiority to other citizen males and the ascendancy of Rome's military might over barbarian enemies. At the same time, the Roman army paradoxically required of the ordinary soldier – in the interests of military discipline – what would under other circumstances be construed as a degrading and effeminizing submissiveness to physical violence. With the special exceptions noted below (pp. 8–9), the army was the only context in which a citizen might legitimately be subjected to summary physical chastisement.[15] In the first place, the citizen-soldier might be flogged – a penalty normally associated with slaves – by his superior officers; but the harshness of Roman military discipline is of course most famously embodied in the practice of decimation, which again has analogies with collective penalties prescribed under extreme circumstances for slaves.[16] Here we can see in an arresting way the ambiguity of a soldier's status, and a correspond-ing duality in the exemplary quality of the violence which a soldier had to be prepared to face. To quote Jonathan Walters, the soldier's battle scars 'are conceptually placed as the polar opposite of scars from a servile beating. They are ... the signifier, permanently inscribed on his body, of his social status as a full man.'[17] War wounds, then, are the mark of masculine courage and free male status: the warrior-hero is the ultimate *exemplum virtutis*. By a kind of inversion, the corporal and capital punishments peculiar to the military context fulfilled a similarly exemplary, but this time deterrent, func-tion in offering to the fellow-soldiers of the condemned a graphic represen-tation of the consequences of insubordination.[18]

---

[15] See Walters 1997: 37–40; cf. Konstan/Raval, Chapter 1, p. 48 below.

[16] The analogy is made explicit by Cassius Longinus in Tacitus' account of the senatorial debate concerning the punishment of Pedanius Secundus' slaves (*Ann.* 14.44; see below). On decimation, and Roman military discipline in general, see esp. Polyb. 6.37–8; specific instances are recorded at, e.g., Tac. *Ann.* 3.21, *Hist.* 1.37; Plut. *Crass.* 10.4, *Ant.* 39.9; Suet. *Galb.* 12.2; App. *B Civ* 1.118.

[17] Walters 1997: 40.

[18] On the inherent ambiguity of scars, which may be signifiers of (honourable) endurance and courage or of (dishonourable) servility or insubordination, and may be susceptible of different interpretations, see Roller 2004: 12–14; as Roller notes (13 n. 24; cf. Leigh 1995: 196–7, Glancy 2010: 27–37), the ambiguity may sometimes be resolved by appealing to the location of the wound (scars on the front connote military courage, whereas those on the back are indicative of cowardice or servile status). The symbolism of wounds and scars may be related in turn to a more general

Even more than in the case of soldiers, the physical punishments inflicted on slaves possessed a powerfully spectacular quality.[19] The scars left behind by whip or cudgel are invoked in the literary sources as the distinguishing marks of the slave,[20] while it is in the nature of crucifixion – the servile punishment *par excellence*[21] – to expose the body of the victim to the view of the passer-by. After the crushing of the revolt of Spartacus, 6,000 captured rebels are said to have been crucified along the Appian Way:[22] on a rough calculation, and assuming for the sake of illustration that the figure of 6,000 is accurate and that the crosses were erected in facing pairs on either side of the road and at equal distances from each other all the way from Capua to Rome, the traveller would have passed two of these tortured bodies every sixty or seventy metres for two hundred kilometres – a vivid demonstration indeed of the slave's subjection to the authority of free citizens. In an episode from AD 61 recounted by Tacitus (*Ann.* 14.42–5), the punishment meted out to the household slaves of the city prefect L. Pedanius Secundus, who had been murdered by one of them, possesses a similarly spectacular quality, linked to the exemplary nature of the punishment emphasized by C. Cassius Longinus in the senatorial debate which preceded the slaves' execution. Tacitus reports that the fate of the slaves – 400 of them, all of whom were by ancient tradition liable to the death penalty in consequence of the crime – aroused considerable sympathy among the people of the city and some members of the Senate; Cassius, however, argued in favour of the collective punishment, essentially on the ground that the slave population could be kept in check only by the deterrent effect of such harsh measures.[23] Tacitus' account concludes with the memorable image of the slaves led off to execution along a route lined with soldiers, to prevent popular resentment at the senatorial decision from erupting into further violence.

tension in Roman ideology between different ways of conceptualizing (im)passivity, incisively discussed by Bartsch 2006: 174–82; as she points out, *patientia* may be construed either as unmanly 'subjection' to sexual and other demeaning acts or as admirable indifference to bodily suffering and physical pain. For the deterrent effect of decimation and associated punishments in the military context, see Polyb. 6.38; cf. App. *B Civ.* 1.118–19.

[19] On the physical punishments and general abuses to which slaves could be subject, see Bradley 1987: 113–37, esp. 118–23, 131–3; on the use of torture, Bradley 1994: 165–70.

[20] See, e.g., Plaut. *Amph.* 446, (with servile status implicit) Catull. 25.10–11, Hor. *Epod.* 4.3; for discussion, Saller 1991: 153–4, 1994: 137–9; Fitzgerald 2000: 32–41.

[21] See, e.g., Hengel 1977: 51–63; Cantarella 1991: 187–9; Aubert 2002: 110–30, esp. 113–14.

[22] App. *B Civ.* 1.120.

[23] For deterrence as an aim of judicial punishments in general and capital punishment in particular see, e.g., Sen. *Clem.* 1.22.1, *De ira* 1.19.7; [Quint.] *Decl. min.* 274.13; Gell. *NA* 7.14.4; *Dig.* 48.19.28.15 (Callistratus); K. M. Coleman 1990: 48–9; Harries 2007: 37.

In general, then, physical violence in civil contexts may be said to mark a clear line of demarcation between the slave – whose body, as the property of his or her master, could legitimately be subjected to flogging and similar punishments – and the free citizen, whose body was, at least in theory, inviolable.[24] Yet the reinforcement of hegemonic structures in the Roman world through the use of violent treatment goes beyond the distinction between slave and free. In later Antiquity, spectacular penalties such as flogging and crucifixion were extended to lower-class citizens or *humiliores*, reinforcing the social stratification of the citizen body.[25] Already at earlier dates the right to physical inviolability could be held not to apply to certain categories of free person: prostitutes and mime-actresses seem to have received little protection against sexual *vis*,[26] and actors continued to face flogging even after Augustus removed the power of magistrates to impose such punishment without restriction.[27] In the domestic context women and children were, within limits, subject to physical chastisement at the hands of the *paterfamilias*, and even, in the case of children, by social inferiors such as the schoolmaster, notorious in Roman literature for his frequent resort to corporal punishment of his pupils.[28] Notionally, the father's authority over his children – even as adults – was absolute: *patria*

---

[24] See Saller 1991: 151–7, (with fuller detail) 1994: 134–42.

[25] See, e.g., Walters 1997: 38; Harries 2007: 36; Fagan 2011a: 28, 170; and on the general increase in judicial violence through the period of the Empire, MacMullen 1986. Garnsey 1970 traces in detail the relationship between social status and legal privilege/disadvantage, including the application of differential penalties, from the first century BC to the third century AD and beyond.

[26] See Gardner 1986: 246–7; McGinn 1998: 326–7.

[27] See Suet. *Aug.* 45.3–4; further, C. Edwards 1997: 74–5; Lintott 1999: 94–5.

[28] On women as objects of domestic violence, see esp. P. Clark 1998, J. A. Schroeder 2004, both with late-Antique focus; on the treatment of pupils by schoolmasters, Bonner 1977: 143–5, Fagan 2011b: 475–6. The complexity of the situation within the household is well brought out by Clark, who shows, for example, how the normative slave/free polarity could be inverted through the exercise by older slaves of disciplinary authority over the children of the master and mistress (cf. Fitzgerald 2000: 56–7), while aggression arising from intrafamilial tensions between the women of the house might be displaced on to (female) slaves (cf. Schroeder 2004: 422–3). Clark also notes the ambiguous attitudes attending violence on the part of the *paterfamilias*, who was expected to keep his household in order, and yet at the same time demonstrate self-control and not display irascibility; Harris 2001: 321–36 argues that a similar ideological imperative encouraged the exercise of restraint in the treatment of slaves. For wives subject to violent treatment by their husbands divorce was an option, but 'domestic abuse was seldom acknowledged to exist and could even be praised' (Harries 2007: 86, citing the exemplary tale of Egnatius Mecenius (Val. Max. 6.3.9), who, after beating his wife to death for drinking wine, was agreed to have made a salutary example of the offending woman), and in practice unilateral divorce was not always straightforward (see Treggiari 1991b; P. Clark 1998: 129 n. 21; Schroeder 2004: 416–17). Among children, the evidence for physical punishment of girls as well as boys is slight: see Saller 1994: 152; P. Clark 1998: 129 n. 36.

*potestas* embraced the right not only to beat children but even to have them put to death.[29]

Here, however, we encounter some uncertainty or complexity in Roman attitudes towards physical violence. The sources strongly suggest a degree of ambivalence around the unfettered exercise of such rights as those associated with *patria potestas*. Even the proverbially stern elder Cato is said to have been critical of husbands who beat their wives and children (Plut. *Cat. Mai.* 20.3: 'he said that the man who beat his wife or child laid hands on the most sacred of holy things'[30]); and Quintilian similarly condemns the practice of beating schoolchildren, on the ground that corporal punishment is not only inappropriate to the status of a freeborn youth but ineffective anyway (*Inst.* 1.3.14).[31] Again, the ambivalence displayed by the elegists in relation to physical abuse of their (non-citizen?) *puellae* no doubt reflects to a certain extent the values of society at large: while the *rixa*, or violent quarrel, is clearly regarded as titillating, and Propertius apparently considers himself fully within his rights to man-handle a girl who refuses to remove her clothes, both he and Tibullus depict the tearing of hair and breaking down of doors as the actions of a *rusticus*.[32] In the public sphere, we have already considered Tacitus' account of the senatorial and popular unease surrounding the collective punishment imposed on the slaves of Pedanius Secundus; and even in the context of war, certain acts of violence might be regarded as excessive.

---

[29] Note, however, that Shaw 2001: 56–77 adduces powerful arguments to question whether the so-called *ius vitae necisque* was ever in fact enshrined in law, let alone widely exercised; cf. Saller 1994: 115–17. On *patria potestas* in general see, e.g., Crook 1967a; Gardner 1993: 52–84; Saller 1994: 102–5, 114–32; Arjava 1998.

[30] τὸν δὲ τύπτοντα γαμετὴν ἢ παῖδα τοῖς ἁγιωτάτοις ἔλεγεν ἱεροῖς προσφέρειν τὰς χεῖρας.

[31] *caedi vero discentis, quamlibet id receptum sit et Chrysippus non improbet, minime velim, primum quia deforme atque servile est et certe (quod convenit si aetatem mutes) iniuria: deinde quod, si cui tam est mens inliberalis ut obiurgatione non corrigatur, is etiam ad plagas ut pessima quaeque mancipia durabitur: postremo quod ne opus erit quidem hac castigatione si adsiduus studiorum exactor adstiterit* ('I am strongly opposed to the beating of pupils, however, although it is common practice and Chrysippus has no objection to it, first because it is base and slavish and certainly insulting (as is agreed in the case of adults); secondly because, if a boy's mind is so ignoble as not to be corrected by reproof, he will merely become hardened to blows like the worst kind of slave; and finally, because there will not even be a need for such a punishment, if the master acts as a constant overseer of the pupil's studies'); cf. [Plut.] *De lib. educ.* 12. Saller 1994: 142–50 (cf. 1991: 157–64) affords a nuanced discussion of differential attitudes to the physical disciplining of free children and slaves.

[32] See Tib. 1.1.73–4, 1.10.61–4, Prop. 3.8, Ov. *Am.* 1.7.11–18 (*rixa* and/or marks of physical violence as titillating); Prop. 2.15.17–20 (refusal to remove clothing invites violence); Tib. 1.10.51–60, Prop. 2.5.21–6 (physical violence associated with *rusticitas*). Cf. also Tib. 1.6.73–4, where the lover both contemplates the possibility of beating his girl and imagines his subsequent regret; Ov. *Ars am.* 2.169–76 (a send-up of elegiac ambivalence). On the dynamics of violence in elegy, see further Cahoon 1988; Fredrick 1997 and 2012: 430–6; Greene 1998: 84–91; James 2003a: 184–97; Kennedy 2012: 189–95; O'Rourke, Chapter 4 below.

Thus Cicero, while implicitly justifying the annihilation of 'cruel' or 'savage' enemies, betrays evident discomfort in regard to the destruction of Corinth,[33] and debate about the end of the *Aeneid* has shown just how difficult it can be to distinguish between what, in Roman thought, constitutes justifiable brutality and what is to be seen as a manifestation of uncontrolled, and thus non-approved, battle-frenzy or *furor*.[34]

In all this, the characteristically Graeco-Roman virtue of self-control (*sophrosune/temperantia*) may be seen as paramount. In many contexts, the judicious application of physical force or corporal punishment is held to be crucial to the maintenance of discipline (whether in the household, the army, or the state), and may be positively valued. Yet an excessive or uncontrolled propensity towards violent action (or the viewing of violent spectacle) typically meets with criticism; in Suetonius' *Lives*, for example, 'bad' emperors are characteristically violent, even towards their wives or other members of the imperial family, and manifest an excessive interest in gladiatorial shows, torture, and execution.[35]

Certain kinds of violent act were of course also regulated, at least in principle, by law.[36] It should be observed, however, that the *leges de vi* promulgated in the late-Republican and Augustan periods were predominantly concerned with violence in the public sphere, and more specifically with the maintenance of public order.[37] The Republican *lex Lutatia* and *lex Pompeia de vi* were passed at times of political crisis (the insurrection of Lepidus in 78 BC and the extended period of rioting following the murder of Clodius in 52), and dealt mainly with acts of sedition; the *lex Plautia* is more controversial, but seems likewise to have been concerned primarily with crimes perceived as directed against

---

[33] Cic. *Off.* 1.35 *parta autem victoria conservandi ii qui non crudeles in bello, non immanes fuerunt, ut maiores nostri Tusculanos Aequos Volscos Sabinos Hernicos in civitatem etiam acceperunt, at Carthaginem et Numantiam funditus sustulerunt; nollem Corinthum, sed credo aliquid secutos ...* ('when victory is won, those who have not been cruel or savage in war should be spared: thus, our ancestors went so far as to grant citizenship to the Tusculani, Aequi, Volscians, Sabines, and Hernici, but utterly destroyed Carthage and Numantia; I could wish that they had not done so in the case of Corinth, but I believe that they had some end in view ...').

[34] For a range of views, see Galinsky 1988 and 1994; Putnam 1990; Stahl 1990; M. R. Wright 1997; Tarrant 2012: 16–30.

[35] See, e.g., Suet. *Tib.* 53.2, 61–2, *Calig.* 32–3, *Claud.* 34, *Ner.* 35, *Vit.* 14, *Dom.* 10; according to Tacitus (*Ann.* 1.76), Drusus was said to have been reprimanded by Tiberius for displaying an excessive taste for blood in the arena. For the ideological premium set on the control of anger in classical Antiquity see Harris 2001, with the 'angry ruler' discussed at 229–63.

[36] Harries 2007: 106–17 affords a broad-ranging survey of remedies for violence in the Roman world.

[37] On the *leges de vi*, see Nippel 1995: 54–5; Lintott 1999: 107–24; Harries 2007: 107, 110–11.

the state.[38] The Augustan (or Caesarian?) *leges Iuliae* were somewhat more comprehensive, making provision against the formation of gangs,[39] forcible seizure of property, wrongful imprisonment, and abuses of power by magistrates, as well as actions which threatened public security, but they still appear to have allowed fairly broad scope for the kind of 'self-help' remedies that were traditional in the Roman system of justice. In particular, the concept of self-defence had wide application, and included the right to employ armed force and kill in certain circumstances.[40] Andrew Lintott observes that 'in the late Republic we find an increasing belief among those concerned with the law that violence, especially that involving gangs and arms, is in itself a bad thing'; yet he also notes that the use of private force in, for example, bringing an unwilling defendant to court or 'deal[ing] with men who were morally considered outlaws' was regarded as entirely proper, sometimes even necessary.[41] Issues of definition would appear to be crucial in reconciling the implicit contradiction here: categories of violent act prohibited by law will self-evidently be those that are socially disapproved, while those that are positively regarded remain beyond the scope of such legal sanctions.

Many of the foregoing points are illustrated with particular clarity by an institutionalized form of violence which we have not yet considered: the gladiatorial shows and other violent spectacles of the arena.[42] Here, the Roman world can be seen to be represented in microcosm: the citizen body seated in the *cavea* views the products of empire – slaves and exotic animals – brought into the city and symbolically subjected to its collective control.[43] Yet, as has often been observed in recent scholarship on the *munera*, the experience of the audience must have been strongly ambivalent. The spectacle of war-captives and criminals, abjected from 'Rome', fighting to the death on the sand below is likely to have fostered a sense of group solidarity, the audience being spatially and symbolically separated from the 'other';[44] but at the same time, as a number of Roman writers attest, gladiators were widely regarded with admiration, as exemplars of

---

[38] For detailed argument see Lintott 1999: 109–21.   [39] Lintott 1999: 126.

[40] On 'self-help' and the recognition of certain forms of violence as legitimate, see Nippel 1995: 35–9; Lintott 1999: 22–34; Harries 2007: 106, 118.

[41] Lintott 1999: 130, 66.

[42] The bibliography is extensive. Notable items include Ville 1981; Hopkins 1983: 1–30; K. M. Coleman 1990; Wiedemann 1992; Barton 1993, esp. 11–81; Plass 1995, esp. 13–77; Edmondson 1996; Gunderson 1996; Futrell 1997; Kyle 1998; Fagan 2011a.

[43] Cf. Gunderson 1996: 133.

[44] See Edmondson 1996: 81–4; Fagan 2011a: 121–54, esp. 141–2.

courage and fighting skills, and as objects of desire.[45] The dialectic of scorn and admiration is further complicated by the possibility – hinted at especially in the philosophical writings of Cicero and Seneca – of identification with the gladiator as an exemplar not of mastery but of impassivity in the face of defeat and death.[46] Like the soldier, whose honourable wounds are the visible marks of his *virtus*, the gladiator demonstrates that, under certain circumstances, the capacity to endure as well as to inflict violence may be regarded as admirable. It is striking, however, that several ancient authors express concern about the potential effects of gladiatorial *munera* on the viewer, a concern that has points of similarity with the modern 'media-effects' debate, on which we shall touch in Section V. As we have noted,[47] Suetonius depicts an excessive taste for the violence of the arena as characteristic of the tyrannical disposition; rather differently, Seneca and Augustine both represent arena spectacle as something dangerously seductive, which enables vice to 'steal upon us under cover of pleasure' (*per voluptatem . . . vitia subrepunt*, Sen. *Ep.* 7.2) and intoxicates Augustine's young friend Alypius to such an extent that he develops a kind of addiction to its bloodthirsty thrills.[48]

The spectacularity of arena violence is of special relevance to the concerns of this volume. The violent acts of the arena, like those of the

---

[45] Gladiators as exemplary figures: (e.g.) Livy 41.20.12, Plin. *Pan.* 33.1; as objects of desire: (e.g.) Juv. 6.103–12, Tert. *De spect.* 22 (a passage which outlines particularly sharply the ambivalent attitude within Roman culture towards gladiators and other public performers). For further references, and bibliography, see Gale, Chapter 2 below, p. 69 nn. 20–1. It should be noted that some gladiators were free (or freed) volunteers, though the numbers are hard to estimate; these *auctorati* (contract gladiators), however, whatever their original status, were in consequence relegated to the fringes of society, sharing with prostitutes, pimps, and actors the stigma and degraded legal condition of *infamia*. See further C. Edwards 1997; Kyle 1998: 87–90.

[46] See, e.g., Cic. *Tusc.* 2.41, Sen. *Ep.* 30.8, with illuminating discussion of this aspect of the gladiator's symbolic role in the Roman imaginary in C. Edwards 2007: 66–8.

[47] P. 10 above.

[48] August. *Conf.* 6.8.13 *ut enim vidit illum sanguinem, immanitatem simul ebibit et non se avertit, sed fixit aspectum et hauriebat furias et nesciebat, et delectabatur scelere certaminis et cruenta voluptate inebriabatur. et non erat iam ille qui venerat sed unus de turba ad quam venerat, et verus eorum socius a quibus adductus erat. quid plura! spectavit, clamavit, exarsit, abstulit inde secum insaniam qua stimularetur redire . . .* ('when he saw the blood, he drank in savagery together with it, and did not turn away, but gazed fixedly and drained the cup of frenzy unawares; and he delighted in the viciousness of the combat and became drunk on bloodthirsty pleasure. He was no longer the man who had come there, but one of the crowd which he had joined, and the true companion of those who had brought him. In brief: he watched, shouted, caught fire, took away from there the madness that spurred him to return . . .'); on such Christian critique, see Castelli 2004: 112–17. For the crowd psychology implicit in *non erat iam ille qui venerat sed unus de turba* cf. Sen. *Ep.* 7.6 *subducendus populo est tener animus et parum tenax recti: facile transitur ad plures* ('the delicate soul, whose hold on rectitude is weak, should be kept away from the crowd: it is easy to go over to the many').

literary texts discussed here, are offered for the sake of the viewer's (reader's) pleasurable consumption. While this is true of all kinds of arena spectacle, it is particularly evident in the case of what Kathleen Coleman terms 'fatal charades', in which condemned criminals are forced to play the role of mythical characters such as Orpheus or Hercules, and torn to pieces or burned to death before the watching eyes of the crowd.[49] What on a practical level is a terrifying, agonizing, and humiliating form of punishment destined to conclude in death simultaneously offers a pleasure-seeking audience a dramatic and spectacular re-presentation of events from the rich and culturally loaded repertoire of myth.

## II Violence, Myth, and Literature

For the impresarios who laid on these remarkable spectacles, stories suitable for re-enactment as 'fatal charades' were not far to seek. Graeco-Roman myth is filled with violent acts, with tales not only of war on both the cosmic and the human scale, but of bodies swallowed up, mutilated, or ripped apart. Even before humans come on the scene, the gods are busy castrating (Ouranos and Cronos), devouring (Cronos and his children), and warring with themselves or other beings (the Titanomachy and Gigantomachy).[50] Zeus/Jupiter is infamous for his sexual violation of nymphs and human females alike: a striking instance is that of Callisto, who is doubly victimized, first raped and then transformed into a bear, only to be hunted to death – or nearly so – either by Artemis or by her own unknowing son.[51] The intrafamilial element in the story of Callisto and Arcas is readily paralleled: Oedipus kills his father, while Medea, Athamas, Procne, and Atreus slaughter their own children or those of a sibling, the last two proceeding to butcher the corpses and feed them to the children's father. Tantalus, similarly, attempts to trick the gods into feasting on the flesh of his dismembered son, Pelops; and many other myths and legends culminate in the dismemberment of the central figure or a comparable act

---

[49] See K. M. Coleman 1990, esp. 60–6; the nature of the pleasure derived by Roman audiences from deadly arena spectacles is considered at 57–9.

[50] Ancient critics of myth and its allegedly impious representation of the gods frequently draw attention to such episodes. See esp. Pl. *Resp.* 2.377–8; also Xenoph. fr. 1.21–3 Diels–Kranz (cf. fr. 12); Pind. *Ol.* 1.28–53; Isoc. *Bus.* 38.

[51] See, e.g., Callim. fr. 632 Pfeiffer, Paus. 8.3.6–7, Apollod. *Bibl.* 3.8.2 (Artemis); [Eratosth.] *Cat.* 1.1 (Hes. fr. 163 Merkelbach–West), Ov. *Met.* 2.409–507, *Fast.* 2.155–90 (Arcas). In the latter version, Callisto's death at the hands of Arcas is standardly averted at the last minute by Zeus/Jupiter, who sets her among the stars as the constellation of the Bear.

of brutality (Orpheus and Pentheus torn limb from limb by maenads, Marsyas flayed alive by Apollo, Mettius Fufetius ripped to pieces in punishment for oathbreaking).[52] Other mythical or legendary figures inflict violence upon their own persons: Oedipus blinds himself, Attis castrates himself, Mucius Scaevola burns away his right hand,[53] Ajax, Jocasta, and numerous others commit suicide.

Of the major mythical cycles, that revolving around the Trojan War is particularly noteworthy, both for its central place in the Greek and Roman literary canon and for its instantiation of violence in many forms. In addition to the countless warrior-heroes wounded or killed on the battlefield itself, the prelude to the war and its conclusion and aftermath offer a catalogue of violent deaths. The Trojan expedition is bracketed by two episodes of human sacrifice, those of Iphigenia and Polyxena; the murders of Astyanax, Polydorus,[54] Agamemnon, and Penelope's suitors are all entailed by it. The lesser Ajax is, in one account,[55] struck by lightning and impaled upon a rocky peak in revenge for his rape of Cassandra, Laocoön and his sons are strangled by monstrous snakes. And, as Roman writers emphasize, the war brings further conflicts in its wake, between Aeneas and the native Italians, and ultimately – in Virgil's version – between Rome and Carthage.

Graeco-Roman myth might thus be described as a rich repository of narratives involving violence of both more and less culturally validated kinds, from heroic warfare to rape, murder, and dismemberment. The higher genres of literature, which in general draw their subject matter from the mythological corpus (and at the same time reformulate it), tend accordingly to work out their own thematic concerns through the depiction of violent incidents of one kind or another. This is most obvious in the case of Greek and Roman epic, to which *reges et proelia*, 'kings and battles', whether mythical or historical, are traditionally central: the epic hero is, first and foremost, a warrior, whose heroic status derives in large part from his courage and skill on the field of battle. But from Homer on, classical epic juxtaposes its celebration of heroism with emphasis on the destructive and wasteful aspect of warfare; the conventions of ancient battle-narrative, with its close-up depiction of wounding and mutilation,

---

[52] For Mett(i)us, see Livy 1.23–8; Virg. *Aen.* 8.642–5.    [53] See Livy 2.12.

[54] In the version of the story familiar from Euripides' *Hecuba* and Virgil's *Aeneid* (3.19–68), Polydorus is treacherously killed by Polymestor of Thrace, to whose care he has been entrusted as a child; in Homer, however, he dies on the battlefield by the spear of Achilles (*Il.* 20.407–18). For other variants, see R. D. Williams 1962: 57.

[55] Virg. *Aen.* 1.39–45; cf. Hom. *Od.* 4.499–511, Sen. *Ag.* 528–56, Quint. Smyrn. 14.530–89.

may be seen as crucial to this dialectic.[56] Even didactic epic, though less directly concerned with violence and with mythological themes than its narrative cousin, inherits something of this focus on conflict and warrior-heroism: from Empedocles to Lucretius to Virgil, didactic poets have a tendency to frame their lessons, whether theoretical or practical, in terms that recall the battlefields of the mythological/historical epics. The worlds of the *De rerum natura*, the *Georgics*, and even the *Ars amatoria* are, in their different ways, violent ones.[57]

In Greek tragedy, acts of violence are by convention not normally represented on stage,[58] but they are nevertheless a central focus of many plays. The messenger-speeches in which news of violent death or mutilation is standardly conveyed to the characters of the drama are notable for their *enargeia* – the technique of rhetorical description which brings events vividly before the mind's eye.[59] This means of representation allows for a sharper focus on the detail of torn and bleeding flesh and on the victim's agonized sufferings, with a correspondingly greater immediacy of impact, than the inevitably stylized mimesis of theatrical violence would permit.[60] The blinding of Oedipus in Sophocles' play and the gruesome deaths of Pentheus and of Creon and his daughter in Euripides' *Bacchae* and *Medea* are all described in excruciating detail.[61] Senecan tragedy – on the assumption that the plays were in fact staged[62] – does not show the same reluctance as its Greek models to present violent acts directly (Seneca's Medea kills her sons in full sight of the audience, Jocasta

---

[56] On the relationship between heroic ideals and the disfigurement of the enemy corpse in the *Iliad*, see Vernant 1991, a brilliant essay. On wounding and mutilation in Homeric battle-narrative more generally, see, e.g., Friedrich 2003, Mueller 2009: 78–83; and for Roman epic, e.g., Kroll 1924: 305–7, Heuzé 1985: 67–206, Most 1992: 397–400.

[57] On war and military imagery in Lucretius and the *Georgics*, see Gale 2000: 232–40, 243–69. In the case of the *Ars amatoria*, this tradition intersects with the elegiac topos of *militia amoris*, on which see O'Rourke, Chapter 4 below, with bibliography at p. 111 n. 8.

[58] Cf. Finglass 2011: 377 (arguing against the view that the suicide of Ajax in Sophocles' play was staged before the audience): 'There is no precedent for a violent death, or even severe wound, being inflicted on the fifth-century tragic (or even comic) stage'; Konstan/Raval, Chapter 1, pp. 44–5 below. The audience may, however, be directly confronted with the results of such action: typically the dead body, as (for example) in the first two plays of Aeschylus' *Oresteia*, but cf. also Kennedy, Chapter 7, p. 227 below, on Euripides' *Bacchae*.

[59] Cf. in general de Jong 1991, esp. 172–7. On *enargeia* (Latin *evidentia*), see Lausberg 1998: 359–66, with copious testimonia; Webb 2009, esp. 87–130.

[60] Cf. Hor. *Ars P.* 182–8: violent actions such as Medea's infanticide and Atreus' butchery of his brother's children will be more convincing to the audience if reported rather than represented directly, and should therefore take place offstage (a precept which Seneca later pointedly ignores: see below, with Kennedy, Chapter 7, p. 238).

[61] Soph. *OT* 1265–79; Eur. *Bacch.* 1095–1143, *Med.* 1167–1219.

[62] For sensible comment on the debate, see Boyle 2014: xli–xliii.

in the *Oedipus* stabs herself similarly), and exceptionally horrific consequences of such acts are somehow put on display in the *Phaedra* and
*Thyestes* (the fragments of Hippolytus' ravaged corpse, the severed heads
of Thyestes' sons); but in the reporting of such violence too Seneca raises
the stakes considerably, piling on 'extraordinarily precise, abundant, and
ghastly detail' in the extended accounts of dismemberment and mutilation which he assigns both to messengers and to other characters.[63]
Indeed, as has been pointed out, 'there is not a single tragedy in the
Senecan *corpus* in which the mutilation and amputation of human bodies
does not play a significant role'.[64]

The representation of violence, then, might well be claimed as a
defining characteristic of works at the higher end of the generic spectrum.[65] Yet acts of violence are also frequently depicted in the less
elevated genres, often in a more intimate, domestic setting. This is
particularly obvious in the case of Roman, especially Plautine, comedy,
where a key source of humour is the body of the slave, with the scars he
bears as traces of past beatings, and the ever-present menace of similar or
worse punishment hanging over him.[66] Roman love-elegy – a genre more
closely related to comedy than has generally been recognized – is similarly
concerned in various ways with violence in the domestic sphere. Elegiac
passion goes beyond playful rough and tumble: Propertius, who refers to
his erotic engagements with Cynthia as 'battles' (*proelia*, 2.1.45, 3.5.2),
likes to make her cry (3.8.23–4; cf. Tib. 1.10.63–4) and even responds to
her desertion with threats of murder (2.8.25–8), while Ovid goes so far as
to assert that women like to be raped (*Ars am.* 1.673: *vim licet appelles:*
*grata est vis ista puellis*[67]). The element of aggression embodied in such
passages appears at first glance starkly at odds with the 'softness' (*mollitia*)
standardly attributed by the poets both to their own *personae* and to the
style of their verse. This duality, and the ambivalent attitude towards
violence directed against female victims noted above (p. 9), may be
connected with the characteristically slippery terms in which the elegists

---

[63] See Most 1992: 391–6 (quoted phrase at 391); Boyle 1997: 133–4, 2014: xlix–l.

[64] Most 1992: 395. For critical analysis (and analysis of the criticism) of the dismemberment of
Hippolytus in the *Phaedra*, see Kennedy, Chapter 7 below.

[65] As Kennedy notes (Chapter 7, p. 216 below), Ovid assigns the epithet *violenta* to his personification
of tragedy at *Am.* 3.1.11.

[66] On the physical chastisement of slaves as a source of humour in comedy see, e.g., E. Segal 1987:
137–69; H. N. Parker 1989; Fitzgerald 2000: 36–41; Konstan/Raval, Chapter 1 below.

[67] 'You may call it force, but that kind of force girls like'; Ovid goes on to illustrate his point with a
(disturbingly?) witty excursus on the rape of Deidamia by the disguised Achilles (discussed by
O'Rourke, Chapter 4, pp. 138–9 below). Cf. also *Am.* 1.5.13–16; *Ars am.* 2.713–16.

reflect on the generic status of love-poetry. Explicit rejection of military values and the desire for *gloria* (as, for example, in Propertius 2.7 and 3.5, or Tibullus 1.10) serves on one level to indicate a self-conscious distancing from the lofty style and martial themes of epic; yet the overt modesty with which elegy embraces its generically 'lowly' status is clearly disingenuous. In this context, the lover's violent treatment of his *puella* can be understood either as a recuperation of masculinity, a kind of erotic equivalent to the battlefield exploits of epic, or as manifesting a lack of self-control and so reconfirming the unmanly characterization to which the poets elsewhere give their ironic assent.[68]

A similar equivocation between (often violent) self-assertion and self-deprecating confessions of *mollitia* or (literary or sexual) impotence is evident in iambic poetry and satire.[69] To be sure, a clear progression can be traced in this regard from the poetry of the (aristocratic, Republican) Lucilius to that of his (socially dependent, Triumviral/Imperial) successors; but despite the self-conscious toning down of satiric discourse from the end of the Republican period on, the poets continue to use the language of assault – 'biting', 'wounding', and the like – in characterizing the satiric genre.[70] This aggressive posture is still more striking in the invective poetry of Catullus and Martial, who repeatedly employ the threat of sexual assault in expressing their hostility to those who have insulted or wronged them, or merely incurred their disapproval;[71] and both have recourse to the common trope whereby iambic poetry is figured as a missile or other weapon, with which the writer aims to 'wound' his addressee.[72] The punitive violence threatened in personal contexts in these epigrams of Martial is actualized on the grand scale in his *Liber spectaculorum*, celebrating the inauguration of the Flavian Amphitheatre in AD 80.[73] Brutal punishments inflicted on human

---

[68] On *militia amoris* and elegiac ambivalence with regard to traditional values and generic hierarchies, see further Gale 1997; O'Rourke, Chapter 4, pp. 113–18 below.

[69] The *locus classicus* is Juv. 1, where the violent indignation of the moralizing satirist (tellingly troped as a 'drawn sword' in the apologetic reference to Lucilius at 165) collapses bathetically at the poem's end, as the speaker resolves to attack only the dead. The theme of (sexual and political) impotence is particularly prominent in Horace's *Epodes*; for metapoetic readings of this motif see, e.g., Fitzgerald 1988, Watson 1995, Oliensis 1998: 64–101, Henderson 1999b.

[70] See Miller, Chapter 3 below.

[71] The most famous instance is Catull. 16.1 *pedicabo ego vos et irrumabo* ('I'll bugger you and make you suck my dick'); see also, e.g., Catull. 15.18–19, 21.7–8, 37.6–8; Mart. 3.82.33, 3.96.

[72] Catull. 36.5 *truces vibrare iambos* ('to hurl savage iambics'), 116.8; Mart. 7.12.5–6 *cupiant cum quidam nostra videri, | si qua Lycambeo sanguine tela madent* ('when there are those who wish to foist on me shafts dripping with the blood of Lycambes'). Cf., e.g., Hor. *Ars P.* 79; Ov. *Rem. am.* 377–8, *Ib.* 53–4; Stat. *Silv.* 2.2.115.

[73] A convenient simplification; for full discussion of the problems, see K. M. Coleman 2006: xlv–lxiv.

bodies[74] and the slaughter of ferocious animals are here presented as both entertaining and edifying, at once subjecting the marvellous and the exotic to the gaze of the arena crowd (and Martial's readers) and demonstrating Rome's, or the emperor's, civilizing power.[75]

While prose genres are rather more difficult to comment on in general terms, violence in various forms is prominently represented in many texts. War-narratives are central to Roman historiography, as (not coincidentally) to epic.[76] Both Livy and Tacitus appear to take it for granted that war and empire are the proper or ideal subjects for the historian;[77] and, as Bruce Gibson points out in Chapter 9 below (pp. 271–2), while Tacitus contrasts the apparently trivial and uninspiring nature of his own subject matter with that of earlier historians, who were in the fortunate position of being able to deal with *ingentia … bella, expugnationes urbium, fusos captosque reges* ('great wars, the sack of cities, the defeat and capture of kings', *Ann.* 4.32), he elsewhere delineates his own project in terms which lay a marked emphasis on violence (*opus adgredior opimum casibus, atrox proeliis, discors seditionibus, ipsa etiam pace saevum*,[78] *Hist.* 1.2.1). Other prose genres have their own violent preoccupations. Murder, rape, torture, and mutilation all form part of the stock-in-trade of practitioners of declamation, while Christian martyr-literature, in its very nature, regularly focuses on the torture and violent deaths of its exemplary heroes and heroines. In Latin prose fiction, too, both inside and outside the traditional canon of 'the novel', violence may play a prominent part: *The Story of Apollonius King of Tyre* begins with an act of incestuous rape, while the hapless hero of Apuleius' *Golden Ass* both repeatedly suffers cruel treatment himself and witnesses (or hears of) acts of violence inflicted upon others.[79]

This brief survey suggests something of the range and variety, as well as the sheer volume, of representations of violence in Roman literary texts.

---

[74] Including the 'fatal charades' mentioned above (p. 13), for which the *Liber spectaculorum* is our main source.

[75] Cf. Gunderson 1996: 133–4; Lorenz 2002: 55–82, esp. 78–81.

[76] Cf. esp. Ash 2002, who traces mutual influences between epic and historiographical battle-narratives (Sallust, Virgil, Tacitus), and (255–6) notes the suggestive similarity between the titles of historical monographs such as Caesar's *Bellum Gallicum* and Sallust's *Bellum Iugurthinum* and the historical epics of, e.g., Naevius (*Bellum Punicum*) and Lucan (*Bellum civile*); also Rossi 2004, who considers the use of historiographical schemata in Virgilian battle-narrative. On the relationship between historiography and epic more generally see, e.g., Wiseman 1979: 143–53; Woodman 1988: 1–5 (Herodotus), 28–38 (Thucydides), 168–76 (Tacitus); Leigh 2007.

[77] See, e.g., Livy, pref. 7–9, 21.1.1–2; Tac. *Ann.* 4.32–3.

[78] 'I assail a narrative rich in disasters, grim with battles, torn by insurrection, cruel even in peace.'

[79] For episodes of violence as a prominent feature of the *Golden Ass*, see (in addition to the discussion by Fitzgerald in Chapter 10 below) Fagan 2011b: 470–4, 478–85.

While it would be absurdly simplistic to see this phenomenon as straight-forwardly reflecting the institutionalized violence of Roman society considered above,[80] common patterns in the spheres of social practice and literary representation can nonetheless be perceived. The ideology of violence embedded in institutions such as the army or the arena can offer a helpful framework for the interpretation of literary texts; conversely, critical analysis of literary representations of violence may contribute towards a fuller and more nuanced understanding of Roman ideology in the sociocultural sphere. Here, we would argue, the hermeneutic circle is not altogether a vicious one.

At this juncture, two broad tendencies in what we might call the cultural functioning of Roman literary violence may be identified. First, like the institutionalized forms of violence we have discussed, the literary representations may be said in general to reinscribe prevailing social hierarchies and power-relations, in so far as those against whom the violence is perpetrated are, on the whole, 'other' in relation to the norma-tive male citizen reader. As we have seen, violence, or the threat of violence, may serve to underline the division between slave and free, female and male, animal and human,[81] the former category in each case representing (within certain limits) the legitimate or accepted target of violence. Again, satiric and invective violence may serve to stigmatize those who violate social or moral norms; while the 'other' may himself (or herself) be depicted as uncontrolled in the use of violence, transgressing the Roman ideal of self-restraint.[82] This construction also has its shadow side. Certain depictions of violence may be seen to reflect anxieties, relating either to the individual citizen's supposed immunity to violent treatment or, more symbolically, to the instability of social norms.[83] The

---

[80] As Henderson points out (Chapter 6, p. 181 below), we should beware of assuming that traffic between literature and 'the real world' is unidirectional: the fictive or symbolic violence of declamation – and other genres – may supply scripts for action in concrete historical situations. Further, as Kennedy indicates (Chapter 7, pp. 231–2 below), the opposition between literature and life is in any case fallacious, in the sense that there is no position outside ideology from which violence can be apprehended in a 'pure', unmediated state. Cf. also p. 5 above, with n. 13.

[81] For the animal/human polarity in Apuleius' *Golden Ass* as emblematic of hierarchical social structures in general, see Fagan 2011b: 480–1.

[82] An obvious illustration of this is the opposition in the *Aeneid* between Aeneas' proto-Roman restraint and Turnus' 'archaic' excess (problematized, of course, both by the fact that the native Italians are also, in a sense, proto-Roman, and by Aeneas' surrender to *furor* at key moments in the poem): see, e.g., Otis 1964: 345–82, esp. 380–2; R. D. Williams 1967: 34–6 (= 1990: 28–30). For violence and lack of control as characteristic of barbarians in general, see Dauge 1981: 428–31, 460–1.

[83] See p. 8 above, and p. 22 below, on Plautus. More broadly, Konstan and Raval, Chapter 1, p. 47, suggest that the violence in Plautine comedy may be regarded in part as a reflection of 'the general atmosphere of violence and insecurity in the last decades of the third century BC', informed by the huge losses sustained in the Second Punic War.

mutilations, dismemberments, and visceral imagery of Senecan tragedy, for example, have been interpreted by some as dramatizing a deep-seated sense of alienation, or an unease in regard to personal autonomy and identity, seen as characteristic of the Neronian age,[84] while elegy and satire, with their images of effeminization and castration, have similarly been understood as pointing to a sense of political disempowerment on the part of the elite, and related insecurities concerning masculinity and social status.[85]

Secondly, like the violence of the arena or the battlefield, literary violence has in many cases a clear exemplary function. This is most obviously true for epic, with its central role in Roman education: the study of such texts in school facilitates the internalization by boys of the links between violence and masculinity noted in Section I.[86] Yet, as we indicated in our discussion of arena spectacle (pp. 11–12), victims as well as perpetrators of violence may under certain circumstances be exemplary figures: this is especially evident in the case of martyr-literature, where the martyr's endurance of violence and indifference towards, or even exultant welcoming of, pain and death are (like the exemplary fortitude of the gladiator invoked by Cicero and Seneca[87]) held up for the reader's admiration and emulation.[88]

## III   Violence, Language, and Power

To this point, we have been employing the word 'violence' as though it were a neutral and transparent term.[89] Yet, as Bruce Gibson makes clear in his discussion of Tacitus' deployment of the term *vis* in Chapter 9, the very concept of 'violence' is in itself problematic and ideologically determined. In Gibson's words, 'violence is what other people get up to, never one's own side' (p. 269).[90] The English word has strongly negative connotations, as a glance at the *OED* entry bears out: violence is 'the exercise of

---

[84] See C. P. Segal 1983, esp. 172–3 (= 2008: 136–7), Most 1992; cf. also Bartsch 1997: 40–7, on Lucan.

[85] On elegy, see esp. P. A. Miller 2004, who relates elegiac discourse to crises of both masculinity and political authority at the transition from Republic to Principate; for connections between emasculation and political disempowerment in Catullus and the elegists, see also Skinner 1997, Fear 2000: 237–8. On satire, see Miller, Chapter 3 below.

[86] On the role of epic in the Roman educational system, with special regard to gender-construction, see Keith 2000: 8–35.

[87] See p. 12 above.       [88] On Christian martyrs as gladiators, see Cobb 2008: 33–59, esp. 54–5.

[89] Cf., however, n. 2 above.

[90] Cf. Bryen 2013: 74 'Violence is not so much a thing to be defined as it is a label used in a process of defining the actions of another'; see also 66–7 for helpful discussion of the conceptual and linguistic problem, with reference to Weber.

physical force *so as to inflict injury on, or cause damage to*, persons or property', '*undue* constraint applied to some natural process, habit, etc.'; to do violence to someone is to '*outrage* or *violate*' them (our emphases).[91] Particularly striking are the popular and journalistic usages quoted in section 1d. On the one hand, 'Only 35 percent of American men define "police shooting looters" as violence and only 56 percent define "police beating students" in this manner' (*Science*, June 1972); on the other, 'Mr Scargill ... said: "... My facts show to me ... that the people guilty of intimidation and violence in this dispute have been the police"' (*The Times*, July 1984). Also instructive is comparison with near-synonyms, such as 'force', 'coercion', and 'cruelty'.[92]

Of the nearest Latin equivalents, *violentia* is similarly negative in its connotations, *vis* more neutral (closer to English 'force').[93] Yet the semantic openness and complexity of the latter term offers in itself broad scope for implicit distinctions between officially sanctioned, and thus legitimized, uses of 'force' or 'coercion' (as in the perceptions of the police actions in the quotation from *Science* magazine above), and unauthorized acts of 'violence' (as in Arthur Scargill's unambiguously pejorative phrase 'guilty of intimidation and violence', as reported in *The Times*). Gibson's study indicates that while *vis* may be positively conceived as an expression of Roman imperial power, the ambiguity of the term lends itself, in Tacitus' hands, to a subtly critical account of that power, in which military might or the emperor's authority can easily 'slide into acts of force or violence' (p. 285).[94] The threat of physical coercion may serve the interests of peace, stability, and good government; but the unchecked use of *vis* is associated with tyranny, oppression, and mutiny.

Such slippages notwithstanding, it is clear that violence, language, and power are intimately interrelated. For Tacitus, *vis*, whether positively or negatively conceived, is 'the embodiment of power';[95] and the use of violence maps similarly on to various sociopolitical hierarchies in other

---

[91] *Oxford English Dictionary*, 2nd edn. (1989), s.v., sects. 1a, 1d, 1b.

[92] On the neutral or positive connotations of the term 'force', see Gibson, Chapter 9 below, pp. 269 n. 3, 273; on 'cruelty', cf. Fitzgerald, Chapter 10, p. 288. Arendt 1970: 43–7 attempts to make categoric distinctions between 'force' (as 'the energy released by physical and social movements'), 'violence' (as inherently instrumental in nature), and related terms ('power', 'strength', 'authority') as (they should be) applied within the language of political science, without, however, appearing to take account of the ideologically loaded character of the terminology as commonly used.

[93] See Gibson, Chapter 9 below, esp. pp. 272–3, 284.

[94] Cf. p. 284: 'The potential for *vis* to be something negative is always there.'

[95] Gibson, p. 284 below.

texts discussed in this volume. In many, though by no means all, cases, this mapping tends – as suggested above – to reproduce and naturalize the power-dynamics of contemporary society. Thus comedy – in spite of its sympathetic presentation of slave-characters – may be seen ultimately to legitimize the differential use of violence in demarcating the citizen from the slave. Although, as David Konstan[96] shows in Chapter 1, a number of Plautine plots involve threats to the physical inviolability of characters who are, or turn out to be, of citizen status, there is a crucial distinction between these instances of (potential) abuse and the casual and inconsequential violence which is simply an accepted part of the comic slave's life. Though contained within the comic framework of the drama, the former are represented as a much more serious matter, a source of 'legitimate indignation at an offence to [the free citizen's] civic identity' (p. 49). Even the exceptional case of the soldier Pyrgopolynices in Plautus' *Miles gloriosus*, who *is* the victim of on-stage violence at the end of the play, can be accommodated to this pattern: Pyrgopolynices' violation of the sanctity of his neighbour's house – 'emblematic', according to Konstan, 'of the inviolability of the citizen's body' (p. 51) – is appropriately punished by a violation of *his* bodily integrity, and the social order threatened by his transgressive act thereby restored.

A similar kind of pattern is evident in Lucilian and Horatian satire. Paul Allen Miller's study in Chapter 3 lays emphasis on the tendency of the satiric genre to punish deviation from social norms with symbolic violence: the satirist traditionally seeks to inflict pain on his victim using the 'weapon' of public censure. For Miller, Lucilius' elite status offers a key to understanding the genre's origins and development: the satirist adopted 'an intellectual and aristocratic style . . . exemplified both in the censure of others and in the establishment of standards of behaviour that serve as models of aristocratic comportment' (p. 99). In the changed conditions of the Triumviral period, the freedman's son Horace turns his satiric scrutiny inwards, introjecting Lucilian violence and paradoxically combining satiric aggression with images of disempowerment and self-censorship. For the earlier satiric discourse of 'violent spectacle and admonition' (p. 109), Horace substitutes a kind of interior monologue, in which the speaker models ideals of self-examination and self-mastery. If the post-Lucilian satirist is both aggressor and victim, however, it remains clear that his weaponry is deployed (however ironically) in the service of normative social and moral

---

[96] References in this Introduction to Konstan as the author of Chapter 1 should be taken as shorthand for 'Konstan and Raval'. See editors' note on Chapter 1, p. 44 below.

values; this is clearer still in the case of Juvenal, whose targets include women, *cinaedi*, foreigners, upstart freedmen, and other social climbers.[97]

Such a clear-cut model of the relation between violence and status-hierarchies is not, however, implied by all the texts explored in this collection. In Chapter 5, Carole Newlands argues that the many graphically represented episodes of violence in Ovid's *Metamorphoses* invite the reader to interrogate the power-relations obtaining in Augustan Rome. Seeking to move the debate away from the narrow focus on rape and gender that has dominated discussion of this subject,[98] she considers instead the poem's most notorious and detailed account of sexual violence – the rape of Philomela in Book 6 – in the context of two episodes where the victims are male, the metamorphosis and death of Actaeon and the flaying of Marsyas. Observing that all three cases involve inequalities of status and power, whether between male and female or god and mortal, she characterizes the representation of violence as 'a way of talking about power-relations' (p. 142). In her analysis, the vulnerability of mythical bodies to maltreatment by those of superior status and authority dramatizes anxieties arising from the reconfiguration of power-structures under Augustus. Unlike Plautus and the satirists, Ovid tends to divorce physical violence from moral authority: Diana and Apollo are presented as being as cruel and arbitrary as the barbarous Tereus, the spectacularly horrific punishments inflicted on their victims as (to say the least) excessive. Newlands shows how Ovid's narrative technique in the *Metamorphoses* – his use of landscape-description, focalization-shifts, internal audiences, narratorial intervention, and allusion – draws attention in different ways to the moral and political complexities of the violent acts narrated: the unsettling combination of idyllic setting and bodily mutilation in the Actaeon episode, for example, 'exposes the brutality and contradictions that lurk behind the most civilized veneer' and 'invite[s] the reader to engage with the narrator in questioning the violent exercise of divine (or imperial?) authority and justice' (p. 150). At the same time, these episodes can be seen to prompt reflection on the role of the artist, and of language itself, in confrontation with institutions of power. Attempts at silencing may fail, the victim's speech, or art, withstanding repression and surviving to become an instrument of resistance or even (as in the case of Philomela's tapestry) an instigator of violence in its turn.

---

[97] Cf., e.g., Walters 1998; Keane 2006: 42–5.

[98] See, e.g., Curran 1978; Richlin 1992c, esp. 162–6; C. P. Segal 1994; Enterline 2000: 1–11, 31–5, 74–90.

An analogous interrogation of normative power-relations can be seen to be implicit in Apuleius' *Golden Ass*. In his reading of this text (Chapter 10), William Fitzgerald argues that the shifts in narrative perspective entailed by the metamorphosis of the first-person narrator, Lucius, into an ass emphasize status-differences, and call into question the right of the more powerful to abuse the disempowered (animal or slave) victim. Because Lucius both does and does not identify himself with his animal form, his matter-of-fact accounts of and even jokes about the violence repeatedly inflicted on him are startling in a way that Plautus' gallows humour is not: as narrator, he both takes for granted the cruelties perpetrated upon 'his' ass, and invites a horrified sympathy by means of his detailed, first-person accounts of torture and beatings. Again, the fates of slave-characters are typically made light of or taken for granted in Apuleius' novel; but the fact that the narrator is himself in a similarly subordinate position tends to ironize this lofty indifference.

Violence and power are associated in a rather different way by the Epicurean Lucretius, who, on Monica Gale's analysis in Chapter 2, tends to connect physical suffering and bodily mutilation not with the enforcement of normative values or the abuse of power but with competition for political office, social status, and material goods. Like the poets of narrative epic, Lucretius confronts his reader with strikingly detailed images of wounding and dismemberment; in pursuit of his Epicurean message, however, he portrays warfare and other kinds of conflict not as heroic enterprises inspired by the quest for glory, but as pointlessly destructive consequences of a desire for these ultimately empty goals. In this context, Lucretius' graphic vignettes appear designed to elicit a viscerally negative reaction, inviting an empathetic participation in the victims' suffering. Yet, at the same time, the poem seeks to impress on us that the death and decay of our own bodies is something we must all learn to face with indifference; furthermore, the convinced Epicurean disciple will *ipso facto* be removed from situations in which violence is likely to occur. In the rhetorical economy of the *De rerum natura* (Gale argues) violent spectacle thus plays a dual role, alternately engaging and distancing the reader: the poet demands that we both identify with and objectify the victims and indeed the perpetrators of violence, as exemplars of the kind of self-destructive behaviour in which the unconverted reader remains caught up, but from which he is urged to separate himself. Gale sees a suggestive analogy in arena spectacle: if the gladiator invites both hostility (as low-status other) and admiration (for his exemplary display of courage, skill, and endurance), so too Lucretius' reader should experience the contrary pulls of objectification and identification. But in Lucretius the gladiatorial model is inverted, in the sense that the 'other' in question is the overtly successful public figure, and the *exemplum* is a negative one, showing the reader how *not* to live. In this respect, as in others, the *De rerum natura* is iconoclastic, rejecting the conventional role of violence in Roman male self-definition, and idealizing instead a heroism based on 'words, not arms'.[99]

Taken together, these various perspectives suggest a more complex relation between textual violence and hegemonic social structures than that posited earlier. While in general it may be said that the kind of relation outlined on p. 19 is borne out by the texts investigated in this volume, it is clear that at least some works of Latin literature lend themselves to a more oppositional reading: violent acts may be depicted in such a way as to challenge or at least call into question the social hierarchies, power-relations, and dominant ideology of Roman society. This observation will be of some significance when we come to consider the potential impact of textual violence on the reader in Section V.

## IV  Violence, Gender, and Sexuality

As we have already seen, violence in Roman ideology and in Latin literature is closely correlated with gender. With some notable exceptions, the power to inflict violence lies with the man, while women figure in the passive role as objects or victims of violence.[100] Yet, as we have also observed, the gendering of violence is complicated by the premium laid in the Roman value-system on restraint and self-control: ungoverned or excessive violence may thus be perceived as characteristic of the tyrant or the barbarian, in contrast to the exemplary male citizen.

Several contributors draw attention to various deviations from the normative alignment of violence and gender and normative models of male and female behaviour. In Chapter 6, John Henderson considers the 'pornotopic' aspect of Roman declamation, as framed within the master-narrative of the elder Seneca's *Controversiae* with its all-male cast of declaimers, male narrator (Seneca himself), and male narratees (Seneca's sons). Henderson

---

[99] Lucr. 5.50 *dictis, non armis*. Cf. Gordon 2002, who reads Lucretius' attack on *amor* in the finale to Book 4 as a critique of aggressive male sexuality, and suggestively relates this to the cultural construction of Epicurean philosophy in general as effeminate.

[100] Female agents of violence tend, as we have noted, to be found in contexts where other kinds of social hierarchy cut across gender-categories: thus women may inflict physical punishment on their slaves, and both male and female characters in Ovid's *Metamorphoses* are the victims of vengeful goddesses. Tragic or epic heroines who take on the masculine role as perpetrators of violence are in general marked as transgressive: we may think here of Clytemnestra, Medea, or (more ambiguously) Virgil's Camilla.

argues that the father-son relationship as presented in this text is emblematic of the coercive and censorial role that Seneca constructs for himself as author: the reader, along with the internal audience, is allowed only carefully controlled glimpses of the declaimers' 'exquisitely gross' handling of their violent subject matter, in what Henderson terms a 'managed economy of rhetorical libido' (pp. 188, 213). The fragmented and discontinuous character of the work, accompanied by the narrator's often disapproving commentary on the style and technique of the declaimers he quotes, has the effect of constantly offering and yet repeatedly withholding the prospect of 'sadistic drooling over body-tearing and excruciation' (p. 188). While the violence thematized within the declamations from which Seneca quotes is often gendered (women feature notably as rape- and torture-victims, their violated bodies verbally displayed for contemplation by the audience[101]), so too is the framing emphasis on (male) (self-)control: the repeated admonition against unrestrained indulgence in such voyeuristic pleasures – represented as tasteless at best – is, on Henderson's reading, central to Seneca's purposes. Again, as Henderson shows, Seneca lays emphasis on the rivalry between declaimers: in this respect the practice of declamation may be said to instantiate the aggressively competitive character of Roman elite culture in general, but, at the same time, Seneca's critique suggests the ever-present risk of straying into an un-Roman (and unmasculine) excess.

By contrast, Propertius, Tibullus, and Ovid overtly present themselves in just such an uncontrolled, excessive posture, self-consciously adopting the culturally devalued role of the effeminized male, subservient both to his passion and to the *puella* who is its object. Yet, as Donncha O'Rourke demonstrates in Chapter 4, the recurrent episodes of threatened or actual violence that punctuate the elegiac love affair may serve to normalize the disruption of gender- and status-hierarchies paraded by the poems' speakers. Even in such poems as Propertius 3.8 and 4.8, where the lover appears at first glance to accept or even celebrate the unmanly role of victim of his girl's violent rage, an underlying appeal to norms of masculinity can be glimpsed: the lover wears his mistress' bites and scratches with pride, as quasi-heroic 'war wounds' (3.8.21–2), while the authority apparently arrogated by Cynthia in 4.8 is tellingly described as 'granted' to her (*imperio . . . dato*, 4.8.82) – a phrase which (O'Rourke argues) implies a deliberate concession by the lover 'for his own titilla-tion' (p. 123). And yet (again), if this renders the elegists' self-presentation less provocative and more ideologically conservative than

---

[101] See esp. *Controv.* 2.5, discussed by Henderson, Chapter 6, pp. 191–4 below.

it initially appears, Ovid in particular suggests a further perspective, in which issues of interpretation are foregrounded, with the opening up of a marked gap between poet and speaker, addressee and reader. The near-juxtaposition, for instance, of *Amores* 1.5 (in which Corinna is described as putting up a *show* of resistance to her lover's attempts to disrobe her) and 1.7 (a hyperbolical expression of contrition for having assaulted her) invites the reader to ask just how 'real' the resistance of the former poem, or the regret of the latter, should be taken to be. Similarly, the account of the rape of the Sabine women at *Ars amatoria* 1.89–134 thematizes viewing, in a way that challenges us to interrogate our own role as consumers of the titillating spectacle of female terror. Arguably, then, Ovid's (to us) startlingly direct assertion that 'no' means 'yes' (*Ars am.* 1.673–6) invites deconstruction, and the Ovidian corpus as a whole may be read as either critiquing or reinforcing Roman gender-norms – a dilemma that is not, in O'Rourke's view, susceptible of any final resolution.

The elder Seneca and the elegists, then, in their different ways, hold up the (damaged) female body as an object of desire for the male reader; and something similar turns out to be the case, more startlingly, in the Christian texts analysed by David Scourfield in Chapter 11. The persecuted heroines of Jerome, *Letter* 1, and Prudentius, *Peristephanon* 14, both exemplify the central Christian virtues of chastity and faith in God: one a wife falsely accused of adultery, the other a consecrated virgin, they refuse to yield to secular authority, even when faced with torture or execution. As Scourfield shows, the violence to which both women are subjected is strikingly sexualized through the use of metaphorical language: one heroine renders her executioner symbolically impotent, her body proving impene-trable by the sword; the other goes eagerly to meet her own metaphorical deflowering at the hands of her killer, who will (paradoxically) deliver her up, through her death, to 'marriage' with Christ. In both cases, these quasi-sexual assaults are connected with an arresting thematization of the gaze. While Jerome's unnamed heroine is presented, more conventionally, as the object of the male gaze – that of the bloodthirsty governor who orders her torture and execution – Prudentius' Agnes may be seen to appropriate it, directing her own assertively desiring look towards her executioner. The two texts thus problematize the relation between violence, gender, and desire in a Christian context. The prurient, voyeuristic appeal implicit in Jerome's account of his tortured heroine's sufferings appears at variance with the didactic purpose of the letter; Agnes in Prudentius' poem is presented as at once a model of chastity and – disturbingly, in the Roman context – a female with her own desires, who actively welcomes the highly sexualized violence with which she is confronted.

As Scourfield notes in the course of his discussion (p. 317), the metaphorical equation between the penis and the sword is frequently found in Latin literature.[102] A connection between sex and violence is thus embedded in the very language in which sexual acts are commonly described, particularly in humorous or euphemistic contexts. Both (active, penetrative) sex and the capacity for certain kinds of violence connote masculine potency; in Foucauldian terms, Roman constructions of sexuality and violence map on to each other, each constituting a vehicle for the expression of normative power-relations. Yet, as we have seen, this straightforward paradigm is subject in various ways to disruption and interrogation. Even while Seneca in the *Controversiae* recalls the salacious depictions of female victims in Roman declamation, he seeks to impose limits on the representation of violence and its reception by (male) audiences. In a similar way, both elegy and the Christian texts discussed by Scourfield can be read as simultaneously challenging and accommodating, or even reinforcing, the discourses of Roman patriarchy.

## V   Violence and the Reader

Scourfield's analysis of the narrative complexities of the two texts he examines opens up some broad questions of obvious relevance to all literary representations of violence and their potential impact on the reader. To what extent might it be claimed that readers are invited to share the sadistic pleasures enjoyed by such figures as Jerome's provincial governor, to experience a vicarious thrill at the depiction of female torture-victims? How far can the pressures which literary texts exert on their readers to adopt a particular perspective on the actions represented be resisted? Alternatively, is it possible for literary texts to impose limits on their own reception? Here we touch on issues which have been central to both scholarly and popular discussion of media violence in recent decades: Why is it that readers and viewers find depictions of violence appealing? What does the popularity of such depictions say about modern Western

---

[102] Cf. O'Rourke, Chapter 4, p. 131 below, Adams 1982: 19–22; Adams notes that 'this [sc. the penis-as-weapon] is the largest category of metaphors of our general type [sc. those involving sharp or pointed instruments, itself the most extensive of Adams' categories]' (19). Similarly, Adams' discussion of 'The Vocabulary Relating to Sexual Acts' (chapter 5) includes several categories indicative of a connection between sex and violence: '"Strike" and the like' ('one of the largest semantic fields from which metaphors for sexual acts were taken', 145), 145–9; '"Cut, split, penetrate" and the like', 149–51; 'Wound', 152; 'Wrestle, fight', 157–9; 'Kill, die', 159.

(and other) societies? And, perhaps most pressingly of all, what effect, if any, does repeated exposure to such depictions have on audiences?

Contributors to this volume respond to these questions in a variety of ways, which may usefully be considered in conjunction with modern work on cinema and television in particular. It is in these fields that the relation between 'text' and reader has been most fiercely contested, and the battle-lines most clearly drawn between proponents of different theoretical positions; moreover, film- and cultural theory have typically concerned themselves more directly and in more general terms with violence and its representation than have literary studies. At the same time, our strategy of applying such models to classical texts finds justification in ancient reading practices: Graeco-Roman literary and rhetorical theory indicates not only that vivid visual impact (*enargeia*) was something sought after by orators and other writers, but that visualization was widely understood as a crucial element in the experience of the reader or audience, and one inculcated in the young in the course of their education.[103] In this light, the apparent gap between literary and cinematic or televisual texts is minimized, if not closed altogether.

Modern theorists have generally approached the relationship between representations of violence and the pleasure experienced by spectators/readers from two distinct but convergent directions.[104] One line follows the highly influential theory of viewing pleasure and the gaze established by the film-theorist Laura Mulvey, who draws on Freudian psychoanalysis to construct a model in which the viewer is very strongly gendered as male, and the object of the gaze as female.[105] Focusing on classic Hollywood

---

[103] On the importance of visualization in ancient reading practice and theory, see Webb 2009: 19–25, 95–6. We might also think in this connection of the Epicurean therapeutic practice of 'setting before the eyes', discussed by Gale, Chapter 2, pp. 65–6 below.

[104] On psychoanalytic and ideological models in film-theory see, e.g., Mayne 1993: 13–52.

[105] Mulvey 1975; cf. Berger 1972: 45–64 on the gendered gaze in European painting, esp. 47 '*Men act and women appear*. Men look at women. Women watch themselves being looked at.' Mulvey's argument has been much challenged and modified in more recent work on spectatorship and the gaze, but her influence remains profound. Criticism has been directed in particular at her marginalization of the female spectator, associated with the connection posited in her essay between (cinematic) scopophilia/voyeurism and Freudian theories of castration anxiety, and the monolithic quality of her model, which fails to allow for other possible forms of cinematic pleasure or a more mobile subject-position; see, e.g., Studlar 1988, esp. 1–8, Clover 1992, esp. 205–30, Mayne 1993: 70–6, Stacey 1994: 19–48, as well as Mulvey's own 'afterthoughts' on female spectatorship in Mulvey 1981. A helpful overview of more recent theory may be found in Sturken and Cartwright 2009: 130–6. Among others, Studlar and Clover explore the possibility that the (male or female) viewer may under certain circumstances identify masochistically with screen victims, linking this with the flexibility of subject-position characteristic of fantasy; the theory of a 'submissive' or 'reactive' gaze developed by these critics has suggestive resonances with the line of approach taken by several contributors to this book. Fredrick 2002b, esp. 13–16, considers the applicability of Mulvey's and

cinema, Mulvey identifies two forms which such pleasure may take. One form, which she terms 'fetishistic scopophilia', consists in the pleasure derived from looking at idealized objects. In the other form, sadistic voyeurism, pleasure and violence are intimately related. Here, pleasure arises from the degradation and punishment of the female, as a means of allaying unconscious anxieties relating to gender-difference. Mulvey argues that the viewer is typically invited to align himself (or herself; on Mulvey's model, the female viewer's only option is complicity with the gender-paradigms offered by the cinematic text) with the male protagonist, often a figure of authority; the pleasures of spectatorship are thus constituted both by a vicarious satisfaction of fantasies and repressed desires and by the reconfirmation of socially constructed hierarchies of gender and power.

Alongside Mulvey's psychoanalytic mode of interpretation are approaches informed by theories of ideology, particularly Althusserian Marxism. On this view, the cinema functions as an ideological apparatus which serves (along with other such institutions) to strengthen and per-petuate existing social structures and their ideological underpinnings. A number of recent studies of media violence accordingly emphasize the direct relationship between audience enjoyment and the confirmation of normative values: depictions of violence are enjoyable when its victims are those who have offended against the moral norms espoused by the audi-ence, so that their punishment may be viewed as justifiable.[106] To put this differently, the audience is invited to form affective bonds ('identify')[107] with characters whose behaviour ultimately tends to confirm rather than disrupt the existing social and moral order, whose violent acts – however extreme – can be seen to serve the interests of the community or society at large.[108] Again, it has been argued that the victims of screen violence are typically representatives of groups that are in some way 'other': in this

other modern theories of the gaze to the Roman world; for constructive engagement with such theories in the reading of particular Latin texts see, e.g., Benton 2002, Eldred 2002, Salzman-Mitchell 2005, Lovatt 2013, Scourfield, Chapter 11, pp. 321–4 below. On the complexity of 'scopic paradigms' and different kinds of gaze (evaluative v. assaultive/penetrative, one-way v. reciprocal, etc.) in Roman culture, see Bartsch 2006: 115–64.

[106] See in particular Zillmann 1998, esp. 199–209; also Plantinga 1997: 387–9. Cf. Fagan 2011a: 174–88 on 'ingroup' attitudes among Roman arena crowds, noting his emphasis on the importance of 'legitimacy in victim-selection' (175) in shaping the response of spectators to the punishment of the condemned.

[107] We do not here address the complexities of the concept of 'identification', which is generally held to involve affective (empathetic/sympathetic) responses but is not reducible to such terms *tout court*. For helpful observations, see Stacey 1994: 130, Gervais 2013: 139 with n. 3, Lovatt 2013: 121, with further bibliography.

[108] Cf., e.g., Carter and Weaver 2003: 81–7 on the representation of 'legitimate' and 'illegitimate' violence in television crime shows.

connection we may think of the female victims conventional in horror and crime drama alike.[109] Such conventions, by normalizing certain kinds of violence and by confirming the sense that certain groups, or types of people, are either legitimate targets of violence or vulnerable and in need of protection by those in positions of power, arguably serve to reinforce the hierarchical relations that structure society.

Common to both these approaches is an implicit perception that the emotional appeal of cinema, television, and similar media has a powerful and insidious effect upon the audience – a perception that finds interesting parallels in ancient theories of literature and spectatorship. In the Graeco-Roman context, such judgements are clearly related to the intellectualism, and the predominantly negative attitude towards emotion in general, displayed by all the major philosophical schools. Plato's critique of myth and poetry in the *Republic* (2.376e–3.402a; 10.595a–608b) turns in part on the argument that the mimesis of strong emotions, or of individuals of bad character, will impact negatively on the moral constitution of performer and audience: drawn by the charms of poetry into a kind of empathy or imaginative identification with models of inappropriate behaviour, we ultimately internalize a false set of values, and through the vicarious experience of emotion weaken the rational part of ourselves, with deleterious consequences.[110] In the Roman context, such anxieties are compounded by a sense that the pleasure derived from spectacular entertainments is itself damaging. Such entertainments are not infrequently referred to under the general rubric of *voluptates*, and the sensual pleasure they convey represented as corrupt and corrupting.[111] An important

---

[109] The director Brian de Palma is explicit about the gendering of victims in the thriller genre: 'I'm always attacked for having an erotic, sexist approach – chopping up women, putting women in peril. I'm making suspense movies! What else is going to happen to them?' (quoted in Carter and Weaver 2003: 42); similar sentiments are expressed by Alfred Hitchcock and the slasher-movie director Dario Argento, as quoted by Clover 1992: 42. We might also recall in this connection Poe's commonly quoted assertion that 'the death ... of a beautiful woman is, unquestionably, the most poetical topic in the world' (Poe 1846: 165 = 1984: 19, discussed by Bronfen 1992: 59–75); with this as epigraph, Keith 2000: 101–31 explores the prominence of the (frequently violent) deaths of beautiful women in Roman epic. On female victims of violence in film, see further Clover 1992, esp. 32–41, Carter and Weaver 2003: 52–3, 55–8, 63–4; following de Lauretis 1987: 42–4, Clover argues (12–13) that feminine gendering is inherent in the narrative function of the victim, in contrast to the active, masculine role of hero, while Bronfen 1992, in the course of a wide-ranging study of death and femininity in both visual media and written texts, considers the image of the dead or dying woman as a symbol for the radical 'otherness' of death itself. For the victim as other, see also Sontag 2003: 63–5, who points to a tendency on the part of news media to depict the dead, dying, and seriously injured in full frontal view only in the case of enemy casualties or of inhabitants of 'remote or exotic' locations.

[110] See the fine discussion of Ferrari 1989, esp. 108–11 and 134–41; also Ford 2002: 216–26.

[111] See, e.g., Cic. *Mur.* 73–4, Tac. *Ann.* 14.20–1, Tert. *De spect.* 1, August. *Conf.* 6.8.13 (quoted in part above, n. 48); for further discussion, Wistrand 1992: 11–14, C. Edwards 1997: 83–5, Benton 2002:

witness to this characteristically Roman suspicion of visual pleasure is Seneca's *Letter* 7, mentioned briefly above (p. 12).[112] In this letter, Seneca describes with distaste a recent visit to the arena, where he witnessed bouts to the death between condemned criminals unequipped with protective armour – in effect, public executions.[113] The issue in this passage is not the violence itself (Seneca states explicitly that the victims deserve to die); rather, what he condemns as a source of corruption is the sadistic pleasure that the crowd derives from the show (*mane leonibus et ursis homines, meridie spectatoribus suis obiciuntur*, 'in the morning men are thrown to the lions and bears, at midday to their own spectators', 7.4). To take delight in killing for its own sake is, for Seneca, a mark of inhumanity;[114] the individual audience-member becomes crueller and less human(e) (*crudelior et inhumanior*, 7.3) as a result of this shared experience. Here the Stoic philosopher presents the group solidarity of the arena crowd in a negative light, as something that exacerbates the individual's vulnerability to pleasure in general.

On the whole, Roman writers do not extend their strictures against the pleasures of spectacle to literary texts, the pleasures of which are apt to be classified as intellectual rather than sensual.[115] As we noted above, however, the visual element is strongly emphasized in ancient literary and rhetorical theory, and many of the texts under consideration in this book accordingly draw on the techniques of *enargeia*, or make prominent use of internal audiences and the inscribed gaze. The anxieties relating to the pleasure derived from witnessing acts of violence to which Seneca attests may thus legitimately be taken to extend into the literary sphere, even if Seneca did not himself make this connection: if the experience of the spectator in the arena renders him (or her) 'crueller and less human(e)', it is reasonable to think that consumers of textualized violence might be affected similarly.

For both Plato and Seneca, it is the potentially antisocial effects of literary mimesis or spectacular entertainment that are especially disturbing: for these theorists, the seductions of myth and poetry, or the attractions of

---

40–1, Bartsch 2006: 155, 160–3. Frequenting the games is habitually treated in our elite sources as a low pleasure, in contrast to the more refined attractions of (especially) literature and philosophy; see, e.g., Cic. *Fam.* 7.1, Hor. *Epist.* 1.14.15 (cf. 21–6), Sen. *Ep.* 80.2, 88.21–3, Plin. *Ep.* 9.6.

[112] Note the explicit reference to *voluptas* at 7.2.

[113] Sen. *Ep.* 7.2–5. For the distinction between gladiators proper and *noxii* destined for execution, see Kyle 1998: 91–4.

[114] A recurrent theme in Seneca's writings: see, e.g., *Ep.* 95.33, *Clem.* 1.25.1–2, *De ira* 1.6.4, 2.5.

[115] For the opposition between *ludi/spectacula* and *artes liberales* see n. 111 above; cf. also Hor. *Epist.* 2.1.182–213 (theatrical spectacle downgraded in contrast to poetic *psychagogia*).

sensational sights and sounds on stage and in the arena, have a tendency to weaken the individual's sense of moral rectitude and so to undermine normative values. In this respect Seneca, in particular, seems closer to proponents of behavioural-effects theories in the modern debate on media violence than to ideological critics, who, by contrast, see most screen violence as reinforcing existing power-relations and social structures. Numerous sociological and psychological studies have set out to examine the (possible) impact of screen violence on viewers; though the issue remains highly controversial, one prominent school of thought holds that repeated exposure to depictions of violence is apt to result in increased aggression and/or desensitization to the suffering of 'real-life' victims.[116] The debate has gained a particular urgency from the supposition that it is possible to trace a direct causal relationship between particular violent acts in the real world and the prior viewing habits of the perpetrators, with accompanying calls for the imposition of more rigorous censorship on the cinema and other media.[117]

A criticism which has been raised against both the ideological and the media-effects model of spectatorship is that the approach in each case tends to flatten out the diversity of individual response to the viewing experience, portraying the audience as passively positioned by the representational strategies of the cinematic text. To be sure, ideological critics regularly distinguish between the cinematic *subject* – a position constructed *by* a particular film and the cinematic apparatus in general – and the *individual* viewer. Yet this distinction has not always given sufficient recognition to the capacity of the individual to read critically, to exercise a faculty of choice between different possible subject-positions.[118] In this connection, we might invoke – in opposition to the Platonic model, according to which literary and visual texts operate *on* the reader/spectator – Aristotle's rather different understanding of the relationship between text and receiver as expressed in the *Poetics* and elsewhere. As is well known, Aristotle relegates the spectacular aspect of tragedy to a position of relatively minor importance (*Poetics* 6 (1450b), 14 (1453b)), emphasizing instead a more active intellectual engagement on the part of the audience. For Aristotle, literary or viewing pleasure is above all a matter of recognition, where the

---

[116] For discussion of media-effects research and its associated controversies, see, e.g., Berkowitz 2000; Felson 2000; Prince 2000b: 19–25, 39–40; Barker and Petley 2001a; Carter and Weaver 2003: 1–17.

[117] Cf. Scourfield, Chapter 11, p. 337 below, on putative connections between Oliver Stone's *Natural Born Killers* and the Dunblane massacre.

[118] Cf. Mayne 1993: 53–102; Plantinga 1997.

audience's enjoyment is derived not from the intrinsic appeal of what is represented, but from the skill with which it is represented, and from our perception of the relationship between the thing represented and its representation. Extrapolating from Aristotle's explicit statements, Duncan Kennedy suggests (Chapter 7, pp. 217–19 below) that on this model the pleasure of tragedy (and, by the same token, of tragic violence) lies in the way in which pain and suffering are rendered meaningful and intelligible by the framework of the drama.[119]

Alongside theories that represent spectatorship as a one-way process, in which the viewer is positioned as subject by the conventions of the spectacle itself, we may, therefore, place a more dynamic model of critical interaction between film and audience, text and reader. Naturally, critical engagement on the part of the reader or viewer is not itself situated 'outside' ideology; but it seems important to recognize that ideology is not in itself something monolithic, and that our response to a film or other work of art will be conditioned by our specific cultural context and our character as individuals, as well as by the subject-position(s) offered to us by the cinematic or literary text. As Carl Plantinga puts it, 'audience response lies at the intersections of individual and general spectator characteristics, specific context, and textual cues'.[120]

Questions relating to the pleasures of spectatorship, and more specifically the pleasures of violent spectacle, are addressed directly by several of the contributors to the present volume. The theory of cinema as ideological apparatus and of cinematic spectatorship as a vehicle for the reinforcement and legitimation of the dominant ideology has its counterpart in the tendency discussed above for representations of violence in Latin literature to align themselves with normative values and social hierarchies. Thus the violence of comedy is entertaining rather than disturbing because on the whole its victims are slaves, whose bodies are legitimately subject to the physical chastisement from which citizens are exempt. Yet David Konstan's analysis identifies further, complicating factors which – though ultimately converging with this legitimation of cultural norms – point to a rather different model for the experience of the audience. Konstan offers a suggestive parallel between the conventions of Roman comedy and the modern cartoon: Wile E. Coyote or Tom and

---

[119] Generally helpful is Belfiore 1992: 45–70.

[120] Plantinga 1997: 382. Fagan 2011a: 124–5, 136–7, similarly stresses that the experience of ancient arena crowds should not be thought of as uniform and unvarying, but as dynamically shaped by a range of factors.

Jerry invite our laughter rather than our sympathy because the violence to which they are endlessly subjected is without consequences – the flattened, electrocuted, or otherwise mangled character is miraculously restored in the next frame, and the chase continues.[121] Our familiarity with the conventions of genre, then, will to a considerable extent condition our experience of textualized or screen violence, and our reactions to it. Further, as in the case of Sceledrus in Plautus' *Miles gloriosus* or Tranio in the *Mostellaria*, violent treatment is on the whole a *threat* held over the slave, rather than an *act* perpetrated on him during the course of the drama.[122] Following Erich Segal's influential study, much informed by Freud,[123] Konstan suggests (p. 54) that the pleasure of comedy is founded in part on the vicarious satisfaction of repressed desires, as the audience is invited to respond positively to the clever slave's triumphant flouting of patriarchal authority and his evasion of punishment. Yet this element of carnivalesque inversion is, arguably, contained by the strong demarcation between theatre and ordinary life, holiday and workday, and subsumed by the shared assumption that, despite the temporary deferral of the threatened punishment, the slave's body is nevertheless legitimately subject to violent treatment.[124]

If, for Konstan, the pleasure of comedic violence lies at once in its temporary inversion and its confirmation in the longer term of existing social hierarchies and power-relations, other works examined in this book may be seen to deploy violent episodes in ways that are more unsettling and challenging for the reader. Newlands, Kennedy, and Fitzgerald, in particular, advance interpretations of their text's construction of its reader which suggest a model very different from Mulvey's (envisaging the vicarious satisfaction of desire) or from those espoused by certain media-effects theorists (for whom violence in film and television drama tends in practice to affirm group solidarity and reinforce hegemonic power-structures, while appealing to the audience's appetite for emotional

---

[121] Compare the distinction posited in McKinney 2000 between 'strong' and 'weak' portrayals of cinematic violence: the former have regard for the consequences of violent acts, and seek to arouse the empathetic involvement of the viewer, while the latter 'by refusing a full commitment to their own content . . . resist a viewer's emotional investment' (108). Cf. also the suggestive discussion by Charney 2001: 58–60 of 'the cartoonish quality of violence [sc. in action movies] and the violent quality of cartoons' (59).

[122] Cf. E. Segal 1987: 141: 'Plautus abounds in threats; tortures are enumerated with minute specificity – and then never carried out.' For Sceledrus and Tranio, see Konstan/Raval, Chapter 1, pp. 48–9, 51–4 below.

[123] E. Segal 1987.

[124] Cf. H. N. Parker 1989: 246: 'The wish for rebellion is indulged, but the fear of rebellion is pacified'; McCarthy 2000, esp. 17–29; Stewart 2012: 95–116.

stimulation).[125] These three scholars all represent the texts which they investigate as setting out in various ways to discomfort the reader: experiencing fictional violence through reading and visualization may, they suggest, be painful rather than (or as well as) pleasurable.

Thus Newlands draws attention to the interplay, in Ovid's vivid depiction of violence in the *Metamorphoses*, between spectacularity and interiority. Various features of style and narrative technique – including the often comic and/or highly stylized treatment of violent episodes, and the aestheticization of violated bodies and of the idyllic settings in which such episodes commonly occur – tend to distance the reader and objectify the victims of the violence; yet the poem's 'shifting perspectives' (p. 141) often seem, equally, to invite or encourage the reader to empathize with the suffering hero or heroine. On Newlands' reading, the voyeuristic pleasures of violent spectacle serve here not (just) as an end in themselves, but as a lure or sweetener by which the reader is drawn in, only to find him- or herself compelled to confront difficult issues in the sphere of power-relations and the sociopolitical order.

We may note in passing that the dialectic between objectification and involvement posited by Newlands finds intriguing parallels in texts considered by other contributors. Gale, for instance, argues that the rhetoric of Lucretius' *De rerum natura* relies on a kind of alternation between the spectacular presentation of violence, in which those on whom it is inflicted are distanced and objectified, and passages in which we are invited to feel empathy with its victims.[126] Similarly, the heroines of the Christian texts discussed by Scourfield are both objects of the gaze and *exempla* whose subjective experience of faith and suffering is critical to their ideological impact. In all these cases, the *pleasurable* viewing of violence seems to depend on spectacularization, whether the enjoyment involved is something approaching *Schadenfreude* (as in Lucretius, who celebrates the

---

[125] Goldstein 1998b offers a helpful synoptic survey of sociological theories concerning the attractions of violent entertainment. It should once again be noted in this connection that Mulvey is explicitly addressing classic, Hollywood cinema, as opposed to the avant-garde; media-effects studies, similarly, tend, for obvious reasons, to be concerned primarily with the mass consumption of popular entertainment. Roman literature, in contrast, was – as has often been observed – created in the main both by and for the cultivated elite (Plautus and Terence representing a partial exception in this regard). It should thus come as no surprise that the relation of our texts to ideological norms is more complicated and self-conscious than in the case of (much) modern cinema or television; this does not of course invalidate the application of modern theories of media violence to ancient texts, but we need to exercise a degree of caution in comparing what are not after all wholly compatible bodies of material.

[126] For analysis along similar lines of spectatorship in Lucan's *Pharsalia*, see Leigh 1997, esp. 234–91.

observer's gratifying awareness of the gulf that separates him from the sufferings of others[127]), or more closely resembles the pleasures of fetishistic scopophilia and sadistic voyeurism theorized by Mulvey (the aestheticized violence of Ovid's *Metamorphoses*; Jerome's sexualized torture-victim). Yet in each case these spectacular pleasures destabilize, or are destabilized by, a contrary pull towards the vicarious experience of pain and suffering.

In the *Golden Ass*, Fitzgerald sees Apuleius going further in the same direction, 'persecuting' his reader by piling on one gruesome incident after another while focalizing the entire novel through the eyes of the sometimes detached but frequently suffering Lucius. Fitzgerald relates the dynamics of the picaresque fiction to those of the torture-chamber: inherent in torture is a tension between the urge to destroy the victim and a desire to preserve him or her in order to prolong the suffering; so, in an episodic narrative where closure is often achieved through the death and even complete obliteration of the protagonist, the reader longs simultaneously for the cessation and the continuation of the narrator's sufferings. The cruelty of Lucius' experiences, Fitzgerald argues, is both emblematic of the violence that characterizes the world in which the story is set and at the same time an arbitrary choice on the part of the author, with whom the reader is compelled to collude: the role of Fortuna as Lucius' persecutor tropes that of the writer but also in part that of the reader. And yet the first-person narration uncomfortably precludes a straightforward objectification of the hero: Apuleius' reader is both persecutor and persecuted, aligned alternately with the torturer and the victim of violence.

Taking a rather different line, Kennedy (Chapter 7) interprets the infamous final scene of Seneca's *Phaedra* as denying the audience any comfortable resolution. If the pleasure of tragic violence is indeed derived from the tendency of tragedy to impose form and meaning on what might otherwise appear senseless and unintelligible, such pleasure is in this case refused to us. The concluding scene offers itself as a metatheatrical trope for the work's resistance to closure. Theseus' inability to make sense of the fragmentary remains of his son's body can be read as an emblem of our

---

[127] Lucr. 2.1–13. With regard to this passage, Lucretius has been both charged with and exculpated of a callous delight in the sufferings of others (see, e.g., Barigazzi 1987; D. Fowler 2002: 37–41; Konstan 2008: 29–37); it should, certainly, be noted that the passage conveys nothing of the malice usually implied by the German word (or its Greek equivalent *epichairekakia*), and that Lucretius in fact responds in anticipation to such a criticism at vv. 3–4. For the notion that the spectacle of suffering may serve as, among other things, a kind of foil or intensifier with respect to our own sense of well-being, cf. Sontag 2003: 88–9.

own confusion and puzzlement with regard to the narrative itself. The consequent discomfort we experience may partly explain why critics have often found the play's ending absurd, as anxiety is displaced into laughter and derision. At the same time, Theseus' attempts to reassemble Hippolytus' dismembered corpse mirror the critic's (inevitably incomplete and frustrated) attempts to 'anatomize' the text and 'reconstitute' it in his or her own terms: the conclusion of the play figures the inadequacy and provisionality of all literary interpretation.

These three chapters taken together, then, suggest that Latin texts across a broad generic and chronological range exploit representations of violence as a means of challenging the reader and impelling us to confront and interrogate the nature of our own reactions to textualized (and societal) violence. In Chapter 8, in contrast, Efrossini Spentzou draws on theories of the abject and the sublime to suggest that the discomfort experienced by the reader of Lucan's *Pharsalia* (*De bello civili*) may constitute a kind of pleasure in itself. Lucan's Caesar, she argues, is a troubling figure because of his transgression of cultural norms as well as of physical and psychological boundaries – a kind of metaphorical violence, perhaps co-ordinate with the poem's very marked emphasis on the mutilation and destruction of human bodies. Caesar's excess and unpredictability almost defy representation; so central to his identity are conflict and the desire for conflict that he might even be understood as an embodiment of violence in the absolute. For Spentzou, the violent emotions aroused in other characters by Caesar's words and actions may be held to shape and direct those of the reader: the appropriate reaction is one of mingled horror and amazement, a combination characteristic of the (Kantian) sublime. Lucan's hero is thus 'catastrophic and irresistible at the same time' (p. 267), offering, in Lacanian terms, a glimpse of the Real lurking beneath the veneer of the Symbolic. Far from affirming normative values, the *Pharsalia* represents a kind of collapse into meaninglessness, as Caesar annihilates the moribund polity of the Republic (perhaps even Law itself), and ushers in the 'dazzling emptiness' of the Imperial era (p. 268).

While, therefore, we may accept that textualized violence plays to the reader's unconscious desires and anxieties, it seems clear that we should resist the assumption that its effects are simply and solely the vicarious satisfaction of those desires or allaying of those anxieties. By the same token, while ancient literature, like the modern cinema, may function in part as an ideological apparatus, individual works may equally prompt interrogation of, rather than reiterate and reinforce, prevailing cultural assumptions. A pressing question which has been raised most explicitly in Ovidian studies[128] is the extent to which the reader/critic is necessarily complicit, through the very act of reading, with the violence inflicted on characters – particularly women and representatives of other disempowered groups – within the diegetic world. A different kind of relationship between implied author and reader – more disjunctive, even antagonistic – may, however, be observed in some of the texts examined in this volume; at the extreme, the reader may even be cast as the *victim* (figuratively speaking) of discursive violence. Such a relationship is posited most explicitly in Fitzgerald's study of Apuleius, but we should note too the observation of Newlands (p. 142), following Garth Tissol, that the 'aggressive linguistic, emotional, and ethical demands' imposed by Ovid on his reader may themselves be troped as violence. Again, far from inviting complicity between author and reader, Seneca's *Phaedra* seeks (on Kennedy's interpretation) to engage the reader actively in the (re)construction of meaning, as we join with Theseus in attempting to reassemble the dissociated *membra* of the textual body.

Kennedy's metatheatrical reading of the conclusion of the younger Seneca's drama displays interesting affinities with John Henderson's dissection of the elder Seneca's *Controversiae*. Here, the fragmented accounts of physical violence which Seneca *père* reports and the concomitant discontinuity of the text as a whole are linked to the coercive relationship between author/narrator and reader ('forcing declamation through his shredder, while vetting it positively and negatively for (un)Roman tendencies, amounts to a violent psycho-graphematic project', p. 184); violence features in yet another way in the aggressive competition *amongst* the declaimers themselves, which may itself be troped in terms of armed combat ('this "off-duty" jousting between courtier glitterati and gurus', p. 179).[129] Henderson teases out Seneca's self-fashioning throughout (what remains of) the work as an icon of patriarchal authority: the narrator's role is not only to comment on, but to regulate his internal and external readers' consumption of, the often violent tableaux created and elaborated on by the declaimers he quotes. The fragmented and disjointed character of this text 'makes for instructively painful reading' (p. 183): for Henderson, Seneca is decidedly not in the business of allowing us to linger over the voyeuristic pleasures that were, it seems, the declaimers' stock-in-trade. If declamation 'knowingly skirts,

---

[128] In relation to the *Metamorphoses*, first by Richlin 1992c; cf. C. P. Segal 1994, and, for a more general discussion of spectacularity and (the problematics of) resistant reading, Sharrock 2002.

[129] Note especially the comparison between declaimers and (pairs of) gladiators at *Controv.* 4.*Pr.*1. The style of certain declaimers is also characterized by Seneca as 'violent', or represented as 'assaulting' the audience: see Henderson, Chapter 6, p. 183 n. 21.

impinges, and abuts on the fundamental values, taboos, and nightmares at the heart of cultured identity-formation' (p. 214), the same is true, *a fortiori*, of the *Controversiae* itself; yet Seneca, as Henderson shows, exercises a rigorous and self-advertising censorship over the genre's more salacious extremes. The *Controversiae* thus shares with the classic Hollywood cinema analysed by Mulvey a concern with the maintenance of cultural norms, but goes beyond it in its explicit policing of those norms. Further, while the declamations reported by Seneca may serve in part to normalize certain kinds of violence, the narrator's framing commentary marks the voyeuristic pleasures which this genre holds out to its audience as deviant in themselves.

As a whole, then, this collection suggests that a number of determining factors, including genre conventions, narrative techniques, and the roles of narrators and internal audiences, are variously at work in guiding audience response to the texts considered. Representations of violence may be reassuring (in their confirmation of normative values and existing social structures), or discomforting and even painful for the reader; the appeal of the text may lie, in some cases, in intellectual provocation no less than in the vicarious satisfaction of desire.

Some parallels from film and television may usefully be considered in this connection. Probably the most controversial exponent of aestheticized violence in contemporary cinema is Quentin Tarantino; a striking example is his two-part ('two-volume') *Kill Bill* (2003–4), which overtly strives (particularly in Volume 1) for a pictorial and anti-naturalistic presentation of its extremely violent narrative. The self-consciously balletic arrangement of the fight sequences and the deployment of intertexts from the comic-book to the martial-arts movie to the Japanese print (along with distancing techniques such as the use of chapter titles) serve to stylize the entire narrative in such a way that the viewer's attention is continually drawn away from the action itself to the representation as representation: crudely put, we are asked to enjoy the director's brilliance, rather than to engage emotionally with his characters.[130] At the same time, the camera's repeated lingering on the damaged body of the female lead suggests something similar to the kind of voyeuristic appeal described by Mulvey. At the opposite end of the spectrum, we might think of Lee Tamahori's harrowing *Once Were Warriors* (1994), a film that aims for maximum

---

[130] Cf. Gervais 2013, esp. 147–9 on intertextuality as a 'distancing device' in the long final sequence of *Kill Bill: Volume 1*. The phrase 'distancing device' is Tarantino's own; the director continues: 'There's never a moment when I'm telling you this is happening in the real world, when you're not aware you're watching a movie' (quoted by Gervais (148) from a *Sight & Sound* interview, Olsen 2003: 15).

naturalism and goes out of its way to depict domestic violence as in every way repellent: the physical appearance of the heroine following a savage beating is explicitly presented as sexually *unappealing*.[131] Moreover, while the frustration of the abusive husband and his inability to express himself other than through violence are sympathetically explored in the film, it is the abused wife whose viewpoint we are invited to share throughout.

Between these two poles lies an extensive catalogue of movies which seek, overtly or implicitly, to probe, critique, or even condemn the use of violence, while at the same time offering violent acts as spectacle for the audience's gratification. Prominent examples include movies by Sam Peckinpah (*The Wild Bunch*, *Straw Dogs*) and Martin Scorsese (*Taxi Driver*, *Gangs of New York*), both of whom have been attacked for glamorizing violence in spite of the overtly declared aim in each case to deglamorize and critique its use in both cinema and society,[132] and Oliver Stone's self-reflexively satirical *Natural Born Killers* (1994), in which the portrayal of the vicious protagonists may be felt ultimately to buy into the very fascination with gangsterism and serial killing that the film purports to attack.[133] A slightly different but comparable case is afforded by Mel Gibson's *The Passion of the Christ* (2004), which was widely criticized on its release for a prurient interest in torture and physical suffering superficially legitimized by its representation of events at the heart of the Christian gospel-story.[134] To turn from film to television, the legitimacy of state-sponsored violence is itself at stake in the long-running action series *24* (2001–14), with its close-up depictions of torture[135] by US counter-terrorist agents, including the central, essentially approved and heroic, character, Jack Bauer. Torture and other acts of violence are here portrayed as both justified by the urgency of the situation (itself a crucial factor in the

---

[131] Contrast the scene in *Kill Bill: Volume 1* where the central character, the Bride, lying in a hospital bed apparently still in a coma after surviving a murder attempt, is offered by an orderly to a trucker for his sexual use. Gazing at her lecherously, the trucker accepts – with (as it turns out) catastrophic violent consequences for *him*.

[132] See Prince 2000c, esp. 175–8, 197–9; cf. also Chong 2004.

[133] See Scourfield, Chapter 11, pp. 335–6 below, with n. 119.

[134] Thus Kermode 2004 writes of 'a fetishised adulation of super-masochistic screen violence', characterizing the film as a whole as 'an accomplished test of cinematic endurance, a work of low-brow exploitation inspired by the sublimations of high art ... that attempts to trample the audience underfoot while keeping their eyes turned ever heaven-ward'. Especially telling is Gibson's elaboration of the scourging of Jesus from a passing comment in the Gospels (at Matt. 27:25 and Mark 15:15, a minimalist participle) to a brutal eight-minute sequence.

[135] A recurring device in *24* is the display of the torture instruments to the camera and the sight of the victim immediately before their use (see, e.g., Season 4, episodes 3 and 18); with this compare Sen. *Ep.* 14.6, and see further the illuminating discussion of Scarry 1985: 27–8.

creation of suspense so central to the show's appeal) and morally questionable, particularly in the later seasons where Jack himself is increasingly
damaged, psychologically and emotionally, by the harm he inflicts on
others.[136] Depending on how closely the viewer identifies with Jack's
pressing need to deal with an immediate and always dire terrorist threat,
the series might be interpreted either as sanctioning or as problematizing
the use of violent methods in extreme circumstances.[137]

Comparison with modern media helps to make clear, on the one hand,
that (verbal or visual) texts may situate the reader in a variety of positions
with respect to violent subject matter, but, on the other, that textual cues
are not the only factor at work. While many of the contributors to this
volume adopt an approach that represents the text as manipulating the
reader and his or her reactions, others lay more emphasis on the reader's
capacity to exert (more or less conscious) control over his or her response.
Newlands, as we have seen, interprets Ovid's *Metamorphoses* as an open
text, which invites a range of possible responses, while Scourfield similarly
emphasizes the possibility of reading with or against the grain of his
Christian texts; again, Gale, briefly considering the reception history of
Lucretius' poem, argues that the work's didactic aims – like those of
Peckinpah or Scorsese – will not necessarily have their intended effect on
actual readers. Audience reactions are not straightforwardly predictable,
and may indeed be determined in large part by factors external to the text
(including, in the case of Lucretius' post-classical reception, ideologies
incompatible with the poem's Epicurean message). Thus, however much
we might seek to hypostasize the implied reader or cinematic subject, the

---

[136] In a highly critical preview of the show's fifth season, Žižek 2006 objects to what he calls 'the lie of
24: that it is not only possible to retain human dignity in performing acts of terror, but that if an
honest person performs such an act as a grave duty, it confers on him a tragic-ethical grandeur'. But
in the later seasons, Jack's moral stature and 'human dignity' appear increasingly precarious, as his
psychological defences begin to crumble under the recurrent pressure of the violent acts he
commits. For the view that the series' depiction of violence and torture is not straightforwardly
legitimizing, but rather invites exploration of complex and problematic ethical issues, see, e.g.,
Sutherland and Swan 2007, de Wijze 2008, O'Mathúna 2008; a more ironic reading is offered by
Orr 2006.

[137] On the big screen, David Fincher's *Fight Club* (1999) similarly places the viewer in an ambiguous
and unsettling position, with its representation of the viewpoint character's attempts to recuperate
his masculinity from the effeminizing effects of consumer culture through the experience and
infliction of physical violence. Critics are tellingly divided as to whether the film offers itself as a
*celebration* or a *critique* of the homosocial bonding and hypermasculine violence it depicts, and to
what extent we are invited to approve the increasingly violent methods adopted by Jack and Tyler
in their assault on the capitalist 'system' (for a range of views, see Windrum 2004; Giroux 2006:
205–25; Diken and Laustsen 2007: 71–89). Further complexity arises from the combination of
sadistic and masochistic elements, observed by both Windrum and Diken and Laustsen, in the
film's depiction of hand-to-hand combat and physical injury.

individual's response to textualized violence will also depend upon his or her own predispositions, tastes, and even conscious choices.

This volume, then, points to a deep complexity in Roman representations of violence. Some broad tendencies are certainly evident across the spread of material, but it is also apparent that both generic forces and the choices made by authors shape the ways in which violence is depicted and prompt (though do not wholly determine) different reactions to different texts; considerable variation results. Several of the works discussed can be read as offering something closely analogous to the scopophilic and sadistic pleasures analysed by Mulvey, though voyeurism may be combined with empathetic alignment (if not masochistic identification) with the victims of violence (Scourfield),[138] or with an implicit critique of, and attempt to impose control over, viewing pleasure (Henderson). The victims of violence may be objectified or aestheticized, or their subjectivity emphasized in such a way that the reader is invited to empathize with their suffering – sometimes within the same text (Gale, Newlands, Fitzgerald). Representations of violence may serve to confirm and legitimize normative values and hegemonic social structures, appealing to the gender and class solidarity of an (implied) elite male audience (Konstan, Miller); or act as a kind of coping mechanism for dealing with 'real-world' anxieties (Kennedy on the Aristotelian interpretation of tragic pleasure). Yet they may also unsettle, dismay, or repel us, acting as a provocation to critical engagement with, rather than comfortable acceptance of, existing ideological structures or cultural norms (Newlands, Kennedy, Fitzgerald; compare also O'Rourke, Gibson). Again, the unease experienced by the reader may be a source of pleasure in itself, because the violence is 'made safe' by its framing as fiction – an experience familiar to devotees of the modern horror film;[139] or it may contribute to the unsettling yet not unpleasurable impact of an encounter with the sublime (Spentzou). Many of these observations will apply, *mutatis mutandis*, to the reception of media violence by modern audiences. Our hope is, then, that this book will make a valuable contribution to the contemporary debate, as well as enriching our understanding of Latin literary texts and their relation to each other, to Roman ideology and cultural forms, and to readers both ancient and modern.

---

[138] Cf. Castelli 2004: 133: 'The cultural production of Christian martyrdom as performance and spectacle ... transforms the readers and consumers of this tradition into uneasy voyeurs of the suffering of others even as it calls them into identification with that suffering.'

[139] Cf. McCauley 1998.

# CHAPTER I

# Comic Violence and the Citizen Body

### David Konstan and Shilpa Raval*

That violence is compatible with comedy is no surprise. One need only think of the pratfalls and farcical horseplay of the Three Stooges, or the spectacle of Wile E. Coyote, in the popular Road Runner cartoons, falling off a cliff and leaving an impression of his splayed body in the ground. These scenes are 'painless and not harmful', in Aristotle's phrase, because we do not believe that the characters are really suffering: they are cardboard figures, not vulnerable to genuine pain; they emerge unscathed, and Wile E. Coyote will rise seconds later from the canyon floor to pursue the honking bird yet again.[1] But New Comedy (in contrast to Old) was distinguished for its apparent naturalism (as in the famous comment by Aristophanes of Byzantium, 'O Menander and Life, which of you imitated the other?'), which suggests that the audience might in fact have pitied or sympathized with the distress of characters on stage. Even tragedy tended to eschew the explicit representation of violent acts.[2] A scholion, or marginal note, in the manuscripts of the *Iliad* (*ad* 6.58–9 Erbse), commenting on the passage in which Agamemnon counsels his brother Menelaus to slay every last Trojan, even the unborn infant in his mother's womb, observes that 'the audience, being human, detests the excessive harshness and inhumanity'[3] of Agamemnon's words, and goes on to suggest that this is why, in tragedy, such brutal deeds are hidden offstage,

---

* *Editors' note.* This chapter was planned as a collaboration between David Konstan and Shilpa Raval. Raval died when the project was still at an early stage, but she and Konstan had already talked through how they would approach the subject and divide up the work between them; she had seen an initial draft of his section, and he knew what plays she had selected to discuss. It fell to Konstan to complete the chapter alone, but Raval is properly credited as co-author; it may stand as the final publication of a gifted scholar.

[1] Arist. *Poet.* 5 (1449a34–5) defines comedy as an imitation of the ridiculous or laughable, and the ridiculous as 'a kind of error and ugly quality that is painless and not harmful' (ἁμάρτημά τι καὶ αἶσχος ἀνώδυνον καὶ οὐ φθαρτικόν).

[2] Cf. Introduction, p. 15, with n. 58.

[3] ὁ δὲ ἀκροατὴς ἄνθρωπος ὢν μισεῖ τὸ ἄγαν πικρὸν καὶ ἀπάνθρωπον.

and revealed only through cries from within or messenger-speeches (of course, such descriptions can be every bit as harrowing as viewing the events themselves). And yet the on-stage representation of physical aggression, or the threat of it, was not foreign to New Comedy. How, then, are we to evaluate its impact? In this chapter, we argue that violence in New Comedy is a function of status roles: to be sure, slaves are, as might be expected, more exposed to mistreatment, but violence is particularly thematized just when the inviolability of the citizen body is called into question.

For all their civility, the surviving comedies of Menander stage or allude to some surprisingly brutal scenes. In the *Perikeiromene*, a soldier in a jealous rage cuts off the hair of his concubine – symbolically a violent enough deed, since it assimilates her appearance to that of a slave; slave she is not, but she does lack citizen credentials, and this exposes her to such abuse. Most likely, this episode was not represented on stage, but took place prior to the dramatic action.[4] In the *Samia*, a slave is threatened with whipping and branding by his master, and escapes the punishment only by taking flight. He returns later and reflects: 'Though I'd done nothing wrong, I was afraid and ran away from my master' (643–4); he admonishes himself: 'So why did you run away, you idiot, you total coward?' (653–4), and immediately answers his own question: 'He threatened to brand me. It makes not a whit of difference whether you suffer this justly or unjustly, it's not a pretty thing in any way' (654–7).[5] Indeed, his pessimistic vision is soon borne out, when he presumes to offer advice to his master's son and is struck on the mouth for his pains (679). Even in Old Comedy, such direct violence is rare. In the *Dyscolus* (81–97), the misanthrope Cnemon pursues the slave of the romantic protagonist, Sostratus, hurling stones and prickly pears at him.[6] Sostratus himself wonders for a moment whether the old brute will strike him, but not even Cnemon is so far gone as to assault a fellow-citizen. A number of Greek comedies took as their point of departure the rape of a citizen woman, for instance, Menander's *Epitrepontes*. In this case, as often, the rape occurs prior to the action, but it is described later in the play in terms that invite sympathy for the victim, who is a

---

[4] Cf. Arnott 1988; Gomme and Sandbach 1973: 467–8, however, argue the contrary.
[5] οὐθὲν ἀδικῶν ἔδεισα καὶ τὸν δεσπότην | ἔφυγον … | … τί οὖν οὕτως ἔφυγες, ἀβέλτερε | καὶ δειλότατε; γελοῖον. ἠπείλησ' ἐμέ | στίζειν· μεμάθηκας· διαφέρ[ει δ' ἀ]λλ' οὐδὲ γρῦ | ἀδίκως παθεῖν τοῦτ' ἢ δικαίως, ἔστι δὲ | πάντα τρόπον οὐκ ἀστεῖον. Text of Menander according to Sandbach 1990. All translations from Greek and Latin texts are ours.
[6] Cf. the beating of the cook in Plautus' *Aulularia* (406–14), again by a misanthropic figure.

citizen girl: 'She ran up to us suddenly, alone, crying and pulling out her hair',[7] her dress reduced to shreds (487–90).[8]

One instance in which Menander's treatment of violence seems extraordinarily casual is found at the beginning of the *Aspis*, or *Shield*. The plot of the play depends on the belief that a young man who is in love with the heroine of the comedy has been killed while fighting abroad as a mercenary soldier. In the opening scene, his slave, Davus, returns home with a pile of booty and slaves acquired in battle. This is how he describes the events leading up to this moment to Smicrines, the soldier's uncle:

> There is a river in Lycia called Xanthus; near it, at that time, we were doing well and having good luck in numerous battles, and the barbarians had run away and abandoned the plain. But it seems this was one of those occasions when it's advantageous not to be lucky in all things, for when someone slips up he's also careful. Our contempt for them led us in disorder toward what was coming. For many of us left the palisade and began pillaging the villages, cutting down the fields, and selling captured slaves, and each of us had lots of goods as we left.[9]

'Great!', says Smicrines. Davus resumes: 'My master collected six hundred gold pieces, a fairly large number of cups, and this crowd of captured slaves you see over here, and he sent me to Rhodes and told me to leave these things with a foreign friend of his and return to him again.'[10] But the enemy got wind of the scattered state of the Greek troops, and in the evening, when the Greeks were luxuriating and drinking in their camp, the barbarians attacked. The Greeks managed to regroup, but many men were lost (23–68). What is striking about this passage is the way a raid by mercenary soldiers, involving the destruction of whole villages and the reduction of their populations to slavery, is treated as an unexceptional state of affairs, to be applauded when it turns out well and deplored only if one's own side loses. The plight of the prisoners of war who stand silently

[7] εἶτ' ἐξαπίνης κλάουσα προστρέχει μόνη, | τίλλουσ' ἑαυτῆς τὰς τρίχας.
[8] Cf. Omitowoju 2002: 174: 'The girl's sudden arrival, her weeping and the emphasis on her torn cloak all seem to suggest events which we are supposed to perceive as both violent and traumatic.'
[9] Men. *Aspis* 23–33 ποταμός τις ἐστὶ τῆς Λυκίας καλούμενος | Ξάνθος, πρὸς ᾧ τότ' ἦμεν ἐπιεικῶς μάχαις | πολλαῖς διευτυχοῦντες, οἵ τε βάρβαροι | ἐπεφεύγεσαν τὸ πεδίον ἐκλελοιπότες. | ἦν δ' ὡς ἔοικε καὶ τὸ μὴ πάντ' εὐτυχεῖν | χρήσιμον· ὁ γὰρ πταίσας τι καὶ φυλάττεται. | ἡμᾶς δ' ἀτάκτους πρὸς τὸ μέλλον ἤγαγε | τὸ καταφρονεῖν· πολλοὶ γὰρ ἐκλελοιπότες | τὸν χάρακα τὰς κώμας ἐπόρθουν, τοὺς ἀγροὺς | ἔκοπτον, αἰχμάλωτ' ἐπώλουν, χρήματα | ἕκαστος εἶχε πόλλ' ἀπελθών.
[10] Men. *Aspis* 33–9 [Sm.] ὡς καλόν. | [Da.] ......] ὁ τρόφιμος συναγαγὼν χρυσοῦς τινας | ἑξακοσί]ους, ποτήρι' ἐπιεικῶς συχνά, | τῶν τ' αἰχ]μαλώτων τοῦτον ὃν ὁρᾷς πλησίον | ὄχλον, ἀπο]πέμπει μ' εἰς Ῥόδον καί τῳ ξένῳ | φράζει κ]αταλιπεῖν ταῦτα πρός θ' αὐτὸν πάλιν | ...... ἀ]ναστρέφειν.

by on stage and are doomed to permanent slavery is evidently not incompatible with the comic spirit of the occasion.

Menander's slaves, nevertheless, are marginal to the action as a whole.[11] The situation is quite different with Plautus, who both made slaves more central and seems to have delighted in exposing them to the most terrible threats and punishments.[12] Given our poor knowledge of the Greek plays on which Plautus based his comedies, it is impossible to be certain to what extent such scenes were current in the Greek theatre as well, but it is universally accepted that Plautus at least amplified such episodes, even if he did not always invent them himself.[13] Scholars formerly were inclined to attribute Plautus' penchant for violence in the treatment of slaves and others to the low taste of the Roman audience, conceived as rural bumpkins lacking the refinement of the cultivated Athenians.[14] It is perhaps more relevant to recall that Plautus began composing comedies during the long Second Punic War, when the enemy, under the command of Hannibal, was seen at the very gates of Rome. Roman losses during these campaigns were enormous, even by the standards of twentieth-century warfare.[15] It is not implausible that the general atmosphere of violence and insecurity in the last decades of the third century BC contributed something to a taste for violent episodes on the stage, even in comedy. War exposes the vulnerability of the human body to pain and injury, and may render this condition a matter of obsessive anxiety.[16] But it was not

---

[11] For further discussion of slaves in Menander's comedies see Konstan 2013.

[12] Mercury's treatment of Sosia in the *Amphitruo* is a case in point; cf. Christenson 2000: 14.

[13] Cf. Fraenkel 1960: 223–41.

[14] For a nuanced expression of this view, see Pociña 1997: 35–6, who affirms that Plautus' chief objective was to make 'the manifold and variegated Roman people' laugh, and so put in play 'the most varied comic devices of a popular sort'. Hostility to the theatre as lowbrow entertainment is common among Roman writers; for attitudes in the first century AD, especially in connection with violence, see Wistrand 1992: 30–40. Anderson 1993: 135–51 takes a more generous view of Plautus' creative adaptation: 'Plautus deconstructs the Greek plays to make them fit his own and his Roman audience's sense of positive humor' (150); cf. E. Segal 1987, who emphasizes the carnivalian nature of Plautine comedy, and especially Marshall 2006: 79, who observes that there were different publics for different events, and 'that of the *palliata* was for the most part urban, with the level of sophistication that entailed'.

[15] David 1997: 60 estimates that Roman losses in the Second Punic War were 'in the region of 50,000 citizens', which (69) 'corresponded to 6 per cent of the total civic population'. Cf. Rosenstein 2004: 107–40, 191–9; Rosenstein concludes of a slightly later period: 'To win the republic its empire in the second century, tens of thousands of young Roman and Italian men paid the ultimate price . . . Death on this scale over so many years cannot but have profoundly affected the farms and families from which these men came' (140).

[16] Cf. Leigh 2004: 26: 'I am convinced that the Plautine moment and the Hannibalic moment coincide'; Leigh concludes that Plautus' comedies thus 'persistently touch the rawest of nerves in the audience for whom he writes'.

only the harm inflicted by the enemy that threatened Roman soldiers in times of war. There was also the fear of corporal punishment by their own superiors, for it was only in the army that a Roman citizen was formally subject to physical discipline.[17] In these conditions, violence might undermine the very basis of citizen identity, since the boundary between citizen and non-citizen was on one level defined precisely by the integrity of the body and its immunity to assault.[18] The dividing-line between citizen and slave, then, will have been particularly susceptible to being blurred under conditions of military discipline, not to mention the ever-present possibility of capture by the enemy. Comic violence may have been in part the expression of an otherwise repressed anxiety in the citizen audience.

In Plautus' *Miles gloriosus*, a young Athenian named Pleusicles has taken up lodgings in the home of Periplectomenus, a rich citizen of Ephesus, next door to that of the mercenary soldier after whom the play is named. The soldier, Pyrgopolynices, has acquired possession of a courtesan, Philocomasium, with whom Pleusicles is in love. Thanks to a hole that has been bored in the wall between the two houses, Philocomasium can pass secretly from the soldier's place to the neighbour's and see her former lover. But the arrangement is in danger of being exposed when one of the soldier's slaves, Sceledrus, who is charged with guarding Philocomasium, climbs on to Periplectomenus' roof in pursuit of a monkey and chances to spy her in the neighbour's courtyard. To prevent Sceledrus from revealing this to the soldier, a plan is concocted to convince him that he saw not Philocomasium herself but rather her (fictional) twin sister. This is not a very plausible ruse, and it depends for its effectiveness more on a series of threats than on argument. Thus, Sceledrus is warned that if he does not conceal the information, he will die doubly: for either he will be laying a false charge against Philocomasium, and hence die, or else he will have failed to guard her adequately, and die for that (295–8). When Philocomasium emerges from Periplectomenus' house in the guise of her ostensible twin sister, Sceledrus seizes her physically, but she escapes and again slips back into the soldier's house. Now, Sceledrus is truly in a pickle: not only has he accused his master's concubine of infidelity, he has also laid hands on a free woman (as he supposes) who is the guest of his citizen neighbour (472). Periplectomenus himself enters, feigns rage at Sceledrus' boldness (486–90), and threatens him with a day-long whipping (501–10). Sceledrus confesses that he deserves the worst of tortures (547–8), and Periplectomenus pardons him, acknowledging that he acted out of

---

[17] See Walters 1997; Gunderson 2003: 154.     [18] Cf. duBois 1991: 37–45.

ignorance. But Sceledrus is certain that Periplectomenus will denounce him to his master, and he decides to lie low for a few days – this is the last we hear of him in the play.

Sceledrus is of course right about the behaviour of his master's concubine, but the confrontation with Periplectomenus revolves entirely about the status-difference between free person and slave. A free person's body, like his property, is inviolate; a slave, who is the property of another, is subject to corporal chastisement. Sceledrus has both intruded upon the sanctuary of Periplectomenus' home by peering into his courtyard and committed assault against a free woman who is his guest. The threats of crucifixion and lashing are the sign of Sceledrus' servile status, just as Periplectomenus' rage is the mark of a free citizen's legitimate indignation at an offence to his civic identity.[19] The violent cowing of Sceledrus, by which he is induced to deny the evidence of his senses, reproduces that annihilation of self in the slave that Orlando Patterson has called 'social death'.[20]

At this point, the strategy of the play shifts gear, as Palaestrio, the slave who is loyal to Pleusicles and is the chief tactician in the play, is asked to come up with a scheme to extract Philocomasium from the soldier's possession. The plan is to hire a couple of courtesans to play the part of Periplectomenus' supposed wife and her maid and persuade the soldier that the 'wife' is in love with him (775–802). Now, Pyrgopolynices is not so fatuous as to be insensible to the risks entailed in seducing a citizen's wife, and he inquires: 'Is she married or a widow?' (964). 'Both', Palaestrio replies: she's young but wedded to an old man. The courtesan playing Periplectomenus' wife is to pretend she wants to marry the soldier (1164; cf. 1239, 1275), and Palaestrio suggests she specify that the house is hers and that her husband has already left her, lest Pyrgopolynices balk at entering another man's home (1165–8). The soldier in fact proves anxious at the thought of being apprehended with a married woman, and has to be assured that she has really expelled her husband and is the owner of the property (1276–8). No sooner does Pyrgopolynices enter his neighbour's house than he is set upon by Periplectomenus and his slaves, who carry him out and bind him, beat him, and prepare to castrate him (1394–1408). The soldier pleads that he was deceived and believed that the woman was divorced (1409–10), and Periplectomenus consents to release him, on the condition that he promise that he will not take vengeance for what he has suffered. The slaves beat him again for good

---

[19] Cf. Allen 2000: 50–72.     [20] Patterson 1982.

measure, demand he hand over gold along with his sword and cloak, and finally let him go. In the closing verses of the play, Pyrgopolynices cautions the audience: 'If this should happen to other adulterers, there would be fewer adulterers: they'd be more afraid and less eager for such things'[21] (1436–7).

The cudgelling of a free man on stage is a shocking event in New Comedy, even in the antic form that Plautus and his Roman contemporaries adopted.[22] Here the violence is actual, not threatened, as it was in the case of the befuddled slave Sceledrus. The abuse of Pyrgopolynices goes well beyond the humbling of the comic lover's rival: the soldier is not just defeated, he is thrashed.[23] What motivated this stunning display of force at the conclusion of the drama? To begin with, we may observe that Pyrgopolynices is not just an ordinary soldier. Rather, he is a professional mercenary, not a native of Ephesus (where the action unfolds) but in town for the purpose of raising troops to fight in the service of foreign kings (75–7, 948–50). Thus, he is not only a figure of power, of the sort that comedy delights in bringing low (compare Lamachus in Aristophanes' *Acharnians*), but an outsider who represents not city-states such as Athens or Ephesus, but rather the interests of the powerful monarchs who inherited the territories conquered by Alexander the Great and who relied to a great extent on hired armies to defend or extend their realms. In this, Pyrgopolynices differs from the soldier in Menander's *Perikeiromene*, who to all appearances resides permanently in Corinth, where the action takes place; in the finale, he will marry the woman he abused, who turns out to be a Corinthian citizen. Glenn Hugh observes that Menander's soldier 'is not a good model for Pyrgopolynices, and Menander's real-life mercenaries have been replaced by Plautus' glorious caricatures'.[24] This is true, but we must add that Pyrgopolynices is not just a mercenary but a high-ranking commander, with no allegiance to the communities he visits in the course of recruiting.

Eleanor Winsor Leach has argued that Pyrgopolynices embodied the threat represented by Hannibal in the Second Punic War, and that the exceptional trouncing to which he is subjected in the finale of the play was Plautus' way of providing comic relief for the anxiety that the war had generated among the Romans.[25] The Carthaginians did depend heavily on

---

[21] *si sic aliis moechis fiat, minus hic moechorum siet,* | *magis metuant, minus has res studeant.* Text of Plautus according to Leo 1895–6.
[22] See J. Wright 1974; E. Segal 1987.
[23] On the surprising cruelty of the punishment of Pyrgopolynices, see Pansiéri 1997: 716.
[24] Hugh 2004.    [25] Leach 1980; cf. Pansiéri 1997: 717–18.

mercenary soldiers, whereas the Romans relied on legions composed of citizen-soldiers and allies, and the connection Leach suggests between the violence in the comedy and the Romans' experience of the war has much to be said for it.[26] But the emphasis of the play falls more particularly on the threat to the citizen household and its potential exposure to an unwelcome intruder. Sceledrus' trespassing and manhandling of a guest anticipate precisely the action of his master in entering Periplectomenus' home without permission and attempting to have an affair with his 'wife'. The sanctity of the house may be seen as emblematic of the inviolability of the citizen's body: for compromising the basis on which a citizen was distinguished both from a slave and from a foreigner, Sceledrus and Pyrgopolynices are subjected to corporal punishment (or the threat of it), which in turn is the sign of their diminished civic condition. Violence in the *Miles gloriosus*, then, serves as an indicator of social status, and is employed to re-establish the social order when the boundaries that define it are endangered.

The analogy between the embodied self and a house is not as far-fetched as it may seem. In Plautus' *Mostellaria*, Philolaches, the young lover of the play, declares, 'I think that a man, when he is born, is like a new house'[27] (91–2), and he develops the comparison to the point of a conceit: parents are like builders (120), but the edifice, however well constructed, is vulnerable to corruption through the neglect of its owners. So too, Philolaches says, he ceased to take care of himself once he fell in love (141–3), and is now a mere vestige of his former self; erotic passion is the rot that destroys the structure. The house will indeed be a central image in the play.[28] The *Mostellaria* begins with an exchange of blows between two slaves. As Grumio drives Tranio, the clever schemer of the comedy, out of the house, Tranio responds by beating him publicly (9–10). With this, Grumio breaks into a lament over the decadent state of the household since the master, Theopropides, went abroad and its management was left to Theopropides' son, Philolaches, whose carousing and lavish dinners, abetted by Tranio, have brought the estate to the verge of ruin (77–81). Philolaches had fallen in love with a slave whom he freed at considerable cost (204), and he has since been supporting her in the manner of a

---

[26] If Pyrgopolynices is a Carthaginian general, then we might see in the strategic leadership of Palaestrio his Roman counterpart; but Leigh 2004: 52–3 remarks that 'the identification of the wily slave of comedy with the figure of the contemporary Roman general was inherently unstable because, for all the Roman airs adopted by the slave, his tactics belonged to the category identified as un-Roman and Carthaginian'.

[27] *novarum aedium esse arbitror similem ego hominem, | quando natus est.*      [28] Cf. Leach 1969.

high-priced courtesan. When Theopropides suddenly returns, Tranio is terrified: 'Is there anyone', he asks the audience, 'who wants to make some easy money and might suffer being crucified today in my place?'[29] (354–5), and he specifies the procedure as the nailing of both feet and both arms (360). Philolaches is equally disconcerted, and declares, 'I'm dead' (*occidi*, 369; cf. 375, 387); but in his case it is only a metaphor.

Tranio comes up with a scheme to save the day: he will pretend the house is haunted, owing to a murder that had been committed there. The ruse drives Theopropides off in terror, but things soon become complicated and test Tranio's powers of improvisation. The former owner of the house denies there was a crime, and simultaneously the moneylender by whom Philolaches financed his extravagances turns up, demanding payment. Thinking fast, Tranio pretends that Philolaches borrowed the money to buy the house of a neighbour, named Simo. Theopropides is delighted that he obtained it so cheaply, agrees to pay off the debt – and immediately proposes to inspect the new premises. Luckily, Tranio intercepts the neighbour as he is stepping out, and persuades him that Theopropides merely wants to look around to get some ideas for new construction in his own place. Simo agrees, indifferent to the fact that his wife is inside (808). Up to now, the scam succeeds. But this trick too is soon exposed, and Theopropides asks the neighbour for the use of several slaves with whips (1038). Tranio, aware that he is done for, takes refuge at an altar, but Theopropides threatens to burn him alive. After a series of dire threats, a friend of Philolaches arrives and intercedes on Tranio's behalf, promising that he and Philolaches will pay off their debts out of their own resources (1160–1; what these resources might be is hard to imagine). Convinced that his son is now ashamed of his behaviour (*si hoc pudet*, 1165), Theopropides relents but is still determined to take out his anger on Tranio. Tranio, in turn, brazenly asks: 'Even if I'm ashamed?' (*tamen etsi pudet?*, 1167). This is sheer defiance, and Theopropides responds, 'I'll kill you, so may I live!' (*interimam hercle ego <te>, si vivo*, 1168). As Robert Kaster writes, 'No slave is ever described as experiencing *verecundia*, presumably because slaves – at least according to the ideology of Roman slavery – have no autonomous volition, hence no actual self, hence no face to maintain or lose: there is accordingly no need for an emotion to draw a line that the non-existent self cannot cross.'[30] But

---

[29] *ecquis homo est, qui facere argenti cupiat aliquantum lucri, | qui hodie sese excruciari meam vicem possit pati?*

[30] Kaster 2005: 23.

Philolaches' friend insists that Tranio be pardoned, and Tranio provides the final flourish: 'What are you complaining about? As though I won't commit some new offence tomorrow! Then you'll be able to avenge both of them, that one and this one, quite nicely'[31] (1178–9). The humour lies in Tranio's bravado and the insouciant way in which he manoeuvres at the edge of danger. It is clear that he will somehow get off scot-free, and so his is, in Aristotle's phrase, an error that is 'painless and not harmful' in the mind of the audience.

In the *Mostellaria*, the threat to the house does not come from outside, as it did in the *Miles gloriosus*, but from within the family. A son's misbehaviour, however, is exonerated by virtue of his shame, the sentiment that marks a citizen. Although Tranio is pardoned in the end, the difference in the way Theopropides treats him and his own son marks the distinction between the body of a citizen youth and that of a slave: the one is spared physical assault, and his self is constituted as a moral entity, while the other is vulnerable to corporal punishment, with no claim to a moral identity. Violence sets the boundary between the two. Further, a citizen's place in the community depends on the maintenance of his estate: if he squanders his inheritance, he loses status and reputation.[32] The integrity of the household is thus a function of the integrity of the householder. Tranio's scheme causes a citizen to be deprived of his own house (on the pretext that it is haunted) and has him believe he is the owner of another to which he has no title and which he enters under false pretences. The threat to the family's assets caused by a wastrel son thus gives way to a slave's reckless disregard for the conventions of property. While the son is rehabilitated in the end,[33] the slave risks being flogged and crucified in one of the more violent scenes in the Plautine corpus. Here again, the connection between the citizen body and the body of the citizen is manifest.

Why is the brash slave Tranio spared punishment at the end of the *Mostellaria*, whereas the free soldier Pyrgopolynices is subjected to physical chastisement on stage? Part of the reason may be that Tranio is closely

---

[31] *quid gravaris? quasi non cras iam commeream aliam noxiam:* | *ibi utrumque, et hoc et illud, poteris ulcisci probe.*

[32] Cf. Catull. 41 on Mamurra as a *decoctor*, i.e., one who has 'boiled away' his fortunes; Cic. *Quinct.* 49–50; discussion in Crook 1967b (my thanks to Monica Gale for these references).

[33] Had he not been, he would have been subject to corporal punishment; in this respect, sons under the authority of their fathers (*in patria potestate*) were somewhat like slaves (cf. Fitzgerald 2000: 78–81). Comedy, however, avoids such an assault on the dignity and civic integrity of its young protagonists.

associated with his young master Philolaches, just as, in the *Miles gloriosus*, Palaestrio is connected with Pleusicles, the young Athenian who is in love with Philocomasium. Youths who conceive a passion for a courtesan are themselves behaving in a transgressive way, squandering a fortune that is not theirs to spend, and it is part of the charm of the genre of New Comedy that they are permitted to indulge such whims, generally at the expense of their fathers, without suffering serious consequences. Holt Parker has argued that the clever slave represents the 'other self' of the *adulescens*, the self that enables and openly abets the libidinous desires of the son.[34] We may also see the adolescents in comedy, and the slaves who serve as their pliant and rascally sidekicks, as stand-ins for the repressed desires of the adult male Roman audience, who get to enact their own fantasies via the wild boys on stage.[35] Those slaves who are aligned with the passionate young men of comedy against their stern fathers get off lightly, partaking of the forgiving spirit of the genre toward wayward sons.[36] Those slaves, however, who take the part of the father and protest against the dissolute son's ruin of his patrimony do not fare so well: in the opening scene of the *Mostellaria*, it is precisely Grumio, the upright servant who attempts to defend the integrity of his master's estate, who is subjected to physical abuse.

The most violent treatment of a slave in Roman comedy is that of Tyndarus in Plautus' *Captivi*, who is sent to work in a quarry with the expectation that he will soon die of exhaustion – as nearly happens, before he is redeemed at the end of the play.[37] In this case, however, the punishment of the slave coincides with that of the son. For Tyndarus, the slave of Philocrates, has been captured in war along with his master, and both are now in the possession of Hegio, who hopes to trade them for a son of his who was taken prisoner by the other side in the same battle. Tyndarus and Philocrates have switched identities, however, so that when Hegio sends the slave, as he imagines, to negotiate the exchange while retaining the master in his possession as a hostage, he has really released Philocrates himself. Hegio discovers the ruse, and it is in fury over the deception and, as he believes, the loss of the crucial bargaining chip that he consigns Tyndarus – now stripped of his disguise as Philocrates – to hard labour. Philocrates, however, lives up to his promise to Tyndarus that he will return, and brings with him Hegio's son Philopolemus, together with

---

[34] H. N. Parker 1989: 242–6; cf. Fitzgerald 2000: 10–11, 41–7.     [35] See McCarthy 2000: 17–34.

[36] Cf. E. Segal 1987: 155: 'In general … we may say that the Plautine slave … never suffers for his rascality.'

[37] Cf. E. Segal 1987: 154: 'Here, for once, the dire threats seem to be carried out, although the text leaves some doubt as to what hardship Tyndarus actually does experience.'

a runaway slave, Stalagmus, who many years before had sold another son of Hegio's into slavery. Philocrates' good faith, together with Philopolemus' own plea, induce Hegio to recall the loyal Tyndarus from the quarry. In the meantime, it emerges that the man to whom Stalagmus sold Hegio's son is none other than Philocrates' father – and so Tyndarus turns out to be Hegio's own long-lost son, whom he has unwittingly subjected to mortal torture. Tyndarus enters lamenting the suffering he has endured: 'I've often seen many paintings of the torments that go on in Hades, but truly no hell is equal to where I've been, in the quarry'[38] (998–1000). The play ends with the removal of the shackles that bind the feet of Tyndarus and their transfer to the still brash Stalagmus.[39] Here again, the infliction of corporal punishment is closely connected to the question of citizen status. The audience, which has been tipped off as to the actual state of affairs by the prologue, knows that Tyndarus is Hegio's son, and Plautus would seem to be deliberately highlighting the role of accident in distinguishing a free person from a slave, at the same time that he asserts a moral distinction between the noble Tyndarus and the sleazy Stalagmus, who deserves, according to the logic of the play, the punishment he will receive in the end.[40] But it is just when the boundaries between free and slave are blurred that physical violence is employed to define and reassert the essential difference between the two.

It is a curious fact about New Comedy that only citizen women are raped, although such rapes are normally, in Aristotle's phrase, outside the action (ἔξω τοῦ δράματος) represented on stage, and serve to launch the plot of the play.[41] There is a logic to the formula. Courtesans sell their favours, and where a young man has fallen in love with one, the plot centres on how he will acquire the cash to purchase her (the *Mostellaria* belongs to this general type). A citizen woman who is raped, however, gives rise to the kind of complication that New Comedy is designed to resolve. For it is a given of the plot that she will bear a child, and so,

---

[38] *vidi ego multa saepe picta, quae Acherunti fierent | cruciamenta, verum enim vero nulla adaeque est Acheruns | atque ubi ego fui, in lapicidinis.*

[39] For a nuanced view of the construction of Stalagmus as the vicious counterpart to Tyndarus, see Leigh 2004: 90–7. Leigh argues that the *Captivi* illustrates the anxiety that any citizen must have endured over the possibility of becoming a prisoner of war and hence a slave: 'If the realization that you yourself can become a slave is perhaps the first step to questioning the ethical validity of the institution, the realization that men as admirable as Tyndarus and Philocrates can suffer such a fate must be the next' (90).

[40] For discussion, see Konstan 1983: 70–1.

[41] See Lape 2004: 102; for a full survey of rapes in Greek and Roman comedy, Pierce 1997; cf. Omitowoju 2002: 228: 'In Menander, rape always leads to marriage', the reason being that the women always prove to be citizens in the end.

according to the conventions of the genre, she will be ineligible for marriage with anyone but the father of the baby – that is, the rapist himself.[42] The recognition that the girl's suitor and her rapist are one and the same permits the plot to end in marriage and restores the woman's status, which was diminished precisely by the rape.

The one surviving example of New Comedy in which a rape occurs during rather than previous to the action represented on stage is Terence's *Eunuch*, in which Chaerea rapes a girl who has been newly introduced into the establishment of the courtesan Thais (he chanced to see her when she was being moved in). Chaerea's brother, Phaedria, is a client and lover of Thais, and has sent her a eunuch as a gift. Chaerea seizes the opportunity to disguise himself as the eunuch, and thus gains admission to Thais' house. When Thais learns of the rape, she reprimands Chaerea for his lack of consideration; she has reason to believe that the girl is in fact of free birth, and was in the process of gaining recognition of her status from her brother, Chremes. Chaerea's act has spoiled her plans, because once it is determined that the girl has been raped, the brother is unlikely to acknowledge her (he will not be able to offer her in marriage, and she will simply be a burden to him).[43] The problem that results from the girl's violation, then, is from Thais' point of view mainly a practical one. As for Chaerea, he coldly declares that he did not commit the offence intentionally, since it was merely a matter of one slave raping another – a witticism, of course, but the implication is that this kind of violence among slaves is of no social consequence. The only protest comes from Pythias, another slave of Thais, who reacts vehemently to Chaerea's remark – Terence's way, it would appear, of signalling that slaves are not devoid of feeling and dignity. Once Chaerea realizes that the girl is a citizen and, prior to being assaulted by him, was a virgin, he declares his intention to marry her, and with this she regains her status. The offence against social mores implied by the rape of a

---

[42] I have argued that male sexual anxiety in classical Athens was focused at least in large part on the question of illegitimate birth, and not exclusively or predominantly on sexual penetration of the female as such: see Konstan 1995: 141–52. Cf. Pierce 1997: 166 on Menander's *Epitrepontes*: 'It is the production of a child that has caused the problems and distress. And it is Charisios' acceptance of being father to a bastard that is pivotal in his change of opinion'; also 178; Omitowoju 2002: 178–82; contra: Ogden 1996: 138 n. 10 and 1997: 38 n. 44.

[43] In this play, where the rape occurs during the action, the question of a possible illegitimate child resulting from the deed is moot; in fact, no clear reason is given for why Chremes would not acknowledge his sister in the event of her having been raped, or even why it is necessary to inform him of the fact. It would have been perfectly reasonable to conceal it, even if she were to give birth, for example by exposing the child, as the wife does in the *Epitrepontes*, or by giving it away: cf. Plaut. *Truc.* 848–9, where Callicles' daughter has been betrothed to a relation, having concealed the fact that she bore a child to Diniarchus.

citizen woman, and against dramatic propriety by having it occur during the course of the drama, is mitigated by casting the girl as a slave – which she will remain if her brother refuses to acknowledge her. The audience is spared the scene of a man consciously violating a citizen woman, as happens in the lead-up to the action in Menander's *Epitrepontes* and *Samian Woman*, Plautus' *Asinaria* and *Truculentus*, and Terence's *Andria, Adelphoe,* and *Hecyra*.

The one Plautine play in which physical violence is offered on stage to a woman of arguably citizen status is the *Rudens (The Rope)*, based on an original by the Greek playwright Diphilus. The story concerns an old Athenian named Daemones, who is living with his wife on the coast of Cyrene. Daemones had lost his daughter when she was three years old. Ultimately she came into the hands of a procurer named Labrax, who brought her and another girl, named Ampelisca, to Cyrene. Here, he had agreed to sell Palaestra, as Daemones' daughter is called, to Plesidippus, also an Athenian, who is in love with her. But Labrax falls in with a Sicilian named Charmides, and decides to abscond by sea with the girls and Plesidippus' deposit into the bargain. As he sets out for Sicily, however, a storm sinks the ship. All four make it to shore, where the women take refuge in a temple of Venus; Labrax, however, desires to reclaim them as his property and is not deterred from attempting to seize them by force. Daemones, unaware of Palaestra's true identity, nevertheless intervenes to protect them, as does Trachalio, a slave of Plesidippus; while Daemones and some slaves of his restrain Labrax, Trachalio fetches his master, who arrives and hales Labrax off to court for breach of contract. The girls are safe at this point, but Palaestra has lost the little casket in which she kept her birth tokens. By good fortune, this too washes up on shore, and reveals that she is Daemones' long-lost daughter. In the end, her father gives her in legitimate marriage to Plesidippus.

The episode that concerns us is the struggle over Palaestra and Ampelisca in the temple of Venus. It is one of the more explicitly physical on-stage disputes in Plautine comedy – indeed, the only one in which the words *violare* (648) and *violentia* (839) occur, along with the abundant use of *vis* ('force') and *tangere* ('touch', 'seize').[44] Trachalio summons the aid of neighbours in defence of the girls and the priestess of the temple: 'Let this be a place where people live by law and not by violence',[45] he cries (621).

---

[44] *vis*: 621, 673, 680–1, 690, 729, 733, 774, 839; *tangere*: 720–1, 759, 762, 776, 784–5, 793, 796–7, 810.
[45] *facite hic lege potius liceat quam vi victo vivere.*

He explains to Daemones that two innocent women are being mistreated in the temple 'contrary to law and justice' (*advorsum ius legesque*, 643), and that the priestess herself is being manhandled. 'Who is it', Daemones asks, 'who deems the gods so worthless?' 'A procurer', Trachalio answers (650, 653).[46] At this, Daemones orders his slaves to come to the rescue, and they are heard beating Labrax (661). Several issues are at stake in the scuffle: the sacrilegious treatment of a priestess in her own temple and the offence against the gods; the status of the procurer, who by virtue of his profession is considered inimical to decency and deserving of chastisement;[47] and the question of law, which, according to Trachalio, Labrax is violating in laying hands on the girls. The audience might suppose that Trachalio's claim rests on the contract that Labrax has made with Plesidippus: he is attempting to seize property that belongs to another. Alternatively, Trachalio may be implying that the girls are free and therefore not subject to seizure. Of course, the spectators know that Palaestra is indeed freeborn, but since she was legitimately sold to Labrax, it is not clear whether she is entitled to assert her freedom in the present circumstances. The audience would have to wait to see whether the girls' claim to immunity from Labrax rests on some technicality of the local code.[48]

Let us look first at the question of law, which seems initially to involve the matter of sacrilege. The girls, at Trachalio's prompting, take hold of the altar, from which they pray that Venus may protect them against the impious aggressors (694–9). Daemones appears and summons Labrax to come out; after accusing him of an attack against the deities, Daemones orders his slaves to punch him in the face (709–10).[49] Labrax retorts that his rights (*ius*) are being violated, since his slaves are being seized against his will (711–12). Trachalio, however, proposes to bring the case to trial in

---

[46] *quis istic est qui deos tam parvi pendit? . . . lenost.*

[47] Cf. Ter. *Ad.* 155–82; Terence borrowed this scene from Diphilus' *Synapothneskontes*, and inserted it into the Menandrean model for his play. E. Segal 1987: 162 observes that 'not every character on the Plautine stage enjoys the clever slave's immunity from punishment. There *are* blows struck in retribution for misdeeds, and sometimes they are delivered right before the audience's eyes.' Segal cites three such exceptions: Labrax; the pimp Dordalus at the end of the *Persa*; and Pyrgopolynices in the *Miles gloriosus*. All three, according to Segal, are 'justly punished'. Pansiéri 1997: 639–64 discusses fathers, pimps, and soldiers as 'oppresseurs', and sees Plautus' hostility towards them as the 'expression d'un subconscient vindicatif'.

[48] Neither Athenians nor Romans would have had much knowledge of the laws of Cyrene. The best discussion of the legal issues is Scafuro 1994: 409–19; see also Paoli 1976: 119–23; Lefèvre 1984: 27–8. Gratwick 1982: 108–9 suggests that the Greek comic playwrights made sure *not* to clarify the legal status of a kidnapped girl in a foreign city, precisely so that the revelation of her origins would not be 'sufficient to ensure her release and her owner's punishment'; cf. Scafuro 1994: 410.

[49] For the assignment of the verses, see Garzya 1967: 43 (*ad* 709).

Cyrene, and he puts the question to the procurer: 'Are these your slaves?' 'Yes.' 'Go on, touch either of them with the slightest finger.' 'What if I touch them?'[50] With this, Trachalio threatens to beat him to a pulp (721–2). 'Am I not permitted to remove my own slaves from the altar of Venus?' asks the procurer. 'You are not: we have a law', replies Daemones. 'I've no business at all with your laws', Labrax cries.[51] But Daemones threatens that if Labrax attempts the least violence against the girls, his slaves will thrash him. Labrax protests that Daemones is treating him violently (733). Trachalio intercedes to say that the women are free Greeks, and one of them an Athenian of citizen parents. At this, Daemones exclaims that he too is Athenian, and Trachalio bids him defend his countrywomen. But Labrax stands firm: he paid their master for them, and thus it makes no difference what city they come from (745–6).

What is the law to which Daemones has appealed? It is impossible to know, though it would seem at first to have something to do with the inviolability of Venus' temple and her priestess, and the right of refuge at the altar.[52] In this case, the issue for Daemones is Labrax' conduct in seizing the girls, not his right of possession. But Trachalio then avers that the girls are freeborn. Even if this were the case, however, it is not clear that Labrax would have to cede possession of them: many freeborn people were reduced to slavery, for example in war, as in the *Captivi*. In the end, the case will be decided on the basis of the agreement Labrax made with Plesidippus, and which he sought to violate; on these grounds, however, Palaestra should belong to Plesidippus, and the question of her freedom would still remain undecided. The conflict goes on for many more verses, with a crescendo of threats of fisticuffs, while Trachalio sets off to get Plesidippus, leaving the girls under Daemones' protection (773–5). When Plesidippus arrives, he demands to know whether the procurer tried to drag his girlfriend[53] from Venus' altar by force (839–40), insisting that Trachalio should have killed him in that case. It is only now that Labrax

---

[50] Vv. 719–21 [Tr.] *suntne illae ancillae tuae?* | [La.] *sunt.* [Tr.] *agedum ergo, tange utramvis digitulo minimo modo.* | [La.] *quid si attigero . . . ?*

[51] Vv. 723–5 [La.] *mihi non liceat meas ancillas Veneris de ara abducere?* | [Da.] *non licet: est lex apud nos –* [La.] *mihi cum vestris legibus* | *<nil quicquamst> commerci.*

[52] On this scene, Naiden 2006: 375 observes: 'Plautus has reported a typical Greek procedure of slave refuge followed by priestly evaluation, and capped it with an unusual, but certainly not unprecedented, act of improper expulsion.' The subsequent complications involving the repossession of the girls and expulsion of the pimp are also 'common practice', and the scene as a whole, Naiden concludes, 'is not a parody'.

[53] *amica* (839) suggests a courtesan rather than a proper fiancée; see Konstan 1997: 91, 146.

becomes truly nervous (*perii*, 844; cf. 877), and the reason clearly has to do with his breach of contract. Plesidippus hauls him off to court, where Labrax will lose his case (1283).

Finally, Daemones realizes that Palaestra is his daughter (1173), and the play ends with her betrothal to Plesidippus and a general reconciliation among all – including even the now chastened Labrax. In the process, however, the question of Palaestra's status is elided. Was she free, as Trachalio had claimed? Or was she of servile condition, whether the property of Labrax or of Plesidippus? The situation is in this respect as ambiguous at the end of the play as it was in the beginning. But the ambiguity is precisely what lends dramatic interest to the threatened violence to the two girls on the part of the procurer. If they are in fact free, then the assault on them is criminal; if they are slaves, then the question is reduced to whether they belong to Labrax or to Plesidippus.

If we accept Trachalio's claim that the women are Greek and free, the case bears a certain resemblance to that of the *Miles gloriosus*: an outsider to the community – there, a mercenary soldier and his slave, in the *Rudens* a procurer or brothel-keeper – intrudes upon a privileged space, whether a citizen's home or a temple whose sanctity is protected by law, and does violence to an inhabitant who is herself of ambiguous status – in the one instance, the supposed free sister of the courtesan Philocomasium (and later the pretended wife of Periplectomenus), in the other, the enslaved Palaestra, who is actually the daughter of the Athenian citizen Daemones. In both comedies, the outsider is subjected to corporal punishment and deprived of the girl in his power. For all the radical differences of context between the two, they share a common preoccupation with citizen status and its construction as immunity to physical assault. The *Rudens* takes a more light-hearted view, in the end, of the aggression on the part of Labrax than does the *Miles gloriosus* of Pyrgopolynices' invasion of the house of a private citizen: Labrax is spared the severe indignities endured by the mercenary soldier, and is accepted into Daemones' home for the feast that concludes the comedy. But in its own way, the *Rudens* exhibits a comparable anxiety over the vulnerability of the citizen household to violence, and takes equal delight in the cudgelling and humiliation of those who threaten its integrity. It seems fair to say that violence on the Roman stage, at least in the comedies of Plautus, bears a special connection to the idea of the citizen body.

Unlike characters of dubious status, such as procurers, or threatening foreigners, such as mercenary captains, adult male citizens are normally spared direct pain and humiliation in New Comedy; but here too there are exceptions.[54] The most outrageous example is Plautus' *Casina*, in which a husband seeks to have an affair with a slave-girl (the Casina of the title), whom his wife has lovingly raised, by marrying her off to his bailiff (also a slave), who will concede to him sexual privileges with the girl. After a series of ploys to derail the old reprobate's plan, his wife arranges to have a slave loyal to her disguise himself as Casina so that both her husband and his bailiff believe that they are consummating the marriage with her. As they attempt to have sex with the fellow, he beats them thoroughly, and they run out of the house, in pain and utterly humiliated. The slave exclaims: 'But I, fool that I am, am now doing something new – I'm ashamed, I who've never been ashamed before' (*sed ego insipiens nova nunc facio: pudet quem prius non puditum umquamst*, 878) – this slave, at least, is capable of shame, though the point would seem to be to underscore the brazenness of his master. The husband in turn is reduced to begging his wife's pardon, which she grants 'so as not to make a still longer comedy out of this long one' (*hanc ex longa longiorem ne faciamus fabulam*, 1006).[55] In this most farcical of conclusions, the errant husband is reduced to the status of a slave, and the slave achieves a modicum of moral stature by virtue of his susceptibility to shame. Casina herself will prove to be freeborn, and will wed the old man's son. Status roles will fall back into place, but the lesson will remain that the head of household who violates the obligations of his position may end up being treated as a slave, and the ultimate sign of his fall is that he becomes subject to the violence of others.

Violence on the comic stage was a source of humour, but the humour was not all of a piece. Citizens in the audience might delight in watching the humiliation of a slave, which reaffirmed their sense of superiority and civic identity. They might also enjoy the discomfiture of figures who threatened the integrity of their households, such as mercenary soldiers or brothel-keepers who gained control of women who had been born free. But the ever-present possibility of being reduced to slavery might lend a special poignancy to the representation of characters subject to corporal abuse: the fate of Tyndarus in the *Captivi*, or of Palaestra in the *Rudens*, was a reminder that citizenship was a fragile shield in times of war, piracy, or general lawlessness, and identities were never entirely secure. Finally, citizens might behave in ways that violated the norms of their own

---

[54] So Demaenetus, the father in Plautus' *Asinaria*, is made to behave in absurd and servile ways (though without the infliction of pain).

[55] For discussion and bibliography, see Konstan 2014. Beacham 1991 has some suggestive observations on how the violent scenes in the *Casina* might be staged.

households, thereby threatening from within, as it were, the barrier that separated them from the status of slaves, who had no legal family. These are the cases in which free adult members of the community might be shown suffering physical assault – a reminder that adultery with a married woman, as in the *Miles gloriosus*, or even an untoward affair with a slave-girl raised almost like a daughter in the home, might expose a man to the kind of violence that was normally inflicted only on the servile class.

# CHAPTER 2

# Contemplating Violence
## *Lucretius'* De rerum natura

### *Monica R. Gale**

## I

A man is eaten alive by a wild animal: he looks on in horror as his own limbs are devoured. Another man's leg is sliced off by a scythed chariot-wheel, and lies on the ground with its toes still twitching; nearby is a severed head with open eyes gazing blankly. Eyeballs are lacerated or torn out by the roots; a rotting corpse 'breathes out' maggots, which seethe within the bloated limbs.

This gruesome catalogue is derived not from one of the 'video nasties' which so alarmed the self-styled 'moral majority' of the 1980s and 1990s, or even from the more lurid pages of Silver Latin epic; it is culled, rather, from a work which explicitly aims to recommend a philosophy of tranquillity and peace of mind, the *De rerum natura* of Lucretius.[1] Lucretius' poem is, indeed, surprisingly rich in graphic images of violence and bodily mutilation. The proem to Book 1 includes an extended account of the sacrifice of Iphigenia (1.84–101), and the final book ends with the families of Athenian plague-victims pointlessly brawling over the corpses of their nearest and dearest (6.1283–6). Severed limbs and dead bodies recur in different contexts throughout the poem, which is punctuated too by scenes of catastrophic convulsion on the cosmic scale, reflected in microcosm by the effects of disease on the human body.[2]

---

* I am grateful to David Scourfield, David Konstan, and Pamela Zinn for very helpful comments on earlier drafts of this chapter.

[1] Living victim of predatory animal: 5.990–8; mutilation by scythed chariot-wheels: 3.642–56; lacerated/torn-out eyeballs: 3.408–15, 563–4; maggoty corpse: 3.719–21. Cf. also 3.170–1, 403–5, 551–3, 657–63; 6.1208–12.

[2] For the microcosm/macrocosm analogy in general, see esp. Schrijvers 1978, Schiesaro 1990: 73–83; for comparison between cosmic upheavals and human diseases, see 5.338–50, 6.591–607, 6.655–69, with C. P. Segal 1990: 94–114, Kany-Turpin 1997. In the finales to Books 1 and 2, there is a similar analogy (explicit in the one case, implicit in the other) between cosmic and human ageing and death: see Segal 1990: 96–7, 102–4. For other images of natural cataclysm, see 2.592–3; 3.842; 5.91–109, 394–415; 6.122–3, 561–7, 585–607.

Leaving aside the once-popular theory that the poet was psychologically unbalanced,[3] there are several ways in which we might attempt to account for the prominence of such scenes and to analyse their potential impact upon the reader. In particular, it seems reasonable to ask whether the depiction of violence has a role to play in what we might call the didactic economy of the poem, a role that would set Lucretius' violent episodes apart from those of writers in other genres. What, I will ask, does the vivid depiction of violent death and bodily mutilation contribute to the poem's protreptic purpose, that is, to its declared aim of converting its late-Republican readership to the philosophy of Epicurus? Three lines of approach suggest themselves, one based upon the poem's Epicurean affiliations, one on its Roman context, and one on its relation to the traditions of epic poetry. In what follows, I pursue each of these in turn, beginning with a brief exploration of the relationship between Lucretius' graphic depiction of violence and mutilation and Epicurean psychological theory and therapeutic practice. Next, I turn in somewhat greater detail to specifically Roman aspects of the poem's rhetorical strategy, suggesting that its representation of violence can be fruitfully considered in the context of the spectacular entertainments that formed so prominent a part of the communal experience of Lucretius' original readership. Finally, I examine the poet's appropriation of elements derived from the closely related genre of heroic epic: graphic accounts of wounding and dismemberment, conventional in epic battle-narrative from Homer onwards, are redeployed (I will argue) in support of a position in most respects diametrically opposed to the ideology of the heroic warrior.

## II

When considered in the light of Epicurean psychology and therapeutics, the vivid quality of Lucretius' depictions of wounds, mutilation, and violent death is somewhat less surprising than it might initially appear. By the first century BC, the Epicureans had developed a systematic theory

---

[3] The ultimate source of this theory – most memorably embodied in Tennyson's 'Lucretius' (1868) – is the *Chronicle* of St Jerome, who records in his entry for the year 94 BC: *Titus Lucretius poeta nascitur, qui postea amatorio poculo in furorem versus, cum aliquot libros per intervalla insaniae conscripsisset, quos postea Cicero emendavit, propria se manu interfecit, anno aetatis XLIV* ('birth of the poet Titus Lucretius, who later – having been driven mad by a love potion, and having in the intervals between bouts of insanity composed several books, which Cicero later edited – died by his own hand in his 44th year'). For reverberations in twentieth-century criticism, see, e.g., Rozelaar 1941, esp. 66–76 and 130–6; Logre 1946; Perelli 1969, esp. 13–52.

of philosophical pedagogy, which was apparently put into practice in the Garden at Athens and other Epicurean schools or communities, and sought above all to deploy physical and ethical doctrine as tools for the 'healing' of the pupil's more destructive emotions.[4] Two fragmentary works of Philodemus, our main source for Epicurean therapeutic practice, emphasize the need for frank and even harsh treatment in the case of recalcitrant pupils, and more particularly recommend the practice of visualization – of 'setting in view before the eyes' (τιθέναι πρὸ ὀμμάτων, ἐν ὄψει) – as a means of detaching the disciple from his or her false beliefs and damaging patterns of behaviour.[5] In both the *De ira* and the *De libertate dicendi*,[6] Philodemus explains that the Epicurean disciple must be made, almost literally, to see the error of his or her ways: desire for a 'cure' can begin only when we acknowledge our 'sickness', and this realization is to be brought about by placing the nature and consequences of such negative emotions as anger vividly before the mind's eye.[7] Similarly, Lucretius' graphic imagery of bodily mutilation may be understood as a means of surfacing our unacknowledged fear of pain and death, which can then be addressed openly and rationally, as the poet seeks to do at the end of Book 3.[8] While this process is not identical with that outlined by

---

[4] See, e.g., Nussbaum 1994: 115–36; Tsouna 2007: 74–87.

[5] On 'visualization' in Epicurean therapy, see Nussbaum 1986: 39–41; Tsouna 2003 and 2007: 80–7, 204–9; F. M. Schroeder 2004.

[6] Phld. *De ira* col. III.13–18 Indelli (cf. cols. I.20–7, IV.15–19); *Lib. dic.* fr. 42 Olivieri (where, however, πρὸ ὀμμάτων is an editorial supplement); cf. also *Lib. dic.* fr. 26 Olivieri for the related practice of visualization on the part of the mentor.

[7] The purpose and intended effects of Epicurean 'visualization' are most clearly described in the *De ira*, where Philodemus explains that the practice is designed to produce 'a great shudder' (μεγάλην ... φρίκην, col. III.14–15 Indelli) in the pupil; at the same time the pupil is to be reminded that it is within our power to free ourselves from the emotions that tend to produce the repellent effects which the mentor has conjured up. Philodemus goes on in cols. VII–XXXI to exemplify the technique by cataloguing in some detail the physical, legal, and social consequences entailed by outbursts of anger.

[8] The fear of pain (as opposed to death) is not in fact directly tackled by Lucretius at any point in the poem, and indeed would seem to present some difficulties for Epicurean ethics: on the one hand, pain is defined as the one true evil, which we should strive on principle to avoid, and might therefore be regarded as something genuinely fearful; on the other, fear, as a species of psychological pain, is itself something to be shunned. Epicurus' rather unsatisfactory solution to this problem appears to lie in the contention that physical pain is either short-lived or mild (οὐ χρονίζει τὸ ἀλγοῦν συνεχῶς ἐν τῇ σαρκί, ἀλλὰ τὸ μὲν ἄκρον τὸν ἐλάχιστον χρόνον πάρεστι ... αἱ δὲ πολυχρόνιοι τῶν ἀρρωστιῶν πλεονάζον ἔχουσι τὸ ἡδόμενον ἐν τῇ σαρκὶ ἤπερ τὸ ἀλγοῦν, 'continuous pain in the flesh does not last long; at its most acute it is present for a very brief time ... whereas those sicknesses that are protracted allow pleasure in the flesh even to predominate over pain', *Principal Doctrines* 4; cf. *Ep. Men.* 133), and is therefore (presumably) not to be regarded as something genuinely terrible. Elsewhere, he implies that mental pleasure can compensate for physical pain (the famous 'deathbed letter', preserved by Diogenes Laertius at 10.22, = Epicurus fr. 52 Arrighetti). See further Warren 2004: 12–15.

Philodemus (Lucretius is concerned to make us recognize the hidden *roots* of our more destructive emotions,[9] Philodemus their negative *consequences*), the resemblance is nevertheless clear.

Lucretius' vivid representation of human bodies as liable to piercing, mutilation, and decay – as, in short, fragile, vulnerable, and permeable – may be connected with Epicurus' well-known dictum that, so far as death is concerned, 'we live in a city without walls' (πόλιν ἀτείχιστον οἰκοῦμεν, *Sent. Vat.* 31). Because the body's boundaries are in their nature penetrable (like all other physical objects), there is no way that we can protect ourselves against the forces that attack them from both without and within, and so ward off death. For the Epicurean, of course, death is not an evil (*nil igitur mors est ad nos neque pertinet hilum*, 'death is nothing to us, and does not matter to us in the least', Lucr. 3.830);[10] but before this contention can take its full effect, the potential convert needs to be made to recognize – to 'see' – that the fear of extinction and the futile desire to keep our fragile bodies permanently intact ironically underlie many or even most of our more self-destructive patterns of behaviour.[11] This line of interpretation is developed at length (on the basis, however, of modern rather than ancient psychological theory) by Charles Segal, in his subtle and penetrating study *Lucretius on Death and Anxiety*.[12] Segal shows in detail how the poet employs images of 'boundary violation' as a means of bringing to the surface our unconscious fears of dying, of annihilation and 'the total extinction of one's self',[13] which can then be directly grappled with and overcome.[14]

---

[9] For the theory that depression, anxiety, and aggression are, ultimately, rooted in the fear of death, see especially the proem to Book 3 (37–93), where Lucretius represents the fear of death as a poison or pollutant that infects all our pleasures and prevents us from enjoying them fully (*metus ille ... | ... humanam qui vitam turbat ab imo | omnia suffundens mortis nigrore neque ullam | esse voluptatem liquidam puramque relinquit*, 'that anxiety ... that unsettles human life from its depths, polluting everything with the blackness of death, and leaves no pleasure pure and unalloyed', 37–40), even – or especially – if we claim to feel no such fears (41–58). Lucretius returns to the notion of unconscious motivation at the end of the book, with a powerful evocation of the sense of ennui afflicting the contemporary elite (3.1053–75).

[10] Lucretius' principal argument here is that extinction should not be regarded as an evil because a being that does not exist cannot suffer harm (3.830–69); cf. Epicurus, *Ep. Men.* 124–5, *Principal Doctrines* 2.

[11] Lucretius suggests that political ambition, competition for power, violation of blood-ties, civil war, and even – paradoxically – suicidal tendencies can be attributed to the futile desire to protect ourselves against the (ultimately inescapable) forces of destruction (3.59–93); cf. 5.1120–35 for a similar analysis of the roots of political ambition and civil conflict. An equivalence between the fear of death and the desire to maintain the physical body intact is established particularly at 3.870–93, where the poet confronts anxieties relating to the body's posthumous destruction.

[12] C. P. Segal 1990.        [13] C. P. Segal 1990: 12.

[14] Cf. also Nussbaum 1994: 240–79, esp. 259–64.

On one level, then, the graphic depiction of bodies as subject to violence, mutilation, and decay may be interpreted as an instance of the kind of 'shock tactics' recommended by Philodemus in the treatment of pupils who are resistant to the Epicurean message: the reader needs to be startled out of his or her complacency and made to realize how desperately s/he needs Epicurus' help.[15] Thus, in general terms, the poet's deployment of such images is in itself rhetorical. As I suggested above, however, the passages in question also repay a more detailed rhetorical analysis: in particular, we might want to ask how the poet tailors his argument to a specific (elite Roman) readership.

## III

My starting-point here is one of the most notorious and problematic passages of the poem, an episode of apparently quite gratuitous horror introduced towards the end of Lucretius' history of civilization at 5.1308–49. The poet has been tracing prehistoric developments in military hardware: this section of the book begins soberly enough with the transition from bronze to iron weaponry, which is followed by the use of war-horses and two- and four-horse chariots, and finally the introduction of scythed wheels. Then comes the training of elephants for use in warfare. At this point, the poet's imagination appears to get the better of him: from the historically attested use of war-elephants, he extrapolates doomed attempts to employ bulls, boars, and even lions on the battlefield. There follows a surreally vivid and nightmarish account of the consequences: lions run amok, seizing indiscriminately on the bodies of friend and foe; horses are gored by bulls or hamstrung by boars, while their riders are trampled underfoot. The passage concludes with what sounds like an odd about-face:

> si fuit ut facerent. sed vix adducor ut, ante
> quam commune malum fieret foedumque, futurum
> non quierint animo praesentire atque videre;
> et magis id possis factum contendere in omni,
> in variis mundis varia ratione creatis,
> quam certo atque uno terrarum quolibet orbi.
> sed facere id non tam vincendi spe voluerunt,

---

[15] Cf. Schrijvers 1970: 73 (on Lucr. 5.1198–1240): 'les vers . . . doivent inspirer au lecteur l'horreur des phénomènes cosmiques afin que celui-ci se cramponne, tel un naufragé à une bouée, . . . à la doctrine épicurienne, porteuse du vrai bonheur'. On the need for 'shock tactics' in the case of recalcitrant pupils, see Phld. *De ira* col. III.13–18 Indelli, *Lib. dic.* frr. 7 and 10 Olivieri.

> quam dare quod gemerent hostes, ipsique perire,
> qui numero diffidebant armisque vacabant.[16]

If indeed they really did these things. But I can scarcely believe that, before so shameful a disaster befell both sides alike, they could not foresee and anticipate in their minds what would happen; and you could more easily assert that this occurred somewhere in the universe, among the many different worlds created in many different ways, than on any one particular planet. But they wanted to do it not so much in the hope of winning, as to make their enemy suffer before they themselves perished; for they had no faith in their numbers and lacked strength of arms.

(5.1341–9)

Bailey calls 1308–49 'the most astonishing paragraph in the poem', and subsequent commentators appear similarly bemused.[17] If, as the lines quoted above seem to suggest, Lucretius had his doubts about the validity of his own historical speculations – which have no parallel in any other ancient author – why include them at all?

In an article published as long ago as 1964, K. L. McKay suggested that the detail of the passage may have been inspired by the poet's experience of watching *venationes*:[18] certainly, the idea of combat between human beings and animals would seem far less outlandish to a Roman reader than it does to us, given the frequency with which increasingly spectacular wild-beast fights were laid on for the late-Republican audience.[19] I want to suggest

---

[16] All quotations from the *De rerum natura* follow the text of C. Bailey 1922, with occasional changes to punctuation; translations are my own.

[17] C. Bailey 1947: III.1529; cf. Beye 1963: 167 ('an exciting poetic fantasy of an intelligence fevered, perverted and cancerous'); McKay 1964: 127 ('the poet has triumphed over the philosopher'); Perelli 1969: 49–50 ('essa rivela il carattere allucinatorio dell' immaginazione lucreziana'). For more sympathetic accounts, see Schrijvers 1970: 296–305; Kenney 1972; Saylor 1972; Feeney 1978; C. P. Segal 1990: 188–95; Nussbaum 1994: 271–3; Shelton 1996: 58–64; Gale 2009: 206–8; Massaro 2010: 269–75.

[18] McKay 1964. Courtney 2006 considers McKay's theory 'far-fetched' (152), and finds what he regards as a more plausible source in hypothetical early versions of the Alexander Romance; my contention, however, is that – wherever the poet 'got his idea from' – the contemporary reader will almost inevitably have been prompted by the detail of Lucretius' account to think of the *venationes*.

[19] Ville 1981: 88–92 (cf. Jennison 1937: 42–59) lists fourteen *venationes* known to have taken place in Rome between 105 and 55 BC, eight of which are dated to the period 65–55. The series culminates in Pompey's spectacularly lavish games of 55, the probable approximate publication date of the *De rerum natura* (on the dating of the poem, see most recently Hutchinson 2001, with the persuasive rebuttal by Volk 2010). While exotic animals had probably been exhibited at the *ludi* since at least the beginning of the second century BC (so Jennison 1937: 44–5), the period under discussion is characterized by beast-fights of unprecedented scale and the introduction of species never before seen in Rome. Sulla's games of 93 featured 'for the first time' 100 maned lions (Plin. *NH* 8.53); M. Scaurus' of 58 included 150 leopards, along with a hippopotamus and five crocodiles (Plin. *NH* 8.64, 96); and Pompey's in 55 incorporated a five-day spectacular (Cic. *Fam.* 7.1.3, Dio 39.38),

that this insight may in fact be much more productive than McKay's own limited objective – to find a plausible historical 'source' for this particular passage – would imply. I will argue that the gladiatorial *munera* can be seen to act as a controlling metaphor which surfaces on several occasions at different points in the poem: the Epicurean sage's experience of the world is depicted as analogous to (if, in crucial ways, different from) that of the spectator in the amphitheatre.

A recurrent theme in much of the recent scholarship on the *munera* is the paradoxical combination of scorn and admiration, alienation and identification, in the attitudes of Roman writers (the anonymous writers of graffiti as well as poets and philosophers) towards the gladiator.[20] The accomplished fighter who risked his life again and again for the audience's pleasure was at once the lowest of the low and the glamorous object of desire. My contention is that Lucretius seeks to exploit this paradox via the implicit evocation of gladiatorial spectacle, which can be seen to underlie not just the 'beasts of battle' digression but many of the scenes of violence and mutilation to which I have referred.

The gladiator is, in different ways, an *exemplary* figure. From one perspective, he offers the audience an admirable example of courage and skill in combat – a function remarked upon by Cicero and Seneca, amongst others.[21] From another, his physical separation from the watching crowd is emblematic of his alienation from them: the slave, criminal, or war-captive belongs to a different order of existence from the citizen body, whose solidarity is reinforced by the citizens' common participation in

---

with elephants, 600 lions, 410 leopards, a Gallic lynx, Ethiopian monkeys, and a rhinoceros, the last three species all new to Rome (Plin. *NH* 8.53, 64, 70–1). Somewhat later than our period (probably second century AD), but strikingly similar in detail to Lucretius' account of this hypothetical animal/human conflict, are the *venatio*-mosaics from Zliten in Libya and El Djem in Tunisia, reproduced by K. M. Coleman 1990, plate II, and S. Brown 1992: 196. The Zliten mosaic shows lions, leopards, boars, and bulls engaged in combat both with each other and with human antagonists or victims (*bestiarii* and bound prisoners); in common with the El Djem mosaic, it also includes a detail of a man in the process of being mauled by a leopard, which might almost serve as an illustration of the scene described at Lucr. 5.1318–22. Like Lucretius' lionesses, which 'launched their furious bodies in a leap ... and attacked the faces of any who approached them, or dragged down their unsuspecting victims ... grasping them with strong jaws and hooked claws' (*irritata ... iaciebant corpora saltu | ... et adversum venientibus ora petebant | et nec opinantis ... deripiebant, | ... | morsibus adfixae validis atque unguibus uncis*), the leopard in the visual images springs upon its prey, simultaneously sinking teeth into the man's face and claws into his chest.

[20] See esp. Ville 1981: 329–44; Hopkins 1983: 21–7; Wiedemann 1992: 26–47; Barton 1993, esp. 15–25; Futrell 1997: 49–50; Kyle 1998: 79–90; C. Edwards 2007: 47–53, 68–77; Fagan 2011a: 270–2. Cf. also Introduction, pp. 11–12.

[21] Cic. *Tusc.* 2.41, *Phil.* 3.35 (cf. *Mil.* 92); Sen. *Ep.* 30.8, *Constant.* 16.2, *Prov.* 2.8, 3.4, *Tranq.* 11.4–5; also Plin. *Pan.* 33.1.

what Paul Plass calls 'a ruthlessly simple microcosm' of Rome's imperial domination.[22] The wild animals destroyed in the *venatio* may be seen as emblematic, likewise, both of Roman conquests (hence the predominance of exotic, foreign species, particularly in the shows of the early and mid-first century BC), and more broadly of human domination over the natural world.[23] The audience was at once emotionally engaged with and ideologically distanced from the participants in the *munera*: to quote Plass again, it 'represented the body politic secure from the actual carnage down on the sand, though deeply involved in the symbolic victory or defeat they had assembled to view'.[24]

Lucretius' exploitation of graphically violent images relies on a similar dialectic of involvement and distancing. The 'beasts of battle', for example, are separated from us as readers by their remoteness in time; yet, as Lucretius emphasizes throughout this part of the culture-history, nothing really changes, and the present in many ways resembles the past.[25] The curious lines which conclude the passage have a similarly double-edged effect. The poet seems at first to be drawing back, suggesting that these macabre events may never have taken place at all (1344–6); yet he appears, on reconsideration (1347–9), to find a satisfying psychological explanation, reflecting that the self-defeating experiment must have been motivated ultimately by a desire to harm the enemy at whatever cost (*voluerunt* | ... *dare quod gemerent hostes, ipsique perire*). Rhetorically, the lines serve in effect to magnify the horror of the preceding scenes, the self-destructive violence of which, Lucretius implies, makes them almost incredible; yet by offering a recognizably human motivation for the actions of his primitive warriors, the poet reminds us that they are, in the end, not so very different from his modern readers.[26] The fleeting suggestion that the whole episode was perhaps no more than fantasy may afford us a momentary relief; but

---

[22] Plass 1995: 42.

[23] For this interpretation of the symbolic significance of the *venatio* see, e.g., Wiedemann 1992: 62–7; Plass 1995: 53–4.

[24] Plass 1995: 42–3. For 'ingroup solidarity' amongst arena audiences, see also Fagan 2011a: 121–54.

[25] Continuity between past and present is stressed at 5.1133–5, 1183–1225, 1408–11, 1423–4; note also the repeated use of analogies between past and present (5.1030–2, 1094–1100, 1339–40, 1376–8). Further, the use of the (generalizing) second-person *videres* at 5.1332 may be said to bring the reader closer to the action described, however chronologically remote: compare Lucretius' use of the same technique in his account of the plague of Athens (6.1163 *nec* ... *posses* ... *tueri*, 1257 *posses* ... *videre*, 1268 *videres*), well analysed by Clay 1983: 262–3, who comments that 'unlike Thucydides, Lucretius forces his reader into close contact with the distant Athenians ... Lucretius' reader is placed in Athens as an observer and even as an actor'. On the rhetorical impact of second-person verbs in the proem to Book 2, see pp. 72–5 below.

[26] Cf. Kenney 1972: 23.

the immediate withdrawal of this short-lived consolation redoubles the disturbing impact of the argument, as we are forced to confront the motives that inspire such devastating and ultimately futile actions – motives that will no doubt have seemed all too plausible to Lucretius' original audience, encountering this text at a period when Rome seemed bent on tearing itself apart through civil and political strife.

Similarly, the images of mutilation which recur in Book 3 and in the plague narrative at the end of Book 6[27] are at once coolly clinical and directly relevant to the reader, in so far as it is ultimately *our own* death that Lucretius wants us to contemplate: the maggoty corpse and severed limbs are, in an important sense, *the reader's*. The gruesome detail of 3.719–21, for example, is strictly impersonal in its focus: we are invited to contemplate this decomposing body, in the immediate context of Lucretius' argument for the mortality of the soul, as evidence for the posthumous disintegration of the *anima* (the scattered remnants of which are perhaps understood to contribute to the spontaneous generation of maggots in the corpse):

> . . .
> unde cadavera rancenti iam viscere vermis
> exspirant atque unde animantum copia tanta
> exos et exsanguis tumidos perfluctuat artus?

[If the soul is immortal and exits intact from the dying body] how comes it that corpses breathe out maggots from their now putrid entrails and that so great a multitude of boneless, bloodless creatures makes the bloated limbs seethe?

Yet the stomach-churning detail of these lines may serve to anticipate the satirical attack in the book's finale on the – as Lucretius sees it – absurd conventions of funerary ritual and associated fears for the posthumous fate of the body (3.870–93). Caring about what happens to our remains after death is for the Epicurean quite illogical, since the dead body is no longer 'us'. This contention may prompt us to re-examine our reactions to the earlier passage: if the poet's vivid evocation of posthumous decay makes our skin crawl, is that because we, too, have failed to separate ourselves fully from the inert and senseless corpse?

The sketch earlier in the same book of bodies dismembered in battle (3.642–56) creates a similar effect through subtle shifts in focalization, inviting us at first to adopt the detached perspective of the contemplative philosopher, but soon drawing us in to empathize with the experience of the mutilated soldier. The argument in this section of the book is that the

---

[27] See p. 63 and n. 1 above.

soul must be mortal because it can be divided into separate parts (indivisibility being for Lucretius a necessary condition for indestructibility): the
poet adduces as evidence the way that body-parts severed in battle allegedly
continue to twitch as though still animate. At the beginning of the passage,
the tone is detached and clinical: the severed body-parts are initially
referred to merely as *membra* ('limbs', 642) or – still more impersonally – *id
quod decidit abscisum* ('the part that has been severed and fallen away',
644–5), without reference to the living individual to whom they so
recently belonged. Immediately, however, the poet turns to the perceptions
of the adrenalin-fuelled soldier, who in the heat of battle is momentarily
unaware of his own mutilation (*mobilitate mali non quit sentire dolorem | et
simul in pugnae studio quod dedita mens est*, '[the victim] cannot feel any pain
owing at once to the swiftness of his injury and to his mental absorption in
the heat of battle', 646–7). Finally, the focalization shifts once more and we
are left with a vivid but once again impersonal image of a head 'severed from
the warm and living torso' (*caput abscisum calido viventeque trunco*, 654)
staring open-eyed as the last vestiges of life depart (654–6).

The rhetorical strategy underlying the paradoxical combination of engagement and alienation in these passages can perhaps be most clearly illustrated
by looking briefly at the movement of the proem to Book 2, where the use
of second-person verbs and pronouns repays close scrutiny. In the opening
lines of the book, poet and reader are imagined as occupying a detached high
point – the 'citadel of philosophy' – from which they can look down calmly
on the pointless struggles of the unenlightened:

> suave, mari magno turbantibus aequora ventis,
> e terra magnum alterius spectare laborem;
> non quia vexari quemquamst iucunda voluptas,
> sed quibus ipse malis careas quia cernere suave est.
> suave etiam belli certamina magna tueri
> per campos instructa tua sine parte pericli.
> sed nil dulcius est, bene quam munita tenere
> edita doctrina sapientum templa serena,
> *despicere* unde *queas* alios passimque *videre*
> errare atque viam palantis quaerere vitae,
> certare ingenio, contendere nobilitate,
> noctes atque dies niti praestante labore
> ad summas emergere opes rerumque potiri.

It is pleasant, when winds are stirring the surface of the mighty sea, to watch from
ashore another man's great struggles; not because there is delightful pleasure in
anyone's suffering, but because it is gratifying to observe evils from which you, for
your own part, are exempt. It is pleasant too to view the mighty conflict of war
arrayed on the field of battle, without any danger to yourself. But nothing is

sweeter than to occupy the peaceful, well-fortified dwelling of the wise, raised high on foundations of philosophy, whence *you can look down* on others and *see* them wandering everywhere, straying in search of the path of life, vying with their talents, competing in nobility of birth, struggling night and day with the greatest labour to reach the heights of wealth and power.

(2.1–13)

In lines 40ff., however, the reader is treated as one of the unenlightened. Lucretius personifies our fears of the gods and of death as demonic spirits, which cannot be deterred by the vain trappings of political or military power: 'if your fears are not frightened away by displays of military might,' the poet asks, 'how can you doubt that this power belongs to philosophy alone?'

> . . .
> si non forte *tuas* legiones per loca campi
> fervere cum *videas* belli simulacra cientis,
> subsidiis magnis †epicuri† constabilitas,
> ornatas armis †itastuas† pariterque animatas,
> fervere cum videas classem lateque vagari,
> his *tibi* tum rebus timefactae religiones
> effugiunt animo pavidae mortisque timores
> tum vacuum pectus linquunt curaque solutum.
> quod si ridicula haec ludibriaque esse videmus,
> re veraque metus hominum curaeque sequaces
> nec metuunt sonitus armorum nec fera tela
> audacterque inter reges rerumque potentis
> versantur neque fulgorem reverentur ab auro
> nec clarum vestis splendorem purpureai,
> quid *dubitas* quin omni' sit haec rationi' potestas?

[Wealth and political prestige benefit neither body nor mind] – unless perhaps when *you watch your legions* surging over the Campus and enacting mock-battles, reinforced with plentiful reserves, equipped with arms and all alike eager for action, when *you see* your fleet surging and ranging far and wide, superstition is frightened off by these things and flees in terror from *your* mind, and the fear of death leaves *your* heart free and released from anxiety. But if we see that these things are absurd and a mockery and that in truth the fears of men and the anxieties that dog them have no fear of the clash of arms or fierce weapons and stroll boldly amongst kings and potentates, showing no reverence for the gleam of gold or the bright sheen of purple robes, how can *you* doubt that this power belongs to philosophy alone?

(2.40–53)

I suggest that, in the context of the direct address to and exhortation of the reader, the poet's use of the second person in these lines should not be dismissed as a generalizing 'one'. Rather, the juxtaposed images of viewing in the passages quoted offer alternative models for the reader's engagement

with the text and the world it portrays, particularly the world of violent
struggle and ambition backed by military might embodied in the *belli
certamina magna* ('mighty conflict of war') of line 5 and the legions of
40–3.[28] The philosophical detachment of 1–13 contrasts sharply with the
fear and anxiety that characterize the unenlightened (44–53); and there is a
marked opposition too between the 'distant view' afforded to the convinced Epicurean[29] and the more immediate involvement of the anxious
and fearful person in the spectacle presented in the second passage (these
are 'your legions' so futilely on display, and failing to frighten away the fear
of death from 'your heart'). Another way of conceptualizing these alterna-
tives might be in terms of a shift from a generalized (though still individual) second-person addressee – Lucretius' ideal reader – in the opening
lines to exhortation directed more specifically at Memmius, the nominal
recipient of the poet's didactic lesson, from line 40 onwards. While the
poem's dedicatee remains (perhaps tactfully) unnamed in this passage, we
might well be put in mind in such a context of the *Memmi clara propago*
('noble offspring of Memmius') – the statesman of the proem to Book 1,
who cannot absent himself from public service at a time of national
emergency (1.41–3).[30] On this reading, the intratextual addressee
plays the role of benighted philosophical beginner, from whom we, the
readers-in-general, are invited to separate ourselves as we come to share the
enlightened gaze of the Epicurean sage. Whichever way we analyse it, this
double perspective is crucial to the protreptic purpose of the *De rerum
natura*: if Lucretius' poem is going to succeed, it must show us both the

---

[28] The double perspective offered by Lucretius here, and his exploitation of the gladiatorial model in
general, has both intriguing similarities with and distinctive differences from the practice of Lucan,
as discussed by Leigh 1997: 234–91. Leigh argues that the epic poet – like Lucretius, on my
analysis – exploits gladiatorial imagery in order to construct alternative models of readership/
spectatorship, whereby the audience is invited both to sympathize/empathize with his characters,
and to view them with a detached, sadistic/voyeuristic pleasure in the often sensational or bizarre
scenes of violence he depicts. For Leigh, Lucan's strategy is disruptive, simultaneously inviting and
stigmatizing a 'guilty voyeurism' on the reader's part; Lucretius, in contrast, can be seen to
manipulate the duality between engagement and detachment as a means to a quite specific
ideological end. Cf. also Lovatt 2013: 283–302 on the 'play of alienation and identification'
(297) in Homer, Virgil, and Flavian epic.

[29] For the Epicurean as detached spectator, in the proem to Book 2 and throughout the poem, see De
Lacy 1964.

[30] For the didactic addressee as a figure 'over whose head' the poet addresses an ideal or implied reader,
see Konstan 1994 and (on Lucretius specifically) Mitsis 1994. As David Konstan points out to me
(*per litteras*), Lucretius' tact in not addressing Memmius by name in this passage is consonant with
the therapeutic strategy recommended by Philodemus, who emphasizes the importance for the
Epicurean teacher of sensitivity to the different predispositions and temperaments of different
pupils: at *Lib. dic.* cols. XXIIb–XXIVa Olivieri, in particular, he warns that people of rank are apt to
be touchy and to stand on their dignity.

tranquillity that we *can* attain, and the horror of the world in which we *actually* live – we have to be persuaded that we *need* Epicurus' salvation.[31]

I suggested above that the corpses and severed limbs of Books 3 and 6 belong to 'us'; but in another, equally important sense, they belong to 'them'. Just as the gladiator is both an exemplar of Roman values and an embodiment of otherness, so the plague- and war-victims described in such vivid detail by Lucretius are both Everyman and – specifically – representatives of the non-Epicurean world. The contexts in which the majority of these images occur are important here. Warfare, as Lucretius implies at several points in the poem, is something alien to the Epicurean, who will see that nothing is really worth fighting for.[32] Hence, both the 'beasts of battle' and the limbs severed in war serve a symbolic purpose, as emblems of futility, in addition to their immediate function in the poet's argument.[33] This is particularly clear in the case of the 'beasts of battle', because the whole digression harks back to the much briefer but equally vivid scene, near the beginning of the history of civilization, in which a primitive human is eaten alive by a predator:[34]

> unus enim tum quisque magis deprensus eorum
> pabula viva feris praebebat, dentibus haustus,
> et nemora ac montis gemitu silvasque replebat
> viva videns vivo sepeliri viscera busto.
> at quos effugium servarat corpore adeso,
> posterius tremulas super ulcera taetra tenentes
> palmas horriferis accibant vocibus Orcum,
> donec eos vita privarant vermina saeva
> expertis opis, ignaros quid vulnera vellent.

For at that time, more than nowadays, one or other of them would be captured and provide living food for wild beasts, devoured by their teeth, and fill the groves and mountains and woods with screams as he saw his living flesh buried in a living tomb. And even those who had saved themselves by escaping with mangled bodies would afterwards call upon Death with dreadful cries, holding their trembling

---

[31] For a similar 'stick and carrot' approach in Epicurean therapeutics, see Phld. *Lib. dic.* frr. 14–15, 63–4, 68 Olivieri, with Nussbaum 1986: 41–2.

[32] See n. 55 below. On Lucretius' representation of warfare, see further Gale 1994: 117–19 and 2000: 232–40.

[33] Cf. Schrijvers 1970: 303–5; Saylor 1972, esp. 310–14; C. P. Segal 1990: 118–36, 226–7; Nussbaum 1994: 271–3.

[34] In addition to the general similarities of content, note esp. the phrase *dentibus haustus* ('devoured by their teeth', 5.991), which is reworked with reference to the bulls and boars of 5.1323–9 (*hauribant … cornibus … caedebant dentibus*, 'gored with their horns … slashed with their tusks'). Cf. C. P. Segal 1990: 120–1, 206–7.

hands over gruesome wounds, until cruel agony took away their lives, unable to help themselves in their ignorance of what their injuries required.

(5.990–8)

The fact that the later passage forms a kind of climax in the culture-history points to a certain circularity: once, the poet suggests, human beings could not avoid the attacks of wild animals; by this point, they have the technology which would allow them to do so, but instead deliberately direct the animals' attacks at each other. The brief analogy between past and present at 1339–40 – the 'beasts of battle' run amok as elephants often do 'nowadays' (*ut nunc*) – suggests that Lucretius' contemporaries are no more able to escape the cycle of violence than were their distant forebears. For the Epicurean poet, the human-animal conflict played out in this passage, with its overtones of contemporary arena spectacle, symbolizes not so much the triumph of civilization over the natural world as the inevitable failure of technological progress to free us from pain and suffering.

The plague of Athens at the end of Book 6 is another of the most controversial parts of the poem. The long account of the aetiology, symptomology, and social effects of the disease serves overtly to exemplify the preceding discussion of epidemics; but the length and detail of Lucretius' treatment has led many critics to detect symbolic significance. An interpretation that has gained wide currency sees the plague-victims as, on one level, representative of the mass of unenlightened humanity.[35] Certainly, as Lucretius implicitly reminds us, they are *pre*-Epicurean: the philosopher's birth, celebrated at the beginning of Book 6, did not occur until some sixty years after the end of the Peloponnesian War. If we compare Lucretius' version of the plague with Thucydides' eyewitness account,[36] it is clear that the poet has exaggerated and sought to focus the reader's attention on the *psychological* effects of the disease, in particular the despair induced in the sufferers as a result of their pathological fear of death.[37] It is this fear, Lucretius tells us, that drove people to amputate their own hands and feet, eyes, and even genitalia (a significant distortion of the equivalent passage in Thucydides, which merely suggests that the

---

[35] See esp. Commager 1957; Schrijvers 1970: 312–24; Bright 1971; C. P. Segal 1990: 228–37; Gale 1994: 223–8.

[36] Thuc. 2.47–54.

[37] Note esp. *cor maestum* ('sorrowing heart', 1152), *anxius angor* ('anguished anxiety', 1158), *timore* ('in fear', 1179), *perturbata animi mens in maerore metuque* ('the mind in a turmoil of sorrow and fear', 1183), *vitai nimium cupidos mortisque timentis* ('too eager for life and fearful of death', 1240); as Commager 1957 shows in detail, all these phrases are additions to, or represent 'mistranslations' of, the equivalent passages in Lucretius' Thucydidean model.

*loss* of these diseased parts allowed some victims to survive).[38] Again, then, the horror of the passage is designed in part to distance us (as potential Epicurean converts): an Epicurean disciple would not, of course, have been able to avoid catching the plague, but would have been immune from its more psychologically damaging effects, and from the pathetic clinging to life so sharply satirized in the lines I have just discussed.

The impact of such passages is, I suggest, analogous at one level to the unifying effect that – it has been argued – gladiatorial spectacles would have had on the audience. The gladiator, or *a fortiori* the criminal condemned *ad bestias*, is a kind of scapegoat: the effect of watching his death is to strengthen the audience's sense of solidarity, to reinforce the cohesion of the community from which the combatant or victim in the arena is symbolically separated.[39] Similarly, Lucretius seeks to create a sense of solidarity between the didactic speaker and the reader, as potential Epicurean recruit. *We* are offered a means of escape from the violence that inevitably dominates the world of the non-Epicurean. At the same time, there is a striking inversion with respect to the amphitheatrical model: whereas, in the latter case, the gladiator or criminal is the outsider, while the watching crowd represents the imperial might of Rome, Lucretius' contemplative philosopher is himself the outsider. The Epicurean 'escapes' the violence on show before him precisely by rejecting the values embraced by the community as a whole: in the proem to Book 2 and elsewhere, Roman society is itself the spectacle at which the poet's detached gaze is directed.[40]

It is also important for the poet to remind us, however, that – unless and until we accept Epicurus' teachings – we recross the boundary between *cavea* and arena, becoming once again participants rather than spectators, as soon as we lay the poem aside. This idea is hinted at in two passages with which I conclude this part of my discussion. Towards the end of Book 4, in the course of an examination of the mechanics of dreaming, the poet catalogues the anxiety dreams suffered by those whose minds 'with great labour bring forth great deeds' (*magnis ... motibus edunt | magna*, 4.1011–12). The phrase is presumably used with some irony to designate non-Epicureans:

---

[38] Lucr. 6.1208–12; Thuc. 2.49.8. The moralizing phrases that frame the Lucretian lines (1208 *graviter ... metuentes limina leti*, 'greatly fearing the doorway of death', and 1212 *usque adeo mortis metus his incesserat acer*, 'to such an extent had the bitter fear of death overcome them') have no counterpart in Thucydides, and should be seen as an Epicurean gloss added by the poet to his Greek source.

[39] For the gladiator as scapegoat see, e.g., K. M. Coleman 1990: 69–70, Plass 1995: 25–8, 58–61; cf. also Introduction, p. 11.

[40] See esp. 2.1–19; 3.41–86, 1053–75; 5.1120–35, 1198–1203, 1226–35.

there is certainly a strong contrast with the experience of the *praeceptor* himself, who dreams peacefully of composing the poem (4.969–70). The dream which particularly concerns me is that described at 1015–17:

> porro hominum mentes, magnis quae motibus edunt
> magna, itidem saepe in somnis faciuntque geruntque,
> reges expugnant, capiuntur, proelia miscent,
> tollunt clamorem, quasi si iugulentur, ibidem.
> multi depugnant gemitusque doloribus edunt
> et quasi pantherae morsu saevive leonis
> mandantur magnis clamoribus omnia complent.

Furthermore, men whose minds with great labour bring forth great deeds often act the same way and perform the same deeds in sleep: kings sack cities, are captured, join battle, raise a shout as though their throats were being cut then and there. Many engage in combat and give cries of pain, and – as though they were being mauled by the bites of panther or savage lion – fill the whole place with loud screams.

(4.1011–17)

In view of the 'bites of panther or savage lion', which suggest a *venatio*, the verb *depugnant* should be taken in its technical sense, 'fight in the arena (as gladiator or *bestiarius*)'.[41] Lucretius has already told us that dreams reflect our daily activities (4.962–86); the dream here arises, one assumes, from the experience of *watching* rather than taking part in gladiatorial shows. Yet at another level, the dream might also be taken as a symbolic reflex of the struggles that characterize the life of the non-Epicurean, in pursuit of the goals ironically designated as *magna* in 1012. The great and good are paradoxically equated with the lowly beast-fighter,[42] putting on a show for the Epicurean convert who watches – with a certain pleasure – from the safe distance of philosophy's 'citadel' (2.7–13).

The image of the non-Epicurean as *bestiarius* recurs in the proem to Book 5, where an extended comparison between the achievements of Hercules and those of Epicurus culminates in a series of rhetorical

---

[41] *OLD* s.v., sect. 2.

[42] As one of Cambridge University Press's anonymous readers points out to me, the equation is underlined by the parallel phrasing in lines 1011 and 1017 (*magnis ... motibus edunt ~ magnis clamoribus ... complent*). I owe to Pamela Zinn the intriguing suggestion that Lucretius additionally gestures in this passage at the hierarchically stratified seating arrangements of the Roman amphitheatre: the reader simultaneously experiences the close-up view of the action which would normally be reserved for the privileged elite in their ringside seats, and, as detached Epicurean spectator, the more distant prospect of the lower-class spectators high up at the back of the *cavea*, while the high-status individual becomes interchangeable (figuratively speaking) with the social outcast fighting for his life in the arena. Considered in these terms, Epicurean enlightenment transcends mere social distinction.

questions, in which the pangs of fear and desire are implicitly likened to the monsters slain by the hero:

> at nisi purgatumst pectus, quae proelia nobis
> atque pericula tumst ingratis insinuandum!
> quantae tum scindunt hominem cuppedinis acres
> sollicitum curae quantique perinde timores!
> quidve superbia spurcitia ac petulantia? quantas
> efficiunt clades! quid luxus desidiaeque?
> haec igitur qui cuncta subegerit ex animoque
> expulerit dictis, non armis, nonne decebit
> hunc hominem numero divum dignarier esse?

But unless we purify our hearts, what battles and dangers must we then enter whether we will or no? How great then the fierce torments of desire, how great too the fears that tear an anxious man apart! What of pride, filth, and wantonness? What devastation they wreak! What of profligacy and idleness? The man, therefore, who has conquered all these and expelled them from our minds, by words, not arms, will he not fittingly be thought worthy to be numbered amongst the gods?

(5.43–51)

If we do not 'purify our hearts', with the help of Epicurus' teachings, we will be condemned, metaphorically speaking, *ad bestias*. It may be significant that – amongst the many other associations of this most polyvalent of heroes – Hercules seems to have had a particular connection with the arena.[43] Yet there is one crucial difference: Epicurus' followers have no need to emulate their hero's figurative battles, as the gladiator or *bestiarius* emulates those of Hercules. Epicurus has, in a way, already killed the 'monsters' of fear and desire: all we need to do to win our freedom is to accept his 'truth-speaking words' (*veridicis . . . dictis*, 6.24).

For Lucretius, then, the gladiator or *bestiarius* is by implication a negative rather than a positive *exemplum*, embodying the non-Epicurean's condemnation to psychological pain and conflict, rather than the Stoic fortitude celebrated by Cicero and (especially) Seneca.[44] Whereas Seneca holds up the gladiator's willing acceptance of the fatal stroke as a model of impassivity in the face of death – which will inevitably come to all, sooner or later – the Epicurean, espousing a philosophy of pleasure, takes as his or

---

[43] See Wiedemann 1992: 178–80, citing Hor. *Epist.* 1.1.5 (the retiring gladiator dedicates his weapons to Hercules); as Wiedemann notes, implicit or explicit comparisons between Hercules and the gladiator or *bestiarius* can also be found in the pseudo-Senecan *Hercules Oetaeus* (1457, 1472) and in Martial (*Spect.* 8 and 32 Carratello). Cf. also Ville 1981: 333.

[44] For the gladiator as an exemplary figure in the writings of Seneca, see n. 21 above and C. Edwards 2007: 72–7.

her model the experience of the amphitheatrical spectator. The reader is offered a choice: either to fight it out with the psychological monsters of Books 4 and 5, to engage in the 'combat' for wealth and power that characterizes the life of the non-Epicurean (2.11–13), or to become part of a philosophical audience watching these spectacles with a certain detached enjoyment (2.1–13). Yet Lucretius' rhetorical strategy relies (with considerable subtlety) on a dialectic between distancing and identification comparable to the tension between superiority and empathy that his original readers are likely to have experienced in viewing the gladiatorial *munera*. As I have argued, Lucretius' depiction of scenes of violence appears to be designed both to involve and to repel the reader, holding up a mirror to our own vulnerability, and then offering us a way of escape.

## IV

The gladiatorial model, then, can help us to appreciate the function of violent images in the rhetoric of Lucretius' poem. A further, perhaps more obvious, source for these images, which can be seen in Lucretius' hands to converge with the violence of the arena, is the graphic depiction of wounds in the battle-scenes of Homeric and Ennian epic.[45] Lucretius' gruesome account of the havoc wrought by scythed chariots seems, in fact, to be based directly on Ennius' narrative of the Battle of Magnesia,[46] while the primitive man devoured by predators is perhaps modelled on the fate of Mettius Fufetius as recounted in the *Annales*,[47] though the horrifying twist that the victim is still alive seems to be Lucretius' own contribution.[48]

The unflinching depiction of wounds and physical mutilation in the epic tradition seems, on the face of it, to be designed to underline the cost

---

[45] The convergence noted here is not exclusive to Lucretius, in so far as single combat on the field of battle is not infrequently figured as gladiatorial spectacle by Roman epic poets and other writers: see Leigh 1997: 236–40. As noted above (n. 28), however, Lucretius exploits the disruptive potential of the analogy between gladiator and warrior-hero in a manner which is distinctively different from that of (say) Virgil or Lucan.

[46] Lucr. 3.642–56; Enn. *Ann.* 483–4 Skutsch *oscitat in campis caput a cervice revolsum* | *semianimesque micant oculi lucemque requirunt* ('a head torn away from the neck gapes upon the plain, and dying eyes twitch and seek the light'), with Skutsch 1985: 645–6. The opening phrase of Lucretius' account, *falciferos memorant currus* ('they relate that scythed chariots …', 642) would appear to function as an 'Alexandrian footnote', directing the reader to the Ennian intertext.

[47] Lucr. 5.993 *viva videns vivo sepeliri viscera busto* ('as he saw his living flesh buried in a living tomb'); Enn. *Ann.* 125–6 Skutsch *volturus in †spineto† miserum mandebat homonem:* | *heu quam crudeli condebat membra sepulcro* ('in the ?thicket a vulture devoured the poor man; alas, in how cruel a tomb his body was buried').

[48] Here, again, the detail is perhaps evocative of arena spectacle: the victims of mauling both in the mosaics detailed at n. 19 above and in Mart. *Spect.* 9.3–5 Carratello are similarly compelled to *watch* the mangling of their own bodies (cf. K. M. Coleman 1990: 54).

and brutality of war, as a counterweight to the genre's emphasis on the glamour and glory of the heroic warrior.[49] Yet the hero's immortal *kleos* is intimately bound up with his determination to endure as well as inflict wounds and death, not just in the sense that – as Sarpedon memorably proclaims in the *Iliad*[50] – this is the risk he must take in order to 'earn' the honours bestowed on him by the people, but also in so far as the 'beautiful death' in battle 'fixes' the warrior at the peak of his youthful strength. The graphic – if at times anatomically implausible – depiction of wounds serves as a constant reminder that the hero's body, for all its godlike beauty, is in fact eminently fragile, liable as it is to piercing, crushing, and dismemberment; but, paradoxically, it is only through the endurance of such physical damage that his youthful perfection can achieve a kind of permanence, thanks to the memorializing institutions of the aristocratic funeral and epic song. In one sense, then, the rupture of the hero's body renders him more, not less, beautiful: thus, the wounded Menelaus is compared in a famous simile to a horse's cheek-piece of ivory, embellished with scarlet dye.[51] As J.-P. Vernant has shown,[52] however, the flip side of the 'beautiful death' is defilement and decay: the dead warrior's hair dragged in the dust, the dismembered body, the corpse exposed as food for carrion birds and beasts.[53] As Vernant argues, the threat that constantly hangs over the Iliadic warrior, but is never carried through to fulfilment (at least in the case of the major heroes), is that of utter annihilation, the simultaneous destruction of physical form and immortal *kleos*: the warrior whose body is ingloriously defiled also and simultaneously forfeits the right to live for ever in epic song. The duality inherent in Homeric epic's portrayal of violence inflicted on the body is, arguably, of a piece with its ambivalent presentation of war in general, as both the arena in which heroes strive to outdo each other in prowess, and the 'wretched', 'lamentable', or 'painful'[54] struggle in which young manhood is wasted and destroyed. To hazard a broad generalization, this duality – this sharp focus on *both* the *dulce et decorum and* the wanton wreck of youth and beauty – is characteristic of ancient epic in general.

---

[49] So, e.g., J. Griffin 1980: 90–100. On the ideology of Homeric warfare in general, see also M. W. Edwards 1987: 154–7; Vernant 1991; van Wees 1992, esp. 168–82.

[50] Hom. *Il.* 12.310–28.    [51] Hom. *Il.* 4.141–7.    [52] Vernant 1991.

[53] See, e.g., Hom. *Il.* 22.401–3 (hair dragged in the dust); 11.146–7, 13.202–4 (dismemberment); 1.4–5, 21.122–7, 22.335–6, 348–54 (exposure of the corpse). At 16.638–40, Sarpedon's body is rendered unrecognizable by dust and grime, as the two armies struggle for possession. On the themes of mutilation and exposure of the corpse, see also C. P. Segal 1971; Redfield 1994: 183–203.

[54] Silk 1987: 73–4 notes that the standing epithets of πόλεμος (οἰζυρός, πολύδακρυς, ἀργάλεος, and the like) are overwhelmingly pejorative.

Lucretius, it can be argued, exploits this tradition too for quite specific rhetorical purposes. His method is essentially to enforce a radical separation between the two elements – violence and glory – which, I have suggested, are mutually implicated in the ideology of epic warfare. For Lucretius, there *is* no beautiful death: rather, descriptions of wounding and death in battle serve only to illustrate the fragility of the mortal body and the finality of its destruction, and implicitly – as we have seen – to emblematize the futility of warfare. In addition to the primitive warriors savaged by imperfectly tamed animals and the victims of attack by scythed chariots in the passages discussed above, graphic accounts of wounding and dismemberment serve illustrative purposes in a number of other places, particularly in Book 3. At 3.170–6, the poet comments on the way that the mind is affected by a physical wound that 'uncovers bones and sinews' (*ossibus ac nervis disclusis*, 171); at 402–5, the fact that a body can still live even when shorn of arms and legs (*circum caesis lacer undique membris | truncus*, 403–4) illustrates the crucial role of the *animus* (concentrated in the chest, in contradistinction to the *anima*, or 'life force', which is spread through the whole body) in maintaining life; at 551–3, conversely, the rapid decay of amputated body-parts – hands, eyes, or nose – is used as a parallel for the inability of the *animus* to survive outside the body. In all these instances, the victims are notably anonymous: while these detailed accounts of bodily mutilation recall the conventions of Homeric battle-narrative, the decontextualization and depersonalization of the bodies and wounds described are striking. Even in more extensive vignettes such as 3.642–56 or the 'beasts of battle', no individual is identified: the scythed chariots of the former passage may evoke the Battle of Magnesia, but there are no winners and no losers, no heroes or conquerors in the brief glimpse of the battlefield that Lucretius offers us. The focus instead is purely on the physical damage inflicted on interchangeable human bodies.

The clinical tone adopted by Lucretius in such passages is of course in keeping with his argument that 'death is nothing to us' (3.830), and that the posthumous fate of the body is, or should be, a matter of indifference: there is no more reason to shrink from the prospect of being devoured by scavengers than from that of burial or embalming (3.870–93). The Homeric hero's greatest terror is something that the Epicurean recruit must learn to contemplate without a shudder. At the same time, graphic images of wounding and mutilation have their uses for the Epicurean poet: stripped of its heroic aspect, no longer the field for the exercise of martial *virtus* and the royal road to immortality, war becomes for Lucretius the ultimate emblem of the pointless and self-destructive patterns of behaviour engendered in the non-Epicurean by the false values of his society.[55] From this perspective too it is important that Lucretius' warriors are anonymous victims rather than immortal heroes: for the Epicurean, fame is meaningless and the desire to dominate others stems from a faulty understanding of the world and our place in it (3.59–86, 5.1113–35). True heroism does not, then, require us either to inflict or to expose ourselves to violence: when, at the end of Book 3, Lucretius offers his own miniature parade of heroes, its two climactic figures are the philosophers Democritus and Epicurus, who died not in battle but by suicide and disease respectively (3.1039–44).

Thus, the ideal of immortal glory is displaced from the warrior onto the philosopher, whose metaphorical triumph over the passions is portrayed as far superior to any military victory. Epicurus 'surpassed the whole human race in intelligence and outshone them as the rising sun dims the stars' (*genus humanum ingenio superavit et omnis | restinxit, stellas exortus ut aerius sol*, 3.1043–4); he 'conquered all the passions and expelled them from our minds, by words, not arms' (*haec ... cuncta subegerit ex animoque | expulerit dictis, non armis*, 5.49–50), and returned like a conquering hero from his defeat of the 'monster' *religio* (1.68–79).[56] The last-mentioned victory is strikingly juxtaposed with the first of several satirical allusions to the Trojan War: the cruel and impious slaughter of Iphigenia by the 'chosen leaders of the Greeks, foremost of heroes' (*ductores Danaum delecti, prima virorum*, 1.86) contrasts tellingly with the bloodless 'triumph' of Epicurus.[57]

---

[55] In addition to the 'beasts of battle' and the wounded warriors of 3.642–56, see esp. 5.1416–35, where the futility of fighting for control of non-essential resources is explicitly spelt out, and 5.1129–30, where peaceful subjection is (provocatively) declared to be preferable to the exercise of *imperium*; in a number of other places, the poet implicitly condemns the pointless destructiveness of warfare and the deluded pursuit of military *gloria* (see, e.g., 1.84–100 and 471–82 on the Trojan War; 2.40–6 and 323–32 for military manoeuvres as emblematic of the trivial and futile; 5.999–1001 on the wanton destructiveness of modern war as compared with accidental deaths amongst primitive humans; and 5.1221–35 on the *imperator* (perhaps modelled on another Ennian hero, Pyrrhus of Epirus: so C. Bailey 1947: 1519, *ad* 5.1228) whose military might cannot save him from shipwreck). On these passages, see Gale 2000: 237–40.

[56] Note esp. *animi virtutem* ('the courage of his spirit', 70); *pervicit* ('triumphed', 72); *victor* ('in triumph', 75); *pedibus subiecta* ('crushed underfoot', 78); *victoria* ('victory', 79). On military and triumphal imagery in this passage, see Sykes Davies 1932: 33–4; West 1969: 57–60; Buchheit 1971; Hardie 1986: 194–5.

[57] For other references to the Trojan War, see 1.471–82, where Lucretius implicitly presents his own subject matter, the interaction of atoms in the infinite void, as something of more universal and pressing importance than the *res gestae* of heroic warfare (so Gale 1994: 109–10; cf. Wardy 1988: 118); and 6.1278–86, where Peta Fowler persuasively detects an Iliadic intertext (P. G. Fowler 1997: 126–9). As Fowler observes, the dismal scrapping over the cremation of diseased corpses with

The intertwining of violence and heroism which characterizes the epic tradition is, then, carefully unpicked by the Epicurean poet, and its separate strands opportunistically redeployed in support of a radically different ideal. Epic's intense focus on the piercing and mutilation of the body serves for Lucretius a double purpose, both reminding us of the fragility of *all* human bodies (and thus of our need for Epicurean philosophy, with its consoling doctrine that death is not to be feared), and pointing the poet's satirical condemnation of the futility of human conflict. While the gruesome detail of these passages serves – as in Homer – to illustrate the costly and destructive aspect of war, there is no compensating pay-off, no sense that the exposure of the body to wounding and death is desirable or worthwhile. Posthumous reputation is not something the Epicurean should care about, and whether we die old or young makes no difference (3.1087–94); what should matter to us is the here and now, and we can best enjoy a life of true pleasure and tranquillity if we reject the desire for immortal fame that motivates the epic hero. In so far as glory means anything to the Epicurean, it is a paradoxical kind of glory, achieved 'by words, not arms' (5.50).

## V

To this point, I have been exploiting for my own ends the seductive rhetoric of authorial/textual authority, according to which the text manipulates or even compels its reader to adopt particular positions and attitudes *vis-à-vis* its subject matter. In concluding, however, I want to come clean and admit that the argumentative strategies I have attributed to Lucretius have not, in practice, always proven as effective as I have perhaps

which Lucretius' poem ends conflates Hector's funeral (*Il.* 24.782–804) with the earlier struggles over the body of Patroclus (*Il.* 17–18): for Fowler, the Lucretian echoes constitute a 'travesty' of Homeric ideology, in that – by scrupulously eliminating any heroic quality from the mourners' actions and motivation, and substituting the chaotic violence of the earlier episode for the orderly closural rituals of *Il.* 24 – Lucretius implicitly dismisses the concern for proper burial so prominent in Homer as 'an aberration of the irrational mind' (128). Also relevant here is the Homeric echo at Lucr. 6.4–8: Epicurus' posthumous fame, derived not from any military victory but from the words which he 'poured forth from his truth-speaking lips' (*veridico . . . ex ore profudit*, 6), fills the world and is 'borne up to heaven' (*ad caelum gloria fertur*, 8, echoing *Od.* 9.20 (Odysseus speaking), μευ κλέος οὐρανὸν ἵκει, 'my fame has reached the heavens'). Ennius comes in for similarly satirical treatment at 3.834–5, where Lucretius' argument that events that follow our deaths will affect us as little as those that happened before our birth is illustrated by an impressive-sounding reference to the Punic Wars, *omnia cum belli trepido concussa tumultu | horrida contremuere* ('when all things trembled, shuddering and shaken by the fearful tumult of war'). The phrasing here recalls Enn. *Ann.* 309 Skutsch, *Africa terribili tremit horrida terra tumultu* ('the shuddering land of Africa trembled in dreadful tumult'), with the implication that all this (epic) sound and fury ultimately signifies nothing.

implied. Not every reader of the *De rerum natura*, after all, comes away from the text as a convinced Epicurean.[58] Indeed, as the reception history of the poem suggests, the rhetorical strategy I have outlined carries very high risks from the perspective of Lucretius' Epicurean mission.[59] I have argued that the deployment of violent and graphic images is double-edged. If he is going to succeed in converting the reader, Lucretius needs both to show us the error of our existing ways and to hold out the hope of salvation. Thus, the persuasive force of Lucretius' argument relies – on my analysis – upon a carefully calibrated alternation, or equivocation, between involvement and distancing of the implied reader; and this effect is based, in turn, on subtle textual cues guiding our responses. But any actual reader may resist these cues, or simply fail to pick them up: while episodes of violence, in literary texts as in (say) the modern cinema or the ancient arena, carry an undeniable emotional charge, we all know from empirical experience that different audience-members are likely to have different reactions, depending upon their ideological and other predispositions.[60]

There is of course a danger of circularity here (having identified the poem's rhetorical strategy on the basis of my own reading, I then critique the readings of others as failures to appreciate that strategy); but if my analysis of Lucretius' depiction of violence and its contribution to the poem's didactic economy carries conviction, the striking fact remains that critics have often been simply puzzled by the presence in this Epicurean

---

[58] Cf. O'Hara 2007: 67: 'At times critics seem to think that identifying a poet's rhetorical strategy or goals is the same as identifying how the poem in reality does work rhetorically on its readers, as though all rhetorical or poetic strategies were immediately successful (unlike, say, military, political, or courtship strategies). We tend to assume that this poet whom we love has been successful, and then work backwards from that posited success to come up with an explanation of how it has been achieved, almost like a high school chemistry student "fudging" an experiment to achieve the desired result.'

[59] A dominant trend in Lucretian criticism, particularly prominent in the late nineteenth and earlier twentieth centuries, detected in the poem a strong note of pessimism and/or a grim fascination with pain and suffering, supposedly at odds with the poet's advocacy of Epicurean *ataraxia*. For analysis along these lines of Lucretius' depiction of violence specifically, see esp. Regenbogen 1932: 80–7, Rozelaar 1941: 66–72, Perelli 1969: 25–6, 262–5; and for the more general critical tendency to understand Lucretius' equivocation between empathy with and distancing from the troubled life of the non-Epicurean as a reflection of his uncertain psychological state or a lack of complete conviction in the philosophical system he professes, W. R. Johnson 2000: 103–33, Gale 2007: 1–3.

[60] Here I record a partial disagreement with G. B. Conte's fine essay 'Instructions for a Sublime Reader' (Conte 1994: 1–34). Conte speaks of 'the text's *construction* of an ideal reader' (31, my emphasis; cf. xviii–xx on the 'reader-addressee'), whereas I am suggesting that the implied reader is not something wholly *encoded within* the text, but is rather constructed by each individual reader from materials *supplied by* the text, as well as the reading community of which he or she is part. Cf. Hinds 1998: 47–50.

text of disturbingly violent images, or even seen them as working *against* the poem's overt message. This observation has potentially far-reaching implications for the issue of authorial (lack of) control over the reader's reception of this – or any – literary text.

In the case of a reader who is from the outset unsympathetic to Lucretius' world-view, or who approaches the text with a determination to read against the grain, in pursuit of internal inconsistencies or signs that the author himself lacks full conviction in the message he preaches, the scenes of violence that I have examined in this chapter are unlikely to elicit the reaction that, on my interpretation, they are designed to provoke. Such a reader may choose (as, historically, many critics have done) to construct an authorial voice that is itself fractured, uncertain, and inconsistent: rather than respond to Lucretius' emphasis on violence and conflict as an effective rhetorical strategy, he or she may instead interpret it as the trace of unconscious anxiety, or even neurosis,[61] on the poet's part. Again, a reading that puts more weight upon the gruesome and macabre element in these episodes, and ignores the exhortation to emotional detachment that explicitly or implicitly accompanies the vivid and spectacular detail, would perhaps tend to feed rather than allay fears of boundary violation; Lucretius' insistent focus on the body's fragility might well be experienced as a source of terror or despair by one unable or unwilling to accept the consoling thought that 'death is nothing to us', and that a life of security and peace is easy to achieve.[62] For some readers, scenes of wounding and dismemberment might even be a source of sadistic or masochistic pleasure, rather than repulsion. Just as many viewers find cinematic representations of violence exhilarating rather than horrifying, even when the director has aimed explicitly at a negative and deglamorized portrayal of violent acts or individuals,[63] so *mutatis mutandis* any particular reader of Lucretius' poem may take away a very different message from the one we may assume its author to have intended.

---

[61] Thus Logre 1946 'diagnoses' Lucretius as a manic-depressive (see esp. 248–61 for the prevalence of images of natural and human conflict in the poem as a symptom of the author's 'depressive anxiety'); cf. Perelli 1969: 13–52. As recently as 2004, Jantzen (admittedly, a non-specialist) could write: 'Although there is no independent evidence, it would seem from his descriptions that [Lucretius] is writing from traumatic personal experience that has left deep scars' (Jantzen 2004: 263).

[62] Cf. Jantzen 2004: 262–3: 'Lucretius' accounts are so lurid that unless a reader is utterly convinced by his argument, their anxieties are at least as likely to be heightened as to be alleviated.'

[63] As, for example, in the cases of Sam Peckinpah and Martin Scorsese; see further Introduction, p. 41.

# CHAPTER 3

# Discipline and Punish
## Horatian Satire and the Formation of the Self

### Paul Allen Miller*

> Horace clearly states that the undisciplined Lucilian satire could have
> no place in the Augustan period.
>
> (Ramage, Sigsbee, and Fredericks 1974b: 4)

Satire presents itself as a violent genre. Its descriptions in Lucilius, Horace, Persius, and Juvenal are filled with images of slashing, biting, rubbing salt in wounds.[1] It is a discourse that, as Horace says in *Satires* 1.4, is widely perceived as an assault and stands to earn an equally violent riposte from its victims (1.4.23–38). Juvenal, therefore, will only write about the dead (1.165–71). Persius will whisper his caustic truth in a hole dug in the ground (1.114–21).

The origin of this imagery can be traced to the genre's founder, Lucilius. His satire not only ridiculed vice but also directly assaulted the political enemies of his patron, Scipio Aemilianus.[2] Lucilian satire was a weapon in the political, ideological, and cultural warfare that sought to define what it meant to be a *civis Romanus*, a *bonus*, a *nobilis*. It was a discourse of positive exemplification in so far as the satirist demonstrated knowledge of social codes, cultural refinements, *virtus*, and *urbanitas*. But it was also a discourse that sought to punish deviations from those perceived norms and did not shrink from naming names.[3]

Horatian satire is different. It seldom attaches the names of prominent citizens to its objects of attack and protests that it does not seek to attack at all.[4] It worries about the response of its victims (*Sat.* 1.4, 1.6, 1.10, 2.1), and is often the butt of its own jokes.[5] In this chapter, I argue that

---

* Many thanks to David Larmour, who read and commented on an early version of this chapter. The comments and criticisms of Monica Gale, David Scourfield, and the Cambridge University Press readers have made this a much better, more precise chapter.

[1] See M. M. Winkler 1991: 24; Gunderson 2005: 233–4; Schlegel 2005: 4, 126; Keane 2006: 4, 45, 49–64.

[2] See Marx 1904–5: I.cxxviii–cxxix; Goldberg 2005: 162.

[3] See Freudenburg 2005b: 5; Goldberg 2005: 165–6; Muecke 2005: 42; Keane 2006: 46.

[4] See Coffey 1976: 90–1; Schlegel 2005: 6, 8–9.      [5] See Plaza 2006: 169–70, 208.

Horatian satire represents an internalization of the genre's traditional
violence to produce a discourse of self-formation and self-discipline. Just
as Michel Foucault argues in *Discipline and Punish* that in the eighteenth
century there was a shift from a culture of admonitory public punishment
to one of internalized discipline and that this shift gave rise to the modern
concept of the self, I contend that Horatian satire seeks to effect a similar
transformation of aristocratic discourse from that of public rhetorical
violence to one of internalization and self-surveillance whose emblematic
images are, as we shall see, withdrawal, castration, and self-admonition,
but are presented under the guise of polish, irony, and sophistication.

By violence in this context, I do not mean just physical assault, but the
deployment of coercion and differentials of power and force.[6] This can be
verbal as much as corporeal, and satiric irony can be one of its primary
modes. Ironic discourse, as I have argued elsewhere,[7] does its work
through the interposition of a moment of non-meaning – a moment of
discursive violence – that creates a breach in the continuity of the existing
symbolic fabric. Such moments of discursive transgression can be
deployed in countless ways. They can be wielded in the form of ridicule
that uses rhetorical force to police a perceived conformity to a set of
norms. This type of irony marks or delimits the territory of the acceptable
by establishing the border that has been crossed and turns the violence of
the moment of division against that which has now been cast as other. At
the same time, in as much as the moment of doubling or difference that
irony marks is in itself non-signifying, it creates a point of discursive
leverage that is inherently labile and may equally be turned back against
the self.

In both cases, 'Violence', as David Konstan and Shilpa Raval argue in
Chapter 1 when considering the comedy of Plautus, '. . . is employed to re-
establish the social order when the boundaries that define it are endangered'.[8] This was never truer, perhaps, than in the collapse of the Republic
and the birth of the Principate. The present chapter extends these insights
to contend that this same coercive power, which is often deployed against
others, manifests as a form of self-curtailment and even mutilation when
used to re-establish social order through the creation of a new formation of
the self.

---

[6] On the difficulties of defining violence see Introduction, pp. 20–1; Gibson, Chapter 9, esp.
pp. 269–70, 272–3.
[7] P. A. Miller 2004: 228–32 and 2009. On the related distinction between satire and carnival, see
P. A. Miller 1998a.
[8] Konstan and Raval, Chapter 1, p. 51 above.

## The Foucauldian Moment

> In the ceremonies of torture, the chief actor is the people, whose real and immediate presence is required for their accomplishment. A torture which had become known, but whose actual execution would have been a secret, would have hardly made sense. An example was made not only to produce the recognition that the least infraction ran the grave risk of being punished, but also to produce terror through the spectacle of power's rage against the offender.
>
> (Foucault 1975: 69–70)[9]

The opening of Michel Foucault's *Surveiller et punir*, translated into English as *Discipline and Punish*, is deservedly famous. It features an account from the *Gazette d'Amsterdam* in 1757 of the public drawing and quartering of Robert-François Damiens, parricide.[10] The detail is excruciating. His flesh is first ripped. Then molten lead and sulphur are poured into the wounds. After that, six horses are attached to his arms and legs in an attempt to rip him limb from limb, before finally an axe is used to hack him to pieces in a public square. The presumed purpose of this torture, and of the crowd's voyeuristic participation in it, is, Foucault argues, precisely that of exemplarity and admonition. The message is clear: this is what happens to parricides and those who commit acts of similar gravity. Public violence aims not at the reform of the offender nor at the systematic eradication of a given social ill by fostering the creation of a new citizen who will police himself, but at the display of behaviour that is deemed transgressive and the spectacle of the consequences that ensue. It is focused on the suffering body of the offender, not the re-creation of his soul. As such, it is a line of punitive reasoning the Romans would certainly have understood. It is essentially the same as that which authorized the crucifixion along the Appian Way of the 6,000 survivors from Spartacus' army (App. *B Civ.* 1.120): i.e., this is what happens to slaves who revolt.[11]

Yet, for Foucault and for us, it is not the scenes of public torture *per se* that are of interest, but the fact that a few years later everything changed. Indeed, by 1791 in France, Russia, Prussia, Tuscany, Austria, and parts of the United States the penal codes had been radically transformed. What once had been a regime of punishment based on the spectacle of the body in pain had become a system of imprisonment, surveillance, and reform. The age of discipline had been born.[12] The desired effect was no longer the

---

[9] This and all other translations are my own.    [10] Foucault 1975: 9–12.

[11] On the reasons for Roman public spectacles of punishment and exemplary violence, see further K. M. Coleman 1990, esp. 45–9.

[12] See Foucault 1975: 12–30.

production of order emanating from the sovereign display of power in the public square but the construction of a body of self-surveilling citizens and workers who internalized the expected norms of behaviour, reported on themselves to themselves, and confessed their deviations and perversions to the instances of authority.[13] They exerted coercive power against themselves, shaping and tailoring their souls with the same rigour that the authorities deployed against Damiens' suffering body. Indeed, Foucault's thesis is that the new regime is not less violent than the old, but all the more so, since the new violence is universal and self-administered. This self-disciplining subject of the factory and the reformatory was also the sexual subject whose erotic life was structured by a cognate set of diffused and self-regulating power-relations, which Foucault would seek to describe in Volume 1 of the *History of Sexuality*,[14] and whose genealogy he would trace in Volumes 2 and 3 and the unpublished fourth volume.[15]

An analogous change in the discourse of elite self-formation during the transition from the Roman Republic to the Principate, alluded to above, has already been charted by a variety of scholars – with either explicit or implicit reference to the Foucauldian model.[16] To summarize the work of these researchers in a schematic fashion, which will have to be further nuanced in our readings of individual texts, there is a shift during this period in the fundamental model of elite self-formation. There is a move from an ideological model of competitive combat, self-assertion, and the public destruction of rival factions and consequent rival norms of elite behaviour, to a model that encourages the production of a self-disciplining elite that seeks the validation of its prerogatives through the practice of a concept of duty.[17] We move from a discourse of spectacle and admonition towards one of irony and restraint. If we cannot all be *pius Aeneas*, we can be Horace's country mouse and avoid becoming either Turnus or the unrestrained Lucilius (*cum flueret lutulentus, erat quod tollere velles*, 'when he flowed muddily there was much you would want to remove', Hor. *Sat.* 1.4.11).

Of course, the analogy between the shift in structures of discourse and power that Foucault chronicles and that of the period between the generations of Lucilius and Horace should not be pushed too far. The

---

[13] See Foucault 1975: 228–64.

[14] See Dreyfus and Rabinow 1982: 105–6, 135; Gros 2003: 12. Compare the description of the 'microphysics of power' in *Surveiller et punir* (Foucault 1975: 34–8) with that of the 'analytic of power' in *La volonté de savoir* (Foucault 1976: 121–35).

[15] See J. Miller 1993: 323–4, 340, 346–7; Rouse 1994: 94–109; Larmour, Miller, and Platter 1998b: 22–33; Vizier 1998: 67–8, 71.

[16] See Wyke 1989: 41; Habinek 1997: 23 and 2005: 197–8; Wallace-Hadrill 1997: 6.

[17] See Foucault 1984b: 57; Joshel 1992: 68; C. Edwards 1993: 195.

Principate did not do away with the spectacle of violence inflicted upon the non-citizen subject body through crucifixion nor did it end grotesque executions in the arena. By the same token, despite Habinek's very reasonable claim that a discourse of sexuality – as opposed to that of the 'use of pleasures' – was elaborated in first-century-BC Rome,[18] no one should confuse Ovid with Krafft-Ebing. In addition, Foucault himself has been criticized for being overly schematic and for paying too little attention to details that do not fit his *grands tableaux*, while ignoring the causal factors that produced the dramatic shifts he chronicles.[19] It is also clear that Roman culture during the periods under discussion was nowhere near as homogeneous as the structures described within the classical Foucauldian *épistémè*.[20]

Nonetheless, the analogy retains its heuristic value. And just as the shift Foucault describes at the beginning of *Surveiller et punir* really did occur, even if not perhaps as neatly and uniformly as portrayed there, so there is a clear shift in the discursive structures of elite self-formation[21] in Rome during the period under discussion. It is thus widely accepted that the collapse of the Republic produced a crisis of elite self-identity and that this both involved a fundamental restructuring of the discourse of the aristocratic subject and made possible new forms of experience and literary genres.[22] In the past, I have charted some of these shifts by examining the conditions of possibility for the development of Catullan lyric consciousness, and the history of the elegiac genre as a form of subjectivity made possible by a crisis in the Roman Symbolic.[23] Others have examined the ideological struggle among the competitive elite for the control and interpretation of traditional Roman culture, defined as the *mos maiorum*,[24] as well as the collapse of traditional markers of status and identity with the dissolution of

---

[18] Habinek 1997; 'use of pleasures': Foucault 1984a.

[19] See, e.g., Dreyfus and Rabinow 1982: 27; Kremer-Marietti 1985: 49, 61; Bannet 1989: 79; Sedgwick 1990: 46–7; Macey 1993: 165, 176, 432; P. A. Miller 1998b. On Foucault's early contention that only a single *épistémè* (see below, n. 20) existed at a given time and his indefinite postponing of an investigation of causal factors, see Foucault 1966: 64–5, 171, 179; Laqueur 1990: 21; Macey 1993: 163.

[20] *Épistémè* is the term Foucault used to describe the ensemble of discursive practices of a given period that produced and legitimated knowledge.

[21] We know far less about how the collapse of the Republic affected the ideological structures of those people whose identities were not tied either to the *cursus honorum* or to the cultivation of equestrian *otium*. The main effects for the average resident of Rome may have been a more uniform application of the rule of law, the end of civil violence, and a more dependable food supply. In short, the crisis experienced by the senatorial and equestrian elite in terms of how they defined their identity in relation to the state and the other orders of society may well have had no analogue among the *populus Romanus*.

[22] See Barton 1993: 37, 46; Gunderson 1997: 228; Janan 2001: 49.

[23] P. A. Miller 1994 and 2004.    [24] See Wallace-Hadrill 1997.

the Republic,[25] and a generalized crisis of the aristocracy's forms of self-legitimation.[26]

One of the ideological values most in need of redefinition as a consequence of this crisis was *libertas*, the very quality that Horace uses to describe Lucilian satire's relation to Old Comedy at the opening of *Satires* 1.4 (see pp. 100–1 below). On one level, *libertas* is the quality that defines the *civis Romanus* (Roman citizen) as opposed to the *servus* (slave), *libertinus* (freedman), or any foreigner who does not enjoy citizens' rights.[27] On another, *libertas* denotes a set of prerogatives that can only be exercised fully by the aristocratic elite.[28] The most noted of these rights is freedom of speech.

*Libertas* also signifies a fundamental notion of self-determination. This is commonly understood as the ability to be subject to the will of no one else and hence implies the capacity to enforce one's will upon others: to be violent but not to suffer violence, especially from those of lesser status. *Libertas* was actualized most concretely by traditional Roman elites through their participation in competitive politics and the governance of the state.[29] It was a value of the elite that was understood to carry with it the power to shame those who were not members of that elite as well as those who deviated from its expected norms. Yet what constituted freedom for the *boni* was *licentia*, or 'transgressive licence', when practised by the *populus* (Cic. *Dom.* 130–1).[30]

Thus, at the beginning of *Satires* 1.4, Horace defines *libertas* as the power of speech Lucilius exercised over others whose behaviour was worthy of censure. Lucilius' poetry was a form of public display, a kind of exemplary and admonitory violence exercised in the name of the aristocratic values and faction he supported. *Libertas*, as such, named the sum total of his aristocratic prerogatives and his ideology, as well as the discourse that sought to enforce and reproduce them. Lucilian *libertas* named less the free expression of an inner self than a form of discursive violence that was excessive by nature, and that through its excess sought to establish and sustain its own vision of what constituted normative *Romanitas* (cf. Hor. *Epist.* 2.1.145–55).[31] As such, it represents an aristocratic

---

[25] See Barton 1993: 189.     [26] Cf. C. Edwards 1993: 185–6.
[27] See, e.g., Cic. *Verr.* 2.1.7 *agunt eum praecipitem poenae civium Romanorum, quos partim securi percussit, partim in vinculis necavit, partim implorantes iura libertatis et civitatis in crucem sustulit* ('the punishments he exacted from Roman citizens are now driving him mad, those he beheaded, those he bound and executed, those he crucified even as they cried out for their *rights of freedom and citizenship*'); cf. *Verr.* 2.5.162.
[28] See Stampacchia 1982: 207.     [29] See Syme 1939: 155; Wirszubski 1950: 38.
[30] Cf. Wirszubski 1950: 8; de Ste. Croix 1981: 366; Joshel 1992: 28.
[31] Cf. Wirszubski 1950: 7; Robinson 1953: 35; Habinek 1998: 45 and 2005: 8; Freudenburg 2005b: 5.

textual practice that appropriated and worked to control the traditional prerogatives of poetry and song.[32]

In other contexts, *libertas* often means 'free speech',[33] but it is the free speech of those who have the right to exercise it. In this sense, it is expressly associated with satire as practised by Lucilius. Satirical *libertas* is the ability to define proper behaviour, to exercise one's prerogatives, and to censure those who either deny one the ability to exercise those prerogatives or violate the norms of conduct. It thus becomes a word in which legal and political rights, artistic licence, and aristocratic privilege all come into play. The following passage from a letter to Cicero dated 25 May 44 BC, by Trebonius, the conspirator who detained Antony outside the Senate-house on the Ides of March, displays the presence of these different levels of meaning, even as it connects *libertas* directly with satire in the Lucilian mode:[34]

> I heard that there was a certain disturbance, which I certainly hope to be false, so that we may at some point enjoy untroubled freedom (*libertate*); which I have had very little experience of to this point. Nonetheless, having procured a bit of leisure while we sailed, I put together a little gift for you ... In these verses if I seem to you rather plain-spoken in certain words, the vileness of the person [Mark Antony] whom I am assailing rather freely (*liberius*) will vindicate me. You will also forgive my anger, which is just against men and citizens of this type. Moreover, why should it have been more permissible for Lucilius to take up this sort of liberty (*libertatis*) than for us, since even if his hatred for those he attacked was equal to our own, he certainly had no worthier targets to assail with such freedom (*libertate*) of language.[35]

This letter is a virtual fugue on Republican *libertas*. In the first use, the term means freedom from political strife. It refers to the existence of a stable constitutional order and political leadership. The comparative adverb *liberius* refers to the freedom of speech one aristocrat had to assail another in the traditional politics of competitive elites that characterized the Roman Republic. The very use of the comparative implies that there were degrees of this freedom and that the possibility of tipping over into *licentia* had to be

---

[32] See Habinek 1998: 117 and 2005: 108–9.      [33] See, e.g., Cic. *Clu.* 118.

[34] See Freudenburg 1993: 87.

[35] Cic. *Fam.* 12.16.3 *audiebam quaedam turbulenta, quae scilicet cupio esse falsa, ut aliquando otiosa libertate fruamur; quod vel minime mihi adhuc contigit. ego tamen nactus in navigatione nostra pusillum laxamenti concinnavi tibi munusculum ... in quibus versiculis si tibi quibusdam verbis* εὐθυρρημονέστερος *videbor, turpitudo personae eius in quam liberius invehimur nos vindicabit. ignosces etiam iracundiae nostrae, quae iusta est in eius modi et homines et civis. deinde qui magis hoc Lucilio licuerit adsumere libertatis quam nobis? cum, etiam si odio par fuerit in eos quos laesit, tamen certe non magis dignos habuerit in quos tanta libertate verborum incurreret.*

guarded against.[36] The last two uses refer specifically to Lucilius' exercise of this aristocratic freedom of speech in satiric verses directed against the poet's political enemies, who are portrayed as no more worthy of public censure than Mark Antony. It is here explicitly a form of attack. Yet the world in which Trebonius was operating was no longer that of Lucilius. By 43 BC, Trebonius had been killed by the Caesarians' henchman, Dolabella. Cicero would die later the same year as his reward for attacking Mark Antony in the *Philippics*. The rules were changing, and *libertas* needed to be redefined in the context of nascent autocracy.[37] The freedom to attack those of equal or lesser status became the freedom to live one's life in quiet retreat (cf. Hor. *Sat.* 2.6). The violence aimed at curtailing the perceived excess of others became a wall of defence around, and hence the creation of, an inner self, whose own excesses needed to be monitored and pruned away (cf. Hor. *Sat.* 1.4.133–7).

## Lucilian Admonition

> nempe incomposito dixi pede currere versus
> Lucili. quis tam Lucili fautor inepte est
> ut non hoc fateatur? at idem, quod sale multo
> urbem defricuit, charta laudatur eadem.

Indeed, I have said that the verses of Lucilius run on an undisciplined foot. What partisan of Lucilius is such a fool as not to confess this? But this same one is praised on that same page because he scrubbed down the city with a great deal of salt.

(Hor. *Sat.* 1.10.1–4)

> secuit Lucilius urbem,
> te Lupe, te Muci, et genuinum fregit in illis.

Lucilius slashed the city – you, Lupus, you, Mucius! – and he broke his molar on these.

(Pers. 1.114–15)

> ense velut stricto quotiens Lucilius ardens
> infremuit, rubet auditor cui frigida mens est
> criminibus, tacita sudant praecordia culpa.

As many times as burning Lucilius raged, as if he had a drawn sword, the listener whose mind is cold with crimes blushes, and his heart sweats with silent guilt.

(Juv. 1.165–7)

---

[36] See Corbeill 1996: 16–20, 105–6.
[37] Cf. Newlands, Chapter 5 below, on Ovid's response in the *Metamorphoses* to the Principate's curtailment of free expression. The grotesque image of Philomela's severed tongue might well serve as an emblem for this chapter as well.

In the later satiric tradition, Lucilius becomes the image of discursive violence. For Trebonius, Lucilius is the licence for his invective verse against Mark Antony, an unfortunate rhetorical strategy that perhaps sealed the conspirator's fate, as the *Philippics* did Cicero's.[38] For Horace, Lucilius scrubs down the city with both wit and salt: an allusion to the medical practice of using astringent rubs. Satire is a salutary abrasive that stings and cleanses.[39] For Persius, Lucilius has been transformed into a biting mouth that both slashes the city and attacks by name individuals of consular rank. The sadistic pleasure of satiric violence is, it seems, integral to its healing mission.[40] In Juvenal, Lucilius is *indignatio* personified and armed with a sword. He could do to the living what Juvenal dares only try against the dead.[41] In short, Lucilius' personal attacks upon the personages named or indirectly alluded to in these and other passages – for example, Q. Caecilius Metellus Macedonicus (consul 143 BC, censor 131, political opponent of Scipio Aemilianus), L. Cornelius Lupus Lentulus (consul 156, censor 147, *princeps senatus* 131–124), and Q. Mucius Scaevola (praetor 120) – became the icons of the genre's original satiric *libertas* (see Hor. *Sat.* 2.1.67–8; Pers. 1.115; Juv. 1.154).[42]

A sense of the kind of invective referred to by the later tradition can be derived from what Krenkel labels the first fragments of Satire 2 in Book 26. These lines concern a set of gladiatorial games offered by Metellus:

rediisse ac repedasse, ut Romam vitet, gladiatoribus
........................................................................

sanctum ego a Metellorum <Anxur> iam repedabam munere
........................................................................

coniugem infidamque, pathicam familiam, inpuram domum

to have returned and gone back, so as to avoid Rome, with the gladiators
........................................................................

I returned to holy Anxur from the games of the Metelli
........................................................................

and an unfaithful wife, a perverse family, and impure house

(Lucilius, frr. 631–3 Krenkel)

All three major editors of Lucilius[43] are agreed that these fragments derive from the same satire, and while the exact nature of the poem remains unclear, a move from the merely *ad hominem* attack (I avoided the city when Metellus was giving his games) to a more savage invective (the entire

---

[38] See Knoche 1975: 71; Coffey 1976: 63.
[39] See Kiessling and Heinze 1921: 160 ad loc.; Morris 1968: 132 ad loc.; Keane 2006: 45.
[40] See Keane 2006: 49–50; P. A. Miller 2007.   [41] Cf. Keane 2006: 4, 46.
[42] See Muecke 2005: 46.   [43] Marx 1904–5; Krenkel 1970; Warmington 1979.

family is sexually perverse) seems clear, even if the precise relation between the fragments remains in dispute.[44]

Another example can be found in Book 1, actually the sixth book published (frr. 1–55 Krenkel). Here we find a parodic council of the gods convened to try the recently dead Lupus on charges of luxury, debauchery, and gluttony.[45] In Book 28, the same Lupus is mockingly portrayed as a hanging judge in the trial of Lucilius and his accomplices for an assault on the house of a courtesan (frr. 778–98 Krenkel). The attack is described in terms of an epic battle, while the trial scene contains parodies of Greek philosophical language used to describe the extreme punishment Lupus proposes for what Lucilius appears to consider rollicking good fun. Lupus is portrayed in Lucilius' satires as a pretentious hypocrite, worthy of public mockery and censure even in death.[46]

Finally, we know that Book 2, the basis for Horace, *Satires* 1.7, was devoted to the trial of Mucius Scaevola in 119 BC on charges of extortion.[47] The accusations made by the prosecutor, however, in typical invective fashion, appear to focus more on Scaevola's supposed sexual insatiability than his actual crimes. The goal of such invectives, as explicitly acknowledged by rhetorical theorists and by the poets, from the early Greek iambists through Old Comedy and beyond, was to inflict pain upon, if not to destroy, one's opponent.[48]

> si natibus natricem inpressit crassam et capitatam
> ..................................................................................
> —ᴗᴗ —ᴗᴗ in bulgam[49] penetrare pilosam
> ..................................................................................
> —ᴗᴗ —ᴗᴗ —ᴗᴗ paedicum iam excoquit omne
>
> if he inserts between the buttocks a thick and headed water snake
> ..................................................................................
> to penetrate into the hairy bag
> ..................................................................................
> he boils off all his lust for boys
>
> (frr. 69–70, 73 Krenkel)

Scaevola's sexual acts are described in terms no less graphic than those used in Persius' later description of Alcibiades' anal depilatory practices

---

[44] Note the cautionary remarks of Goldberg 2005: 169.
[45] See Goldberg 2005: 158–9; Muecke 2005: 46.     [46] See Goldberg 2005: 159; Muecke 2005: 44.
[47] See Coffey 1976: 42.
[48] For an important conspectus of ancient views on the purpose and function of invective, see Nisbet 1961: 192–7.
[49] I prefer here the conjecture of Marx to the colourless *vulgam* of the manuscripts, which Krenkel follows.

(4.35–41). But whereas the latter is framed in terms of philosophy and history, the former belongs to the more immediate context of contemporary politics. Lucilius is not the foe of abstract vice, but of historical men whose politics and behaviour opposed them to the standards of *Romanitas* conceived by the circle of literary and political figures gathered round the house of Scipio Aemilianus.

In sum, Lucilius, as he depicted himself in his satires, was an ally of Scipio and C. Laelius Sapiens in the political and cultural conflicts that were reshaping Roman life at the end of the second century BC.[50] His poetry was a rhetorical weapon designed to wreak violence on his foes. This was a period that, in the wake of Rome's defeat of Carthage and its rapid imperial expansion, was widely perceived as a time of cultural crisis. Lucilian satire was one response to that crisis.[51]

Lucilius, of course, did not invent satire out of whole cloth. He formalized a native tradition of ribald invective, by combining its resources with those of the emerging genre of *satura* developed by Ennius and Pacuvius as a type of miscellany for the display of wit and personal observation, and with Greek traditions from Archilochus and Old Comedy. The result of this hybrid construction was an elite literary discourse whose aim was to define a model subject-position and to stigmatize deviations from it.[52] The satirist created a personality and cleared a space for that personality's exercise and assertion, which implied a certain autonomy or *libertas*.[53] The position of the Lucilian satirist was, thus, an aggressive posture. It produced a discourse of self-formation that was at once urbane and unforgiving, and also, in Quintilian's famous formulation, 'wholly Roman' (*tota nostra, Inst.* 10.1.93).[54]

Lucilius explicitly recognized satire's violent nature in a series of fragments from Book 30. The witty back-and-forth of this passage can be paralleled by similar interchanges in Horace, *Satires* 1.4 (e.g. 65–80), where the latter tries to define his own ideal of satiric *sermo* in relation to that of Lucilius and the problem of satiric violence. My reconstruction of the passage as a sequence, presented below, is speculative, as all such

---

[50] See Hor. *Sat.* 2.1.16–17, 62–79.

[51] See J. W. Duff 1936: 43–4; Krenkel 1970: I.20–3; Knoche 1975: 33–6; Coffey 1976: 35–8, 50; Freudenburg 2001: 61 n. 7.

[52] The beginning of this paragraph represents a synthesis of the views found in J. W. Duff 1936: 39, Nisbet 1961: 193, Ramage 1974a: 8, Knoche 1975: 22, 31–4, and Coffey 1976: 28, 31, 38. Cf. P. A. Miller 2005: 1–34; and on Ennius and Pacuvius, see Courtney 1993: 7–8.

[53] See Gunderson 2005: 224 n. 2; Habinek 2005: 56.

[54] See Ramage 1974b: 27–8; Barchiesi and Cucchiarelli 2005: 214; Gunderson 2005: 225–6; Keane 2006: 75–6.

reconstructions must be, but it in no way contravenes the evidence. In Krenkel's edition, this sequence is assigned to the fifth satire of the book and is introduced by the fable of the fox and the lion, in which a sickly lion asks the fox why he does not approach more closely, and the latter replies that it is because the tracks around the lion's den point in only one direction (frr. 1074–83). It is unclear to which predator the satirist is himself compared, though it is reasonable to assume he is the clever fox rather than the sickly lion.[55] On any view, however, the satirist in Book 30[56] is self-described as a predator, who attacks those whose behaviour falls short of his requirements,[57] whether that description occurs in the context of an attack on the performance of a certain 'baldy' (*calvus* or Calvus?) in the recent Palantine campaign (Marx, Warmington) or of a more general reflection on the nature of satiric invective (Krenkel).

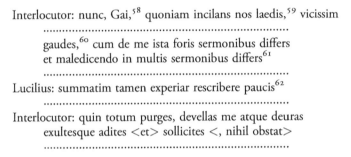

Interlocutor: nunc, Gai,[58] quoniam incilans nos laedis,[59] vicissim
.............................................................................
gaudes,[60] cum de me ista foris sermonibus differs
et maledicendo in multis sermonibus differs[61]
.............................................................................
Lucilius: summatim tamen experiar rescribere paucis[62]
.............................................................................
Interlocutor: quin totum purges, devellas me atque deuras
exultesque adites <et> sollicites <, nihil obstat>
.............................................................................

---

[55] Other editors reconstruct the passage differently. Both Marx and Warmington separate the fable (Satire 30.1, frr. 980–9 Marx; Satire 30.6, frr. 1111–20 Warmington) from the programmatic lines (Satire 30.2 Marx; 30.4 Warmington).

[56] We are secure in our knowledge that all these fragments come from Book 30, because they are cited as such by the late-fourth-century grammarian, Nonius Marcellus, who is the source for around 50 per cent of the surviving fragments of Lucilius (see Chahoud 2007: 87 n. 32).

[57] Cf. frr. 1057–8 Krenkel *inde canino ricto oculisque | involem* ('then let me attack with the snarl and glare of a dog'); also frr. 767–8 (Book 28), where the interlocutor is given the opportunity to give a speech to save himself from a beating.

[58] I.e., C. (Gaius) Lucilius.      [59] Cf. Hor. *Sat.* 1.4.78; 2.1.21, 78.      [60] Cf. Hor. *Sat.* 1.4.78.

[61] Plaza 2006: 50–2, following Griffith 1970, in contrast to Marx, Krenkel, Warmington, and Keane 2006: 45, allocates these lines to Lucilius (responding to his interlocutor) rather than to the interlocutor himself. This attribution is based on a reading of Juv. 1, but there are two persuasive counter-arguments. First, the parallels which have already been cited from Horace, and those which are cited from Persius below, lead to the opposite conclusion. Second, the relevant Juvenal passage read in context precisely explains the shift in the image of the satirist from aggressor to victim. Juvenal fears winding up like one of Nero's party-torches if he exercises the prerogatives of the Lucilian satirist (1.153–7). In short, the shift from the late Republic to the Imperial period necessitated a fundamental rewriting of the concept of *libertas* and shifted the terms of the debate about its nature and appropriateness. Juvenal concludes by stating he will only attack the dead (1.170–1). Lucilius, of course, makes no such concession. See Anderson 1960: 258 (= 1982a: 148).

[62] Cf. Hor. *Sat.* 1.4.38.

Lucilius: omnes formonsi, fortes tibi, ego inprobus: esto[63]

.........................................................................

nolito tibi me male dicere posse putare[64]
et muttonis[65] manum perscribere posse tagacem

.........................................................................

Interlocutor: quod tu a\<utem\> laudes culpes,[66] non proficis hilum

.........................................................................

quid servas quo eam, quid agam? quid id attinet ad te?

.........................................................................

Interlocutor: Now, Gaius, since through blame you harm us, in turn

.........................................................................

You love it when you spread around those things about me in your satires, and you spread me wide open by attacking me in many satires.

.........................................................................

Lucilius: Nonetheless, I shall try to respond briefly in a few words.

.........................................................................

Interlocutor: Nothing keeps you from cleaning me out altogether, plucking me bare, singeing me, and insulting me, going after and harassing me.

.........................................................................

Lucilius: To you everybody is fine and brave, and I'm the reprobate: fine!

.........................................................................

Please don't think I'm capable of slander and that I'm able to describe a hand that's a penis-grabber.

.........................................................................

Interlocutor: Moreover, what you praise, what you blame, gets you nowhere.

.........................................................................

Why do you keep watch over where I go and what I do? What business is it of yours?[67]

(frr. 1089–95, 1102, 1096–8 Krenkel)

Lucilian *sermo* and *libertas* define an intellectual and aristocratic style that is inherited, adapted, and problematized by each of its satirical inheritors. It is exemplified both in the censure of others and in the establishment of standards of behaviour that serve as models of aristocratic comportment. With Lucilius' generation – that of the elder Cato, Terence (a freedman), and the orator Laelius (consul 140 BC) – the self-conscious elaboration of an aristocratic literature that seeks to form and enforce codes of conduct, define *Latinitas*, and establish a properly Roman identity comes into being. Roman satire as an

---

[63] Cf. Hor. *Sat.* 1.4.90–3; Pers. 1.110.    [64] Cf. Hor. *Sat.* 1.4.65–70.

[65] Marx and Warmington print *Musconis*, the reading of Nonius. Marx's speculations on the identity of the said Muscon, a name attested only in Thucydides and Xenophon, are, however, unconvincing. Krenkel's *muttonis* ('penis') follows the readings of Festus and Paulus, who also quote this passage.

[66] Cf. Hor. *Sat.* 1.4.25.

[67] The general drift of the passage is reproduced almost exactly by Pers. 1.107–11.

institution for the production and policing of cultural legitimacy is a product of this ideological and political challenge to the traditional Roman elite.[68] As Habinek observes: 'At Rome literature participates in the "formation" of the aristocracy in both senses of the word, that is by defining, preserving, and transmitting standards of behavior to which the individual aristocrat must aspire and by valorizing aristocratic ideals and aristocratic authority within the broader cultural context.'[69] Lucilian satire presents one such model of the aristocratic speaking subject, even as it dramatizes the subjection of the individual to the norms that must be presumed to make that model possible.

## Horatian Discipline

> Eupolis atque Cratinus Aristophanesque poetae,
> atque alii, quorum comoedia prisca virorum est,
> si quis erat dignus describi quod malus ac fur,
> quod moechus foret aut sicarius aut alioqui
> famosus, multa cum libertate notabant.
> hinc omnis pendet Lucilius, hosce secutus
> mutatis tantum pedibus numerisque . . .

The poets Eupolis, Cratinus, Aristophanes, and other writers of Old Comedy marked down with great freedom anyone who deserved to be written about because he was a criminal and a thief, because he was an adulterer or an assassin or in some other way infamous. Lucilius wholly descends from here, having followed them with only the metre and rhythms changed.

(Hor. *Sat.* 1.4.1–7)

> nunc mihi curto
> ire licet mulo vel si libet usque Tarentum
> . . .
> hoc ego commodius quam tu, praeclare senator,
> milibus atque aliis vivo. quacumque libido est,
> incedo . . .

I can, if I want, ride a castrated[70] mule all the way to Tarentum . . . In this and a thousand other ways, my life is more pleasant than yours, famous senator. I go wherever I want.

(Hor. *Sat.* 1.6.104–5, 110–12)

---

[68] See von Albrecht 1997: I.253     [69] Habinek 1998: 45.

[70] Although the practice of translating *curto* in this passage as meaning 'bobtailed' remains common, this interpretation was refuted more than fifty years ago. The practice of bobbing tails is nowhere found in Antiquity, whereas the castration of domesticated farm animals to render them docile was common. See Ashworth and Andrewes 1957; Freudenberg 2001: 59–60. Moreover, the castrated mule as an emblem of the poet's impotence, relative to the powerful senator, clearly has more point than would a bobtailed mule.

Poem 1.4 is Horace's first and most explicit programmatic satire. It begins with the invocation of Lucilius and compares the *libertas* he enjoyed with that of the Greek poets of Old Comedy. They acted, he says, in the manner of a traditional Roman censor, who would place a mark (*nota censoria*) next to the names of those who failed to exemplify the public and private behaviour expected of the senatorial elite. In this manner, Lucilian satire becomes a fusion of traditional Roman norms with Greek literary precedents. Poem 1.4, however, also negotiates Horace's departure from his Lucilian model. He both explicitly embraces and distances himself from his great forebear. This new satire will be urbane and polished. Its image is the pure stream of Callimachus' *Hymn to Apollo* (108–12), as opposed to the great muddy river of Lucilius (1.4.9–13). It will come closer to the comedy of manners we associate with Menander, Plautus, and Terence (1.4.45–56) than to the tradition of personal attack associated with the Old Comedy of Aristophanes.

In Horace's hands, satire is no longer a discourse of the competitive oligarchic elite in which humour is a political weapon. It represents instead a version of refined speech (*sermo merus*, 1.4.48)[71] and social intercourse that underwrites an as yet undefined, but ultimately very different, political vision, which will become the Principate and then the Empire. Horace claims to have learned this discourse from his freedman father who was constantly pointing out (*notando*, 1.4.106; cf. *notabant*, 1.4.5) examples of virtue and vice to him. 'As a grown man, the son dutifully internalizes his satiric father, becoming his own ever present moral instructor.'[72] It is a discourse of self-surveillance. It seeks less the domination of others than the formation and disciplining of an internalized self.

Of course, none of this is straightforward autobiography. The scenes with his father, as has been amply demonstrated, derive directly from Terence's portrait of Demea in the *Adelphoe*.[73] This is not to say that Horace's father never did the things attributed to him. Rather, it is to note that the personal, the political, and the generic are so presented as to form a seamless whole. Horace's satire is not the direct reflection of his experience, but the refined product of a poet, who labours endlessly to make his poetry look effortless (cf. *Sat.* 1.10.67–71). His freedom is that of a mastery created within himself, a craft and a discipline, an aesthetics of existence, more than a direct assertion of power over others. The poet not

---

[71] See Marchesi 2005: 400–1. Cf. Cic. *Off.* 1.132–7. This is not everyday speech, but the witty and refined speech of the cultivated aristocrat, notable for the purity of his diction and the sparkle of his wit.

[72] Oliensis 1998: 25.

[73] See Kiessling and Heinze 1921: 84; Leach 1971; Freudenburg 1993: 34–5.

only files[74] his verse but in a very real sense through his verse he creates and files down a soul of precisely the dimensions the Augustan Principate demanded.[75] The biting mouth of Lucilius is turned against the satirist as he chews his nails to the quick (*Sat.* 1.10.71).

The first book of Horace's *Satires* is in many ways very different from the work of Lucilius. *Satires* 1.1, 1.2, and 1.3, which borrow heavily from the tradition of diatribe, are the most Lucilian in tone. After 1.3, no living person of note is lampooned, and even in the opening satires there is no real political combat.[76] As Coffey observes, 'In the 30s it would have been dangerous, especially for a freedman's son, to write political lampoons.'[77] What Maecenas and Octavian needed, and what Horace sought in *satura*, was a poetic form in which fundamental Roman values could be redefined. Horace produces a satire that is both politically and aesthetically disciplined, shorn of the Republican excesses that, from the perspective of Octavian, Maecenas, and their circle, had led the Republic to collapse in blood and fire. To this end, Horace relies more on paradox and self-deprecating irony than on the full-frontal assault of traditional invective. In 1.5 he portrays himself as oblivious to the great political events surrounding him, even as he soils himself in a wet dream that underlines his impotence (83–5).[78] In 1.9, he pays a subtle compliment to Maecenas while portraying himself as the hapless victim of a tasteless bore. Horace's *sermo* 'others' this nameless, social-climbing pest, even as it establishes the implicit discursive rules for what constitutes the 'same'.[79] He produces a satire of containment, of internalized limits: *iam satis est.*[80]

*Satires* 1.4 confronts the problem of how to redefine Lucilian satiric *libertas* for a different political and discursive context. *Libertas* in this period was a topic much debated in both political and philosophical circles. It was the rallying cry for both Caesar and his assassins. It could be defined as broadly as the right to engage in invective in the manner of Lucilius or Catullus without fear of reprisal, or as narrowly as the Epicurean commitment to give frank, but discreet, advice to a friend or social superior.[81] Yet, while the debate was ongoing, in the wake of the civil wars and the proscriptions the traditional conception of satiric and political *libertas*, as unbridled aristocratic licence, was clearly becoming anachronistic. Horace's labour in 1.4 to redefine it and the genre most closely associated with it was

---

[74] Cf. *Sat.* 1.10.65.    [75] See Henderson 1999c: 220.
[76] See Rudd 1982: 149–52; Freudenburg 1993: 52.    [77] Coffey 1976: 90–1.
[78] See S. Braund 1992: 19; Freudenburg 2001: 53.
[79] See Rudd 1982: 82–3; DuQuesnay 1984: 52; Henderson 1999c; Schlegel 2005: 120.
[80] See Gowers 1993: 126.    [81] See Freudenburg 1993: 79–88.

both necessary and deliberate. Moreover, insofar as 1.4, as will be recalled from our earlier discussion, alludes both directly and indirectly to Lucilius' own programmatic poem from Book 30, the intertextual relation with Lucilius is probably even denser than we know. Horace in 1.4 seeks not so much to polemicize with Lucilius as to remake him.

Poem 1.4 performs this labour of redefinition and consequent self-fashioning by tracing a trajectory from Lucilian Old Comedy to Horatian New Comic satire. It does so by examining various vignettes concerning approved and rejected forms of *libertas*.[82] Our argument will profit from taking a look at several examples.

Thus after an opening contrast between Lucilius' robust Old Comedy and Horace's refined Callimachean *sermo merus* (undiluted, and hence potentially intoxicating, speech),[83] Horace sketches a secondary contrast between the uncontrolled party-guest under the influence of too much *Liber* (Bacchus, wine), who abuses his host, and the better-mannered satire of Horace, which, while not hesitating to lampoon lower-class buffoons, clearly knows its limits:[84]

> saepe tribus lectis videas cenare quaternos,
> e quibus unus amet quavis aspergere[85] cunctos
> praeter eum qui praebet aquam; post hunc quoque potus,
> condita cum verax aperit praecordia Liber.
> hic tibi comis et urbanus liberque videtur,
> infesto nigris. ego si risi quod ineptus
> pastillos Rufillus olet, Gargonius hircum,
> lividus et mordax videor tibi?

Often you may see groups of four dining on three couches, one of whom loves to speak ill of all the others, except the dinner's host. Afterwards, when he is drunk and truthful Liber opens the secret recesses of the heart, he goes after him too. This fellow seems witty, urbane, and free to you, who are the scourge of black hearts. If I laughed because ridiculous Rufillus smells of breath mints and Gargonius like a goat, do I seem hateful and biting to you?

(Hor. *Sat.* 1.4.86–93)

---

[82] Cf. Schlegel 2005: 47–8.

[83] Cf. Catull. 13.9, where *meros amores* clearly refers not to everyday love, but to pure, unmixed, and hence potentially intoxicating love. *Merus* almost always bears the connotations of unmixed wine, which is what the adjective refers to when used as a substantive.

[84] There may also be an allusion here to the so-called debate between sober Callimachean water-drinkers and their wine-inspired opponents. For the evidence, see Crowther 1979.

[85] Acron glosses this verb as *notare sermonibus vel veneno* ('to mark with words or paint (or another noxious liquid)'; Hauthal 1864–6: II.83 ad loc.). It is tempting to think this gloss was current in Horace's time and so the parallel with *notabant* (1.4.5) was intentional, though the scholiast is probably making the same connection to line 5 as we are.

The passage begins with an image of excess. Roman dining-couches, which would normally hold three diners, are here packed with four, one of whom plays the part of the *scurra*, the lower-class jester who amuses his betters with jokes and pranks, often at the expense of the others present.[86] Practical good sense initially restrains the *scurra* from attacking his host until wine loosens his tongue.

The use of *Liber* here for Bacchus is significant. The guest who seems *liber* and *urbanus* in the next line, two qualities elsewhere associated with Lucilius (1.4.5; 1.10.65), is merely drunk and his *libertas* nothing more than *licentia* (see above, pp. 92–4), harming guest and host indiscriminately.[87] The *scurra* is the negative image of Lucilian satire. He sows discord rather than internalizing the norms of proper behaviour through a sense of the restraint inherent in *libertas* as Horace redefines it in the *Satires*.[88] Nonetheless, Horace complains that because he lampooned two otherwise unknown fops, Gargonius and Rufillus, in an earlier satire (1.2.27), he is said to transgress satiric decorum, to become a biter (*mordax*). One man's *libertas* is another's *Liber*.

Our next passage concerns Horace's own proclivity to speak too freely. His speech is inspired by the Lucilian practice of his father, who pointed out images of vice from the surrounding population, so he would know what behaviour to avoid:

> *liberius* si
> dixero quid, si forte iocosius, hoc mihi iuris
> cum venia dabis: insuevit pater optimus hoc me,
> ut fugerem exemplis vitiorum quaeque notando.[89]

If perhaps I say anything a bit too freely, a bit too teasingly, you will grant me this privilege with indulgence; my excellent father accustomed me to this, so that by marking out every vice by means of examples I might flee them.

(1.4.103–6)

---

[86] The Roman table was surrounded on three sides by couches, with three diners normally reclining on each. This banquet is marked as excessive, though not unusual (*saepe*), by the inclusion of a fourth diner on each couch. See Gell. *NA* 13.11.12. The *unus* is the *scurra*, a hanger-on of his aristocratic host, who would amuse the party as jester and buffoon. The accumulation of numbers (*tribus, quaternos, unus*) gives emphasis to the implication that the *scurra* is the *unus* in excess. In the strict order of hierarchy of a Roman party he would normally recline in the final position (*imus*) on the last couch (*imus*), with the host. He marks the transgression of decorum that Horatian satire refuses. Implicit is a denial that Horace occupies the position of *scurra* in Maecenas' household, a barb aimed at Horace's relatively low social status. Such a charge could never have been made against Lucilius.

[87] On the problem of the satiric transgression of *urbanitas* in this poem, see Keane 2006: 47.

[88] See Anderson 1982b: 14–17.     [89] Cf. 1.4.5.

*Liberius* here is a loaded term. It should be taken in both its literal and its social sense. 'If I speak a little bit too freely, in the manner of one who is *liber*, it is because of my father (who is a *libertus*).' The idea on one level is perfectly transparent, but, in terms of Roman social hierarchy, it presents a paradox. Horace's freedom, even in those aspects that some might term excessive, is predicated upon the practice of his father, who we later find out was not fully free, but merely 'freed' (*Sat.* 1.6.6), and who therefore still bore the social and legal marks of his one-time servitude. Horace's father reinterprets Lucilian satire for those who are not free. He observes the behaviour of others not to reprove them, but to improve himself and his son. This is something new. To say the same of Lucilius' attacks on Lupus, Metellus, and Scaevola, or Trebonius' attacks on Mark Antony, or even Catullus' attacks on Memmius and Mamurra, would border on the absurd.

Later in *Satires* 1.4, this freedom to observe the vice of others, so as to correct oneself, is compared to the criticism of a frank friend:

> ex hoc ego sanus ab illis,
> perniciem quaecumque ferunt, mediocribus et quis
> ignoscas vitiis teneor; fortassis et istinc
> largiter abstulerit longa aetas, *liber* amicus,
> consilium proprium: neque enim, cum lectulus aut me
> porticus excepit, desum mihi: 'rectius hoc est:
> hoc faciens vivam melius.'

On account of this [practice of my father] I am kept safe from all the vices that bring harm, and I am held only by those moderate ones you could forgive; and perhaps long life, a *frank* friend, and my own thought will free me from most of these too. For I am never absent from myself, whether lying on my writing couch or strolling through the colonnades: 'This thing is more correct: I will live better doing this.'

(1.4.129–35)

The external criticism of the father and the frank friend is internalized as the voice of the poet to himself. He is never absent from himself, but always on the lookout, always observing, critiquing, and disciplining the self. Satiric *libertas* has been redirected and internalized as the care of the self.[90]

> haec ego mecum
> compressis agito labris; ubi quid datur oti
> illudo chartis. hoc est mediocribus illis
> ex vitiis unum.

[90] For Foucault's exploration of a similar dynamic in the Greek term *parrhesia* in his 1982–3 seminar, 'Le gouvernement de soi et des autres' (Foucault 2008), see P. A. Miller 2006 (with special relevance to Roman satire).

I turn these things over in my mind with lips closed tight; when I have the time
I play around on paper. This is one of those moderate vices.

(1.4.137–40)

Unlike Lucilian *libertas*, this practice of self-formation takes place with the
poet's biting mouth closed. He does not recite in public halls, but speaks
to himself or a few friends, and then only when forced (1.4.70–6; cf.
1.10.71–92). He speaks to form himself and thus he, unlike the pest of
1.9, comes to have a place, his own particular place, in the circle of the elite
(1.9.51–2).

The result of this internalized practice of satirical self-formation will be
Horace's assertion in 1.6.110–12, quoted at the beginning of this section
(p. 100), that he is freer even than a famous senator, though born from a
*pater libertinus*.[91] This statement would have been absurd in the mouth of
Lucilius. Horace is free, however, precisely because he has no pretensions
to public honours, because he does not seek to wield power over others,
because he cultivates himself, and because he is happy in his own skin
(1.6.19–22).[92] In short, Horatian satire redefines *libertas* as the virtual
opposite of its normative meaning in Republican literature, without at the
same time overturning the fundamental social distinction between free and
slave (1.6.7–8).[93] His is not the power to speak his will and to enforce it
upon others, but to go where he wants on a gelded mule, an image of
lower-class emasculation, a freedom which he contrasts with the enslave-
ment of the *praeclarus senator* to the demands of public life.[94] By the
standard of the previous generation, this is *libertas* as self-mutilation.

In sum, Horatian satire redefines not only the genre but also the
fundamental nature of what it means to be free, to be *civis Romanus*, by
moving from a set of externalized values to their fundamental redefinition
as a set of internalized strictures that require the self-surveillance and self-
disciplining of the newly emergent subject of the incipient Principate.[95]

---

[91] On the relation between 1.4 and 1.6, as well as their central position in the collection, see Sigsbee
1974: 73.

[92] See Classen 1993: 117. The continuing presence of Lucilian *libertas* and the efforts to redefine it
present numerous paradoxes that Horace is able to exploit for poetic effect. One example is the
contradiction between the praise of being comfortable in one's own skin and the heroic efforts
Horace's father undertook to procure his son an education equal to that of the sons of the senatorial
class (*Sat.* 1.6.72–80; cf. Plaza 2006: 285–6). In fact, Horace is every bit as much a social climber as
those he denounces. Cf. Henderson 1999c: 208–16.

[93] Cf. Stampacchia 1982: 208.      [94] See Freudenburg 2001: 59–60.

[95] Cf. Rudd 1982: 51–2. For more on the Horatian redefinition of freedom, see Citti 2000: 127;
Bowditch 2001: 150.

Satiric violence is thus both ironized and directed as much at the self as at the other. Invective now becomes internal monologue.[96]

In the process of this redefinition, Horace seeks to move *nobilitas*, *ingenuitas*, and *libertas* from their traditional Roman definitions as external public virtues towards a new vision of them as internal ethical values cognate with Hellenistic popular philosophy. An anecdote will help to illustrate this relationship. In response to a question from King Antigonus about his family and city of origin, Bion the Borysthenite, the main exponent of the diatribe form and one of Horace's acknowledged models in satire (*Epist.* 2.2.60), replied, 'examine me for myself'.[97] Bion thus declares the irrelevance of inherited status, wealth, or prestige in terms that directly anticipate the opening of *Satires* 1.6, which ends with a direct quotation from him:[98]

> non quia, Maecenas, Lydorum quidquid Etruscos
> incoluit finis, nemo generosior est te,
> nec quod avus tibi maternus fuit atque paternus
> olim qui magnis legionibus imperitarent,
> ut plerique solent, naso suspendis adunco
> ignotos, ut me libertino patre natum.

Maecenas, despite the fact that no one among the Lydians who settled in Etruscan lands is more nobly born than you, and that your maternal and paternal grandfathers once commanded great legions, you do not, as most people do, turn up your nose at those of obscure birth, like me, the son of a freedman father.

(1.6.1–6)

This idea that one's primary worth was not predicated on ancestry and inherited wealth but on abstract virtue was a position not common to the traditional Roman aristocracy. It was, however, as Bion knew, completely at home with learning the language of self-criticism and of ethical self-fashioning from your freedman father.

---

[96] Cf. Schlegel 2005: 79, 101, 112.    [97] Diog. Laert. 4.46 σκόπει δέ με ἐξ ἐμαυτοῦ.

[98] Fiske 1920: 316–18 argued that 1.6 is indebted to Bion. The key phrase is *libertino patre natum* (1.6.6). Little is known about Horace's father. He appears to have been a man of some education and wealth since he sent his son to the best teachers in Rome. The circumstances under which he became a slave and later a freedman are unknown. The phrase, which is repeated throughout the satire both verbatim (45, 46) and with slight variation (29, 36, 58), is a direct translation of Bion (see Freudenburg 1993: 205; Plaza 2006: 201). For other philosophical influences on what seem to be autobiographical elements in 1.6, particularly in relation to 111–15, see the description of the teaching methods of Aidesius of Pergamum by Hadot 1995: 328. See also the ingenious speculation of G. Williams 1995 that Horace's father had been captured during the Social War, and had thus technically been a 'slave' in need of manumission, only to be subsequently fully enrolled as a Roman citizen. This argument makes excellent sense of the available data while doing justice to the poetic complexity of these texts.

Of course, no overly strict dichotomy should be established between the public and the private. These new definitions of traditional Roman virtues only became operational to the extent that others recognized them. The proof of Horace's personal *ingenuitas* was its public recognition by Maecenas. The coalition of forces centred around Octavian and Maecenas, which would emerge as the Augustan regime, had not substituted the private for the public, but had increasingly sought to replace the public recognition of externally determined virtues such as aristocratic birth, wealth, and the competition for political and military honours, with the public promotion of internally determined ethical values such as modesty, duty, honour, and fidelity, as exemplified most notably by *pius Aeneas*.[99]

## Conclusion: Practices of Subjection

> Our society is not that of the spectacle but of surveillance; beneath the surface of images, we invest bodies with a certain depth ... the interplay of signs defines the anchor points of power; the actual totality of the individual is not amputated, repressed, altered by our social order, but the individual is carefully fabricated, according to a tactics of bodies and forces. We are a good deal less Greek than we believe.
>
> (Foucault 1975: 252–3)

> To analyse what is designated as 'the subject' required an examination of what are the forms of relation to the self through which the individual constitutes itself and recognizes itself as a subject.
>
> (Foucault 1984a: 12)

In the period between Lucilius and Horace, the satiric subject's relation to itself, and hence its relation to others and the government of others,[100] changed fundamentally. As I noted at the beginning of this chapter, this shift parallels other changes in the constitution of the Roman subject, Roman knowledge, and the Roman state.[101] What this specific argument traces, however, is the way in which the verbal violence inherent in Lucilian satire and its aggressive relation to political opposition, cultural deviation, and alternative forms of elite subjectivity is turned (in a certainly incomplete but

---

[99] See DuQuesnay 1984: 45–52.    [100] See Kremer-Marietti 1985: 278.

[101] These shifts have been charted most systematically in Wallace-Hadrill 1997, who describes a series of parallel and mutually implicated changes taking place at the end of the Republic in political culture, morals, and the conceptualizations of law, time, and language. The structure of Wallace-Hadrill's observations follows that of Foucault in *Les mots et les choses* (Foucault 1966), though in the latter the focus is on the birth of the 'human sciences' at the beginning of the nineteenth century. For a similar shift in the construction of erotic and sexual discourses during this same period, see Habinek 1997. For the crisis of the Roman subject, see P. A. Miller 2004, esp. 1–30.

nonetheless significant fashion) against the satirist himself. There is, as I have shown, a fundamental shift from a satiric discourse of violent spectacle and admonition to one of internalization and self-discipline.

A final set of images will help concretize this change. In *Satires* 1.4 the satirist is compared to a raging bull whose horns must be wrapped in straw to keep him from goring innocent passers-by (1.4.34). In the same poem, the satirist is also both positively and negatively compared to the *scurra*, the hanger-on who entertains his aristocratic host by abusing others. In poem 1.5, the figure of the *scurra* has been transformed from the drunken dinner-guest (1.4.86–9) to the Oscan buffoon Messius, whose rustic high jinks with the freedman Sarmentus provide an evening's entertainment for Horace, Maecenas, and their friends during the journey to Brundisium (1.5.51–70). Messius, we are told, bears a scar on his forehead, which Sarmentus says makes the Oscan recall a unicorn whose horn has been removed. Hence what once might have been a source of fear has been tamed. Like the Lucilian bull of 1.4 and the castrated mule of 1.6, Messius and the satirist have effectively been emasculated. Indeed, as 1.4 acknowledges, *libertas* has been transformed into the space of self-criticism: a discourse we speak *labris compressis*. Thus, Catherine Keane has argued, 'the scar on Messius' forehead that attracts such attention ... is a fitting metaphor for' Horace's own satiric castration. 'It is a permanent reminder of past injury; similarly, the perform-ance [in 1.5] conjures the whole realm of the poet's experience, including aspects that are suppressed in his current identity.'[102] Messius' scar is, then, the sign of Horace's own self-mutilation.

Of course, what makes Horace so pivotal a figure in both the history of the satiric genre and the creation of Augustan culture is precisely his ability to present this caricatural image of his satiric and social castration while simultaneously asserting his mastery by placing himself in the aristocratic audience. He is both watcher and watched, and hence asserts a fundamen-tal control over both self and that self's relation to the other by means of the very interiorization of discursive violence that this new form of satire demands. Horatian satire is, in fact, a set of mirrors through which the subject is constituted by means of its own self-observation and irony: its reflection on and self-reflection through the other. The introjection of Lucilian violence becomes, thus, the ground for a new form of self-mastery and subjective depth. In the end, it is a moment of simultaneous self-mutilation and -fabrication: a birth that leaves a scar.

[102] Keane 2006: 54–5.

# CHAPTER 4

# Make War Not Love
## Militia amoris *and Domestic Violence in Roman Elegy*

### Donncha O'Rourke*

## I

> deripui tunicam; nec multum rara nocebat,
> pugnabat tunica sed tamen illa tegi;
> quae, cum ita pugnaret, tamquam quae vincere nollet,
> victa est non aegre proditione sua.[1]

I ripped off her dress – its material was not to her (dis)advantage,[2] but still she fought for her dress's protection. Fighting like one who was unwilling to conquer, she was conquered without difficulty through her own betrayal.

> I have pretended to rape my wife (ripped the clothes from her body; however, I know she was very willing and put up a token resistance) . . . It was only play, acting rough (tough on clothes) but being very careful *not* to hurt her. She got a big thrill from this if it was not expected and on rare occasions.

The quotations above juxtapose Ovid, *Amores* 1.5.13–16, with a response drawn from a survey of male sexualities in the late twentieth century.[3] The similarities (and differences) between these two texts invite consideration of the relationship between elegiac violence and the contexts in which it

---

* I thank the editors for their numerous helpful suggestions in relation to the issues and argument of this chapter; also Jane Burkowski for her insightful reflections on an earlier draft and for advance access to what is now Burkowski 2013; and Cybelle Greenlaw and Fiachra Mac Górain for valuable discussion and feedback. This research was facilitated by a British Academy Postdoctoral Fellowship.

[1] The elegists are quoted from the editions of Kenney 1961, Maltby 2002, and Heyworth 2007a. Translations are by the author.

[2] Is *nec multum* to be construed with *rara* ('her tunic, none too diaphanous, marred her looks') or with *nocebat* ('her diaphanous tunic little marred her looks') as most readers prefer (e.g., Barsby 1973: 66; McKeown 1989: 113–14; P. A. Miller 2002: 254)? In the ambiguity and its interpretation there is much at stake. For the colloquial use of *multum* to modify an adjective, McKeown 1989: 113 cites Bömer 1969–86: II.62–3 on Ov. *Met.* 4.155 (*o multum miseri*). For *nec multum* modifying an adjective see, e.g., Juv. 12.66–7 (*modica nec multum fortior aura | ventus adest*); Stat. *Theb.* 6.583.

[3] Hite 1981: 746.

was produced and consumed. The question whether represented violence reflects or affects society is one that exercises analysts of modern media,[4] but it pertains urgently also to Latin elegy as the product of a culture that knew violence as a quotidian reality. From the first poem in each extant collection, the elegiac genre is saturated with violence.[5] The Propertian corpus opens by Romanizing and militarizing an epigram by Meleager (*Anth. Pal.* 12.101) to present Amor in the pose of a victorious combatant (*et caput impositis pressit Amor pedibus*, 'and Love crushed my head under his feet', Prop. 1.1.4).[6] Tibullus 1.1 is a soldier's prayer for a peace that manifests, apparently quaintly, in the lovers' tiff: *nunc levis est tractanda Venus, dum frangere postes | non pudet et rixas inseruisse iuvat* ('now is the time to get to grips with light-hearted love, while there's no shame in breaking down doors and there's pleasure in starting quarrels', 73–4). The first line of Ovid's *Amores* encodes elegy's propensity for violence (*arma . . . violentaque bella*, *Am.* 1.1.1) paradoxically in the moment of rejecting it: rereading as a programmatic statement the violence that opens the Propertian corpus (*pressit Amor pedibus*, Prop. 1.1.4), Ovid's Cupid filches a metrical foot (*unum surripuisse pedem*, 4) to reconfigure the epic 'arms and violent wars' of the opening hexameter as the elegist's allegedly non-violent conflict with Amor and his girlfriend.[7] The lover's conscription in the 'warfare of love' (*militia amoris*) is thus a generic marker that imbricates the elegiac text with the historical context of Rome in the first century BC.[8]

In undertaking an analysis of this imbrication, the present chapter recognizes from the outset that to reconstruct a context against which to read a literary text is to engage in a hazardously circular enterprise. As Duncan Kennedy has argued specifically in relation to Roman love-elegy, the historical reality outside the text, (re)constructed by the reader as context, is, no less than the world within the text, a representation. Accordingly, to read the sexual 'victory' in *Amores* 1.5 as, for example, an act of violent sexual role play such as that described by the survey

[4] See Barker and Petley 2001b for a thought-provoking analysis of this debate.

[5] For overviews of violence in elegy, see Fredrick 1997; James 2003a: 184–97 and 2003b; Caston 2012, esp. 93–112; Fredrick 2012. On Ovid's *Ars amatoria*, see Desmond 2006: 35–54.

[6] On Amor's pose, see Stahl 1985: 30–3; Kennedy 1993: 48; Greene 1998: 41. On the Meleagrian intertext, see Fedeli 1980: 62–7; Booth 2001; Keith 2008: 45–6.

[7] On *Am.* 1.1 as a reading of Prop. 1.1, see Keith 1992.

[8] For overviews of *militia amoris*, see Spies 1930; Lilja 1965: 64–8; Fantham 1972: 26–33; Murgatroyd 1975; Lyne 1980: 71–8; Adams 1982: 158–9; Estévez Sola 2011. For angled interpretations and studies of individual poems, see E. Thomas 1964; F. Cairns 1984; Cahoon 1988; Bellido 1989; Kennedy 1993: 53–61; McKeown 1995; Gale 1997; Alston 1998: 213–14; Greene 1999; Wyke 2002: 42–5; Drinkwater 2013.

respondent is merely to read one kind of representation against another. Within both texts, however, an urgent distinction between representation and reality is being negotiated: in the survey response, the husband's distinction between 'rape' and rape (his alleged care not to cause injury discloses awareness of another kind of 'reality') restates only more prosaically the Ovidian lover's assumption that 'no' means 'yes' ('token resistance' thus has its counterpart in *tamquam . . . nollet*). A further documentary text from the same source will illustrate just how blurred this line between representation and reality can be:

> I just went ahead with it one time because I thought she just wanted to be 'taken' (nothing at all brutal though). Afterward, I realized that I had really forced her and I felt really bad.[9]

The potential for this kind of misreading (or misrepresentation?) reveals what is at stake in the interpretation of a lover's version of events. To the extent that this second respondent gives the lie to the marital 'thrill' described in the first quotation, *Amores* 1.7, in which Ovid admits to having assaulted his girlfriend (*at nunc sustinui raptis a fronte capillis* | *ferreus ingenuas ungue notare genas*, 'but now I went so far as to rip the hair from her brow and, iron-hearted, to mark her noble cheeks with my nail', 49–50), suggests that the 'rape' in *Amores* 1.5 might be more accurately described as such without the use of scare-quotes. The texts from the survey are, of course, the only ones that can be said to have outside them an objective reality according to which their claims are true or not, but Ovidian elegy might nevertheless be said to present an analogous situation within its fiction. In this sense, elegy implicates its readers in processes of evaluation parallel to those which obtain in real life and, by extension, invites reflection on the extent to which its violence is to be considered metaphorical.

Reader-response is itself staged within *Amores* 1.7, which opens with the aggressor's appeal to any bystanding friend (*si quis amicus ades*, 2) to clap him in irons. Not all readers, however, have responded accordingly: those who take Ovid's remorse as sincere[10] deny, or do not see, the irony which for others culminates in his request to Corinna in the final couplet to put her hair back 'at its post' (*in statione*, 68).[11] The spectrum of interpretation

---

[9] Hite 1981: 721.
[10] So Fränkel 1945: 18; Wilkinson 1955: 50; Luck 1959: 149; McKeown 1989: 197.
[11] Degrees of insincerity, humour, and irony are detected by Khan 1966; D. Parker 1969: 84–7; Stirrup 1973; Lyne 1980: 249–51, 254–6; Cahoon 1988: 296–7; Boyd 1997: 123–4; Caston 2012: 105–8. Greene 1998: 84–92 reads *Am.* 1.7 as an implicit critique of moral indifference. On the violence of *Am.* 1.7, see also Fredrick 1997: 184–6, 189, and esp. Greene 1999.

elicited by *Amores* 1.7 illustrates how empirical readers will necessarily bring to elegiac violence their individual, historically located preconceptions and reading practices. In the same way, classicists who read according to genre, metapoetics, narratology, or feminism, for example, have found in *Amores* 1.5, respectively, elegiac playfulness,[12] a poet exercising control over his *materia*,[13] an allegory of the desire to read to the climax,[14] and an endorsement or critique of masculinist scopophilic domination.[15] Thus, in a paradox of the kind that exercises contemporary analysts of violent entertainment media, Ovid's aestheticization of his assaults on Corinna seems to gloss over what would otherwise be plainly unappealing scenes.[16]

Despite the non-metaphorical value of violence in the Roman world, then, readers of elegy are more often inclined to distance the genre's *violenta bella* from literal signification. To be sure, the conceit of *militia amoris*, whereby *amor* is described in terms of *militia*, is an apt paradox with which to characterize the elegiac relationship. As Lyne observes, 'love is both violent and supremely non-violent'.[17] The readiness of the Roman imagination to describe this situation in military terms can be witnessed in Lucretius' description of the phenomenon of physical attraction:

> namque omnes plerumque cadunt in vulnus et illam
> emicat in partem sanguis unde icimur ictu,
> et si comminus est, hostem ruber occupat umor.
> sic igitur Veneris qui telis accipit ictus,
> sive puer membris muliebribus hunc iaculatur
> seu mulier toto iactans e corpore amorem,
> unde feritur, eo tendit gestitque coire
> et iacere umorem in corpus de corpore ductum.

For generally everyone falls towards a wound, and blood spatters in the direction from which we are struck by the blow, and, if it is hand-to-hand, the red fluid covers the enemy. In this way, then, he who receives blows from Venus' weapons (whether a boy with feminine limbs is shooting him or a woman who hurls love from her whole body) inclines in the direction from which he is smitten and strives to couple and to expel into that body the fluid drawn from his body.

(Lucr. 4.1049–56)

---

[12] So, e.g., Lyne 1980: 260–2; Booth 2009: 70 (with 64–5 and 70–1 for other views).

[13] See the seminal discussions collected in Wyke 2002: 11–77, 115–54; cf. also Keith 1994: 29–31; Boyd 1997: 154–7; Holzberg 2002: 49.

[14] See Kennedy 2008; Salzman-Mitchell 2008.

[15] See Greene 1998: 77–84. Contrast, e.g., Luck 1959: 153–7, esp. 154 'There is little need for violent action.'

[16] Cf. McCauley 1998: 46: 'It is not obvious why viewing fictional violence should be attractive when viewing real violence is not.'

[17] Lyne 1980: 72.

For the Epicurean, military imagery offers a powerful means of communicating to a Roman audience the injurious consequences of erotic infatuation. In elegy, however, the subordination of *militia* to *amor* assumes a sociopolitically and generically countercultural dynamic.[18] Thus Propertius abnegates his responsibilities to Roman militarism (*non ego sum laudi, non natus idoneus armis: | hanc me militiam fata subire volunt*, 'I was born suited neither for glory nor for arms: this is the kind of "soldiering" destiny wishes me to undertake', 1.6.29–30; cf. 4.1.137)[19] and opts to write of heroic battles fought in the bedroom with Cynthia (*seu nuda erepto mecum luctatur amictu, | tum vero longas condimus Iliadas*, 'or if she wrestles with me naked, her dress ripped off, then truly we compile long *Iliads*', 2.1.13–14). Tibullus writes from the perspective of a soldier who yearns to trade the long road of Messalla's campaigns for a quiet life in which the only battles he fights are with Delia (*hic ego dux milesque bonus*, 'here I am a fine general and soldier', 1.1.75). In the most sustained example of the figure, Ovid rejects the stereotype of the indolent lover to argue that his exertions are in every respect comparable to those of the soldier (*Am.* 1.9).[20] When *militia amoris* is read metaphorically, then, elegy may be taken to be a peaceable genre in which the rejection of warfare typically sees supreme command transferred to the female beloved in a way that appears to invert the normative power-dynamics in Roman gender-relations.

On closer inspection, however, the 'ironies of elegy' collapse the apparent polarities of mainstream discourse:[21] the elegist's elevation of *amor* (and elegy itself) is absurdly overblown, and the 'warfare of love' requires for its conceit the prior acknowledgement of *militia* (and epic) as normative and respectable. The elegist's abstraction from soldiery, moreover, is incomplete. Tibullus' elegies construct as their interpretative context the 'reality' of a *militia* that engenders the poet's yearning for Delia.[22] The conflation of lover and soldier is witnessed historically in the career of Cornelius Gallus, the putative 'founder' of love-elegy. The alternating verses of the Qaṣr Ibrîm papyrus fragment ascribed to his authorship, like the swansong of Virgil's Gallus in *Eclogue* 10, attest to the intertwining of *militia* and *amor* from the inception of the elegiac genre.[23]

---

[18] See the classic discussion of Hallett 1973.       [19] For this view of Prop. 1.6 see Stahl 1985: 72–98.
[20] See McKeown 1995.       [21] See Gale 1997.       [22] See Kennedy 1993: 13–15.
[23] See *Ecl.* 10.42–9. On the question whether the papyrus preserves a single elegy or a series of separate poems or extracts, see Hollis 2007: 250–1, with further references. On Gallus as precursor of *militia amoris*, see Lyne 1980: 266 n. 16. On *militia* in Gallus, see F. Cairns 2006: 87–90.

If lovers really are soldiers, then, there is a sense in which metaphorical *militia* also has non-metaphorical potential. This is a point with serious implications for elegiac violence. In Propertius' picture of the late Gallus laving his wounds in the underworld (*et modo formosa quam multa Lycoride Gallus | mortuus inferna vulnera lavit aqua*, 'and recently deceased for fair Lycoris, how many wounds did Gallus wash in the water below', 2.34.91–2) there is unsettling ambiguity between the elegist's metaphorical and literal *vulnera*, between the figurative *miles amoris* and the historical soldier who paid the ultimate price for military insubordination.[24] As Gallus' wounds oscillate between figurative and literal signification, so the 'warfare of love' is a paradox only for those whose ideology of love is, indeed, non-violent. It is worth remembering that Lucretius' description of the mechanism of erotic attraction, quoted above, employs a military analogy not merely to commit to the Epicurean view of *amor* as a source of violent psychological upheaval: on the atomic level, the violence of love is no paradox or metaphor in that attraction and anguish result from a physical process in which the lover's sensory organs are quite literally bombarded by *simulacra* (effluences) emanating from the beloved.[25] For the Epicurean, as for Propertius' Gallus, the metaphorical *vulnus* turns out to be something all too tangible. The 'wound of love' famously made flesh by Dido, Virgil's elegiac interloper in the *Aeneid*, implicitly recognizes the Lucretian analogy as a comparison between two phenomena that are essentially the same at the material level.[26] At *Heroides* 7.189–90 (*nec mea nunc primum feriuntur pectora telo; | ille locus saevi vulnus amoris habet*, 'nor is this the first time my breast is smitten with a weapon: that place bears the wound of savage love'), Ovid's Dido knowingly conflates the figurative and literal wounds that occur separately at *Aeneid* 4.67 and 689 in the repeated line-ending *sub pectore vulnus* ('a wound beneath the breast').

These examples indicate how the perception of metaphor may be ideologically conditioned, dependent as it is on essentializing linguistic compartmentalizations whereby, in the case of *militia amoris*, love and war are perceived as mutually exclusive categories. As Kennedy's discussions of elegiac metaphor suggest,[27] the violence that pervades elegy threatens to

---

[24] For a convenient summary of the circumstances that may have precipitated Gallus' disgrace and suicide, see Raymond 2013: 60–1.
[25] See R. D. Brown 1987: 64, 72 ('like weapons, *simulacra* too are physical projectiles'), 180–4, 191–6.
[26] See Hardie 1986: 219–33.    [27] Kennedy 1993: 51–7 and 2012.

diminish the figurative value of *militia amoris* to the point at which it
might be wondered whether *amor*, rather than *militia*, is the metaphor
'carried across', so to speak, into a domain where the default setting is
militant rather than erotic. The potential for such inversion of elegiac non-
violence can have far-reaching implications. In Propertius 2.14, a rare
occasion of erotic requital is equated with a military triumph (*haec mihi
devictis potior victoria Parthis,* | *haec spolia, haec reges, haec mihi currus erunt,*
'this victory is worth more to me than Parthia conquered: this will be my
booty, this my parade of kings, this my chariot', 23–4). So far, so elegiac.
The next elegy continues the celebration of the lovers' *rixa* (2.15.4–5),
arguing according to elegy's countercultural code that the real warfare
witnessed at Actium could have been avoided had all parties signed up
to the amatory lifestyle (41–8).[28] However, the Propertian lover's insistence that 'our cups have hurt no gods' (*laeserunt nullos pocula nostra deos,*
48)[29] is undercut by his less pacific disposition towards Cynthia some
lines earlier:

> quod si pertendens animo vestita cubaris,
>     scissa veste meas experiere manus.
> quin etiam si me ulterius provexerit ira,
>     ostendes matri bracchia laesa tuae.

But if you insist on going to bed with your clothes on, you'll have your dress
ripped and you'll feel my hands. Moreover, if anger pushes me over the edge, you
will be showing your mother the arms I hurt.

(Prop. 2.15.17–20)

The use of the verb *laedere* ('to hurt') in both contexts hints that the life of
love is not necessarily as harmless as its advocate maintains, and so
threatens to collapse the polarity that gives elegiac *militia amoris* its
countercultural value. Read in sequence, *bracchia laesa* and *laeserunt . . .
deos* might rather suggest that the man who cannot control his passions
privately is liable to do violence to society, too. In the context of the 20s
BC, this liability might have been taken as one of the many inflections in
the Propertian persona of the historical (or historiographical) Mark
Antony,[30] to whose allegedly ungovernable lust the recent crisis was

---

[28] For an 'anti-Augustan' reading of Prop. 2.15, see Stahl 1985: 215–33, esp. 226–33; see also Gurval
1995: 180–2.

[29] Most editions print *pocula* as transmitted, but the preference of, e.g., Giardina 2010: 172 for *proelia*
(Fontein) points to the underlying contrast with non-amatory battles.

[30] On Propertius and Antony, see P. A. Miller 2001: 128–31; also J. Griffin 1977; Stahl 1985:
228–30.

ascribed. On this reading, then, Propertius 2.14–15 are more violent and less straightforwardly oppositional than they might at first appear.

A sequence of Ovidian poems (*Am.* 2.12–14) exposes the hypocrisy of elegiac non-violence with rather different ideological implications. As in Propertius 2.14, a night of lovemaking is hailed 'a victory worthy of a triumph' (*victoria digna triumpho*, *Am.* 2.12.5): Corinna has been 'captured' on an Ovidian campaign (*ductu capta puella meo*, 8). The conventional paradox of *militia amoris* is rehearsed as Ovid dissociates his glory from that of the soldier (*at mea seposita est et ab omni milite dissors* | *gloria*, 'but my glory is separate and not shared by any soldier', 11–12) and rejects the wars of Graeco-Roman mythology (9–10, 17–24), while at the same time appropriating military terminology to valorize his own exploits (*me duce ad hanc voti finem, me milite veni;* | *ipse eques, ipse pedes, signifer ipse fui*, 'as general and soldier I came to this my prayer's fulfilment; I myself was cavalryman, I myself footsoldier, I myself standard-bearer', 13–14). Like Propertius, the Ovidian lover appears to wave the elegist's 'make love not war' banner: Corinna is bloodless booty (*sanguine praeda caret*, 6) and Ovidian *militia* is purely metaphorical (*sine caede*, 'without slaughter', 27). These comfortable convictions, however, are undercut in the next elegy, which opens with Corinna's life hanging in the balance following an abortion (*Am.* 2.13.1–2). The recriminations which follow her recovery ignore, and thereby draw attention to, Ovid's responsibility for her plight:[31] levelling against Corinna the hypocrisy that women are spared warfare only to wage it against themselves (*Am.* 2.14.1–4), and declaring that the first woman to abort a child ought to have died by her own *militia* (5–6), Ovid imports into his condemnation the very lexicon he had employed to celebrate his 'victory'. That women are suspected of following this course of action to preserve the bodily aesthetic Ovid elsewhere admires (cf. *Am.* 1.5.21) merely exposes the *puella*'s impossible situation as an elegiac commodity: *scilicet ut careat rugarum crimine venter,* | *sternetur pugnae tristis harena tuae?* ('Is it really so that your tummy might avoid the accusation of wrinkles that the unhappy arena of your fight will be scattered with sand?', 7–8).[32] The gladiatorial violence of which Ovid accuses Corinna is therefore an act with which his own hands are implicitly bloodied. The inescapable conclusion that *militia*

---

[31] For a 'female' reading of the gaps and silences of *Am.* 2.13–14, see Gamel 1989. Contrast, e.g., Laigneau 1999: 263–6, who argues that the Ovidian persona sides with Augustus as *curator morum* by reducing female sexuality to procreation.

[32] For this and other motivations for abortion in Antiquity, see Kapparis 2002: 97–132. James 2003a: 173–83 rereads *Am.* 2.14 and several other elegies in this light.

*amoris* is non-violent only for Ovid bankrupts the metaphor of its idealistic – indeed of its metaphorical – pretensions.

These examples suggest that allowance should be made for a degree of permeability between elegy's violent text and contexts. In the three sections which follow, then, the limits of *militia amoris* as a metaphor will be tested against three realities of violence familiar to readers ancient and modern: domestic violence; the seepage of military violence into civilian life; sexual violence in military conflicts.

## II

In 2005 the World Health Organisation (WHO) published a report illustrating the extent of domestic violence against women, or 'intimate partner violence' (IPV), in today's world.[33] The parameters of the survey encompassed 'acts of physical, sexual and emotional abuse by a current or former intimate male partner, whether cohabiting or not', 'controlling behaviours', and violence against females by non-partners.[34] Statistics for the prevalence of IPV in Antiquity are irrecoverable, but disclosures of violence against women in non-poetic texts are an important element of the cultural context within which elegiac representations of such violence are to be assessed.[35] Rhetorical theory and declamation frequently mention extramarital rape and present wives suing husbands for emotional or, less frequently, physical *mala tractatio* (maltreatment).[36] This term nuances the inaugural moment of Tibullan *militia amoris* (*nunc levis est tractanda Venus*, 'now light-hearted love must be taken in hand', 1.1.73), though the poet-lover differs from his counterparts in the fictive legal scenarios in tending to imagine rather than to inflict violence.[37] The exceptional case of Ovid's assault on Corinna in *Amores* 1.7 therefore comes across as an exaggeration or parody of elegiac tradition,[38] though it might also be said to expose a pre-existing propensity in the genre. The WHO reports a correlation between physical and non-physical violence as the lived

---

[33] García-Moreno *et al.* 2005. The report surveyed 24,000 women across ten countries.

[34] See García-Moreno *et al.* 2005: 13.

[35] For an overview of the evidence, see Seifert 2011. For an extended case study, see Pomeroy 2007.

[36] On the emphases of these texts *vis-à-vis* IPV, see Treggiari 1991a: 430–1. For cases of non-physical *mala tractatio* of wives, see, e.g., Sen. *Controv.* 3.7, 4.6, 5.3; Quint. *Inst.* 4.2.30, 9.2.79–80; [Quint.] *Decl. mai.* 8.6, 10.9, 18.5, 19.5, *Decl. min.* 363. For physical *mala tractatio* of wives, see, e.g., Sen. *Controv.* 1.2.22; Quint. *Inst.* 7.8.2; [Quint.] *Decl. min.* 383.

[37] The elegiac lover's restraint is well discussed by Caston 2012: 93–112 and Burkowski 2013: 92–126.

[38] See Barsby 1973: 91; Lyne 1980: 249–51; Boyd 1997: 156–7.

experience of all too many women in modern life.[39] The fine line between the two phenomena is witnessed also in ancient texts – more obviously, for example, in a declamation pertaining to a woman who opted to marry her rapist only later to sue him for jealous harassment ([Quint.] *Decl. min.* 383),[40] but elegy too, for all the lover's purported restraint, abounds in parallels for the WHO's 'operational definitions' of controlling behaviour.[41]

The elegiac lover's controlling behaviour thrives in the environment of conservative moral entrenchment under construction, at least officially, from 18 BC.[42] The *leges Iuliae* introduced in that year criminalized adultery primarily by regulating female sexuality: married men could apparently pursue affairs with unmarried women with impunity, but women, married and unmarried, risked loss of property, status, and, at least in theory, life.[43] The legislation seems to have been aimed at the upper classes, but the social and marital status of the elegiac *puella* is sufficiently indeterminate[44] to render it difficult to disregard the numerous references to her fear (e.g., *Am.* 3.4.31–2 *iuvat inconcessa voluptas:* | *sola placet, 'timeo' dicere si qua potest*, 'illicit pleasure is delightful; she alone charms who can say, "I'm afraid"').[45]

It is perhaps not coincidental that Propertius' celebration of the failure of an Augustan marital law (Prop. 2.7) is couched within a sequence of elegies marked by escalating intimidation.[46] In elegy 2.5, the *amator* warns

---

[39] See García-Moreno *et al.* 2005: 36 and appendix, table 8.

[40] For the interpretation of her complaint (*nimio amore et sollicita inquisitione hic offendit uxorem*, 'he wronged his wife by his excessive love and anxious questioning') see Winterbottom 1984: 584–5.

[41] García-Moreno *et al.* 2005: 14 (box 2.1) set out the following 'operational definitions' for controlling behaviours: keeping the woman from seeing friends (cf. Tib. 1.6.17; Ov. *Am.* 2.19); restricting contact with her family of birth (cf. Prop. 2.6.7–14); insisting on knowing where she is at all times (cf. Tib. 1.6.21–3); ignoring or treating her indifferently (cf. Prop. 2.5.5–8, 2.11, 2.22.37–40, 3.24–5, 4.7.23–34); getting angry if she speaks with other men (cf. Tib. 1.6.39–42; Ov. *Am.* 2.5); often accusing her of being unfaithful (cf. Tib. 1.6; Prop. 1.15.2, 2.5.3, 2.6.14, 2.8, 2.9.28, 2.18.19, 2.29b.31–42); controlling her access to health care (cf. Tib. 1.6.13–14; Ov. *Am.* 2.13.3 and 27–8, 2.14.43–4). On jealousy in elegy, see Caston 2012. See also James 2003b on elegiac tears, genuine as a reflection of emotional dependence, feigned as a strategy of emotional control.

[42] On elegy and the *leges Iuliae*, see Laigneau 1999: 337–67. On *amor* and the law in Ovid's *Ars amatoria*, see Sharrock 1994; R. K. Gibson 2003: 25–32.

[43] On the inequalities of the law, see Gardner 1986: 127–31. For further particulars, see Dixon 1992: 78–83; C. Edwards 1993: 37–42; Galinsky 1996: 128–40; McGinn 1998: 140–215.

[44] On the minimized identity of the elegiac *puella*, see Wyke 2002: 29–31. More determinative investigations are undertaken by, e.g., Lilja 1965: 35–42; Laigneau 1999: 193–207.

[45] Cf. Tib. 1.6.59–60, 2.6.49–50; Prop. 2.23.19–20, 3.14.23–4; Ov. *Am.* 2.19.20, 3.8.63, *Ars am.* 3.603–10.

[46] On this sequence, see Fredrick 1997: 180–2; James 2003a: 190–3.

Cynthia that she will pay the penalty for her perfidy (*dabis mihi, perfida, poenas*, 2.5.3), and though he ostensibly eschews physical violence – tearing clothes, smashing doors, pulling hair, bruising – he also describes it in detail (21–4); in the following elegy, jealousy is said to make explicable the crimes of the Centaurs against the Lapiths and Romulus against the Sabines (2.6.17–22); having claimed decapitation as preferable to the failed legislation in 2.7, Propertius resumes the intimidation in 2.8: *sed non effugies: mecum moriaris oportet; | hoc eodem ferro stillet uterque cruor* ('But you'll not escape: you should die with me. From this same blade the blood of us both will drip', 25–6). In this sequence, one wonders whether Cynthia might not have been protected by a law making her relationship with Propertius illegal.

Jealousy, possessiveness, and violence are illustrated in the last elegy of Tibullus' 'Delia cycle' (Tib. 1.6), in which the poet-lover suspects that his girlfriend Delia is deceiving her *vir* ('man', ?'husband')[47] with a paramour other than himself. Fearless of exposing his own entanglement in this erotic quadrangle, Tibullus disabuses of his delusions the man he has hitherto cuckolded, urging him to adopt a range of strategies (15–24) to keep his promiscuous *coniunx* under lock and key (*quid tenera tibi coniuge opus, tua si bona nescis | servare? frustra clavis inest foribus*, 'What good is a tender wife to you if you don't know how to guard your goods? In vain the key is in the door', 33–4). This comic paradox was later developed by Ovid,[48] but the humour is double-edged in that Tibullus' self-recommendation as Delia's chaperon (37–42) hints not merely at the lover's *servitium*, but at the oppressive guardianship to which Delia is subject, too (*at mihi servandam credas*, 'but you should entrust her to me for safekeeping', 37).[49] Tibullus goes on to warn of retribution both for the parvenu rival and for Delia herself, quoting as his authority a self-mutilating priestess of Bellona, goddess of war and, accordingly, an apt patroness for the *miles amoris*:[50]

> haec, ubi Bellonae motu est agitata, nec acrem
>   flammam, non amens verbera torta timet.
> ipsa bipenne suos caedit violenta lacertos
>   sanguineque effuso spargit inulta deam,

---

[47] Here, as elsewhere in elegy, the status of the rival is ambiguous: the terms *vir* (8) and *coniunx* (15) do not necessarily indicate a marital relationship. For discussion and references, see James 2003a: 41–52; cf. p. 119 above, with n. 44. On 'irregular unions', see Dixon 1992: 90–5.

[48] On Ov. *Am.* 2.19 and 3.4, see Greene 1998: 99–108.

[49] On this line, see Fitzgerald 2000: 75; Maltby 2002: 271.

[50] See Putnam 1973: 113; Maltby 2002: 272.

statque latus praefixa veru, stat saucia pectus,
 et canit eventus quos dea magna monet:
'parcite quam custodit Amor violare puellam,
 ne pigeat magno post tetigisse malo.
attigerit, labentur opes, ut vulnere nostro
 sanguis, ut hic ventis diripiturque cinis.'
et tibi nescioquas dixit, mea Delia, poenas;
 si tamen admittas, sit precor illa levis.

When she is spurred by Bellona's impulse, she fears not the searing flame nor, in her frenzy, the knotted whip. With a double-edged blade she violently slashes her own arms and, unharmed, spatters the goddess with her streaming blood. She stands, pierced in the side with a spike, she stands, wounded in her breast, and proclaims an outcome of which the mighty goddess warns: 'Forbear to violate the girl whom Love guards, lest later you regret having touched her to your great cost. Anyone who touches her will see his wealth ebb away like the blood from my wound, as this ash is scattered by the winds.' For you, too, my Delia, she prescribed punishments of some kind; if, however, you should be guilty, I pray that she be lenient.

(Tib. 1.6.45–56)

Following Tibullus' endorsement of Delia's oppression, this description of female violence is all the more conspicuous for the fact that, as the commentators note, Bellona's priests were usually male.[51] The gender of the acolyte might also allude to the sacred prostitutes that served the temples of Bellona's Cappadocian counterpart Ma, a touch of erudition that lends the prophecy a further degree of suitability as an erotodidactic warning to Delia.[52] The description of ritual violence might thus be said to displace onto the priestess-prostitute the 'menacingly indefinite'[53] punishment (*nescioquas . . . poenas*, 55) Tibullus claims to hope the meretricious object of his erotic worship will escape. Tibullus himself, however, seems not to be immune to the *furor* for which the priests of Bellona were notorious:[54] his earlier admission to the husband that he is not his own master where Delia is concerned (*non ego te laesi prudens*, 'I did not offend against you on purpose', 29) undermines his asseveration that he wishes to spare Delia not on her own account (*non ego te propter parco tibi*, 57) but in deference to her mother. This in turn gives the lie to his rejection of violence, prepared though he is to suffer it himself:

---

[51] See Putnam 1973: 113; Murgatroyd 1980: 198; Maltby 2002: 273.
[52] See F. Cairns 1979: 40–1; Murgatroyd 1980: 198.
[53] Maltby 2002: 274; cf. Murgatroyd 1980: 197: 'intimidating indefiniteness'.
[54] Lee-Stecum 1998: 193–5 draws out the parallels between Tibullus and the priestess.

> et, siquid peccasse putet, ducarque capillis
> immerito pronas proripiarque vias.
> non ego te pulsare velim, sed venerit iste
> si furor, optarim non habuisse manus.

And if she thinks I have sinned, let me be dragged by the hair and undeservingly cast headlong down the streets. Nor would I wish to hit you, but if that madness did come, I'd pray to have no hands.

(1.6.71–4)

Making its third appearance in the elegy, the hexameter opening *non ego te* (which occurs nowhere else in Tibullus) contrasts the active *amator* with the objectified *puella* in the context of a *furor* which the accompanying denials (*non ... prudens*; *non ... te propter*; *non ... velim*) hint may ultimately be ungovernable.

The restraint, or appropriate channelling, of anger is an ancient discourse in which the elegists can be seen to offer positive and negative paradigms.[55] For her part, the wife of an irascible husband was encouraged, according to the analogy that structured their relationship as that of master and slave, to suffer his outbursts and mollify his temper by adopting a demeanour of patient submissiveness.[56] Livy's Valerius famously argues in favour of repealing the sumptuary *lex Oppia* in 195 BC on the conviction that, faced with the choice, women would prefer their *servitus muliebris* ('womanly servitude') to the freedom conferred by widowhood and orphanhood, however much their husbands and fathers might avoid keeping them *in servitio* (Livy 34.7.11–13).[57] Augustine's account of his mother's subservient 'management' of her abusive husband shows the persistence of this analogy in fourth-century Africa (August. *Conf.* 9.9).[58] Although elegy concerns itself with extramarital relations, its inversion of the analogy through the figure of *servitium amoris* ('the slavery of love') can be seen as a component in the genre's wider inversion of the normative Roman household.[59] Propertius 4.8 presents a sustained travesty of marital fidelity and domestic *concordia* in which Cynthia takes on the role of an

---

[55] On ancient anger management, see generally Harris 2001 and, in relation to IPV in late Antiquity, Dossey 2008. On restraint (and lack thereof) in elegy, see R. K. Gibson 2007, Caston 2012: 93–112.

[56] On the analogy and its limits, see P. Clark 1998; Saller 1998; also Shaw 1987: 11–12, 28–9.

[57] See Treggiari 1991a: 212–14; P. Clark 1998: 118.

[58] See esp. P. Clark 1998: 110–17; also Shaw 1987: 31–2; Dossey 2008: 12–13.

[59] On the dynamics of the Roman *domus*, see Shaw 1987. On *servitium amoris* in elegy, see Copley 1947; Lyne 1979; Murgatroyd 1981; Kennedy 1993: 73; McCarthy 1998; Fitzgerald 2000: 72–7; Fulkerson 2013.

Odysseus who returns to a rather less than faithful Penelope.[60] Having expelled the 'suitors', she focuses her epicizing violence on Propertius and her slave:

> Cynthia gaudet in exuviis victrixque recurrit
>   et mea perversa sauciat ora manu;
> imponitque notam collo morsuque cruentat
>   praecipueque oculos, qui meruere, ferit;
> atque ubi iam nostris lassavit bracchia plagis,
>   Lygdamus ad plutei fulcra sinistra latens
> eruitur, geniumque meum prostratus adorat.
>   Lygdame, nil potui: tecum ego captus eram.

Rejoicing in her spoils, Cynthia dashes back in victory and slaps my face with the back of her hand, stamps her mark on my neck and draws blood with her bite, and, above all, pounds my eyes (served them right). And when at last her arms were worn out from beating me, Lygdamus is rooted out from his hiding-place at the couch's left-side headrest, and prostrate he pleads for my protection. Lygdamus, I was powerless! I was her prisoner like you.

(Prop. 4.8.63–70).

The scene is redolent of the mimic stage, but the redirection of Cynthia's violence from Propertius to Lygdamus is no laughing matter. Despite the lover's protestation that he and the slave are in the same boat, the juxtaposition of Cynthia's *servus amoris* with her *servus* proper underlines the difference between the violence each experiences: the one will conclude with an 'armistice' in bed (*toto solvimus arma toro*, 88), the other with a slave in shackles and back on the market (79–80). The power Cynthia wields over these men is by no means analogous, therefore, and a truer reflection of the domestic hierarchy is revealed as Lygdamus pleads to Propertius, rather than to Cynthia, for mercy. The master's blithe response of solidarity reveals a less sympathetic Propertius than many readers are accustomed to acknowledge, and his insouciant capitulation to Cynthia's demand for Lygdamus' resale (which, from 4.7.35, we can infer he cancelled) suggests that he enjoys jurisdiction over her chattel, too. By the end of the poem, then, as at the end of a comedy, norms are reaffirmed as it becomes clear that Cynthia enjoys only the power that Propertius concedes to her for his own titillation (*risit et imperio facta superba dato*, 'she laughed, made haughty by the power she was granted', 82). Cynthia's 'abuse' of Propertius is a farcical inversion of the normative hierarchy (cf. *perversa ... manu*, 64), but her abuse of Lygdamus draws attention

---

[60] See Evans 1971; Hubbard 1974: 152–5.

to the fact that in reality she can vent her frustrations only on those below her own impotent status.

In Roman elegy, then, depictions of the *domina*'s abuse of her lover should not be taken as recognition that the perpetrator of domestic violence is not always male: the bruising with which Propertius threatens Cynthia if she goes to bed clothed (2.15.17–20, quoted above, p. 116) is not symbolically equivalent to that which elsewhere he invites as a token of her true love (3.8.5–10) and displays, or wishes to display, to his peers as manly 'war wounds' (3.8.21–2). The prospect of Cynthia's violence, interpreted as *signa caloris* ('evidence of her passion', 3.8.9), proffers the Propertian lover the emotional requital he so sorely wants. To this extent, the lack of aggression on the part of Tibullus' Delia, though such aggression is authorized in the final elegy addressed to her (1.6.71–2, quoted above, p. 122), may be understood to provoke the violence of the lover whose passion she refuses to reciprocate. Inversely, Cynthia's all-out display of violent passion in Propertius 4.8, as the ultimate emotional requital in the final elegy in which she features, signifies the death of elegiac love much more substantively than does the appearance of her ghost in elegy 4.7.[61]

Ultimately, then, the marks of physical violence in elegy, whether (imagined) on the male or the female body, always betoken male dominance and female servitude. The marks of corporal abuse illustrate the domestic hierarchy that informs *Amores* 2.7 and 2.8, which see Ovid on the defensive against Corinna's accusation that he has been sleeping with her hairdresser.[62] Although in the first poem, addressed to Corinna, Ovid protests that, as a free man, he is neither turned on by a contemptible slave's scarred back nor so foolhardy as to trust his mistress' confidante (*Am.* 2.7.19–26), in its sequel, addressed to the hairdresser, he threatens to expose the affair unless she accedes to his further demands for sexual intercourse (*Am.* 2.8.21–8; cf. *Ars am.* 1.375–98). The contrast in 2.7 between freedom and scar-tissue and the comparison in 2.8 of the slave-girl to Briseis and Cassandra (11–14) explain why Ovid's calculation is likely to be as effective after the diptych as it appears to have been in its prehistory (*quid renuis fingisque novos, ingrata, timores?*, 'Why are you shaking your head and inventing fears *anew*, you ungrateful girl?', 2.8.23).[63]

---

[61] Cf. also Ov. *Ars am.* 2.451–4. For a similar reading of these texts, but with attention also to the risk of the male lover's public humiliation, see Caston 2012: 95–102.

[62] On literal and metaphorical *servitium* in *Am.* 2.7–8, see Fitzgerald 2000: 63–7.

[63] See further James 1997.

## III

The possibility that elegy's soft-focus snapshots of *militia amoris* partake of the hard reality of Roman militarism has extra bite for a twenty-first-century audience made aware, by sociological research and media coverage, of a connection between military service and IPV.[64] The first major study to control for socio-demographic differences between military and civilian populations found that the former reported a 'significantly higher' rate of severe (though not of moderate) husband-to-wife spousal aggression.[65] Quantitative psychology has also established duration and type of deployment as factors which exacerbate post-deployment aggression,[66] while more discursive research points to a correlation between the degree to which a society is militarized and the prevalence therein of IPV.[67]

Of interest to the present discussion, therefore, are the detailed statistics marshalled by social historians to illustrate the extent of Rome's militarization during the Republic and Empire.[68] The picture is more complicated in the latter period in that, under Augustus' reforms, the army was downsized and remobilized to the provinces and frontiers, with the result that the Italian peninsula was considerably demilitarized (a pacification that neatly complemented the projected imperial image).[69] At the same

---

[64] In the popular media see, e.g., E. Schmitt, 'Military Struggling to Stem an Increase in Family Violence, *New York Times*, 23 May 1994; A. Travis, 'Revealed: The Hidden Army in UK Prisons', *The Guardian*, 24 September 2009; H. Smith, 'One in Eight War Veterans Is Violent on Return Home, Reveals Study', *Metro* (London), 24 July 2012; also 'The War at Home', *Sixty Minutes* (television broadcast), CBS News, 17 January 1999 (which I have not seen). Until recently, most scientific research in this area has been conducted in the United States. MacManus *et al.* 2012 is a major study of post-deployment violence (including IPV) among British veterans of the Iraq War; Williamson 2012 is a more anecdotal study. A report by the National Association of Parole Officers ('Armed Forces and the Criminal Justice System', accessed 2 August 2012 at www.napo.org.uk/about/news/news.cfm/newsid/39) links insufficient support for veterans, especially those suffering from post-traumatic stress disorder (PTSD), to the fact that more than 20,000 military personnel were in the UK criminal justice system in 2009 (accounting for 8.5 per cent of the total prison population and 6 per cent of those on probation or parole), often for violent offences in a domestic setting (thirty-nine cases out of a sample of ninety). For a clinical study of PTSD as a significant contributory factor in cases of domestic abuse, see Sherman *et al.* 2006.

[65] Heyman and Neidig 1999; cf. also MacManus *et al.* 2012: 1665 (of the 12.6 per cent of veterans who reported violent behaviour, one-third reported IPV).

[66] See McCarroll *et al.* 2000 (*non vidi*), summarized in McCarroll *et al.* 2003; MacManus *et al.* 2012.

[67] See Adelman 2003 for an analysis of domestic violence and militarism in Israel, and n. 73 below for comparative figures for military spending in Israel, the United States, and the United Kingdom as a proportion of GDP.

[68] For the Republic, see the tables of Brunt 1971: 425 and Hopkins 1978: 33; on the 'militarization of the Roman citizenry during the principate', see Scheidel 1996: 93–7.

[69] On Augustus' reform, see Keppie 1984: 145–71; Gilliver 2007 (185 for the view that 'Italian society swiftly became demilitarized').

time, however, with the establishment of nine cohorts of the Praetorian Guard (each initially 500 strong), four urban cohorts, and seven cohorts of *vigiles*, the city of Rome saw a permanent military presence for the first time in its history.[70] On the basis of the census figures for 8 BC (also the *floruit* of love-elegy) and the size of the Roman armed forces at the time, it has been estimated that more than one-fifth of all Roman male citizens in their twenties and early thirties would have been enlisted; with the extension of regular (i.e., not senatorial or equestrian) service in the legions ultimately to twenty-five years, not more than half of these recruits, even in peacetime conditions, would have made it to retirement.[71] In this respect, it can be argued that 'the militarization of Roman citizen society during the early principate may even have intensified compared to the 2nd c. B.C.'.[72]

Notwithstanding the vast differences between ancient and modern warfare, then, ancient Rome, like some modern societies, can be described as militarized.[73] The scientifically attested relationship between the military and IPV is therefore suggestive in a discussion of the non-metaphorical potential of elegiac *militia amoris* as an expression of love in a militarized society. For example, in the context of the Republican practice, which Augustus initially continued, of settling veterans on the land,[74] Tibullus' dream of returning from war to the countryside and to Delia, from *militia* to *militia amoris*, is a rural fantasy with considerable contemporary relevance.[75] The apparent innocence of the scenario presented at the end of elegy 1.1 is undercut, however, at the inverse position in the book, where the peace born of war gives way to a new kind of war born of that peace:[76]

---

[70] See Keppie 1984: 153–4, 187–9.    [71] See Scheidel 1996: 93–4.    [72] Scheidel 1996: 94.

[73] Military expenditure as a share of GDP is taken by Stålenheim *et al.* 2009: 213 as 'an indicator of the economic burden of military expenditure' in modern states; the economic 'guesstimates' put forward in Hopkins 2002: 199–201 suggest military expenditure in the region of 3.5 per cent of estimated actual GDP for the Roman empire in the mid-first century AD, though the unseen or incalculable costs of the Roman army (on which see Herz 2007) in a pre-industrial economy may imply a significantly greater burden (to which, e.g., Agrippa's speech at Dio Cass. 52.6 bears witness). Stålenheim *et al.* 2009: 237–46 (table 5A.4) give figures of 8.6 per cent (estimated) for Israel, 4 per cent for the United States (= 45 per cent of the total world spend), and 2.4 per cent for the United Kingdom.

[74] Cf. Aug. *RG* 3.3 (more than 300,000 soldiers settled in colonies or paid off), 16.1 (soldiers settled on Italian and provincial land for which Augustus personally disbursed 860 million sesterces in 30 and 14 BC), 28 (ten provincial and twenty-eight Italian colonies established during Augustus' lifetime), with Brunt and Moore 1967: 41–3, 57–9, 72–3. See generally Keppie 1983.

[75] On veterans as farmers, see Keppie 1983: 122–7.    [76] See Gaisser 1983: 71–2.

Pace bidens vomerque nitent, at tristia duri
   militis in tenebris occupat arma situs.
rusticus e luco revehit male sobrius ipse
   uxorem plaustro progeniemque domum.
sed Veneris tunc bella calent, scissosque capillos
   femina perfractas conqueriturque fores.
flet teneras subtusa genas, sed victor et ipse
   flet sibi dementes tam valuisse manus.

Through Peace's agency the axe and ploughshare gleam, but in the darkness rust attacks the tough soldier's grim weapons. Out of the wood the yeoman, barely sober, drives his wife and child back home in the wagon. But then the wars of Venus glow, and the woman bewails her torn hair and broken doors. She cries, her tender cheeks all bruised, but the victor himself cries too, that his mindless hands were so strong.

                                           (Tib. 1.10.49–56)

Modern psychology might relate the sequence of tension, violent outburst, and remorse witnessed here, as above in Propertius and Ovid, to the 'cycle of violence' described by L. E. Walker in her 1979 book *The Battered Woman*.[77] As the Tibullan collection effects its ring-composition, then, so a 'cycle of violence' completes itself, dragging into its orbit the violence disclaimed by the poet-lover in the centre of the book at the close of the 'Delia cycle' (*non ego te pulsare velim, sed venerit iste | si furor, optarim non habuisse manus*, 1.6.73–4: see above, pp. 121–2). Recollection of that instability here (*tam valuisse manus*, 56) will destabilize Tibullus' ensuing attempt to distance himself from the iron-hearted *rusticus* (51; cf. 1.1.8 of Tibullus himself) and problematize his distinction between the torn hair, smashed doors, and bruised cheeks (*subtusa genas*, 55)[78] of a violent sexual assault and the ripped clothes, dishevelled hair, and tears of a titillating *rixa* (1.10.61–6).[79] Propertius distances himself from similar acts of assault and battery in elegy 2.5 (see above, pp. 119–20), but the apparent attempt to deny the Tibullan lover his moral high ground (*rusticus haec aliquis tam turpia proelia quaerat*, 'let some *rusticus* pick such shameful fights as these', 2.5.25)[80] proves short-lived as Propertian elegy

---

[77] See now L. E. Walker 2009: 85–106.

[78] On *subtusa*, see Murgatroyd 1980: 293, to which add Adams 1982: 148 for possible sexual connotations.

[79] Cf. Murgatroyd 1980: 291: 'T. openly identifies the violent lover with the soldier and states his preference for Peace.' F. Cairns 1984: 213–14 (= 2007: 300) discusses the etymological play (*kat' antiphrasin*) of *duri | militis* (49–50; a *miles* is *durus* because he is not *mollis*).

[80] On Propertius' response to Tibullus here, see Solmsen 1961: 273–6; Lyne 1998: 524–44; Keith 2008: 69–73; Caston 2012: 104–5.

effects a violent cycle of its own. In an erotodidactic coda to this tradition, *Ars amatoria* 3.565–72 assures women that the 'old soldier' (*vetus miles*), unlike the 'new recruit' (*tiro*), will not break down doors, attack his girlfriend's cheeks with his nails, rip her clothes, or pull her hair. In this last example, as elsewhere, it is not entirely clear whether Ovid is talking of real or metaphorical soldiers.

## IV

The slippage between the metaphorical and literal aspects of *militia amoris* is facilitated not only by elegy's militarization of love and sex, but also by its eroticization and sexualization of war. In the most common form of this inversion, elegy exploits the erotic aetiologies and subplots of the Trojan War to 'elegiacize' Homeric epic.[81] This game of generic one-upmanship is not necessarily as innocuous as it may appear from, to cite a representative example, Propertius' reading of the *Iliad* as a tale of stolen love (Prop. 2.8.29–38): 'he [i.e., Achilles] suffered everything for fair Briseis' sake' (*omnia formosam propter Briseida passus*, 35). The scale of sexual violence in the military conflicts of the twentieth century[82] has made it more apparent than ever before that rape in war is not so much an act of opportunism on the part of individual soldiers as a tactic or weapon specifically deployed to assert hegemony within socially constructed matrices of gender, ethnicity, and status.[83] In the founding statute of the International Criminal Court, adopted in 1998, the perpetration of sexual violence in international armed conflict was declared both a 'crime against humanity' and a 'war crime';[84] in 2008 the United Nations Security Council demanded 'the immediate and complete cessation by all parties to armed conflict of all acts of sexual violence against civilians with immediate effect', and noted 'that women and girls are particularly targeted by the use of sexual violence, including as a tactic of war to humiliate, dominate, instil fear in, disperse and/or forcibly

[81] See Berthet 1980; Dalzell 1980; Levin 1983; Benediktson 1985.
[82] See Brownmiller 1975: 31–113 on sexual violence and war in World War I and II, Bangladesh, and Vietnam. The United Nations Development Fund for Women (UNIFEM) estimates that 500,000 women were raped in the Rwandan genocide, 60,000 in the wars in Bosnia, Herzegovina, and Croatia, and 64,000 in Sierra Leone: see Leatherman 2011: 2.
[83] See Skjelsbæk 2001 for a survey and analysis of the literature on this subject. See further Leatherman 2011.
[84] See Articles 7 and 8 of the Rome Statute, available at www.un.org/law/icc.

relocate civilian members of a community or ethnic group'.[85] On occasion, aspects of this reality come into view in elegy and challenge the insouciance with which the poet-lover eroticizes warfare. To back up his assertion that sexual adroitness is an instinct (rather than an *ars*), Ovid cites Briseis' experience:

> fecit et in capta Lyrneside magnus Achilles,
>     cum premeret mollem lassus ab hoste torum.
> illis te manibus tangi, Brisei, sinebas,
>     imbutae Phrygia quae nece semper erant?
> an fuit hoc ipsum quod te, lasciva, iuvaret,
>     ad tua victrices membra venire manus?

Mighty Achilles rose to the challenge, too, with his captive from Lyrnessus, when battle-weary he reclined on her soft bed. Briseis, did you allow yourself to be touched by those hands which were forever stained with Phrygian slaughter? Or was this just what turned you on, you wanton girl, the conqueror's hands returning to your limbs?

*(Ov. Ars am.* 2.711–16)

The candour of this apostrophe exposes the extent to which Propertius' perspective on Achilles' war-captive domesticates epic violence.[86] The war-crimes associated with Achilles seem not to be lost on Propertius, however: when he tells Cynthia his tomb will be as renowned as 'the blood-soaked mound of the Phthian hero' (*Pthii busta cruenta viri*, 2.13.38), the allusion to the sacrifice of Polyxena is hardly incidental.

When elegy finds a legendary exemplar of the *miles amoris* in the figure of Romulus, the implications of sexual war-crimes come closer to home. Propertius 2.6 restyles the proto-Augustan *auctor urbis* ('founder of the city') as a proto-Propertian *criminis auctor* ('instigator of crime', 19), driven to violence by elegiac jealousy: *tu rapere intactas docuisti impune Sabinas; | per te nunc Romae quidlibet audet Amor* ('you taught how to rape the Sabine virgins with impunity; because of you Love now stops at nothing in Rome', 2.6.21–2).[87] This view of Romulus may seem to subvert his appropriation by Augustus, but the memory of the founder's rape of *intactas . . . Sabinas* in the later anticipation of the emperor's conquest of 'virgin Arabia' (*intactae . . . Arabiae*, 2.10.16) hints at structural similarities

---

[85] United Nations Security Council Resolution 1820, available at www.un.org/en/sc/documents/resolutions/2008.shtml. All resolutions on 'Women, Peace and Security' are collected at www.peacewomen.org/security-council/WPS-in-SC-Council.

[86] Compare the *faux-naïveté* of the *praeceptor*'s perspective on the tragic heroines Andromache and Tecmessa at *Ars am.* 3.517–24, on which see Green 1982: 395–6 for Ovid's 'covert sympathy'.

[87] See Caston 2012: 146–51.

between the erotic and imperial conquests of Romulus' Augustan successors. Far from being a countercultural symbol, elegiac sex has a stake in
Roman imperialism: subjugated territories export prostitutes to placate the
frustrated *amator* (Prop. 2.23.21–2) and luxury commodities to gratify his
mistress (Tib. 2.3.49–58; Ov. *Am.* 1.14.45–6); the Roman triumph is a
spectacle at which the lover and his *puella* gaze from the sidelines
(Prop. 3.4; Ov. *Ars am.* 1.213–28). To no small degree, the elegiac lifestyle
is implicated in Roman militarism.[88]

Similar issues arise in Ovid's reading of the Sabine rape as an aetiological
exemplum for the contemporary practice of 'capturing' girls in the theatre
(*Ars am.* 1.89–134).[89] Whether or not Ovid's closing remarks amount to a
jibe at recruitment difficulties in the legions,[90] they play on the idea that a
campaigning soldier might expect or wish to have ready access to sexual
gratification: *Romule, militibus scisti dare commoda solus:* | *haec mihi si dederis*
*commoda, miles ero* ('Romulus, you alone knew how to give your soldiers
perks: give me these perks and I'll be your soldier', 131–2). This implication
is anticipated in the 'epic' simile (117–19; cf. Hom. *Il.* 22.139–40) which
likens the Sabines to doves and lambs fleeing the predation of eagles and
wolves, symbols respectively of Roman militarism and Romulean barbarity.[91] Here, then, the soldier reveals the aggressive sexuality of the lover only
to the extent that the lover reveals the sexual aggression of the soldier.

The rapprochement of opposite semantic fields is all but complete in
*Amores* 1.9, where Ovid justifies his claim that 'every lover is a soldier'
(*militat omnis amans*, 1, 2) by arguing that lovers and soldiers embody
identical virtues of wakefulness (7–8), endurance (9–16), and valour:

> ille graves urbes, hic durae limen amicae
>     obsidet; hic portas frangit, at ille fores.
> saepe soporatos invadere profuit hostes
>     caedere et armata vulgus inerme manu;
>
> . . .
>
> nempe maritorum somnis utuntur amantes
>     et sua sopitis hostibus arma movent.

---

[88] See esp. Keith 2008: 139–65; more generally, see Bright 1978: 38–65 on Tibullus' relationship with
Messalla.

[89] Labate 2006 reads Romulus here as an 'anti-exemplum' from the unsophisticated past, in contrast
to the positive exemplar of Ovidian *ars* constituted by Achilles at *Ars am.* 1.681–704 (see
pp. 138–9 below).

[90] See Hollis 1977: 52, 57. Pliny the Elder (*NH* 7.149) lists *iuventutis penuria* among Augustus'
complaints; on recruitment difficulties in Italy, see Brunt 1971: 413–14, Keppie 1984: 152–3.

[91] See Eidinow 1993. For a simile with similar implications, see Virg. *Ecl.* 9.13 with R. Coleman
1977: 259.

One besieges great cities, the other his harsh girl's threshold; one breaks down city-gates, the other house-doors. Often it has been advantageous to make an assault on the slumbering enemy and to slay their unarmed throng with armed hand ... Lovers, too, take advantage of husbands' sleep, and ready their weapons while the enemy dozes.

(Ov. *Am.* 1.9.19–22, 25–6)

The second and final couplets quoted here deploy several lexically similar components (*soporatos ... hostes* ~ *sopitis hostibus*; *armata ... manu* ~ *arma movent*) in what ought to be the mutually exclusive domains of war and love, respectively. The word *arma* and its cognates are particularly unstable terms, however, such that the common figuration of the male genitalia as weaponry[92] can be readily inverted, as in the case of the coarsely inscribed sling-bullets of the Perusine War (41–40 BC)[93] or the euphemisms of today's 'defence intellectuals'.[94] Thus Ovid's remark that Virgil *contulit in Tyrios arma virumque toros* ('brought *Arms & the Man* into a Carthaginian bed', *Tr.* 2.534) is a pun that has a more literal thrust for Dido, as discussed above (p. 115). Although elegy rarely descends to the obscenity associated with satire,[95] the *arma* of *Amores* 1.9 oscillate between the semantic fields of love and war in a way that suggests a militarized psychology liable to behave with like rapacity in both military and non-military settings. The same connotations have been doubted in the drunken 'night raid' recounted in Propertius 1.3 (*subiecto leviter positam temptare lacerto | osculaque admota sumere et arma manu*, '... slipping my arms gently under, to essay her as she lay, and to take kisses and my weaponry in my assailing hand', 15–16),[96] but the similarities with *Amores* 1.9 (cf. *inerme manu*, 22; *arma movent*, 26) suggest that the Propertian lover can be understood as so 'armed'[97] and

---

[92] Adams 1982: 19–22 discusses weapons as the largest category of metaphor for *mentula*: 'The frequency of *ad hoc* metaphors both in Greek and Latin shows that the sexual symbolism of weapons was instantly recognisable in ancient society' (19). See further Introduction, p. 28 n. 102; Scourfield, Chapter 11, pp. 317–18.

[93] On the sexual aggression of the *glandes Perusinae* and the Octavianic epigram preserved by Mart. 11.20, see Hallett 1977; and on inscribed slingshots in Antiquity, A. Kelly 2012.

[94] See Cohn 2004.

[95] For this difference, see Richlin 1992a: 44–7; on the paucity of anatomical double entendres in elegy, see Adams 1982: 224. In addition to the examples discussed here, see Prop. 3.20.19–20, 4.8.88; Ov. *Am.* 1.8.47–8.

[96] Editors have mistrusted the *textus receptus*, but the context of sex and violence suggests that Scaliger's *tarda* (preferred by, e.g., Butler and Barber 1933: 159) is a bowdlerization. In defence of *arma*, see Richardson 1977: 154; Heyworth 2007b: 17.

[97] By zeugma, *sumere* governs both *oscula* (cf., e.g., Ov. *Am.* 1.4.63 *oscula iam sumet, iam non tantum oscula sumet*) and *arma* (cf., e.g., Ov. *Ars am.* 3.492 *armaque in armatos sumere*). The violent connotation of *manus admovere* (see *OLD* s.v. *admoveo*, sect. 4d) combines with *arma* to bring out the darker aspect of *temptare* (*OLD* s.v., sects. 9a, 9b): see Heyworth 1992: 59.

that his purpose is to play out the charade in which he has cast himself as Bacchus stealing upon Ariadne (1.3.1–2, 9, 14; cf. Ov. *Ars am.* 1.525–68). The lover of Propertius 1.3 may be less physically aggressive than his counterpart in *Amores* 1.5, but his monstrous gaze (1.3.19–20) subjects Cynthia to the analogous violence, if not rape, of fetishistic scopophilia (cf. *Am.* 1.5.17–24).[98]

## V

The foregoing sections suggest that it is difficult to disconnect the literary 'warfare of love' from more literal forms of sexual violence. It remains to be considered whether or not elegy interrogates its own imbrication with these realities. As several of the passages discussed above illustrate, erotic violence goes hand in hand with erotic viewing in ways that can implicate the reader as onlooker. This kind of meta-spectatorship might be activated by any context of intensive representation or objectification, but the theatrical and amphitheatral settings of *Ars amatoria* 1 bring the relationship between art and audience to centre stage. By locating the Sabine rape, contrary to tradition, in the theatre,[99] Ovid pointedly stages Rome's inaugural act of *militia amoris* in a locus that, by definition, entails spectatorship (*spectatum veniunt, veniunt spectentur ut ipsae*, 'the women come to gaze, they come to be gazed at themselves', *Ars am.* 1.99) as well as issues of aesthetics (*scena sine arte fuit*, 'it was an artless scene/stage', 106) and audience response (*in medio plausu*, 'in the midst of the applause', 113). Moreover, the theatre at Rome was not merely a venue where drama was acted, but one where social drama was enacted: through its hierarchical seating arrangements and the potentially unstable superiority of the audience over the *infames* on the stage,[100] the Roman theatre was 'a site of contesting identities and power, a place where the elite might be praised or attacked, where status was defined and defended, where social and sexual identity was proved and challenged'.[101] It augurs ill from the start, therefore, that

---

[98] See the influential discussion of Brownmiller 1975: 392–6. For contrasting perspectives on the male gaze and implicit violence of Prop. 1.3, see Greene 1998: 51–9, Fredrick 2012: 428–9; on *Am.* 1.5, cf. Scourfield, Chapter 11 below, p. 322 with n. 63.

[99] See Wardman 1965. The 'original' setting in the circus can be glimpsed in lines 101 (*ludos*), 105 (*nemorosa Palatia*), 107 (*gradibus ... de caespite factis*).

[100] On the 'penetrability' of actors, gladiators, prostitutes, and other public performers, see C. Edwards 1993: 130 (quoting Tert. *De spect.* 17), H. N. Parker 1999: 164–6; for other similarities, see C. Edwards 1997.

[101] H. N. Parker 1999: 163.

the Sabine women 'come to behold and to be beheld' in a theatre where the 'fourth wall' is so permeable: Ovid's theatrical staging effectively converts the rape into a mime-show in which the Sabine women take on the role of actresses, the *infames* whose bodies are subject to the penetrating gaze of soldiers who act out a scene of 'theatrical' violence that is all too real (*respiciunt oculisque notant sibi quisque puellam* | *quam velit*, 'the men glance about, and with his eyes each notes to himself the girl he wants', 109–10).

As the text summons its own audience, complex tiers of spectatorship are set up. At the most basic level, the audiences within the text – the Sabine victims and the Roman aggressors – figure potential audiences outside the text. Between the reader and rape, however, stand other intermediary audiences. First, there is the *praeceptor*, through whom the narrative is focalized, and his addressees, against whose combined reactions the reader can gauge his or her own response. Second, there are the historical Ovid(s) and the Roman audience(s) with the subjectivities ascribed to them by the reader. Thus, when Ovid is reclaimed as an author who critiques underlying assumptions concerning rape and imperialism, the shift of focalization from the apparently sympathetic snapshots of Sabine fear, grief, and vulnerability (121–6) to Roman male delectation therein (*et potuit multas ipse decere timor*, 'and their fear could be fetching for many of them', 126) opens up an ironic distance between Ovid's literary persona and historical personality.[102] Against this view, however, it has been argued that female fear remains an aesthetically pleasing component of the plot, and that Ovid's Sabine rape is but one more example of a poetry that 'depends for its elegant existence on the exposure of violence'.[103] The theory of effective oratorical 'performance' in Antiquity understood that the relationship between performer and audience is not necessarily a one-way communication, and that 'transgressive behaviors on the part of the orator respond to the transgressive desire of the audience'.[104] This is a view that certainly complicates the reader's attempt to assess his or her own spectatorship of *militia amoris*.

---

[102] See Hemker 1985.

[103] Richlin 1992c: 165; (on the Sabine rape) 166–8. For illustration of the point, see, e.g., Hollis 1977: 51 ('It is one of his most pleasant creations'), 56 ('Ovid achieves clarity and sharpness of visual detail, combined with the utmost economy of words'); Dimundo 2003: 78 ('straordinaria pregnanza espressiva').

[104] Connolly 2007: 164; cf. esp. 145–8, 163–5.

Given the potential of Ovid's theatre to thematize the interpretation of elegiac violence in this way, it is notable that Ovid also recommends the *tristis harena* of the gladiatorial spectacle as a 'cruising-place' for the prospective *amator* (*Ars am.* 1.164–70). The evocation here of the figurative *tristis harena* of Corinna's abortion (*Am.* 2.14.8; see p. 117 above) suggests an implicit connection with Ovid's prior discourse on elegiac violence. Now Ovid warns that the lover is not invulnerable to Cupid's shafts: *illa saepe puer Veneris pugnavit harena | et, qui spectavit vulnera, vulnus habet* ('in that arena Venus' boy has often fought, and he who watches wounds gets wounded', *Ars am.* 1.165–6). The polyptoton *vulnera vulnus* shifts from literal to metaphorical discourse, from the bodily wounds of gladiatorial combat to the psychological 'wound' inflicted on the elegiac prospector who succumbs to *militia amoris*. An allegorical significance for the reader, too, may be suggested by the parody in these lines of philosophical misgivings about the deleterious effects of gladiatorial entertainment:[105] as Seneca departed the arena 'a crueller and more inhuman person' (*crudelior et inhumanior, Ep.* 7.3) and Augustine's young friend Alypius 'was struck with a more severe wound in his soul than the man, whom he desired to see, was in his body' (*percussus est graviore vulnere in anima quam ille in corpore quem cernere concupivit*, August. *Conf.* 6.8), so Ovid's reader might be alerted to the militarizing influence of elegy as an arena of love.[106] The coexistence of literal and metaphorical meanings here is facilitated by the ways in which violence was fused with the erotic at gladiatorial spectacle. Ancient graffiti attest that gladiators themselves were objects of desire,[107] and a mosaic depicting 'Cupid gladiators' recommends a more literal interpretation of Ovid's *puer Veneris*:[108] the borders between literal and figurative violence, between militarized *amor* and eroticized *militia*, are especially permeable down in the arena, where 'fatal charades' of this order invited viewers to 'interpret reality as myth, thereby translating myth into reality'.[109] A similar gladiatorial pageant may lie behind the wound of love visualized at *De rerum*

---

[105] For this suggestion, see Hollis 1977: 62.

[106] Cf. Leigh 1997: 234–91, esp. 282–91, on meta-spectatorship in Lucan's allusions to gladiatorial spectacle.

[107] On 'the close link ... between gladiatorial fighting and sexuality', see Hopkins 1983: 22–3.

[108] See Hollis 1977: 62. For the mosaic (from Bignor in West Sussex, *c.* AD 300), see P. Johnson 1982: 33 with plate 24.

[109] K. M. Coleman 1990: 73, invoking Mart. *Spect.* 5.2 (*accepit fabula prisca fidem*, 'the ancient myth won credence').

*natura* 4.1049–56 (quoted above, p. 113), but if Lucretius recommends that we assume the detached and inviolable perspective of the audience (see Gale, Chapter 2, pp. 77–80 above), Ovid seems to suggest that, in the end, we cannot but find ourselves fighting it out in an arena of physical as well as psychological violence (*saucius ingemuit telumque volatile sensit | et pars spectati muneris ipse fuit*, 'wounded he [i.e., the *amator*] groaned and felt the flying shaft, and himself was part of the spectacle', *Ars am.* 1.169–70).

Through the specularity of violence in the theatre and arena, then, the reader is challenged to notice where metaphor breaks down and reality bites. Consciousness-raising does not of itself lead to liberation, however, as Pierre Bourdieu has argued in his analysis of that everyday 'symbolic violence' which structures the dominated to participate in the system of their own domination, always violently and sometimes physically:

> Because the foundation of symbolic violence lies not in mystified consciousnesses that only need to be enlightened but in dispositions attuned to the structure of domination of which they are the product, the relation of complicity that the victims of symbolic domination grant to the dominant can only be broken through a radical transformation of the social conditions of production of the dispositions that lead the dominated to take the point of view of the dominant on the dominant and on themselves.[110]

The wresting of the elegiac genre from male control by Sulpicia opens up a space where this transformation is theoretically possible, and her elegies have been shown to harness the destabilizing potential of intertextuality to challenge the patriarchal system in which they are situated.[111] Yet one of Sulpicia's greatest challenges has been the right to her own gender,[112] and further uncertainty hangs over the poems to be included under her name. If the Sulpician corpus begins at [Tibullus] 3.8,[113] rather than 3.13 as generally accepted, one may wonder whether it is an indication of Sulpicia's participation in or appropriation of the system of her own domination that she begins with an appeal to 'violent' Mars not to drop his *arma* as he admires her:

> Sulpicia est tibi culta tuis, Mars magne, kalendis;
> spectatum e caelo, si sapis, ipse veni;
> hoc Venus ignoscet; at tu, violente, caveto
> ne tibi miranti turpiter arma cadant.

---

[110] Bourdieu 2004: 342.  [111] See Keith 1997; Hallett 2009.  [112] See Skoie 2002.
[113] So Hallett 2002; *contra*: Stevenson 2005: 39–41.

Sulpicia is decked out for you, mighty Mars, on your kalends: come yourself from
the sky to look, if you're wise. Venus will forgive it; but you, violent one, be
careful that your *arma* don't fall shamefully as you admire.

([Tib.] 3.8.1–4)

# VI

It might be said that to read elegiac metaphor *as literally as possible*
ignores much of the genre's humour. This is undeniably true, but
laughter tells its own story. The conjunction of sexual humour with
virile aggression is, in Amy Richlin's analysis, personified in the
'minatory figure' of Priapus and characteristic particularly of satire,
the priapic genre *par excellence*, but it is not entirely alien to elegy.[114]
Symbolic of elegy's affinity with satire is the statue of Priapus which
Tibullus erects over the dreamscape of his opening poem (1.1.17–18)
and which takes voice in elegy 1.4 to advise the pederast that coercion
is not only necessary, but welcome (*rapias tunc cara licebit | oscula:
pugnabit sed tamen apta dabit*, 'then you can snatch dear kisses: he'll
fight, but still he'll give them readily', 53–4). If the transmitted text is
accurate,[115] the rerun of this scenario in *Amores* 1.5, with *pugnabat
tunica sed tamen illa tegi* at v. 14 (see p. 110 above), takes its lead
from Tibullus' Priapus. Ovid may be having fun, but, as Richlin's
analysis of priapic humour powerfully argues, laughter in this context
operates according to, reflects, and consolidates pre-existing structures
of power.

The reader's readiness to collaborate or resist in the depiction and
perpetration of violence is put directly to the test when the Ovidian
*praeceptor* finally confronts the issue of a lover's use of force (*Ars am.*
1.663–80). Like Tibullus' erotodidactic Priapus, Ovid insists that
kisses are always on offer since, in another possible inflection of the
*sed tamen* motif, 'in her struggle she nonetheless wants to be conquered' (*pugnando vinci sed tamen illa volet*, 666).[116] Once again, then,
the masculinist focalization of 'token resistance' recurs with startling
candour:

---

[114] See Richlin 1992a, esp. 58–9 (on Priapus as a symbolic figure), 156–63 (on Ovid's satiric leanings
and their influence on Martial).

[115] Maltby 2002: 231 defends Santen's conjecture *tibi rapta* (for *tamen apta*).

[116] The parallel favours *sed* (*ς*) over *se* (*ROAω*, printed by Kenney 1961: 138), though it should be
noted that at *Am.* 1.5.14, too, the MSS transmit both *sed* (*Pς*) and *se* (*Sω*).

> vim licet appelles: grata est vis ista puellis;
> quod iuvat, invitae saepe dedisse volunt.
> quaecumque est Veneris subita violata rapina,
> gaudet, et inprobitas muneris instar habet.

Use 'force', if you like; that kind of force is welcome to girls. The unwilling are often willing to have given what appeals. Any girl who has been assaulted by a sudden onslaught of passion rejoices, and the impudence has the status of a favour.

(1.673–6)

It is likely that this question of consent became particularly urgent after 18 BC, since the criminalization of adultery will have required a legal distinction between *stuprum* (illicit sexual relations in general) and *per vim stuprum* (a technical term for rape).[117] The *Digesta Iustiniani* in which the *leges Iuliae* are embedded preserves evidence of a legal exemption that radically transforms the way in which depictions of rape in Augustan texts can be understood:[118]

> si quis plane uxorem suam, cum apud hostes esset, adulterium commisisse arguat, benignius dicetur posse eum accusare iure viri: sed ita demum adulterium maritus vindicabit, si vim hostium passa non est: ceterum quae vim patitur, non est in ea causa, ut adulterii vel stupri damnetur.

> If anyone should prove clearly that his wife committed adultery when she was in enemy hands, it shall be decreed more liberally that he can accuse her by his right as a husband; but the husband will avenge the adultery in this way only if she did not suffer force from the enemy; she who suffers force, however, is not in the situation that she can be condemned for adultery or unchastity. (*Dig.* 48.5.14.7 [Ulpian])

The military context in which the exemption comes into force reflects the association of rape and war in the Roman imagination,[119] a point with implications for *militia amoris* in the light of the military realities discussed above. The exemption also suggests that the Ovidian *praeceptor*'s caveat at *Ars amatoria* 1.667–8 (*tantum, ne noceant teneris male rapta labellis* | *neve*

---

[117] On the terminology, see Gardner 1986: 118–25; Moses 1993: 45–9; Domínguez and Martos Fernández 2011.

[118] See Moses 1993 for a detailed treatment of the legal context behind Livy's account of the rape of Lucretia (1.58). On approaches to the *Digest* and the other sources for the *leges Iuliae*, see Richlin 1981.

[119] Noting that the phrase *per vim stuprum* (*vel sim.*) occurs in literary texts most frequently in a military context, Moses 1993: 58 n. 75 concludes: 'For the Romans, then, it seems, forcible sex happened in a war context (or a context that had the attributes of war) and was significant for the power and violence of the perpetrator.'

*queri possit dura fuisse, cave,* 'just take care that no roughly taken kisses hurt her tender lips and that she is not able to complain that they were rough') is issued with the law in mind. Given the legalistic implications at stake here, it is worth pointing out with Kennedy that the ethics of the Ovidian passage trade on the ability of the phrase *vim licet appelles* (673) to mean both 'although you term it force' and 'you are permitted to use force'.[120] Only readers less willing to subscribe to the teacher's assurances that elegiac *vis* is mere play-acting will consider the latter interpretation.

Ambiguity of this kind can also be seen to operate in the ensuing narrative of Achilles and Deidamia on Skyros (*Ars am.* 1.681–704) with which Ovid illustrates the precept that sexual violence is welcome. Achilles' transvestism, emblematic of the outwardly effeminate appearance of the elegiac *amator*,[121] thematizes the subtext that appearances can be deceptive. The narrator's attempt to use the myth as a test-case to reclassify the crime of *per vim stuprum* as *stuprum* is equally specious:

> forte erat in thalamo virgo regalis eodem;
>    haec illum stupro comperit esse virum.
> viribus illa quidem victa est (ita credere oportet),
>    sed voluit vinci viribus illa tamen.
> saepe 'mane' dixit, cum iam properaret Achilles:
>    fortia nam posito sumpserat arma colo.
> vis ubi nunc illa est? quid blanda voce moraris
>    auctorem stupri, Deidamia, tui?

As it happened, the royal virgin was in the same bedroom: through *stuprum* she discovered that he was a man. She was won by force, indeed (so we're supposed to believe), but she wanted to be won by force nonetheless. Often she cried 'Stop!' when Achilles was in haste: for he had put down his knitting and taken up his powerful *arma*. Where is that force now? Why are you delaying the agent of your *stuprum*, Deidamia, with your sweet-talk?

(1.697–704)

The narrator's needling inquisition interprets Deidamia's sole word (*mane*, 701) as an admission of consent (cf. *quid … moraris?*, 703), but the slippage of *arma* between military and erotic connotations surely invites a more unsettling interpretation.[122] In the history of the reception of elegiac violence, it is notable that no authoritative translation or

---

[120] Kennedy 1993: 55. Kennedy 2012: 193–4 adds that Ovid here and elsewhere puns on *vis* as both noun ('violence') and verb ('you want').

[121] For similar issues in Prop. 4.9, see Lindheim 1998.

[122] Heyworth 1992 reads *arma* and *properaret* (after *hasta*, 696) as double entendres in the context of the ancient discourse on 'slow' sex; so too Holzberg 2002: 9.

commentary attempts to reflect this alternative.[123] Here, then, as else-where, elegy teaches not only that there lurks beneath the outwardly effeminate *miles amoris* a militant rapist, but also how easily *militia amoris* may be mistaken for something more benign and less violent than it actually is. This exposé of the use and abuse of language and law is a powerful reminder of the subjectivity of interpretation and explains why the jury will always be out in cases of elegiac violence.[124]

---

[123] See Dryden 1709: 51, who lingers on the point: 'With tears her humble suit she did prefer, | And thought to stay the grateful ravisher. | She sighs, she sobs, she begs him not to part; | And now 'tis nature what before was art. | She strives by force her lover to detain, | And wishes to be ravish'd once again'; Mozley/Goold 1979: 61: 'Stay'; Green 1982: 188: 'Don't go'; Melville 1990: 106: 'Oft, "Stay", she cried'; Pianezzola 1991: 59: 'Resta!'; Michie 1993: 42: '"Stay", she begged him again and again, "please stay"'. Brandt 1902: 58 compares *Ars am.* 2.125 (*o quotiens illum doluit properare Calypso*, 'how often Calypso grieved at his rushing off'); Hollis 1977: 141 and Dimundo 2003: 255 cite F. Cairns 1972: 138 for the propemptic bid to stall the departing traveller (cf. Stat. *Achil.* 1.931–55).

[124] Desmond 2006 argues that zero-irony reception of the *Ars amatoria* in medieval texts had a lasting effect on heterosexual ethics in the West. For comparison and contrast of Roman and modern (US) law *vis-à-vis* violence against women, see Nolder 2001.

# CHAPTER 5

# Violence and Resistance in Ovid's Metamorphoses

## Carole E. Newlands*

When I saw Mary Zimmerman's play *Metamorphoses* a few years ago I was rather disappointed because, despite the brilliant use of the central pool of water that the living and the dead slip into, it seemed to me non-Ovidian in that, for the most part, it lacked the poem's jarring violence. Ovid's great epic of change and flux, desire and cruelty, had been transformed into a drama about the transcendent power of love; the play achieves redemptive closure with the introduction of Apuleius' 'Cupid and Psyche', followed by the story of Baucis and Philemon, whose transformation into trees here symbolizes the immortality of true love. By contrast, in Ovid's *Metamorphoses* the story of Baucis and Philemon occurs in the middle of the poem (8.611–726) and is followed by the story of Erysicthon, which reveals that not even a sacred tree is immune to the violence of the axe (8.726–878).

The experience of watching Zimmerman's play made me realize, in short, how central violence is to the themes and verbal texture of Ovid's *Metamorphoses*. True, love has often been seen as central to the poem.[1] But although the body is a central image of the poem, it affords little joy;[2] and metamorphosis, the process of sudden change in physical bodies, is often enacted by violent means.[3] Indeed, the poem's presentation of grotesque forms of punishment and death and its *stylization* of violence – the

---

* I wish to thank W. S. Anderson, J. F. Miller, and G. P. Rosati for their helpful suggestions on this chapter; also the faculty and students at Baylor University and the University of Pennsylvania for their responses to earlier versions; and Monica Gale and David Scourfield for their comments and for inviting me to write on this topic in the first place.
[1] Thus Holzberg 1997: 123–58 argues that many of the themes of the *Metamorphoses* approximate those of the Greek erotic novel.
[2] Thus C. P. Segal 1998: 37.
[3] See, e.g., Farrell 1999; Enterline 2000: 1–11; Rimell 2006: 27–36. Feldherr 2010: 7 appositely comments: 'Metamorphosis, as a tool for deception, as the immortalization of the subject, as justified punishment, or as cruel victimization, confronts characters with the fact of their vulnerability or power and its conflicting meanings and consequences.'

rhetorical exuberance, elegance, and even wit with which scenes of brutality are described – have been regarded as problematic aspects of Ovid's epic, and yet they also give the poem much of its energy and dynamism. Ovid lays bare a cruel universe, but he does so voluptuously.[4]

Sometimes the violence in the *Metamorphoses* is comic; thus traditional epic heroes clash at weddings rather than on the battlefield and mixing-bowls serve as weapons along with swords.[5] But more often, violence takes place *outside* a heroic context and is troublingly directed against those who are particularly vulnerable, whether because of their gender, their profession, or their beauty. Given the poem's interest in visual and verbal spectacle, such scenes of violence have been understood as symptomatic of a decadent Roman aesthetic and a culture of bloodletting.[6] The many scenes of specifically erotic violence have been criticized, moreover, as perpetuating a male bias with respect to female sexuality; the reader is dangerously enticed by the spectacle of violence into the morally dubious role of voyeur.[7] Yet such critical positions run the danger of being reductive, influenced moreover by an outmoded perception of Ovid as a superficial writer and by a narrowly gendered construct of readership. As many scholars have pointed out, Ovid's text characteristically offers shifting perspectives for narrator and reader on the violence it describes.[8] Moreover, the male gaze does not necessarily victimize the female but can be manipulated by her.[9] The poem's vivid interest in spectacle invites a variety of responses within the poem as well as on the part of the reader; graphic scenes of violence thus need not preclude an empathetic response. The role of voyeur can at least be resisted, if we are to read the poem with any sense of ethical responsibility;[10] indeed, the poem often establishes its own critique of the voyeuristic role.

Tissol has provided the most sustained defence of the poem's often exquisitely poised tension between the cruelty of the event and the pleasure of its rhetoric. Indeed, as he argues, violence itself is ultimately a trope for

---

[4] Thus Richlin 1992c: 176.    [5] On such comic elements see Horsfall 1979; Keith 1999.

[6] See Galinsky 1975: 110–57; Most 1992. On Ovid's interest in visual and verbal spectacle see esp. Rosati 1983: 95–173; Feldherr 2010 explores the theatricality of the narratives of violence.

[7] See Richlin 1992c; cf. also Scourfield, Chapter 11 below. Curran 1978 first drew attention to rape rather than love as a major issue of the poem.

[8] See, e.g., C. P. Segal 1994; W. R. Johnson 1996.

[9] On female manipulation of the masculine gaze and the importance of Medusa as an ambiguous figure of both creative and destructive power see Rimell 2006; cf. also Liveley 1999.

[10] On the influence of Judith Fetterley's model of the resisting reader on classical scholarship see Liveley 1999.

the relationship between the artist and his readers, on whom he makes aggressive linguistic, emotional, and ethical demands.[11] But Tissol in a sense naturalizes violence; on his reading unintelligible suffering is part of a cruel and arbitrary world ruled by metamorphosis and flux. Missing from this account is one salient and recurrent feature of Ovid's poem: gods and rulers often inflict such suffering. Central to the Ovidian universe, then, are unequal relations of power. The problem of violence rests not so much upon gender *per se* as upon hierarchy. The poem's persistent violence provides a way of talking about power-relations – between the sexes, between gods and humans, and between the emperor and Ovid. The pleasures of the text keep us engaged; but the poem's cumulative effect drives us to consider the moral and political complexities of a metamorphic world often supported by the violent exercise of power.

The poem's opening account of the Golden Age looks towards the Iron Age world in which the events of the poem take place, providing for the epic a broad political framework that includes Rome (*Met.* 1.91–3):

> poena metusque aberant, nec verba minantia fixo
> aere legebantur, nec supplex turba timebat
> iudicis ora sui, sed erant sine vindice tuti.[12]

Punishment and fear were absent, and no threatening words were read fixed upon bronze, and a suppliant crowd did not fear the face of its judge, but people were safe without a prosecutor.

The legalistic language of these three lines refers to the Roman system of justice; Ovid imagines the Roman practice of publicly posting laws on inscribed tablets of bronze.[13] The phraseology, however, suggests that fear, threats, and intimidation are the concomitants of law. By presenting the Golden Age in this oppositional way, Ovid introduces the inequality in power-relations that is fundamental to the poem's dynamic at the start where we might least expect it. Rome, moreover, is the striking embodiment of the Iron Age. The start of the poem invites scrutiny of

---

[11] Thus Tissol 1997: 89, 129 talks of 'the aggressive power of wordplay' made by Ovidian wit which, by disarming readers, forces them to pay attention and be emotionally and intellectually engaged in the narrative; the 'assault on the readers' sensibilities' made by the intrusion of witticisms into scenes of intense suffering likewise does not invite emotional withdrawal from the story but if anything intensifies the horror. For a similar construction of the relationship between textual violence, author, and reader, in Apuleius' *Golden Ass*, see Fitzgerald, Chapter 10 below.

[12] I cite the *Metamorphoses* according to the text of Tarrant 2004, though here I follow Barchiesi 2005 in reading *legebantur* at 92 for Tarrant's *ligabantur*; translations of Latin texts are my own throughout.

[13] See Barchiesi 2005: 168–9, on *Met.* 1.91–2.

contemporary, Augustan Golden Age ideology; this is a work deeply implicated in its own times, as well as all time.

Directly after Ovid's account of the four ages of the world, the poem's introduction of Jupiter in the myth of Lycaon (1.162–252) provides a suggestive link between autocratic cosmic rulership and Augustan political order. The primary emotion of Jupiter, who is compared to the emperor Augustus (1.168–76, 199–205), is anger (1.166).[14] Jupiter rules by intimidation, and he wipes out the entire human race for the impiety of Lycaon, despite the obvious piety of those who worship him when he visits earth (1.220–1).[15] Although the punishment of mankind is vastly out of proportion to the crime, there is little protest from his cowed, self-interested fellow-gods, a divine senate that has abandoned its civic responsibilities (1.199–203). The story of Jupiter and Lycaon seems to express anxieties about power that is unrestrained by any other governing body; the other gods are portrayed as ineffective and weak. To be sure, according to long-established mythic patterns, the crime of one person causes a ritual pollution among the community, which must then as a whole be punished. But the collapse in time between the myth of Lycaon and the Augustan age, engineered by the witty allusions to the Augustan political hierarchy and by the analogy between Jupiter and the emperor, makes deeply disturbing the unequal relations of power violently on display in heavenly politics. Moreover, the *Metamorphoses*, along with the *Fasti*, is one of the first Roman poems to address systematically claims to divinity on the part of Rome's rulers: what are the implications for mortals if their earthly rulers assert the lineage and rights of gods? And what is the scope of power for such rulers who blur the boundaries between the earthly and the divine? As Feeney observes,[16] by taking at face value Augustus' claims to semi-divinity, Ovid opens up a limitless discourse about the status and power of the imperial ruler. Such troubling questions about the implications of absolute rule will be raised again and again, implicitly or explicitly, in the *Metamorphoses*, a poem in which violence and suffering are frequently displayed as the consequences of

---

[14] On the puns on *Caesar* that reinforce the comparison between Jupiter and Augustus and destabilize any sense of semantic certainty see Ahl 1985: 74–92. *Ira* is the dominant characteristic of Augustus in Ovid's exile poetry; see Syme 1978: 222–5, Feeney 1991: 221–4, who points out that the comparison Jupiter/Augustus in panegyric is a slippery one capable of multiple interpretations.

[15] The specific crime that prompts Jupiter's drastic decision is Lycaon's serving him human flesh (*Met.* 1.226–31). We can compare Tantalus, who served the gods the cooked flesh of his own son Pelops, but suffered (only) individual punishment while the child was put back together (*Met.* 6.401–11).

[16] Feeney 1991: 24.

unrestricted power on the part of gods or their earthly counterparts.[17] Indeed violence, central to the heroic ideology of the epic battlefield, is here intricately explored through its impact on human communities and individuals; as the main instrument of a ruler's control in this poem, violence is shown to shatter social relationships and unhinge individual identities, rather than honour them. While the poem is interested in the emotional issues involving the mythic victims of violence, the very 'modernization' of myth also brings moral and political issues to the fore. Although violence is often connected with the psychological depths of the human heart, including sexual desire, Ovid's poem also shows how and why his rhetoric and aesthetics cannot be separated from the questioning of Roman politics and ethics.

My chapter has a double focus, first to explore how the poem's aestheticization of violence disrupts the possibility of a complacent reading and thus opens the poem up to multiple perspectives and interpretations from a presumably diverse readership.[18] I will suggest, however, that the text, through the devices of authorial intervention and allusion, often seeks to guide the reader towards a particular reading, while not foreclosing the possibility of other interpretations. Secondly, I will explore how key actors in the poem are often victimized by those in a position of power over them, a theme which in Ovid's exile poetry emerges as highly pertinent to the artist's relationship to the state and to posterity. I will focus upon three myths, those of Actaeon (*Met.* 3.131–259), Procne, Philomela, and Tereus (*Met.* 6.424–674), and Marsyas (*Met.* 6.382–400 and *Fast.* 6.693–710), where the violence of gods and rulers against their victims seems particularly cruel and excessive and where, perhaps not coincidentally, the conjunction of violence and aesthetics has been found particularly problematic. All three myths concern physical mutilation, linked to loss of the power of speech: Actaeon, transformed by Diana into a stag (but still with a human mind fully capable of feeling pain and suffering), is savaged to death by his own hounds; Philomela, after repeated rape, loses her tongue to a human tyrant; Marsyas loses his skin to a god. Physical mutilation is a potent symbol of an unjust political order; the sickness of the body politic is etched on to the material bodies

---

[17] Cf. Feeney 1991: 222, who comments: 'It is a god-like prerogative to be beyond the limits of human behaviour, an insight which the *Metamorphoses* explicates more systematically than any other ancient poem.'

[18] For a recent discussion of Ovid's relationship to his own changing culture see Feldherr 2010, esp. 4–9, who cautions that Ovid's readership was diverse, and his poetry therefore capable of arousing diverse responses.

of its victims, reifying the intimate connection in the *Metamorphoses* between violence and injustice.

I have chosen to focus on these three myths, moreover, because in them language, a crucial feature of human identity, plays a prominent role as an instrument of resistance to the inequities of cruel and excessive punishment, thus serving as a double-edged weapon against the erasure of memory in the face of social and political repression. Double-edged, for language can engender violence as well as resist it. Moreover, the physical setting of these myths, while it may invite our pleasure as well as, perhaps, our fear and horror, plays an important role in drawing our attention to the moral, emotional, and political complexities of the violent deeds enacted there and to our complicity in the 'pleasures of the text'. For, as Schiesaro comments in his study of Seneca's *Thyestes*, 'a debate about the role and function of the poetic word . . . lies at the heart of works such as Ovid's *Metamorphoses*'.[19] For Ovid, such debate had a particular point, for not only does he lay bare a violent universe with great imaginative power and skill, but in exile he depicts himself as suffering within it.

The troubling interconnection of rhetoric, violence, and politics in these myths does not preclude an empathetic or ethical response to them, nor should it make us overlook the aesthetic achievements of the *Metamorphoses* in particular. Scarry argues that all language is ultimately inadequate to describe human suffering.[20] The *Metamorphoses* perhaps provides an important exception. In one regard the poem is a great aesthetic experiment that, with strong emotional and psychological impact, pushes the bounds of language into largely uncharted realms of representation. It may be that sometimes Ovid fails or goes too far, yet he always provokes.

## Actaeon (*Met.* 3.131–259)

The setting in which violence takes place is often an important narratological element of the *Metamorphoses*. This is particularly the case in the first five books of the poem, whose beautiful landscapes with their groves and glinting springs have delighted and intrigued generations of poets,

---

[19] Schiesaro 2003: 7; cf. Kennedy, Chapter 7 below, p. 222 n. 32. See also Scourfield, Chapter 11, p. 337, who argues that the 'politics of pluralism' precisely allows this debate to continue to take place today; that 'if we accept pluralist principles, then far from demanding to be silenced, textual violence can be claimed as both an intellectual and a political good'.

[20] See esp. Scarry 1985: 3–11; at 4 and 10 she cites Virginia Woolf's complaint that there are so few literary representations of the experience of pain.

painters, and landscape gardeners.[21] These *loci amoeni* are the playgrounds of the gods, who demand beauty from the earth and its inhabitants. Indeed, after the great flood and fire Jupiter creates the first *locus amoenus* when he repairs Arcadia with flowing water, fresh grass, and shade (*Met.* 2.401–8) – but he thus also provides the setting for his seduction of the unwilling nymph Callisto (2.409–532). As Parry first emphasized, these landscapes are also dangerous and are often the site of sexual violence perpetrated by divine beings. They inevitably fail to protect the innocent outsiders who come to them seeking shelter and comfort, for here the gods freely exercise their divine prerogatives of unbridled lust – and anger, when their earthly pleasance is transgressed. Lured into a sense of safety by the peaceful, beautiful surroundings, their victims find their trust in the protection of the landscape misplaced as they are pursued, raped, or transformed by gods.[22] As Hinds too has argued, Ovid's landscapes raise in acute form the question of the aesthetic appeal of the poem.[23] There is a violent disjunction between the beautiful appearance of the landscape and the violence that takes place there. The beauty of the setting moreover complements the beauty of god and victim; acts of cruelty are thus all the more shocking. Sometimes, in addition to their fatal yet deceptive allure, the landscapes help to provide the means for the victim's destruction; the water of Diana's pool, for instance, transforms Actaeon into a stag (*Met.* 3.189–90). Our appreciation of these landscapes is thus complicated by the fact that their very artistry often provides a seductive veneer overlying their violent or deceptive properties. As Hinds concludes, we cannot deny the irresistible appeal, the guilty pleasure of the landscapes and their transmutations in the visual arts.

All the same, even as they seduce, these attractive settings reveal the limitations of a purely aesthetic response. The very idea of landscape implies a degree of separation and observation.[24] But the role of art in these landscapes is ambiguous, for they *always* have a deceptive element, making them collusive with the violence that takes place there and with their gods; their artistic features promise a garden, but prove a wilderness for the victims. Generally the *locus amoenus* is connected to a morally or

---

[21] The setting for the rape of Callisto by Jupiter programmatically provides the paradigm of the *locus amoenus*: a beautiful landscape with water, soft grass, and shade, and, in this case, set in Arcadia (*Met.* 2.405–8, 417–21). See Hinds 2002: 122.

[22] On this pattern of reversal see Parry 1964; C. P. Segal 1969; Newlands 2004. Feldherr 1997 emphasizes the particular transformation of the victim from spectator of the landscape to spectacle.

[23] Hinds 2002.      [24] Cf. R. Williams 1973: 120.

socially ambiguous context as the victims may, though unwittingly, trespass on a god's terrain or refuse to co-operate with divine needs and power; but the degree of culpability, if it exists, is outweighed by the act of violence committed against them. Shifting, elusive, and illusionary, often poised between art and nature, between cultivation and primeval power, Ovid's idyllic landscapes reify the moral and emotional ambiguity of the text – and of the reader's ambivalent position, situated between aesthetic pleasure and moral dismay.[25]

The moral – and political – ambiguity of the *locus amoenus* as a setting for violence is strikingly apparent in the grove of Diana, where Actaeon unwittingly trespasses. True, Diana inhabits sacred space, not to be violated, yet the excessive nature of her vengeance is called into question from the very start of the narrative. Ovid, following Callimachus in refusing earlier versions of the myth that made Actaeon a voyeur,[26] attempts to guide the reader's ethical response to the narrative with his initial question, 'What crime was there in a mistake?' (*quod enim scelus error habebat?*, 3.142). The poet was to ask this question again in exile, revisiting the myth of Actaeon in Tomis as an example of unjust punishment to be compared to his own (*Tr.* 2.103–8).[27] Indeed, the preceding story, that of Cadmus' founding of Thebes, is endowed by Ovid with Roman political relevance,[28] and here too an unwitting offence is visited with extreme punishment. The *locus amoenus* where Cadmus' men go to collect water for a sacrifice to Jupiter is similar to Diana's in its deceptive appeal, for it harbours a serpent of Mars which kills the men for trespassing (*Met.* 3.28–49); the inviting landscape is complicit with the violence that takes place there. To be sure, sacred space in Graeco-Roman religious and political thought had to be carefully guarded from pollution; but Cadmus' men were on a sacred mission. The *locus amoenus* here troublingly dramatizes the contrast between the innocence of the men and the savage power of the serpent, and draws attention to the tragic inequities in the relations between gods and humans.[29]

---

[25] Cf. Hinds 2002: 128; also Newby 2012: 350, who argues that landscape can often act 'as a potent force expressing the powers of nature and the gods, challenging human control of the natural world and implicating the viewer in the dangerous world of myth'.

[26] Callim. *Hymn* 5.111–18; for earlier versions see Forbes Irving 1990: 197–201.

[27] See Theodorakopoulos 1999: 155–6.

[28] See Hardie 1990, who argues persuasively that Ovid's Theban books (*Met.* 3–4) are constructed with constant reference to the history of Rome as unfolded in Virgil's *Aeneid*.

[29] Cf. Barkan 1986: 43: 'Holy mystery is no longer equated with virginity and benevolence but with corruption and unmotivated violence.'

The realm of what Girard calls 'savage sacredness'[30] is particularly problematized by the exaggerated anthropomorphism of Ovid's deities. Actaeon, who is Cadmus' grandson (*Met.* 3.138), encounters Diana, not a monstrous serpent, but the consequence of his encounter is equally deadly; the violence affecting the origins of the Theban race continues in the fates of the descendants. The description of the sacred grove where Diana takes her bath again plays an important role in suggesting the moral ambiguity of Diana's punishment of Actaeon, for its deceptive artistry is pronounced, as too is the sophistication of her ablutions (3.155–62):

> vallis erat piceis et acuta densa cupressu,
> nomine Gargaphie, succinctae sacra Dianae,
> cuius in extremo est antrum nemorale recessu
> arte laboratum nulla: simulaverat artem
> ingenio natura suo, nam pumice vivo
> et levibus tofis nativum duxerat arcum.
> fons sonat a dextra tenui perlucidus unda,
> margine gramineo patulos succinctus hiatus.

There was a valley called Gargaphie, thick with dark pine and bristling cypress, and sacred to girded Diana. In deep seclusion at its far end was a woodland grotto, fashioned without art; nature had imitated art by its own cunning; for it had created a natural arch of living pumice and light tufa. A translucent fountain bubbled from the right with slender stream, its open pools girded by a grassy rim.

Here we have the basic features of a *locus amoenus*: water, shade, and trees. The uncut wood and the thickly shaded valley might arouse some suspicions that this is a sacred landscape, to be approached with caution. At the same time, as we move, like Actaeon, further into the grove, the landscape aims for an aesthetic effect, with an attractive grotto (157–60) and a clear spring (161–2). Here, we are explicitly told, by its own cunning, nature had imitated art (*simulaverat artem* | *ingenio natura suo*, 158–9).[31] The striking inversion of this phrase boldly draws attention to the deceptiveness of Diana's grove, which has a garden's sensuality; it seems made for love, not virginity. Diana, 'girded' (*succinctae*, 156) for the hunt and now for the bath, is complemented by the sexually suggestive 'girding' (*succinctus*, 162) of her pool.[32] The beauty of this place conceals its primeval power, for the pure water will be the instrument of Actaeon's transformation into a stag,

---

[30] See Girard 1977: 276–7.
[31] On the effects of this inversion in the poem, where art becomes the norm, see Solodow 1988: 210–15.
[32] Hinds 2002: 132, following C. P. Segal 1969, interprets the complicity of Ovid's landscapes with violence as a symbolic figuration of sexual desire.

cruelly hunted by his own hounds (3.189–90). We approach this landscape with a sort of double vision, seeing it both through Actaeon's
innocent eyes, as an ideal place of refreshment after the hunt, and through
our knowing, wary eyes, as readers of the *Metamorphoses* who have
encountered other such ambiguously artistic, sacred landscapes in the
poem and who have already been told the tragic outcome by the narrator
(3.138–42).

Diana is the goddess of boundaries, of physical rites of passage; as Cole
has shown, her sanctuaries are often associated with mountain passes that
are both secluded and vulnerable to enemy penetration.[33] Yet the interplay
with contemporary culture in this ambiguous sacred space is a crucial
aspect of the landscape here that brings Diana's violent actions within the
human and moral sphere. Like Renaissance paintings, which often set
Ovidian myth in contemporary surroundings, Ovid's landscapes draw on
contemporary garden imagery to appeal to his readers' cultural as well as
artistic sensibilities. A favourite feature of the Roman garden was the
grotto, tastefully adorned; throughout the garden, statues of divinities
blurred the division between art and nature, the divine and the human.[34]
With its garden décor, then, this *locus amoenus* makes a deceptive appeal to
contemporary sensibilities as well as to Actaeon's; peace, relaxation, and
refinement are what this grove seems to promise. Indeed, so sophisticated
is this environment that Diana herself, like a Roman matron, does not
bathe in the pool but rather has skilled nymphs attend to her with urns of
water drawn from the pool (3.171–2): we might expect that a refined code
of behaviour operates here. Instead, this 'Roman matron' savagely commits
Actaeon to mutilation and death by his hounds; the gap between Diana's
sophisticated setting and her uncompromising exercise of power dramatizes her vengeance as excessive. Segal finds the juxtaposition of refined
*locus amoenus* with the brutal punishment of Actaeon an aspect of Ovid's
'baroque' style, and an unsettling shift of tone.[35] But refinement and
violence are not juxtaposed but rather interwoven; violence resides *within*
the beautiful landscape, in the deceptiveness of a nature that, in a startling
inversion, imitates art (158–9).

The physical ambiguity of the idyllic setting of Diana's grove is thus
closely tied to the moral ambiguity of the victim's position as innocent

---

[33] Cole 2004: 184–5.
[34] On grottos and garden sculpture, see Farrar 1998: 61–2 and 97–129 respectively; on the shared
 sensibility in Ovidian landscapes and Roman gardens, Hinds 2002: 140–9. Newby 2012: 356–7
 considers Ovid's evocation of Roman garden landscapes in the Actaeon episode specifically.
[35] C. P. Segal 2005: lxii.

trespasser into a sacred domain. The narrator's initial query about divine justice prompts the reader towards sympathy with Actaeon. Actaeon suffers not only metamorphosis but also a savage death by his own hounds; the violence is horrifyingly incremental. The scene of his mutilation (3.235–52) has been regarded as grotesquely reminiscent of wild-beast hunts in the Roman amphitheatre or of the mauling of humans by animals there; Actaeon's fellow-huntsmen ironically deplore that Actaeon is not there for the 'spectacle' (245–6).[36] But Ovid's text does not describe in detail this spectacle, the mutilation of Actaeon; rather, its focus is upon the psychological and physical horror of his predicament, a fully sentient human being trapped in an animal body and unable to communicate. As in the description of the grove, the passage emphasizes the deceptiveness of vision: the hounds and Actaeon's companions think they see a stag because they cannot recognize its true human identity (243–6), while Actaeon wishes to see his hounds, not feel them (247–8); what the hounds tear apart is their master concealed by the image of a false stag (*dilacerant falsi dominum sub imagine cervi*, 250).[37] The complicity of the Romanized grove with the holder of power, Diana, thus exposes the brutality and contradictions that lurk behind the most civilized veneer. Ovid's idyllic landscapes confuse the issue of divine and human responsibility and invite the reader to engage with the narrator in questioning the violent exercise of divine (or imperial?) authority and justice. The story ends in open-ended fashion with a divided response among the local inhabitants to Actaeon's terrible death, some criticizing the goddess for excessive violence, others approving her defence of her virginity (3.253–5). As at the start of the myth, the issue of divine equity is brought to the fore; the narrator's point of view (3.141–2) is now seen to be shared as well as denied by many others.

The description of Diana's grove is centred on a startling conceit, the dangerous reversal of the normal mimetic relation between art and nature (158–9). Yet nature in the end does not trump art – at least, not the art of language. The telling of Actaeon's story is in a sense a defeat of Diana's desire for secrecy and of her angry words depriving him of the power of human speech, *nunc tibi me posito visam velamine narres,* | *si poteris narrare, licet* ('now you may *tell* the story of how you saw me without my clothes on – if you can *tell*', 3.192–3); here repetition of the verb 'tell' emphasizes the story that will survive Actaeon's individual metamorphosis and at least

---

[36] See Galinsky 1975: 133–4.

[37] Solodow 1988: 208–9 points out that Ovid often uses *imago* with latitude, to mean 'false image'.

through other voices challenge Diana's vengeful speech-act. Actaeon, though deprived of speech, ironically now has stories told about him.[38] The varied internal response to the story (*rumor in ambiguo est*, 3.253) points to the freeing of the narrative from its divine censor; thus the story is opened up to a range of other possible meanings and responses, and, appropriated by the community at large, escapes from the repressive power-plays of Ovid's seductive landscapes.

Occasionally in the *Metamorphoses*, however, there is no apparent moral ambiguity about either the crime that a person commits or the punishment that he or she suffers for it. In such situations, the setting for violence lacks the deceptive allure of art. An example is the sacred grove that harbours a ravaging wolf sent to bring vengeance upon Peleus for the murder of his half-brother (*Met.* 11.359–64):

> templa mari subsunt nec marmore clara neque auro,
> sed trabibus densis lucoque umbrosa vetusto:
> Nereides Nereusque tenent . . .
> iuncta palus huic est, densis obsessa salictis,
> quam restagnantis fecit maris unda paludem.

There is a temple near the sea that is not bright with either marble or gold but rather is shaded by thick beams and an ancient grove; Nereids and Nereus inhabit it . . . Adjacent is a marsh, beset with thick willows, which brackish sea-water has made a swamp.

This landscape represents the inversion of an ideal landscape. It has the key ingredients of water and trees, but the water, far from being clear, is a sluggish marsh thick with willows (363–4). Architecture is not contemporary Roman garden chic but an ancient temple lacking all rich adornment (359–60); the ambiguity of *trabibus*, 'tree branches' or 'roof beams', links the temple closely with its uncultivated environment. There is no appeal to art to call to mind a more complex moral code than the one on which this primal act of revenge is based. Unlike Actaeon, Peleus has already committed a crime, fratricide; the moral stakes are clear, and a monstrous wolf comes to take vengeance. As the landscape lacks physical ambiguity, so the violence that takes place there is both clearly motivated and morally unambiguous.

Lack of moral and physical ambiguity also characterizes the landscape in which the rape of Philomela takes place, but in this instance the wildness of the setting emphasizes the barbarity of her attacker and the savagery of

---

[38] See Theodorakopoulos 1999: 155.

the events that take place there. Coming as it does shortly after the
beautiful landscapes that characterize the narratives comprising the myth
of the abduction of Proserpina (*Met.* 5.385–96, 585–91), the grim setting
for the rape of Philomela, a hut in ancient woods (*Met.* 6.521), represents a
dramatic break from the previous beautiful settings for divine rape that
have occupied the first five books of the *Metamorphoses*. The uncultivated
landscape complements the violent assault in its lack of ambiguity and
emphasizes the myth's powerful transgression of social and cultural boundaries; here the country stands in sharp contrast to the city, the hut to the
palace, but in the end, as we shall see, these separate categories dissolve in a
symbolic wilderness.[39]

## Procne, Philomela, and Tereus (*Met.* 6.424–674)

The myth of Procne, Philomela, and Tereus is one of Ovid's most
disturbing narratives both in its graphic violence and in its dramatic shifts
in moral authority among its violent agents. Boundaries involving familial,
sexual, and culinary codes are violated, and hierarchical relations are
overturned. Tereus, king of Thrace, makes a political alliance with the
king of Athens through marriage to the king's elder daughter Procne;
however, Tereus subsequently rapes and mutilates his sister-in-law Philomela, Procne's sister; in revenge the two sisters kill Tereus' son and serve
him up as a meal to the tyrant.[40] The myth has often been taken as a
supreme example of Ovid's delight in gratuitous cruelty,[41] and readers
have been so disturbed by its ending that authors and critics from Chaucer
to contemporary feminist writers have omitted the myth's final, female act
of revenge.[42] But the myth is also perhaps Ovid's most disturbing and
extreme exploration of the devastating consequences of tyrannical power,
exercised without restraint. Tereus acts like a god in indulging his appetites; lacking sacred status, he exposes the sheer brutality of such

---

[39] The opposition between the house and the wilds is characteristic of stories involving metamorphosis
into birds; see Forbes Irving 1990: 107, and his full discussion of the myth of Procne, Philomela,
and Tereus at 99–107.

[40] On the confusion of familial and social categories in this myth see Barkan 1986: 59–63. Oliensis
2009: 78–81 also points out the incestuous subtext in the myth; for instance, as Philomela embraces
her father, Tereus burns to be in Pandion's situation (6.482). Incest of course is another divine
privilege – but Tereus is no god.

[41] Thus Galinsky 1975: 129–32.

[42] In the seventh story of *The Legend of Good Women* Chaucer makes Philomela refuse revenge; see the
discussion in Saunders 1997: 259–63. Very influential has been Joplin's 1984 article calling for the
rewriting of the myth in a way that foregrounds the importance of Philomela's weaving as a positive
creative act.

unrestrained exercise of power. Violence here shatters political alliances and kinship communities while destroying individual identities; even retribution is deprived of justice. In his extensive reading of this narrative, Feldherr has argued that 'the anguished redefinition of family roles' in the poem must have raised questions for Ovid's audience about what it meant to be Roman.[43] In addition to its problematic presentation of physical and psychological violence, a particularly striking feature of this myth is its troubling exploration of the role of art as a weapon of resistance against physical and political repression.

The lack of moral ambiguity about Tereus' rape of Philomela is complemented by the absence of aesthetic ambiguity in its location in a hut in the midst of uncultivated woods (6.521). Indeed, whereas the beauty of the ideal landscapes complicates the reader's moral response to scenes of violence, here the striking disjunction between the setting and the Athenian princess starkly heightens the horror of her predicament and the brutality of her assailant: *in stabula alta trahit, silvis obscura vetustis* ('he drags her to a remote hut, shaded by ancient woods', 6.521). 'Ancient woods' suggests the absence of human intervention in the form of cutting, trimming, planting, or even settling the area; their darkness allows for secrecy rather than shade. This is no pleasant grove. The hut, the word *stabula* evoking primitive accommodation for cattle, further suggests the bestial nature of Tereus' rape and mutilation of Philomela. Tereus, as Segal has pointed out, exemplifies the tyrant *par excellence*, with his uncontrolled appetites.[44] Moreover, Tereus' homeland is Thrace, known for the wild, martial behaviour of its inhabitants; the mutilation of Philomela provides a powerful material sign of the barbarity of this state under its violent, passionate ruler.[45] The wild setting, far from the city and civilization, not only emphasizes the villainy of the deed and of Tereus' character, both tyrant and barbarian, but also sympathetically emphasizes Philomela's isolation from her privileged Athenian background. Unlike Actaeon, she is not a trespasser in the woods; rather, Tereus 'drags' (*trahit*) her there and drives home upon her body the contrast between her cultured Athens and his barbaric Thrace. Unequal relations of power are displayed here in their most uncomplicated form. Tereus' betrayal of his marriage and of his

[43] Feldherr 2010: 217; full discussion of the narrative at 199–239. Oliensis 2009: 77–88 also demonstrates the Roman and political associations of the Philomela myth.
[44] C. P. Segal 1994: 259.
[45] On the proverbial wildness of Thrace see Nisbet and Hubbard 1978: 257, on Hor. *Carm.* 2.16.5 *bello furiosa Thrace*. On the racial tensions in Ovid's version of this myth see C. P. Segal 1994: 268–9.

in-laws' trust in him is starkly set against a landscape that lacks both the complexity of human encounters with deities and the sensuous, if problematic, glamour of the landscapes of the gods' seductions. There is no moral ambiguity here about the setting or the deed – that comes later in the tale.

The text here echoes Virgil's description of the grove to be cut down for Misenus' funeral pyre: *itur in antiquam silvam, stabula alta ferarum* ('they entered an ancient wood, the deep lairs of wild beasts', *Aen.* 6.179). But whereas the *Aeneid* presents a grove to be cut down in a communal heroic ritual, here the 'cutting' will rupture all social bonds. Thus the sinister aspects of the wooded site are developed, presenting the 'cutting' of Philomela as a familial, secret, and brutal act by the brother-in-law turned rapist: who are the *ferae*, the wild beasts, here? This is the first rape in the poem that involves human beings. Yet the change in type of setting is not simply a function of the distinction between the mortal Tereus and the gods for whom the world is a playground. Rather, even as it enables the rape, it communicates its particular barbarity as the sole rape in the poem accompanied by physical mutilation – the latter, moreover, a form of violence endured only by men elsewhere in the *Metamorphoses*.[46] And even after Philomela's tongue has been torn out, Tereus repeatedly rapes her (6.561–2). Her mutilated body, stripped of the accoutrements of Athenian civility, becomes a potent symbol of the effects of tyranny, pierced through and through and left without a voice.

This setting for the rape is ironically anticipated earlier by the simile comparing Philomela, as she first arouses Tereus' desire, to beautiful woodland nymphs (6.451–4):

> ecce venit magno dives Philomela paratu,
> divitior forma; quales audire solemus
> Naiadas et Dryadas mediis incedere silvis,
> si modo des illis cultus similesque paratus.

Look, Philomela enters, rich with grand adornment, but richer in beauty; like the Naiads and Dryads that we hear walk in the middle of the woods, if you were to give them similar sophisticated style and adornment.

Hardie has noted that a complex clustering of Virgilian allusion and Ovidian self-allusion in this simile draws the reader into an uneasy collusion with Tereus' scopophilic gaze at the female body; the first-person plural (*audire*) *solemus* marks our collusion with Tereus and other literary

---

[46] Cf. C. P. Segal 1994: 258; 2005: lv.

representations of sexual violence.[47] Tereus is in Athens at his wife's behest, to request that Philomela visit her sister. Once smitten with desire, he plays fully the role of elegiac lover in his attempt to 'court' Philomela and persuade her father to entrust her to him.[48] Yet the text also critiques the common cultural sanctioning of the male sexual gaze.[49] Although we see Philomela in part through Tereus' controlling gaze, the narrator, in an ethnocentric move, offers an immediate critique of that gaze as typical of *others*, not his readers – *pronumque genus regionibus illis | in Venerem est* ('the people from those regions are inclined to lust', 6.459–60). Thus the reader is directed towards an ethical, critical response to Tereus' lustful gaze, even as Philomela's beauty is acknowledged. Furthermore, Tereus' elegiac strategies of eloquent speech and tears receive the narrator's condemnatory exclamation *pro superi, quantum mortalia pectora caecae | noctis habent* ('ye gods, how much black night human hearts contain', 6.472–3), followed by an emphasis on Tereus' desire as crime (*scelus*, 473; *crimen*, 474).

The simile of the nymphs, however, ominously anticipates the setting of Philomela's rape. She is distinguished from nymphs by her rich adornment, material symbols of her urban culture and royal status. The repetition of *dives* ('rich') in *divitior*, and of *paratu* ('adornment') in *paratus*, both at line-end, along with *cultus* ('sophisticated style'), presents her as a beautiful work of art, to be gazed at in admiration. Indeed, her arrival is like a divine epiphany; thus Corinna appears to Ovid in the numinous midday hour (*Am.* 1.5.9).[50] But normal divine/human relations are brutally reversed in the barren landscape to which Philomela is dragged; here her wealth and artistic refinement are of no avail. Rather, she becomes like the nymphs to whom she was compared, beautiful to be sure, but like them the object of violence. Nymphs, however, sometimes have divine resources for escape or physical change; for instance, Syrinx, pursued by Pan, is turned into reeds (*Met.* 1.689–712). Lacking such magical resources, Philomela instead undergoes a psychological change. The woods, a site without definite cultural or physical boundaries, emerge as

---

[47] Hardie 2002: 260–2.     [48] Thus Holzberg 1997: 141.

[49] In her study of representations of sexual violence and rape in contemporary film, Projansky 2001: 135–7 notes that frequently – for instance, in the film *Thelma and Louise* (1991) – the seriousness of sexual assault can be undermined by the spectator's complicity with, and social sanctioning of, the masculine gaze.

[50] On the phrase *ecce venit* (6.451) as signalling a divine appearance see McKeown 1989: 109–10, on Ov. *Am.* 1.5.9.

an important liminal place that engenders Philomela's shift from innocent victim to murderess.[51]

It is characteristic of Ovid's narrative strategies that the act of rape is not narrated in any detail; rather, the focus is on its aftermath, when Philomela threatens Tereus that she will let the whole world know of his crime (6.533–48). Philomela's speech, writes Oliensis, is 'unconventional in the extreme. It is regularly the woman, not the man, who suffers the stigma of rape; once her modesty has been violated, the woman's part is to repair the damage by covering herself back up, not to exacerbate it by making her injury public.'[52] Already, therefore, Philomela is changing. Her concluding words, *implebo silvas et conscia saxa movebo* ('I shall fill the woods and move the rocks with this knowledge', 547), construct her as an Orpheus figure, who can rouse the inanimate with the power of his voice (*Met.* 11.1–2); Orpheus too suffers mutilation, decapitation. But in a brutal act of verbal castration, Tereus deprives Philomela of her speaking voice by cutting out her tongue, whereas Orpheus' powerful voice survives (11.50–3).

At this point in the narrative the apparent sympathy of the narrator for Philomela, constructed by the grim setting for her rape, is for some readers crudely dispelled by the grotesque image of Philomela's excised tongue, squirming like a snake's mutilated tail on the ground (6.557–60):

> radix micat ultima linguae,
> ipsa iacet terraeque tremens immurmurat atrae,
> utque salire solet mutilatae cauda colubrae,
> palpitat et moriens dominae vestigia quaerit.

The stump of the tongue's root pulsates, the tongue itself lies quivering and murmuring into the black earth, and as the tail of a mutilated snake usually jerks in spasms, so the tongue throbs and in its death-throes seeks the footsteps of its mistress.

'There is no more gruesome picture in Ovid's entire work', comments Fantham.[53] For Galinsky, the image typifies Ovid's penchant for gratuitous violence in its cruelty and his ghastly indifference to the pathos of Philomela's plight; thus 'Ovid replaces Philomela with the gyrations of her tongue.'[54]

---

[51] Thus Joplin 1984: 42, drawing on Girard's notion of the woods as 'undifferentiated wilderness'.
[52] Oliensis 2009: 81.     [53] Fantham 2004: 66.
[54] Galinsky 1975: 130–1. A different point of view is represented by C. P. Segal 1994, who argues that Ovid's tale, by its dramatic shift in narrative positions and the incorporation of the perspective of a female reader, critiques the very violence that at the same time it seems to enjoy.

Certainly, from an anatomical perspective, Ovid's simile of the snake is gratuitous and incorrect; Galen tells us that after excision the tongue is decisively *without* movement.[55] Moreover, sexual connotations are at play here: *salire* is a technical term for 'mount'; *cauda* can denote the penis; *morior* ('I die') is likewise a sexual euphemism.[56] Indeed, the shocking personification of the tongue, seeking the footsteps of its mistress, its *domina*, ironically plays upon a common fantasy of love-elegy: the tongue plays the role of rejected or exhausted lover expiring in front of his mistress, and of the phallus itself, all sexual potency expended. The image of erotic exhaustion substitutes for the act of rape itself in a particularly grotesque way and seems to unhinge the moral certainties of the preceding part of this story; in a sense, even a part of Philomela's own body is infected with lust. We might remember that Tereus himself, before he returned to his woods, played the role of elegiac lover. At the same time, with the emphatic word *domina*, almost the hallmark of Ovidian elegy, the text moves beyond the bounds of Greek myth to engage in a critical way with Ovid's own world and poetry. The amatory image suggests the ability of the language of love to move beyond its restricted realm of amatory experience and encompass the dangers and potential tragedy of violent passion.[57]

The image of a severed body-part seeking its owner also derives from an epic context, specifically from a noted Virgilian passage: *te decisa suum, Laride, dextera quaerit | semianimesque micant digiti ferrumque retractant* ('your severed right hand seeks you, Larides, its master, and the half-dead fingers pulsate and grasp for the sword', *Aen.* 10.395–6). The severed hand is a striking image of the loss of power, of an individual's inability to act with personal or political effect.[58] Furthermore, the Virgilian context is that of the battlefield: the body-part is an arm, not a tongue; the owner a hero, not a woman; the killer the youthful Pallas.[59] Tereus, we are told at the myth's beginning, had garnered a distinguished name from military conquest (*clarum vincendo nomen habebat*, 6.424). Here, however, the transposition

---

[55] Gal. *Anim. pass.* 11.10.129.

[56] See Adams 1982: 36–7 (*cauda*, with reference to Hor. *Sat.* 1.2.45, 2.7.49), 159 (*morior*), 206 (*salire*). Cf. generally Scourfield, Chapter 11, pp. 316–18, 329–31 below, on the sexual metaphors latent in the violent punishment of female martyr-figures in Jerome and Prudentius, with comment on the Ovidian narrative at 321–2, 323–4.

[57] Cf. O'Rourke, Chapter 4 above, esp. pp. 110–18, for slippages between metaphorical and literal violence within elegiac discourse itself.

[58] See Rowe 1999: 4.

[59] Even here the image may occasion discomfort; thus S. J. Harrison 1991: 174 on *Aen.* 10.395–6 hedges, 'this grotesque and *almost comically* gruesome description' (my emphasis). Virgil's main model is Enn. *Ann.* 483–4 Skutsch.

of Virgil's gruesome yet heroic image to the sexual arena shockingly foregrounds the degradation of the warrior[60] while putting Philomela in the role
of epic hero, in anticipation, perhaps, of her assumption of her aggressive
role in revenge. That revenge, however, will follow a tragic script.

We can also approach this image as a response to the problem of
representing an unspeakable act.[61] The dissonance between the grotesque
image and the human tragedy dislodges readers from an easy and neutral
spectator's position. The difficulty of communicating human pain
necessitates the transforming of the real body experience of physical
violation into an objectified form;[62] but while this mitigates the horror
posed by assault, a moral or empathetic response is not thereby excluded.
The controversy over this image not only draws attention to Philomela's
lack of speech but also confirms the strain on language caused by the
difficulty of conveying Philomela's experience. Thus the Ovidian narrator
comments on Tereus' repeated rape of Philomela, *vix ausim credere* ('I
could scarcely dare believe it', 6.561) – a comment also on the strain on his
powers of representation.

Moreover, Philomela is not 'dismembered' or divided into constituent
parts, as often happens in contexts where the female body is objectified and
subject to male control.[63] Her mutilation is limited to the tongue alone. Bal
has commented that the depiction of rape is often displaced through the use
of metaphor.[64] *Lingua* of course means language itself as well as the physical
organ of speech. Philomela's loss of voice is expressed *literally* through the
independent movement of the tongue in its dying moments,[65] while the
death of the tongue is also a metaphor for the attempted destruction of her
subjectivity. The attribute of speech is fundamental to human identity;[66]
we see the despair of the transformed Actaeon, unable to communicate who
he truly is as he lifts 'his silent face' (*tacitos . . . vultus*, 3.241) to his ravening
hounds. In particular, as Bal has argued,[67] the semiotic behaviour surrounding rape involves the difficulty the survivors have in recounting their
experience; the cutting out of Philomela's tongue is an extreme

---

[60] Thus Tereus degrades military language by crying *vicimus* (6.513) as his ship, with Philomela
aboard, moves away from Athens and her father's protection.
[61] Thus Enterline 2000: 11: 'Ovid's emphasis on Philomela's "os mutum" and writhing tongue tells us
that such an experience exceeds any words its victim can utter.'
[62] See Bronfen 1992: 46; also Scarry 1985: 3–11.
[63] Cf. Scourfield, Chapter 11 below, pp. 322–3. As he indicates, this does not happen in the Philomela
myth but in, e.g., *Am.* 1.5.
[64] Bal 1991: 68.     [65] Cf. Bate 1993: 116.
[66] As C. P. Segal 2005: lxxx notes, the loss of human speech is always catastrophic in this poem.
[67] Bal 1991: 60–93.

representation of their traumatized silence. Yet as a metaphor for language, the tongue also points the way towards successful resistance and revenge and indeed to the poem's broader obsession with the power and vulnerability of both spoken and written language. Oliensis observes that Philomela does not produce a child, the conventional result of rape in ancient myth; instead, she produces eloquence through her tapestry. Indeed, Oliensis suggests that we can, if we wish, find political allegory in this episode, a reminiscence of Cicero's silenced tongue that inspired other forms of eloquence.[68] Ovid's very emphasis upon *lingua* foreshadows Philomela's subsequent change in character, her shift from victim to agent as she weaves the story she can no longer speak. At the same time, the association between the snake, creature of the wilds, and the tongue – as the organ of speech, the primary mark of distinction between humans and animals – problematizes that psychological change, pointing towards Philomela's assimilation to the wilderness in her eventual abandonment of human laws.

The image of the disembodied tongue, centrally located within the myth, thus marks a pivotal moment in the narrative, the change in Philomela from *virgo* to *virago* and the accompanying shift in the balance of power from men to women along with the dislocation of moral authority, for the women now act like male aggressors. As Fantham has noted, Philomela has the dubious honour of being the first woman in the *Metamorphoses* to commit murder, and the first of a series of women in the poem who dare criminal acts.[69] The women's violence is troublingly motivated by acts of writing and reading. The central image of *lingua* thus connects with the text's exploration of the problematic relationship between art and violence.

In captivity Philomela regains the power of language through weaving her tale in an artful, allusive manner. Weaving as a form of cunning writing transcends the extremity of her circumstances and allows her to elude the control of the tyrant (6.576–8):

> stamina barbarica suspendit callida tela
> purpureasque notas filis intexuit albis,
> indicium sceleris.

Cunningly she hung threads upon a foreign loom and interwove purple marks with white threads, evidence of crime.

---

[68] Oliensis 2009: 82–3. She points to the kinship of the story with that of Lucretia, a kinship emphasized both in Ovid's *Fasti* and in the Roman cultural imagination. See also Feldherr 2010: 217–21.

[69] Fantham 2004: 66.

Book 6 is thus framed by two myths in which a woman's weaving plays an important role in her resistance to tyrannical repression: Arachne defies Minerva's threat to her genius by weaving her own perception of the gods and exposing their violence, rather than their benevolence, towards humans (6.1–147), while Philomela weaves the story of her horrendous rape. Unlike Arachne's tactless tapestry, which arouses Minerva's anger and leads to her punishment, Philomela's tapestry is subtly woven. This is suggested by Philomela's description as *callida*, and by the *notae*, marks which form an attractive design on the cloth in purple and white *and* provide a powerful representation of her rape. These 'marks' surely cannot be pictures of her rape, for that would give the game away to her custodians. Rather, I suggest, she weaves the story in her native language of Greek; the purple 'marks' are Greek letters, which make a design appealing to the barbarian viewer, but represent a legible script to her Athenian sister.[70] In addition, these marks carry further layers of signification in that they also suggest sexual violence as both bloodstains and 'love-bites', a common meaning of *notae* in love-poetry.[71] Philomela thus writes with signs that only her sister – a 'learned' reader who knows Greek – can understand. As Oliensis observes, *notae* can suggest a private code; 'individual ingenuity will always find a way to circumvent tyrannical censorship, no matter how violently imposed'.[72]

Ovid draws here upon the long classical tradition of weaving as a metaphor for poetic composition.[73] Here he explores this metaphor further, as Philomela's textile is also, literally, a *cunningly* made text. Procne unrolls it like a papyrus scroll and reads its pitiable 'song': *evolvit vestes saevi matrona tyranni | fortunaeque suae carmen miserabile legit* ('the savage tyrant's wife unrolls the tapestry and reads the piteous song of her misfortune', 6.581–2). Writing overcomes the silencing of the voice through subtle, allusive, and visually attractive means. The phrase *carmen miserabile* recalls the nightingale's song at the end of Virgil's *Georgics* (*miserabile carmen*, 4.514); thus it not only signifies the

---

[70] Rosati 2009: 339 on *Met.* 6.577 points out that *notae* frequently carries the sense of secret writing.

[71] Thus, e.g., Ov. *Am.* 1.8.98 *factaque lascivis livida colla notis* ('your neck black and blue from passionate love-bites'); see further McKeown 1989: 185.

[72] Oliensis 2009: 82. Cf. also Rimell 2006: 13: 'Violent male desire . . . energizes a compulsive cycle of competition and retaliation which animates much of Ovid's poetry, forcing the hand of female creativity.'

[73] See Scheid and Svenbro 1996. Rosati 1999 argues that in the *Metamorphoses* Ovid revives what had become a conventional, lifeless metaphor; thus the myths of Arachne (6.1–145) and the Minyeids (4.1–415) illustrate the metaphor of the text as textile in all its narrative complexity.

power of Philomela's text but also prefigures the women's transformation into birds.[74] The word *carmen* actualizes her earlier projected association with poetry through Orpheus (*Met.* 6.547), a sign of the power of her written voice and a link with the *Metamorphoses* itself, which has represented already the story of her rape.[75] It draws attention to the debate over the poetic word: read correctly by its destined primary reader, Procne, this woven poem provides material as well as emotional testimony to the violence done to Philomela and thus triggers her escape and successful revenge. At the same time, by arousing powerful emotions in Procne, who in the guise of a bacchant makes a frenzied rescue of her sister (6.587–600), the textile/text generates further violence.[76] Cixous, confronting, like Scarry, the representational problem posed by extreme human pain, writes that in such circumstances, 'il faut inventer l'impossible chant'.[77] Yet although Philomela miraculously finds a way to communicate by weaving in writing her 'impossible song', her new language does not solve the problem of violence and provide the peaceful solution that Cixous' feminist writings seek; rather, it sparks a terrible revenge that destroys the moral authority of the women.

In the last scenes of this tragic narrative woods and palace are conflated as Procne and Philomela, both in the garb of bacchants, return within the city walls (6.587–600); together they repeat and double the original crime by not only mutilating Procne's innocent son Itys but also killing him and then boiling his dismembered body as a horrendous meal for Tereus (6.636–66). These acts of violence take place within the palace, yet they may as well be in the wilderness. Procne is described as more savage than a tigress (636–7) as she drags off her young son in a reminiscence of Tereus' 'dragging' of Philomela into the woods.[78] Indeed, the tigress (unlike Procne here) was proverbially most protective of its young.[79] The

---

[74] Although *carmen* has been judged suspect (see Tarrant 2004: 174, app. crit. ad loc.), *miserabile* programmatically describes elegiac lament: see Hor. *Carm.* 1.33.2, with Nisbet and Hubbard 1970: 371.

[75] See Feldherr 2010: 229–30.

[76] The violence done to Philomela is not unmade by this act of weaving, as Joplin 1984: 48 suggests: see the critique of Joplin by Linklater 2001, esp. 255–6. As Linklater argues, the tapestry gives the rape concrete material form, while providing a powerful image of female agency and resistance.

[77] Cixous 1988: 28.

[78] Compare 6.521 *in stabula alta trahit silvis obscura vetustis* ('he drags her to a remote hut, shaded by ancient woods') – reversed by Procne's actions at 6.660 *attonitamque trahens intra sua moenia* ('dragging her [Philomela] in a dazed state within her city walls') – with 6.636 *nec mora, traxit Ityn* ('without delay, she dragged off Itys').

[79] See Plin. *NH* 8.66.

innermost part of the house, which should be the safest and most protected from the wilderness outside, drips with blood (*manant penetralia
tabo*, 646), a visible sign of the corruption of the family from within.[80]

The myth ends with a perpetuation of the cycle of violence (6.667–74).
The two sisters are transformed into the swallow and the nightingale. Birds
are often associated with escape from the sorrows of earthly life,[81] yet in
this myth they are hunted by Tereus, transformed into the predatory
hoopoe with 'outsized beak, extremely long at the tip' (*immodicum prae-
longa cuspide rostrum*, 673), a permanent figure of violent, tyrannical excess
and immoderate sexual appetites.[82] Segal suggests that the poem's commitment to metamorphosis dilutes the moral force of the tale, and that
patriarchal power is troublingly reasserted at the end through these
metamorphoses.[83] Yet the birds provide a memorable visual representation
of the skewed power-relations of this myth and of the women's guilt as
well as Tereus'. The purple and white signs, *notae* (6.577), that Philomela
weaves into her fateful tapestry anticipate the *notae* of blood that permanently mark the breast of her sister,[84] a sign of the causal link between
sexual and intrafamilial crime in this story; the 'love-bites', proof of sexual
abuse, are now transferred to the sister and conflated with the stains of
murder (669–70):

> neque adhuc de pectore caedis
> excessere notae, signataque sanguine pluma est.

And to this day the marks of murder have not left her breast, and her plumage is
marked with blood.

The move at the narrative's close from the textual to the extratextual, from
letters to physical marks again, also connects the indelible stain of crime
with the dangerous power of language.[85] At the same time, *notae* have a
further quite common specialized meaning in Roman culture – they are

---

[80] Cf. Konstan/Raval, Chapter 1, pp. 51–3 above, for analogy between the house and the embodied
self in New Comedy.

[81] See Forbes Irving 1990: 113–27.

[82] See Adams 1982: 20, 77 on the sexual symbolism of *cuspis* ('tip of the sword'), and 19–22 on
weapons in general as sexual metaphors.

[83] C. P. Segal 1994: 277.

[84] The swallow has red colouring on its breast. Although there was confusion in classical literature
about which sister became which bird, Rosati 2009: 351 on *Met.* 6.668–9 suggests convincingly
that Philomela becomes a nightingale, for she seeks out the woods familiar to her, whereas the
domestic Procne becomes a house-haunting swallow.

[85] See here particularly Enterline 2000: 5, who argues that the figure of *notae* as well as that of the
tongue refuses any ultimate distinction between body and language, matter and idea.

the Roman censor's marks of condemnation.[86] Propertius plays upon the double meaning of *nota* as the 'scarlet letter' of sexual shame when he writes to Cynthia, *nunc in amore tuo cogor habere notam* ('now, through my love of you, I am forced to bear a mark of shame', 1.18.8). From the bold use of language, Procne and, by extension, Philomela become stamped forever with the marks, *notae*, of a guilty text. Thus the final image of hunt and flight, coupled with the enduring reminders of tragic crime, implicates all three in a seemingly unending cycle of fear and intimidation; as we leave the birds suspended in the air – *corpora Cecropidum pennis pendere putares;* | *pendebant pennis!* ('you would think the Athenians' bodies were suspended on wings; they were suspended on wings!', 667–8) – so too final moral judgement has to be suspended.[87] The impact of Tereus' tyranny remains imprinted on the natural world with, moreover, the original inequality of power-relations still in place, as the predatory hoopoe pursues the gentle nightingale and swallow.

The central image of the tongue in Ovid's version of this myth, then, draws attention to a key concern, the seductive power of language, the freedom of the word to resist physical and political violence and at the same time its responsibility in engendering it. Philomela's tapestry is thus a powerful, paradigmatic image for the poem as a whole, for it reflects the ambiguous status of writing as a form of communication that can both express and engender violence in an aesthetically pleasing form; it reveals art's dangerous power. Shakespeare played up the tension between violence and aesthetics in this myth when he wrote his early, supremely violent play *Titus Andronicus*,[88] translating Ovid's narrative into gruesome dramatic performance.[89] Its central scene of rape is characterized by its horrific doubling of the Philomela myth: two villains, Demetrius and Chiron, rape the heroine Lavinia and cut out her tongue. Having read Ovid too well, they also cut off her hands, so she cannot weave her tale. But Lavinia knows her Ovid! She finds a copy of the *Metamorphoses* and with her bloody stumps gestures to the passage telling the myth of Philomela so as to explain her condition and prompt a revenge that goes well beyond the one specified by Ovid. Bate suggests that the Ovidian text seemingly

---

[86] See *OLD* s.v. *nota*, sect. 4a.

[87] On the frequent ambiguity of myths involving metamorphosis into birds, which are more remote from humans than other animals and often point to an alternate state of being, see Forbes Irving 1990: 112.

[88] On the relationship between Shakespeare's play and the Ovidian myth see the fine discussion in Bate 1993: 101–17.

[89] See Kennedy, Chapter 7, pp. 222–3 below.

*licenses* the Elizabethan play's violence and thus problematizes the playwright's relationship to the classical past.[90] Shakespeare exposes Ovid's double game – the conjunction of gorgeous language with sickening violence – by critiquing the humanist education of his day in which Ovid's *Metamorphoses* was central; but his criticism of imitation of Ovidian myth and its language is ironically accompanied by an expansion of its repertory of violence beyond words into grotesque spectacle – a move further capitalized upon by Julie Taymor in her cinematic interpretation of Shakespeare's play.

The confrontation between art and institutional power leads me to the final narrative I wish to discuss, that of Marsyas, whose fate, I shall suggest, is interwoven with that of the poet himself in its dramatization of the political threat of violence to artistic memory.

## Marsyas

> along a gravel path
> hedged with box
> the victor departs
> wondering
> whether out of Marsyas' howling
> there will not some day arise
> a new kind
> of art – let us say – concrete
>
> suddenly
> at his feet
> falls a petrified nightingale
>                    (Zbigniew Herbert, 'Apollo and Marsyas')[91]

The *Metamorphoses* and the *Fasti* provide us with the first extant poetic versions of the story of Marsyas, the satyr who dared to compete with his flute against Apollo with his lyre and was flayed alive for his presumption (*Met.* 6.382–400; *Fast.* 6.693–710). As Herbert's poem suggests, the myth of Marsyas is linked to that of Philomela through its exploration of the double-edged nature of art, its civilizing but also its destructive power; correspondingly, both myths examine the precarious role of the artist in

90  Bate 1993: 107.
91  Herbert 1968: 83. For a detailed discussion of Ovid's myth in relation to Herbert's poem see Niżyńska 2001. Niżyńska offers a political reading of Ovid's two versions of the Marsyas myth, tying them explicitly to Augustus' adoption of Apollo as his patron.

confrontation with higher authority, particularly when, unlike Actaeon, he or she knowingly transgresses socially prescribed roles or expectations.[92] The episode of Marsyas is the final tale in *Metamorphoses* 6 concerning those punished for blasphemy. In his second appearance in Ovid's works, the Marsyas of the *Fasti* emerges also as a figure of resistance to the erasure of poetic memory.

Like the Philomela myth, in the *Metamorphoses* the Marsyas myth is marked by a shocking image of horrific violence, the flaying of the satyr, and again the scene of bodily mutilation emphasizes the gruesome in sound and image while here at first inviting a certain clinical detachment on the part of the reader (*Met.* 6.388–91):

> nec quidquam nisi vulnus erat; cruor undique manat
> detectique patent nervi trepidaeque sine ulla
> pelle micant venae; salientia viscera possis
> et perlucentes numerare in pectore fibras.

Nor was there any part that was not a wound; the blood flows everywhere, the sinews lie bare and the veins, trembling, stripped of any skin, throb; you could count the innards spasmodically jerking and the organs transparent and glistening in the chest.

The graphic verbs – *micant venae; salientia viscera* (390) – anticipate the language describing the mutilation of Philomela, where the tongue's root flickers (*micat*, 557) and resembles the jerking in spasms (*salire*, 559) of a snake's tail. As in the case of Philomela's tongue, aesthetic distancing – the separation of the body from the human subject – makes the unbearable bearable, even as we experience the violence via its textual representation. Characteristically, however, the text plays with the reader's involvement as well as detachment. The poet's abandonment of the past for the immediate present tense (*erat . . . manat*, 388), and of the epic third-person narration for the second-person *possis* (390), draws the reader after all into the horrifying spectacle of Marsyas' flayed flesh; we are invited to count his quivering guts. But if *possis* demonstrates the reader's complicity in an extreme spectacle of violence, it surely does not preclude compassion among the variety of possible emotions the scene arouses.[93] At the same time, Marsyas' flayed body is described with musical terminology that

---

[92] Cf. Theodorakopoulos 1999: 156: the myth of Marsyas provides 'one of the most notoriously brutal passages in the poem [sc. the *Metamorphoses*] and . . . also one of the most important treatments of the problems of human authority and creativity'.

[93] I agree here with Niżyńska 2001: 155, who challenges the claim of Galinsky 1975: 134 that these lines reflect a typical Roman delight in cruelty; see also G. D. Williams 1996: 83.

evokes Apollo's lyre, the instrument of Apollo's triumph (*nervi* can mean lyre-strings), while *perlucentes* suggests the brilliance of the sun.[94] Marsyas' body has ceased to be human; Apollo's triumph over him is symbolized by his ghastly metamorphosis into the victorious instrument, a bloodstained image that implicitly comments on the cruelty of Apollo's victory. In the glistening, throbbing, visceral 'lyre', the poet graphically thematizes the problematic conjunction of aesthetics and violence. Feldherr comments that 'the poet Marsyas comes to merge with the voice of the god'[95] – or is it the voice/instrument of the god that comes to merge with Marsyas?

In his great painting of the flaying of Marsyas, Titian, unlike Ovid, makes Marsyas' fellow-satyrs direct participants in the flaying, and they do not mourn but rather show a chilling, mundane detachment. A satyr collects in buckets the bodily fluids flowing from Marsyas and a dog laps some of the spill; Orpheus, detached, plays the violin while Apollo with cool surgical precision peels back the satyr's skin. Midas sits beside the flayed body deep in contemplation. The synchronic representation of events and the very detachment of the participants concentrate the horror of the scene; Ovid by no means holds a monopoly on violent effects.[96] Titian seems to have understood from Ovid's text the paradoxical power of detachment to provoke a moral and intellectual response to the problem of the artist's punishment by the more powerful god. What is curious about this painting too is that Titian has included himself in it, as a figure in a black hat, coolly flaying a leg. Why has Titian done this? I suggest that he offers here a double identification for himself. As artist he has created a sympathetic portrait of a cruelly punished musician. But he also recognized that human suffering can paradoxically create wonderful, even sublime art. Hence he has included himself in the painting, since as artist he is complicit in creating a powerful image of suffering. In particular he depicts here the artist in the process of producing the kind of anatomical image known as an écorché, that is, a figure drawn, painted, or sculpted showing the muscles of the body without skin. Of great influence for artists at this time was the anatomical compendium of Vesalius, *De humani corporis fabrica*, which displayed meticulous illustrations of the human body in all its layers of muscle and skin. With a dark type of Ovidian wit, Titian blurs

---

[94] See Feldherr and James 2004: 82–3; Feldherr 2010: 104.
[95] Feldherr 2010: 105. See in general his stimulating discussion of the myth at 99–105.
[96] Thus for a long time art critics denied that the painting was a work of Titian: see, e.g., Panofsky 1969: 171 n. 85; cf. Neumann 1962. Puttfarken 2005: 193–6 rejects Neumann's allegorical reading based on Neoplatonic ideas of the divine nature of art; rather, he puts divine injustice at the heart of Titian's exploration of Ovid's text.

the boundaries between painting the flayed skin and flaying the skin for painting. By including himself in this painting Titian does in paint what Ovid does with words, that is, thematize the complicity of the artist in the depiction of violence and its complex emotional effects.

Significantly, in Ovid's version of the Marsyas myth in the *Metamorphoses* there is no contest, usually a key element of the myth.[97] The lack of explanation for Marsyas' punishment is an example, Tissol observes, of Ovid's 'audacious neglect of what traditionally gave the story its meaning and made Marsyas' agony comprehensible'.[98] As a result, the god's violence is made to seem all the more arbitrary and excessive, Marsyas' suffering all the more stark and cruel. The resemblance of the flayed body to Apollo's lyre may exalt Apollo's power, but as a hideous, bleeding parody of the god's instrument and a monstrous symbol of revenge, the body again also dramatizes the cruelty of the god. Read as a portrait of the artist cut out and cut away by absolute power, the story of Marsyas here represents in extreme form the artist's vulnerability when confronted by authoritarian powers. Ovid's Marsyas is not so much punished as persecuted.

Critics, however, have also been disturbed by Marsyas' slick speech as he hangs dying, for it seems to indulge in a species of wit more appropriate to the poet than to the flayed victim:[99] *'quid me mihi detrahis?' inquit;* | *'a! piget, a! non est' clamabat 'tibia tanti'* ("Why do you tear me from myself? Ah! it is disgusting, ah! it is not", he kept shouting, "worth so much, the flute"', *Met.* 6.385–6). As Dryden objected in the preface to *Fables, Ancient and Modern* (1700), 'Was this a Time to be witty, when the poor Wretch was in the agony of death?'[100] But, as Tissol points out, the personal pronoun *me, mihi,* used in two different cases, reflects the physical division of Marsyas as he is being flayed, the cleavage of his identity.[101] His agony echoes throughout the next line in the repetition of the monosyllable *a!* The broken flow of words, disrupted by the two cries of pain and then by the intervention of *clamabat,* also represents Marsyas' dismemberment; as his body is torn apart so too are his words. What increases the horror is that Marsyas can still speak in the midst of such desperate circumstances – a sign, I suggest, of the heroism of the artist that exposes the disproportionate nature of divine vengeance.

---

[97] See the discussion in C. P. Segal 2005: lx–lxii. The contest is an important element in artistic representations of the myth, popular on Greek vases and Roman sarcophagi; see Wyss 1996: 19–25.
[98] Tissol 1997: 126.
[99] See Bömer 1969–86: III.109 on *Met.* 6.385–6 as an instance of 'black humour'.
[100] Cited in Tissol 1997: 11.        [101] Tissol 1997: 59.

Marsyas is not permitted the metamorphosis granted to others in the poem. Instead he undergoes complete bodily dissolution. This is a reversal of the usual type of transformation in the *Metamorphoses*, where new material covers up old identities; here no body in any form is left. The obliteration of the self, the compounding of violence in the description of the punishment, and the clinical detachment of the description are striking features of the bailiff's tale in Apuleius' *Golden Ass*, which Fitzgerald analyses in Chapter 10 below as paradigmatic of the intrinsic violence of this text, and as a demonstration of how closely narration itself comes to cruelty.[102] In Ovid's *Metamorphoses*, however, the scene of intense cruelty modulates into pastoral, with the narrative turn to the rustic mourners, fauns, satyrs, nymphs, and herdsmen (6.392–400). Their tears become the river that bears the name of Marsyas, 'the clearest of rivers' (*liquidissimus amnis*, 400). In other versions of the myth, Marsyas' blood itself becomes the river;[103] here it is the tears of *others*. *Liquidus* is not often applied to rivers *per se*; moreover, the superlative is unusual and, in thus stressing rarity and purity, the word suggests that in Callimachean terms a new refined fount of poetry is associated with Marsyas' name.[104] Significantly, his immortality is embedded in language alone.

The story conforms in some ways to the mythical pattern of scapegoating outlined by Girard:[105] the violent punishment of the scapegoat Marsyas is followed by the solidifying of the pastoral community through the shared emotion of grief; indeed, the community is renewed through the creation of a new river providing the water so essential for a pastoral landscape – and metaphorically for pastoral song. Girard sees such violence as beneficial as opposed to destructive, for the sacrifice of Marsyas bears positive fruit for the community.[106] The epic song of violence is thus 'dismembered', metamorphosing into pastoral, which is often, like elegy, the poetry of lament. The creativity of mother earth here, turning the tears of Marsyas' mourners into a pure stream, plays a variation upon Lucretius' vivid account (1.250–64) of the mating of the sky and earth; a new poetic genre, along with a new river, comes into being. Landscape literally and metaphorically makes a place here for consolatory lament – a genre that

---

[102] Fitzgerald, Chapter 10, pp. 291–5.
[103] See Feldherr and James 2004: 92, 98; also Theodorakopoulos 1999: 156–7.
[104] *Liquidus* is associated with clarity of sound as well as of water: see *OLD* s.v., sects. 6 and 5a respectively. Bömer 1969–86: III.112 on *Met.* 6.400 points out that the superlative *liquidissimus* occurs only twice in Ovid's poetry; its connection with *amnis* is also unusual.
[105] See, e.g., the definition of the scapegoat in Girard 1996: 11–15.
[106] On the notion of two types of violence see Girard 1977: 1–38.

Ovid would aggressively make his own in exile. Thus we have a reversal of the pattern found in the story of Actaeon, for here a beautiful, peaceful landscape emerges from the sorrow and suffering of the local inhabitants. Yet, as Feldherr notes, the pastoral overtones of this passage ironically underscore the gap between the Virgilian pastoral world of peaceable poetic competition and the Ovidian world, where the cruel stakes are a matter of life and death.[107] Typically, too, in Ovid's world the boundaries between horror and beauty are never firm; the pastoral landscape carries a reminder of the violence of Marsyas' punishment. *Liquidissimus*, the unusual epithet used to describe the river, conveys the residual memory of the liquefaction of Marsyas' body, the absolute transparency of his vital organs (*perlucentes fibras*, 6.390).[108] The clarity of the water, a prized feature of the *locus amoenus*, is associated not only with grief but also with the particular form of Marsyas' punishment. The ambiguity in the beautiful landscape again plays upon the paradox that beauty can emerge from this horrifying exercise in divine power on the part of the god of poetry.

Book 6 of the *Metamorphoses* contains overall some of the most horrible accounts of physical torture in the poem. Williams has argued that the myth of Marsyas depicts the poet as he displays himself in the *Ibis*, as fascinated with psychological states involving enormous cruelty and their effects.[109] But the myth of Marsyas is also particularly concerned with the role of art in confrontation with political power.[110] The book programmatically opens with Minerva's punishment of the brilliant weaver Arachne for her truth-telling about the gods, for *her* 'Metamorphoses' (6.1–145).[111] The survival of art, particularly non-conformist art, as the purveyor of knowledge and truth is perilous under autocratic rule. As Rosati argues, the myth of Arachne is both an essay on the ideological partiality of the producer of a text and also a fable about the problematic relationship between the artist and power.[112] These indeed are the themes

---

[107] Feldherr and James 2004: 83. Feldherr further argues (83–4) that the text is uncomfortably split between the hymnic (worship of Apollo) and the bucolic – a form of generic dismemberment.

[108] For the association of *luceo* with water and transparency, cf. *Met.* 4.297–8 *lucentis . . . lymphae*, 4.313 *perlucenti . . . amictu* (of the pool and dress of the water-nymph Salmacis).

[109] G. D. Williams 1996: 81–91.

[110] The theme of the failed artist punished for challenging the gods was first extensively explored by Leach 1974; see now P. J. Johnson 2008, with a particular focus on the myths of Arachne and Orpheus.

[111] On Minerva as 'resisting reader' of Arachne's text see Smith 1997: 54–64. On this myth see also Rosati 1999: 248–52.

[112] Rosati 1999: 251–2.

of the myth of Marsyas in Ovid's *Fasti* (6.693–710), a version of the tale
that has generally garnered less attention than its epic counterpart.[113]
While the version of the myth of Marsyas in *Metamorphoses* 6 makes only
passing reference to Minerva's complicity in Marsyas' fate,[114] here in the
*Fasti* Minerva plays a prominent role both as the narrator and as the
traditional inventor of the flute, which the satyr makes his own after she
discards it for spoiling her beauty when played.[115] In the contemporary
Roman context Minerva is the poet's patron deity, for Ovid's birthday fell
during her festival of the Quinquatrus in March (*Tr.* 4.10.13).[116] Ovid's
personal link with the goddess blurs the boundary between history and
myth and makes possible a troubling alignment between the Roman poet
and Marsyas.

A comparison of the two narratives in the *Metamorphoses* and *Fasti*
suggests that they are meant to be read together. Structurally, the two
tales are similar; both occur in the sixth book of the relevant poem; they
are of comparable length, nineteen and eighteen lines respectively; both
avoid an account of the musical contest that led to Marsyas' defeat; and the
focus of both narratives is the satyr's punishment, although the *Fasti*
account lacks the detailed description of the satyr's suffering – as an elegiac
poem, the *Fasti*, unlike the *Metamorphoses*, is generically devoted to
brevity. A major concern of the *Fasti*, however, is the curbing of speech;
as Feeney points out, the very title of the poem, *Fasti*, draws attention to
the restrictions upon speech operative not just in myth but in Roman
society.[117] The *Fasti* and the *Metamorphoses* intersect over this troubling
issue. While the relative dating of the two poems remains a somewhat
vexed problem, there is extensive cross-referencing between the two.[118]
Indeed, as I shall argue, the version of the Marsyas myth in the *Fasti* seems
to have been a late composition by virtue both of its location in the poem's
final book, and of Ovid's nostalgic reference at the episode's start to a

---

[113] See, however, Newlands 1995: 196–201; G. D. Williams 1996: 81–3; Barchiesi 1997: 89–92 on
the lesser Quinquatrus (see below).

[114] The flute is referred to as Minerva's (*Tritoniaca ... harundine, Met.* 6.384).

[115] The relationship between Minerva and Marsyas was long established in myth. Thus a pair of lost
statues by the famous Athenian sculptor Myron on the Acropolis depicted the goddess cursing the
flute and Marsyas stooping to pick it up; on these and other early artistic depictions of the myth of
Minerva, Marsyas, and Apollo see Wyss 1996.

[116] Thus special point is given to his invocation to Minerva in his first account of the Quinquatrus,
*si mereor, studiis adsis amica meis* ('if I am deserving, come propitious to my endeavours', *Fast.*
3.834).

[117] Feeney 1992: 9.      [118] See Hinds 1985: 10–11.

happier, earlier period when exile meant only relocation to Tibur (*Fast.* 6.666).[119] This late version of the Marsyas myth thus engages in an act of reception – and consequently interpretation – of the version in the *Metamorphoses*. It provides a contemporary Roman gloss on the Greek myth, confronting and indeed, to some extent, circumventing its pessimism about artistic achievement. In the *Fasti* Marsyas is more obviously a figure of artistic resistance to violence, not merely its victim.

The setting for the Marsyas myth in the *Fasti* is a city festival; the myth is embedded in a discussion of the lesser Quinquatrus, at which the flute-players' guild honoured Minerva as their patroness (6.649–710). The importance of the flute-players' guild to the festival is explained by a historical tale involving the state's *failed* attempt in the fourth century BC to control the freedom of the flute-players in Rome (6.653–92); issues of artistic censorship therefore impinge upon the Marsyas myth, which, significantly, Ovid probably composed in exile in Tomis. The episode is marked by Ovid's newly deferential relationship with authority, the opening *iubeor*, 'I am ordered' (651), suggesting the compulsion under which he now writes. Minerva is interviewed by Ovid in his new didactic role of city poet and researcher into Rome's ancient rites, but she herself tells the story of her discovery of the flute and Marsyas' subsequent punishment;[120] by contrast, a nameless nobody tells the tale in the *Metamorphoses*, *nescioquis Lycia de gente virorum* ('someone from the Lycian race,' *Met.* 6.382). As patroness of the flute-players' guild, a body that was regulated by the state, Minerva represents official authority over the arts in Rome. But she seems to care little about its music beyond the honour that it brings her, specifically from the flute-players' worship: *sum tamen inventrix auctorque ego carminis huius: | hoc est cur nostros ars colat ista dies* ('however, I am the inventor and originator of this song: this is why that art honours our festival days', *Fast.* 6.709–10).[121] Her narrative is thus self-defensive and partisan.

Not surprisingly, Minerva glosses over the punishment of Marsyas in a line and a half (6.707–8). Even so, her words carry great rhetorical power: *Phoebo superante pependit; | caesa recesserunt a cute membra sua* ('with Phoebus' victory he hung; his limbs, sliced open, peeled away from their

[119] On this remark see Barchiesi 1997: 89–90. Fantham 1986 has argued that important sections of the *Fasti* were rewritten in exile (after AD 8, therefore); Herbert-Brown 1994: 229–33 argues that the poem was not begun till late in AD 4.
[120] On the divine narrators in Ovid's *Fasti* see J. F. Miller 1983; also Newlands 1995: 51–86.
[121] For the *Fasti*, I follow the text of Alton, Wormell, and Courtney 1985.

skin').[122] The keen assonance, and the possible pun *a cute/acute* ('from the skin', 'sharply'), draw attention to the suffering of the satyr. In addition, we might see a similar pun, based on word-division, in the first two words of line 708, *caesa re/Caesare*, a momentary insertion of 'Caesar' into the scene of suffering that subtly links imperial power and the inflicting of punishment.[123] Politics, as I said at the start, are inevitably involved with aesthetics; at issue here is not only who speaks, but also what is spoken, and how. In the forfeiting of poetic authority here to Minerva as representative of the state and narrator of this story, the goddess might seem to have the final word. Yet the cunning wordplay in line 708 perhaps invites a contemporary, critical reading of this episode, the Caesar behind the cruel Apollo, the exiled Ovid behind the persecuted artist. Let me pursue this further.

First of all, a striking instance of triple verse repetition draws retrospective attention to key moments in Ovid's poetic career. At line 701 Minerva's words of rejection of the flute, *'ars mihi non tanti est; valeas, mea tibia' dixi* ('"art is not worth so much to me; farewell, my flute", I said'), closely echo both her own words rejecting the flute in the *Ars amatoria, 'i procul hinc,' dixit, 'non es mihi tibia tanti'* ('"go far away from here," she said, "you, flute, are not worth so much to me"', *Ars am.* 3.505), and also Marsyas' agonized words in the *Metamorphoses, 'a! piget, a! non est' clamabat 'tibia tanti'* ('"ah! it is disgusting, ah! it is not", he kept shouting, "worth so much, the flute"', *Met.* 6.386).[124] The triple verse repetition here operates on dissonant registers: the echoing of Marsyas' scream in Minerva's dismissive words implicates her more closely in the consequences of her rejection of the flute than her partisan account admits.

Minerva's invention of the flute was closely linked from early Antiquity with Marsyas' flaying.[125] Minerva, as narrator of the story in the *Fasti*, detaches herself from responsibility for the satyr's terrible death; he was, she comments dismissively, *inter nymphas arte superbus* ('proud in his art among the girls', *Fast.* 6.706). Yet her smooth words casually rejecting the flute grimly mark the violent, tragic consequences of that rejection through their echo of Marsyas' desperate cry in the *Metamorphoses*.[126] The allusion

---

[122] G. D. Williams 1996: 81–2 argues that the intransitive verbs suggest tact on Minerva's part about the punishment inflicted by Apollo. Equally, her succinctness can be seen to convey callous indifference to the satyr's fate.

[123] On Ovid's punning on *Caesar* elsewhere see n. 14 above.

[124] On another such instance of triple verse repetition at *Pont.* 4.4.32 see J. F. Miller 1991: 160 n. 29; Hinds 2005: 226–8.

[125] See n. 115 above.      [126] See Bömer 1958: 382 on *Fast.* 6.694.

in the *Fasti* to Marsyas' extreme agony chillingly marks the chasm between Minerva, the wielder of state authority, who tosses aside the flute out of personal vanity, and the committed artist. Indeed, in this dissonant echo of Marsyas' scream, two different views of art tragically confront one another: the utilitarian but powerful view of Minerva, tied to the Roman state, and the idealistic view of the individual Marsyas. Despite Minerva's control of the narrative, the allusion to Marsyas' scream offers another line of interpretation, one that implicates the goddess in Marsyas' fate and again raises the question of the justice of the satyr's punishment. Indeed, by taking us back to Book 6 of the *Metamorphoses* Ovid reminds us of Minerva's controversial role there in the punishment of Arachne.

The pastoral setting, the perfect site for flute-playing, is also the perfect site for this type of echoic allusion. The reflection of Minerva's face in the clear stream finds its aural correspondence in the words that echo her own earlier speech and Marsyas' scream.

> faciem liquidis referentibus undis
> vidi virgineas intumuisse genas.

As the clear waters reflected my face, I saw my virgin cheeks puffed out.

> *(Fast.* 6.699–700)

The duality of the *locus amoenus* is here exposed as the clear water mirrors not beauty but ugliness; it reveals the two faces of Minerva, goddess of arts and of war. As Rimell suggests, Minerva sees in the water the face of her martial talisman, Medusa.[127] Likewise, the verse repetition reveals two voices echoing one another; as the water betrays Minerva's monstrous side, so too her words are implicated in Marsyas' hideous suffering, thus marking her complicity. The clear stream, *liquidis ... undis* (699), perhaps recalls the river Marsyas, *liquidissimus amnis* (*Met.* 6.400); if so, then the story's beginning and end are further jarringly conflated as Minerva's casual rejection of the flute is here yet again intimately connected with Marsyas' terrible fate.

As we have seen, Minerva also echoes her own words at *Ars amatoria* 3.505, again in connection with her rejection of the flute: '*i procul hinc,*' *dixit,* '*non es mihi tibia tanti*' ("'go far away from here," she said, "you, flute, are not worth so much to me"').[128] The verb *dixi* in the *Fasti* (6.701) marks her self-citation; she remembers the words that Ovid gave her in the

---

[127] Rimell 2006: 20–1.

[128] On the relative dating of the two passages see Feldherr 2010: 101 n. 73; R. K. Gibson 2003: 37–45 finds unconvincing the evidence for a late date for Book 3 of the *Ars amatoria*.

*Ars*. Thus the quotation here in the *Fasti* essentially spans Ovid's entire poetic career, from the earlier didactic *Ars amatoria* through the epic *Metamorphoses* to the late didactic *Fasti*. The repetition reveals how Ovid's poetic strategies change over time, for the poet who preferred in his *Ars amatoria* (1.25–9) to rely on his own experience rather than divine assistance now in his late didactic poem defers to the goddess Minerva and prays for her aid (*Fast.* 6.652). Changed social and artistic circumstances call for a different kind of art.

Barchiesi suggests that Ovid through self-quotation in the story of Marsyas hints at his personal remorse for his elegiac *Ars amatoria*.[129] The *Fasti* indeed has been read as Ovid's apologetic answer to the *Ars amatoria*, in effect a belated attempt in didactic poetry to conform to the prevailing civic discourse of morality and religion. The overdetermination of the triple rejection of art might seem to support this view. Yet at the same time the text makes sure that the *Ars* will be remembered. The self-quotation in the *Fasti* contains one significant alteration. Whereas in both the *Ars* and the *Metamorphoses tibia* serves as the subject of the verse – *non es mihi tibia tanti* and *non est ... tibia tanti* respectively – the *Fasti* substitutes *ars*: *ars mihi non tanti est*. Minerva's rejection of the flute is here made to encompass art in general, not just the flute. At the same time, of course, the word *ars* signals an allusion to the *Ars amatoria*, whose words she is quoting – Ovid's most controversial poem, which, after his exile, was banned from the libraries in Rome, including that of Palatine Apollo.[130] Possibly in response to this act of Augustan censorship, the story of Marsyas in the *Fasti* incorporates a powerful reminiscence both of the *Ars amatoria* and of the *Metamorphoses*, in particular Book 6, which begins with Minerva's troubling punishment of the artist Arachne. Ironically, the memory of the banned poem and the memory of Marsyas' terrible punishment in the *Metamorphoses* are preserved in Minerva's remembering words; the triple verse repetition thus links Ovid's fate (through his *Ars amatoria*) with that of Marsyas.

The myth of Marsyas in the *Fasti* draws attention to the issues of artistic authority and poetic memory, issues that were crucial for imperial literature.[131] By embedding the memory of the *Metamorphoses* and the *Ars amatoria* within its seemingly official discourse, the Marsyas myth in *Fasti* 6 can also be read as transcending punishment, dismemberment, and the scattering of words and books to dissolution. Although the Marsyas of the

[129] Barchiesi 1997: 89–92.      [130] See Ov. *Tr.* 3.1.59–82; Newlands 1998: 67–73.
[131] See Gowing 2005.

*Metamorphoses* is silenced, the iterative imperfect *clamabat* (*Met.* 6.386) has an interesting afterlife in the *Fasti*, for there Marsyas' words of pain are repeated and remembered. When Minerva quotes herself from the *Ars amatoria* and simultaneously alludes to the *Metamorphoses*, the tenacity of the poetic word infiltrates the very institutions that censure written works but can also crucially disseminate their memory.

Ovid's introduction of the Marsyas myth to his discussion of the festival of the lesser Quinquatrus is worth special attention precisely because it is *irrelevant* to the aetiological exchange between poet and goddess: there is a mismatch between the poet's question to Minerva, 'Why is the Quinquatrus so called?' (*Fast.* 6.694), and her reply, in which she explains why the flute-players' guild worships her (despite her dislike of the instrument) and in this context tells the story of Marsyas.[132] Rather, the story, placed towards the end of the *Fasti*, provocatively suggests an alignment between the figures of the poet Ovid and Marsyas that reinterprets the gods' violence against mortals as an attribute of state power. The gods, and the powers-that-be on earth, may demonstrate arbitrary cruelty, their punishments may be far out of proportion to the crime, but the poet's words survive through their complex, skilled, and allusive art.

The reinterpretation of the Marsyas story in Ovid's Roman poem may have been influenced by the important Roman cult of Marsyas, which, contrary to Greek myth, supposed that the satyr, having escaped Apollo's torment, fled to Italy, where he became ancestor of the Marsi.[133] As such, he survived in a bodily, sculptured form to signify Republican freedoms; his statue had stood prominently in the Roman forum since (apparently) the fourth century BC (and many copies were distributed throughout Italy and the provinces). Wiseman emphasizes the long association between the satyr and both liberty and the god Liber, citing Servius: *in liberis civitatibus simulacrum Marsyae erat, qui in tutela Liberi Patris est ... est in civitatibus in foro positus libertatis indicium* ('in free cities there was a statue of Marsyas, who is under the protection of Liber Pater ... he is placed in the forum in cities as a symbol of freedom', Serv. *A.* 3.20, 4.58).[134] As Small observes, the statue of Marsyas displays 'the tenacity with which figures held on to their monuments in Rome. They could not be destroyed.'[135] Thus in Roman tradition Marsyas lived on as an emblem of Republican freedom, claiming an important place in the topographical

---

[132] An explanation for the festival's name – a reference to its five-day span – has already been offered at *Fast.* 3.810.
[133] See Plin. *NH* 3.108.    [134] Wiseman 2000: 274.    [135] Small 1982: 110.

heart of Rome. His vitality only began to be eroded during the Augustan Principate, in part because his patron Liber was the god of Augustus' rival Antony.[136] And, as Niżyńska has argued, Augustus' Apollo essentially usurped the prophetic powers of augurs such as Marsyas. Augustus emphasized Greek accounts of Apollo's victory over the barbaric satyr, dooming the symbol of civic freedom eventually to oblivion.[137]

For the Roman reader of the *Fasti*, Marsyas therefore had powerful associations with Republican freedoms. That Marsyas, opponent of Apollo, the god who was Augustus' new artistic director, appears towards the end of the extant *Fasti* is surely significant. Indeed, the juxtaposition of *Phoebum* and *Phoebo* at *Fasti* 6.707 (*provocat et Phoebum. Phoebo superante pependit*, 'he even challenged Phoebus; with Phoebus' victory he hung') draws attention to Apollo's role as Marsyas' punisher (and indeed to his unusual prominence in Book 6 compared to the rest of the poem). The complex associations of Marsyas, emblem of Roman political freedom and tragic victim of Apollo, draw Ovid's own fractured poem to a close with a troubled reflection on the relationship between the artist and the state. Generally poets accrue literary authority throughout their poetic career. The reverse was true for Ovid. Indeed, his late poetry reflects a poet struggling to regain the cultural capital he has lost. The Marsyas myth plays a key part in this coded attempt to reclaim authority, to create a bulwark of memory against the threat to his art, the expunging of his poetry from the main libraries in Rome – even as he rewrites himself in the *Fasti* into a more deferential role.

The curious fact that Ovid never names Marsyas in either the *Metamorphoses* or the *Fasti*[138] – although he does, in the *Fasti* version, name Apollo twice – might be understood in two ways. The first would imagine what Ovid the poet most feared: the very erasure of the name could mark the complete dissolution not only of the body but also of artistic memory. A second possibility hands the question of survival to the reader, who must figure out who the satyr is, and with this act of readerly remembrance, reclaim his name as a reminder, in a time of waning freedoms, of the enduring and transformative power of language itself to circumvent the violence of the state against the individual; thus Ovid ends *Tristia* 5.3 with

---

[136] See Wiseman 2000: 290–7.
[137] See Niżyńska 2001: 157–60. Small 1982: 83 argues that Marsyas' association with civic freedom only came later, with the Principate; all the same, at 85–6 she makes reference to the Censorinus denarii of 82 BC (minted in the midst of the conflict between Marius and Sulla) that show Apollo on the obverse, Marsyas on the reverse wearing a freedom cap.
[138] At *Met.* 6.400 only the derivative name of the river is given.

an appeal to his fellow-poets to do what the regime allowed, preserve his name: *quod licet, inter vos <u>nomen</u> habete <u>meum</u>* ('as is permitted, keep *my name* among you', 58).[139] In the *Fasti* the power of allusion keeps Marsyas' words (and name) alive. In a similar way, it was not by confrontation but by cunning and by coded language that Philomela gained her ill-used freedom from captivity – and her 'name'. The Marsyas of the *Fasti*, like Philomela, points to the poetics of the Imperial age, where art draws its power from allusion, myth, and symbolic language. M<u>a</u>rsyas, then, whose name encompasses both the title of Ovid's censored poem and art in general, is a fitting figure for the concluding book of the *Fasti*, which looks towards 'a new kind of art' that is crafted both in deference to Rome's new 'gods' and in resistance to their propensity for violence and injustice.

To conclude: the tension between aesthetics and violence should be seen as vital to the dynamic power of Ovid's poetry; indeed, the two crucially converge in the poet's late representation in the *Fasti* of his brilliant but fractured career. We may not be able to remove an element of delight or pleasure in Ovid's depictions of violence. But, as Tissol has commented, critics who emphasize or see only the pleasure (or the brutality) of these scenes seriously underestimate the emotional range of the poem.[140] Indeed, Eagleton offers us a way to have (as he puts it) 'our humanist cake and eat it too' when he argues that tragic drama caters to our sadism, our masochism, *and* our moral conscience all at once.[141] Violence in the *Metamorphoses* has a formal purpose, to create novel and striking conjunctions and disruptive juxtapositions; at the same time, as I have tried to argue, violence as a property of speech and of the culture that produced it is a major concern of the poem, exposing its readers to ethical, political, and intellectual issues. The *Metamorphoses* and the *Fasti* respond to a crucial period of change in the Roman state with the establishment of the Julio-Claudian dynasty and its ideology of divinity. Ovid's poetry explores not only the cruelty and violence of Roman society but also the implications of the new configurations of political power, with a *princeps* transmuting into autocrat, dynast, and semi-divine ruler.

The personal, semi-autobiographical element in the *Metamorphoses*' reflection on the conjunction of aesthetics and violence emerges in its beginning and end. In the proem the poet hopes for a co-operative and

---

[139] Cf. also the proud assertion of the famous epilogue to the *Metamorphoses*, <u>nomenque</u> erit indelibile <u>nostrum</u> ('*my name* will be indestructible', 15.876).
[140] Tissol 1997: 125.    [141] Eagleton 2003: 176–7.

beneficial relationship with the gods: *di, coeptis (nam vos mutastis et illa)* |
*aspirate meis* ('gods, breathe on my enterprises, for you have changed them
too', *Met.* 1.2–3). While acknowledging the power of the gods over his
literary career and poetic memory, the poet seems, in the tension between
*aspirate* and *mutastis*, to be requesting a stance of non-belligerence on the
part of the gods. Yet such hopes for inspiration and protection are
drastically undermined by Jupiter's discourse on power in Book 1, where
the unchecked exercise of violence is revealed as the prerogative of autocratic rule (1.177–252). The epilogue of the *Metamorphoses* applies the
'anger of Jupiter' (*Iovis ira*, 15.871) – the first emotion attributed to the
god in the poem (1.166) – to Ovid's own poetry, thus thematizing political
opposition and aggression as a potential threat to Ovid's poetic memory.
But although transgressive speech all too often in the myths of the
*Metamorphoses* results in violent punishment, by predicting his immortality and that of his poetry (15.875–9) Ovid leaves his material body behind
in one of the poem's rare upward metamorphoses, soaring beyond the stars
and the instruments of violence – Jove's anger, the thunderbolt, the sword,
even corrosive age (871–2). The poet imagines survival 'in his better part'
(*parte . . . meliore*, 875), freed at last from the tyranny of violence and its
seductive power. Ovid's epic poem of crime and punishment may present
an often harsh view of human existence, ruled over by punitive and
arbitrary powers, but art, and particularly poetry, for all its seeming
vulnerability and flaws, provides a current of defiant, transcendent joy.

# CHAPTER 6

# Tales of the Unexpurgated (Cert PG)
## Seneca's Audionasties (Controversiae 2.5, 10.4)

### John Henderson*

*quidquid antiqua saevitia invenerat, quidquid et nova adiecerat*
('Ancient sadism's every hit, plus modern supplements', 2.5.6)

*intuemini debilia infelicium membra*
('Gaze upon the poor creatures, their useless limbs', 10.4.3)

## Let Id Go

Expect spectacular themes of sadistic violence within Seneca's corpus of excerpted snatches of mock-debate recalled from Augustan and Tiberian Rome. We do. So we should. In the fourscore years between the deaths of Cicero and Caligula, Roman declamation modelled a performative culture that spilled into writing and politics, through theatricality and theory, all over entertainment and education. Across the range of genres, texts took on declamatory colour and avowed the intermedial pollination. The elder Seneca's first-person anthologization of contributions from the celebs' debating club in the cosmopolis tells an eloquent story of the centring of the new world culture around this 'off-duty' jousting between courtier glitterati and gurus. He knew it full well.[1] His bioscript's import(ance) would be to have launched his family from the edge of beyond in swish hicksville Roman Spain, and straight into an intimate matrix of super-power at play.[2] Informed and empowered by philosophically modulated

---

* All unspecified references are to *Controversiae*; they come at you in sequence. Texts are from Winterbottom 1974 (rare exceptions indicated), translations mine. *Pr.* = *Praefatio*. I bellow thanks to both eds. for their meticulous incisions. *exposita tormenta sunt* . . .

[1] Seneca ushers himself in as a 'continuator' of Cicero: detained in 'my colony' (Corduba) from joining those declamation sessions self-immortalized in the grand *novus homo*'s writings (cf. Dugan 2001: 72–5), but perfectly timed to join the new party of post-Ciceronian *controversiae* at Rome (1.*Pr.*11–12): 'Nowt simpler than knowing from the cradle a wotsit born since my time.' On *declamatio* for real, see Stroh 2003; on the 'rhetorical habitus', Bloomer 2011: 170–91.

[2] Spanish backwater rising: Latro and 'that brave redneck Spanish character' (1.*Pr.*16). See 10. *Pr.*14–16; M. T. Griffin 1972.

coaching,[3] Seneca writes himself, through a dozen sound-bite samplers of *Greatest Hits* with counterfoil commentary, enfolded within editorial dubbing, into paradigmatic status as the declamatory father whose glory will be the reward bestowed on him retrospectively by his stake in interpreting *success* in the environs of the Julio-Claudian establishment.[4]

Yes, Seneca's three sons are set to model the range of lifestyle opportunities available in this future:[5] the eldest, Novatus, will be invested in the market for political honours, adopted by the hotshot declaimer, orator, and senator Gallio,[6] and himself bound for provincial governorship and consulate; Mela, the youngest, will be spared rant and cant, 'retained in port' for running family estates and business between Italy and Spain, fully imprinted with memories shared with fellow-graduates, and hooked into the same formative thinking-patterns and mindset pragmatics as the administrative fraternity;[7] and the median figure of self-transcendence, second son *Seneca*, will manage to combine the portfolios of a statesman – orator, senator, and eventually consul – and advisory interface between business, administration, and palace, with the fullest realization of his father's model of writerly expert on rhetoric and supportive presence at court: a boy Caesar's teacher, ghost writer, and counsellor, and also author of authors for the new order, declaiming philosophy through epistolary, suasory, scientific, and epideictic modes, and besides detonating tragedy to death. Co-opt Mela's son Lucan, and this household is wired to blast 'historical epic' into declamatory explosion, and complete the coup. In (*non-performing* recording angel) Seneca the Eldorado's nostalgia-trip, the lead soloist Porcius Latro does the business for Augustan logomachy that gives his long-lived friend the stand-in superhero he needed to guide posterity

---

[3] Papirius Fabianus as tutor to Seneca Jr.: see esp. Sen. *Ep.* 100 (with Henderson 2003: 154–5; cf. 16). Both father-figures far too good to declaim – to declaim only dysfunctionally.

[4] See Bloomer 1997b and esp. Gunderson 2003: 29–58 for the ideation of Senecan paternality (with index s.v. Seneca the Elder, 'as a father (literally) . . . (metaphorically)').

[5] The three sons: 1.*Pr.*1, and esp. 2.*Pr.4 fratribus tuis ambitiosa curae sunt foroque se et honoribus parant* ('the political ladder is your brothers' focus, readying themselves for forum and successive appointments'); cf. 9.*Pr.*1. At 10.*Pr.*14–16 the boys will acquire a compositionally significant fourth brother and amigo by authorial adoption.

[6] Iunius Gallio: 1.1.4, 14, 25; 1.2.11–12; 1.5.2; 1.6.8, 10; 1.7.12; 1.8.9; and *passim*. See esp. 10.*Pr.*8 ('your' G., *vester*, owns a fun book to cadge); *Suas.* 3.6–7 (friend of Ovid). He *may* have presided over Book 5, 6, or 8 (where prefaces have not survived).

[7] *Mela . . . melioris ingenii* ('superior flair') – 'readied by declamation for . . . whatever came next' = 'free . . . to obey orders: "(1) follow inclination, (2) *paterno contentus ordine* ('content with father's rank') withdraw a majority stake of selfhood from fortune's control"!' (2.*Pr.*3–4; cf. 10.*Pr.*9).

through the contrary debating game, pioneering the trail out to boss the empire.[8] Verbal pyrotechnics internalized for outdoing all-comers in leaving a mark on a favourite fictive theme already supply real court-rooms with honed skills in ingenious sensationalism: declamation fuels delation, and knows it.[9] Routinized scenarios of tyrannicide will play through the actualized assassination of crazed Caligula, just as Senecan scripts will soon enough translate Greek tragedy into vehicles for palace-watching Roman dread. Twenty years on, and Seneca's prize pupillage will have trained his someday prince to butcher father, brother, and sister, sp(l)icing matricide with incest and for finale bringing the polis crashing down about its ears – torchery, blood flood, geno-suicidal world's end ...

Such is the poisonous gift wrapped up for Roman cataclysm in Seneca's *Controversiae* and *Suasoriae*. The denunciation of declamation as a *histor-ical* fable of doomed descent, through purposive customizing of Greek pedagogy, to pathological habituation, to imperial histrionics.[10] Where we come in, declamation is going great guns – blowing a gale. But as we read on, the boys need a good shaking, and before the writing dies away *pater* has despaired of the lot of them (us). The cardinal sin? – to lap it up.[11] So concerned with telling on his own topic is this traitor to debating that he constantly interposes between memory and reader his own take on the parade of performers, and infiltrates, under dissembling cover of the formless precariousness of memory-dredging,[12] a fatal *narrative*[13] of

---

[8] Porcius Latro: 1.*Pr*.13–24, and generally first contributor thereafter, as well as dominant impresario of *divisiones*, *passim*: Seneca's friend to the grave, and his point of departure (1.1 the first effort he ever heard from a Latro in short trousers: on disinheritance for disobedience by a son/a brother's son).

[9] Declaiming *delatores*: Romanius Hispo, *accusatoria usus pugnacitate* ('making hay with prosecutor-style combativeness'), 1.2.16; Cassius Severus, 3.*Pr*.1, 5, 17; Vinicius, 7.5.11–12; Vallius Syriacus, 9.4.18; cf. 7.*Pr*.6, Albucius.

[10] 'Downhill all the way ... Roman eloquence ... Greek hubris ... that sinking feeling ...' (1.*Pr*.6–7). Establishing what will be Seneca's characteristic trajectory at every compositional level: the mindset of *cata-chresis*.

[11] Seneca's downhill narrative of declamation's degradation kicks in from the start: already we give 'more on Latro than the boys bargained for'; skip his *argumenta* for the *sententiae*, 'or risk boring them'; get the show on the road, 'no warm-up-act teasing' (1.*Pr*.20, 22, 24; cf. 4.*Pr*.1–2, 7.*Pr*.1, 10. *Pr*.1).

[12] See 1.*Pr*.5 *necesse est ergo me ad delicias conponam memoriae meae quae mihi iam olim precario paret* ('So I suit myself to my memory's whims – it's long since been obeying me only when it feels like saying yes'), with Gunderson 2003: 34.

[13] *Ordo* features as crucial to the memory feat ('2,000 names repeated back in order', 1.*Pr*. 2; 'a market day's sales invoices listed *ordine suo* ('in order')', 1.*Pr*.19), and as the principle of organization in any classroom (1.*Pr*.24 *cum iam coepisset* [sc. *Latro*] *ordinem ducere*. ||, 'when he'd begun leading the line-up'; cf. 1.*Pr*.4 *mittatur senex in scholas*, 'Back to school, crumblies', with Fordyce 1952). But

stigmatization, and recommended abstention and displacement in favour of the traditional powerhouses of philosophy, epic, and history.[14]

It is no use looking for a definitive authorial standpoint on his subject, for Seneca is himself a counterpunching performer, on paper.[15] His text is *not* itself 'declamatory' stylistically – let alone compositionally. Hardly a *text* at all? A puzzle for all scribes, editors, and readers, this 'unreadable' author writes into note form snippets of talk from counterposed quibblers who themselves used memorized, mental, or shorthand notes,[16] and we shall never know how far we are kept from what he wrote because the insufferability of his non sequiturs and abruptnesses defeated copyists, nor how far the nose-to-tail jam of choking excerpts faithfully delivers Seneca's version of cut-and-thrust reportage in an improvised idiom devised to reproduce the improvisational noise of this anti-literary rapping.[17] But yes (chiz), Seneca the Elder is *a pain*.

He sets out to be. A deliberately cutting 'Cato' counterpart.[18] The compilation strategy is to collect, for each in the series of miscellaneous themes shoehorned into each volume by the half-dozen (if not ten at a time): (1) runs of juicy cuts gathered per participant, whether in character as litigant or *in propria persona* as counsel (*sententiae*); followed by (2) (miserly-to-vanishing-point dribs from) shots at pleading the counter-claim; then (3) we are led backstage, beyond sound-bites, to the thinking behind lines of argument, and on stage through criticism of them, in bouts of discussion (*divisiones*, with *quaestiones*, 'issues', and *colores*, 'tonal approaches'); and (4) we finally wind up, with (usually scathing and minimal) Greek anticipations and inspirations of the sound-bites, petering out in contretemps, contradiction, and bathetic diminuendo.[19] The *writing* that Seneca does produce is concentrated into the fun of sparky

---

'you mustn't want for me to follow *quasi certum aliquem ordinem* ('some virtual fixed order') in gathering things that occur to me' (1.*Pr*.4). For *Controv.* as system(atization): Cappello forthcoming.

[14] Seneca's abusive displacement of declamation by philosophy: 2.*Pr.*, 7.*Pr.*1; epic: 2.2.8–12, 3.7, 7.1.27, 9.5.17, 10.4.25; history: 7.2, 9.1.13–14, 10.*Pr.*8, 10.5.22; add a burst of mime: 7.2.14, 7.3.8–10, 7.4.8.

[15] See Gunderson 2003, index s.v. Seneca the Elder, 'as an orator/declaimer'.

[16] See esp. Latro (1.*Pr.*18): 'he'd made notebooks superfluous – claimed he wrote in his mind'. Yet books of published *colores* ('stylistic approaches') already existed (1.3.11, 2.1.33), so Seneca's crossover play with oral-textual dynamics was no one-off, but engrained in declamatory culture. Regular schoolboys would learn to jot down highlights (Quint. *Inst.* 2.11.7).

[17] Compare Seneca's skeletal excerpts – the standard textual footprint for declamation – with his dramatically multidimensional discourse (however mauled), to see why his showcase of declamation is at once our most authentic and our least transparent witness to the institution.

[18] See 1.*Pr.*9, with Gunderson 2003, esp. 39–40.

[19] Cf. Fairweather 1981: 27–49, 'The Declamatory Anthology'.

prefatorial coaxing and scolding of the addressees,[20] and the successive write-ups introducing high-profile participants to be featured in the book(s) ahead, a restricted eloquence which carries over into the anecdotal 'asides', remarks, and morals attached both to these character-sketches and to some of the bursts of lines of counter-argument, when they arrive. Seneca is not about to elaborate on his own extremist stylistics, but the violence of representation bodied forth in his staccato, asyndetic flurry of citation and attribution makes for instructively painful reading.[21]

In most senses of the word, he makes sure he cannot be *read*. Which is to say (climb in), this specially customized writing superimposes an extra level of demand on top of regular norms for legibility.[22] Just as the three sons already know the declamation game perfectly well, and at first hand, but (a hard ask) are pressing pops for any fossils or dinosaurs he can rescue from his memory-bank,[23] so all readers must take this walk down memory lane, and there attune to the renascent moment. Appreciative glosses and countermanding health-warnings are sparsely attached to *mots* and *pas* (no time, not the place), and we are told, as well as obliged, to decide for ourselves whether they are *bons* and *faux*.[24] What does make them unforgettable and unerasable? (The time *and* the place.) Similarly, when it

---

[20] Cf. Bloomer 1997a: 120–5, 'The Ambition of the Prefaces'.

[21] Often re-marked in the text, e.g. 1.1.25 *schema . . . – sed, ut Latroni placebat, schema quod vulnerat, non quod titillat* ('a figure . . . – but, as Latro preferred, a figure that *wounds*, not tickles'); 9.2.22 *in . . . schemata minuta tractationem violentissime infregit* ('*really brutally smashed* the treatment into . . . pulverized figures'); 10.*Pr*.5 *quia . . . homines . . . laniabat, Rabienus vocaretur. animus . . . violentus . . .* ('for . . . butchering . . . folks, was nicknamed *Rabiesness*. A mind . . . *brutal . . .*'); 10. *Pr*.11 *dicebat violenter, sed dure* ('spoke *brutally* but rugged'); 10.4.17 *vehementissime dixit* ('spoke *powerfully*'); and *passim*. For *murder* by rhetoric, cf. 5.2 *extra*. *Saenianus rem stultissimam dixit: dives me semper contempsit, numquam nisi pro mortuo habuit. ut aliquid et ipse simile Saeniano dicam, post hanc sententiam semper Saenianum pro mortuo habui* ('Aside: Saenianus said the stupidest thing: "The rich guy always scorned me, treated me exclusively as though dead." To say something Saenianus-like myself, since that gem I've always *treated him as dead*'). I take it as read that my subject, the violence of representation in the representation of violence (see Armstrong and Tennenhouse 1989, and nn. 73, 79 below), nails us to the reading of Latin and, make no mistake, that's what I'm here to do. For a welter of fresh attempts to impact violence out there, see Six-Hohenbalken and Weiss 2011.

[22] First-century Latin prose saw all manner of experimental anti-stylistics: e.g. the crash-and-burn jotting of the elder Pliny's thirty-six-books-long continuously annotational grunge (see Henderson 2011, cf. 2002: 89–101; Book 19 Englished in Henderson 2004: 67–101, 'Nature's Miracles in Pliny's Encyclopaedia').

[23] 1.*Pr*.1, 4; 10.*Pr*.2 (calling foul!), 9, 13.

[24] The reader as jury: esp. *Suas.* 1.16 *utrorumque faciam vobis potestatem. et volebam vos experiri non adiciendo iudicium meum nec separando a corruptis sana; potuisset enim fieri ut vos magis illa laudaretis quae insaniunt. at nihilo minus poterit fieri quamvis distinxerim* ('I'll give you control either way. I wanted to test you by neither attaching my verdict nor blocking off sound from corrupt, since it could have happened that you'd approve of the lunacies – yet, that can still happen even if I've set them apart!'), 2.10 *ipse sententiam <non> feram; vestri arbitrii erit utrum explicationes eius luxuriosas*

comes to the *divisio* (editorial bridge) Seneca veers between giving his own analysis of the line being floated and (so) trumped, and reporting what the star gave as his own thinking and/or the critique voiced from a rival piping up from the audience. Between the *sententiae* (*mots*) and the *quaestiones* (issues), we are left to imagine (as if it matters) how we'd go about setting verbal brilliance into a sustained as well as distinctive cognitive coherence. Often enough, we are notified of, not just subjected to, the overdub track telling us what was *really* at stake on the day – that what counted was *not* the conducting of the fictive case, but the occasion it afforded for ulterior reflection or extrinsic consequence. What made an incident memorable can be its leakage to the course of history, its linkage to understanding how power works.

For, as the elder Seneca substitutes his own tiered programme of *Declamation: The Golden Years* for any textualized exemplar, he does so not only to strike a declamatory pose towards the collage of samples within his reach, but also to *police* the culture editorially.[25] While showing us how it was and should ~~not~~ be done, Seneca lays down a heavy frame of containment and construal to screen the performances from us. Mapping the range of oratorical virtuosities available, and theorizing their dynamics, is one preoccupation. Figuring out how the club activities interarticulated with the rest of the ensemble of Roman institutions is another. Forcing declamation through his shredder, while vetting it positively and negatively for (un)Roman tendencies, amounts to a violent psycho-graphematic project. A creatively complex lesson in upfront suppressive textuality.

## Keeping Mum (Books 1–2: 2.5)

Containment/release of pornotopic violence plays an ever-morphing role as Seneca's collection unfolds. In Book 1, *controversiae* 2-through-8:

> 2, *the pirate-prostituted priestess has killed her soldier rapist;*
>
> 3, *the fallen woman must go over the cliff – better luck second time around;*
>
> 4, *son would not lend pa a hand and kill adulteress ma;*
>
> 5, *a double rapist must marry and die;*
>
> 6, *the pirate daughter's husband will not swap her for the orphan stipulated by pa;*
>
> 7, *a double fratricide – a tyrant and an adulterer respectively – discards the dad who would have paid to disarm him;*
>
> 8, *dad disowns suicidally heroic son.*

*putetis an vegetas* ('I'm not going to declare my vote, it'll be your decision whether you think his fanfares baroque or healthy!').

[25] See esp. Bloomer 1997a: 119–24.

All strong fare fit for swashbuckling Latro to take the lead – a temperamental genius lurching through cycles of frenzied output and blockage (from 1.*Pr*.13 *vehementi viro*, 'power hero', through 1.1.15 *vehementer pressit*, 'he powered on', to 1.8.15 *vehementer egit*, 'his power-play').[26] Passages of voyeuristic cruelty are lacking, *and Seneca tells why*:

> dicendum est in puellam vehementer, non sordide nec obscene. sordide, ut Bassus Iulius, qui dixit: 'extra portam hanc virginem' et: 'ostende istam aeruginosam manum,' <vel> Vibius Rufus, qui dixit: 'redolet adhuc fuliginem fornicis.' obscene, quemadmodum Murredius rhetor, qui dixit: 'unde scimus an cum venientibus pro virginitate alio libidinis genere deciderit?'

> Invective at the girl must be power-packed, not grubby or filthy. Grubby: Iulius Bassus' phrasing, 'this girl – beyond the city-gate', and 'show us your copper-stained hand'; Vibius Rufus', 'she still stinks of her pitch'. Filth: e.g. Prof. Murredius' *mot*, 'how can we know if she traded with her callers – her virginity for lust under some other head?' (1.2.21)

To be sure, this prohibition is a loophole for the smuggler in Seneca as he sports to and fro across the faffing line of decency.[27] Dysphemism-euphemism rules some more, as ton-of-bricks Scaurus flattens praetorian X's tomfool fancy of imagining the groom's wedding-night trick of going easy on the panicky bride – by 'playing next-door to the spot' (*vicinis . . . locis ludunt*): 'quoth Ovid, "out of place" [*inepta loci*]!' 'It's all the Greeks' fault – writing themselves a blank cheque and passing it off!' (1.2.22). Thus, too, 'Hybreas' lived up to his name and culture by having his cuckold check the lover was a guy, not a dildo, while a speculative compatriot summoned up a shemale fucker . . . And back in the scene with Murredius – *he* quipped, 'just as obscenely' (23): *fortasse dum repellit libidinem, manibus excepit* ('maybe while she fended off his lust, she took it in her hands'). Upon which Seneca rounds:

> longe recedendum est ab omni obscenitate et verborum et sensuum: quaedam satius est causae detrimento tacere quam verecundiae dicere.

---

[26] Cf. 1.*Pr*.15 *quotiens ex intervallo dicebat, multo acrius violentiusque dicebat . . . nesciebat dispensare vires suas, sed inmoderati adversus se imperii fuit . . .* ('Every time he spoke after a time-out, he spoke far more incisively and *powerfully* . . . no idea of how to regulate his strength, his self-control was *unrestrained* . . .'). From the first, declaimers are idiosyncratic eccentrics whose portraits must be caricatures, their quirks of style a gift for Seneca's (to shadow).

[27] See Langlands 2006: 253–64 for detailed analysis of 1.2, 'The Prostitute Priestess'; esp. 257 n. 30, 'he is teetering on the line himself'. For the thesis that Seneca shows violence controlled – 'mediated' through storied verbalization/discussion – see Bloomer 2011: 198.

Back way off. You *must*. Away from all filth, verbal *or* conceptual. Some
things you're better off not saying to the detriment of the case than saying
them to the detriment of propriety. (1.2.23)

Characteristically, this smidgen of explicit expostulation lapses into the let-
down tease of a coda that tugs the rug from under us: 'Vibius Rufus
seemed to have exploited ordinary language but avoided abuse/and fash-
ioned a *bon mot* [*non male dixisse*]': *ista sacerdos quantum mihi abstulit.* ||
('That priestess walked away with all that off me. ||', 23).[28]

But Latro himself led this crudity charge into verbal GBH: 'Reckon
you're a virgin, but manhandled with the world's kisses – even though
you're this side of Ruin (*stuprum*), still you've rolled 'n' tumbled with
guys . . .'.[29] Contrary to a persistent misperception, *he* was a speaker *both*
brave *and* spot-on – 'in fact, if any strong point was his, being spot-on
was'.[30] And no further assault on the girl slips through the net. Nothing to
touch senator X's plunge into deplored folly as the next theme has him
'bounce *the condemned girl*'s doped-up boulder of a body back up off the
rocks' – outdone by lemming copycats with 'a body harder than rock', a
'virgin trampolinist', and 'maybe she'd trained for it, mastered the art of
cadence' . . . (1.3.11). The fact of sniggering mockery of *the hero with no
hands* to grip his 'blade' is *reported*, but not palmed off on us – rather,
fingered as deserving the death penalty (*ridebant adulteri truncas viri fortis
manus, circa sua arma labentis*; . . . *quem adulteri tunc riserunt cum deberent
mori*, 'The adulterers *laughed at* the hero's stump hands fumbling his
weapons'; '. . . the one the adulterers *laughed at* when they ought to have
been dying', 1.4.3). Here Latro evidently counter-attacked with full *repraesentatio* (graphic reportage) of the boy frozen in fright at the primal scene:

> *descripsit* stuporem totius corporis in tam inopinati flagitii spectaculo, et
> dixit: pater, tibi manus defuerunt, mihi omnia. et cum oculorum caliginem,
> animi defectionem, membrorum omnium torporem *descripsisset*, adiecit:
> antequam ad me redeo, exierunt.

> He *described* his whole body frozen at the sight of such an unexpected
> outrage, and said, 'Father, hands let you down, the whole lot let me down.'
> And when he'd *described* the fogged eyes, faint mind, and stunned limbs one
> and all, he added, 'Before I came back to myself, they'd scarpered.' (1.4.7)

---

[28] Punning (on) forensic slang: 'Daylight robbery – I ask you – she *waltzed off* with the case!'
(cf. 2.1.35 *paene causam abstulit*).

[29] 1.2.13 *puta enim virginem quidem esse te, sed contrectatam osculis omnium; etiamsi citra stuprum, cum
viris tamen volutata es.*

[30] 1.Pr.20 *in illo, si qua alia virtus fuit, et subtilitas fuerit*; amplified in 21, and applied to compositional
structure at 1.1.13, *divisio . . . subtil[is]* ('a spot-on analysis').

But *we* are spared the somatic ecphrasis,[31] instead treated to a gallery of 'pretty' variants on the comic situation of the guy 'who couldn't do it', including both the Greek-buster peach, 'When he'd described himself fighting at the front, he said, "Woe's me, the hands that lover-boy escaped!"', and the superlative idiocy of 'I left hands fighting at the front!' (12).

So too the *twice in one night rapist* has his horrific punishment pared down, 'stuck in the public gaze, chopped for ages, and dying all day for offending all night' (1.5.2). Otherwise, we find Latro rooting for 'not pointing straight at everywhere suspicion can be sprayed', matched by Seneca deploring 'Albucius' "Let him mince over to *les boys*" – how no flaw lacks its lover, so there are people to rate this as silver-tongued!' (9). Best friend Latro fittingly brings down the curtain (and the house?) on our serial rapist, with: 'Next he was getting set for No. 3 – only the night ran out! ||' (9).

Contrariwise, *Captain Hook's daughter* fails to ignite, perhaps because 'no tussle has arisen – nearly all agree' (1.6.8). Most notable item? Haterius' neck-tingler beauty of a 'technorama set-piece' (*describere*), hosing out rhetoric 'as if he caught the noise of trouble in the distance – 100% devastation and pillaging, burning farms incinerated, countryfolk running for it . . . – and, when he'd saturated the whole picture with panic, he added, "Why the alarm from you, sonny? It's just your wife's dad on his way!"'[32]

*The killer released by the pirates* makes a perfect invitation to wring the changes on the declaimers' own hand-signals (try gesticulating through 1.7.3),[33] and when it comes to the prosecution case, pa capitalizes by holding up his hands to wallow for our pleasure in imaginary, exhibitionist, masochistic self-mutilation:[34]

> quidquid passus es, quidquid timuisti, patiar: posce flagella, scinde rugas. ustus es? subice ignes, semimortuam hanc faciem, *quae tantum in contumeliam suam spirat*, quia extingui non potest, exure. si parum est, fac quod ais ne piratas quidem fecisse, manus praecide. *exhibeo tibi*. hae sunt illae quae quidlibet scribunt.
>
> hae nempe scripserunt epistulam manus: praebeo; praecide et ale.

---

[31] *Pace* the important dissection of this body as spectacle by Connolly 2009.

[32] 1.6.12 . . . *quasi exaudiret aliquem tumultum, vastari omnia ac rapi, conburi incendiis villas, fugas agrestium; et cum omnia implesset terrore, adiecit: quid exhorruisti, adulescens? socer tuus venit.* At 1.6.10, our friend Gallio fills a gap left by *omnes scholastici* ('pedants united') – as if this declaimer is not one.

[33] Cf. S. Butler 2002 *passim*.

[34] Denigration of the breed of declaimer hits a new low in the minimal note at 1.7.15, 'I recall Sparsus also declaimed in this vein, a sane person among pedants, a pedant among the sane' (*hominem inter scholasticos sanum, inter sanos scholasticum*). How crazy is that – coming from sane-scholar-pedant Seneca?

All you've suffered, your every fear, I'll suffer: call for whips, rip my wrinkles. You were branded? Apply the heat. Take this half-dead form, *that breathes only for its own abuse*, and since it cannot be put out, burn it up. If that's not enough, do what you claim even the pirates didn't – chop off my hands. *I hold them out for you to see* – here are those hands, there's nothing *they* won't write . . .

These hands for sure wrote the letter. I hold them out: chop them off – and feed me. (1.7.9, 10)

By contrast, Book 1's final piece on *the thrice hero* is a vehicle for Roman back-slapping (v. craven Hellenic wimps, 1.8.7, 11, 15) and uplift (Gallio's patriotic paradox from pa, 'This I command, for the republic's sake, for your sake, for my sake . . .', 9). Our first parade bows out at 16 with 'a *sententia* that could be a winner not merely in declamation but even in some more substantial genre of writing', and, *also in Greek*, 'a rather too stratospheric effort for regular civil speech-making – but an exceptionally emotive portrait of a father's consternation', concluding with the befuddled earth-shaker, 'I fear for our planet . . . Son, what's this babble from me?'[35]

The second gathering *will* feature *controversial* melodramas of sadistic drooling over body-tearing and excruciation, on parade at 2.5. Which reads as an invitation to *go there*, pick up on the pleasurable ingenuity of exquisitely gross representation; the opportunity, then, to undercut declamatory extravagance, to condemn the febrile excess of graphic brutality lured out into articulated audibility. Such attention-seeking provocation (featuring no father and no son) is bound to test the limits of the (s)exploitation script. In broaching this traffic within the discursive setting of this Senecan corpus, this essay will be myth-analysing (its) declamatory discussion and exploration of parameters within declamation for licit and transgressive imagination in regard to the practice of verbalized violence in valorized public discourse. (I move.)

In most respects, the host did not break ranks with his declaimers in Book 1. The second preface at once pops up the whipper-snapper *Fabianus philosophus* for its avatar, and his trajectory leads away from debut *in declamando* to fame *in disputando*. Learning to critique his teacher and training taught *him* how to graduate: 'fast'. Jettisoned the hype, clung to the obscurantism, 'all the way to philosophy' (2.*Pr*.1–2).[36] *His* take on

---

[35] These *mots* are preceded by a (Greek) warning to a son in imminent danger (1.8.16): 'A father reads a son's future chances best of everything there is.'

[36] Only negligible hints of division between debater and egghead precede: at 1.3.8, it was a declaimer's denigration to represent a performance as tackling details 'as though philosophical cruces' (*tamquam*

soapbox spiel drives a wedge into the biz. Expect from *this* compilation the counter-attraction of Fabianesque deficiency in combative adrenalin and edge, regularly compensated by the sweet-phrased Jeremiad lambasting Modernity, plus the verbal tsunami for panoramic vistas of planet Earth (2–3).[37] Seneca's readers-in-the-text diverge accordingly: passing *his* declaimer's test 'will suit' Mela, *fili carissime* ('dearest son', 3), 'the senior intellect of the brothers three', 'same as it suited Fabianus' (4). And the *principle* instated here extends wide, wider, widest:

> video animum tuum a civilibus officiis abhorrentem et ab omni ambitu aversum hoc unum concupiscentem, nihil concupiscere. tu eloquentiae tamen studeas: *facilis ab hac in omnes artes discursus est; instruit etiam quos non sibi exercet.*

> I see your temperament as not getting on with public service and incompatible with politicking, with one solid desire – to desire nothing. See you work on your oratory, all the same: *spin-off to all the skills is easy from this one, it tools up even those it's not training for itself.* (2.Pr.3)

Yes, all are welcome to Seneca's holiday camp. Each to his own, satisfaction guaranteed. For the duration, this modulated course will cater for mixed abilities, mixed motives. Turn students on, help them get on, or ... help them turn off.

The promised all-out spree of Fabianus (2.Pr.5), proxy for the Seneca quartet, starts (ahem) promisingly, with 2.1 *rich pa disowning all three sons – then a pauper's son refuses adoption.* Perfect vehicle for the budding philosopher's catascopic panorama and vitriolic pasquinade on Mankind and Strife, Madness and Luxury (2.1.10–13). Uncontentiously conventional stuff – nobody gets hurt – so no call for *divisio*, just lots of ingenuity (nature/nurture/adoption), and (so) extra-prolific coloration (24–32; *Fabianus philosophus* at 25, true to form, *in divitias dixit, non in divitem*, 'spoke against riches, not the rich man').[38] Generous, genial coverage stays in the Fabian groove,

---

*problemata philosophumena*), leading associatively to invocation of 'the will of the gods' and 'the immortal gods' in the next items (9, 10). At 1.7.17, Albucius again, this time the psychoanalyst, 'dragged in a philosophical topos' (*philosophumenon locum introduxit*). The book's penultimate entry at 1.8.16 rose above the genre, 'when he did the set-piece on fortune's unpredictability' (*cum de fortunae varietate locum diceret*).

[37] *quotiens inciderat aliqua materia quae convicium saeculi reciperet, inspirabat magno magis quam acri animo. deerat illi oratorium robur et ille pugnatorius mucro ... locorum habitus fluminumque decursus et urbium situs moresque populorum nemo descripsit abundantius ...* ('Every time any subject cropped up allowing for excoriation of decadence, he heaved with epic rather than acid mentality. He had none of the orator's oak or the classic killer's edge ... nobody *described* more volubly the feel of places, spate of rivers, locations of cities, character of populations ...').

[38] For the rich/poverty-stricken declamatory discourse on Riches/Poverty, see Tabacco 1978.

room for excursus within excursus, on funny (dreamy, suspicious) Iunius Otho, who one time actually *declaimed in open court* against Vallius Syriacus, and now 'reads the newspaper into your ear' (33–9)![39]

In second place, *the spousal suicide pact turns sour* (2.2): plenty of spats – "'I love you more" ... "No, I do" ... "Can't live without you" ... "No, *I* can't without *you*" ... "Our oath was the peacemaker, works every time"' – but nobody dies (2). No call, again, for *divisio*, just scope for fuss over the trouble with oaths. Fabianus has his flicker, but this time he loses out to Ovid, no less (8–12): the king of declamatory elegy and epic (quoted) had started out as fan of Latro, and no mean declaimer – apart from the 'waywardness' (*sine certo ordine*, 9). Which three verses would you erase and he save? (Seneca starts us off with *two*!) So that's *another* way a son could go, after debating society.[40]

Next, *a rapist son drives his dad mad*, licensing lurid vituperation of the victim and impersonation of the demented, offset by plea-bargaining for forgiveness, and remorse (2.3).

In 2.4, *adoption of the orphaned whoreson nephew spells another dad gone mad, claims his other son*, in what opens as a drama of comedic routinization and laddish innuendo, but turns into an entrée for another giant of oratory, and world politics, Messalla. Seneca takes time out (11–12) to satirize the infected carrier and blue-blood Fabius Maximus, 'who first inflicted on the Roman forum this new-fangled disease which now besets it': *haec autem subinde refero quod aeque vitandarum rerum exempla ponenda sunt quam sequendarum* ('I frequently recount these stories because *negative lessons* need laying down just as much as *positive*'). Messalla had jousted with Latro and awarded Fabianus full marks (8, 10); but reality bites hard when Latro's *controversia* 'is counterproductive for counsel not case' (12–13): Augustus and Agrippa are there, see, large as life, so royal family adoption and self-acquired pedigree hang in the air – an accident waiting for a loose gun. Maecenas sees to it that our pal's goose is truly cooked. Seneca ticks off anyone 'who thinks losing their head beats wasting a wisecrack'; but *the point for a Novatus or Seneca Jr.* must be that declamation does not merely lead through the courts to

---

[39] Seneca's narrative descends: Fabianus' antithesis Vibius Gallus at 2.1.25–6, '*en route* between great eloquence and later insanity' (he was to method-act himself into madness): 'like some crooner, he'd tell you over and over when about to describe love, "I want to describe love." He made us hate (the cliché topos of) Riches by chorusing "I want to describe riches"! ... Just a sliver of lunacy ... "I love dad for free"!' At 2.3.19, thunderous applause from the *scholastici* automatically, I think, curls the doyen Pollio's lip.

[40] No lawyer, Ovid, no fear – good grief to his father (*Tr.* 4.10).

court; no, the court and courtiers already drop in for the show, and are liable to drop you in it.

Past our re-fabricated torture-chamber of 2.5, Book 2 will wheel on with *a dad as mad as his lad*. Bitching as usual: so, for example, first Fabianus cashes in some more on his hobby horse: 'Refuse to covet material wealth . . .' (2.6.2), then he scuppers the other side: 'You're sinking the ship – in harbour . . .' (4). The band plays on, to the perfect ending: *rem ab omnibus dictam celerrime Syriacus Vallius dixit: fili, quando vis desinamus?* || ('Vallius from Syria said fastest what everyone said: "Son, when, please, can we stop?" ||', 13).

Just one more, then stop: *the thrice-denied merchant ruined the chaste wife's marriage by leaving her the lot – and witnessing her chastity* (2.7). Uninterrupted coverage of Latro heartily scourging modern sexual *mores*, all the way.[41] But then the paradosis gives up the ghost – after the most sustained cameo in the whole of Seneca *pater*. (*If* we can tell [. . .])

Now. Now for *torta a tyranno pro marito* ('The woman tortured by the tyrant for her husband's sake', 2.5), who comes coated in protective blasé.[42] Arrest is (what else?) a package, a routine:

> (Latro) '*quid moraris? . . . iam exposita tormenta sunt.*'

> *What you waiting for?* The torture kit is *set up for action.* (2.5.1)

We all know tyranny talk:

> (Cestius) *trahebantur matronae, rapiebantur virgines; nihil tutum erat.*

> Respectable wives manhandled, girls raped, nothing safe. (2.5.2; cf. 4)

There is a torture-chamber (standard format). So let rip:

> (Cestius) *inposita in eculeum . . .*

> (Fuscus) *explicatur crudelitatis adversus infelicem feminam adparatus* et *illa instrumenta virorum quoque animos ipso visu frangentia ad excutiendam muliebris pectoris conscientiam proponuntur . . . flagellis caeduntur artus, verberibus corpus abrumpitur exprimiturque ipsis vitalibus.*[43]

> She was stuck on the rack . . .

> The *apparatus* of cruelty is unfurled against the poor woman, *those* proverbial tools that smash even heroes' morale on sight *are set out* for screwing secret knowledge out of a female breast . . . whips slice limbs,

---

[41] See Langlands 2006: 71.

[42] An 'especially vivid [digression]': Sussman 1978: 116. Pagán 2007–8 now brilliantly *teaches* this didactic packaging of torture as representational ambivalence, meshed into traditional Roman reality and not safely contained within fascinating fiction.

[43] Gertz supplies *sanguis* as a normal subject for *exprimitur*, accepted by editors including Winterbottom; but this dulls the Latin just when grotesque violence is on our hands.

beatings snap the body, squeezed out of its own organs. (2.5.3, 4; cf. 8 *caeditur . . . uritur,* 'slashing . . . branding'.)

Give it the works:

> (Hispo) *nullum tormenti genus omisit;* omnia membra laniata, omnes artus convolsi sunt, scissum corpus flagellis, igne exustum, convulsum tormentis.

> He *passed up on no category of torture:* all body-parts butchered, all the limbs torn away, body chopped by whips, branded with fire, torn apart by tortures. (2.5.5)

Pulled out all the stops? Then change the (rhetorical) record:

> (Cornelius Hispanus) adsidue tormenta *variantur;* accenduntur extincti ignes; tortor vocatur sub quo mariti uxores prodiderant.

> The tortures are constantly *shuffled,* fires that have gone out are re-lit, the torturer is called for in whose hands husbands had betrayed wives. (2.5.5)

One more (X-rated) failure:

> (Albucius) vicerat saevitiam patientia; deerat iam sanguis, supererat fides. aliquando proiecta est; deserebatur distortis manibus, emotis articulis; nondum in sua membra artus redierant. *talem* uxorem tortor dimisit ad partum.

> Endurance had sadism licked. Blood was now running out; plenty of faith was still left. Finally she was chucked out and abandoned, with mangled hands, fingers out of sockets, limbs still not back in their joints. *In that condition* the torturer let a wife go, to give birth. (2.5.9)

But for one hustling moment, the visceral sexual sadism at the core of this uxoricidal theme cuts clean through the counterfeit clichés:

> (Gallio) instabat tyrannus: torque: *illa pars* etiam potest; subice ignes: *in illa parte* iam exaruit cruor; seca, verbera, oculos lancina, fac iam *ne viro placeat matrix.*[44]

> No respite from the tyrant: on with the torture. *That bit*'s still working – apply heat; *in that bit,* the blood has dried – carve, beat, razorblade the eyes, see *this womban turns her husband on no more.* (2.5.6)

---

[44] This abusive *matrix* is the one-word condensation that hits the spot, but *covers* the muted theme: 'breeding animal' – 'womb' – '*the body-part* that makes men want, and impregnate, women'. See Pagán 2007–8: 176–8 for Seneca's demolition here of literariness as security blanket. Real Roman students (must) need this lesson: Bernstein 2012. On this (and the) heroic wife of declamation: Larosa forthcoming.

It (this?) triggers, too, a concentrated/expansive page of the gruesome, graphic ecphrasis we have come to expect we shall be spared:

> (Fabianus) *describam nunc ego* cruciatus et *miram corporis patientiam inter tyrannica tormenta saevientia*: extincti sanguine refovebantur ignes; *in hoc desinebatur torqueri aliquando ut saepius posset. exquisita* verbera, lamnae, eculeus, *quidquid antiqua saevitia invenerat, quidquid et nova adiecerat – quid amplius dicam?* et tyrannus torquebat et cum de tyrannicidio quaereret. o nos felices quod nullis exhausta puerperiis fuit! tacuit ac silentio tyrannicidium fecit, certe tyrannicidam. convolsis laceratisque membris nec adhuc sufficientibus non dimissa est ex arce sed proiecta . . .

> *Now let me describe* the agonies, *the miracle of endurance amid tyranny's tortures.* Flames put out by blood were re-kindled, *from time to time came a stop to the torture to make sure it could happen more often. Rustled up* were whips, metal plates, rack, *ancient sadism's every hit, plus modern supplements – why say more?* Not only was a tyrant a-torturing, but his interrogation was on the topic of tyrannicide. How lucky are we that she'd not been worn out by bearing children! She said nothing and by her silence she committed tyrannicide, or at least committed *a* tyrannicide. Limbs torn and chopped to bits and holding up no more, she was, not let go from the castle, but chucked out . . . (2.5.6)

The philosopher warms to scolding 'today's in' Pretty Women (*ut saeculi mos est, 7*); sermonizing that nat(ur)al mystery, fertility; and pressing the husband's outstanding debts – his wife's condition (*publica est*, 'all over the street',[45] 'tortured – and barren', 7). Still he rants in shorthand précis, protectively couched in formulae and layered by self-advertising commentary. And this must be Seneca's proposition: the debater is his own internal policeman. Screening, cutting, masking, muting: this was an institution of *re*clamation, recalling the tongue, recoiling from un~~repression~~.

So the excrescence in 2.5 must be the fault of 'Fabianus'. The caustic frankness of prating from the 'philosophical' tendency. An opening salvo counterbalanced and compensated by the wisdom it fronts. It's Seneca's doing – turning on his topic at this point in the *grand récit*. Factor in the

---

[45] For (doubted) *publica* here (Winterbottom obelizes), cf. Sen. *Ep.* 88.37 *an Sappho publica fuerit, et alia quae erant dediscenda si scires* ('whether Sappho was a people's princess on the streets – and more of the ilk that you'd have to unlearn if you knew it'). Wife was manhandled up to the top of the hill (2.5.1, 3 *bis*), then chucked back down again (6, 9). Now she is stained and profaned by *their* phrase, by *our* gaze. Under denial: *'bene est,' inquit mulier, 'ad stuprum ~~non~~ vocor'* ('"Phew," said the woman, "at least I'm ~~not~~ being called in for defilement"', 1).

temptation to shout for a muted hero(ine).[46] OTT body-ripping rep and mater melodramatics, they are down to transported fantasy. No one, so everyone, shares responsibility for these deep-and-fast metaphorics of gendered violence. It is my fault for hunting down the outer limit to this praxis of Rome, there to turn up the silenced declamatrix.[47]

## Save the Children Fun (Books 3–10: 10.4)

One leg at a time will do nicely. *Controversiae* clocks up plenty more mileage between Books 2 and 10. The hulking star of 3, Cassius Severus, twinned imperious oratory with declamatory mediocrity: the surprise *tour de force* apologia he gave Seneca (3.*Pr*.8–18) espouses specialized excellence, and roundly depreciates chinwag: *in scholastica quid non supervacuum est, cum ipsa supervacua sit?* ('Academia? What's not surplus to requirements there, when that's just what academia *is*?', 12).[48] These shadow-boxers belong in their counterfactual closet, kids' stuff for fans of Cestius – i.e. Seneca's own teacher – above Cicero, 'virtually a species apart' (13, 15, 18).[49]

---

[46] *tacet . . . tacet . . . tacet* ('she is, stays, is, mum', 4; cf. 18). Tyranny (see Dunkle 1967, Tabacco 1985) clamps mouths and wombs. Muttering, mumbling conspirators have their 'babies', their weak spots, their (pre)occupations.

[47] In the 'natural' discourse of birth control, where husbands are not *not* torturer tyrants (*uxor*, passim, cancelled as *infelix*, 3, 4; *inutilis*, 1; *fessa*, 5; *sterilis*, 5, 7, and esp. 13–15; so ~~occupata~~/*vacua*, 4, 9, 14).

[48] Cassius' string of insults includes bilious sarcasm at the *scholastici* and the gauntlet of litigation thrown down for Cestius to run (3.*Pr*.12–17).

[49] The body of Book 3 is known only through meagre excerpts virtually shorn of personnel and bare of editorial input. No sign of sadistic splurge anywhere; but no chance of that. So too Book 4. So too Books 5, 6, 8 – but they lack prefaces too. The *themes* we pretty well know. They comprised/included:
Book 3.1–9:
1,  *a lottery blinding;*
2,  *parricide;*
3,  *(un)fraternal (dis)inheritance;*
4,  *pa disowns his saviour son;*
5,  *the raped daughter kept home by pa;*
6,  *the house burned down with the tyrant inside;*
7,  *the self-harming son handed poison;*
8,  *the immigrant caused a riot that incinerated eleven lads including his son;*
9,  *the slave faces crucifixion for refusing to mercy-kill master.*
Book 4.1–8:
1,  *the mourning pa was forced to party;*
2,  *blinded Metellus cannot serve as priest;*
3,  *the homicide's boy advised his raped sister's suicide;*
4,  *the hero half-inched weapons from a dead hero's tomb;*
5,  *the disowned son healed pa, but won't treat stepmother;*
6,  *two boys, from two mothers – one pa, and he's not telling;*
7,  *the lover caught in flagrante killed the woman's husband the tyrant;*
8,  *the freedman's former owner reneges on the deal struck when he'd lucked out in the civil war.*

If anyone missed this stunt, 4.*Pr.* sets them straight: Seneca is no random jotter – he's the *ringmaster*, running the programme of acts so as to keep punters happy and coming back for more:

> quod munerarii solent *facere*, qui ad *expectationem* populi detinendam nova paria *per omnes dies* dispensant . . . hoc ego *facio*: *non semel omnes produco*; aliquid novi semper habeat libellus . . .

> A regular *ploy* of amphitheatre promoters is to buoy up the crowd's *suspense* by paying out new duellists each and *every day* . . . It's my *ploy*, too. *I don't bring them all on at one go*: a book shall always have something new. (4.*Pr.*1)

For an instant *example*:

> non tamen *expectationem* vestram macerabo *singulos producendo*: liberaliter *hodie* et plena manu *faciam*.

> I'm not going to string you out in *suspense by bringing them on one at a time* – my *ploy* for *today* is to be generous and open-handed! (4.*Pr.*2)

Back we go to the orator, statesman, and reciter Pollio, as the iron man who declaimed three days after his son died; and his opposite, and butt, the out-of-control 'muddy river in spate' Haterius, the declaimer who never got over losing his [son? – the text is uncertain] – which enhanced his potential for pathos, as in his method acting of the piece placed first in the book, where a father mourning three boys is forcibly partied by yob kidnappers (4.*Pr.*6, 11; 4.1).

Book 5 did push ahead, our first excerpt starting: *tres, inquit, liberos perdidi* ("'I", he said, "lost three children"') – but we can only jump to Book 7, where normal broadcasting is resumed.

Book 5.1–8:
1, *the saved suicide who'd lost three children, wife, and ship, knows no gratitude;*
2, *pauper pa returns to find son married to rich enemy's daughter;*
3, *two all-in wrestling brothers die in the ring, and it's pa's fault;*
4, *brother framed for parricide locks brother up;*
5, *moneybags burned pauper neighbour's tree in his way, plus the house;*
6, *raped in drag on a bet, the lad wants to address the public;*
7, *the general locked out the escapee POWs for butchery at the gates;*
8, *the stepped-down tyrant wants to stand for election.*
Book 6.1–8:
1, *father meddles with the legacy as both sons are disowned;*
2, *son shut out pa exiled for manslaughter, daughter let him in;*
3, *pitting half-brother's slave mother against his inheritance;*
4, *the outlawed couple drink poison, but he survives;*
5, *Iphicrates' Thracian bodyguard pressurized the Athenian jury;*
6, *the wife who poisoned daughter engaged to her lover-boy;*
7, *pa lets the son dying of love for stepmother have her;*
8, *what did the Vestal Virgin's poem in praise of marriage mean?*

*Instatis mihi cotidie* ... ('You squeeze me, 24/7', 7.*Pr.*1). No more teasing. The boys want Albucius, and Albucius they shall have. Endlessly rambling, mistimed philosophy, incomplete, unstoppable performances. No rival for Latro or even Fabianus here, the over-egged arguments were 'a drag, never spot-on', and his fatal flaw was to rig every single response to enquiry as a full palaver in its own right: 'No limb is serviceable if it's the same size as the body' (1–2). The portrait is a queen of puddings, mind, pulling magnificent contortions from Seneca's Latinity. Not least, on the theme of Albucius' stunning non-match of shine on shite (3), we learn 'he didn't want to seem a *scholasticus* – or rather, he didn't try not to be a *scholasticus*, only not to seem one!' (4). Like mine, his penchant for vulgarity actually worsened with age. People regretted hearing him, but always wanted to. A grim bag of nerves, he had renounced courtroom reality, ever since he'd had a rhetorical conceit taken at its word, and it cost him the case. But ridicule pursued the refugee into the debating society, where jokerman Cestius first mocked his whimsy, then, when (in the course of the very next theme ahead) he was dying on his feet too, he turned the mockery back on the audience (4–9). In short, Seneca has sunk to making a joke of declamation with jokes about declamation. The boys are taking it all more seriously than pa – so, the question looms, *should they?*:

> video quid velitis: sententias potius audire quam iocos. fiat: audite sententias in hac ipsa controversia dictas.
>
> I see what you boys are after: to hear *mots* rather than jokes. So be it – hear *mots* voiced in this debate. (7.*Pr.*9)[50]

So to it (7.1): *when pa handed one parricidal son to the other to punish, he let him go become a pirate who captured pa and has let him go.* A full company pushes the boat out on this one, and the climax has the native Greek-speaker Cestius stuck for words, caught out trying to do a Virgil – imitating the epic flourish *nox erat* ... ('Nightfall, and ...'), just where Virgil had successfully built on Varro's epic, and Ovid too had seen a way to rethink the Varro phrase (27). So it is that declamation's crossed (s)words start to open out, through bungled debate, to play host to 'literary criticism'.[51] Here hot post-Augustan intertextuality can be caught at the drawing-board stage. Seneca countersigns his first scoop for everybody on their way up to epic, or who never left.

The next theme does the same for (to) Roman historiography. *Once defended by him on a count of parricide, Popillius brought Antony Cicero's head* (7.2). The invitation to enjoy dismembering Cicero in style, limb by rhetorical limb, has but a modest yield:

---

[50] On this, see C. Schneider forthcoming.   [51] See esp. Mannering forthcoming.

(Latro) abscidit caput, amputavit manum, effecit ut minimum in illo esset crimen quod Ciceronem occidit.

(Albucius) caedit cervices tanti viri et umero tenus recisum amputat caput. i nunc et nega te parricidam.

(Capito) fertur adprensum coma caput et defluente sanguine hunc ipsum inquinat locum in quo pro Popillio dixerat.

(Latro) necesse certe non fuit manum caputque praecidere mortuo.

Cut off his head, lopped off his hand, made it so his slightest crime was in killing Cicero.

Hacked the great hero's neck-muscles and lopped off the head, hacked away right to the shoulder. Now try going and saying you're no parricide!

The head is fetched grasped by the hair and as the blood cascades stains the very spot where he'd spoken in defence of Popillius.

One thing's certain: it was *not* mandatory to chop the hand and head off Cicero's corpse. (7.2.1, 2, 7, 9)

Surely no wrangling declaimer worth the name could let this one pass without plunging into a panto season's worth of ghastly gore. Mucky Murredius didn't:

non est passus hanc controversiam transire sine aliqua stuporis sui nota. *descripsit* enim ferentem caput et manum Ciceronis Popillium et Publilia-num dedit: Popilli, quanto aliter reus Ciceronis <tangebas caput> et tenebas manum eius! ||

He didn't let this debate go by without a mark of his gaga self: no, he *described* Popillius fetching Cicero's head and hand, and came out with this Publilius-like offering: 'Popillius, how different the way you touched Cicero's head and held his hand when you were in the dock.' || (7.2.14)

For sure, Cicero's thinking head and writing hand are eternally the essential props for every Roman speaker to mime, and Seneca will from here on station him centre stage, as cult icon, rather than as his own unglimpsed forerunner as Professor of Declamation. The collective imagination in debate, he underlines, has created a Cicero to outbid historians (8). And that is his own preoccupation: the usual filters have axed the butchery, thinned the bloodshed.

*For round four of their feud, the son pours away the poison he's caught mixing, claiming it was meant for himself* (7.3). 'In line with the rest of his gaganess', Murredius repeats the dose of Publilianesque panto (8), this time sparking another 'lit. crit.' debate on the (un)wisdom of improving on *his* pithy/pissy one-liners, as championed by Cassius Severus, implacable enemy of the one-worder – the pun epidemic caught from pre-Publilian mime, spread by Cicero and Laberius, and now pundemic across *tout le monde romain.* (Gasp.) From now on, then, the declaimer's punceptual sound-bite will come complete with built-in sub-literary yardstick:

> Otho Iunius ineptam sententiam videbatur dixisse: non multum interest mea; aut enim me aut filium meum voluit occidere. ||
>
> Iunius Otho seemed to have uttered an incompetent *mot*: 'It doesn't make any odds to me – he meant to kill either me or else my son.' || (7.3.10)

If it were vaudeville, we'd laugh. *Is* declamation so very different?

When *tears of grief for pirated pa blind ma, and son deserts her to ransom him* (7.4), Seneca dredges up thoughts (theory and practice) on 'how to conclude' (5, 6: the *epilogus*). Into the ever-catantiphrastic declamationist memory pops the diminutive figure of Calvus, acerbic orator and miniaturist poet, complete with the demonstration and lesson of Pompey the Great cut down to size in a one-couplet epigram, but a lamb, a smoothie, a girlie, in a famously gentle epilogue: *credite mihi, non est turpe misereri* ('Trust me, there's no shame in pitying') (6–8). Which puts neoteric poetry in the loop, set beside more Publilianesque declamation, such as assorted *sententiae*, from ... the equally diminutive platform-speaker Festus: *'captus est, inquit, pater.' si te capti movent, et haec capta est* ('"My father", he said, "has got robbed." If getting robbed makes you feel for people, well, *she's* robbed, too', 8). A weak play on the phrase *captus oculis* ('robbed of eyesight') which – typically – he marred by (needless) over-explanation. For (enter the paragon) 'a nicely tripping *sententia* has imposed on so many' (10): Latro once upbraided *scholastic* nonchalance in non-attention to such trilling cadences by concluding a passage that surfed the wave with the vacuous *inter sepulcra monumenta sunt* ('among the tombs, there lie monuments/warnings', 10). To ringing applause, and the trap sprung. They'd be slower to clap mindlessly in future, for fear of an ambush!

*Five years old, the witness to pa's murder and ma's battering accuses the live-in manager, who accuses the (step)son renting next-door the other side of the tunnelled-through party-wall* (7.5). Scope for atrocity, 'We watch the sword forced into the heart' (*videmus adactum in praecordia gladium*, 2),[52] but spotlight on 'some prettiness, some, no, bags of, silliness, over the

---

[52] No need to specify *whose* heart here (with Gertz's supplement *in <patris> praecordia*, adopted by Winterbottom).

stepmother's wound' (*circa vulnus novercae quidam belle res dixerunt, quidam ineptas, immo multi ineptas*, 8).[53]

*Lad's dad was mad to wed sis to the slave who did not take up the tyrant's permission to rape her* (7.6) gets hitched to ... philosophical jawing on freedom as social construct (18: Albucius; cf. 20). 'Surprised that all the speakers were *compos mentis* on this one? *They weren't!*' (24).

*The captured general lives long enough on the cross to denounce dad: 'Beware betrayal'* (7.7) prompts denunciation (by Cestius) of the 'echo' cliché that simply cuts a phrase from the theme and pastes it for the finale (19). To one student who started and ended advising Alexander to sail Ocean with 'How long, invincible?', he quipped 'I'll end with you, I'll start from you', and another he rapped with: 'And *you* – how long?' Seneca takes just long enough to explain (20): 'The general must have meant the envoys to think *they* were in danger – *that*, finally, is why he said "Beware betrayal."' ||

Finally, *the rape-victim wants to change plea from marrying the suspect to choosing his execution* (7.8) kicks in with Albucius getting us there:

> *proponite vobis illam* supplici *invisam faciem*, carnificem, securem: hoc semel licere nimium est.

> *Stand up before you all that hateful scene* of execution, the executioner and axe: this being allowed once is too many. (7.8.1)

The rest argue(s) the toss on the rape. But nothing graphic reaches *us*.[54]

'Job done?' Book 9 (pro)poses that Seneca was running a final check to see nothing has passed him by – when the boys came up with Montanus (9.*Pr*.1): 'Keep the names coming.' This Votienus Montanus turn, then, is *their* fault – and he at once earns his *ex*clusion: '*Never once declaimed* for exhibition – or even for exercise!' His explanation releases as fully rehearsed and as fully authorized a declamatory indictment as Seneca can muster. It's 'out to please, not to win. Selling self, not the case. And (so) the flaw

---

[53] First Saenianus, logo for 'diligent idiocy', ships derision (11). Next, 'a grave disease has plagued the *scholastici*' (12–13). Then a string of sound-bites – foul, applauded, inane (and the pantomimic kind) – lapse into aridity and self-confutation from a miserable pair of Greeks (14–15, 'Not one of ours.' ||).

[54] Gutted Book 8.1–6 once handled:

1, *the third son has saved ma, who lost husband and two sons, from the rope, and must now foil her suicidal confession;*

2, *Elis cuts off the sacrilegious temple-robbing sculptor Phidias' hands, and won't pay the insurance;*

3, *a son must marry his brother's widow, but what is pa's game?;*

4, *a suicide is denied proper burial;*

5, *two heroes can't bury their father-son hatchet;*

6, *moneybags took pauper's daughter to wife under duress when castaway on his land: let her choose!*

follows declaimers into the courthouse' (1–2). Without applause for punctuation and propulsion, they deflate under pressure. Why, the story goes (yours to verify) that Latro – yes, Latro, *declamatoriae virtutis unicum exemplum* ('one-and-only paragon of perfection in declamation'), in your own backyard, once boobed in the opening salvo for the defence, thrown by being *en plein air* (3)!

> usque eo ingenia in scholasticis exercitationibus delicate nutriuntur ut clamorem silentium risum, caelum denique pati nesciant.

> To such an extent are talents mollycoddled in academic exercises that they have no idea how to stand racket, hush, mockery, even the sky above. (9.*Pr*.4)

Softie graduates come blinking into the sun (5): 'they need hardening into orators by breaking in with insult after insult, toughen up immature minds wilting through *scholastic* nambying – some *real* work!'[55] Some devil's advocate for the *Controversiae*, this: one over the eight? The spitting image of *contrariness*.

*Cimon has killed his unfaithful wife despite her pa Callias having saved his life* (9.1) works up a fine lather from this remotest of themes, until the final sound-bite se(le)ction delves deeper into the pitfalls of imitation poetics, plagiarism, translation (12–14).[56] The payload (of the fifth-century detour) drops when Fuscus' apologia bundles provocative declamation in with high culture: *multa oratores, historici, poetae Romani a Graecis dicta non subripuerunt sed provocaverunt* ('The orators, historians, and poets of Rome have not stolen but challenged many of the *mots* of the Greeks', 13). Let the big guns roll: Thucydides *reformé* in Sallust? Enter Livy to pick holes in the technique, bitching for Imperial History.[57]

So to Rome and the Republic, with *the proconsul Flamininus inviting a condemned man to a beheading, all to give a whore a thrill* (9.2). With Salome, sadistic spectacle. Surely:

> (Iulius Bassus) inter temulentas reliquias sumptuosissimae cenae et fastidiosos ob ebrietatem cibos modo excisum humanum caput fertur; inter purgamenta et iactus cenantium et sparsam in convivio scobem humanus sanguis everritur.

> (Fulvius Sparsus) contactam sanguine humano mensam loquor, strictas in triclinio secures.

---

[55] The fulmination fades all too soon/late: in lacuna [...

[56] The currency and fuel of Senecan declamation: see Bloomer 1997a: 142–53, 'Declamatory [Im]propriety'.

[57] Livy will butt in again, dogmatic on *oratory*, at 9.2.26.

(Florus) refulsit inter privata pocula publicae securis acies; inter temulentas ebriorum reliquias humanum everritur caput.

Midst sottish relics of a bankrupting banquet, food squeamish through drunkenness, a fresh chopped human head is brought in. Midst refuse, stuff chucked by banqueters, and sawdust carpeting the dining-room human blood gets swept up.

A table polluted by human blood is my theme, naked axes in the dining-room.

Midst private goblets flashed the edge of the public axe. Midst drunkards' sottish relics a head is swept away, a human head. (9.2.4, 5, 24)

Truly, Montanus' (superfluous) gathering is where Roman declamation definitively curdles. Seneca lets us savour just these nauseating gobbets of drivel, concentrating instead on letting us know how good this theme *was* to salivate with: we are told how Albucius *video*ed *praetorem amatorem, scortum avidum caedis* ('lover mayor, hooker thirsty for slaughter', 7). See the prisoner stood up before the governor's gaze, thinking he's to be freed and thanking him for it, while diners weep or giggle, and the order comes to stand still and keep a stiff neck, while glasses are primed (7–8). Learn that Capito 'described the so very different scene when there's a proper public chopping in the forum. *Not* my description of a joke at a feast!' (10). Plenty was said back, both good and rotten (21–2): 'in the description of the execution, anyway, those who wanted to echo all the execution phraseology in their *sententiae* fell into one flaw or another'. His old buddy must save Latro from being saddled with Florus' stinking *sententia*. Instead:

> ille, cum in hac controversia *descripsisset* atrocitatem supplicii, adiecit: *quid exhorruistis*, iudices? meretricios lusus loquor.
>
> In this debate, when he'd *described* the brutality of the execution, he added: '*Why'd you shudder*, gentlemen of the jury? I tell of call-girl fun and games.' (9.2.24)

But vulgarity rules in these parts, and it's not Seneca's job to cover up the lunacy. Now the time has come to say it loud:

> omnia autem genera corruptarum quoque sententiarum de industria pono, quia facilius et quid imitandum *et quid vitandum* sit docemur exemplo.
>
> I stick in all known species of depraved *mot* on purpose. Why? Because we're taught by example more easily what to copy *and what to avoid.* (9.2.27)

Aggravated taste lives here: more from nutty Saenianus – and notice of a 'long description' from him (28: cut). Greek bullet-points quietly close down this grab-bag of nails in declamation's coffin. Had almost enough?

*Will the father who abandoned the baby boys give one to the father who saved both their lives?* (9.3) works Cestius into bossing further rumination on translation, imitation, and pupils *apeing* teacher (12). *The tyrannicide who had gone along with whipping pa's ass when brother jumped to his death should instead forfeit his hands* (9.4) invites demonstrative father-beating to a tyrant coach's satisfaction:

> (Triarius) haec vulnera *quae in ore videtis meo* postea feci quam dimissus sum.
>
> (Iulius Bassus) conpressas fili manus in os meum inpegi, caedentem consolatus sum.
>
> (Blandus) [manus] tenent *ecce* cruentum tyranni caput; nunc illas praecidite.
>
> (Cestius) tyrannus iubet caedere, *exposita tormenta sunt; quid faciat?*

> These wounds *you see on my face* I caused after I was let go.
>
> My son's clenched fists I slammed into my face, me consoling him slashing.
>
> [The hands] – *see* – hold the tyrant's bloody head: now go lop them off.
>
> The tyrant ordered him to get slashing, *the tortures were out on parade: what could he do?* (9.4.1, 3, 4, 16)

That is all the haul we are vouchsafed. (How they *must have* hammed!) Attention detours instead to tales of inveterate jokester Asilius Sabinus (17–21). On his feet here, in the dock, from his cell – still wisecracking among the Sejanus mob of billionaires behind bars: 'Send me to break rocks – no break, and doesn't rock!' (*in lautumias . . . minime lauta res*, 21). It's debating today, debacle tomorrow.

*Two sons are dead, the third kidnapped by his mother's father for safe-keeping* (9.5) tries gramps *de vi* ('for GBH'), but ends up molesting your very own Montanus, Scaurus' 'Ovid among orators', for his 'fatal flaw – magnified when debating' (15–17): *iteration*. And declamation – I repeat, *Declamation* – gets *its* own back, big time:[58]

---

[58] Seneca's counter-offensive first recalls the telltale figure of *kuklos*: <u>erras</u>, inquit, pater, et vehementer <u>erras</u> ('you're wrong, pa, and way wrong at that', 16). Seneca's counter-offensive then repeats the telltale figure of *antimetabole*: quos perdidisti non quaeris, quem quaeris non perdidisti ('the ones you've lost you're not looking for, the one you're looking for, you haven't lost', 16). Make no mistake, memory is all re-call, in the round – *la recherche de non perdu*.

memini illum ... non fuit contentus; adiecit ... etiamnunc adiecit ... ne sic quidem satiare se potuit; adiecit ... et plura multo, quae memoria non repeto ... et alia plura ... adiecit ...

idem in hac declamatione fecisse eum memini ... deinde ... deinde ... deinde ... et deinde ... et deinde ... repetendo ... non est contentus unam rem semel bene dicere ... ne multa referam quae Montaniana Scaurus vocabat, uno hoc contentus ero ... poterat hoc contentus esse; adiecit ... nec hoc contentus est; adiecit ...

I remember he ... wasn't satisfied: he added ... now he also added ... even so he couldn't glut himself: he added ... and much much more than I recover from memory ... plus more different points ... he added ...

I remember he did the same thing in this debate ... then ... then ... then ... and then ... and then ... by repeating ... he wasn't satisfied to say one thing once well ... not to repeat the many things Scaurus would call 'Montanusesque', I'll be content with just this one ... he could have been content with this: he added ... he wasn't content with this: he added ... (9.5.15–16, 16–17)

*Enfin*, Seneca seizes the chance to enact, and portend, termination:

aiebat autem Scaurus rem veram: non minus magnam virtutem esse scire dicere quam *scire desinere*. ||

Scaurus used to speak this truth: it's no less great a virtue to know how to speak than to *know how to stop*. || (9.5.17)

But not yet content Seneca passes up t/his chance to finish: *he* adds.

One more stepmother to torture. And a stepdaughter for the chop: *Was the stepdaughter her mother's accomplice in poisoning pa's son?* (9.6) reveals-reveils-relives-reviles-relieves Latro's tableau of shame:

dixerat, *cum descripsisset tormenta*: instabam super caput non accusator sed tortor; ipse ignes subiciebam, ipse ad intendendum eculeum manus admovebam. ego non bibam sanguinem istius, non eruam oculos?

He'd said, *in describing the tortures*: 'I stood over her head as torturer not prosecutor. 'Twas I brought the flames underneath her, 'twas I set hands to stretch the rack. Shall I not drink her blood, gouge her eyes out?' (9.6.18)

To wind up, we get to catch Gallio pushing speculation at breaking-point:

fortasse, inquit, hanc nominavit ut veros conscios celaret, fortasse ut, quia acerrume instabat accusator, hoc metu territus finem tormentis inponeret, fortasse nimio dolore tormentorum stupefacta nescit quid loqueretur.

'Maybe', he said, 'she named her to hide the true accomplices. Maybe, as the prosecutor was pressurizing with maximum pain, to scare him this way

and so bring the torture to an end. Maybe frazzled by too much hurt from
the tortures she didn't know what she was saying.' (9.6.20)

Amen. Seneca's *storyline*, however, uncorks Montanus one last time, 'most
elegantly deriding the botchery of the rhetoricians': '"Mummy, what *is*
poison?" went the kindergarten's infantile refrain!' (10).

The barrel is scraped, the dregs drained. Seneca has had enough second
childhood, and says so. But . . . – by way of a tenth preface:

> quod ultra mihi molesti sitis non est . . . fatebor vobis, iam res taedio est . . .
> iam me pudet, tamquam diu non seriam rem agam.
>
> No call for you guys to bother me further . . . I'll admit to you, this stuff's a
> bore . . . I'm now ashamed for spending so long on something so short of
> seriousness. (10.*Pr*.1)

A little of the scholastic goes a long way, he determines, so one last request,
and he will have 'told his truth, whole, and nothing but' (1).[59] First pick in
the game, and lesson, of reluctance will hit on – irrelevance! (2). Two sorts:
'(a) the outlived; (b) the familiar', e.g. the wasted talent Scaurus, lucky his
speeches were burned by decree (2–3). Hard to disappoint himself, but he
managed it. But then there's mad-dog Labienus-Rabienus, for whom
Imperial book-burning was actually invented (5–7: 'rehabilitated later,
when used on its inventor'). So *Cicero* got lucky, proscribed, but still in
circulation, declaims Seneca with gusto, finally presented with a fit cue for
outrage at *crudelitas* and *saevitia*. For *Controversiae*, the casually introduced
Labienus proves in fact to incarnate the project (7–8): a memory to
memorialize, of a hero who entombed himself so as not to outlive his
incinerated work, who left a legacy of history only to be read after his
death, who now lives on animating Seneca's every memoir.[60]

---

[59] Fordyce 1938 spotted Seneca's courtroom wording here, as he asseverates all he has said in Books
1–9 – and all he will have said in 10.

[60] The 'Timagenes' digression at 10.5.22 will dwell some more on book-burning and history in
conflict with autocracy. But the sequel of *Suasoriae* (two books to make an 'epic' dozen? Or more –
so, e.g., Migliario 2007: 45, but *Suas.* 6.27 suggests a single book) has been signalled long since
(2.4.8), and here horizons open wider still and wider:

> *Suas.* 1, *world-conquering Alexander faces Ocean* (with Roman civil war stories inset, 5–7);
> *Suas.* 2, *Leonidas at Thermopylae faces Xerxes;*
> *Suas.* 3, *Agamemnon becalmed at Aulis faces Iphigenia;*
> *Suas.* 4, *Alexander faces Babylon – and a warning;*
> *Suas.* 5, *Athens faces Xerxes – again.*

In the end, Rome takes over:

> *Suas.* 6, *will Cicero face Antony on his knees?;*
> *Suas.* 7, *Cicero faces Antony – his books or his life?*

Next, Musa. For there *is* another next. Now Musa is another case of (b), the already familiar, wheeled on for his put-down *just* when Seneca has declared, as if drawing a line, 'Nothing left to declare!' (9). Musa (Mela must take it on the chin) was the limit, beyond bearing. The boys inflicted him on broad-minded pops, so if he ever did say anything tolerable (not much) – *they* can supply it! The new deal doesn't stop Seneca running down his list some more, though. Moschus: spoiled himself, everything a conceit (beyond metaphor, *bad*), ace at the nailing insult that stuck; Sparsus: gruffian and wannabe Latro; Bassus: Sparsus' eloquent rival, vinegary and graceless poseur of a mock-orator; turns out to be another (b), so maybe that's three in a row, plus Capito – that pseudo-Latro from 7.2 above – . . . makes four?

He hasn't lost his touch. Seneca's Capito pulls us onto a punch from nowhere, for with the small talk in the listing – *bona fide scholasticus erat* . . . – we learn that on his day Capito *'belongs ahead'* of all the declaimers in the book bar the leading quartet (. . .*praeferendus*, 12). 'What *leading quartet* is that?', he has the boys ask. Handing out the prizes at the end, to the Big Four of Latro (gets the glory), Fuscus, Albucius, and Gallio (gets the win), is

More (and more) scornful tales of our posse of mad, foolish declaimers (Romans, Greeks, but forget the Spanish contingent – Latro and Gallio, etc., of course, apart). An inside line goading the boys on: *Suas.* 1.16, 2.10, 2.21–3 ('. . . when you reach my age; but in the meantime, I have no doubt the flaws that will irk will now delight you'), 3.7, 4.5 ('You're such pains about *Fuscus, Fuscus, Fuscus* . . . I'll tip his flourishes over you') (see Sussman 1977; cf. 6.16, 6.27). But most decisive, *the point* of *Suasoriae* will be to push the capacity of declamation to interface with the grand world of the imperial library the whole way and up front: (a) Epic: 'the worst rot since men lost their minds' was a Homeric allusion: cue Maronolatry (*Suas.* 1.12–13; cf. 2.20, 3.4–5, 4.4–5); Pedo's *Ocean-going* page beats the declaimers hands down (quoted in full, 1.15; cf. Cornelius Severus' tribute to Cicero, 6.26); (b) History/Oratory: 'a historian booby', this time (2.22); 'a gem worthy of inclusion in history or oratory' (5.8). Cicero recycled for counselling Cicero sparks a takeover of declamation by historians memorializing him (6.14–27, reclaimed by Roller 1997, Kaster 1998, esp. 254, Richlin 1999, S. Butler 2002): whence the theme of 7 (6.14; cf. Migliario 2007: 121–49). With this 'metapoetic' finale, as anticipated at *Controv.* 10.*Pr*.5, on Rabienus, *res nova et invisitata supplicium de studiis sumi* ('a first for modernity: punishment exacted from representation'), the entire Declamation narrative comes full circle back to Seneca's initial role as 'continuator' of Cicero (cf. Wilson 2008), only now his task is to push readers on past argy-bargy, and aim higher. A surreal envoi gaily entraps the boys, *and tells 'em so*: 'As I've happened on *Suasoria* 6, I think it's OK [*non alienum!*] to point up how historians handled his memory . . . Don't frown, I'll make it up to you. But . . . maybe . . . I'll manage . . . once you've read these diamond gems . . . to get you away from the *scholastici*. As I shan't get there straight up, I'll have to trick you, (very) like somebody getting medicine down the kids' necks. So. "Raise your glasses, please!" . . . (*Thinks afterwards*) If I stop here, though, I know you're going to stop reading back where I quit the *scholastici*. So. To get you to feel like unrolling the book right to the end . . . I'll add a piece, just like the *Suasoria* next door!' (*Suas.* 6.14, 16, 27, Baraz forthcoming; cf. Bloomer 2011: 316). Thus (from the hearse's mouth): *will Cicero burn his boats or his books?* is only there as bait to get readers to plough through the grand Obits of History to the bitter end. Just so long as the feel of the volume tells you there's one more treat to come, *anything* would do the trick . . . And it has. Just as, at this pyre to share with his *alter ego*, Seneca fades (. . . on us, at 27). [. . .

no casual afterthought, and at once readers are told plainly to 'rank the rest as you see fit: *I have put them all in the palm of your hand*' (13). So at the last gasp, this ultimatum of an editorial contrives a postscript injunction to (have) read these compilations *together*, as a single running competition between contenders for All-Time Champ of Declamation.[61]

Meritocracy was the contract, all along. The flip side? No use for mediocrity. 'Paternus, Moderatus, Fabius, and the like are surplus to requirements' (13). Now the boys have had their fill of Seneca –

– there is one more request to deal with. *This time*, his own ... *More* 'declaimers you never knew'. Neither (a)s nor (b)s, but no stars of *Roman* Declamation. No. *Their* claim to fame is that they have been cheated of it. *Not* by lack of talent, but by *geography* (*defuit* ... *locus*). Here Book 10 commits, and shows its hand: it will be a *Spanish* supplement.[62] Did we never spot how Seneca was holding out on us all along? Holding back, along with traces of those mediocre *refusés* just noticed in order to give them their notice, all mention of Gavius Silo, who comes with Augustus' recommendation, and of Turrinus Clodius, who listened hard to Latro, took no risks, and revived his household from civil war setback to climb the social Everest (*ita ad summam ... dignitatem ut, si quid illi defuerit, scias locum defuisse*, 'so to the highest ... office – if he had anything missing, bound to be geography missing', 16).[63] Now's when Seneca will return to his roots in order to write the future. *The empire strikes back*. In the end, 'We shall find these provincials' *sententiae* are ~~not~~ showcased out of warped judgement or overdone devotion – a match for the biggest names' best, if not belonging ahead' (*aut pares ... aut praeferendas* ‖). Now Turrinus' son can match his cagey father's rise, *if* he goes for it (*adulescens summae eloquentiae futurus nisi ... ad summa evasurus iuvenis nisi ...*, 'a lad destined for the top, eloquence-speaking, but for ... sure to scale the heights, but for ...', 14, 16). And *he is, always has been, Seneca's fourth son: cuius filius fraterno vobis amore coniunctus est ... filius quoque eius, id est meus – numquam enim illum a vobis distinxi ...* ('his son is linked to you

---

[61] By contrast, considered as a unit of composition in its own right, each piece has *always* contrived to secure progression through the narremes sequenced by the theme, distributed among its multi-author co-operative of fragmented narrators at each other's throats.

[62] See esp. Migliario 2007: 11–31, stressing the 'sociology' of the declamatory community and the ongoing and retroactive figured relationship of their busyness to Roman politics (with Henderson 2010).

[63] The civil wars that kept Seneca from getting to Cicero (1.*Pr*.11) also brought Spain into the Roman world, with Pompey's son at Munda and Julius Caesar billeted *chez* the Turrini – and now Augustus regularly sits in at Tarraco declamations (*Suas*.1.5; *Controv*. 10.*Pr*.16, 14): the sob story of 10.3 will register there, as everywhere in the (Roman) world.

boys by a brother's love . . . and his son, too – *my* son, that is – you see, I've never split him from you . . .', 14, 16).

In *this* leading quartet, there may be another Novatus or Seneca in the making – '*if* he chooses to chase all he can get rather than apply all he has' (14) – or else there may be a second Mela – '*if* he is content with modest means, and so in with a good chance of satisfaction guaranteed for modest desires' (16). Just as Seneca overcame geography to write declamation for Rome, so his Clue to Success in Latin will see his extended family of readers climb whatever peaks they choose. Spaniards growing up on the *Declamationes* will be no also-rans in some afterthought supplement. Never again. Seneca will have fixed that, for the empire (of Quintilian and Martial, and of Trajan and Hadrian).[64]

Within Book 10, metropolitans – Big Four and the rest – and proud provincials share the autocue, at *unspecified location, location, location.*[65] And that's the point, as the sequence unfolds (10.1–6):

> 1, *the pauper's son stalks pa's loathed moneybags to ruin his chances with the voters;*
>
> 2, *court rules son the greater hero, pa disowns him;*
>
> 3, *brother claims dad was mad to tell sis go hang for coming home as a civil war widow, after sticking by her husband on the other, losing, side – she did, at the front door;*
>
> 4, *exposed babes are collected, maimed, and sent out to beg – proceeds to go to their saviour;*
>
> 5, *Parrhasius bought a POW to model for a painting of Prometheus' pain to hang in the temple of Athena – he died for Art;*

and finally (just a start is preserved, 10.6):

> *the thief who stole proof of treason is debarred from addressing the assembly.* [. . .

Hammed-up horrorshow is barely notified (as usual) at 10.3.3:

> (Sparsus) filia ante limen paternum in cruore suo volutatur. *quid exhorruistis?* paterna satisfactio est.

> The daughter before her father's threshold rolls in her own blood. *Why'd you shudder?* This is to satisfy a father.

---

[64] In Seneca's world, where *our* Latro and *our* Gallio hold court, backed up by Cornelius Hispanus and Statorius Victor, the Greeks have had their day (see esp. 10.4.18, 21; 10.5.19–28, esp. the sarcastic close on *Greek Art* . . .!). There to improve and eschew, they tail off at the back, barely a whimper between them. (Or so the paradosis leaves us to conclude.)

[65] Silo: 10.2.7, 16; 10.3.14; 10.4.7; 10.5.1. Turrinus: 10.1.5; 10.2.5–6, 10, 14; 10.3.2, 9, 12, 14; 10.4.6, 16; 10.5.2; 10.6.1.

But our *Death Drawing Class* gloats *much* more like the heart's still in it:

> (Gavius Silo) caeditur: 'parum est' inquit; uritur: 'etiamnunc parum est';
> laniatur: 'hoc ... nondum [satis est]'.

> (Argentarius) aiebat tortoribus: 'sic intendite, sic caedite, sic *istum* quem
> fecit cummaxime *vultum servate*, ne sitis ipsi exemplar.'

> (Musa) *narraturus sum* Olynthi senis ignes, verbera, tormenta ... pinge
> Philippum crure debili, oculo effosso, iugulo fracto, per tot damna a dis
> immortalibus tortum.

> (Sparsus) *statuitur* ex altera parte Parrhasius cum coloribus, ex altera tortor
> cum ignibus, flagellis, eculeis ... 'torque, verbera, ure': sic iste carnifex
> colores temperat.

> (Hispo) ignis, ferrum, tormenta: pictoris ista an Philippi officina est?

> He's slashed: 'Not enough', he says. He's branded: 'Still not enough.' He's
> butchered: 'This? Still not [enough].'

> He'd say to the torturers, 'Stretch him like so, slash him like so, *keep the face
> he's making* looking exactly like so – or *you*'ll be modelling for me.'

> *I shall now tell the tale* of an old man from Olynthus' fire, beatings,
> torture ... Picture Philip, one leg useless, an eye gouged out, throat
> shattered – racked by the immortal gods through this catalogue of loss.

> On one side *is posed* Parrhasius plus palette, on the other the torturer plus
> heat, whips, racks ... 'Rack, beat, brand' – that's how that executioner
> blends paint.

> Fire, steel, torture kit: is this a/the painter's workplace – or (a) Philip's?
> (10.5.1, 3, 6, 9–10, 23)

But we know (we're told) we've been spared both *descriptio picturae* and
*descriptio tormentorum* (23, 26), and twinning of this snuff techno piece
with its ~~Dickensian~~ predecessor (same *actio*, with 5.7 alone in Seneca; plus
back-reference at the *divisio*, 10.5.13) serves to underline the relative
restraint – yes, *restraint* – of this reportage, sticking to the restricted palette
of 'torturer's apprentice' formulae featured in 2.5.[66]
    It's Seneca's doing – turning on the fresh infusion of Spanish steel at
this point in his *grand récit*. Factor in the temptation to shout for
silenced waifs. OTT body-ripping rep extends imported fantasy into a
frightful supplement. This textual violence is your fault for reading this
far. For *a Fagin gone to the bad twists his dodgers for Cripplegate* (10.4)

---

[66] See Morales 1996 for excruciation.

in-controvertibly cries out for artful *repraesentatio* (graphic writing), as
Seneca notes:

> (Bassus) *intuemini* utramque partem, et ei succurrite quae miserabilior est.
> *liceat videre* mercedarios tuos: hic caecus est, hic debilis, hic mutus.

> Cassius Severus dixerat: *ostende* nobis captivos <tuos>. Iulius Bassus
> dixerat: *ostende* mercedarios tuos. Labienus commodius videbatur dixisse:
> *ostende* nobis alumnos tuos.

> *Gaze upon* both sides and assist the one that is the more pitiful. *Allow us to
> see* your financial backers: this person's blind, this one's a cripple, this
> one's dumb.

> Cassius Severus had said, '*Show* us your prisoners', Iulius Bassus, '*Show* us
> your backers'; Labienus seemed apter when he said, '*Show* us your mouths
> to feed.' (10.4.5, 25)

A custom-built vehicle for ecphrastic horrorshow:

> (Vibius Gallus) *intuemini debilia infelicium membra* nescio qua tabe con-
> sumpta, illi praecisas manus, illi erutos oculos, illi fractos pedes. *quid exhorres-
> citis?* sic iste miseretur. tot membra franguntur ut unum ventrem impleant . . .

> (Latro) cum *descripsisset* debiles artus omnium et alios incursantes, alios
> repentes, adiecit: *pro di boni!* ab his aliquis alitur integer?

> *Gaze upon the poor creatures, their useless limbs*, perished through some pox,
> hands lopped off *him*, eyes gouged out of *him*, feet smashed on *him*. *Why'd
> you shudder?* This is how he expresses pity. All these limbs smashed to fill
> one stomach . . .

> Once he'd *described* the useless limbs of them all, some dashing up, others
> crawling, he added: '*Good gods!* Somebody in one piece getting fed by *this
> lot?*' (10.4.3, 21)[67]

Latro at once heralds 'sadistic inventiveness' (*crudelitas . . . novo more*, 1),
and it falls to Severe, lean and hungry, Cassius Severus this time to be
caught on tape chilling spines with a hideous page to put us through the
fiendish mutilation of the foundlings, in an opening salvo which will prove
to broach fundamental principles of humanity and community, while
harbouring hypocrisy and callosity. In all its gory:[68]

---

[67] Cf. 10.4.3 *eruantur, inquit, oculi illius, illius praecidantur manus* ('"Have *his* eyes gouged out," he
said, "have *his* hands lopped off"'); 10.4.5 *deme huic oculos, illi manus* ('Take away this one's eyes,
that one's hands').
[68] Cf. Fairweather 1981: 280 for the rhetorical techniques.

hinc caeci innitentes baculis vagantur, hinc trunca bracchia circumferunt, huic convulsi pedum articuli sunt et extorti tali, huic elisa crura, illius inviolatis pedibus cruribusque femina contudit: aliter in quemque *saeviens ossifragus iste* alterius bracchia amputat, alterius enervat, alium distorquet, alium delumbat, alterius diminutas scapulas in deforme tuber extundit et *risum in crudelitate*[69] *captat. produc*, agedum, *familiam* semivivam, tremulam, debilem, caecam, mancam, famelicam; *ostende nobis* captivos tuos. *volo* mehercules *nosse illum* specum tuum, *illam* humanarum calamitatium officinam, *illud* infantium spoliarium. *sua cuique calamitas tamquam ars adsignatur.* huic recta membra sunt, et, si nemo naturae . . .[70] proceritas emicabit: ita frangantur ut humo se adlevare non possit, sed pedum crurumque resolutis vertebris reptet. huic [. . .][71] extirpentur radicitus. huic speciosa facies est: potest formonsus mendicus esse; reliqua membra inutilia sint, ut Fortunae iniquitas in beneficia sua *saevientis* magis hominum animos percellat. *sine*[72] *satellitibus tyrannus calamitates humanas dispensat.*

Over here the blind wander propped on sticks, there they cart round arm stumps, this one has torn feet-joints and ankles screwed out of sockets, this one has legs shattered away, that one's feet and legs are undamaged, but he crushed the thighs. Finding different *sadisms* for each individual, *this bone-breaker* chops arms off one and severs the sinews of a second's, rips one apart and castrates another, hammers somebody's squashed shoulder blades into an ugly hump, and *goes for laughs over a case of brutality. Bring on* – just do it – *the family staff,* half-alive, shivering, useless, blind, crippled, starving. *Show us* your prisoners. *I want* for Chrissake *to know intimately that* cave of yours, *that* workplace turning out ruination of human beings, *that* yard for stripping baby carcasses. *Each one has his own ruination assigned him, as if this were a craft*: this one has straight limbs and if no one [does anything to] the way he's growing, towering height will shoot up: so have them smashed so he can't lift himself up off the ground but will crawl round once we've undone the sockets of his feet and legs. Whereas this one [. . .] – get them pulled out by the roots; and this one has a good-looking face, potential there for a beaut beggar, but the rest of the limbs shall be useless so that Fortune's injustice, so *sadistic* against her own blessings, will slam humanity's minds all the more. *The tyrant with no bodyguard metes out ways to ruin human beings.* (10.4.2)

The incorporated ameliorations here include self-labelling as a freak variant on the topos of atrocity, and as *locus horridus* designed to generate fantasy re-designation, in both respects spinning the writing as but a rhetorical routine. One sop is assimilation to the comedic turn of bringing on a line-up of 'mangy' slaves for an earful – a volley of abusive depersonalization, in a

---

[69] Winterbottom prints *e crudelitate* (Gertz), which would slightly alter the 'point' here.
[70] Text uncertain here. Winterbottom prints Müller's *moratur* for *naturae*; I welcome aposiopesis.
[71] Text uncertain here.
[72] No need for Bursian's conjecture <*sic*> *sine*, adopted by Winterbottom.

predicative spree that gets from *family* to *famished* in six moves and as many words – half-dead, quivering, weak at the knees, can't see what's coming, helpless, and hungry for more? – ; another is final affiliation of *this* verbal 'cave', *this* rhetorical 'factory', *this* declamatory 'unit for corpse-stripping used baby gladiators', to that old stand-by, 'the tyrant's castle'. But the frivolity is (also) worn on the sleeve, first poetically imagining a flight-of-fancy caption for 'today's sadist' as no mere hawkish bird of prey but 'literally the first osprey worthy of its name of "bone-breaker" (ossifrage)'; then displaying 'laugh-in' gusto – 'What's up? Got the hump?' – so openly that we'll overlook it; and finally giving it up for the disfigured set-piece as the ~~forbidden~~ fruit of ~~perverse~~ 'desire' for ~~bad~~ 'knowledge'.

First, we got a grotesque pair of lame props – 'the *blind*, on crutches?' Whatever next? 'Armless kids waving stumps – look, no hands'; but then, most bruising of all, were the purple passage's *pièces de résistance*, the ~~clinical~~ anatomization of mutilation.[73] Precision body-mapping lumped this nobbled ward caught full of wards of court into a single body scheduled for systematic dismemberment. Rhetorical articulation moves us limb by limb down through that first sentence, as surgical dislocation tears limb from limb upwards – from feet, ankle, shin, thigh, arm, groin, shoulder, to … kaput. Captious and captivated alike cop the assignment without mincing of words: the patients were treated with 'a customized *technology* of affliction', and we are treated to a sensitized *artistry* of inflection fit to challenge the brushstrokes (of a Parrhasius, as in 10.5). Fiends are the original ergonomists, so 'the tall will crawl, the [ ] vanish without trace, the disabled body highlight a pretty face'. This crack-pot audit pays out a jack-pot for every punter. This game show plays self-appointed ~~god~~ – all this '*without* a despot's squad of minders'.

It got everybody talking, so it was uncharitable of Seneca to flash up just Labienus' *sententia* for re-run:[74]

> sedet ad cotidianum diurnum et mendicantium quaestus *recognoscit*: 'tu hodie minus attulisti: cedo lora; gaudeo me non omnes emancasse. quid fles? quid rogas? plus rettulisses si sic rogasses.'

> He sits beside his daily chart and runs over the beggars' takings: 'You brought in less today: gimme the belt; so glad I didn't lame the lot of

---

[73] For detailed (fiendish) ana-lysis of the representation of such morselization, see Kennedy, Chapter 7 below.

[74] It *shouldn't* come as a shock when Sententica winds the piece down with some choice persecution of the Greeks for passing on the foul taste of their conceits (19–25). Translates into Latin all too easily – 'anything that can be well said speaks across linguistic frontiers' – but Latin has tighter controls (23).

you. Why you crying? You begging or what? You'd have fetched back more
if you'd begged like that.' (10.4.24)

*Isn't it a pity* charity culture is like that. Patriotic icons are for cashing in
(ask any Victorians, no don't),[75] but underage suffering jerks tears and
dollars best on a universal basis. Common humanity begging LOUD for
attention. Yes, it's a worldwide scandal. Exposed for a start by Latro:

> aestimate quale sit scelus istius, *in quo laesi patres*, ne liberos suos aut
> agnoscant aut recipiant, *etiam confessas iniurias tacent.*
>
> Reckon up what sort of crime is his, *in which victim fathers keep mum about
> even confessed crimes* so they don't have to recognize, let alone retrieve,
> their kids. (10.4.1)

The case is brought in the name of society; it indicts society (18, 'today's'
hush-up 'vice' of displacing *saeculi vitia* from attention). Giving this traffic
in misery the publicity it courts damages the public courts and the city by
prosecution for damaging society. An issue of public welfare (11, 16).
Exposé of exposure puts parents in the dock, guilty of buying off their
guilt. A social conscience should recognize no mechanism for writing off
human life. 'A fate worse than death' is a ready phrase (3, 4, 7), but are
these crippled beggars crippled to beg worse off than any gladiator, any
prostitute (11)? Brats. In a busy world, no time to stand and stare,
certifying non-persons is a licence not to care:

> vacare homines huic cogitationi, ut curent quid homo mendicus inter men-
> dicos faciat! . . . *curare vobis in mentem venit* quis ex solitudine infantes
> auferat perituros nisi auferantur; non curatis quod [V], non curatis quod [X]:
> in mentem vobis venit misereri horum quod [Y]; quidni *illorum* quod [Z]?
>
> To think there are people with spare time for meditating on this, on bothering
> with what a beggar does among beggars! . . . It's entered your minds to bother
> who's removing babes from where they're abandoned, on their way to death
> if not removed: when *you aren't bothered* by W, *you aren't bothered* by X,
> and it has entered your minds to take pity on this lot, because Y, but not *that
> lot*, because Z? (10.4.17–18)

In humane society, fundraising is a career. Run by (for?) carers, people who
bother. More showbiz, pricing pity by capacity to shock. It's an individual
thing, choosing a personal charity, finding a favourite affliction. Exploitation is
wired into the system, too. Respect a personal mission to salvage society's
rejects; but understand that no one person can save the whole of its refuse tip.[76]

---

[75] Declaimers bounce ideas off the she-wolf that saved baby Romulus and baby Remus, or the empire
   wouldn't be here, orating in Latin (3, 4, 5, 9).
[76] The declaimers abusively calibrate 'one v. many' in divers sick limb-counts (23). They knew their
   game is to dismantle the body politic in style, ripping yarns for the hell of it.

Desperate need calls for desperate shifts. What goes down with the public. And why. 'A fine balance', indeed.[77]

It still works, *scholastici*.[78] Stirs up violent emotions. Heated debate. *Controversy*. Eminently worth a defaced page of execrable taste in anyone's copybook. *We turned Fagin into Geldof.* 10.4.[79]

## Where It Was (L'Ego)

It should now be clear that *and wherefore* clips of descriptive salivation in unleashed violence of language and representation litter the *Controversiae*, but regularly play as remarkably sparing components in a managed economy of rhetorical libido. They are being deployed, and they are being *policed* – subjected (it is held) to the logonomy intrinsic to textual power. The governing narrative frame presents the collection as the scrambled

---

[77] On set in today's India, the Beggarmaster's fine-tuned sociorhetorical imagination enhances his clients' pulling-power between cradle and grave. With designer mutilation on palette, let the magisterial artist enthuse: "'But there has to be a unique feature about the candidates. Let me show you." From the briefcase, he removed a large sketchbook containing the notes and diagrams relating to the dramaturgy of begging. He opened the book to an old pencil drawing titled Spirit of Collaboration. "Here's what I have been trying to create for a long time ... The blind man will carry the cripple on his shoulders. A living, breathing image of the ancient story about friendship and cooperation. And it will produce a fortune in coins ... because people will give not only from piety or pity but also from admiration'" (Mistry 1997: 445, q.v.).

[78] Editor Scourfield cues John Chrys. *Hom. 21 in I Cor.* 5 (PG 61.177) ratcheting up the dire poverty in Antioch, where 'some were forced to maim [specifically, to blind] their still unfullgrown kids in order to get past our compassion fatigue' (cf. P. Brown 1989: 310, who in turn cues (n. 26) a medieval beggar ganglord, 'the Improver', 'who made children better able to act as beggars by crippling them', *ap.* Bosworth 1976: I.37–8). But, yes, it works a treat: 'As portrayed so vividly in the Oscar winning film, *Slumdog Millionaire*, some of the children are deliberately maimed. Arms and legs are forcibly amputated, others are cruelly blinded. The gangs also pour acid on to children's bodies leaving them with suppurating wounds. The more they are tortured or tormented, the more sympathy they gain when they beg. Children are trained to approach certain kinds of people and use certain mannerisms, to extract even more money. There are many child beggars who are not mutilated, but those with the worst injuries make the most money, earning up to ten times the amount that millions in India survive on each day' (Dalit Freedom Network UK, 'Child Beggar Gangs in India', accessed 12 August 2016 at www.dfn.org.uk/childbeggargangs). Our storyline from fetid Roman sensationalism is now a WWWebfodder mash-up of apokrypha with testimonia: for Bangladesh, China, India ... – google 'child beggars, mutilation'.

[79] (Police and Citizens Band.) Underageism in Rome: Rawson 2003. Child-trafficking, and exposure of babies in Rome: Harris 1994, esp. 8, 12, 16; Corbier 2001, esp. 68 (on 10.4), 'no more than a declamatory exercise in which mutilations are invoked to support the most paradoxical arguments'; Bernstein 2009 (esp. on 2.1, 9.3). The alms trade in Antiquity: Hands (*sic*) 1968; the Charity Business in Modernity: Lloyd 1993; Brougham 1818 to Henderson Administration 1994–6 and *Reward Group* 1994–5. With Sanders, Oyewole, and Mboup 1998:

> Save our childrens | that are dying
> Lovers mothers | brothers fathers
> Now's the moment | for salvation
> All we need | is inspiration.

See Registered Charity No. 213890: savethechildren.org.uk.

contents of a vast database of verbatim citations stored as memory together
with quoted bites from discussions at particular performances, with their
overdub of authorial analysis, remark, and musing.

The series of prefaces to the books styles the album of reminiscences as a
father's response to prodding from his three sons, budding imperial
citizens who between them promise to realize their first-generation Spanish
father's bid for assimilation into the inmost echelons of the Roman elite.
Across the range of *vitae* from political engagement to business management. Bleeding between narrative frame and inset tableaux has been, more
than frequent and marked, a structural condition for the montage of the
whole text: entry to Rome = advance to go.[80]

Paternal know-how is imparted to Seneca's sons, and through them to
every Roman family nucleus: in the process, the imparting of normative
knowledge is modelled and a claim to paradigmatic power showcased; and
Roman paternity is rehearsed in a complex of multi-layered, self-referential
imaging that simultaneously risks and polices an etiquette of rhetorical
performance that courts off-duty, non-serious, relaxed badinage but knowingly skirts, impinges, and abuts on the fundamental values, taboos, and
nightmares at the heart of cultured identity-formation.[81]

This structure is the constant that is played across by the narrative that
develops through the collection. Initial enthusiasm for the educative project,
which will anchor the aspiring adolescent to a proper cultivation of the
proprieties of class(y) selfhood, deteriorates, wastes, and eventually self-
disgusts, as investment in the facetious hothouse of declamation reaches
the advisory ceiling announced by the controller. The memory-hoard
touches bottom long before the graduands know they have had enough
for their own good: the gallery declares itself replete, so complete, and
declaims a retrospective protocol for proper engagement with this activity.[82]

Seneca has written a kind of inverted epideictic performance of his own
onto the institution of declamation, arguing inexorably from enthused trans-
mission of his own exultation in this memorable socializing scene all the way
to sated persiflage excoriating its show-business dimension, and worse. Suitability for an advanced syllabus yields to critical discrimination and distancing
from the diminishing returns of an etiolated career-setting. The traditionally
privileged textual forms of philosophy, epic, and history are finally reinstated,
announced as the Senecan family legacy of declamatory glory – post-
declamatory, and yet, and so, propter-declamatory. Violent tableaux called
for regulatory backgrounding to near (in)audibility. Ours to hear the cry of
one barren womb (2.5) and a chorus of maimed innocents (10.4). Wipeout.

---

[80] Seneca's hustle, or mission: see Bloomer 1997a: 119–20.     [81] Cf. Gunderson 2003 *passim*.
[82] Van den Berg forthcoming unpacks this 'decline' within declamation.

# CHAPTER 7

# Dismemberment and the Critics
## Seneca's Phaedra

### Duncan F. Kennedy

Violence has a disturbingly mesmeric effect on the observer. In exploring his reaction to witnessing '(domestic) "scene[s]"', for him 'a pure experience of violence . . . always inspir[ing] *fear*', Roland Barthes attributed his feelings to the way in which 'violence always organized itself into a *scene*: the most transitive of behaviour (to eliminate, to kill, to wound, to humble) was also the most theatrical'.[1] Witnessing such violence, he feels himself compelled to take on the role of *spectator*. Conversely, spectacle, in the sporting arena or the cinema or theatre, frequently focuses upon *scenes* of violence. In *Mythologies*, Barthes offers an engaging discussion of all-in wrestling, which, he asserts, is not a sport such as boxing, in which a story of the rise and fall of fortunes culminating in victory or defeat is constructed as it happens before our eyes, but a *spectacle*, where the spectator is rather looking for 'the transient image of certain passions'.[2] Wrestlers take on the roles of Hero or Villain, instantly identifiable as such to the spectators through their physique, dress, attitudes, and gestures, which make the intention of each move transparent:

> Each moment in wrestling is therefore like an algebra which instantaneously unveils the relationship between a cause and its represented effect. Wrestling fans certainly experience a kind of intellectual pleasure in *seeing* the moral mechanism function so perfectly . . . What is thus displayed for the public is the great spectacle of Suffering, Defeat and Justice. Wrestling presents man's suffering with all the amplification of tragic masks.[3]

This is but one of a number of occasions in his essay when Barthes impishly compares wrestling with ancient drama. Tragedy, it might be objected, is not the same thing at all; it is a serious genre, in which, since the time of Aristotle, spectacle has always been the least regarded component (cf. Arist. *Poet.* 6 (1450b15–20)), and it presents suffering, and causation, in a more complex way than Barthes' wrestlers.

[1] Barthes 1977: 160; emphases in original.　　[2] Barthes 1973: 16.　　[3] Barthes 1973: 19.

In seeking to define the idea of the tragic in a recent book, Terry Eagleton points out the paradoxical character of that complexity:

> To expect a play to reward the virtuous and punish the vicious, as Thomas Rymer demands, would be painfully unsophisticated. Tragedy must be, after all, an imitation of life in all its moral chequeredness. But this is not the issue. The question is why a form that shows the innocent being torn limb from limb should be acclaimed as the highest expression of human value.[4]

Rymer's view of tragedy is hardly adequate for Barthes' wrestling fans – for whom their spectacle provides an explicitly *intellectual* as well as moral pleasure – and emphatically not for Eagleton. When Ovid – one of the form's practitioners – personifies the genre, he does so as *violenta Tragoedia* (*Am.* 3.1.11), and Eagleton's remarks are indicative of the way that dismemberment, arguably the most extreme manifestation of violence perpetrated on the human body, has become emblematic of the tragic. The apparent pleasure taken in such spectacles of violence, and the anxiety that they are morally corrupting, have since ancient times been matters of ethical and social concern, whether those spectacles are 'games' or 'plays'. The younger Seneca notoriously condemns the former (*Letter* 7) and writes the latter. For Eagleton, the tragedies of Seneca are hardly the highest expression of human value. He speaks of 'the splendid extrava-ganzas of Seneca – *Thyestes, Medea, Phaedra* and the rest – with their bombast and carnage, their vision of the world as vile, bloody and chaotic and of men and women as betraying a bottomless capacity for cruelty. In this theatre of the grotesque,' he continues, 'action takes precedence over meaning, rather as it does when comedy tilts over into farce.'[5] Eagleton's insouciant tone signals his sense that (though there is nothing much to shock us here these days in their representation of cruelty and violence) Seneca's plays can claim a place at best only on the very margins of tragedy – a faded ancient equivalent, perhaps, of the modern slasher movie.[6] Eagleton is only the latest to associate the tragedies of Seneca with extreme carnage and cruelty, and to marginalize them formally and aes-thetically as a result.

---

[4] Eagleton 2003: 134–5.    [5] Eagleton 2003: 8.
[6] A genre scholarly studies have not sought, hitherto at least, to analyse in terms of tragedy. Typically such studies concentrate anxiously on the gendered nature of the representation of violence and its effect on audiences; see, e.g., Sapolsky, Molitor, and Luque 2003, and cf. Introduction, pp. 30–1 with n. 109.

So, tragedy's long association with violence has not been to its detriment – unless the author is Seneca, it seems. The title of Eagleton's book, *Sweet Violence*, can be traced back through Sir Philip Sidney to an anecdote about the tyrant Alexander of Pherae in Plutarch's *Life of Pelopidas*: 'Once when he was watching a tragic actor performing Euripides' *Troades*, he left the theatre abruptly, but sent a message to the actor telling him not to be afraid and not to put any less effort into contending for the prize as a consequence, for he had not left out of contempt for his acting, but because he was ashamed to have the citizens observe him, who had never pitied any of those whom he had murdered, shedding tears over the sufferings of Hecuba and Andromache.'[7] In *An Apology for Poetry*, Sir Philip Sidney recounts this 'notable testimony of the abominable tyrant Alexander Pheraeus' to draw this moral: 'so as he that was not ashamed to make matters for tragedies, yet could not resist the sweet violence of a tragedy'.[8] The anecdote exemplifies the tradition beginning with Aristotle that has seen the key to the pleasure taken in such spectacles, and indeed the potential benefits derived from them, precisely in their status as *representations*. For Aristotle, the instinct for imitation is innate in human beings, as is the enjoyment of works of imitation. 'Evidence of this', he says, 'is what happens in actual experience: we enjoy looking at the most accurate representations of things which in themselves we find painful to see, such as the forms of the lowliest of animals and of dead bodies.'[9] The pleasure – for philosophers and others alike – is an *intellectual* one: 'They enjoy seeing likenesses because as they look they learn and deduce (*manthanein kai sullogizesthai*) what is represented, for example that this is such-and-such a person.'[10] He makes a very similar point in the *Rhetoric*: 'Since learning is pleasant, and the feeling of wonder, then such things as acts of imitation must necessarily be pleasant (for example, painting, sculpture, and poetry), and every product of skilful imitation, even if that which has been imitated is not itself pleasant; for the enjoyment is not in the object

---

[7] Plut. *Pel.* 29.9 τραγῳδὸν δέ ποτε θεώμενος Εὐριπίδου Τρῳάδας ὑποκρινόμενον ᾤχετ᾽ ἀπιὼν ἐκ τοῦ θεάτρου, καὶ πέμψας πρὸς αὐτὸν ἐκέλευε θαρρεῖν καὶ μηδὲν ἀγωνίζεσθαι διὰ τοῦτο χεῖρον, οὐ γὰρ ἐκείνου καταφρονῶν ἀπελθεῖν, ἀλλ᾽ αἰσχυνόμενος τοὺς πολίτας, εἰ μηδένα πώποτε τῶν ὑπ᾽ αὐτοῦ φονευομένων ἠλεηκώς, ἐπὶ τοῖς Ἑκάβης καὶ Ἀνδρομάχης κακοῖς ὀφθήσεται δακρύων. All translations in this chapter are my own.
[8] Maslen 2002: 98.
[9] Arist. *Poet.* 4 (1448b9–12) σημεῖον δὲ τούτου τὸ συμβαῖνον ἐπὶ τῶν ἔργων· ἃ γὰρ αὐτὰ λυπηρῶς ὁρῶμεν, τούτων τὰς εἰκόνας τὰς μάλιστα ἠκριβωμένας χαίρομεν θεωροῦντες, οἶον θηρίων τε μορφὰς τῶν ἀτιμοτάτων καὶ νεκρῶν.
[10] Arist. *Poet.* 4 (1448b15–17) διὰ γὰρ τοῦτο χαίρουσι τὰς εἰκόνας ὁρῶντες, ὅτι συμβαίνει θεωροῦντας μανθάνειν καὶ συλλογίζεσθαι τί ἕκαστον, οἶον ὅτι οὖτος ἐκεῖνος.

itself, but rather one makes an inference that "this is such and such a thing", and thus learns something.'[11]

Aristotle's analysis draws a sharp distinction between the 'object itself' (*auto to memimemenon*, the thing imitated or represented) and its representation, but this is a distinction that is far from simple, as we shall see. Witnessing violence can be a traumatic experience, but the mesmerizing sense of spectatorship of domestic scenes to which Barthes draws attention suggests how the configuration of what is happening *as* a representation, a 'scene', marks the desire to understand a painful and seemingly inexplicable phenomenon that is difficult to come to terms with; it also serves to suggest that the 'reality' of violence (the 'object itself') may not be theoretically as easy to disentangle from its representation as Aristotle would have it. When Barthes draws attention to the way that wrestling 'unveils the relationship between a cause and its represented effect' and allows its spectators to 'experience a kind of intellectual pleasure', his analysis may appear impeccably Aristotelian, but is subtly different. That difference is epistemological: does reality precede its representation, as Aristotle would have it, or is our apprehension of the reality of violence inextricably conditioned in its (various forms of) representation, as Barthes would? This will lead us to explore how different forms of the representation of violence – including the representations we encounter in scholarship – condition our responses. On the other hand, in comparing the representation of violence in different forms, we may also want to move towards a sense of what is distinctive about its representation in tragedy. Can Seneca's dramas help us to think through these problems? In this chapter, I consider how violence is represented in Seneca, and examine in detail the dismemberment of Hippolytus and Theseus' attempt to put together the pieces of his body in the *Phaedra*. I then analyse how critical responses to these scenes go about trying to understand these and similar scenes, and explore how the very process of analysis and the search for intelligibility is repeatedly troped in terms of the human body and its

---

[11] Arist. *Rh.* 1.11.23 (1371b4–10) ἐπεὶ δὲ τὸ μανθάνειν τε ἡδὺ καὶ τὸ θαυμάζειν, καὶ τὰ τοιάδε ἀνάγκη ἡδέα εἶναι οἷον τό τε μιμούμενον, ὥσπερ γραφικὴ καὶ ἀνδριαντοποιία καὶ ποιητική, καὶ πᾶν ὃ ἂν εὖ μεμιμημένον ᾖ, κἂν ᾖ μὴ ἡδὺ αὐτὸ τὸ μεμιμημένον· οὐ γὰρ ἐπὶ τούτῳ χαίρει, ἀλλὰ συλλογισμός ἐστιν ὅτι τοῦτο ἐκεῖνο, ὥστε μανθάνειν τι συμβαίνει. For Jacques Derrida, the perception of similarity and difference links metaphor and mimesis, and the pleasure both offer has the same rationale: 'A dividend of pleasure, therefore, is the recompense for the economic development of the syllogism hidden in metaphor, the theoretical perception of resemblance. But the energy of this operation supposes, nevertheless, that the resemblance is not an identity. *Mimēsis* yields pleasure only on condition of giving us to see in action that which nonetheless is not to be seen in action, but only its very resembling double, its *mimēma*' (Derrida 1982: 239).

dismemberment. In the metatheatrical reading of the closing scenes of the *Phaedra* which I then go on to construct, I return to the dominant reading of tragedy, with its roots in Aristotle, which requires of the form that it render intelligible the traumatic events it represents, and suggest that these scenes set themselves up as a challenge to that reading. In what follows, I readily endorse what John Henderson wrote in the previous chapter: 'I take it as read that my subject, the violence of representation in the representation of violence ... nails us to the reading of Latin, and, make no mistake, that's what I'm here to do.'[12] And, I would add, not only the reading of Latin; make no mistake, that's what *I'm* here to do. Some vigorous academic cut-and-thrust will be staged, and you will be the spectators of that scene.

First, however, we need to get a handle on the marginalization of Senecan drama within discussions of tragedy, for it colours responses to the issue of violence, as Eagleton's dismissive comments suggest. This is a comparatively recent phenomenon; for Renaissance tragedians, Seneca stood supreme as a tragic model.[13] However, at the beginning of the Romantic period, a reaction, to the benefit of Greek tragedy, set in, which, for all the critical efforts of the past generation or so, is still manifest. For August Wilhelm von Schlegel in 1809, the character of Seneca's tragedies and what he saw as their lack of any theatrical understanding meant that they were not actually intended for the stage,[14] a statement which initiated a controversy about their performability that still rages in some scholarly quarters today. At the level of plot, their reputation for violence and goriness seems thoroughly justified: butchery and the cooking of entrails followed by cannibalism (*Thyestes*); the gouging of eyes (*Oedipus*); and so on. As long ago as 1927, however, T. S. Eliot suggested that this reputation was not wholly deserved:

> When we examine the plays of Seneca, the actual horrors are not so heinous or so many as are supposed. The most unpleasantly sanguinary is the *Thyestes*, a subject which, so far as I know, was not attempted by a Greek dramatist ... Yet even in the *Thyestes* the performance of the horrors is

---

[12] Henderson, Chapter 6, p. 183 n. 21.    [13] See Staley 2010: 11–12.

[14] von Schlegel 1972: 14: 'sie sind über alle Beschreibung schwülstig und frostig, ohne Natur in Charakter und Handlung, durch die widersinnigsten Unschicklichkeiten empörend, und so von aller theatralischen Einsicht entblösst, dass ich glaube, sie waren nie dazu bestimmt, aus den Schulen der Rhetoren auf die Bühne hervorzutreten' ('they are bombastic and frosty beyond all description, completely unnatural in their characterization and action, shocking in their nonsensical impropriety, and so stripped of all theatrical understanding that I believe that they were never intended to emerge from the rhetorical schools on to the stage').

managed with conventional tact; the only visible horror is the perhaps unavoidable presentation of the evidence – the children's heads in a dish.[15]

Forty years later, C. J. Herington corrected Eliot's assumption that there were no Greek versions of *Thyestes* (he mentions eight), and remarked that, while Eliot quite justifiably protested against the belief that Senecan tragedy is a catalogue of horrors, 'he still cannot shake off the even more widely spread ancestral opinion that at any rate it ought to be gorier than *Greek* drama'.[16] Yet Eliot is right to emphasize that 'visible horror' is rare. There is certainly nothing in Seneca as explicit as the scene in *King Lear* where Gloucester is tied to a chair and his eyes are gouged out (3.7.28–84), let alone the bloody excesses staged in *The Spanish Tragedy*, *Antonio's Revenge*, or *Titus Andronicus*.[17] As Sander M. Goldberg has said, 'Seneca's *Thyestes* actually has none of the bizarre spectacle so vital to the impact of *Titus Andronicus*. Seneca puts the *effects* of these violent actions before us but exhibits none of them. Physical violence remains at a distance in *Thyestes*, as it generally does in Senecan tragedy.'[18] Le Théâtre du Grand-Guignol, with its elaborate and grisly visual effects, Senecan drama is emphatically not, though comparable special effects may have been available to the actors of Roman mime.[19]

Eliot argued that the plays of Seneca were composed not for stage performance but for private declamation, and that this 'attenuates the supposed "horrors" of the tragedies, many of which could hardly have been represented on a stage, even with the most ingenious machinery, without being merely ridiculous'.[20] No firm consensus has emerged on the question of performance, with critics arguing for a range of possibilities from full staging,[21] perhaps in small private theatres as was common practice in the Hellenistic period,[22] to recitation by a single reciter[23] or to a form of recital, unstaged but with a number of voices, in the manner of a concert performance of an opera.[24] The absence of firm evidence

---

[15] Eliot 1951: 80.

[16] Herington 1966: 427; emphasis in the original. Herington cites the Euripidean descriptions of the deaths of Creon in the *Medea*, Hippolytus in the *Hippolytus*, and Pentheus in the *Bacchae*; Sophocles' version of the agonies of Lichas and Heracles in the *Trachiniae*; and Aeschylus' account of the Thyestean banquet at *Ag.* 1587–1602.

[17] See Boyle 1997: 164–6 for an extended catalogue of violent acts represented on stage in Renaissance drama. He concludes: 'Indeed one of the great contemporary appeals of Senecan and Renaissance drama is precisely its use of violence as a dramatic mode.' For a shrewd analysis of the relationship between Seneca and Renaissance English drama, see Goldberg 2000.

[18] Goldberg 2000: 210; original emphasis.    [19] Cf. Suet. *Calig.* 57.4 with Goldberg 2000: 222–3.

[20] Eliot 1951: 67. Note the term 'ridiculous'; we shall see much more of this in what follows.

[21] B. Walker 1969; Herington 1982; Sutton 1986.    [22] Calder 1976; Marshall 2000.

[23] See esp. Zwierlein 1966.    [24] Fantham 1982: 34–49.

makes it likely that speculation on this question will continue, but whatever their views, scholars seem to concur in the belief that central to an understanding of Seneca's plays is their manipulation of *language*, rather than visual effect, that in some sense, as Eliot said, 'the drama is all in the word'.[25] That at least is in keeping with Aristotle's ideas on tragedy: 'For the plot ought to be so arranged that even without seeing them the person who hears of the events which occur shudders and pities as a result of the things that happen . . . Those who create the effect not of the fearful but only of the monstrous through the use of spectacle have nothing in common with tragedy.'[26]

Nonetheless, Goldberg makes the useful point that ancient texts were always in some sense performative: 'Given the Romans' reading habits and their penchant for recitation, it could not be otherwise . . . Though the stage performance of new tragic scripts cannot be assumed or even expected after the time of Accius, the debate in Seneca's case is only over the *kind* of performance he may have envisioned, not the *fact* of performance before an audience.'[27] He suggests that tragedy at this period was 'the verse equivalent of declamation',[28] which was 'a boisterous exercise, with cheers to greet every effective gesture and clever turn of phrase and hecklers ready to deride the unwary and the inept, a spectator sport for highly engaged spectators'.[29] A major aim of rhetoric, realized in declamation, was the use of words to create vivid mental images, what ancient theorists of rhetoric called *enargeia*;[30] violence in Senecan drama is for the most part the object not of visual but of verbal display, realized not to the body's but to the mind's eye. So, whatever answer we give to the question of performance, Senecan tragedy presents us with a particular *form* of representation of violence, verbal rather than visual. *Pace* Eliot, the horrors, if such they simply were, may not have been thereby attenuated for a culture

---

[25] Eliot 1951: 68.

[26] Arist. *Poet.* 14 (1453b3–6, 8–10) δεῖ γὰρ καὶ ἄνευ τοῦ ὁρᾶν οὕτω συνεστάναι τὸν μῦθον ὥστε τὸν ἀκούοντα τὰ πράγματα γινόμενα καὶ φρίττειν καὶ ἐλεεῖν ἐκ τῶν συμβαινόντων . . . οἱ δὲ μὴ τὸ φοβερὸν διὰ τῆς ὄψεως ἀλλὰ τὸ τερατῶδες μόνον παρασκευάζοντες οὐδὲν τραγῳδίᾳ κοινωνοῦσιν. See further Staley 2010: 112–14. Staley's book locates Seneca's tragedies in relation to ancient theories of tragedy, including Aristotle's.

[27] Goldberg 2000: 230 n. 24 (his emphases); cf. also Littlewood 2004: 2–4.

[28] Goldberg 1996: 274. For early-Imperial Rome as a 'performative culture' with special reference to declamation, see Henderson, Chapter 6 above.

[29] Goldberg 1996: 279. He adds (279 n. 20): 'Whether this audience [sc. of Senecan tragedy] was notional or real and whether the plays were written with full stage performance in mind hardly matter, though (as far as I can see) nothing much is added to the effect of a Senecan play by a visual component or lost by its absence.'

[30] See Webb 1997 and 2009.

that was more highly attuned to the effects of this than ours. In a refreshingly defiant contrast to the long and sterile tradition that denigrates Senecan rhetoric, Goldberg sees this concentration on the word as no less than the salvation of tragedy. The growing appetite for visual spectacle, which he sees as destroying tragedy after Accius, was well catered for elsewhere. Action and special effects could become secondary to the manipulation of language, and the loss of a mass popular audience allowed tragedy to take on 'a new life in a new environment by reclaiming its literary heritage and becoming once again a vehicle for serious literary endeavor'.[31]

As a literary endeavour, Seneca's tragedies are now coming to be seen as allied not simply to Greek tragedy, but to Ovid's *Metamorphoses*, Lucan's *Bellum civile*, and the literature of the early Empire more generally, and as sharing a similar range of concerns.[32] Meanwhile, scholars have argued that Renaissance tragedy turns to Seneca rather than the Greeks 'not because Greek is harder to learn, but because of serious interest in the story which Senecan rhetoric is suited to tell'.[33] Lines are even redeployed from Seneca's text, and in *The Spanish Tragedy*, when plotting revenge for the death of his son, Hieronimo enters with a text of Seneca in his hands and quotes from *Agamemnon* and *Troades*.[34] But contrariwise, the extreme violence staged as visual spectacle in Renaissance tragedy has helped retrospectively to colour the modern world's view of Seneca's treatment of violence. The new emphasis in Renaissance tragedy on staging scenes of violence transposes to the level of action and visual spectacle what in Seneca, and in the literature of the early Roman Empire more generally, had been the province of the word. Thus, in *Titus Andronicus*,

---

[31] Goldberg 1996: 283.

[32] Thus for Schiesaro 2003: 7, the *Thyestes* 'pushes to breaking-point a debate about the role and function of the poetic word which lies at the heart of works such as Ovid's *Metamorphoses* and Lucan's *Bellum Civile*. Its exploration of passion, hatred and horror is more concentrated and sustained than in Lucan or Statius; its lumping together of the personal and the political amplifies a line of thought which is central to post-Virgilian literature, as are its preferred forms of expression – self-reflexive, highly charged, bordering on the illogical.' Littlewood 2004: 1 remarks of his study of Senecan tragedy: 'Lucan, Ovid, Virgil, even Horace have been more important figures for me than any tragedian.'

[33] Braden 1985: 68; cf. Herington 1966: 452–3: 'Our cool modern assumption that Greek tragedy must be the ultimate criterion for Senecan tragedy leads, almost every time, to a dead end. Similarly, one of the factors in Western Europe's belated recognition of Greek tragedy was the cool Renaissance assumption that *Senecan* tragedy was the ultimate criterion. Better, perhaps, to avoid either extreme, and to take each type of tragedy, in the first instance, on its own terms.' Cf. also Tarrant 1978: 217.

[34] See Boyle 1997: 143–4; cf. also Newlands, Chapter 5, p. 163 above, who notes the similar way in which Ovid's *Metamorphoses* is introduced in *Titus Andronicus*.

'Shakespeare's mind was captured by the idea of translating to the play-house images of violence he had found in the prototype of this story, Ovid's telling of the rape of Philomel.'[35] Nonetheless, it is to nearly word-for-word quotation of the Latin of Seneca, and specifically of the *Phaedra*, that this drama of violence and dismemberment turns at two crucial moments, 'to preface the rape and mutilation of Lavinia . . . and to express the ineffable pain of Titus on reading the names of those who committed the outrage'.[36]

For arguably the most extreme example of violence in Seneca's tragedies – in the form of a bravura verbal description – is the dismemberment of Hippolytus in the *Phaedra*. The messenger, after an initial show of reluctance, describes how Hippolytus, attacked by the monster from the sea summoned up by the curse of Theseus, gets entangled in the reins of his chariot and suffers effectively a catalogue of extreme injuries. His head is crushed and his face is torn away (1093–6), he is transfixed by a sharp stake (1098–9), his flesh is lacerated by shrubs (1102–3), and he is torn to pieces (1101–4):

> late cruentat arva et inlisum caput
> scopulis resultat; auferunt dumi comas,
> et ora durus pulchra populatur lapis        1095
> peritque multo vulnere infelix decor.
> moribunda celeres membra pervolvunt rotae;
> tandemque raptum truncus ambusta sude
> medium per inguen stipite erecto tenet,
> paulumque domino currus affixo stetit.        1100
> haesere biiuges vulnere – et pariter moram
> dominumque rumpunt. inde semianimem secant
> virgulta, acutis asperi vepres rubis
> omnisque truncus corporis partem tulit.[37]

He stains the fields far and wide with his blood, and his head, colliding with the rocks, bounces off them. The brambles carry off his hair, the hard stones ravage his lovely face, and his ill-fated beauty is destroyed by wound after wound. The speeding wheels tumble his dying limbs, and at length a tree-trunk with a charred stake holds him, taken right through the groin, on its erect stump; and for a moment the chariot stood still, with its driver impaled. The team were brought to a standstill by the wound – and at one and the same moment they put an end to delay and their master. Then the bushes and the prickly brambles slice his half-dead body with their sharp thorns, and every tree-trunk took a share of his flesh.

---

[35] Hattaway 1982: 200.     [36] Boyle 1997: 145; he offers a detailed treatment of the citations.
[37] I follow the text of Boyle 1987.

The description of the injuries is far more lengthy and detailed than in either of Seneca's two main models, the messenger's speech in Euripides' *Hippolytus* (1236–9) and Hippolytus' own description of his death in Ovid, *Metamorphoses* 15.524–8.[38] Any of these injuries could be a sufficient cause of death, and the severity of the mutilation precludes a scene such as we find in Euripides' play, where the mortally injured Hippolytus survives long enough to be carried back and to speak at length with Theseus and Artemis (1347–1461).

However, the particular injuries Seneca's Hippolytus suffers resonate with some of the major themes of the play. The blood with which he soaks the fields (1093) recalls the bloodthirstiness of the hunting which he celebrates in his opening song (1–80). As he is dragged along, two areas of his body are the focus of particular attention, the head and the groin. Hippolytus' beauty has been commented on at length earlier in the play,[39] and its destruction is emphasized rhetorically in 1095 by the intrusion of *durus*, the adjective associated with the noun *lapis*, into the phrase *ora . . . pulchra*. The stake that impales his groin and holds him transfixed has strong sexual overtones in the case of one who has denied his own sexual impulses.[40] As his team, for a brief time halted by their master's impalement,[41] resume their flight, the moment of Hippolytus' dismemberment is ironically marked by a zeugma, the stylistic figure in which one word (*rumpunt*, 1102) is connected with two other words (*moram dominumque,*

---

[38] For a detailed comparison of the death of Hippolytus in Euripides, Ovid, and Seneca, see C. P. Segal 1984. Although in general Seneca is likely to have owed a major debt to tragedy written in the Augustan age, there is no evidence for a treatment of the Phaedra story then (cf. Tarrant 1978: 261); the Ovidian Phaedra's epistle (*Her.* 4) was clearly important for Seneca (cf. Coffey and Mayer 1990: 14; Littlewood 2004: 259–301), but will not have been relevant to the final scenes.

[39] By Phaedra (657–60) and by the Chorus (741–823), which ominously discourses upon its loss.

[40] See C. P. Segal 1986: 128; Boyle 1987: 23. C. P. Segal 1984: 323 n. 36 notes that the injuries caused to Euripides' Hippolytus involve no trees and only rocks, but that there is a branch or stake in Hippolytus' description of his own death at Ov. *Met.* 15.525 (*nervos in stipe teneri*, 'sinews held on a stake'); cf. also Jakobi 1988: 83–9. That the stake is charred (*ambusta*) is a puzzle; Zwierlein reports in the apparatus to his Oxford Classical Text (Zwierlein 1986: 204) a suggestion made to him by Bertil Axelson: '*an abrupta?*' (i.e., 'broken off'). However, Segal suggests that the detail ironically fulfils the invocation of Jupiter and his thunderbolt by Hippolytus at the moment he discovers Phaedra's love for him (680–4): *cur dextra, divum rector atque hominum, vacat | tua, nec trisulca mundus ardescit face? | in me tona, me fige, me velox cremet | transactus ignis. sum nocens, merui mori: | placui novercae* ('Ruler of gods and men, why is your right hand empty, and the world not in flames with your forked lightning? It's against me you should thunder, me you should pierce, me you should drive your swift flame through and burn. I am the guilty one, I have deserved to die: I have become the object of my stepmother's passion').

[41] Zwierlein 1986: 204 deletes line 1100, presumably on the grounds that its sense is largely replicated by 1101, but it could be argued that the time taken in its narration mimics an agonizing pause in the dismemberment.

1101–2) but in a different sense with each.[42] The messenger goes on to report how the servants of Hippolytus are even now scouring the fields for the remnants of his body (1105–14):

> errant per agros funebris famuli manus,                    1105
> per illa quae distractus Hippolytus loca
> longum cruenta tramitem signat nota,
> maestaeque domini membra vestigant canes.
> necdum dolentum sedulus potuit labor
> explere corpus. hocine est formae decus?            1110
> qui modo paterni clarus imperii comes
> et certus heres siderum fulsit modo,
> passim ad supremos ille colligitur rogos
> et funeri confertur.

His servants, a band in mourning, wander through the fields, through those places which Hippolytus, torn asunder, marks out in a long trail with stains of blood, and his sad hounds track their master's limbs. Nor has the careful toil of the mourners yet been able to complete the body. Has the glory of his beauty come to this? He who, just now the bright partner of his father's power and his assured heir, shone like the stars, is being assembled from everywhere for his funeral pyre and gathered together for his rites.

The search of his attendants and his dogs for parts of his body grimly recalls Hippolytus' evocation at the beginning of the play of a chase that ends with guts spilling out as carcasses are cut open and dogs returning with bloodstained snouts.[43]

In the graphic details it gives of the injuries suffered, then, the messenger's narrative goes well beyond what is found in Euripides or Ovid. Moreover, the dismemberment of Hippolytus gains a special emphasis in Seneca's play through the vain attempts of Theseus in the closing scene (1247–80) to reassemble the scattered fragments of the body in preparation for cremation. The chorus requests Theseus to fulfil the rites due to his son

---

[42] *moras rumpere* is a common expression meaning 'to put an end to delay' (cf. *OLD* s.v. *rumpo*, sect. 10c), but the verb *rumpere* is also used of bursting open blisters or wounds so as to let the liquids pour out (cf. *OLD* s.v., sects. 1c and 1d). *Zeugma* denotes a 'yoking', and the ironic use of the figure in this context may be pointed up by the term *biiuges* for the yoked pair of horses earlier in line 1101, as well as by *pariter*, a marker of the figure (cf. Lussky 1953: 285), as in, e.g., Ov. *Met.* 2.311–13 (of Jupiter dashing Phaethon from his chariot with a thunderbolt, arguably a model for Seneca's use both of the figure and of *pariter*), *intonat et dextra libratum fulmen ab aure* | *misit in aurigam pariterque animaque rotisque* | *expulit* ('he thunders and balancing the bolt dispatched it from beside his right ear at the charioteer and tossed him at one and the same moment from his chariot and from life').

[43] *Phaed.* 51–2 *tu iam victor* | *curvo solves viscera cultro* ('you, the victor now, will release their innards with curved knife'); 77–8 *tum rostra canes* | *sanguine multo rubicunda gerunt* ('then the dogs sport snouts red with much blood'). See C. P. Segal 1986: 63.

(*nunc iusta nato solve*, 1245), and quickly to hide away the limbs that have been obscenely scattered by the fierce dismemberment (*et absconde ocius | dispersa foede membra laniatu effero*, 1245–6). However, Theseus lingers long over the preparation of the corpse, a ritual habitually described in Latin by the verb *componere* ('to put together'),[44] and here gruesomely literalized as Theseus tries to put the parts of his son's body together again:

huc, huc reliquias vehite cari corporis
pondusque et artus temere congestos date.
Hippolytus hic est? crimen agnosco meum;
ego te peremi, neu nocens tantum semel                    1250
solusve fierem, facinus ausurus parens
patrem advocavi: munere en patrio fruor.
o triste fractis orbitas annis malum.
complectere artus, quodque de nato est super,
miserande, maesto pectore incumbens fove.                 1255
disiecta, genitor, membra laceri corporis
in ordinem dispone et errantes loco
restitue partes. fortis hic dextrae locus,
hic laeva frenis docta moderandis manus
ponenda; laevi lateris agnosco notas.                     1260
quam magna lacrimis pars adhuc nostris abest!
durate trepidae lugubri officio manus,
fletusque largos sistite, arentes genae,
dum membra nato genitor adnumerat suo
corpusque fingit. hoc quid est forma carens               1265
et turpe, multo vulnere abruptum undique?
quae pars tui sit dubito; sed pars est tui.
hic, hic repone, non suo, at vacuo loco.
haecne illa facies igne sidereo nitens,
inimica flectens lumina? huc cecidit decor?               1270
o dira fata, numinum o saevus favor!
sic ad parentem natus ex voto redit?
    en haec suprema dona genitoris cape,
saepe efferendus; interim haec ignes ferant.
    patefacite acerbam caede funesta domum.               1275
Mopsopia claris tota lamentis sonet.
vos apparate regii flammam rogi;
at vos per agros corporis partes vagas
inquirite.
        istam terra defossam premat,
gravisque tellus impio capiti incubet.                    1280

---

[44] Cf. *OLD* s.v., sect. 4c.

Bring here the remains, here the burden of his precious body; heap his limbs together as they come and give them over into my keeping. Is this Hippolytus? I recognize my fault. I killed you; and so as not to be guilty just once or on my own, when as your father I was about to perpetrate this deed I called on my father's help. Look, here is the fulfilment of my fatherly duty.[45] O the loss of my child, a bitter calamity for my enfeebled years. Clasp these limbs, wretched man, and lay yourself down and clutch what is left of your son in your grieving embrace. Set, as his father, the scattered limbs of his mutilated body in order, and restore to their place the parts that have gone astray. This is where his strong right hand goes, here should be placed his left, skilled in controlling the reins; I recognize traces of his left side. How great a part of him is still wanting to our tears! Stay firm, my hands trembling with this mournful duty, and, my eyes, check these flowing tears and be dry, while a father apportions limbs to his son and fashions his body. What is this piece, misshapen and ugly, severed all around with wound after wound? I do not know what part of you it is; but it is part of you. Put it here, here – not in its proper place, but in a vacant one. Is this the face that shone with fire like the sun, turning his enemy's eyes aside? This far has his splendour set? How dreadful his fate, how cruel the favour of the gods! Is this how a son comes back to his father in answer to his prayers?

Take these the final gifts of your father, you who will often have to be borne out for funeral rites; for now, let the fires bear off these parts.

Open wide the palace made bitter by this grievous carnage. Let all of Attica resound with loud laments. Some of you make ready the flames of the royal pyre, while others search through the fields for parts of his body gone astray.

As for this one here, let the earth crush her buried deep, and heavy may the soil lie on her wicked head.

Such a scene may not be without precedent in Greek tragedy. There is a large lacuna of at least fifty lines in our text of Euripides' *Bacchae* after line 1329, in which Agave seems to have laid out the dismembered limbs of Pentheus for burial.[46] However, the scene in which Theseus attempts to reassemble his son's body-parts has particularly taxed critics of the

---

[45] It is almost impossible to bring out in translation the multiple ironies of *munere en patrio fruor*. *munus* embraces the senses of responsibility and duty. Theseus is aware that in cursing Hippolytus and invoking the aid of his own father Neptune he is guilty in respect of 'what a father should do for a son' (*patrium munus*) not simply once (*semel*, 1250) but twice; the bitter reward (*fruor*) he gets for these perverse displays of paternal *munus* is to exercise that duty here and now (*en*) one last time in respect of the final responsibility due to Hippolytus, his funeral rites (commonly referred to as *munera suprema*; cf. *OLD* s.v. *munus*, sect. 1d).

[46] The full text seems to have been known to Apsines of Gadara (third century AD), and to the author of the twelfth-century *Christus patiens*, which extensively adapts the *Bacchae* to the story of Christ's passion. See Diggle 1994: 352–6 for the testimonia and possible fragments, together with the discussion of Dodds 1960: 234–5 on Eur. *Bacch.* 1329. Apsines recounts how 'in Euripides, the mother of Pentheus, Agave, freed from her madness and recognizing the son whom she has torn apart, accuses herself and moves the audience to pity' (παρὰ τῷ Εὐριπίδῃ ἡ τοῦ Πενθέως μήτηρ Ἀγαυὴ ἀπαλλαγεῖσα τῆς μανίας καὶ γνωρίσασα τὸν παῖδα τὸν ἑαυτῆς διεσπασμένον κατηγορεῖ

*Phaedra*, or, in the words of Michael Coffey, 'occasioned ridicule from Seneca's detractors'.[47] Thus, H. E. Butler thought this scene the 'climax' of absurdity in the 'ghastly and exaggerated account of the death of Hippolytus'.[48] W. S. Barrett from the high ground of his commentary on Euripides' *Hippolytus* seems no less dismissive. He remarks: 'In Seneca Hippolytos is brought on dead; Phaidra, in remorse at the sight, confesses her crime and kills herself; Theseus, after bitter self-reproach, assembles the fragments of the body in a grisly jigsaw (this last is pure Seneca).'[49] Even the normally sympathetic Sander Goldberg seeks refuge in the belief that Seneca wrote his plays for verbal effect rather than full staging: 'Thus even the infamous finale of *Phaedra* (1247ff.), where Theseus reassembles the broken body of his son, is less remarkable for ghoulish display – we do not necessarily see or need to see what Theseus sees – than for the wretched father's (verbal) process of recognition and lament.'[50]

Coffey's co-editor, Roland Mayer, could himself be numbered amongst the detractors, for in his commentary on lines 1256–61 he remarks: 'It may indeed have been a moral duty in Antiquity to reassemble a broken corpse, but how such a scene is described depends on the writer. S[eneca] lacked a sense of humour and he failed to perceive that an over-explicit description becomes funny or wearisome.'[51] Remarkably, he uses the lost scene of the *Bacchae* to denigrate Seneca's efforts: 'What was probably very moving in Euripides is generally deemed laughable in Seneca.'[52] Now, it is undeniable that the representation of dismemberment can be the occasion for humour, as when this famous motif from *Gawain and the Green Knight* forms the basis for John Cleese's Black Knight's show of defiance as he is

---

μὲν αὐτῆς, ἔλεον δὲ κινεῖ); 'Euripides has used this motif wishing to excite pity for Pentheus. For his mother, holding each of his limbs in her hands, laments over it in turn' (τοῦτον τὸν τόπον κεκίνηκεν Εὐριπίδης οἶκτον ἐπὶ τῷ Πενθεῖ κινῆσαι βουλόμενος· ἕκαστον γὰρ αὐτοῦ τῶν μελῶν ἡ μήτηρ ἐν ταῖς χερσὶ κρατοῦσα καθ' ἕκαστον αὐτῶν οἰκτίζεται) (*Rhet. Gr.* IX.587, 590 Walz = I.318, 322 Spengel–Hammer). If the report of Apsines is correct, then this scene must have taken place on stage; cf., however, Barrett 1964: 44 n. 4, who believes that 'holding them in her hands' cannot be a legitimate inference from Euripides' text, apparently on the grounds that all instances of the verb involved (κρατέω) in this sense are late (cf. LSJ s.v., sect. IV.5; Gahan 1987: 385); Willink 1966: 45 suggests that Apsines' phrase is derived from some late stage directions.
[47] Coffey and Mayer 1990: 17.     [48] H. E. Butler 1909: 69–70.
[49] Barrett 1964: 44; the reluctance to Latinize the names of Seneca's characters is a further dig.
[50] Goldberg 1996: 283 n. 21.     [51] Coffey and Mayer 1990: 195.
[52] Mayer 2002: 32; cf. 17 'It might prove laughable in performance'; 69 'An elite Roman audience will have expected that sort of recombination of elements drawn from the dramatic tradition [viz. the incorporation of the scene from the *Bacchae*]. (Of course they may also have felt that it was tastelessly managed in this case.)'

hacked to pieces in the movie *Monty Python and the Holy Grail*; or when Ovid in the *Metamorphoses* puts into the mouth of Hippolytus himself an account of his own mutilation and death.[53] Dismemberment, then, while it is emblematic of tragedy, can be differently mediated to different effect. Nonetheless, Seneca's *Phaedra* has generally been accounted a tragedy. Might we be bold enough to wonder whether Seneca lacks a sense of humour rather less than Mayer lacks a sense of the tragic? In piecing together (I choose my words carefully) the form a specifically 'tragic' reading of the end of the play might take, we need to delve more deeply into how dismemberment is treated in literature – and in criticism.

The dismemberment of Hippolytus is for Glenn Most the prime example of what he sees as a more general fascination on the part of Neronian writers with the theme of dismemberment.[54] Most draws attention to the poems of Martial which take as their subject the savaging of humans by animals in public spectacles. 'Strikingly, these poems use the incidents they recount as the occasion for oddly grim jokes: a hint of discomfort, or of boredom?' he asks.[55] Strikingly, I would remark, Most's article itself contains a number of oddly grim jokes, such as its epigraph from a Tom Lehrer song ('I hold your hand in mine') and, in its description of the dismemberment of Hippolytus, an allusion to Humpty Dumpty ('the combined toil of all his slaves and all of his dogs cannot put him together again').[56] A hint of discomfort, or of boredom? Perhaps the response to dismemberment marks this scholarly article as being generically closer to epigram, or even nursery rhyme, than to tragedy.

---

[53] C. P. Segal 1986: 314 remarks: 'Ovid doubtless took a certain delight in transposing the Euripidean narration from the spectator to the participant. By casting the event as a retrospective narration in the mouth of the dead man himself, he surprises his readers. Even the bloody details gain a certain grim humor when told as first-person present-tense narrative by the deceased.'

[54] Most 1992 offers an extended catalogue of references to dismemberment in Seneca (395–6), Petronius (396), and Lucan (397), with comparative statistics for the types of wounds (cuts, amputations, punctures, crushing blows, and miscellaneous) mentioned in Homer, Virgil, Lucan, Silius, and Statius. He argues of dismemberment that (400) 'a few celebrated passages of Greek tragedy describe similar mutilations of the body, and some of the attested titles of early Roman tragedies, and a small number of the transmitted fragments of these and of early Roman epic give evidence that a similar taste was not foreign to Republican Rome. But neither among the surviving Greek tragedies nor, as far as we can tell from the fragmentary evidence, in early-Republican poetry is there anything like the persistence and emphasis with which this theme is treated in Neronian literature. The only significant precursor of this feature seems to be Ovid, who is responsible for a number of memorable scenes of dismemberment, not only in his account of the death of Hippolytus but elsewhere as well.' For Neronian interest in corporeal imagery and dismemberment see also Quint 1993: 140–7 on Lucan; Connors 1998 and Rimell 2002 on Petronius.

[55] Most 1992: 415 n. 60.   [56] Most 1992: 391–2.

The point is not an entirely flippant one, for scholarly articles can be viewed as rhetorical constructions with their own generic affiliations and constraints, and I shall return to consider this in a moment.

It is possible to find responses which treat the ending of the *Phaedra* as tragic. Tony Boyle, all too briefly, gestures in this direction. He speaks of 'the torture of [Theseus'] guilt, the pathos, horror, futility of his macabre attempt to piece together the shattered fragments of a shattered world, his son's dismembered body'.[57] Does the tragedy reside, then, in an extended consciousness of grief and remorse for which ritual, in the particular circumstances of dismemberment, cannot provide adequate consolation and closure? Theseus finds it difficult to recognize his son in the assortment of body-parts he handles; what he does recognize in them is his *crimen* (1249), and this is expressed not only in the desire for the body-parts that remain lost, but also for the *forma* which those parts represented when they constituted a unity. To observe a grief that can find no prospect of consolation is difficult, and this scene obliges us to do that; 'there is no comfort in this', remarks Boyle.[58] Discomfort, then, may be an entirely appropriate response; and one response to discomfort is displacement, which can be into black humour and grim jokes, or to see the scene as 'ridiculous' or 'laughable'.

But forms of displacement other than into jokes are available. Scholarly articles (including this one) too are modes of representing violence and, more explicitly than tragedy, they seek to 'unveil the relationship between a cause and its represented effect', to recall the words of Barthes; indeed their epistemological pretensions are their *raison d'être*. In seeking to address the phenomenon of dismemberment in Seneca, Most offers the following very explicit methodological statement:

> Of course, the kind of complex and multifaceted phenomenon we are considering here does not admit of simple causal explanation: instead of attempting to reduce the Neronian interest in dismemberment to the direct effect of some specifiable cause, it is surely preferable to try to identify various kinds of contexts for it with which connections of affinity or similarity can be established. To do so is not to aim at a strictly deterministic explanation – compatibility is very far from causality – but at a hermeneutic interpretation in terms of coherence within a larger cultural matrix.[59]

---

[57] Boyle 1987: 35.
[58] Boyle 1987: 24 (= 1997: 66). He continues: 'Phaedra, burdened with guilt, shame and a life bereft of purpose, suicides (1159–98) and Theseus is left (1199ff.) not only with the experience of catastrophic reversal but with the unendurable knowledge of his own role in the perversion and irreversible dismemberment of his world (esp. 1208ff., 1249ff.).'
[59] Most 1992: 401.

There is much going on in this extract, and it will be worth our while to consider it in some detail. Most divides into three the contexts he identifies as potentially fruitful – history, philosophy, and rhetoric – and the historical takes first place in his analysis: 'The most obvious, and the most frequently suggested, context of interpretation for the emphasis upon scenes of cruelty in Silver Latin literature is provided by the notorious circus spectacles which provided audiences throughout the Roman empire with frequent opportunities to enjoy the sight of the many varieties of human suffering.'[60] While Most is hesitant to give simple causal explanations for the violence in Seneca's tragedies, he seems less cautious in respect of the spectacles: 'Indeed, there is abundant evidence that daily life in Imperial Rome supplied a great deal of organized carnage for the delectation of people for whom real warfare had become a remote and negligible possibility.'[61] But are such spectacles – any more than Seneca's tragedies – transparent phenomena with self-evident causes? As Barthes' discussion of wrestling suggests, displays of this kind are amenable to analysis as representations. Indeed, some of the most famously gruesome of such spectacles seem to have had a very clearly defined and explicit mimetic element,[62] and Most himself draws attention to their 'theatricality', though he immediately seeks to move beyond this:

> In Imperial Rome, the line, always thin, that separates theater from life could easily vanish – indeed, transgressing that line seems to have been eagerly performed for its effect upon audiences (until this too eventually became predictable and boring).[63]

Although Most seems mainly concerned here to assert the progressive blunting of people's responses as the levels of violence depicted become more extreme,[64] we may note how strong the temptation is to elide this representational element – to cross 'the line . . . that separates theater from life' – as though we could then get at the 'thing-in-itself', violence as it 'really' is, unmediated, pure, unadorned, *raw*. Most is drawn in this direction as he plots a line that runs from tragedy to circus to 'real warfare'. This is the pull of epistemological realism. Contrast the observation of Barthes with which I began this essay, who even as he regards 'the

---

[60] Most 1992: 401.    [61] Most 1992: 401.    [62] See Barton 1989; K. M. Coleman 1990.
[63] Most 1992: 402.
[64] The contemporary impulse behind this commentary seems clear; in a footnote (415 n. 58) Most remarks: '*Mutatis mutandis*, the same may perhaps be said about the increase in bloodshed in American films over the past decade or so', presumably a reference to the slasher genre, for which see n. 6 above. On desensitization to violence, see also Introduction, p. 33 with n. 116.

(domestic) "scene" as a pure experience of violence' self-consciously puts inverted commas around the word 'scene' that suggests to him that his experience of violence is not, in fact, *pure*, and then goes on to remark:

> In all violence, he [Barthes] could not keep from discerning, strangely, a literary kernel: how many conjugal scenes must be classified under the label of some great genre painting: *the wife cast out* or, again, *the repudiation!*[65]

For Barthes (no unreflective realist he), although we may seek to gesture beyond our modes of representation to pure 'things', our under-standing of those 'things' is differently generated *within* different modes of representation – not least language. From this perspective, 'cause and effect' are themselves plotted within those forms of representation that fall under the rubric of 'realism', the representation of *res*, though it is the claim of realism to elide the means of representation to get at 'the thing itself'.[66] Realism holds out the prospect of explanatory closure that is extremely strong, not to say final, and Most has committed himself methodologically to resisting this.

The second and third contexts into which Most seeks to embed the *Phaedra* are philosophy and rhetoric, but for the purposes of the present discussion I shall resist the division he makes between the two. He makes the interesting observation that 'for a Stoic, human dismemberment could raise awkward questions of personal identity':[67] at what point did mutilation of a body lead to the loss of personal identity of that body's owner? Most relates the issue to Stoic physics, where 'bodies', unlike the indivisible Epicurean atom, can be divided into ever smaller parts. What for the Stoics prevents this from happening is that 'bodies' are held together by a force or tension that permeates them and binds them together 'like glue'.[68] Unlike the Epicureans, for whom indivisibility is the key concept, the central issue for Stoics, then, is the question of *coherence*. Hippolytus' dismembered body has lost that tension and coher-ence, prompting Theseus to ask of its shattered parts, 'Is this Hippolytus?' (*Hippolytus hic est?*, 1249). Most goes on to draw attention to what he calls a 'curious feature' of the language of ancient rhetoric and literary criticism, namely 'the fact that words for the body and parts of the body form an important part of the conceptual vocabulary with which the ancients analyze texts and parts of texts'.[69] Words meaning body, head, limb, foot are used to refer to a variety of grammatical, metrical, and rhetorical

---

[65] Barthes 1977: 160; emphases in original.    [66] See Kennedy 2002: 14.    [67] Most 1992: 405.
[68] Most 1992: 405.    [69] Most 1992: 407.

phenomena.[70] In keeping with his firmly historicizing approach, Most associates his comments with *ancient* philosophy and *ancient* rhetoric, but we should pause for thought. In what way is the feature Most refers to 'curious'?

The term 'body' for us, no less than *soma* or *corpus* for the Greeks and Romans, tropes, to different intellectual ends, notions of unity and wholeness (as, for example, when we trope a set of facts or texts as a 'body' of work or talk about an author's 'corpus' of works or the 'body politic'); and we could recall that it is the role of the critic to analyse or anatomize, to chop up – to dismember: the 'critic' is one who divides up (*krinein*) or discriminates, enacts a *crimen*, indeed. But while critics do indeed do this, they are involved in a more complicated process. An example will be helpful here. In his introductory book on the *Phaedra*, Roland Mayer discusses what he sees as a characteristic of the literature of Seneca's time, a concern with parts rather than the whole:

> Nero's passion was the drama, in which he liked to perform, in the original Greek, roles of a specially pathetic nature, for example, Niobe, Canace's birth pangs, the blinded Oedipus, and the raving Hercules (Suetonius, *Life of Nero* 21.3); the last two were roles recreated for the Roman stage by Seneca. Here too we note the contemporary fashion for 'bleeding chunks', hacked off the body of a play or concert performance, another inducement to focus upon the scene rather than the integrated plot of the whole drama.[71]

The phrase 'bleeding chunks' derives from Sir Donald Francis Tovey's description of the practice of performing excerpts (etymologically, things plucked out) from the operas of Wagner.[72] Violent dismemberment of the body provides a repertoire of images for describing the separation of parts from the whole, and Tovey adds a grimly memorable and much-repeated phrase to this repertoire.[73] But critics do not simply wield a cleaver. Conscious of gaps in their knowledge, they dismember their object of study, whether through excerpting, citation, discussion, or paraphrase, *so as to reassemble* it in an attempt to recover a plenitude of form or meaning they believe to have been lost. They re-present so as to understand.

---

[70] Most 1992: 418 n. 116 has an extensive catalogue, including *caput* (cf. *OLD* s.v., sects. 16a, 16b, 18), *corpus* (*OLD* s.v., sect. 6b), *membrum* (*OLD* s.v., sect. 5c), and *pes* (*OLD* s.v., sect. 11).

[71] Mayer 2002: 12.

[72] Tovey 1935: 71: 'bleeding chunks of butcher's meat chopped from Wagner's operas'.

[73] Mayer, it should be noted, makes no use of this image in relation to the closing scene of Seneca's *Phaedra*.

Let's return to Most's methodological statement we considered earlier, where attempting to 'reduce' Neronian interest in dismemberment to the direct effect of some specifiable cause is rejected in favour of establishing 'connections of affinity and similarity' and aiming at a hermeneutic interpretation in terms of what Most referred to as 'coherence within a larger cultural matrix'. The former approach adopts what we could call an 'Epicurean' style of argument: a realist, reductionist search back along a linear chain of causation for an ultimate cause, aiming at a strictly deterministic explanation. Such a mode of thinking relies upon the notion that ultimately, somewhere back along the chain, there is a thing that is self-evident, requiring no analysis, no 'breaking up', just as, when this theory is applied to matter, there is an ultimate limit to division in a primary particle that cannot be divided further, an atom – a term that Lucretius tropes as 'body' in phrases such as *genitalia corpora rebus* ('the bodies that give birth to things', 1.58) and *corpora prima* ('first bodies', 1.61). The latter we could call a 'Stoic' fashion: unity is sought in terms of a principle of coherence amongst the parts, the glue or tension that holds them together, that makes of the parts a 'body'. The part – dismemberment in Seneca's *Phaedra* – will be understood *within* the whole, what Most (using an image derived from the body) calls 'the larger cultural matrix'. The former mode of thinking is associated in contemporary thought with reductionist physics, and with realism; the latter with anti-realist or constructivist modes of thought.[74] Most's methodological statement signals its willingness to take the latter seriously as plausible modes of explanation. Anti-realist modes of explanation seek to understand the phenomena they are interested in not as they are 'in themselves', but as a function of their representation. Realist modes of explanation are strongly closural, and seek to 'discover' the 'true' explanation; anti-realist modes are more provisional, 'inventing' possible explanations that may well be superseded. With Seneca's help, we may be able to take this argument further, and bring the issue back to tragedy and its explanatory dimension.

What we experience as 'violence' can afflict us with fear and horror, but, as the autobiographical reminiscences of Barthes and the article of Most in their different ways attest, it *simultaneously* challenges our understanding, and a response to that challenge is reflected in our characterization of it as a 'scene' or as 'theatrical'. Furthermore, not only can dismemberment (and violence more generally) be differently represented to different effect, as we

---

[74] See Kennedy 2002: 89–90.

have seen; the matter is also complicated by the fact that dismemberment is itself part of the image repertoire of representation and understanding. Dismemberment in Seneca's *Phaedra*, emphatically mediated, may be profitably explored within its representation as 'tragic'. And if 'the drama is all in the word', then we would do well to heed the words rather than seek, in a realist spirit, to gaze through them at some unmediated 'thing'.

Somewhat belatedly, after pioneering work on English tragedy in the 1960s and 1970s,[75] and its application to Greek tragedy (notably the *Bacchae*) the following decade,[76] a metapoetic approach has come to be applied to Senecan tragedy, most notably in Alessandro Schiesaro's extended reading of the *Thyestes*.[77] Strongly influenced by Jamie Masters' reading of Lucan's epic, in which it is argued that Caesar fighting the civil war is a reflection of the poet writing the civil war,[78] Schiesaro contends that within Seneca's plays, 'at several critical junctures, the actions of certain characters embody a reflection of the text on itself and offer important insights into its poetics'.[79] Is Theseus' assembling of the scattered body-parts of Hippolytus one such 'critical juncture' and could it 'embody' specifically metadramatic insights? Just before this final scene, Theseus, in response now to the death of his wife as well as his son, calls punishment down upon himself (1220–2):

> crudus et leti artifex,
> exitia machinatus insolita effera,
> nunc tibimet ipse iusta supplicia irroga.

Bloody craftsman of death, who has contrived unheard-of and savage modes of destruction, now inflict on yourself just punishment.

The term *artifex* is one that can embrace both the performer on the stage and the figure of the author,[80] and in *machinatus* we may sense the stage

---

[75] Abel 1963; Calderwood 1971.  [76] C. P. Segal 1997: 215–71, 369–78 (original edition 1982).

[77] Schiesaro 2003; see also Littlewood 2004: 172–258. For earlier discussions of Seneca's plays as metatheatrical, see Goldberg 1996; Boyle 1997: 112–37.

[78] Masters 1992.

[79] Schiesaro 2003: 13; he further comments (14): 'As the equivalent in theatrical terms to "metanarrative", "metadrama" can usefully indicate moments when the play, through a variety of devices, reflects on itself and its functioning.' Staley 2010: 22 suggests the limits of this mode of interpretation. In the absence of an explicit Senecan poetics outside of the plays, it is tempting to use the metatheatricality of the plays to articulate that poetics from within; 'the very prevalence of this trope, however, diminishes its interpretive power as a key to Seneca's theory of tragedy. If drama can symbolize politics, psychology, and even the nature of philosophy itself, then theatre need not, even within the plays, represent only or always itself.'

[80] Cf. *OLD* s.v., sects. 5, 6.

machinery (*mechane*) by which the tragedian can engineer his effects.[81] If Theseus' character is a metadramatic reflex of the tragedian, we can also see in *insolita* the topos of poetic originality. More than a century ago, Friedrich Leo drew attention to a characteristic use of the verb *solere* in Seneca, and argued that the products of the rhetorical schools not infrequently make use of a technique whereby, to increase the force of an argument, they touch on something which is well known to have happened only once in such a way as to suggest that it habitually occurs in similar circumstances.[82] As Leo remarks, when Phaedra complains early in the play that 'Theseus shows his wife the faith he is wont to do' (*praestatque nuptae quam solet Theseus fidem*, 92), 'anyone who has read these tragedies will grant that only Ariadne is in mind here'.[83] Quite so; but recently scholars have taught us to regard such expressions as authorial markers of intertextual reference, an invitation in this case to compare Phaedra's lament over Theseus' infidelity with Ariadne's in Catullus 64.132–201. We might see references to the 'habitual' and the 'new' more generally as 'reflexive annotations',[84] metapoetic invitations to consider the relationship of this play to its various intertexts. Theseus has already drawn attention in 1208–9 to the 'novelty' of Hippolytus' dismemberment (*morte facili haud dignus sum qui nova natum nece | segregem sparsi per agros*, 'as one who scattered my son in pieces across the fields in a *new* form of killing, I do not deserve an easy death'), and we might see this and *exitia machinatus insolita* in 1221 as emphasizing the significance of its divergences from the Euripidean *Hippolytus*.[85] Conversely, when Theseus in the immediately preceding line invokes his father Neptune as '*always* readily compliant with my wrath' (*tuque semper, genitor, irae facilis assensor meae*,

---

[81] Cf. Sen. *Med.* 266, where Creo calls Medea *malorum machinatrix facinorum*, a female 'engineer of wicked deeds', a phrase which evokes the use of the *mechane* at the end of Euripides' play, but also calls to mind Wilamowitz's quip that Medea must have read Euripides' tragedy about herself (Wilamowitz-Moellendorff 1919: III.162). Perhaps more than that. Seneca's Medea is conscious that she is fashioning herself to be a 'Medea' (cf. 910 *Medea nunc sum* ('I am now Medea'), which picks up on 171, where the Nurse addresses her as Medea, evoking the response *fiam* ('I shall become her')), and so could be troped not simply as the 'reader' but as the 'author' of her plot.

[82] Leo 1878: 149: 'non raro eo colore rhetores utuntur ut ad augendam vim argumenti rem quam semel evenisse notum sit, ita tangant quasi eadem saepe et adeo semper in simili occasione evenerit.' Note Leo's phrase 'ad augendam *vim* argumenti': competitive rhetorical training is centrally concerned with the force/violence of language.

[83] Leo 1878: 150: 'ubi qui has tragoedias legerit concedet tantum de Ariadna cogitari'.

[84] On such 'reflexive annotations' in Roman poetry cf. Hinds 1998: 1–16; he notes (3–4) that the figure of Ariadne is associated with some of the most prominent instances.

[85] Leo 1878: 155 associates *Phaed.* 1208–9 with descriptions in Seneca and elsewhere of Medea's dismemberment of Absyrtus, but this hardly accounts for *nova*.

1207), the marker underlines the adoption of the motif of the curse from Seneca's tragic predecessor.

When Theseus[86] enunciates his enactment of the *compositio membrorum*, the language used is particularly evocative of *literary* 'composition' (1256–8):

> disiecta, genitor, membra laceri corporis
> in ordinem dispone et errantes loco
> restitue partes.

Set, as his father, the scattered limbs of his mutilated body in order, and restore to their place the parts that have gone astray.

In the words *disiecta . . . membra* we may recall Horace's famous phrase *disiecti membra poetae* (*Sat.* 1.4.62). In lines 38–62 of *Satires* 1.4, Horace denies himself the title of poet for the genre he terms 'conversations' (*sermones*), just as he would deny it to the writer of comedy, albeit that comedy similarly is written in verse. It is not enough to make up a verse out of plain words, he says, and if you were to invert the order of Horace's words and so abolish the metre, it would be a very different matter from breaking up a phrase such as *'postquam Discordia taetra | Belli ferratos postes portasque refregit'* ('"after grim Discord broke down War's gates and portals bound with iron"', 60–1, seemingly a quotation from Ennius), for then *invenias etiam disiecti membra poetae* ('you could still find the limbs of the dismembered poet', 62). The limbs of the dismembered poet primarily evoke the fate of Orpheus, the master-poet torn apart by women in a Bacchic frenzy, but as used by Horace the image powerfully suggests how the body acts as a trope of artistic unity and integrity.[87] If Horace is prepared to be ironically playful in respect of comedy and satire, he is altogether more serious when it comes to tragedy. Seneca's echo of Horace's phrase can set in motion a complex metaliterary discourse in which Horace's *Ars poetica*, Rome's most important theoretical treatise on tragedy, plays a central part.

Calculated defiance of the Horatian tenets of decorum expressed in the *Ars poetica* characterizes the poetry of the later Augustan and post-Augustan

---

[86] Some editors follow MS Florence Laur. 37.13 (E) in attributing these lines to the Chorus rather than Theseus on the grounds of the second-person address; but this would not affect the points I am about to make.

[87] For a stimulating discussion of body imagery in Horace see Farrell 2007. The critic remarks of his own methodology (176): 'I will follow a lexical approach by collecting the different body parts strewn throughout Horace's oeuvre and assembling them into an aggregate Horatian body.'

periods.[88] Thus, when Horace enjoins that certain kinds of tragic action should be reported rather than directly presented (*Ars P.* 179–88), and takes as one of his examples 'that Medea should not slaughter her children in front of the audience' (*ne pueros coram populo Medea trucidet*, 185), this is precisely what Seneca does in his version of the tragedy, and, as if to emphasize the point, she commits murder not just once (*Med.* 969–71) but a second time as well (1018–19).[89] Horatian notions of artistic unity are memorably expressed at the beginning of the *Ars poetica* once more in terms of the human body (1–13):

> humano capiti cervicem pictor equinam
> iungere si velit, et varias inducere plumas
> undique collatis membris, ut turpiter atrum
> desinat in piscem mulier formosa superne,
> spectatum admissi risum teneatis, amici?    5
> credite, Pisones, isti tabulae fore librum
> persimilem cuius, velut aegri somnia, vanae
> fingentur species, ut nec pes nec caput uni
> reddatur formae. 'pictoribus atque poetis
> quidlibet audendi semper fuit aequa potestas.'    10
> scimus, et hanc veniam petimusque damusque vicissim;
> sed non ut placidis coeant immitia, non ut
> serpentes avibus geminentur, tigribus agni.

If a painter were to choose to join a horse's neck to a human head and to spread feathers of different colours on limbs brought together from anywhere and everywhere, so that a woman beautiful on top ended foully in a hideous fish, when admitted to view it, could you restrain your laughter, my friends? Believe me, Pisos, just like that picture would be the book whose parts,[90] like the dreams of a sick man, are imperfectly put together so that neither foot nor head can be combined into a shape that will be a unity.[91] 'Poets and painters have always had a fair liberty to venture whatever they like.' I'm aware of that, and I look for and

---

[88] For example, when Horace criticizes the poet who, from a desire to introduce variety monstrously into a subject that is really one (*qui variare cupit rem prodigialiter unam, Ars P.* 29), 'depicts a dolphin in the woods' (*delphinum silvis appingit,* 30), Ovid, in his *Metamorphoses,* famously engineers an early opportunity to do just that (1.302–3).

[89] Leo 1878: 149 attributes this defiance to the rhetorical training and influence of Seneca's father, remarking that in the tragedies as well as the prose works, 'we will be obliged to bring together father and son so as to understand that no one educated from his earliest years in this discipline could have acquiesced in the rules of the Greeks or of Horace, which Seneca openly scorned in his tragedies, and that, if he were writing tragedies, he could not have written them differently' ('in tragoediis filium cum patre ipsum conferre debebimus, ut intellegamus nec potuisse quemquam hac disciplina a prima aetate instructum in Graecis adquiescere vel in Horatii legibus, quas scilicet Seneca in tragoediis palam contempsit, nec, si tragoedias scriberet, alias scribere potuisse').

[90] For *species* as 'the parts that make up a poem' see Brink 1971: 89 ad loc.

[91] For the proleptic sense of *uni* here, see Brink 1971: 91 ad loc.

grant in turn this licence, but not to the extent that wild creatures are mated with tame, and serpents coupled with birds, lambs with tigers.

There are some significant points of contact between the *Phaedra* and the opening of the *Ars poetica*. The phrase *undique collatis membris* (*Ars P*. 3), albeit that in Horace *undique* connotes 'from any and every animal', is echoed in the messenger's description of the body-parts of Hippolytus 'assembled from everywhere for his funeral pyre and gathered together for his rites' (*passim ad supremos ille colligitur rogos | et funeri confertur, Phaed.* 1113–14).[92] When Theseus arranges his son's remains (*corpusque fingit, Phaed.* 1265), Mayer comments: 'The technical term for arranging a body for burial is *corpus componere*; S[eneca] wittily chooses a synonym for the verb which stresses how unusual this "laying-out" is.'[93] More than that: *fingere*, as line 8 of the *Ars poetica* explicitly attests, is a verb commonly used of a poet 'fashioning' his work.[94]

At the level of plot and characterization, Horace's mixed births are picked up in Seneca by the repeated theme of the monstrous offspring of Phaedra's mother, the Minotaur, which haunts Phaedra throughout the play, and which underlies the imagery used by the nurse to express her fear of the confusion of generations which an affair with Hippolytus would entail: 'Are you preparing to mix the father's marriage-bed with the son's, and to receive in your unholy womb a blended offspring?' (*miscere thalamos patris et gnati apparas | uteroque prolem capere confusam impio?*, 171–2).[95] But how might this intertextual play with Horace operate at a metapoetic level? Horace's focus at this stage of the *Ars poetica* is on unity. One possible approach would be to take it as referring to Seneca's use of his tragic sources: the incorporation (*sic*) of a scene from one Euripidean play, the *Bacchae*, into another, the *Hippolytus* (the equivalent of what modern

---

[92] How, we may wonder, are these to be distinguished if 'everywhere' included the setting for Hippolytus' earlier hunting?

[93] Coffey and Mayer 1990: 195 ad loc.

[94] In this regard, note also the literary resonances of the terms Theseus uses to enjoin the correct disposition of the body-parts: *in ordinem dispone et errantes loco | restitue partes* (1256–7); cf. *Rhet. Her.* 1.3 *dispositio est ordo et distributio rerum, quae demonstrat quid quibus locis sit collocandum* ('[rhetorical] disposition is the sequence and distribution of topics, which indicates what is to be located together in which places'), Cic. *Inv. rhet.* 1.9 *dispositio est rerum inventarum in ordinem distributio* ('disposition is the distribution of the topics you have devised into their sequence').

[95] See Boyle 1987: 143 on *Phaed.* 113 *fatale miserae matris agnosco malum* ('I recognize the fateful evil of my poor mother'). He compares 122, 174ff., 242, 649, 688ff., 1067, and 1170–1, and contrasts Euripides' *Hippolytus*, where no reference is made to the Minotaur and only one to Pasiphaë's love for the bull (337–8), a useful reminder of how much these two plays differ.

critics call, in relation to comedy, *contaminatio*).[96] As Boyle suggests, '[it] seems no accident ... that Theseus' attempt to put together the separated fragments of his dismembered son in the final act of the *Phaedra* is the construct of a scene which is itself an attempt by Seneca to put together the separated fragments of the dismembered *oeuvre* of Euripides – as the Roman dramatist endeavours to bring together fragments of Euripides' *Hippolytus* and *Bacchae* into a new, harmonious whole'.[97] However, Horace's imagery, the coupling of distinct species so as to produce 'unnatural' composites, suggests another possible approach, one based on the notion of *genus*, a term that can embrace both types of animal and types of writing. The tragic tradition is but one 'part' of Seneca's literary tradition, and while it must be assigned its proper 'place' (whatever that is),[98] it is necessary to look beyond the boundaries of the genre of tragedy.

Schiesaro has argued for the importance to the *Thyestes* of epic intertextual reference ('specifically the filter of Ovid's *Metamorphoses* and peculiar aspects of Virgil's *Aeneid* – the epic of violence and *horrida bella* rather more than the celebration of heroic virtues and beliefs'), suggesting that 'it is almost as if tragedy could not refer directly to tragedy, but should necessarily rely on an epic filter and thus testify to the impossibility of an immediate connection, to a hiatus in the continuous tradition of tragic writing. Here again Senecan tragedy highlights its posteriority, its position outside the mainstream of tragic writing.'[99] While commending Schiesaro's use of intertexts to figure Seneca's place within the literary tradition, we might query the rather negative rhetoric of marginality, and see Seneca as reflecting on what happens when tragedy is generically coupled with other forms. In the case of *Phaedra*, the most important 'filter' (though in this context I would be tempted to adopt as more apposite the metaphor Schiesaro uses elsewhere on the same page, 'cross-fertilization') is that of Roman erotic elegy, specifically elegy's use of the imagery of hunting to suggest sexual pursuit, an imagery that when transplanted from an elegiac

---

[96] Cf. C. P. Segal 1986: 215: 'The last scene of the *Phaedra* has a peculiarly complex form of literariness and textuality, for Seneca here "contaminates" Euripides' *Hippolytus* with the *Bacchae*.'

[97] Boyle 1997: 112; he adds: 'Appropriate ramifications of Theseus' failure for the poetics of Senecan tragedy are at hand. What seems involved is not only Seneca's sense of the impossibility of recreating the Attic form in a post-classical age, but also his location of discord at the centre of the new style.' For possible verbal reminiscences of the *Bacchae* in the *Phaedra* see Gahan 1987.

[98] Cf. *Phaed.* 1267–8 *quae pars tui sit dubito; sed pars est tui.* | *hic, hic repone, non suo, at vacuo loco* ('I do not know what part of you this is; but it is part of you. Put it here, here – not in its proper place, but in a vacant one'). For Mayer, line 1267 is 'arguably the worst line in Senecan drama' (Coffey and Mayer 1990: 195 ad loc.). Were Seneca Ovid, one could imagine him claiming it as his best.

[99] Schiesaro 2003: 84.

into a tragic context is gruesomely materialized in Hippolytus' dismemberment.[100] It is also relevant that when the elegiac erotic gaze dwells on the object of its desire, it expresses its appreciation of perfection and beauty by effectively 'dismembering' the body of the beloved.[101]

If Horace provides an intriguing intertext through which the literary and generic affiliations of the *Phaedra* may be explored, we may be encouraged to probe further how the end of the play engages with discourses of the tragic. The closing scene is ostensibly one of tragic recognition (Theseus says 'I recognize my *crimen*' (1249)), but critics have remarked upon how limited that recognition is. 'Emphasis on Theseus' guilt and acknowledgement of guilt in the final scene (esp. 1201ff., 1249ff.) makes the final comment on Phaedra and its simplistic moral judgement abhorrent ... Like Jason in the final lines of *Medea*, Theseus reveals he has understood little', remarks Boyle.[102] Moreover, as we have seen, the recognition accorded to Theseus offers little in the way of consolation or closure. The ending of *Titus Andronicus*, which, as we saw earlier, echoes that of *Phaedra*, provides an interesting contrast. The orgy of gruesome violence complete,[103] Marcus, one of the few survivors, addresses the people of Rome:

> You sad-fac'd men, people and sons of Rome,
> By uproar sever'd, like a flight of fowl
> Scatter'd by winds and high tempestuous gusts
> O! Let me teach you how to knit again
> This scatter'd corn into one mutual sheaf,
> These broken limbs again into one body.
>
> (5.3.67–72)

This encourages the expectation that order may return to a world that has been broken into pieces and dispersed. By contrast, the efforts of Hippolytus' companions and his dogs have not yet succeeded in 'filling out' his body (*explere corpus*, 1110), and Theseus anticipates that the funeral rites

---

[100] For a detailed study of the elegiac associations of hunting imagery in the *Phaedra* see Littlewood 2004: 259–301.

[101] Cf. Ov. *Am.* 1.5.17–22 *ut stetit ante oculos posito velamine nostros, | in toto nusquam corpore menda fuit: | quos umeros, quales vidi tetigique lacertos! | forma papillarum quam fuit apta premi! | quam castigato planus sub pectore venter! | quantum et quale latus! quam iuvenale femur!* ('When she stood before my eyes with her clothes laid aside, there was nowhere on her whole body a blemish: what shoulders, what arms I gazed at and touched! The shape of her breasts – how suited to be caressed! How smooth the stomach beneath her firm bosom! So long and lovely her flank! How youthful her thigh!'), with Scourfield, Chapter 11 below, p. 322 with n. 63.

[102] Boyle 1987: 35.

[103] Hulse 1979: 106: '[*Titus Andronicus*] has 14 killings, 9 of them on stage, 6 severed members, 1 rape (or 2, or 3, depending on how you count), 1 live burial, 1 case of insanity, and 1 of cannibalism – an average of 5.2 atrocities per act, or one for every 97 lines.'

will have to be repeated often (*saepe efferendus*, 1274). The verb *explere* has connotations of completion, finality, closure, and the satisfaction that brings,[104] but the *Phaedra* seems to deny this satisfaction to both Theseus and the audience.

How might this contribute to a sense of *Phaedra* as a *tragic* text? Elaine Scarry argues in her book *The Body in Pain* that pain is a phenomenon that resists representation in language, finding its readiest expression rather in paralinguistic shrieks and yells.[105] Tragedy could be seen as one form of representation that seeks to capture such phenomena, as Terry Eagleton suggests:

> Tragic art involves the plotting of suffering, not simply a *raw* cry of pain. And while this very *mise-en-scène* may endow suffering with a spurious *shapeliness*, lending it an intelligibility which seems to betray the *ragged incoherence* of the thing itself, it is hard to see how we could even use words like 'tragic' outside some such moral or social contextualizing, in life as much as in art. *Tidying up* the tragic may thus be part of the price we pay for articulating it.[106]

The phrases which I have italicized are worthy of note as echoing the themes we have been considering. Eagleton sees tragedy as a way of giving what he calls 'intelligibility' to suffering, but at a cost, in that the closure it can offer runs the risk of endowing it with a 'spurious' shapeliness – 'in life as much as in art'. Roland Barthes is likewise concerned that the 'scene' of violence, the domestic quarrel so terrifying to witness because there seems to be no alternative to escalation in its verbal exchanges, is compromised, when it is dramatized, precisely by this drive to closure:

> Language is impotent to close language – that is what the scene says: the retorts engender one another, without any possible conclusion, save that of murder; and it is because the scene is entirely bent on, aims toward this ultimate violence, which nonetheless it never assumes (at least among 'civilized' people), that it is an essential violence, a violence which delights in sustaining itself . . .
>
> (On stage the scene is domesticated: the theater *humbles* it, obliges it to end: a cessation of language is the greatest violence that can be done to the violence of language.)[107]

---

[104] Cf. *OLD* s.v., sect. 5 for connotations of completion, and sect. 6 for those of satisfaction. An online search of the PHI Latin Texts database indicates that *corpus* is found as the object of *explere* only here.

[105] Scarry 1985: 3–11.     [106] Eagleton 2003: 63.     [107] Barthes 1977: 159; original emphasis.

If Senecan drama is 'all in the word', a violence of representation as well as a representation of violence, the issue of a closure that reassures is a particular challenge.

Alessandro Schiesaro has argued for an intense metapoetic interest in the *Thyestes* in the issue of tragic closure. The play, he suggests, contains a set of internal frames, in which '*Thyestes* isolates an inner core, a deepest level, where Atreus acts out a plot of his own devising and successfully punishes his brother'.[108] However, the strongly closural character of this innermost frame contrasts with the outer ones which 'remain undoubtedly open and portend no shortage of future evils ... In this way *Thyestes* affords its audience both the reassuring satisfaction of closure and the tormenting promise of renewed terrors.'[109] Does – should – tragedy move towards closure? Aristotle's definition of tragedy in the *Poetics*, as 'the representation of an action that is serious and *complete in itself* and has some amplitude ... a whole ... which has a beginning, a middle, and an end', indicates a predisposition towards plots that have closural qualities.[110] Plot for Aristotle, we may recall, is the most important element of tragedy, and of the constitutive parts of plot, *peripeteia*, *pathos*, and *anagnorisis*, Aristotle devotes the most attention to *anagnorisis* (recognition). Given that recognition is so important to Aristotle, what *kind* of knowledge does 'recognition' provide? 'Ana-gnorisis, like re-cognition, in fact implies the recovery of something once known rather than a shift from ignorance to knowledge', suggests Terence Cave,[111] a contrast, we may say, between realist views of knowledge that see it as *discovery* of what was (already) there, but which has been effaced, and the anti-realist *construction* of modes of enquiry (for example, different kinds of writing) that essay understanding

---

[108] Schiesaro 2003: 64.   [109] Schiesaro 2003: 65.

[110] Arist. *Poet.* 6, 7 (1449b24–5, 1450b26–7) ἐστιν οὖν τραγῳδία μίμησις πράξεως σπουδαίας καὶ τελείας μέγεθος ἐχούσης ... ὅλον δέ ἐστιν τὸ ἔχον ἀρχὴν καὶ μέσον καὶ τελευτήν. Aristotle speaks at length of plot in terms of the body (*Poet.* 7 (1450b34–1451a6)), and prescribes that the unified plot should be 'the imitation of a single and unified action, and the limbs of the events should be so ordered that if one limb is differently placed or taken away the whole is dislocated and disturbed' (χρὴ ... τὸν μῦθον, ἐπεὶ πράξεως μίμησίς ἐστι, μιᾶς τε εἶναι καὶ ταύτης ὅλης, καὶ τὰ μέρη συνεστάναι τῶν πραγμάτων οὕτως ὥστε μετατιθεμένου τινὸς μέρους ἢ ἀφαιρουμένου διαφέρεσθαι καὶ κινεῖσθαι τὸ ὅλον, *Poet.* 8 (1451a30–4)). Lucas 1968: 117 observes that διαφέρεσθαι ('dislocated') is 'probably a medical term'.

[111] Cave 1988: 33. Cave further notes of the definition of *anagnorisis* in *Poetics* 11 that 'the phrasing is parallel to that of the definition of peripeteia in that anagnorisis too is said to be a change (*metabolē*) from one thing to or into (*eis*) its opposite, except that what is changed is not the "things being done" but the degree of knowledge. Anagnorisis appears first as the epistemological counterpart of peripeteia.'

in a heuristic spirit but see the pursuit of a full and final truth as an ongoing process, and its achievement as perhaps even infinitely deferred.

It is certainly tempting to see Hippolytus' body as a site for a specifically tragic meditation on knowledge and attempts to understand, and Seneca as reconfiguring this (Aristotelian) tradition of tragic criticism in the tropes and conventions of tragedy itself. However, epistemological pretensions, as we saw earlier when considering Glenn Most's article, link tragedy with what at first sight appears a very different genre, scholarship. In its search for epistemological closure, Most's article diverges quite markedly from the *Phaedra*, and it is hard to read its mode as tragic. Terence Cave sees the prominence given in the *Poetics* to *anagnorisis*, and to texts in which recognition is a key motif (particularly the *Odyssey* and *Oedipus Tyrannus*), in terms of the whole work's interest in 'fictions of knowledge', and wonders whether Aristotle, 'being interested in epistemology, could not help "discovering" epistemological themes and structures in literary works'. He continues:

> Aristotle's poetics is a powerful instrument, not because it provides an accurate account of how tragedies do or should work, but because it absorbs the narrative structure of a group of literary texts into a discourse deeply concerned with modes of cognition, and in the process transforms them: in the context it provides, the plays perform a heuristic role. It is by no means clear that they perform this role anywhere but in the *Poetics* – or, *mutatis mutandis*, in later versions of poetics. There is an important sense in which the things we see in literature are not there until we see them.[112]

When scholarly works are viewed as heuristic constructions, they often appear as recursive mimeses of the tropes of the texts they interact with, reconfiguring the themes and the imagery they appropriate from the texts they study into fresh epistemic and generic settings, as Cave suggests is happening with tragedy in Aristotle's *Poetics*. Might the same be said of *this* present essay, which in an anti-realist spirit similarly configures Seneca's *Phaedra* as a 'fiction of knowledge'? It could, of course, be read under the sign of 'recognition', as 'discovering' things that have 'really' always been there. That would offer a very satisfying sense of historical closure, but would go against the grain of the argument I have been developing. I have represented the closing scene of Seneca's *Phaedra* as a peculiarly brutal commentary, inscribed within the language and conventions of tragedy, on the corporeal images in which we habitually represent to ourselves our

---

[112] Cave 1988: 10.

modes of understanding, including tragic understanding, as *adequate*, so habitually that we take them for granted until disturbed into reflecting upon them. A resulting sense of the inadequacy of our means of representation might well induce feelings of pain which we swiftly move to displace into a joke, a tragedy – or another article.[113]

---

[113] My thanks to the editors and to Cambridge University Press's anonymous readers for their criticisms, which have helped me to put the *errantes partes* of this essay together, though probably not to their entire satisfaction. As author, I can but echo the words of Theseus: *quae pars tui sit dubito; sed pars est tui. | hic, hic repone, non suo, at vacuo loco.*

CHAPTER 8

# Violence and Alienation in Lucan's Pharsalia
## The Case of Caesar

*Efrossini Spentzou*

Lucan's epic of civil war is a (post-)classic(al) locus of violence in ancient literature. Blood gushes, bodies lose their human form, excruciating death stares the reader unblinkingly in the eye, daring one to make sense of a deluge of physical, somatic destruction. Scholarship on the text has offered various accounts of the bleakness and disintegration of Lucan's ailing world.[1] The present study differs from that scholarship in focusing on a kind of violence that is not primarily physical. Time and again in the *Pharsalia* cultural norms are transgressed, boundaries violated, social and political order disrupted, psychological barriers broken, and mental and emotional states fractured through the sheer, unyielding force of a single personality, Caesar, whose bruising grip over the epic is, ultimately, almost 'unthinkable'.[2]

Caesar's first appearance in the *Pharsalia* (1.143–57) follows and parallels that of his enemy, his former friend and son-in-law, Pompey (1.129–43). The descriptions of both men invite comparison with Aeneas and, through him, with each other. But whereas Pompey's introduction involves a painful description of decay,[3] Caesar's brims with barely contained energy, reflecting a fierce desire for action. His reputation is

---

[1] See, e.g., Ahl 1976; Henderson 1987; W. R. Johnson 1987; Masters 1992; Leigh 1997; Hershkowitz 1998: 197–246; Sklenář 2003.

[2] Alston and Spentzou 2011 place Caesar's megalomania alongside other cases of disturbing individuality from other narratives of the period, seeing them all as manifestations of a widespread crisis of political ontology.

[3] A shadow of his erstwhile illustrious self, Pompey is likened to a lofty oak in a fruitful field – conjuring up the image of a steadfast Aeneas, resisting Dido's allure, as an oak with strong roots at Virg. *Aen.* 4.438–46. But unlike the firm Aeneas, who is about to head off to found a new people and embrace a glorious destiny, rejecting the blandishments of a foreign woman, the roots of Pompey's oak have lost their robustness (1.136–9). For a systematic exploration of the inverted formulas we encounter when reading Pompey's journey eastwards in the *Pharsalia* alongside Aeneas' journey westwards in the *Aeneid*, see Rossi 2000, with special reference to the image of the oak at 573–4.

246

matched by his limitless ambition. The description culminates in a comparison of Caesar with a thunderbolt that flashes through the clouds:

> sed non in Caesare tantum
> nomen erat nec fama ducis, sed nescia virtus
> stare loco, solusque pudor non vincere bello
> . . .
> . . . inpellens, quidquid sibi summa petenti
> obstaret . . .
> qualiter expressum ventis per nubila fulmen
> aetheris inpulsi sonitu mundique fragore
> emicuit.[4]

But not so with Caesar: he had not only the name and fame of a general, but restless vigour; his only shame was not to conquer in war . . . striking against whatever might stand in the way of his achievement of greatness . . . Just so flashes out the thunderbolt forced by the winds through the cloud, with the stricken heavens and shattered atmosphere resounding around it.[5]

(1.143–5, 149–53)

The lightning speed and deafening noise evoked here recall the language of cosmic upheaval in the closing scene of Virgil's *Aeneid* when Aeneas hurls his spear at an overwhelmed Turnus:

> telum Aeneas fatale coruscat,
>                   . . . et corpore toto
> eminus intorquet. murali concita numquam
> tormento sic saxa fremunt nec fulmine tanti
> dissultant crepitus. volat atri turbinis instar
> . . . hasta.

Aeneas brandishes his lethal spear and . . . launches it with all the strength of his body from afar. Rocks hurled by a siege engine do not make so great a noise, nor does the crash of the thunderbolt reverberate so loudly. The spear . . . flies like a black tornado.

(Virg. *Aen.* 12.919–24)

The reader is invited by Lucan here to place Caesar and Aeneas side by side. At first sight, the imagery serves to accentuate these heroes' differences: whereas, in the case of Caesar, the thunderbolt is presented as an uncontrollable force of nature (1.155–7), Aeneas' thunderous throw of his spear assimilates the Trojan hero to (vengeful) divine justice, as executed by Jupiter through his sending of the Dira in *Aeneid* 12.853–60.[6] Yet, in

---

[4] I cite the *Pharsalia* according to the text of J. D. Duff 1928.
[5] All translations from ancient texts are mine.     [6] See Hardie 1986: 147–8.

the wake of this simile, Aeneas perpetrates his most controversial act in the
epic: the fatal attack on the wounded Turnus. Fuelled by passion, the blow
Aeneas delivers in the closing scene of the poem seems to hint at a Roman
state into whose fabric destructive (civil) conflict is woven at the very
moment of its foundation. As if unaccustomed to such fury, the *Aeneid*
breaks off leaving a lingering memory of violence.

Caesar's eruption into Lucan's epic calls to mind Aeneas' *furor*, the
spectre of violence which haunts the end of the *Aeneid* and the foundational moment of Rome moving to centre stage in the *Pharsalia*, the epic of
Republican loss and the origins of Empire. Lucan's poem ventures where
the *Aeneid* was reluctant to go and starts where its predecessor left off, with
Caesar ushering the hero's story into an uncharted territory of fury and
violent outbursts. Thanks to Caesar's crazed talent, the epic code is
violated and a new epic born, with a protagonist of unprecedented type
and extraordinary (if abrasive and frenzied) individualism. Caesar is an
empowered and overwhelming individual, terrifying and alluring at the
same time. Trailing after him, the soldiers, as we shall see, are gripped by
that mixture of disgust and morbid fascination that dislocates perception.
By his very unpredictability, Caesar sabotages the expectations of normative expression and representation, pushing characters and readers alike to
the limit of their comprehension. In the rest of this chapter I shall focus on
the bruising nature of Caesar's self-assurance and self-isolation, in an
attempt to formulate a reaction to (though not an explanation of) the
enigma that is Lucan's extraordinary hero. I propose to dwell on the
incalculable effect that Lucan's Caesar has on the world of the epic as well
as on the reader; and to this end I will draw out resonances with modern
philosophical responses to the incomprehensible in life (as manifested in
the Kantian sublime) and in one's own identity (as explored in Julia
Kristeva's discussions of the abject).[7]

### Mutilating the Mind: Caesar's Radical Violence

The ideological and generic solipsism of Caesar as conjured up by Lucan
confronts the reader right from the start. No sooner are we through with
the introductory presentations than Caesar dispenses with 'the anxiety of

---

[7] In Chapter 7 above, Duncan Kennedy observes and engages with a similar critical inadequacy *vis-à-
vis* extreme (physical) violence. Probing the violent corporeal images of Hippolytus' mutilation with
which Seneca's *Phaedra* concludes, Kennedy exposes the fragility of our standardized modes of tragic
understanding and traces the marks of uneasiness and displacement in previous criticism when faced
with this fragility.

influence'. Though the *Aeneid* is hardly a unidimensional work, Aeneas' striving to control the forces of disorder and provide boundaries for his people is an incessant drive in the text that tends to curb people's darkest, impulsive instincts. After all, in spite of the problematic slaughter of Turnus, readers of the *Aeneid* could still, like Venus, find reassurance in Jupiter's first Roman prophecy at 1.257–96: Law (292–3) was to become a foundational element of Roman Republican values. But in the *Pharsalia*, Law could not be more disgraced. Caesar treats with contempt the past, its traditions, and its social ties: in sum, all the constituents of a system that gave to the older epics, and the old Roman world, a moral and collective dimension.[8]

Indeed, at the core of the story of the *Pharsalia* lies a single physical transgression, the crossing of the Rubicon, a gesture that dashes any lingering hope for reconciliation between the factions. Reduced to a meagre brook in the summer, the river in winter is swollen on account of unusually heavy rainfall (1.213–19), so that exceptional efforts are needed for the crossing (1.220–2). Underlining the (symbolically violent) transgressiveness of Caesar's action, Lucan has Roma appear to Caesar in a dream as a dishevelled woman the previous night (1.186–9). After overcoming his initial anxiety about the vision (1.192–4), Caesar is unstoppable. It is at this point, with the crossing of the Rubicon, that the magnitude of Caesar's violation begins to emerge. Unlike Aeneas, whose own feat consisted in containing individuality within a cosmic order of *pietas*, Caesar has placed himself outside the boundaries of a moral code. Lucan writes:

> ut adversam superato gurgite ripam
> attigit, Hesperiae vetitis et constitit arvis,
> 'hic,' ait, 'hic pacem temerataque iura relinquo;
> te, Fortuna, sequor. procul hinc iam foedera sunto.'

When he reached the opposite bank, having overcome the swollen stream, and stood on the forbidden soil of Italy, he said, 'Here, here I abandon peace and violated law; you, Fortune, I follow. Away now with agreements!'

(1.223–6)

Caesar's driving force and (un)ethical map is the 'beyond', the world he sees (perhaps not clearly) extending out there, beyond the Rubicon, beyond the limits and limitations of others' treaties and what he calls the

---

[8] Note, for example, Caesar's careless trampling over the ancient ruins – and history – of Troy at 9.964–79, with further discussion of the passage at Rossi 2000: 588 with n. 74, Alston 2011.

violated laws of Rome. The world of the *Pharsalia* is amoral in the sense that, despite the characters' claims to the contrary, it is devoid of transcendental essences (such as gods) and universalizing moralities. The epic could be described as non-foundational since it shows little sign of defending or arguing for fundamental social or moral values that could provide social grounding. There is no 'moral code of the warrior', no consistent devotion either to state or to some metaphysical ideal. The only force that drives Caesar appears to be his need to break containment and to triumph over all. He is relentless, frenetic, and uncontrolled, raging against delay and seeking never to pause.

In Book 3, as Pompey flees Rome, Caesar is consumed by rage at the temporary postponement of hostilities.

> non illum gloria pulsi
> laetificat Magni: queritur, quod tuta per aequor
> terga ferant hostes. neque enim iam sufficit ulla
> praecipiti fortuna viro, nec vincere tanti,
> ut bellum differret, erat.

Yet the glory of expelling Magnus does not give him any joy. He complains that the enemy has escaped to safety over the sea, for no success is good enough now for the impetuous man, and victory was not for him worth postponing the war.

(3.48–52)

Deprived of this opportunity for destruction, at least temporarily, Caesar sends his envoys to spread warfare to Sicily and Sardinia (3.52–70). Throughout, he refuses to rest. Triumphal processions remain unclaimed, as he presses on in his unremitting campaign of conquest. The narrator cannot help but wonder:

> pro, si remeasset in urbem,
> Gallorum tantum populis Arctoque subacta,
> quam seriem rerum longa praemittere pompa,
> quas potuit belli facies!
> . . .
> perdidit o qualem vincendo plura triumphum!

Alas, if he had returned to Rome with only the peoples of Gaul and the north subdued, what a sequence of achievements, what images of war could he have put forth in the long procession! ... What a triumph he lost by securing more victories!

(3.73–9)

Formal declaration of victory would have been a resolution of the breach in order that is civil war, and Caesar is averse to such closure and any concomitant societal consensus, loath to abandon the encounter with the edge and with the limits of a system and its (false) securities. A key moment in this irresistible urge for trespass comes in Book 5. As a large part of his army is stranded in Brundisium by bad weather, he is prevented from mounting an assault on the Pompeians in Greece. Caesar rages at the delay (5.476–91), and when all threats and cajoling have failed, he takes the crazed decision to cross the Adriatic from Epirus to Brundisium in a small boat with the near-impossible mission of leading his stranded troops back to the Greek coast (5.497–503). In this episode, the fury of the sea challenges the narrator's comprehension,[9] and Caesar's unfathomable daring exercises the comprehension of his soldiers.[10]

Conflict seems to be a constituent feature of Caesar's identity, as he continually strives to deny others either resolution or reconciliation. We are persistently told that the one thing that Caesar fears above all else is a softening of the troops' resolve and frenzy,[11] that brief moment of respite which would allow the soldiers to look around them, reflect, perceive (and connect with) each other. But thanks to Caesar's abrasive but irresistible style of leadership, such respite rarely occurs, and the troops continue to march on under his influence. One of the most striking of his numerous unpredictable moments is his order to the soldiers to spare the desperate Pompeian soldiers of Afranius and Petreius at Ilerda. He explains this unusual act:

> 'en, sibi vilis adest invisa luce iuventus
> iam damno peritura meo; non sentiet ictus,
> incumbet gladiis, gaudebit sanguine fuso.
> deserat hic fervor mentes, cadat impetus amens,
> perdant velle mori.' sic deflagrare minaces
> incassum et vetito passus languescere bello . . .

'Look! Here come young men, holding themselves cheap, hating the light, about to die, to my detriment; they will not feel the blows, they will fall upon the swords, they will rejoice at the shedding of their blood. Let this passion leave their minds, let the demented impulse fade; let the wish to die be lost.' Thus, by refusing battle, he allowed their threats to burn out fruitlessly and lose their force.

(4.276–81)

Their lives spared, the captives are brought before Caesar. Their representative speaks and asks for any punishment which would not compel them to conquer along with the Caesarian army. Caesar obliges; he shows

---

[9] See, e.g., 5.558–600, 605–12, 616–17.      [10] See, e.g., 5.682–99.
[11] Goading, indeed, is a trademark of his leadership, from the very early stages of the civil war (see, e.g., 1.239–41, 393–4) all the way to the battlefield of Pharsalus (7.557–70).

*clementia* when least expected and frees the soldiers, causing bewilderment and a certain admiration in the captives and the narrator (4.344–81). Caesar sees the passion that drives the soldiers and elevates them above the ordinary, and forbids it to them. He allows their emotion to break on the rocks of his troops, and exhausts their passion. In passion, no one can be allowed to compete with Caesar. His refusal to be bound by expectation triumphs: the defeated soldiers are denied the resolution which would have given their madness meaning and narrative force. They return home quietly, their fury rendered meaningless before the greater passion that is Caesar.

Time and again as the civil war unfolds, Caesarian troops despair of the enigma that their leader represents. With Rome almost in sight, Caesar gathers his soldiers for an exhortatory talk. Times are tense and the soldiers are agitated. An uneasy silence spreads across the army as the troops catch sight of their general (1.296–8). Caesar then explains the reasons for the war with the aim of rousing his soldiers for battle, in a speech which startlingly compares his invasion with that of Hannibal (1.304–5). Caesar thus emerges as a second historic threat to Rome, recalling that earliest of Roman foundational epics, Naevius' *Bellum Punicum*. Yet Caesar justifies the war by claiming his personal dues, the blessings of fortune that run with him, and the weakness of the aging Pompey. There is a double motive for turning to arms: the opportunity to seize power, as a response to the 'crimes'[12] of Pompey which Caesar lists, and the rewards in Gaul that the soldiers have the right to demand. The soldiers respond to this history lesson with a mixture of distaste and arousal:

> dixerat; at dubium non claro murmure volgus
> secum incerta fremit. pietas patriique penates
> quamquam caede feras mentes animosque tumentes
> frangunt; sed diro ferri revocantur amore
> ductorisque metu.

He finished; but the doubtful crowd mutters indistinctly with uncertain whispers. Though made fierce by slaughter, their swelling hearts and minds are softened by devotion to their country and their ancestral gods; but they are recalled by their fearsome love of the sword and their terror of their leader.

(1.352–6)

Devotion to (and responsibility for) country is here juxtaposed with something much more uncontrolled and impulsive: addiction to

---

[12] Explicitly referred to as *scelera* at 1.326 and 1.334.

violence. At the same time, the soldiers' respect for the ancestral gods is replaced by fear of their leader. Momentarily, Caesar's soldiers waver between their patriotic feelings and their thirst for blood, between the values of the traditional order (home, family, religion, tradition itself), so obviously represented by the ancestral gods (brought by Aeneas from Troy), and Caesar, who threatens to replace all those values of community, leaving himself as the only object of loyalty. What holds them to Caesar is not love, but terror, an emotion which is not bonding and social, but individual and atomizing. In the soldiers' fear of their leader each man is isolated, locked in a profoundly personal and thus more mesmerizing relationship with the force that is now to rule them. This conflict between society and leader sets up a tension that diverges sharply from the ethos of the *Aeneid*. When every so often Aeneas' personal magnetism somehow fails to inspire his soldiers, the ever-so-distant and yet omnipresent collective goal of the formation of a community is mobilized to rally the troops.[13] In Lucan's epic, however, the moment of doubt – this collective wavering between modes of life, between community and whatever the future holds – ends with a dramatic reassertion of an entranced loyalty to Caesar voiced by the centurion Laelius, ironically described as a man honoured for the saving of Roman lives (1.357–8). Notably, the speech is even more violent, even more excessive than that of Caesar, a demented outburst to marvel at:

> 'si licet,' exclamat 'Romani maxime rector
> nominis, et ius est veras expromere voces,
> quod tam lenta tuas tenuit patientia vires,
> conquerimur. deratne tibi fiducia nostri?
> dum movet haec calidus spirantia corpora sanguis,
> et dum pila valent fortes torquere lacerti,
> degenerem patiere togam regnumque senatus?
> usque adeo miserum est civili vincere bello?
> duc age per Scythiae populos, per inhospita Syrtis
> litora, per calidas Libyae sitientis harenas:
> haec manus, ut victum post terga relinqueret orbem,
> Oceani tumidas remo conpescuit undas,

---

[13] Aeneas' performance in the first instance of crisis we witness in the epic is both telling and programmatic. With their lives in immediate danger, abandoned to the wrath of Juno, Aeneas galvanizes his soldiers with a mention of the grander destiny that awaits them (Virg. *Aen.* 1.187–209). It is significant, in this context, that Aeneas omits what Odysseus, in an equivalent moment of crisis, showers us with: lavish praise of his own self, and especially his personal standing and capabilities as a leader (Hom. *Od.* 12.201–33).

fregit et arctoo spumantem vertice Rhenum:
iussa sequi tam posse mihi quam velle necesse est.
nec civis meus est, in quem tua classica, Caesar,
audiero. per signa decem felicia castris
perque tuos iuro quocumque ex hoste triumphos:
pectore si fratris gladium iuguloque parentis
condere me iubeas plenaeque in viscera partu
coniugis, invita peragam tamen omnia dextra;
si spoliare deos ignemque inmittere templis,
numina miscebit castrensis flamma monetae;
castra super Tusci si ponere Thybridis undas,
Hesperios audax veniam metator in agros;
tu quoscumque voles in planum effundere muros,
his aries actus disperget saxa lacertis,
illa licet, penitus tolli quam iusseris urbem,
Roma sit.'

'If, he exclaimed, 'it is permitted and lawful to speak the truth, mightiest helmsman of the Roman nation, we complain that your prolonged patience has curbed your strength. Did you lack faith in us? While hot blood stirs these bodies and they breathe, and sturdy arms avail to hurl the javelin, will you suffer the degeneracy of civil authority and the tyranny of the Senate? Is it so terrible to win a civil war? Come, lead us through the Scythian peoples, through the inhospitable shores of Syrtis, through the hot sands of thirsty Libya. To leave a conquered world behind, these hands subdued the Ocean's swollen waters with the oar and tamed the Rhine, foaming with icy eddies. To follow your orders I have both the will and the power that I need. Nor can the man against whom I hear your trumpets sounding, Caesar, be a fellow-citizen of mine. I swear by the standards prosperous over ten campaigns, by your triumphs over every enemy, that if you should bid me plunge my sword into my brother's heart or my parent's throat or the womb of my pregnant wife, I will do it all, even with hand unwilling; should you bid me despoil the gods and set alight the temples, the flame of our military mint will melt down the divinities; should you order me to pitch camp by the waters of Etruscan Tiber, I will enter the fields of Hesperia as a bold surveyor; whatever walls you wish reduced to the ground, the battering-ram propelled by these arms will scatter their stones, even if the city which you have ordered to be destroyed is Rome.'

(1.359–86)

Laelius proclaims his personal loyalty to Caesar, who is elevated to a mythical, quasi-divine status as the foremost *gubernator* of the Roman people, and yet is a leader who will not reaffirm the values of community and family but will lead precisely to the destruction of those bonds of family and love in a welter of annihilation and world conquest. Violent death and love are again opposed in the horrific offer of Laelius to kill, if required, his own brother, parent, or pregnant wife and unborn child

(1.376–8).[14] The helmsman of Rome is to be served to the very destruction of Rome and its gods. In Laelius' feverish speech, all are to fall before the triumph of Caesar, a triumph that is to bring the devastated world under Caesar's sway. Immediately, in this spirit, Caesar's troops invade Italy.

The heavy lurch from deep distrust to the intoxication of a powerful allure that we just saw Laelius perform (on behalf of many) is on display again in Book 5 as Caesar's soldiers are being led to Brundisium, where they are to embark on ships and cross the Adriatic in order to pursue Pompey in Epirus. The troops have, however, grown weary. The absence of any resolution to the war and their leader's lack of any limits exhaust them, and they begin once again to waver. In Book 1, Laelius' speech reconfirmed them in their fanatical devotion to Caesar; here, they turn to mutiny. Lucan attempts to explain this puzzling change of heart thus:

> ... seu maesto classica paulum
> intermissa sono claususque et frigidus ensis
> expulerat belli furias, seu, praemia miles
> dum maiora petit, damnat causamque ducemque
> et scelere inbutos etiamnunc venditat enses.
>
> non pavidum iam murmur erat, nec pectore tecto
> ira latens; nam quae dubias constringere mentes
> causa solet, dum quisque pavet, quibus ipse timori est,
> seque putat solum regnorum iniusta gravari,
> haud retinet. quippe ipsa metus exsolverat audax
> turba suos: quidquid multis peccatur inultum est.

Perhaps the short interruption of the trumpet's gloomy sound and the cold, sheathed sword had expelled the fury for war from their hearts; perhaps the troops rejected cause and leader while seeking greater prizes, and again put up for sale their swords still stained with crime.

No longer was there fearful muttering, or anger lurking in the secret heart; for what tends to bind doubtful minds together – each fearing those to whom he causes fear and believing that he alone is oppressed by tyranny's injustice – had lost its grip. The bold crowd had relieved itself of its fears: the transgressions committed by many go unpunished.

(5.244–8, 255–60)

---

[14] As relatives and fellow-soldiers (1.363–4) are referred to in terms of body-parts, life and community bonds are further demeaned. Extreme graphic violence tends to be an interpretative crux for the reader on more than one level. In Chapter 11 below, esp. pp. 316–26, David Scourfield discusses at length the eroticized graphic violence directed against the female torture-victim in Jerome, *Letter* 1, exposing the moral and political ambiguities generated by it, and their effect on our critical readings – specifically, our attempts to understand the power-relations underpinning the text. See also Kennedy, Chapter 7 above, on Seneca's emphatic dwelling on the dismemberment of Hippolytus' body as a site of unresolved critical angst.

Their vast numbers, we are told, embolden the soldiers who, as a crowd, muster the courage – that they lack as individuals – to rage at Caesar. And yet the rebellion unearths a mix of conflicting emotions, hard to decipher and surely even harder for Caesar to respond to: the soldiers are exhausted by his utter indifference to their extreme devotion to him (fuelled by his very limitlessness), which at the same time brings them into contact with absolute freedom, rendering them both uniquely powerful and entirely powerless, delirious and spent all at once. Consider here the soldiers' fevered state of mind:

> imus in omne nefas manibus ferroque nocentes,
> paupertate pii. finis quis quaeritur armis?
> quid satis est, si Roma parum est?
> . . .
> usus abit vitae, bellis consumpsimus aevum:
> ad mortem dimitte senes. en inproba vota:
> non duro liceat morientia caespite membra
> ponere, non anima galeam fugiente ferire
> atque oculos morti clausuram quaerere dextram,
> coniugis inlabi lacrimis, unique paratum
> scire rogum; liceat morbis finire senectam.
> . . .
> nil actum est bellis, si nondum conperit istas
> omnia posse manus. nec fas nec vincula iuris
> hoc audere vetant.
> . . .
> adde quod ingrato meritorum iudice virtus
> nostra perit: quidquid gerimus, fortuna vocatur.
> nos fatum sciat esse suum. licet omne deorum
> obsequium speres, irato milite, Caesar,
> pax erit.

We advance to every crime, causing harm with hand and sword, yet pious in our poverty. What end to warfare are you seeking? What is enough, if Rome is not enough for you? ... Enjoyment of life is a thing of the past, we have consumed our lives in fighting: dismiss us in our old age to die. See how shameless our prayer is: spare us from laying our dying limbs on the hard turf, from striking the helmet with our escaping breath and searching for a hand to close our eyes at the moment of our death; let us slip away amid our wives' tears and know that the pyre is prepared for one body alone; let us end our old age through sickness ... Nothing have the wars accomplished if he has not yet appreciated that our hands are capable of anything. Neither duty nor the bonds of law limit our audacity ... Our valour is wasted when we have a judge who feels no gratitude for our services: whatever we achieve is called 'luck'. Let Caesar learn that we are his destiny. Even though you, Caesar, hope for absolute compliance from the gods, if your troops are angered, there will be peace.

$$(5.272\text{–}95)$$

The ensuing uproar, we are told (5.300), would have frightened the toughest leader. But Caesar, as so often before, shakes his soldiers (and the reader) out of their complacency with his astonishing reaction. The commotion instils new energies in him. The soldiers have plunged him into a crisis that threatens his role, his goal, and even his life, and he, unruffled to the last, sees the crisis as a gift. Caesar, we are told, 'accustomed to cast his fate to the brink, and relishing testing his fortune in the greatest dangers',[15] rejoices in his frenzied troops. He would give them the temples of Rome, and allow them to rape the mothers and daughters of the senators (5.305–7). 'He wants them to beg him for every possible atrocity, to desire the rewards of war' (*vult omnia certe | a se saeva peti, vult praemia Martis amari*, 5.307–8). According to Lucan, Caesar's only fear is that his unbridled soldiers should return to their senses (*militis indomiti tantum mens sana timetur*, 5.309).

Caesar is right to be fearful of a hiatus in the explosive rhythm to which he has marched his soldiers to this point. In the lengthy passage quoted above, we see how the pause in warfare suddenly leads the soldiers to value community once more. They rise up because the respite allows their alienation from each other to disappear, so that they can once again feel part of a community. Moreover, this corporateness gives them new-found confidence. They now desire the pleasures of community which they had rejected at the height of their infatuation. They want the religious rituals of death that negotiate communal and individual loss. They want the caring hand to close their eyes. They want the emotional comfort of and connection to those same wives whom they, swayed by Laelius' words, were willing to slaughter in Book 1. The soldiers have proved themselves to the great Caesar by embracing his excess up to this point, but their communal instinct now wants to limit this excess. Caesar responds not with reconciliation but with violence, since he fears the peace that brings sanity and allows reflection, both of which lead to a restoration of community. As the glorious individual, Caesar lives in extreme incommensurability with a community that cannot accommodate his extraordinary genius. He thus threatens to kill the leaders of the mutiny in a public execution (5.359–64)

---

[15] 5.301–3 *fata sed in praeceps solitus demittere Caesar | fortunamque suam per summa pericula gaudens | exercere . . .*

and to discharge all who wish to give up the fight as he no longer considers them worthy of his cause (5.357–8). His long, goading speech manages to disengage them gradually from each other and ultimately wins them over by proclaiming his personal might and his will to victory and threatening them with exclusion from the great power that he embodies (5.319–36). Before Caesar, each individual is as nothing. The same choice is offered to them as in Book 1: community or Caesar. And the soldiers, defeated before the demonic cunning of a leader far above their rational capacity, surrender. As in Book 1, they embrace Caesar and offer themselves to death on his behalf (5.364–74).

## Encounters with the Sublime and the Abject

There is an 'excess' to Caesar that can hardly be adequately represented. He breaks free of conventions and his extremity means that he can be neither controlled nor understood. His unpredictability can be linked to his refusal to cease activity. It is almost as though, if he were to stop, he would be caught inescapably in the bonds of society and ideology. People might just begin to understand him and his genius; his excess of spirit would not be able to carry all before it. To pause and accept victory would be to allow society to come to an accommodation with the victor and locate the victims within the victory narratives of the new regime, or even within oppositional narratives; Caesar would be incorporated into an ideological order and his story given a conclusion (however disputed). But Lucan's Caesar hates peace, as well as the laws (new or old) that maintain peace. He is never ready to accept a societal resolution. The difference from the values of the *Aeneid* could not be starker: there Aeneas' mission is to comprehend and conform, as well as to assimilate the inchoate individual to an ideal *telos* and an all-encompassing spirit that demands that each separate everyday conflict is subsumed by its essence. In the personality of Aeneas, the ideal strives to incorporate reality, whereas in that of Caesar universality gives in to individuality and the ideal is suppressed in the vicissitudes of the particular moment.

Caesar is an enigma, powerful and alluring. He exists beyond the conventional, a self-sufficient leader whose appeal is neither to the community nor exactly to the individual: in fact Caesar sublimates the ordinary individual within his own greatness. He is ineffable and inexplicable, a crux in the text resisting our efforts to integrate him within an interpretative framework. In this moment of aporia I turn to Immanuel Kant and his famous discussion of the sublime in conjunction with the beautiful.[16] In particular, Kant's insight into the uncomfortable kind of pleasure that is generated through contact with the sublime finds a resonance in the twisted, compulsive attraction of the soldiers to Caesar witnessed in episodes such as the mutiny in Book 5.

> The one liking ([that for] the beautiful) carries with it directly a feeling of life's being furthered, and hence is compatible with charms and with an imagination at play. But the other liking (the feeling of the sublime) is a pleasure that arises only indirectly: *it is produced by the feeling of a moment-ary inhibition of the vital forces followed immediately by an outpouring of them that is all the stronger.* Hence it is an emotion, and so it seems to be seriousness, rather than play, in the imagination's activity. Hence, too, this liking is incompatible with charms, and, since the mind is not just attracted by the object but is alternately always repelled as well, the liking for the sublime contains not so much a positive pleasure as rather admiration and respect, and *so should be called a negative pleasure.*[17]

The paradoxical concept of negative pleasure, the product of an experience that is both compulsive and repellent, begins to address the enigma that Lucan's Caesar represents. Paralysing doubt gives way to demented devo-tion, both in Book 1 (exemplified in the speech of Laelius) and in Book 5, when the soldiers' mutiny ends with them offering their lives to Caesar. The soldiers' mental and emotional exhaustion in the face of the avalanche that is Caesar can in fact be explained to some degree in terms of the Kantian sublime:

> If [a thing] is excessive for the imagination (and the imagination is driven to [such excess] as it apprehends [the thing] in intuition), then [the thing] is, as it were, an abyss in which the imagination is afraid to lose itself.[18]

At the same time the idea of the sublime provides a helpful lens through which to view and comprehend the ambivalence of the soldiers' inevitable surrender to something so irresistible, and yet so destructive in its enor-mity, as Caesar:

---

[16] For a detailed reading of Lucan's poem in terms of theories of the sublime from Longinus to the present, see Day 2013, with 'The Caesarian Sublime' discussed at 106–78; the brief analysis I offer here is my own. It should also be noted, however, that the representational challenge and ethical puzzle of a delirious personality are linked to a wider nexus of ideas, much debated in modern literary criticism. Particularly thoughtful on the wondrous ineffable within the context of Levinas' anti-representational ethics is A. Gibson 1999, esp. 54–81. See also Cornell 1992 on the refusal to assimilate as an ethical stand celebrating what she calls the 'philosophy of the limit', as explored mainly by Adorno, Levinas, and Derrida.

[17] Kant 1987: 98 (= 1913: 244–5); my emphases.     [18] Kant 1987: 115 (= 1913: 258).

A liking for the sublime in nature is only negative (whereas a liking for the beautiful is *positive*): it is a feeling that the imagination by its own action is depriving itself of its freedom, in being determined purposively according to a law different from that of its empirical use. The imagination thereby acquires an expansion and a might that surpasses the one it sacrifices . . . and is indeed seized by amazement bordering on terror, by horror and a sacred thrill.[19]

Amazement blending with terror, and horror mixed with a sacred thrill: this heady cocktail of violent emotions is exactly what Lucan's Caesar instils in his long-suffering troops as he mesmerizes them by means of a near-demonic self-confidence. The biting scorn of his address to the mutinous troops (5.319–64) produces results beyond his own wildest expectations as the soldiers lurch from extreme hostility to extreme devotion. The effect of his bruising attack on their minds and behaviour is made evident in the immediately following passage:

> tremuit saeva sub voce minantis
> volgus iners, unumque caput tam magna iuventus
> privatum factura timet, velut ensibus ipsis
> imperet invito moturus milite ferrum.
> ipse pavet, ne tela sibi dextraeque negentur
> ad scelus hoc, Caesar: vicit patientia saevi
> spem ducis, et iugulos non tantum praestitit enses.

The passive crowd trembled before the ferocity of his threatening voice, and so great an army is cowed by a single man – a man they sought to depose – as if he could command their very swords and wield the steel against the soldiers' wishes. Caesar himself is afraid that weapons and strong right hands may be denied him for this crime: but the troops' compliance surpassed the expectation of their fierce leader and they offered up not just their swords but their necks.

(5.364–70)

The soldiers are overawed by the irresistible force of a sublime spirit that manipulates and dominates them. They are shattered by his abuse and yet lifted almost by force (certainly mental coercion) to a plane above norms and expectations, made to feel that they belong to something mighty, larger than (their) life, worth offering their own lives for, something they are distinctly unclear about and yet somehow part of. Passive to start with, immobilized by his might, they then, in a sudden great release of energy, offer their throats to be cut, providing themselves as victims of the exemplary punishment that he wants to exact. We are reminded here of

---

[19] Kant 1987: 129 (= 1913: 269).

that peculiar, oppressive fascination we encountered in Kant's definition of the pleasure of the sublime, a sensation 'produced by the feeling of a momentary inhibition of the vital forces followed immediately by an outpouring of them that is all the stronger'. In his unfathomable might, Caesar pushes those around him to their own limits – and beyond. Transported by their leader's incomprehensibility, the troops are caught up in the unfettered energy that he seems to represent. His mighty destiny (his imagination) has become their mighty destiny (and imagination), though they barely understand it.

In a lengthy discussion of the aesthetics of the sublime and the avant-garde, Jean-François Lyotard searches for physical manifestations of the sublime:

> In the event of an absolutely large object – the desert, a mountain, a pyramid – or one that is absolutely powerful – a storm at sea, an erupting volcano – which like all absolutes can only be thought, without any sensible/sensory intuition, as an Idea of reason, the faculty of presentation, the imagination, fails to provide a representation corresponding to this Idea. This failure of expression gives rise to a pain, a kind of cleavage within the subject between what can be conceived and what can be imagined or presented. But this pain in turn engenders a pleasure, in fact a double pleasure: the impotence of imagination attests a contrario to an imagination striving to figure even that which cannot be figured ... *Here is then an account of the sublime feeling: a very big, very powerful object threatens to deprive the soul of any 'it happens', strikes it with 'astonishment' (at lower intensities the soul is seized with admiration, veneration, respect).* The soul is thus dumb, immobilised, as good as dead ... The sublime [is] no longer a matter of elevation (the category by which Aristotle defined tragedy), but a matter of intensification.[20]

A 'very big, very powerful object' threatens the terrified citizens of Rome, indeed. Not a storm at sea or an erupting volcano, but unfamiliar stars (1.526) and a 'sky burning with flames, meteors flying sidelong through the void, the tail of a threatening star, and a comet signalling a change in power on earth ... a silent thunderbolt ... strik[ing] the ancient capital of Latium'.[21] And the people of Rome sense the enormity and 'each through his fear gives strength to rumour, and they dread their own unconfirmed imaginings'.[22] The old seer Arruns is asked to study the terrifying signs but even he is hostage to the

---

[20] Lyotard 1991: 98–100; my emphasis.
[21] 1.527–9, 533–5 *ardentemque polum flammis caeloque volantes | obliquas per inane faces crinemque timendi | sideris et terris mutantem regna cometen. | ... tacitum ... | fulmen ... | percuss[ens] Latiare caput.*
[22] 1.484–6 *quisque pavendo | dat vires famae, nulloque auctore malorum, | quae finxere, timent.*

ineffable: 'We fear things that may not be uttered; but worse than our fears will soon come' (*non fanda timemus; | sed venient maiora metu,* 1.634–5). Assaulted by Caesar's terrifying reputation, the people of Rome feel their imagination aroused and captivated by something they, however, barely understand and are thus unable to put into words. Images of doom which they can barely account for or express, yet which numb them with their striking reality, invade their mind.[23] What is worse, they know yet more terror is to come to replace the terror they do not comprehend.

The fear is very real, and close, and all-encompassing, and – very importantly – palpable and material. Burning skies and threatening, fiery stars, or else 'a very big, very powerful object' introduce matter, physical substance, into the attempts to represent, even if always inadequately, the sublime, taking it away from the purely contemplative sphere. The portents stand as a concrete manifestation of Caesar's sublime mental violence, pushing the crowd to the non-land where meaning collapses and there reigns only abjection – to which I now turn, in the final stage of my attempt to conjure the ineffable violence of Caesar.

Embarking on her study of violence in Lucan's epic,[24] Shadi Bartsch focuses on the plight of the ordinary soldiers trapped in the mayhem of the civil war. She is especially interested in the effects of physical violation on the soldiers' subjectivity. Her observations on the physical ruptures that pervade the epic lead to an extended discussion of boundaries – personal as well as social – and their violation. Bartsch reads the somatic violence as a metonym for a generalized breakdown of boundaries that constitutes an irrevocable stage in individual and social collapse.[25] Dwelling on the revulsion caused by some of the most gory descriptions of disembowelling, Bartsch employs Julia Kristeva's notion of the abject:

> The abject [is] a bodily part or product that is and is not identifiable with the self, a thing that is ambiguously positioned between self and other because it has been severed or separated from its origin. The abject thus includes all bodily emissions, all substances that pass from being part of us to being ... 'other' and often taboo ... From the point of view of the individual, [the abject] is neither subject (me) nor object (part of the outside world) but something in between; it disrupts our most basic conceptual categories ... The disturbing quality of the abject arises

---

[23] Cf. here 1.469–71 *vana quoque ad veros accessit fama timores | inrupitque animos populi clademque futuram | intulit* ('empty rumours were added to real fears, and burst into the people's minds with thoughts of future disaster').

[24] Bartsch 1997.     [25] Bartsch 1997: 17–18.

precisely from this uncertain status, for it necessarily confuses our sense of the limits that define us against that which is not-us . . . '[The abject] . . . is what disturbs identity, system, and order, disrupting the social boundaries demanded by the symbolic.'[26]

The power of the abject, the power of the revoltingly disfigured, gaping bodies of the soldiers in Lucan's *Pharsalia* lies in their ability to transgress boundaries and upset the distinctions between inside and outside, subject and object, I and other, victims and onlookers, weakness and power. Excluded by the community and the laws, the repulsive bodies of those slaughtered manage in turn to expel the 'I' in a topsy-turvy world where the passive act and the active passively observe the action. Bartsch notices that time and again strange grammatical formulations underpin this unnatural reversal.[27] One episode in particular prompts a more extensive comment from her. In Book 6, Caesar has encircled the Pompeians near Dyrrachium; fierce battle ensues, and the soldiers' dead bodies pile up in front of the defensive wall. A manic Scaeva, Caesar's centurion, stuns everyone with his superhuman strength. His companions in the lengthy *aristeia* are none other than the bodies of the dead. As Bartsch notes:

> Dead bodies 'move' a wall to the level of the earth, a twisted idiom for the way a growing heap of corpses slowly rises to the height of the city's defenses ('cumulo crescente cadavera murum | admovere solo,' 6.180–181). Here, not only are the cadavers the active subjects of the verb *admovere*, but they are said to move a wall that is in fact constituted of nothing but themselves: the dead are subject and object of their own impossible action . . . And these reversals of agency extend beyond death and violence to encompass geography, society, and *moral responsibility*.[28]

What Bartsch detects in the borderline existence of the abject is a material manifestation of the precariousness of identity that seems to afflict the individuals in Lucan's epic. She speculates about the extent to which this precariousness reflects the fragility of the self in the late Republic, that highly explosive period of vulnerable limits and permeable boundaries.[29] In the context of the present study, I employ the notion of the abject and its liminality not in respect of the mutilated bodies that fill the pages of the epic, but for the insight it can give us into the transgressive nature of mental violence, which, as I have shown, is equally central in Lucan's epic and is fundamental to my reading of his Caesar. In *Powers of Horror*, a study preoccupied with the tenuousness of the 'I' as a unitary self with

---

[26] Bartsch 1997: 19 (concluding quotation from Elizabeth Grosz).    [27] Bartsch 1997: 26–7.
[28] Bartsch 1997: 27; emphasis in original.    [29] Bartsch 1997: 45–6.

clear boundaries, Kristeva is very explicit when describing the mesmerizing and also bruising effect of abjection's in-betweenness on the psyche:

> There looms, within abjection, one of those violent, dark revolts of being, directed against a threat that seems to emanate from an exorbitant outside or inside, ejected beyond the scope of the possible, the tolerable, the thinkable. It lies there, quite close, but it cannot be assimilated. It beseeches, worries, and fascinates desire, which, nevertheless, does not let itself be seduced ... Unflaggingly, like an inescapable boomerang, a vortex of summons and repulsion places the one haunted by it literally beside himself.[30]

Indeed, a 'dark revolt of being' is an apt description when a *matrona*, the paragon of self-restraint and order, bursts into the city at the very end of Book 1 like a bacchant, foretelling future disasters in front of a stunned audience. This astounding image comes straight after Arruns and then Figulus have tried to interpret the unnatural and overwhelming celestial apparitions and other portents witnessed by the people of Rome. As news of Caesar's crossing of the Rubicon and descent towards Rome has spread across the countryside and reached the eternal city itself, a woman literally beside herself (to quote Kristeva), haunted by, and enveloped in, Rome's impending catastrophe, breaks into a frenzied outburst of manic speech (1.673–95). The inverted spectacle of a demented matron instils unspeakable horror in the onlookers' hearts. And yet the speech makes good sense (in its senselessness) as an emblem of Kristeva's 'subject-in-trial', that multiple and heterogeneous subject that is never complete, and does not know itself or its limits.

Primarily interested in all those repressed drives and dark, unrepresentable processes that rupture the unitary subject and the carefully articulated societal law, Kristeva thinks of the abject as a flow, whose energy renders boundaries meaningless: I and other, subject and object, friend and foe, matron and bacchant find themselves implicated in one continuous, volatile, and unpredictable current. In this uncontrollable melding triggered by abjection, the subject finds itself in a shocking and, at the same time, irresistible encounter with the most unfamiliar and uncanny elements of its own inner core. In other words, the abject is significant because it resides inside, just as much as outside, the self, making the self's boundaries porous and thus exposing the fragility of both subject and society with its symbolic economy. That symbolic economy (as

---

[30] Kristeva 1982: 1.

instantiated in the ritual actions of society) seeks to keep the dirty and the dead away from the clean and the living. As Kristeva herself puts it: 'I experience abjection only if an Other has settled in place and stead of what will be "me." Not at all an other with whom I identify and whom I incorporate, but an Other who precedes and possesses me, and through such possession causes me to be.'[31]

In turning against his country in the name of defending it (1.195–203), Caesar places himself in the liminal territory of abjection where respect and contempt, praise and blame, the benign and the sinister collapse into each other. By crossing the Rubicon, Caesar has scorned his own country's intactness, engulfing and haunting all those in contact with him – inside and outside the text. In this world of confusion and refracting mirrors, even when they do not sustain wounds, the soldiers and citizens exposed to Caesar's demonic energy suffer in ways that leave them spent and exhausted. There is, I think, an uncanny affinity between Caesar's over-bearing dominance over the soldiers' (and the Roman people's) minds and Kristeva's description of the despotic perversity of the abject:

> The abject is perverse because it neither gives up nor assumes a prohibition, a rule, or a law; but turns them aside, misleads, corrupts, uses them, takes advantage of them, the better to deny them. It kills in the name of life – a progressive despot.[32]

In Caesar's dark plans, violence (violation) as the cause of abjection is a continuous trespassing of boundaries that leads the characters (and the readers) to a murky place where, as we have seen, meaning collapses. An abject other, Caesar is the terrifying object that horrifies the onlooking soldiers, as well as the repressed other of their own self, blending in with it, without, nonetheless, becoming one with it, a stranger inside their own soul. We have come, I believe, closer to sensing, even if never fully comprehending, the power of Caesar's violation. Caesar's murderous might is unstoppable because it 'touches' the soldiers. They do not know how, and yet his intent becomes their intent, however convulsed by it they may seem to be. Laelius, thus transformed, will kill with unwilling hand his own brother and wife (1.376–7), if he so much as senses that this is Caesar's will. It is as if, seized by unfamiliar drives that, prompted by Caesar's abjection, have lashed out from within the darker recesses of his own self, he is no longer in possession of that self. And as we saw in the case of the mutiny in Book 5, once confronted by Caesar's abjection, the

---

[31] Kristeva 1982: 10.    [32] Kristeva 1982: 15.

army experiences a frightening and yet empowering loss of subjectivity and personal agency, as if Caesar's demonic genius somehow suddenly resides *in* them. As we read earlier: 'So great an army is cowed by a single man – a man they sought to depose – as if he could command their very swords and wield the steel against the soldiers' wishes' (5.365–7).

## Coda: Sociopolitical Considerations

Far from explaining Lucan's Caesar, this study has sought to probe Caesar's destructive lure, and in the process, found that it lies in its very inexplicability. By deploying ideas deriving from the modern philosophical realms of the sublime and the abject, it has invited the reader to succumb to, rather than resist, Caesar's enigma. As incalculable forces that threaten to repudiate the orderly pronouncements of society and the symbolic economy, abjection and the sublime both serve as reminders of the limits, and limitations, of rationality. Lucan's Caesar is neither only sublime nor only abject, but a combination of the two, irrupting violently into the epic and disturbing its meaning. Where the sublime oppresses and terrifies the mind with its very incomprehensibility, the abject confronts the terrified subjects with the realization that at least part of that extravagant strange force that threatens them actually lies, dormant, inside them. In engaging the notions of the sublime and the abject in the study of Caesar's megalomania, I have asked the reader to allow Caesar's violent and isolated existence to remain untamed by explanation: to experience it, rather, as an inexplicable sensation that pierces through the veil of certainties in which we tend to envelop our enlightened world.[33] Lucan's Caesar remains a problem that cannot be dismissed, an enigma that cannot, but also should not, be solved. In his unfathomable attraction, Caesar is also a terrifying measure of the individual's darkest inner drives, the repressed other that resides inside him – the soldier, the citizen, the reliable and compliant member of a firmly articulated society.

And a last word: Lucan's Caesar is far from a common criminal, or a one-dimensional murderous figure (though he is murderous too). Caesar eludes categorization because categories simply collapse in the political and

---

[33] Compare Fitzgerald, Chapter 10 below, who seeks to expose the nonsensical nature of violence as a wayward narrative force that yields very little in terms of explanation to the reader. Fitzgerald focuses on cruelty, as a particular manifestation of violence, in Apuleius' *Golden Ass*. Narrator and reader are spent by gratuitous violence, but, unlike in Lucan, the impasse tends to lead eventually to a change of register, from seriousness to light-hearted comment, which, nonetheless, does not rinse the bitter taste of violence from either Lucius' or the reader's mouth.

social arena of the last days of the Republic. At a time when the Republican political economy and its time-honoured bonds are falling apart, Caesar bursts with superhuman energy into a civic space opened by the collapse of sovereign Law. Terry Eagleton's presentation of the sublime all but depicts the Caesar I have traced above:

> The sublime is one name for the annihilating, regenerating power we have been investigating. A far more important name is freedom ... The sublime is any power which is perilous, shattering, ravishing, traumatic, excessive, exhilarating, dwarfing, astonishing, uncontainable, overwhelming, boundless, obscure, terrifying, enthralling, and uplifting.[34]

In the inverted world where Caesar's abjection reigns, boundaries are eliminated as subject and object blend into each other. Faced with Caesar, the soldiers are repelled by his 'annihilating' and simultaneously 'regenerating' power, and yet the distance between him and them narrows until he overwhelms them and they become enveloped in, and part of, his force. As I read Eagleton's reflection on the impact of the sublime on the soul, I am reminded of the near-epiphany of Caesar on a mound facing down the mutiny in Book 5: 'He stood on a mound of piled-up turf with undaunted countenance, and, fearing nothing, earned the right to be feared.'[35] Towering over them, Caesar crushes the soldiers with his supernatural assertiveness, keeping them trapped in an emotional rollercoaster that sustains in them insatiable hunger for war, while depriving them of any offsetting everyday reality, cares, or pleasures. Eagleton posits that in such circumstances:

> A vulnerable object becomes an infinite subject. By identifying ourselves with the boundlessness of the sublime, we cease to be anything in particular, but thereby become potentially everything. In this dazzling emptiness, all and nothing are closely allied, since both are absolved from limits.[36]

Lucan's Caesar is an overbearing figure precariously perched on the edge, the chaotic moment of transition from the dying Republic to ... something else. His abject perversion makes him catastrophic and irresistible at the same time. Indeed, rousing transitions just before vast historical changes often end as repulsive periods of terror.[37] But Lucan's Caesar is

---

[34] Eagleton 2005: 44.
[35] 5.316–18 *stetit aggere fulti | caespitis intrepidus voltu meruitque timeri | non metuens.*
[36] Eagleton 2005: 45.
[37] The energy that brought the revolution exceeds its proper boundaries under the pressure of its own inexhaustibility and vigour. The French Revolution and the concomitant Terror are perhaps the most obvious example from modern history.

more than an abrasive revolutionary probing exhausted and vulnerable limits at the end of an era. His sublime excess is contagious; everything and everyone in touch with him is 'absolved from limits', to use Eagleton's striking observation. Caesar's unlimited force, his sublime and at the same time abjecting violence, hints at a possible world made devoid of boundaries by his own limitlessness, a world where the allure and the cult of the individual have free, unfettered, anarchic reign. Absolute freedom (and hence absolute terror) offers a glimpse of an unfathomable possibility for Rome, embodied by a delirious general.[38] Could Lucan, more than a century later, be suggesting to us that a boundless Caesar is ushering the exhausted Republic into the 'dazzling emptiness' – to quote Eagleton one last time – of Rome's Imperial era?

---

[38] For an extensive discussion of such conundrums of fear and freedom in the discourses of modernity, see Eagleton 2005: 68–88.

# CHAPTER 9

# Tacitus and the Language of Violence

## Bruce J. Gibson*

> tu regere imperio populos, Romane, memento
> (hae tibi erunt artes) pacique imponere morem,
> parcere subiectis et debellare superbos.

Remember, Roman, to rule the peoples with imperial power (these will be your arts) and add civilized practice to peace,[1] to spare those who have submitted and overwhelm those who are proud.

(Virg. *Aen.* 6.851–3)

When we use phrases such as 'violent crime' or 'domestic violence', our language conveys nothing if not disapproval for the kinds of action described.[2] Violence is what other people get up to, never one's own side.[3]

---

* I am indebted to the editors, and to Rhiannon Ash, Robin Seager, and Tony Woodman, for their invaluable comments on earlier drafts of this chapter. Tacitus' *Annals* and *Histories* are cited according to the text of Fisher 1906 and 1911 respectively, with translations taken from important recent versions: for the *Annals*, A. J. Woodman's Hackett translation (Woodman 2004), and for the *Histories*, David Levene's revision of Fyfe's translation, published in the Oxford World's Classics series (Fyfe and Levene 1997). I have preferred to use these translations rather than provide my own so as to illustrate more objectively the range of possible interpretations of *vis* in Latin.

[1] For the meaning of *pacique imponere morem* see, e.g., Austin 1977: 263–4.

[2] In this connection note the long tradition of the phrase 'men of violence' being used to refer to paramilitaries in Ireland, though for the reverberating complexities of semantics in the context of Northern Ireland see, e.g., Curtis 1998: 133–7. Compare also the subtitle of Kate Kray's monograph on the Kray twins, *The Twins: Men of Violence* (Kray 2002).

[3] Modern governments tend to refer to the use of 'force', and this positive usage of 'force' is also, it should be noted, enshrined in the UN Charter itself: in Chapter VII, entitled 'Action with Respect to Threats to the Peace, Breaches of the Peace, and Acts of Aggression', Article 44, for example, provides that 'When the Security Council has decided to use force it shall, before calling upon a Member not represented on it to provide armed forces in fulfilment of the obligations assumed under Article 43, invite that Member, if the Member so desires, to participate in the decisions of the Security Council concerning the employment of contingents of that Member's armed forces', a passage which also illustrates the linguistic similarity between the singular 'force' and the plural 'forces', referring to military contingents; compare indeed Latin *vis* and *vires*. For a critique of the use of 'force' in recent times, see Chomsky 2000, and note also the 1967 debate featuring Chomsky, Hannah Arendt, and Susan Sontag, on whether or not violence could ever be legitimate (see the transcript on Chomsky's own website at chomsky.info/19671215 (last accessed 17 January 2017)).

The Virgilian epigraph above offers a classic example of this; indeed, the ideological slant of *parcere subiectis et debellare superbos* as an affirmation of the acceptable acquisition and maintenance of power by force against the will of others (here conveniently called *superbos*) scarcely needs comment.[4] For the other side of the coin, contrast Virgil with what Julius Caesar is said to have remarked when Cimber began the attack on him in the Senate-house: *ista quidem vis est*, 'that is violence',[5] which makes quite clear Caesar's own views on the matter,[6] even if the assassins saw themselves as liberators and tyrannicides; Tacitus in fact referred to the event in similar terms, *repentina vis dictatorem Caesarem oppresserat* (*Hist.* 3.68.1).[7]

The role of violence in historiography and works of a similar kind is more complex, since warfare – military violence – is held to offer excellent subject matter for historians, and, from Homer onwards, regarded as an ideal arena in which to obtain glory. Thus Thucydides, and Livy in his twenty-first book, clearly regarded the wars they were writing about as good material for history (Thuc. 1.1.1–2; Livy 21.1.1–2). There is also a tradition of writing on the deaths of individuals: compare Cicero's letter to Lucceius, where Cicero comments on the pleasure of reading about Epaminondas' death at the Battle of Mantinea (*Fam.* 5.12.5), or the

---

[4] For discussion of victory as granting retrospective legitimacy to acts of violence in warfare in Hellenistic times, see Chaniotis 2005. For wider cultural studies of Roman violence see, e.g., Wistrand 1992 on spectacles; Plass 1995: 15–77 on the arena and 81–134 on political suicide; Leigh 1997: 30–40; Kyle 1998.

[5] Suet. *Iul.* 82.1. There may also be some intersection between Caesar's words and legislation *de vi*, which was already in force in the late Republic; for discussion of the complexities involved in reconstructing the *lex Plautia de vi* and the *lex Lutatia de vi*, see Lintott 1999: 110–16, who suggests that the *lex Lutatia* dealt with insurrection (*seditio*), while the *lex Plautia* dealt with acts of violence against private individuals which were judged as being *contra rem publicam* as well. Republican legislation *de vi* is notoriously hard to reconstruct, since the subsequent *leges Iuliae de vi* under Augustus effectively overwrite and obscure our knowledge of their predecessors; see Lintott 1999: 107–9, 126, and also 1993: 117–18. For a general survey of *vis*, concentrating almost exclusively on its legal aspects, see Eisenhut and Mayer-Maly 1961: the *leges Iuliae* (see further *Dig.* 48.6–7) dealt with *vis publica*, which included breaches of the right of Roman citizens to appeal (*provocatio*) against the decisions of a Roman magistrate, and *vis privata*, which dealt with such issues as gatherings of gangs. Tacitus refers to a prosecution *de vi* at *Ann.* 4.13.2. The very existence of legislation *de vi* suggests that in certain contexts *vis* is to be seen as inherently negative.

[6] There are differing versions of what (if anything) Caesar's last words were. Suet. *Iul.* 82.2 goes on to reject the tradition that Caesar subsequently addressed Brutus in Greek with the phrase 'You too, child?', while Dio Cass. 44.19.5 records that the nature of the attack made it impossible for Caesar to say or do anything, before also noting (and rejecting) the story of the words spoken to Brutus. Plut. *Caes.* 66.8 reports a different tradition that Caesar asked Casca in Latin what he was doing, while App. *B Civ.* 2.117 does not report any specific words but simply notes Caesar's angry shouting during the attack. On this topic see Gershenson 1992.

[7] 'The dictator, Caesar, had been the victim of sudden violence.' Heubner 1963–82: III.63 ad loc. compares *repentina vi* at Cic. *Sest.* 140.

younger Pliny's letters to Tacitus on the death of his uncle (*Ep.* 6.16, 6.20).[8] Evidence such as this might suggest an aesthetic of death as suitable subject matter for historical writing; the debates on 'tragic historiography', if it ever existed, are relevant here.[9]

Tacitus himself, at *Annals* 4.32.1, remarks on how it was possible for earlier historians to write about much more exciting subjects – *ingentia . . . bella, expugnationes urbium, fusos captosque reges*[10] – before noting that such writers also had the chance to write about internal political discord in Rome, which featured extensive acts of violence in the last century of the Roman Republic.[11] All this, Tacitus claims, is actually more agreeable to read than the kind of history which he has to write, where emperors were reluctant to extend the frontiers of the empire: *nobis in arto et inglorius labor* (4.32.2),[12] from a passage which implicitly contrasts the failure of the empire to grow under the Principate with Republican Rome's expansion in the Mediterranean from the time of the First Punic War onwards, and the glory that had been won for commanders in the various conflicts which had brought about Rome's rise to power.[13] Yet, although Tacitus associates sometimes violent subject matter such as wars and civil discord with Republican historiography, there is much that is violent in Tacitus' own writing: thus the *Histories* open with an emphasis on deeds of violence – *opus adgredior opimum casibus, atrox proeliis, discors seditionibus, ipsa etiam pace saevum* (*Hist.* 1.2.1)[14] – before listing a whole series of disasters in the period to be covered.[15] And even in the *Annals*, we should not forget that there are foreign wars (albeit sometimes low-key), to say nothing of the

---

[8] On Pliny and historiography, see further Ash 2003.

[9] See, e.g., Walbank 1960; Woodman 1988: 116 n. 151 and 1993: 120 n. 62; Wiseman 1994: 18–21; Leigh 1997: 30–40; Marincola 2013.

[10] 'mighty wars, stormings of cities, routed and captured kings'.

[11] For violence in the late Republic, the classic treatment is Lintott 1999.

[12] 'My work, on the other hand, is confined and inglorious.' Compare also the manner in which peace is signalled as characteristic of Augustus' Principate at *Ann.* 1.3.6: *bellum ea tempestate nullum nisi adversus Germanos supererat, abolendae magis infamiae ob amissum cum Quintilio Varo exercitum quam cupidine proferendi imperii aut dignum ob praemium* ('As for war, none survived at that time except against the Germans, more to erase the infamy of the army lost with Quintilius Varus than through any desire of extending the empire or for some worthy prize'). Keitel 1984 argues that in fact Tacitus' presentation of peace in the Principate is characterized by the evocation of civil war themes, with an overall idea of emperors making war on the state.

[13] The implications of this passage have been considered extensively by Tony Woodman, both in his published inaugural lecture at Durham and in his *Rhetoric in Classical Historiography* (Woodman 1985: 9–13 and 1988: 180–6).

[14] 'The story I now commence is rich in vicissitudes, grim with warfare, torn by civil strife, a tale of horror even during times of peace.'

[15] See further Woodman 1988: 164–7; Damon 2003: 82–7.

various trials and executions and suicides.[16] Arguably, Tacitus' writing
shows a similar interest in the depiction of violence (even if it is deplored)
to that evident in epic poets such as Lucan and Statius (who also regularly
censure the actions they narrate).[17]

However, rather than deal with particular instances of violence in
Tacitus, I shall instead focus on an aspect of the *language* of violence.
This chapter will thus consider the blurring of meaning to be found in the
usage of the word *vis*.[18] I shall concentrate on *vis*, since this term possesses
shades of meaning ranging from 'strength' and 'force' to 'violence', as well
as other meanings such as 'power' or 'influence', 'essence', 'value,
amount',[19] whereas *violentia* and its cognates tend to be used with less
ambiguity, in situations where violence is singled out for censure.[20] It is

---

[16] For the idea of the 'alternative *Annals*', which provides matter of the kind which Tacitus had
affected to be unable to provide, see Woodman 1985: 13–20 and 1988: 186–90.

[17] For warfare as a common interest shared by historiography and epic see Introduction, p. 18 with
n. 76.

[18] On linguistic instability in Tacitus see, e.g., Henderson 1998: 260–5; O'Gorman 2000: 10–22.

[19] See *OLD* s.v., sects. 1 'physical strength exerted on an object (esp. in order to constrain), force,
violence. [b] *vi, per vim*, forcibly, by force'; 4 'violence in politics, public life, or sim.'; 5 'violence
directed against enemy troops, military force; (esp.) [b] *vi*, by force of arms; *vim facere*, to make an
assault, force a passage, etc.'; 11 'ability to control affairs, political weight, power, influence, or sim.';
17 'that which makes a thing what it is, its essence; *sua vi*, in itself, intrinsically'; 19 'value, amount;
*vim habere* (w. gen.), to be equivalent in amount (to)'; 24 (for the plural *vires*) 'military strength,
fighting power'. Cf. Goodyear 1981: 74 on Tac. *Ann.* 1.55.3 *vi Armini*: '*vi*, which T. often thus uses,
may variously denote armed force, strength, power, influence. An exact meaning is sometimes hard to
fix. Here perhaps "Arminius' onslaught"'; cf. also Nipperdey and Andresen 1915: I.116 ad loc.

[20] With *violentia* and its cognates, this negative quality is perhaps explicable in terms of the
etymological connection with *violo*, though one should note too the etymology given by Isidore,
*Etym.* 10.279 *violentus, quia vim infert* ('violent, because he brings force to bear'); compare the
etymology of Vulcan's name given by Varro, *Ling.* 5.70 *ab ignis iam maiore vi ac violentia Volcanus
dictus* ('Vulcan is so called from the force and violence of fire that is on the increase'), and see further
Maltby 1991: 647, 653. *Vis* is of course etymologically linked with Greek (ϝ)ῖς. I give in this note a
full list of instances of *violentia, violentus*, and *violenter* in Tacitus (they are found only in *Hist.* and
*Ann.*; Tacitus does not use *violens*): in all of these, the sense is negative; in a number of cases, the
words refer to natural phenomena. *violentia: Hist.* 3.49.2 *militari violentia* ('by their [the soldiers']
violence'); *Ann.* 1.59.1 *insitam violentiam* ('his innate violence'), referring to Arminius; 1.70.3
*cuncta pari violentia involvebantur* ('everything was engulfed in equal violence'), referring to
difficulties experienced by Vitellius' troops while crossing treacherous ground; 2.6.4 (the violence
of the Rhine's course); 2.63.3 (Tiberius' speech referring to the violence of the peoples who were
Maroboduus' subjects); 3.19.1 (Tiberius warns Fulcinius *ne facundiam violentia praecipitaret*, 'not
to debase his fluency by violence'); 4.36.2 (the people of Cyzicus are accused of violence against
Roman citizens); 4.64.1 (the violence of the fire on the Mons Caelius); 12.51.3 (a reference to the
violence of Radamistus' love for his wife in the context of his plan to prevent her falling into enemy
hands by killing her and committing her body to the river Araxes); 13.1.1 (Junius Silanus' death not
the consequence of any *ingenii violentia*, 'violence of temperament'); 13.15.1 (Nero contemplates
the *violentia* of his mother, Agrippina); 15.18.2 (the violence of a storm); 15.38.1 (the violence of
the fires which had affected Rome); 15.40.1 (the violence of the fire at Rome); 16.13.1 (the violence
of a whirlwind in Campania). *violentus: Ann.* 2.24.1 *quanto violentior cetero mari Oceanus* ('just as
the Ocean is more violent than the sea in general'); 2.43.2 *Cn. Pisonem, ingenio violentum et obsequii*

worth bearing in mind too that *vires*, the plural of *vis*, can denote 'strength' and also military forces.[21] This chapter will examine Tacitus' exploitation of these different shades of meaning, in order to demonstrate that the way in which language is used to represent violence is as worthy of attention as the phenomenon of violence itself.[22] Whereas English more straightforwardly tends to distinguish between acts of 'force', something which might, in spite of occasional examples like 'forced entry', typically be regarded neutrally, and 'violence', which tends to be something viewed negatively, in Latin *vis* reflects a whole range of meanings, as we have seen. As juridical texts such as the following passage from Paulus show, *vis* can in the same sentence have two different shades of ethical meaning:

> qui, cum aliter tueri se non possent, damni culpam dederint, innoxii sunt: vim enim vi defendere omnes leges omniaque iura permittunt. sed si defendendi mei causa lapidem in adversarium misero, sed non eum, sed praetereuntem percussero, tenebor lege Aquilia: illum enim solum qui vim infert ferire conceditur, et hoc, si tuendi dumtaxat, non etiam ulciscendi causa factum sit.

> Those who do damage because they cannot otherwise defend themselves are blameless; for all laws and all legal systems allow one to use force to defend oneself against violence. But if in order to defend myself I throw a stone at my attacker and I hit not him but a passerby, I shall be liable under the lex Aquilia; for it is permitted only to use force against an attacker and even then only so far as is necessary for self-defense and not for revenge.[23] (*Dig.* 9.2.45.4)

*ignarum* ('Cn. Piso, temperamentally violent and a stranger to compliance'); 3.1.1 (Agrippina is *violenta luctu et nescia tolerandi*, 'violent in her grief . . . and unfamiliar with enduring'); 5.4.4 (Sejanus' anger becomes more violent); 12.64.3 (the younger Agrippina and Domitia Lepida are both *impudica, infamis, violenta*, 'immoral, infamous, and violent'); 15.68.2 (Nero considers Vestinus to be *violentum et infestum*, 'violent and hostile'). *violenter*: *Hist.* 3.11.2 (soldiers violently demand the execution of Aponius); *Ann.* 1.31.1 *Germanicae legiones turbatae, quanto plures tanto violentius* ('the German legions were disrupted – all the more violently, given their greater numbers'); 2.55.2 (Cn. Piso reproaches the Athenians for *quae in Macedones improspere, violenter in suos fecissent*, 'their inauspicious actions against the Macedonians, their violence against themselves'); 6.3.1 (Tiberius violently berates Junius Gallio for interfering with a proposal relating to the praetorians); 12.31.1 (the Britons attack more violently because there is a new governor); 15.58.3 (Faenius Rufus acts *violenter*, in a hectoring fashion, in the interrogation of his former partners in the conspiracy against Nero in order to conceal his own involvement). As for *vehemens* and its cognates, the only instances in Tacitus are at *Agr.* 4.3 and *Dial.* 25.4, and neither case refers to violence.

[21] For the several meanings of plural *vires*, see *OLD* s.v. *vis*, sects. 20–8.

[22] On the intertwined quality of violence and its representation in language, cf. Kennedy, Chapter 7 above.

[23] Tr. Watson, in Mommsen, Krueger, and Watson 1985: I.291.

Alan Watson's translation of *vim enim vi defendere omnes leges omniaque iura permittunt* illustrates the difference between English and Latin usage perfectly, with *vis* used twice in the Latin to represent, first, the 'violence' offered by an attacker, and second, the 'force' used in self-defence.[24] One can also compare, from a quite different kind of text, the manner in which Horace speaks of *vis* in *Odes* 3.4.65–8:[25]

> vis consili expers mole ruit sua,
> vim temperatam di quoque provehunt
>    in maius, idem odere viris
>    omne nefas animo moventis.

> Force without wisdom falls by its own weight.
> When force is tempered, the gods also advance it
>    and make it greater. They abhor strength
>    which moves all manner of impiety in the heart.[26]

Here the neutrality of *vis* on its own is indicated by Horace's qualification of the term, *vis* without *consilium* being negatively characterized, whereas a *vis* that is tempered (*temperatam*) can turn out well. Horace then returns to the negative manifestation of the now plural *viris* with the phrase *omne nefas animo moventis* in the fourth line.

A text which is also worth considering from this point of view, before we move on to Tacitus, is Cicero's *De officiis*. This is because the *De officiis* explicitly engages with questions of morality and also deals with the issue of Rome's imperial power and conduct from a theoretical point of view. I began this chapter with the famous injunction in Virgil's *Aeneid* (6.853), *parcere subiectis et debellare superbos*, which should be seen against the background of wider Roman thought on imperial power, such as the idea of the 'just war', *iustum bellum*, discussed by Cicero at *De officiis* 1.35–8, or the view that it is proper to extend the power of the state (*Off.* 2.85). The positive view of imperial conquest that we find in a range of texts such as this might at first sight encourage us to consider the nature of the language of violence as a marginal issue. Nevertheless, it is striking how the

---

[24] Note too how *illum enim solum qui vim infert ferire conceditur* has been blurred in this translation, since a more literal rendering would be 'for it is permitted to strike only that person who has brought to bear violence'. For the notion of self-defence, cf. Eisenhut and Mayer-Maly 1961: 315–23; Lintott 1999: 22–3: '*Vis* was a neutral concept, nearer to our "force" than "violence", so there was no difficulty in applying it to both illegal violence and legal self-help. Cassius thought that by virtue of a law of nature "vim vi repellere licet" [*Dig.* 43.16.1.27].'

[25] On these lines see, e.g., Fraenkel 1957: 282; West 2002: 51–2; Nisbet and Rudd 2004: 75–6.

[26] Tr. West 2002: 43.

ideological qualities of this language come to the fore even in Cicero's famous discussion. Consider, for example, the following:

> nam cum sint duo genera decertandi, unum per disceptationem, alterum per vim, cumque illud proprium sit hominis, hoc beluarum, confugiendum est ad posterius, si uti non licet superiore.

> For since there are two methods of contention, one through dispute, and one through force, and since the former is characteristic of a man, and the latter characteristic of beasts, one must have recourse to the latter only if it is not possible to make use of the former. (Cic. *Off.* 1.34)

Here Cicero indicates that while the use of *vis* is to be avoided if at all possible, it can sometimes serve as a last resort. Another instance occurs shortly afterwards:

> et cum iis quos vi deviceris consulendum est, tum ii, qui armis positis ad imperatorum fidem confugient, quamvis murum aries percusserit, recipiendi.

> The interests of those whom you have overcome by force must be considered, and at the same time those who, after laying down their arms, have recourse to the generals' mercy, even though the battering-ram has struck their walls, must be taken under your protection. (Cic. *Off.* 1.35)

In this passage, we can again see how *vis* is used to characterize action against the state's enemies. The issue here seems to be that *vis* may be used, but acting mercifully and responsibly towards the defeated afterwards is also important: we are not so far away from the Virgilian injunction.

More direct, and unambiguously negative, is Cicero's use of *vis* immediately after a passage on the ill-treatment of slaves:

> cum autem duobus modis, id est aut vi aut fraude, fiat iniuria, fraus quasi vulpeculae, vis leonis videtur; utrumque homine alienissimum, sed fraus odio digna maiore.

> But although wrongdoing may take place in two ways, that is, either through force or through deceit, deceit seems the action of a fox, force that of a lion; both actions are very far removed from a human being, but deceit is worthy of greater hatred. (Cic. *Off.* 1.41)

Rather different, however, is the use Cicero makes of the word *vis* in writing about the role of Scipio Nasica in suppressing Tiberius Gracchus and his supporters:

> nec plus Africanus, singularis et vir et imperator, in exscindenda Numantia rei publicae profuit quam eodem tempore P. Nasica privatus, cum Ti. Gracchum interemit; quamquam haec quidem res non solum ex domestica

est ratione – attingit etiam bellicam, quoniam vi manuque confecta est – sed tamen id ipsum est gestum consilio urbano sine exercitu.

Nor was Africanus, an exceptional man and commander, more advantageous to the Republic in destroying Numantia than was P. Nasica at the same epoch in his capacity as a private citizen, when he killed Ti. Gracchus; although this matter does not only have a domestic dimension – it also has a military one, since it was accomplished by physical force – but all the same the deed itself was done without an army, as a measure for the city. (Cic. *Off.* 1.76)

This passage is of interest for various reasons. In the first place, Cicero strikingly makes an equivalence between the victorious action of Scipio Africanus (Aemilianus) in the war against Numantia and the accomplishment of Scipio Nasica in suppressing Tiberius Gracchus and his followers, an action which Cicero praises elsewhere in his works, for example in the opening of the *First Catilinarian* (*Cat.* 1.3).[27] Second, Cicero uses *vis* to characterize the killing of Gracchus not so much in the moralizing terms that we have seen him use before, but to associate the killing with military activity, even if it was nevertheless essentially the resolution of a domestic political crisis. This instance clearly demonstrates that, even within a text with serious philosophical pretensions, *vis* is not always a firmly rooted concept: its use here is some way off from the passage we have just considered at 1.34 where *vis* is associated with beasts. On the other hand, there are further passages in the *De officiis* where *vis* seems closer to being seen as something negative: there are several instances of the word where it represents a means of forcible control, associated with fear (*Off.* 2.22, 24, 25), and there is also the striking moment at the start of Book 3 where Cicero explains that he has been kept away from involvement in public life *armis impiis vique*, 'by wicked arms and force' (*Off.* 3.1).

This brief survey of examples from the *De officiis*, a text directly concerned with the morality of state actions, is a useful prelude to considering the historical work of Tacitus. Accordingly, the remainder of this chapter will consider four aspects of *vis* in Tacitus: its association with imperial power; with military commanders; with Rome itself and also foreign powers; and finally with the armies.

I shall begin with the association of the word *vis* with imperial power in the *Histories* and the *Annals*. My first example is from early in the *Annals*, 1.9.5, from the pair of chapters which offer verdicts on Augustus. One of the points made in favour of Augustus is that there were occasional

---

[27] See further Dyck 1996: 278–9 on Cic. *Off.* 1.109.

instances of *vis*, so that others might enjoy the benefits of *quies: pauca admodum vi tractata quo ceteris quies esset.*[28] Here one might argue about what shade of meaning to apply to the word *vi*, with Woodman's 'force' as one possibility, whereas another might be to translate as 'violence', placing a more apologetic emphasis on *pauca admodum*. The ambiguity of such language is perhaps pointed to in the next chapter, at 1.10.4, where negative verdicts on Augustus are offered; the passage corresponding to this one, dealing with Augustus' deeds of violence (or force), invites us to resolve the meaning of *vi* in no uncertain terms: *pacem sine dubio post haec, verum cruentam: Lollianas Varianasque cladis, interfectos Romae Varrones, Egnatios, Iullos,*[29] where the adjective *cruentam*, applied to *pacem* (itself picking up on *quies* from 1.9.5), firmly pushes *vi* in 1.9 towards a negative signification.

On other occasions we see emperors referring to their own actions in terms of *vis*, which would seem to preclude a negative intention (at least on the emperor's part). Thus at *Annals* 2.26.3, Tiberius, advising Germanicus on what to do in Germany, recalls his own past there, remarking that he had accomplished more through counsel than through *vis: se ... plura consilio quam vi perfecisse,*[30] where *vi* need not denote something intrinsically bad, but simply military action, something which was not as effective as *consilium*, which presumably implies diplomacy. Similar, if more belligerent, is 12.20.2, where in a letter to Eunones, Claudius remarks that *nec sibi vim ad exequendum deesse,*[31] that he did not lack the military power to capture Mithridates by force and have him executed.

There are also several instances where *vis* is directly linked with imperial power. Striking in this respect is *Annals* 3.60.1, where Tiberius' practice of referring provincial questions to the Senate is described in the following way: *sed Tiberius, vim principatus sibi firmans, imaginem antiquitatis senatui praebebat postulata provinciarum ad disquisitionem patrum mittendo,*[32]

---

[28] Woodman translates: 'Just a few things had been handled by force to ensure peace for the rest.' Tacitus' use of the passive *tractata* is a subtle means of distancing Augustus from these actions.

[29] 'Peace there had been without doubt after that, but gory: there had been the Lollian and Varian disasters, and the killing at Rome of Varrones, Egnatii, and Iulli.'

[30] 'He himself[, sent nine times by Divine Augustus to Germany,] had achieved more by planning than by force'; for this idea Koestermann 1963–8: I.296 compares *Ann.* 2.63.3, 2.64.1, 6.32.1. For *vis* and *consilium*, cf. Syme 1958: 733, who compares Livy 21.2.5; see also the discussion of Hor. *Carm.* 3.4.65–8 at p. 274 above.

[31] 'he himself did not lack the power to follow it through'.

[32] 'Yet Tiberius, while reaffirming for himself the essence of the principate, presented to the senate an old-fashioned image in sending demands from the provinces for investigation by the fathers.' The meaning 'essence' or 'reality' for *vim* (*principatus*) here is already suggested by Woodman and Martin 1996: 433 ad loc., with reference to *OLD* s.v., sect. 17, though they appear to regard the

where Tacitus draws attention as so often to a contrast between the façade
of Republican forms (*imaginem antiquitatis*) and the realities of imperial
power, *vim* pointing to the power that is the essential quality of the
Principate, which eclipses constitutional forms, even if they are occasionally invoked for show.[33] This usage of *vis* can be paralleled elsewhere: thus
at 15.69.1, when Nero takes action against Vestinus, Tacitus writes, *igitur
non crimine, non accusatore existente, quia speciem iudicis induere non
poterat, ad vim dominationis conversus Gerellanum tribunum cum cohorte
militum immittit*;[34] the phrase *vim dominationis* suggests here the naked
potential of imperial power for violence, represented by Nero's decision to
use violence against Vestinus, contrasted with the legal forms of redress
which the emperor eschews on this occasion, unable as he is to assume the
*speciem iudicis*.

There are also passages where *vis* can denote what one might call the
essential, inner nature of imperial power. Thus in the *Annals*, in the
aftermath of the murder of Agrippa Postumus, Sallustius Crispus advises
Tiberius that he should not weaken the *vis principatus* by referring everything to the attention of the Senate: *neve Tiberius vim principatus resolveret
cuncta ad senatum vocando* (1.6.3).[35] After a murder, signalled by Tacitus
as the first event of Tiberius' reign earlier in the chapter (compare the
similarly marked death of Junius Silanus at 13.1.1 at the outset of Nero's
reign),[36] the temptation to see Sallustius Crispus' advice on the *vis principatus* in terms of a potential for violence is irresistible. In the same way, at
*Histories* 4.85.2 Mucianus advises Domitian to remain at Lugudunum and
not involve himself in fighting because of the need to display the *vis
principatus*, here perhaps with more emphasis on strength than on

---

meaning 'power' as predominant, citing *Ann.* 1.6.3 and *Hist.* 4.85.2. The translation of *Ann.* 1.6.3
in Woodman 2004, however, shows a similar shift in emphasis from 'power' to 'essence' (see n. 35
below); all of which serves as a further indication of the slippery nature of the Latin word and the
difficulties it poses for translators. On the proceedings in the Senate relating to the asylum rights of
Greek cities reported at *Ann.* 3.60–3, see B. J. Gibson 2014: 128–33.

[33] Cf. Goodyear 1972: 136 on *Ann.* 1.6.3: 'It is not surprising that *vis* is a favourite word in T.: it
expresses a harsh fact and it readily lends itself to use in contrasts between appearance and reality';
also Ash 2007: 184 on *Hist.* 2.39.1.

[34] 'Since he therefore could not, in the absence of both charge and accuser, assume the role of judge,
he resorted to his despot's power and sent in the tribune Gerellanus with a cohort of soldiers.' See
further the discussion of Koestermann 1963–8: IV.318 ad loc., comparing Arruntius' observation at
*Ann.* 6.48.2 that Tiberius was *post tantam rerum experientiam vi dominationis convulsus et mutatus*
('after so much experience of affairs … unhinged and changed under the influence of being
master').

[35] '. . . and that Tiberius should not dissipate the essence of the principate by calling everything to the
attention of the senate'.

[36] See Martin 1955: 121; Woodman 1995: 266 (= 1998: 35).

potential violence: *ipse Luguduni vim fortunamque principatus e proximo ostentaret, nec parvis periculis immixtus et maioribus non defuturus.*[37] Similar is the account of the behaviour of Mucianus himself at *Histories* 4.11.1: *nec deerat ipse, stipatus armatis domos hortosque permutans, apparatu incessu excubiis vim principis amplecti, nomen remittere*;[38] here, the *vis principis* is closely associated with the potential for violence as a fundamental aspect of imperial power, hence the presence of armed men in Mucianus' entourage. That a potential rival for imperial power might have *vis* is also indicated at *Annals* 11.1.1, where Claudius is warned against Asiaticus' *vim atque opes principibus infensas*;[39] Tacitus' use of *vis* in this passage might again be seen as exploiting a range of possible shades of meaning, with the word suggesting Asiaticus' strength, strength that might be used against the emperor.

Indeed, we find that *vis* in Tacitus is not merely the prerogative of emperors. Other commanders can also be associated with the concept. The significance of *vis* in terms of power is made clear at *Histories* 2.39.1, where command in the absence of Otho is described in the following way: *profecto Brixellum Othone honor imperii penes Titianum fratrem, vis ac potestas penes Proculum praefectum.*[40] There is clearly a distinction being drawn here between *honor* and more real forms of power, but the association of *potestas* and *vis* conveys the fact that power can depend on the potential for violence. This more violent aspect of *vis* is underlined at *Annals* 12.49.2, where we hear how Helvidius Priscus in the east conducted affairs more by his *moderatio* than by *vis*: *moderatione plura quam vi composuerat*[41] (cf. *Ann.* 2.26.3, quoted above, p. 277). Not unexpectedly, we also find that command of the praetorians is associated with *vis*: thus at *Histories* 4.68.2, when Mucianus is about to depose Varus from this post, Varus' situation is described in these terms: *Varus praetorianis praepositus vim atque arma retinebat*;[42] similarly, at *Annals* 4.2.1, Tacitus notes how

---

[37] 'Domitian should stay at Lyons and there show the power and prosperity of the throne from close quarters. By abstaining from trifling risks he would be ready to cope with greater ones.' Cf. Heubner 1963–82: IV.209 ad loc.

[38] '[Mucianus was now the sole object of their flattering attentions,] and he lived up to them. He surrounded himself with an armed escort, and kept changing his house and gardens. His display, his parades, his bodyguard, all showed that he had adopted the power of an emperor while forgoing the title.' For the contrast between *vis* and *nomen* Heubner 1963–82: IV.32 ad loc. compares *Ann.* 6.43.3.

[39] 'might and wealth that were inimical to principes'.

[40] 'When Otho started out for Brixellum, he left his brother Titianus in nominal command, but power and control lay with the Prefect Proculus.'

[41] 'He had settled things down more by moderation than by force.'

[42] 'Varus, as commanding the Guards, still controlled a powerful military force.'

Sejanus enhanced the power of the praetorian prefecture by concentrating the praetorians into a single camp: *vim praefecturae modicam antea intendit.*[43]

If emperors and other commanders can be linked with the idea of *vis*, then so too can Rome itself.[44] Thus at *Annals* 2.4.3 we hear how Roman military force is potentially a critical factor in determining the course of events in the politically unstable region of Armenia: *sed ubi minitari Artabanus et parum subsidii in Armeniis, vel, si nostra vi defenderetur, bellum adversus Parthos sumendum erat, rector Syriae Creticus Silanus excitum custodia circumdat.*[45] Similarly, at *Annals* 3.60.3, in the passage on senatorial discussion of Greek provincial affairs already mentioned (pp. 277–8), there is a reference back to Republican times and the foreign kings who were powerful then, *regum ... qui ante vim Romanam valuerant.*[46] And while such projection of Roman might overseas can easily be integrated into ongoing ideologies of imperial power, it is nevertheless worth probing such passages further. With these two particular examples, indeed, one might feel that *vis Romana* could be construed in terms of power or force, rather than specifically as violence, but other cases show that such sharp distinctions are in fact illusory. This is illustrated at, for instance, *Annals* 4.50.2, where the Thracian Dinis advocates that peace should be made with the Romans. Tacitus' description of Dinis contains the information that he had long been familiar with Roman *vis*: *provectus senecta et longo usu vim atque clementiam Romanam edoctus.*[47] The telling antithesis (or hendiadys?) between *vis* and *clementia* here contrives to present both in a much less favourable light from the perspective of the Thracians.[48] One

---

[43] 'He increased the influence (previously limited) of the prefecture.'

[44] Cf., e.g., Hor. *Epod.* 16.2 *suis et ipsa Roma viribus ruit* ('and Rome itself falls down through its own strength'), where Watson 2003: 489 glosses *viribus* as 'military strength', citing *OLD* s.v., sect. 24; for *vis Romana*, note also Livian examples such as *omnisque vis Romana Veios conversa est* ('and all the might of Rome turned towards Veii'), 6.25.6, 32.15.2.

[45] 'But, when Artabanus [king of Parthia] started menacing and too little support for Vonones [former Parthian king, now in exile in Armenia and elevated to the Armenian throne] was coming from the Armenians (the alternative, if he was to be defended by our might, was taking up war against the Parthians), the governor of Syria, Creticus Silanus, summoned him and surrounded him with guards.'

[46] 'kings who had ruled before the period of Roman might'.

[47] Woodman translates: '[Dinis,] advanced in age and through long experience well taught in Roman might and clemency'. Martin and Woodman 1989: 212 ad loc. note parallels with Sall. *Hist.* 2.87D Reynolds *at illi quibus aetas inbellior et vetustate vis Romanorum multum cognita erat, cupere pacem* ('But those whose years were less suited to war, and who had great familiarity with Roman might on account of their age, wanted peace') and Livy 6.32.7.

[48] For consideration of the ideological dimension of Roman *clementia* see, e.g., Brunt 1978: 183–5 (= 2004: 174–5); S. Braund 2009: 30–44.

can compare this passage with *Histories* 4.69.1, where Julius Auspex urges that the Remi reach an accommodation with the Romans: *at Iulius Auspex e primoribus Remorum, vim Romanam pacisque bona dissertans ...;*[49] the phrase *vim Romanam* might seem to slide between denoting Roman military might as, on the one hand, something to be feared, in contrast to *pacisque bona*, 'the benefits of peace', and, on the other, something that might in the future secure the advantages of peacetime, so that different perspectives here lend the phrase different meanings. Even more direct, however, is *Annals* 13.54.2, where Dubius Avitus, in charge of the province of lower Germania, warns the Frisians in no uncertain terms: *Dubius Avitus, accepta a Paulino provincia, minitando vim Romanam nisi abscederent Frisii veteres in locos aut novam sedem a Caesare impetrarent ...*[50] Here *vis Romana* itself is at the centre of the threat, and the connection with violence is easy to see.

There are also examples where foreign power is expressed in terms of *vis*. Thus at *Annals* 2.3.2 Artaxias, the king of Armenia, is said to have protected himself by recourse to the *vis* of the Parthian royal family: *Arsacidarum vi seque regnumque tutatus est.*[51] And a more wide-ranging use of *vis* in the context of non-Roman nations occurs at *Annals* 15.13.2, where inaction on the part of Romans besieged by Vologaeses is described in terms of their fears of enemy *vis*: *at illi vix contuberniis extracti, nec aliud quam munimenta propugnabant, pars iussu ducis, et alii propria ignavia aut Corbulonem opperientes, ac vis si ingrueret, provisis exemplis cladis Caudinae Numantinaeque; neque eandem vim Samnitibus aut Hispanis quae Romani imperii aemulis.*[52] More complex, however, is *Annals* 2.60.4, where the power of Rameses of Egypt is expressed in terms of lists of tributary goods which Tacitus claims were no less impressive than those levied by Rome or by Parthia: *haud minus magnifica quam nunc vi Parthorum aut potentia*

---

[49] 'However, Julius Auspex, a chieftain of the Remi, enlarged upon the power of Rome and the blessings of peace.'

[50] 'Dubius Avitus, receiving the province from Paulinus, and threatening the Frisians with Roman might unless they withdrew to their old locations or made a successful request for their new abode from Caesar ...'

[51] '... protected both himself and his kingdom by the might of the Arsacidae'.

[52] 'But they could scarcely be drawn out of their billets and did nothing but protect the fortifications, some at the order of their leader, others through personal cowardice or waiting for Corbulo and, if violence threatened, with premonitions of the disastrous precedents of Caudium and Numantia – and the violence of the Samnites or Spaniards was hardly the same as that of the Roman empire's rivals!' For *vis si ingrueret*, Koestermann 1963–8: IV.184 ad loc. compares *Ann.* 14.61.2 *ne ... vulgi acrior vis ingrueret* ('[from her dread] that ... the violence of the public might pose a fiercer threat'). For Tacitean exploitation elsewhere of the resonance of the Caudine disaster, see Ash 1998.

*Romana iubentur.*[53] In this passage the pairing of Parthian *vis* and Roman *potentia* might appear to point to *vis* as something more forcible, and something associated with a foreign people, as opposed to Roman *potentia*, but, as we have seen, Tacitus is not afraid elsewhere to consider Roman power in terms of *vis* as well.[54] Thus attempts to consider Roman power as somehow ontologically different from foreign power are likely to be fraught with difficulty. And it is the same if we are talking of violence. For the potential for violence in Rome to take on a 'foreign' aspect, there is one striking example in the *Histories*. In the first book, at 1.40.2, the Roman soldiers who are about to kill Galba are compared to those who might depose a Parthian monarch from his throne: *igitur milites Romani, quasi Vologaesum aut Pacorum avito Arsacidarum solio depulsuri ac non imperatorem suum inermem et senem trucidare pergerent ...*[55] Here the situation of Roman civil discord in the capital city itself is implicitly compared to the kind of political and dynastic upheaval characteristic of Rome's eastern neighbour, Parthia.[56]

We have seen how the power of emperors, and that of Rome itself, can be expressed in terms of *vis*, with the potential for such power to be enforced through acts of violence. In large part this power could be enforced through the use of the military. I shall show now how Tacitus reflects this through the association of the word *vis* with the armies, but in such a manner as to suggest that such *vis* can have its own dynamic, independent of higher authority. To begin with a simple example, at *Annals* 11.9.1 we hear how Roman troops took part in action against mountain fortresses in Armenia, *vi militis Romani ad excidenda castellorum ardua,*[57] where one might almost say that the use of *vis* with a genitive is merely equivalent to Virgil's *odora canum vis* (lit. 'the keen-scented force of

---

[53] '[contributions] no less magnificent than those that are now at the bidding of the Parthians' might or Roman powerfulness'.

[54] As noted by Furneaux 1896–1907: I.357 ad loc.; cf. Koestermann 1963–8: I.369 ad loc., who comments, 'die Substantiva ohne Unterschied der Bedeutung'. Note also *Germ.* 42.2 *sed vis et potentia regibus ex auctoritate Romana* ('but the might and power of the kings came from Roman authority').

[55] 'Off went the Roman soldiers as if they were going to drag Vologaeses or Pacorus from the ancestral throne of the Arsacids – and not to butcher their own emperor, a helpless old man.' On Galba's death in Tacitus, see Ash 1999: 79–83.

[56] For this notion of Romans behaving in the manner of foreign peoples in Tacitus see Ash 2007: 111 on *Hist.* 2.12.2. Compare the striking and anachronistic simile used by Statius at *Theb.* 8.286–93, where the Greek Thiodamas, who has just replaced Amphiaraus as the seer of the army before Thebes, is compared to an Achaemenid boy anxious at succeeding to his father's throne; see further Hardie 1993: 111; B. J. Gibson 2008: 103.

[57] 'with the might of the Roman soldiery to extirpate the steep strongholds'.

dogs', *Aen.* 4.132) and similar phrases.[58] Other instances are less straight-forward, however. At *Histories* 2.76.4, Mucianus makes a speech which is designed to encourage Vespasian to consider a challenge for the throne. He points out that Otho's demise should not deter Vespasian, since Otho was a victim of his own despair: *ne Othonem quidem ducis arte aut exercitus vi, sed praepropera ipsius desperatione victum.*[59] Notice here the pairing of *ducis arte* and *exercitus vi:*[60] though armies have command-ers, the implication is that the army itself can exert power and determine the result of a battle.[61] The power of the legions and their concomitant potential for violence are indeed a concern of the *Histories*. Thus at *Histories* 1.14.1 Galba, fearful concerning the revolt of the legions in Germany, is said to be *anxius quonam exercituum vis erumperet,*[62] the verb *erumperet* underlining the danger represented to an emperor by unco-operative and potentially violent legions. At *Histories* 3.1.2, those Flavian supporters who favoured a delay in prosecution of the war make much of the power of the German legions: *Germanicarum legionum vim famamque extollebant.*[63] At *Histories* 2.85.1, we hear of how the Moesian legions attempt to draw the army in the nearby province of Pannonia into joining their cause: *ita tres Moesicae legiones per epistulas adliciebant Pannonicum exercitum aut abnuenti vim parabant,*[64] where the threat of violence in case of a refusal does not have any accompanying mention of commanders. And it is no surprise to find in the *Annals* as well that legionary revolts are characterized by references to the *vis* of the legions. At *Annals* 1.19.3, when Junius Blaesus attempts to curb the excesses of the legions, he asks why they are planning *vis* (*cur contra morem obsequii, contra fas disciplinae vim meditentur?*);[65] but such appeals fall on deaf ears, as Tacitus tells us that the *vis* of the troops only became worse (*flagrantior*

---

[58] See further, e.g., Austin 1955: 61 and Paratore 1947: 29 on Virg. *Aen.* 4.132.

[59] 'Even Otho fell not by the generalship of his opponent or the might of his army, but by his own precipitate despair.'

[60] This pairing might be seen as analogous to that of *consilium* and *vis* discussed above in relation to Hor. *Carm.* 3.4.65–8 and Tac. *Ann.* 2.26.3 (pp. 274, 277 with n. 30).

[61] As Ash 2007: 295 on this passage notes, the phrasing is particularly pointed since Vitellius himself was not even present at the first Battle of Bedriacum.

[62] 'fearful as to the extent to which the violence of the troops might spread'.

[63] '[Those who were in favour of waiting for reinforcements and prolonging the war] dwelt on the strength and reputation of the German legions.' Cf. Heubner 1963–82: III.14 ad loc.

[64] 'Accordingly, the three Moesian legions addressed letters to the Pannonian army, inviting their co-operation, and meanwhile prepared to meet refusal with force.' For *vim* with *parare*, cf. Heubner 1963–82: II.286 ad loc.

[65] '... why, contrary to their habit of compliance, contrary to the obligations of discipline, were they contemplating violence?'

*inde vis, plures seditioni duces*, 1.22.1).[66] The potential for the legions to become involved in attempts on the throne is also expressed in terms of *vis* at *Annals* 1.31.1, when Tacitus turns from the legionary mutinies in Pannonia following Tiberius' accession to the legions on the German frontier, and we hear of hopes that Tiberius' adopted son (and nephew) Germanicus might use his troops there against Tiberius in an effort to secure the imperial power: ... *magna spe fore ut Germanicus Caesar ... daret ... se legionibus vi sua cuncta tractaturis*,[67] where it is the *vis* of the legions, not their commander, which is said to have such a decisive potential.

To sum up. While Tacitus uses *violentia* and its cognates in a manner whose negative tone is similar to that of the English word 'violence', he also makes use of *vis*, a word which can require ethical clarification, sometimes provided through qualifying phrases in the Latin or the wider context within the work, and sometimes left more open to the reader's judgement. *Vis*, as the embodiment of power, is something which, as the quotations from Paulus, Horace, and Cicero towards the start of this chapter show, can go either way, in terms of how it is viewed ethically. The pages of Tacitus indicate, however, that the potential for *vis* to be something negative is always there. Thus *vis*, when associated with emperors, can sometimes suggest the power of the Principate, but the *vis principatus* can easily be turned towards violent actions, as at *Annals* 15.69.1, with Nero's decision to act against Vestinus. Other commanders too can be linked with *vis*, which can symbolize their potential and energy, yet at the same time this *vis* can be put to use in a violent cause, as when the Pannonian legions come over to Vespasian (and hence involve themselves in civil war) *vi praecipua Primi Antonii* (*Hist.* 2.86.1).[68] Similarly, Roman imperial power can be described in terms of *vis*, which sometimes straightforwardly signifies Rome's ability to impose force, or violence, on others, as at *Annals* 13.54.2, where the Frisians are threatened with *vis*

---

[66] 'Thereupon the violence burned more feverishly, and the mutiny had more leaders.' On this passage, see Woodman 2006: 315, who argues that *vis* here recalls technical uses of the word in contexts of sickness.

[67] '... with high hopes that Germanicus Caesar [would be unable to suffer the command of another and] would entrust himself to the legions, who would handle everything by their own force'. *tractaturis* is the convincing conjecture of Woodman 2005: 321–2, and preferable to Lipsius' *tracturis* (read by Fisher; the manuscript has *tracturus* here).

[68] '[They lost no time in joining Vespasian's cause,] being chiefly instigated by Antonius Primus.' The word in this passage can be glossed as 'influence' (cf., e.g., Heubner 1963–82: II.287 ad loc. 'vor allem unter den Einfluß'), but the point can be made that such influence occurs here in a context of potential violence.

*Romana*; it is also significant, as we have seen, that Roman *vis* can be paralleled by the *vis* of non-Roman nations. Finally, *vis* is also something which is clearly linked by Tacitus with the power of the legions. It can on occasion denote, quite simply, the military might of the legions in dealing with Rome's enemies; yet the word is also used in contexts such as civil war and mutiny. The uncertain slipperiness of *vis*, often denoting power which can slide into acts of force or violence, as illustrated in this chapter from the pages of Tacitus, is a potent reminder of how terms such as 'force' and 'violence' are never likely to be objective.

# CHAPTER 10

# Cruel Narrative
## Apuleius' Golden Ass

### William Fitzgerald

How does violence become a literary subject? We speak of 'mindless' or 'senseless' violence, and complaints about the ubiquity of violence in contemporary film and television are often accompanied by a lament at the decline of interest in plot, character, and dialogue.[1] Violence might seem to be the quintessentially non- or even anti-literary phenomenon, best accompanied by the 'kerplow', 'splat', and 'boom' of the comic strip.[2] However, in the work that I will be discussing violence is described in some of the most exquisite Latin prose ever written. The *Golden Ass* is a work which invites us to inquire broadly into the relation between narrative and violence, for it is a work to which violence is central in a way that has not been adequately recognized.[3] Admittedly, violence is almost as characteristic of ancient prose fiction as it is of epic, but in the *Golden Ass* it plays a special role, since at the heart of the work lies the story of a man who turns into an ass and suffers all the cruelties that humans mete out to their beasts of burden. Much of the violence in the *Golden Ass* is experienced by Lucius the ass in the form of murderous beatings, but the stories that are interwoven with, or interpolated within, his own are also frequently violent in nature.

Yet the *Golden Ass* is not just a text that contains a great deal of violence; it is a narrative to which violence is intrinsic. Modern audiences are familiar with stories that are given shape or direction by a violence that threatens, escalates, or erupts – Peckinpah's *Straw Dogs*, for instance; or with works in which violence hangs in the air, like the persistent menace of a Pinter play. The modern obsession with violence prompts us to look at

---

[1] For a stimulating collection of essays on screen violence, see French 1996.

[2] Cf. Kennedy, Chapter 7, p. 242 above, quoting Scarry 1985 to the effect that pain is difficult to represent, and is best expressed in paralinguistic shrieks and yells.

[3] J. J. Winkler 1985: 93–8 deals with this aspect of the work under the category of 'sensationalism' and acknowledges that 'If I were trying to give an adequate account of the AA [*Golden Ass*], sensationalism is one of the many lines that would have to be developed' (96).

ancient texts from a new angle. Thus Denis Feeney has argued that in the *Aeneid* violence is promised but constantly delayed, and that when it arrives Virgil draws attention to the reader's complicity by lamenting that it need never have happened (but would we have been disappointed had it not?).[4] The structural role of violence in the *Golden Ass* is quite the opposite of what Feeney describes for the *Aeneid*, for in this case a story that features continual violence breaks out into something quite other in the final book, in which our hero becomes a devotee of the goddess Isis.

I have argued elsewhere[5] that Lucius' conversion, the sudden and overwhelming conviction that Isis rules all things and beings, echoes an earlier, metaphoric 'conversion', in which a sudden and violent beating 'converts' the reluctant Lucius to an obedient slavery, much to the amusement of the human participants (*subita sectae commutatione risum toto coetu commoveram*, 'I roused the laughter of the whole gathering by my sudden change of philosophy',[6] 9.12). That the earlier scene should allude to an initiation, a ceremony that could similarly involve disorientation and violent shock,[7] only enforces the connection. When Lucius wakes on the beach at Cenchreae at the beginning of Book 11, it is sudden fear that wakes him, a fear that is by now instinctual after the repeated violence to which he has been subjected. Lucius' immediate acknowledgement of Isis' total power is a response to the utter powerlessness he has experienced as an ass. Everything he has undergone is condensed in that confession, and this condensation allows Lucius to free himself from the daily cruelties to

---

[4] Feeney 1999: 178–9.  [5] Fitzgerald 2000: 109–10.

[6] I cite the *Golden Ass* according to the text of Hanson 1989; translations are my own except where noted.

[7] Cf. Plut. fr. 178 Sandbach πλάναι τὰ πρῶτα καὶ περιδρομαὶ κοπώδεις καὶ διὰ σκότους τινὲς ὕποπτοι πορεῖαι καὶ ἀτέλεστοι, εἶτα πρὸ τοῦ τέλους αὐτοῦ τὰ δεινὰ πάντα, φρίκη καὶ τρόμος καὶ ἱδρὼς καὶ θάμβος ('first, wanderings and tiring circuits and suspicious journeys through the darkness that go nowhere, then just before the end all things frightful – terror and trembling and sweat and wonder'); Achilles Tatius, *Leucippe and Clitophon* 5.23 ἑλκύσας δὲ τῶν τριχῶν ῥάσσει πρὸς τοὔδαφος καὶ προσπίπτων κατακόπτει με πληγαῖς. ἐγὼ δὲ ὥσπερ ἐν μυστηρίῳ μηδὲν <ᾔδειν> ('Dragging me by the hair he pounded my head against the floor and falling on me he began punching me right and left. I, like one being initiated into a mystery, [knew] nothing at all') (translations from J. J. Winkler 1985: 244–5). Similarly, Lucius' experiences at the mill involve wanderings and circuits followed by sudden violence: *et ilico velata facie propellor ad incurva spatia flexuosi canalis, ut in orbe termini circumfluentis reciproco gressu mea recalcans vestigia vagarer errore certo ... complures enim protinus baculis armati me circumsteterunt atque, ut eram luminibus obtectis securus etiamnunc, repente signo dato et clamore conserto, plagas ingerentes acervatim ...* ('And then with my head covered I was pushed along the curved path of a circular channel, so that, retracing my steps in the cycle of a rounded course that returned them to the beginning, I would wander without deviating ... But several of the men armed with sticks at once took up a position around me, unconcerned as I was because of my blindfold. Suddenly, on a signal, they gave a concerted shout and piled blows on me ...', 9.11).

which he has been subjected. Violence, then, plays a central role in the logic of Lucius' conversion.

I will come back to Lucius' conversion later, but my main concern will be with the structuring role played by violence in the episodic narrative of Lucius' adventures, and for this purpose I want to look at violence as a manifestation of cruelty, which is how it most commonly appears in this story of the experiences of a beast of burden. Cruelty is a richer concept than violence, and can be more easily attached to intentions, though like violence (and unlike revenge, for instance) it has a problematic relation to the notion of plot.[8]

In his much-cited *Reading for the Plot*, Peter Brooks makes a connection between narrative and desire, whether that of the protagonist, the narrator, or the reader.[9] The *Golden Ass* begins with curiosity, Lucius', and, by implication, our own.[10] In fact, one could describe the main arc of the work as the uncovering of a secret, in so far as Lucius' desire to experience magic leads him to initiation into a mystery. But, somewhere along the way, Lucius' quest is waylaid and his curiosity begins to be satisfied ironically. The nosy busybody becomes a passive victim, and this puts him, and us, in a position to undergo many curious experiences.[11] At this point the novel loses the plot, and is reduced to episodes. Lucius the ass is a passive hero who has no goal or desire except survival. Brooks has little to say about episodic narratives such as this, remarking that the picaresque presents the rock-bottom paradigm of the narrative of desire in so far as the *picaro*'s ambition is simply to stay alive.[12] So this section of the *Golden Ass* presents considerable difficulties to a reader who is trying to make out 'the organizing line and intention of narrative', as Brooks defines plot.[13] Chance seems to dominate the succession of events, as we can see from Bakhtin's account of the events that precipitate Lucius' adventures as an ass: 'The witch's maid Fotis *accidentally* took the wrong box and in place of a cream for transforming men into birds gave Lucius the cream for turning men into asses. It was an *accident* that *at that moment* the roses necessary to reverse this transformation were not to be found in the house. It was an *accident* that *on that very*

---

[8] Ancient conceptions of cruelty are discussed in Viljamaa, Timonen, and Krötzl 1992; Lintott 1999: 35–51. Lintott argues that the Romans generally regarded an act as cruel if it was performed to satisfy emotion rather than in pursuit of a particular interest.
[9] Brooks 1984: 37–61.
[10] 1.2 '*immo vero*' inquam '*impertite sermone non quidem curiosum, sed qui velim scire vel cuncta vel certe plurima*' ("'No, don't," I said, "but rather include me in your conversation – not that I am inquisitive, but I am the kind of man who wants to know everything, or at least most things'").
[11] Cf. Fitzgerald 2000: 103–5, where Lucius' curiosity is related to the knowledge of the slave.
[12] Brooks 1984: 38.     [13] Brooks 1984: 37.

night robbers attacked the house and drove away the ass.' Bakhtin comments: 'And in all subsequent adventures of the ass itself, and of its various masters as well, chance continues to play a major role.'[14]

Chance certainly plays a role in Lucius' experiences, but in the form of *Fortuna* it is constantly personified, and this personification serves to give the very episodic quality of the work at this point something in the nature of a plot.[15] Lucius assigns his sufferings to the hand of *Fortuna*, playing the role that the anger of Poseidon plays in the *Odyssey*, the persecution of Priapus in the *Satyrica*, or the anger of Aphrodite in Chariton's *Chaereas and Callirhoe*.[16] Consider the following interjections, all occurring within a fairly short span of the narrative:

> talibus aerumnis edomitum novis Fortuna saeva tradidit cruciatibus, scilicet ut, quod aiunt, domi forisque factis adoriae plenae gloriarer.

> verum Fortuna meis cruciatibus insatiabilis aliam mihi denuo pestem instruxit.

> sed in rebus scaevis affulsit Fortunae nutus hilarior, nescio an futuris periculis me reservans, certe praesente statutaque morte liberans.

> sed illa Fortuna meis casibus pervicax tam opportunum latibulum mira celeritate praeversa novas instruxit insidias.

> sed illa Fortuna mea saevissima ... rursum in me caecos detorsit oculos et emptorem aptissimum duris meis casibus mire repertum obiecit.

> Cruel Fortune handed me over, broken by these afflictions, to new torments; I suppose so that I might, as they say, 'boast of glory achieved by deeds performed at home and abroad'.

> But Fortune, who could not get enough of torturing me, prepared still another plague for me.

> But, just as things were going badly, Fortune shone a happier nod in my direction, perhaps saving me for future perils, but certainly delivering me from a present death sentence.

> But Fortune, persistent in my troubles, pre-empted my recourse to this most convenient hiding-place with marvellous speed and set a new ambush for me.

> But that most cruel Fortune of mine ... again turned her blind eyes to me and came up with a buyer wonderfully suited to my misfortunes, whom she threw my way. (7.16, 17, 20, 25; 8.24)

---

[14] Bakhtin 1981: 116 (emphases his).    [15] Cf. Schlam 1992: 60–2.

[16] *Tuche* also plays a significant role in the Greek novel. In the present context cf. esp. Ach. Tat. 6.13.3, where Clitophon describes *Tuche* as contriving a new plot (*drama*) against him.

The priest of Isis concurs with Lucius' attribution of responsibility and also finds that 'blind' Fortune has a plot (cf. 8.24), albeit unwittingly:

> sed utcumque Fortunae caecitas, dum te pessimis periculis discruciat, ad religiosam istam beatitudinem improvida produxit malitia. eat nunc et summo furore saeviat et crudelitati suae materiem quaerat aliam.

> But anyway, the blindness of Fortune, in the very process of tormenting you with the worst of perils, has brought you, in her thoughtless malice, to this state of holy happiness. Let her go ahead and rage in all her fury and find out some other object for her cruelty. (11.15)

*Fortuna's* plot is, quite simply, to torture Lucius,[17] and this is consistent with Bakhtin's description of the way that unfortunate coincidences accumulate to persecute him. Some of the human persecutors of Lucius, and especially the one usually known as the cruel boy (7.17–24), seem to be incarnations of the abstract *Fortuna*.[18]

In one direction, the stage-managing *Fortuna* points to the cruelties of the 'world' of the *Golden Ass*, the realities of inequality and exploitation that Lucius encounters as an ass. But, in another direction, she points to the author himself, who can gratuitously make life as tough as he wants for Lucius.[19] In this story of cruelty to a dumb animal, the author glories in the fact that he can do anything he wants with his hero. Lucius, resigned at what *Fortuna* has in store for him, is the character at the mercy of his creator, or indeed, the reader at the mercy of the author, for as Lucius passes from master to master we must pass from one episode to another, looking for deliverance from the mere sequentiality of a narrative that takes us from bad to worse and refuses to gather into a plot. The author's frustration of our desire for plot is tied to a certain kind of cruel narrative structure, so that the torment of Lucius is shadowed by a persecution of

---

[17] As Schlam 1992: 61 points out, '*Saeva*, "cruel," is the most frequent epithet of *Fortuna* in the *Metamorphoses*' (see also 144–5 n. 21). This adjective is traditional for *Fortuna*: see Kajanto 1981: 531.

[18] For the cruel boy in this regard, see 7.18 *nec tamen post tantas meas clades immodico sarcinae pondere contentus* ('yet even after all my sufferings he was not satisfied with the excessive weight of my load'); 7.18 *idem mihi talem etiam excogitavit perniciem* ('he thought up yet another way to afflict me, namely . . .'); 7.19 *denique tale facinus in me comminiscitur* ('finally he devised this outrage against me'). Cf. 7.17 *Fortuna meis cruciatibus insatiabilis* ('Fortune, who could not get enough of torturing me').

[19] For a third direction, see J. J. Winkler 1985: 106–8, who is interested in the way the interjections just noted characterize Lucius the narrator. Arguing against those who would link Lucius' complaints to a growing world-disgust that leads to his conversion, Winkler comments (108): 'In the interests of such a connection, the interpreter must also suppress the comedy of Fortuna's unrelenting insidiousness in ever devising new perils and the comedy of the philosophizing ass's shocked innocence.' These remarks on Lucius' part, according to Winkler, represent a 'dereliction of [the narrator's] responsibility for integrating the story as a measured progress toward [its] end'.

the reader. Alternat(iv)ely, our desire to read on is tied to the 'plot' of *Fortuna*, and we become complicit in her cruelty. As we shall see in connection with 7.17 and 7.25, this double perspective is to some extent true of Lucius' own attitude to his adventures. But I do not want to make too much of the metanarrative aspects of cruelty. I will be arguing that cruelty can function as a motivating and structuring principle for an episodic narrative such as the *Golden Ass* because of its inherent complexity. On the one hand, cruelty tends towards the total destruction of its object, and on the other hand, it must always swerve away from the obliteration that will deprive it of its object, preventing that further turn of the screw. This tension is what keeps us hooked on the narrative.

## The Bailiff's Tale: A Cruel Story

Before we turn to the episodic narrative of Lucius' sufferings I want to look at one of the inset tales. The story of the bailiff is an extreme and provocative tale that comes very close to aligning narration with cruelty. It is perhaps the cruellest passage in this cruel work, and not incidentally it is the shortest of the inset tales. Not incidentally also, it has received virtually no attention from commentators. Winkler includes it in his list of inset tales,[20] but it is the only one about which he has nothing to say. It is narratologically interesting primarily because it seems to represent the zero-degree of narration, but not in the same way as the narrative of Lucius. If the episodic narrative of Lucius' sufferings is too loose, this narrative is too tight, and that is not an incidental fact but something it casts in our face. Here, to tell a story means to create a character and then to destroy him.

> servus quidam, cui cunctam familiae tutelam dominus permiserat suus, quique possessionem maximam illam in quam deverteramus villicabat, habens ex eodem famulitio conservam coniugam, liberae cuiusdam extrariaeque mulieris flagrabat cupidine. quo dolore paelicatus uxor eius instricta cunctas mariti rationes et quicquid horreo reconditum continebatur admoto combussit igne. nec tali damno tori sui contumeliam vindicasse contenta, iam contra sua saeviens viscera laqueum sibi nectit, infantulumque quem de eodem marito iam dudum susceperat eodem funiculo nectit, seque per altissimum puteum appendicem parvulum trahens praecipitat. quam mortem dominus eorum aegerrime sustinens arreptum servulum qui causam tanti sceleris luxurie sua[21] praestiterat

[20] J. J. Winkler 1985: 26.
[21] The manuscript from which all other surviving witnesses to the *Golden Ass* descend (Florence, Laur. 68.2, = *F*) has *uxori su(a)e*, but a variant in the margin has been erased and an important group of descendants reads *luxurie sua*, which Hanson prints.

nudum ac totum melle perlitum firmiter alligavit arbori ficulneae, cuius in
ipso carioso stipite inhabitantium formicarum nidificia bulliebant et ultro
citro commeabant multiiuga scaturrigine. quae simul dulcem ac mellitum
corporis nidorem persentiscunt, parvis quidem sed numerosis et continuis
morsiunculis penitus inhaerentes, per longi temporis cruciatum ita, carni-
bus atque ipsis visceribus adesis, homine consumpto membra nudarunt ut
ossa tantum viduata pulpis nitore nimio candentia funestae cohaererent
arbori.

There was a servant whose master had entrusted him with the steward-
ship of his entire household and who acted as overseer of that extensive
holding where we had stopped for the night. He was married to another
servant in the same household, but was passionately in love with a free
woman who lived outside the estate. Smarting at her husband's infidelity, the wife set fire to all his records and everything he kept in the
storehouse and completely destroyed them. Not content with this
damage as satisfaction for the dishonour done her marriage, she next
turned her rage against her own flesh. Knotting a noose around her
neck, she tied the baby she had just borne her husband to the same rope
and hurled herself into a deep well, dragging down with her the little
one attached. Their master was extremely upset at their deaths, and
arrested the servant whose wanton behaviour had provoked this terrible
tragedy. He had him stripped and smeared all over with honey and then
tied securely to a fig tree, inside whose rotten trunk lived a multitude of
nesting ants who marched back and forth in rippling streams. As soon
as they noticed the sweet honeyed smell of his body, they began to
fasten themselves deep in his skin with their tiny bites, small to be sure,
but numerous and ceaseless. After an interminable period of torture the
man died, his flesh and even his innards eaten away, his body so
denuded that only the bones remained, bereft of flesh and gleaming
brilliant white, still clinging to that funereal tree.[22] (8.22)

The story of the bailiff may be untypical in its narrative structure, but it is
thematically well integrated into the narrative at this point: the gleaming
bones and the devouring of a human, for instance, are motifs that recur in
this part of the work.[23] The story also plays its role in the narrative rhythm
of Lucius' adventures, where every deliverance leads to something worse.
Lucius escapes from his captivity among the bandits when his fellow-
prisoner, Charite, is rescued by her fiancé, Tlepolemus (7.13). But Lucius'
reward for his part in the escape, a life of ease in a meadow of mares, is

---

[22] Translation: Hanson 1989.
[23] See Dowden 1993: 107–8. As Kirichenko 2010: 28 points out, the tale introduces a long series of
erotic tales featuring adultery and jealousy, though in this case, uniquely, it is the husband who is
the adulterer.

exchanged for drudgery at the mill when the groom charged with his care by Charite turns him over to his greedy wife. Meanwhile, the joyous reunion and marriage of Tlepolemus and Charite comes to a tragic end when Tlepolemus is murdered in a hunting 'accident' by a jealous rival, Thrasyllus. Charite avenges Tlepolemus by blinding Thrasyllus, and then kills herself. After the death of Charite, Tlepolemus' slaves go on the run and encounter one danger after another. The story of the bailiff is introduced just when the company has fled the scene where one of their number has been found half-consumed by an enormous snake (*pestilenti deserta regione*, 'deserting this pernicious region', 8.21), and is resting for the night in a village. There they hear the story of the bailiff, which drives them away from this abominable resting-place too (*hac quoque detestabili deserta mansione*, 8.23). So, this short, economical, and self-contained story of crime and punishment is itself an episode in the rambling story of Lucius' persecution by a gratuitously cruel *Fortuna*. Is the narrative getting too loose for you? Try this on for size!

From the bare fact of the bailiff's infatuation the narrative leads us through a progressively more horrifying series of responses that culminates in a scene of destruction totally out of proportion to the initial action. In fact, the adultery (or adulterous love) serves merely as the starting-point for the narrative's systematic persecution of the bailiff. This is in stark contrast to the adultery tales of the next book, which take us into the realm of the comic. The clandestine meetings, unexpected returns, concealments, stratagems, and exposures that are the focus of those tales are elided here, and the narrative jumps straight from the fact of love to the revenge of the spouse. It is a narrative that seems to take satisfaction from its own ruthless efficiency, as one protagonist takes over from the other in a series of relative clauses which lead us seamlessly from the adulterous *vilicus* to the man-eating ants: *servus quidam . . . flagrabat cupidine. quo dolore paelicatus uxor eius instricta . . . quam mortem dominus eorum aegerrime sustinens . . . quae [formicae] simul dulcem ac mellitum corporis nidorem persentiscunt . . .* There is minimal interest in the psychology of the principals, and their motives are stripped to the bone; only the details that the bailiff's paramour was free and not part of the same household (*liberae . . . extrariae*) distract from the concentration on the bailiff's sufferings. Ebel, the only commentator who makes anything of this story, claims that it stands alone. 'It is, for one thing, not a tale at all but a synopsis of catastrophe: brief, relentless and mechanical. If the narrative paradigm of the *Metamorphoses* is the unexpected or inexplicable turn of chance, the revelation of universal vicissitude through the flux of events, then this tale is distinguished by the remorseless linear certainty with which its events succeed each other.'[24] This story, then, is a paradigm of what the framing narrative at this stage is not. Ebel puts his finger on something important when he says that this is not a tale at all but a synopsis of catastrophe. I would put it differently, however, and say that this narrative, which suffers from a surfeit of consequentiality, seems to ask us, 'Is this a story?' Not only does its irrevocable forward movement stress the basic narrative fact that actions have consequences, but it does so with a cruel satisfaction. Ebel calls it 'mechanical', and he is right: the bare mechanics of narrative are exposed as starkly as the bailiff's bones. The narrative impulse itself is stripped down to the essential, for the tale is introduced simply with the words 'A most notable crime had been committed there; I would like to tell the story' (*inibi coeptum facinus oppido memorabile narrare cupio*, 8.22). What sort of a desire is it to want to narrate *this*? Or rather to *narrate* this, because Ebel is right to attach an ethos ('remorseless') to the narration. Between the framing narrative of Lucius' adventures and this little tale we have two narrative extremes, tending in opposite directions towards the vanishing point of story, but sharing the principle of cruelty.

But Ebel exaggerates the extent to which this story diverges from the narrative paradigm of the *Golden Ass*. The linear sequence of action and reaction may be untypical, but the compounding of cruelty upon cruelty is not, as we have seen from the descriptions of *Fortuna*. We could analyse the story as a cruel narrative as follows. A certain slave was entrusted with his master's household, but he was in love with an outsider, though he had a wife from the household. His wife took it hard and burned all he had been entrusted with. (End of story? Not by a long chalk!) The next sentence announces the principle of the narrative itself, for the bailiff's wife is another human counterpart to the insatiable (*insatiabilis*, 7.17) *Fortuna*: *nec tali damno tori sui contumeliam vindicasse contenta*. Raging now against her own vitals (*contra sua saeviens viscera*), she hangs herself. But the narrator is *not content* with suicide as the referent for *contra sua saeviens viscera*, and so he has her attach the infant she has *just* borne *the same husband* and plunge herself down the *deepest* well with the little one attached. *Sua viscera*, it turns out, refers to her child.[25] But these deaths, far from being a punishment of the *vilicus*, become themselves a *cause* for

---

[24] Ebel 1970: 166.     [25] Cf. *OLD* s.v. *viscus* 1, sect. 5.

punishment as the master (not the bailiff) takes them very hard (*aegerrime sustinens*). Here the narrative slows down and takes a deep breath. The sensational and violent events of the first half give way to the methodical and almost pedantic destruction of the slave. The slave is tied to a tree just where a colony of ants is going about its business, and the narrator pauses to give us time to realize, with horror, what is about to happen. The final, longest, and most carefully wrought sentence leaves us with bones sticking to a tree, and the story is wrapped up as the nameless slave (*servus quidam*) is methodically consumed and returned to the nothingness from which he emerged. Only here does the narrative become expansive, as though the human detail that had been elided earlier has been displaced to this passage, where it takes on a very dark hue. The master's punishment may be no worse than the wife's but it is certainly more systematic and complete. The bailiff is not just destroyed, he is rendered into matter. If his wife left him widowed (*viduatus*), the ants leave his bones 'bereaved of meat' (*viduata pulpis*), a striking phrase, since *pulpa* is commonly used of animal, not human, flesh (cf. 2.7 *pulpam frustatim consectam*, 'meat chopped into pieces'). We might explicate the phrase as 'bereaved of humanity in becoming meat'. So: 'There once was a slave to whom everything was entrusted, and then everything was taken away from him until there was no him left.' Is this a story? Or is it simply the abstraction of a story, almost a meta-story, in which the creation of a character out of nothing (*servus quidam*) is balanced by the systematic process of returning him to nothing. Closure indeed!

## A Moral Tale?

If this is a cruel tale, in which a character is created merely to suffer and be destroyed, it is nevertheless as ruthlessly coherent as the cautionary tales of *Struwwelpeter*. In the opening contrasts between *familiae, famulitio* on the one hand and *extrariae, liberae cuiusdam* on the other, the slave's transgression against the household is underlined. Everything is entrusted to this slave and, as a result of his adulterous love, everything is taken away; furthermore, the fit between crime and punishment is exquisite. The flame of his illicit love (*flagrabat*) is punished by the fire that burns his records and his master's barn; the consequence of his *luxuries* is to be stripped naked and coated with honey. The trajectory of the story completes a neat ring, as the bailiff's attraction to an external (*extrariae*) woman leads eventually to the point where he becomes a source of attraction to another species; like him, the ants are diverted from their business by something sweet. In the small, continuous, and penetrating little bites we may recognize a hideous version of the love-play of the adulterous couple, for which the narrative, in its sweep to oblivion, had no time.[26] The final image of the gleaming white bones clinging to the tree is another, still more gruesome, vision of the lovemaking that initiated the story. It is appropriate that the ants, whose bites represent the destructiveness of desire, should be associated here, as often, with the virtues of teamwork and steady thoroughness. These, after all, are the same creatures that, in the most famous of the inset tales (4.28–6.24), help Psyche to perform one of the tasks set by a jealous Venus as punishment for Psyche's presumptuous love for her son; Venus comments that Psyche is so hideous that she can only attract a lover *sedulo ministerio* ('by industrious service', 6.10), and Psyche's ants succeed in separating the different grains in the promiscuous pile that Venus has created as a test of her *sedulitas*. Representing the domestic values that the bailiff has contravened and, at the same time, the lovemaking of the bailiff and his paramour, ants are the perfect agents of the bailiff's punishment.

In its general outline, the story of the bailiff may remind us not only of the *zelotupos* plot in mime but also of the 'servant parables' of the New Testament.[27] Matthew's Gospel has two parables of stewards (*vilici*) who fail their master in the trust bestowed on them and are consequently cast into the darkness (where there will be weeping and gnashing of teeth), but not before one of them has been cut into two (Matt. 24: 45–51, 25: 14–30). The New Testament stories are apocalyptic parables of the kingdom of heaven, and the master's overreaction serves as a mark of divinity. In the tale of the bailiff the master is a figure of similarly awesome vindictiveness. Blind *Fortuna* may be random and perverse, but the 'god' of this story is a monster of consequential justice, and these opposites meet under the category of the cruel narrative. Somewhere between the

---

[26] For the use of *inhaereo* in erotic contexts cf., e.g., Ov. *Tr.* 1.6.1–3 *nec tantum Clario est Lyde dilecta poetae ... pectoribus quantum tu nostris, uxor, inhaeres* ('Lyde was not so loved by the Clarian poet [Antimachus] as you, my wife, cleave to my heart'), Petr. 86.5 *basio inhaesi* ('I fastened on him with a kiss'). An erotic version of the scene is played out at 8.29, where the cinaedic priests of the Dea Syria seek to 'devour' a naked youth (*passimque circumfusi nudatum supinatumque iuvenem exsecrandis oribus flagitabant*, 'surrounding the naked and prostrate youth on all sides, they began to press their loathsome kisses on him').

[27] On the bailiff's wife as *zelotupos*, see Kirichenko 2010: 26–9, who compares Herodas 5 and the *Moicheutria*. Bowersock 1994 is a brilliant study of the shared world of the Gospels and pagan prose fiction, though he does not make this particular connection. Fitzgerald 2000: 111–14 has some remarks on slavery in the *Golden Ass* and the Gospels. On Christianity and the ancient romances, see Ramelli 2001 (on Apuleius specifically, 193–219).

gratuitous cruelty of *Fortuna* and the cruel justice of the bailiff's master will fall the mercy of Isis.

## Narration and Obliteration

The bailiff's story attains closure with a vengeance. But it is not the only story where Apuleius' narration seems to equate the satisfactions of closure with the obliteration of the protagonist. Take the story of Charite, who wreaks a terrible vengeance on the murderer of her husband. Charite recounts the whole gruesome business after she has blinded Thrasyllus and just before she commits suicide. The episode is wrapped up with the death of Charite immediately after she has narrated her story, methodically bringing it to an end:

> et enarratis ordine singulis quae sibi per somnium nuntiaverat maritus quoque astu Thrasyllum inductum petisset, ferro sub papillam dexteram transadacto corruit, et in suo sibi pervolutata sanguine postremo balbuttiens incerto sermone perefflavit animam virilem.

> She told in detail everything that her husband had revealed to her in her dream, and how cleverly she had led Thrasyllus on and attacked him, then she drove the sword under her right breast and collapsed. Rolling over in her own blood, she finally stammered out some incoherent words and breathed out the last of her manly spirit. (8.14)

Charite gives out her breath as she brings the story to a close, and meanwhile the narration makes a thorough job of obliterating her (*pervolutata, postremo ... perefflavit, in suo sibi ... sanguine*). All the principals are dead. Or not quite. In a coda that ties everything up, Thrasyllus has himself brought to the same tomb as Charite:

> valvis super sese diligenter obseratis inedia statuit elidere sua sententia damnatum spiritum.

> When he had carefully bolted the tomb doors over himself he resolved to destroy by starvation the life that he himself had judged and condemned. (8.14)

Thrasyllus is condemned to death by his own decision and, as the doors of the tomb close, the last remaining player in this tragedy is on his way to death.

Other stories end with the same denouement. Lamachus, the bandit leader, is pushed from a window by an old woman whom he is in the process of robbing, but has time to tell his tale before he expires:

rivos sanguinis vomens imitus, narratisque nobis quae gesta sunt, non diu cruciatus vitam evasit.

Bringing up rivers of blood from deep inside, he told us what had been done and then departed from life after a brief suffering. (4.12)

The wife of a physician who has supplied a poisoner with the means of murder is double-crossed and herself poisoned, but before she dies she recounts the story of the crime:

> iamque ab ipso exordio crudelissimae mulieris cunctis atrocitatibus diligenter expositis, repente mentis nubilo turbine correpta semihiantes adhuc compressit labias et, attritu dentium longo stridore reddito, ante ipsos praesidis pedes exanimis corruit.

> She painstakingly laid out all the atrocities of that most cruel of women right from the beginning, then suddenly, seized by a black dizziness, she closed her lips, half-open until then, gave out a long whistling sound through clenched teeth, and collapsed lifeless before the very feet of the governor. (10.28)

These examples differ, admittedly, from the story of the bailiff in that it is the death of a *narrator* which brings the story to a close. Winkler takes these dying narrators as participants in Apuleius' game with the reader about the narrative's accountability.[28] How, we are prompted to ask, does the narrator know what he or she is telling us? Again and again in the *Golden Ass*, what we had taken to be a third-person narrative is revealed to be a first-person narrative after all, or knowledge that seems to position a narrator as omniscient turns out to be derived from the personal experience of someone who participated in the relevant event. In the final moments of a story Apuleius proves that he has, in fact, not been 'cheating'. This is a brilliant observation. I would only add that Winkler's focus on issues of truth, knowledge, and authority, itself derived from a particular notion of what conversion is about (belief), blinds him to an important connection between narration and death. When read in relation to the story of the bailiff, these endings have more to do with the way narration persecutes and uses up its characters than with the question of who authorizes the narrative.

The story of Charite ends, as we have seen, with one act of suicidal closure followed by another. A more complex example of layered closure is provided by the story of the *paterfamilias* who invites Lucius' current owner, the market-gardener, to dinner (9.33–9). The market-gardener is

---

[28] See J. J. Winkler 1985: 69–76, esp. 71–3.

perhaps the only one of Lucius' masters who does not mistreat him. In fact, he and Lucius share the same food, but such is the gardener's poverty that their fare is worse than the fodder Lucius has grown used to as an ass. They live a shared misery. When a property owner (*paterfamilias*) from the neighbouring district takes shelter with the gardener on a rainy night, he promises grain, olive oil, and wine in return for this hospitality. The gardener sets off on Lucius' back and arrives at the *paterfamilias'* house, where he is welcomed with a sumptuous dinner. But this remission in their sufferings turns to disaster. The laying of an egg, which the host hails as an appetizer for their dinner, turns out to be a starter of a very different stripe. The hen lays not an egg but a fully formed chick. There follows a succession of portents: a fountain of blood gushes from the ground beneath the table, a weasel drags a dead snake from its lair, and a frog leaps from a dog's mouth, whereupon the dog is attacked and bitten to death by a ram. In this sequence, a humdrum event ushers in a succession of monstrosities which spirals out of control. But these portents are only the prelude to the news that will leave the *paterfamilias* childless and cause him to take his own life, for a slave now runs in to tell him that his three sons have all been killed defending the rights of a poor friend against a rich landowner. Once again, the end of a story (the narration of the calamity by the running slave) is marked by death, in this case that of the narratee, not the narrator. However, the story is more open-ended than this synopsis suggests, for the most striking feature of the narrative at this point is the way that one act of violence compounds another as we move between the tales that are nested within each other. The narration draws attention to this compounding, as we can see from the following summary. The final son, having killed the young landowner, kills himself with a sword *still wet with his opponent's blood* (*confestim adhuc inimici sanguine delibuto mucrone gulam sibi prorsus exsecuit*, 9.38); after the slave's narration has ended, the father imitates his son and stabs himself repeatedly with the blade with which he had just been dividing the cheese, thereby *washing away the blood of the portents with a fresh river of gore* (*ipse quoque ad instar infelicissimi sui filii iugulum sibi multis ictibus contrucidat, quoad super mensam cernulus corruens portentuosi cruoris maculas novi sanguinis fluvio proluit*, 9.38). The gardener, having paid with tears for his meal (*depensis*[29] *pro prandio lacrimis*), wrings his empty hands and returns home. But *even he* did not get home safely (*nec innoxius ei saltem regressus evenit*, 9.39), for on his return journey he is assaulted by a soldier. One act of violence compounds

---

[29] Helm 1931, following *F* (on which see above, n. 21), reads *deprensis*.

another, but the sequence is not contained within a single tale, and it bleeds from the story of the landowner and the three brothers into the scene of the *paterfamilias'* dinner and from there into the context of Lucius' adventures. The phrase *nec ... ei saltem* acknowledges the way that misfortune crosses from one level of the story to another, and it turns the spotlight on the narrative itself, as though to reveal its principle. Like *Fortuna*, who always finds something worse to throw at her victim Lucius, the narrator is not going to let us off the hook. We emerge from one tragic story and come up for air into the main narrative only to find ourselves submerged in disaster again. Our breathlessness may be exhilarating or exhausting, but structurally our experience is not unlike that of Lucius himself.

## Avoiding Death

The continuation of violence across levels of the narrative is one way in which the screw of cruelty can be given another turn, even after an individual story has reached its closure with the death of the protagonist. As far as the story of Lucius is concerned, we know that should he die our story will end.[30] So, counterpointing the alignment of narrative satisfaction with the systematic obliteration of the protagonist(s) is the principle that is enunciated several times in connection with *Fortuna*: the victim is preserved from peril only to be handed over to something worse. One strain of the cruel narrative moves towards the closure of death and the other constantly evades it. Apuleius' episodic narrative proceeds according to the principle that the obliteration with which Lucius is constantly threatened must be constantly avoided, only to plunge Lucius into fresh sufferings. The narrative is kept going by the deferral of death together with changes of register that facilitate the introduction of new torments or threats.

One of the cruelties that Lucius must endure is that, like the victims in de Sade, he must listen to his masters discussing his fate.[31] He may be a

---

[30] Is Lucius' story also spoken from the edge of, or beyond, the grave? Does he recover his human form and voice for long enough to tell his story and die? Is he like Socrates in Aristomenes' story (1.5–19), who seems to have evaded the witches' grasp? It's a speculation we might be encouraged to play with along Winklerian lines.

[31] Mention of de Sade raises the possibility that this material could have been treated under the rubric of sadism. Mulvey 1975: 14 (= 2009: 22) remarks: 'Sadism demands a story, depends on making something happen, forcing a change in another person, a battle of will and defeat, all occurring in a linear time with a beginning and an end.' My conception of the relation between narrative and

dumb animal, but he is not deaf. When Lucius is accused by the cruel boy of assaulting a passing girl, one of the rustics suggests that Lucius be slaughtered. But there is more:

> et 'heus tu, puer,' ait 'obtruncato protinus eo intestina quidem canibus nostris iacta, ceteram vero carnem omnem operariorum cenae reserva. nam corium affirmatum cineris inspersu dominis referemus eiusque mortem de lupo facile mentiemur.'

> And he said, 'You, boy, butcher him right away and throw his innards to our dogs, but keep all the rest of the meat for the workers' dinner. For we will stiffen the hide by sprinkling ashes on it and take it back to our masters; and it won't be difficult to concoct a lie about his death at the hands of a wolf.' (7.22)

From the perspective of the rustics, this sharing of the animal may be a means of articulating the hierarchy of the social body, but now we are reading from the perspective of the victim, and the division of Lucius' body amounts to the ultimate denial of individuality. As the sword is being prepared, another rustic speaks up against the plan with what promises to be a humane objection. But his objection (*nefas . . . sic enecare . . .*, 'it is criminal to kill in this way . . .', 7.23) is followed by an even worse suggestion, which has Lucius contemplating suicide: if the ass were to be castrated there would be no more problems from lover-boy, and he would grow fatter and more docile, fit for service. Violent punishment gives way to a cruel instrumentalization, which entails an equally complete alienation of the body, its urges negated so that it can be used more efficiently.

A similar deliverance occurs after Lucius has exposed the orgies of the cinaedic priests of the Dea Syria with his bray. The priests flee the town and, once they have gained enough distance from it, they gird themselves to slaughter Lucius (*accingunt se meo funeri*, 8.30). They strip him of his tackle, tie him to a tree, and whip him nearly to death. Then one of them threatens to hamstring him. But Lucius' life is spared, not out of pity, but in order to carry the statue of the goddess. At the next town the priests are welcomed by one of its grandees into his house, but Lucius immediately runs into mortal danger. A dog makes off from the kitchen with a huge haunch of venison destined for the master's dinner. The cook is so terrified of the consequences that when his master calls for dinner he says farewell to his son and prepares to hang himself. But his wife persuades him that

---

sadism is quite different, as it focuses on the narration as much as on the relation between characters.

providence has put deliverance in their way in the shape of the ass. All he needs to do is to slit the ass's throat, butcher it appropriately, cook it in a powerful sauce and no one will be any the wiser. As the cook prepares his knives, the book ends. These two consecutive episodes present a neat reversal: Lucius first evades death because he is an animal, and the 'revenge' of the priests gives way to considerations of his usefulness as a beast, but in the following episode the fact that Lucius is an (edible) animal has the opposite effect, and he is once again threatened with death. The individual episodes are cruel, but crueller is the arbitrariness with which Lucius is threatened or preserved by virtue of his form.

## The Cruelty of Perspective

The effect on the reader of these discussions of Lucius' fate depends on a conflict of perspectives: the humans who are in a position to dispose of Lucius speak of him as an animal, but Lucius listens as a human, and the reader listens with him. How far does, or should, this awareness of perspective affect our reading of other passages? For instance, when the priests of the Dea Syria punish Lucius they use a whip knotted with sheep's bones. This gratuitous detail seems to be simply an additional cruelty, but it brings about the grotesque situation that one animal, about to be slaughtered, is tormented with another animal's carcass. If we are sympathizing with an ass, then what about the sheep that provided the bones? The whip is not only an instrument but also the residue of another animal's death, which remains resolutely in the background as we attend to the danger threatening Lucius. It is only because the ass is really Lucius that we are attending to the suffering of animals, which usually passes unnoticed, like the 'story' implied by the reference to sheep's bones.

In the kitchen of the rich devotee of the Dea Syria we are plunged into a drama that recalls the story of the bailiff. The cook is so terrified of his master's reaction to his negligence that he is prepared to hang himself (and we remember the punishment meted out to the bailiff). Were this not the story of Lucius we would share the cook's relief at his wife's scheme, but it is, and we fear that we are about to lose our hero. Nevertheless, Lucius' outrage is so phrased that it rebounds on itself, with the result that we wonder where our sympathies should lie: 'that wicked good-for-nothing decided to ensure his safety at the price of my death' (*nequissimo verberoni sua placuit salus de mea morte*, 8.31). Fair enough, surely – the life of an animal for the life of a man. Lucius' *verberoni* ('whipling') draws attention to the fact that the cook is a slave, but, as an ass, he is hardly in a position to pull rank! As throughout this story of metamorphosis, in which what is normally background becomes foreground, Apuleius here draws attention to the way that narrative cruelly prioritizes one perspective at the expense of another.

The episodic nature of the narrative also entails shifts of perspective that relegate foreground to background, making subordinate what had been primary. Take the sudden switch to the perspective of the poor gardener after the suicide of the *paterfamilias*:

> domus fortunam hortulanus ille miseratus, suosque casus graviter ingemescens depensis pro prandio lacrimis, vacuasque manus complaudens saepicule, protinus inscenso me retro quam veneramus viam capessit.
>
> The gardener pitied the family's misfortune and, groaning heavily at his own ill luck, paid with tears for his dinner. Over and over again he wrung his empty hands, then mounted me at once and started back on the road by which we had come. (9.39)

The gardener's chagrin that he must return without the promised olive oil and wine (and possibly dinner) seems callous in the light of the *paterfamilias'* tragedy. The narrative has shifted instantly and ruthlessly back to the main story of Lucius and his master, and with this goes a shift in perspective and priorities. But it is an even-handed narrative, and the gardener too will be abandoned when his time comes. During his return home from the ill-omened dinner he encounters a soldier who tries to requisition the ass. The gardener fights back, overpowers the soldier, pummels him to a pulp, and leaves him for dead. But the soldier is faking, and when he recovers he gathers a search-party to go after the gardener, who has taken shelter with a friend. When the search-party, tipped off by a treacherous neighbour, reaches the house of the gardener's friend, it fails to find the gardener. The posse is on the point of giving up when the curious Lucius peers out of a window and gives the game away. The gardener is dragged away, 'no doubt for execution' (*poenas scilicet capite pensurum*, 9.42), and everybody jokes about Lucius' peeping, including Lucius himself. The book ends: 'And this is how the common proverb about the peeping ass and his shadow came about' (*unde etiam de prospectu et umbra asini natum est frequens proverbium*).

When the narrative abandons the gardener, the event is signposted by the word *scilicet* ('*no doubt* for execution'). Dowden has remarked on the narratological importance of this word for Apuleius' narrative, which takes great pains to explain the authority for what it knows.[32] Again and again,

---

[32] Dowden 1982: 422–5; see also J. J. Winkler 1985: 66–7.

*scilicet* is used to draw attention to the fact that the narrator does not vouch for anything he has not witnessed. In this particular case, though, it has another narratological role to play, which is to mark the fact that our interest in the gardener has come to an end. He disappears into the machinery of authority, and the chapter ends with a joke about Lucius' irresistible curiosity and the origin of a proverb. Apuleius' 'proverb about the peeping ass and his shadow' is actually a conflation of two proverbs ('the peeping of an ass' and 'about the shadow of an ass'), both of which signify a trivial matter.[33] If the facetious *aition* of these proverbs makes a brutal contrast to the extremity of the gardener's fate, the fact that they both signify a trivial matter compounds the brutality of the shift in register. But the accepted *aition* of one of the proverbs, '(an argument) about an ass's shadow', provides a sharp metanarrative commentary on the reader's, and the narrator's, ruthless shift of focus. According to the ancient paroemiographers, the proverb originated with Demosthenes, who noticed once that the jury was not paying attention to his speech. He broke off to tell his inattentive audience a delightful story. A man once rented an ass for a journey from Athens to Megara, and stopped at noon to rest in the shadow of the ass. The ass's owner remonstrated that he had rented out the ass but not its shadow, and after some argument the two parties decided to go to court to settle the matter. At this point Demosthenes stopped. The audience, naturally, clamoured for him to finish the story and to tell them how the argument was resolved. 'So, you want to hear, gentlemen, about an ass's shadow! But when a man is on trial for his life, you can't bear to listen to my voice?'[34] As for us readers of the *Golden Ass*, we go where the narrative leads us, even if this means abandoning our interest in a man who 'no doubt' (*scilicet*) is about to be executed.

   Clearly, the very nature of this story, in which a human becomes an ass and we become very much interested in a fate that would otherwise pass unnoticed, makes the issue of perspective narratologically significant. At the beginning of the work, the as-yet-untransformed Lucius thanks his travelling companion for telling a story that has lightened the toil of the journey, and adds that his horse is grateful too, since he has ridden all the way not on the horse's back but on his own ears (1.20). This *jeu d'esprit* anticipates the unusual perspective that the narrative will come to adopt.

---

[33] See Otto 1890: 41–2 (s.v. *asinus, asellus* 8).

[34] Zenobius 6.28 ὑπὲρ μὲν ὄνου σκιᾶς ἀκούειν, ὦ ἄνδρες, ἐπιθυμεῖτε· ἀνθρώπου δὲ κινδυνεύοντος ὑπὲρ ψυχῆς οὐδὲ τῆς φωνῆς ἀνέχεσθε; (translation from J. J. Winkler 1985: 121, where Zenobius' account is given in full).

But such a moment of extended sympathy makes us sensitive to its opposite, of which a good example is the passage in Book 7 where Lucius discovers that he has been blamed for the assault on his host Milo's house perpetrated by the bandits who abducted him. One of the bandits recounts the story to his companions in Lucius' hearing, including the detail that, once suspicion had fallen on Lucius (who had, after all, disappeared immediately after the assault), his slave was tortured almost to death, though he admitted nothing (*tormentis vexatum pluribus ac paene ad ultimam mortem excarnificatum*, 7.2). Lucius bewails his own fate and expatiates on the blindness of Fortune, sublimely indifferent to the fate of his slave. If we respond to the irony that the bandit's interest in the news he relates is quite different from that of the listening ass, who has taken the blame for the crimes of the bandits, then we should be struck by the way that the sufferings of Lucius' slave are relegated to the background of his own concern with reputation.

## The Body of the Ass

As I have argued, Lucius' transformation has a complicating effect on narrative perspective, and this begins with Lucius' own attitude to his body. Lucius cannot quite identify himself with his asinine body, though it is the locus of his suffering and the means by which the world gets at him. At one point, considering the advantages that his form has bestowed on him, he refers to his body as 'my ass' (*asino meo*, 9.13), as though it were as separate from him as the horse he refers to in the opening book (*illum vectorem meum*, 1.20). This attitude characterizes those occasions where Lucius jokes about the beatings he endures as an ass, of which this is a good example:

> ceterum plagis non magnopere commovebar, quippe consuetus ex forma concidi fustibus.

> Besides, I was not greatly affected by the blows, since I was accustomed to being beaten with clubs in due form. (7.25)

The phrase *ex forma* means 'in due form of law'.[35] But Lucius is punning on *forma*, and if we take *ex forma* with *consuetus*, instead of with *concidi*, we can translate 'habituated because of my form', a cruelly ironic wordplay directed against 'his' ass on Lucius' part, since it is precisely his form that excludes him from the procedures and rules that govern human society.

---

[35] See *OLD* s.v. *forma*, sect. 12a.

His beatings are violent and cruel, in fact anything but *ex forma*. The pun conveys the callous detachment of one species from the other it exploits ('*they* don't feel it like us, they're used to it'), intensified here by the simultaneous reference to the procedures that protect members of the human race. But this detachment of Lucius from his own body is by no means consistent, and Lucius' descriptions of his sufferings are often horrifyingly detailed and elaborate, calling forth some of Apuleius' most artful prose. Sometimes these descriptions imitate on a smaller scale the broader rhythms of the narrative. Take this description of a beating delivered by the cruel boy:

> coxaeque dexterae semper ictus incutiens et unum feriendo locum dissipato corio et ulceris latissimi facto foramine, immo fovea vel etiam fenestra, nullus tamen desinebat identidem vulnus sanguine delibutum obtundere.
>
> By always striking the blows on the right hip and hitting the same spot he made the hide split and produced a broad hole of a wound, indeed a pit or even a window, but he did not cease at all from his repeated thumping of the wound drenched in blood. (7.17)

In this carefully constructed sentence the syntax opens up like the wound itself. We begin with a dicolon of present participle and gerund (*ictus incutiens* [notice *ic-, inc-*] *et unum feriendo locum*), and this is subordinated not to a main verb but to another dicolon, of ablative absolutes (*dissipato corio et . . . facto foramine*), which is then expanded in a (possibly facetious) parenthesis (*immo . . .*), alliterating with *foramine* (*fovea, fenestra*), and itself taking the form of a dicolon (*vel etiam*). With *nullus . . . desinebat* we finally reach the subject and main verb, and the word *nullus*, semantically if not grammatically, seems to suggest that we have reached an end: eventually suffering comes to a close, when there is nothing left of the sufferer. But *nullus* (here 'not at all') refers to the boy, not to Lucius or his body, and it does not bring the sentence and the torture to a rest, but rather imparts new energy to them (*nullus tamen desinebat identidem . . .*). The word *nullus* engineers an effect that is repeated again and again in the broader narrative, as Fortune proves herself unsatisfied with what she has already inflicted (*insatiabilis*, 7.17). Apuleius brings the sentence to an end with an image that is painful to visualize, though it demands visualization. With the earlier phrase *fovea vel etiam fenestra* we have been given a powerful prompt to look deeply into Lucius' wound. Can we resist it? Apuleius' exquisitely controlled prose is often lavished on scenes of violence and torture (as, for instance, in the punishment of the bailiff), and the carefulness of these descriptions conspires with the cruelty that is being described, to persecute both protagonist and reader.

Lucius' body is not only an object of fluctuating identification but also an important source of narrative tension. The very existence of Lucius as Lucius depends on the survival of 'his' ass. But how much cruelty can the body of an ass endure? Is there a limit to its cartoonish elasticity? In fact, not all of Apuleius' little narratives of torture are unresolved crescendos of cruelty, for the body *in extremis* proves to have its own resources. The 'punishment' of Lucius by the mother of the cruel boy, with which Book 7 comes to a close, is a good example. When the cruel boy is finally destroyed by a bear, his mother blames Lucius for not coming to the aid of his 'fellow-slave and master' (*conservo magistro*, 7.27). She ties his legs together with her bra, takes the bar used to bolt the doors of the stable, and beats him, 'not ceasing to bludgeon me until her strength was overcome by weariness and the club dropped from her hand under its own weight' (*non prius me desiit obtundere quam victis fessisque viribus suopte pondere degravatus manibus eius fustis esset elapsus*, 7.28). Then she picks up a firebrand and shoves it between Lucius' 'loins' (*inguinibus*) until Lucius, responding with the only defence he has left, 'poured out a stream of liquid dung and covered her face and eyes with filth' (*liquida fimo strictim egesta faciem atque oculos eius confoedassem*). The book ends with a joke about Meleager, Althaea, and the firebrand. Just as Lucius' body, driven to its limit, finds release in its ejaculation, so the reader, driven to the limits of sympathetic suffering by this narrative of pain, finds release in laughter. This little episode of cruel revenge concludes not with the death of the victim (as will the tragic version of this scene at 10.24) but with a sudden change of register, from tragedy to comedy.[36]

Let me suggest that the final book of the *Golden Ass*, with its sudden change of register and style, works rather like the end of Book 7, where the tormented body of Lucius responds with the only resource it has, and the narrative, which has reached the limits of cruelty, must turn to something completely different. The suddenness of Lucius' conversion (or, rather, confession of the goddess' power) is both as shocking and as natural a reflex as his evacuation: 'waking in sudden fear' (*experrectus pavore subito*, 11.1) to the sight of the full moon rising from the sea, he pours out a stream of eloquent prayer to the 'queen of heaven' (*regina caeli*, 11.2). The connection I have just made between Lucius' conversion and the violent episode of the mother's revenge can supplement the connection I made at the beginning of this chapter between Lucius' conversion to Isis and the violent 'conversion' of Lucius at the mill. Laughter ensues on the violence

---

[36] Cf. 4.3, where a similarly desperate situation is saved by the same action.

inflicted on Lucius both by the cruel boy's mother and by the mill-hands, but the difference is that in one case he escapes from his fate while in the other he acknowledges it. The conversion to Isis, described by her priest as a form of voluntary slavery (11.15), manages to conflate the two.

Isis, as others have pointed out, is a kind of anti-Fortune, seeing where Fortune was blind, and merciful where she was cruel.[37] But the relation between Fortune and her various human equivalents on the one hand and Isis on the other is not exclusively one of opposition. In some cases, cruelty is a perverse form of caring. Take the baker's wife, who persecutes Lucius with an extraordinary hatred (*miro* . . . *odio*) which gives shape to her (and his) day:

> talis illa mulier miro me persequebatur odio. nam et antelucio, recubans adhuc, subiungi machinae novicium clamabat asinum, et statim ut cubiculo primum processerat insistens iubebat incoram sui plagas mihi quam plur-imas irrogari, et cum tempestivo prandio laxarentur iumenta cetera, longe tardius applicari praesepio iubebat.

> Being the kind of woman she was, she hounded me with extraordinary hatred. For before dawn, while she was still lying in bed, she shouted for the new ass to be hitched to the mill-wheel, and as soon as she had left her bedroom she demanded insistently that as many blows as possible be inflicted on me while she watched. And although the other beasts were relieved in good time for dinner, she ordered me to be returned to the manger much later. (9.15)

Her first thought in the day is for Lucius, whom she wants to see (whipped) the moment she rises. Perhaps she is breaking in the new recruit, softening him up so that he will be a docile worker. But, if so, 'while she watched' (*incoram sui*) is an unnecessary detail. For some unexplained and inexplicable reason, she has taken an interest in Lucius.

Cruelty in the *Golden Ass* is for the most part gratuitous and unmotivated, and it serves by inversion to characterize the similarly unmotivated provi-dence of Isis.[38] Why Lucius? It is a question one might as easily ask of Isis as of the baker's wife, for divine pity, like human cruelty, is gratuitous.[39] As for narration, Apuleius' *Golden Ass* seems to suggest that to tell a story is to pick on someone.

---

[37] See, e.g., Schlam 1992: 64–6.
[38] The gratuitousness of Isis' favour is emphasized by the misinterpretation of the faithful (*felix Hercules et ter beatus, qui vitae scilicet praecedentis innocentia fideque meruerit tam praeclarum de caelo patrocinium*, 'happy, by Hercules, and thrice blessed, he whose uprightness and good faith in his life until now has merited such a splendid inheritance from heaven', 11.16).
[39] On divine pity, see Konstan 2001: 116–22.

# CHAPTER II

# Violence and the Christian Heroine
## Two Narratives of Desire

### J. H. D. Scourfield*

## I

From the beginning, institutionalized violence was a central theme in the stories which the early Christians told about themselves. The infant Jesus escapes the child-massacre ordered by King Herod through the intervention of an angel;[1] the grown man is crucified under a Roman provincial prefect. The Acts of the Apostles records the trial before the Sanhedrin and stoning of Stephen in Jerusalem in the first years after Jesus' death.[2] In the early fourth century, soon after (or shortly before)[3] the official legitimization of Christianity by imperial edicts,[4] Eusebius of Caesarea's pioneering *Ecclesiastical History* placed great emphasis on the persecution of the Church through the ages and the sufferings of Christians martyred for their beliefs, while his contemporary Lactantius turned the tables on its enemies by recounting the divinely achieved, inglorious, and grisly ends of persecuting emperors in *On the Deaths of the Persecutors*.[5] Suffering, and triumph over it, formed a crucial and ineradicable element of Christian self-identity.[6]

Notable for its groundbreaking documentary approach to historical writing, the *Ecclesiastical History* incorporates a number of pre-existing,

---

* I should like to thank Barbara Gold and Carole Newlands for their valuable comments on an earlier version of this chapter; John Curran, for assistance on specific historical points; audiences in Charlottesville, Glasgow, London, Los Angeles, Maynooth, and particularly Swansea and Warwick, where the essential argument was first aired; and Monica Gale, for numerous helpful discussions. Translations of Greek and Latin passages are my own throughout.

[1] Matt. 2: 13–18.    [2] Acts 6: 8–8: 2.

[3] The dating of Eusebius' *Ecclesiastical History* is complicated and disputed; for a summary of the issues see Louth 2004: 271–3.

[4] I use this term as a convenient shorthand, notwithstanding the agitated strictures of Barnes 2010: 98 against the use of the term 'Edict of Milan'; the associated question of the legitimization of Christianity by Gallienus half a century earlier (cf. Barnes 2010: 97) is of no consequence here.

[5] See esp. the account of the death of Galerius (*De mort. pers.* 33, 35.3).

[6] On this theme see esp. Perkins 1995.

essentially contemporary, accounts of Christian martyrdom, such as those of Polycarp, bishop of Smyrna, in the 150s, and the 'Gallic martyrs' of Lyons and Vienne in 177.[7] Such texts represent a significant strand in early Christian literature, though one of a highly heterogeneous character. Court-style records, eyewitness accounts, first-person reports by the martyrs themselves all feature in the mix, and in terms of truth-content the extant material ranges from the strongly authentic (though always editorialized) to the entirely fabricated.[8] At the same time, a common purpose is easily discerned: as their name implies, martyrs gave witness to their faith, and their commitment to God and exceptional courage in the face of death and under torture that was often severe made them exemplary figures within the Christian community.

Persecuting authorities were no respecters of gender,[9] and male and female martyrs alike find their place in the literary record.[10] Of texts describing female martyrdom the best known is the *Passio Perpetuae et Felicitatis*, which deals with an episode of persecution at Carthage in the early third century, focusing on the experiences in prison and deaths in the arena of a young married woman of some rank and education, Vibia Perpetua, and her companion Felicitas.[11] Condemned to die following their refusal to make the required sacrifice, they are brought into the arena naked, only to be recalled and lightly clothed when the crowd reacts negatively to the sight of a 'delicate girl' (*puella delicata*, 20.2)[12] and another with milk dripping from her breasts – Felicitas had given birth to a child only two days previously – in this condition. On being sent back into the arena, they face the assaults of a wild cow; tossed by the animal and her tunic ripped, Perpetua pulls the garment down as best she can to

---

[7] Euseb. *Hist. eccl.* 4.15, 5.1–2. For the full text of the *Martyrdom of Polycarp*, which has been transmitted independently (Eusebius' version is somewhat abbreviated), see conveniently Musurillo 1972: 2–21 (with the Eusebian account of the Gallic martyrs at 62–85). Most of the prose martyr-texts cited in this chapter are most easily accessible in this collection, whatever its shortcomings (on which see, e.g., Barnes 2010: 352–3).

[8] For a helpful summary of the position see Musurillo 1972: l–lv.

[9] Cf. Jones 1993. Women could not, however, legally be executed while pregnant: see *Dig.* 48.19.3 (Ulpian), *Passio Perpetuae et Felicitatis* 15.2, with Jones 1993: 26, Salisbury 1997: 115–16, Heffernan 2012: 306–7.

[10] Male martyrdoms, however, are much more frequently so memorialized – though this of course need not imply that there were more male martyrs: see Shaw 1993: 13 (= 2004: 294).

[11] Latin text, with very full apparatus, in Heffernan 2012: 104–24 (who also prints the Greek version, generally considered to be later, at 445–55). The discussion by Shaw 1993 is outstanding.

[12] The connotations of *delicata* here are hard to pinpoint: physical fragility and social refinement may both be implied. I am less inclined than Sigismund-Nielsen 2012: 114–15 to detect the presence of a strong erotic connotation.

cover her thighs, 'mindful more of her modesty than her pain'.[13] Finally, delivered to an inexperienced gladiator for execution, she assists him by guiding his trembling right hand to her throat; the precise fate of Felicitas is not described.

Against this general background I want in this chapter to discuss two later Latin texts, one prose, one verse, which depict scenes of torture and execution involving Christian women. An important theme in both these texts is chastity, and this theme is brought into close relation with the acts of violence which the texts describe by the use of metaphorical language through which, in different ways, the violence is sexualized. My main interest here lies in how in both cases this use of metaphor, together with other aspects of the narration, in particular the use of the inscribed gaze, cracks open the closed body of a strongly ideological, in essence univocal, text, which then bleeds outside its prescribed channels and beyond the boundaries of its creator's control. As I shall seek to make clear later, struggles for power inside the text thus find reflections outside the text, in ways which evoke questions of personal, social, and cultural responsibility, and which force us even to examine the very practice of criticism.[14]

## II

Around the year 375 Jerome, the future biblical scholar and controversial-ist, wrote a letter (*Letter* 1) to an old friend, Innocentius, recounting an event that had taken place at Vercellae in the north Italian province of Aemilia-Liguria at some unspecified but relatively recent date.[15] A man had accused his wife of adultery, and laid charges against her and her alleged lover with the provincial governor. Torture was applied. The lover, his body lacerated and bloody, confessed. But the woman, unmoved by rack, fire, and blade, steadfastly denied the charge. The governor,

---

[13] *Passio Perpetuae et Felicitatis* 20.4 *pudoris potius memor quam doloris.* As others have observed, the gesture evokes the Polyxena of Euripides and Ovid (Eur. *Hec.* 568–70, Ov. *Met.* 13.479–80), traces of whom can also be seen in Prudentius' Agnes, discussed below: on this see esp. Burrus 1995: 39–42.

[14] Particularly relevant to this chapter's concerns with martyrological violence, eroticism, and the gaze is Frankfurter 2009, whose aims and argument, however, are very different.

[15] A translation and helpful notes may be found in Rebenich 2002: 63–9, 176–80. For a composition date of 375 see Scourfield 1986; others interpret the evidence differently and incline to place the letter in the early 370s (so Rebenich 1992: 70–1 with n. 310, Müller 1998, arguing against Schwind 1997, who makes an unconvincing attempt at a radical redating to *c.* 386). The incident at Vercellae, if historical, is most naturally located in the period when Evagrius of Antioch was in the West, i.e. between 364/5 and 373/4 (for these dates see Rebenich 1992: 71); see further below, with nn. 18–19, 21–2.

considering it 'more plausible that a guilty woman should deny a crime
than an innocent young man confess it',[16] had both parties taken off to
execution. At the first blow of the sword the man's head was lopped off.
But when the woman knelt to face her death, a remarkable thing
happened. Three times the sword, wielded with all the executioner's
might, failed to do more than scratch her neck. Terrified and desperate,
the executioner put the point of the blade to her throat – only to find the
blade bending back to the hilt. Taking his place, a new headsman, with a
new sword, delivered a further three blows; and wounded, finally, by the
third of these – the seventh in all[17] – the woman appeared to die. The
story, however, does not end there. Under cover of darkness, the corpse,
taken off by clerics to burial, suddenly heaved back to life. To keep this
from the authorities, the body of an elderly female, who had died naturally
of old age, was buried in the woman's place, while she herself was cared for
in secret, disguised as a man; and finally the intervention of a notable priest
with the emperor secured her freedom.

For all its miraculous aspects, this story, the veracity of which Jerome
seems to be at pains to emphasize,[18] has commonly been regarded as having
a historical core, though a healthy degree of scepticism has recently begun to
emerge.[19] But the question of the historicity or fictionality of the story is of
little relevance to its main purposes. Though cast in epistolary form, and
purporting to have been written at Innocentius' request (ch. 1), this text is
evidently not intended for its addressee's eyes alone. From one point of
view, it may be regarded as a 'graceful compliment'[20] to another friend,
Evagrius of Antioch, with whom, at the time of writing, Jerome had been
staying, prior to his withdrawal into the 'desert of Chalcis', for a year or
more:[21] he is the priest whose approach to the emperor won the freedom of

---

[16] Jer. *Ep.* 1.6.2 *credibilius reor noxiam ream negare de scelere, quam innocentem iuvenem confiteri.*
Except where indicated, the text is cited according to Hilberg 1996.
[17] Hence the title of the letter given by the manuscripts, 'De septies percussa' ('On the woman struck
seven times') (see Hilberg 1996: 1), derived from the phrase *septies percussa* at 13.2.
[18] See ch. 1, where (in the first sentence of the letter) the events are said to have occurred 'in our time'
(*in nostram aetatem*); ch. 15, where Jerome attributes the eventual happy outcome to Evagrius of
Antioch, linking it to Evagrius' known recent historical activity (see below).
[19] A historical core is assumed by, e.g., Matthews 1975: 63; McLynn 1994: 5–6; Sivan 1998; Harries
1999: 228. For the sceptical position, see, e.g., Arjava 1996: 197 n. 15; Rebenich 2002: 63
('Obviously, it is not Jerome's intention to give a report of a true incident'), marking a shift from
his earlier stance (Rebenich 1992: 63).
[20] J. N. D. Kelly 1975: 39.
[21] See Scourfield 1986, with n. 15 above. Innocentius too was with them; Jerome reports his death at
*Ep.* 3.3.1, while he was still in Antioch. A different view is presented by Rebenich 1992: 71, who
argues that the letter was written before Jerome's departure from Italy for the East and Evagrius'
roughly contemporary return to his home city.

the alleged adulteress of Vercellae. In the final chapter of the letter (15) Jerome not only reports this successful intervention but praises Evagrius for his services to orthodox Christianity in the troubled (and often violent) environment of late-Antique ecclesiastical politics.[22] The letter thus has an encomiastic aim, and at the same time, at an early stage in Jerome's career,[23] both establishes his credentials as a Nicene Christian and provides a platform for the display of his considerable literary talents.[24]

More obvious are the letter's edificatory and exemplary functions. Jerome's account of the events at Vercellae illustrates God's power and his support of those who put their trust in him – it is divine intervention which spares the woman from pain and saves her from death, and which even causes her, helpfully, to seem to die[25] – and simultaneously affords, in the depiction of the woman, an example of how a Christian should behave in the most demanding and physically testing circumstances.[26] It is telling that in certain manuscripts the letter is associated by position with nine of the ten letters of Jerome commonly regarded as consolatory, almost all of which can be seen to have not just (or even mainly) a consolatory purpose but an exemplary one, in some cases even made explicit.[27] In this regard, as in others, the letter strongly echoes martyr-literature.[28] The *mise en scène* of course differs from that of the martyr-accounts in one important respect, namely, that the martyrs face torture and death because they will not

---

[22] Jerome gives few details, but 15.2 clearly refers to involvement on Evagrius' part in (a) the efforts made by prominent orthodox Christians over many years to remove from the see of Milan its Arian bishop Auxentius, (b) the long power-struggle between Damasus and Ursinus that followed their rival consecrations as bishop of Rome in 366 (Evagrius supporting the former). See further Rebenich 1992: 62–6.

[23] It is generally accepted to be the earliest of Jerome's extant works. [24] Cf. Rebenich 2002: 64.

[25] See esp. 5.1, 8.2 (reading *iam igitur et tertium ictum sacramentum frustraverat trinitatis* ('Now the sacred Trinity had made vain the third blow, too'), with Scourfield 1987: 489), ch. 11.

[26] The notion of Grützmacher 1901–8: I.145, that the story symbolizes the conflict between Christianity and the temporal power of the Roman Empire, seems to me rather to miss the point – though of course competing discourses are certainly evident.

[27] So esp. *Ep.* 127.1.1; cf. also *Ep.* 23.2.2, 108.15.4. Burrus 2004: 56–7 interestingly connects *Letter* 1 to *Letter* 108 in particular by placing them within the frame of a developing Jeromian female hagiography. *Letter* 1, together with *Letter* 24 (also explicitly exemplary), is embedded among the consolatory letters (which appear in the order 60, 118, 39, 108, 75, 77, 23, [24, 1,] 127, 66) in at least the following manuscripts: Paris, Bibliothèque Nationale, Lat. 1869 (ninth century); Vatican City, Vat. lat. 355 + 356 (ninth-to-tenth century); London, British Museum, Harley 3044 (twelfth century): see Lambert 1969–72: IA.242, 293, 200 respectively; cf. also Schwind 1997: 175 n. 12, who draws attention to the fact that all the letters in the sequence from 77 to 66 concern exemplary females.

[28] Cf. Müller 1998: 208–9. Coppieters *et al.* 2014 view the letter as, in part, 'subtle propaganda for asceticism by use of martyrological themes' (390; cf. 408); but, whatever the cultural-historical links between Christian martyrdom and the ascetic movement, it is hard to discern here anything so purposive.

renounce their faith, as required by the secular authorities to do, while the woman of Vercellae, though her faith and courage are no less, is (half a century after the end of the age of persecution and martyrdom) tried on a charge which has nothing to do with her religion. But the trial setting, the account of the tortures, and various other features of the narrative are powerfully redolent of the textualized world of the martyrs. The tired torturer (*lassus tortor*) of 6.2, for example, exhausted by the woman's endurance, has his counterparts in the *Martyrs of Lyons and Vienne*, who (1.18) torture the slave-girl Blandina all day long, in shifts, until they are worn out and have to admit defeat. Jerome's governor, a *iudex crudelis* ('cruel judge', 5.2), *ira excitus* ('roused by anger', 6.2), similarly resembles the governor in this martyr-narrative, who treats the Christians with ὠμότης, 'savagery' (1.9), is subject to outbursts of rage (ὀργή) (1.17, 1.50), and is associated with the devil (1.27), a detail transferred in Jerome's letter to the second executioner (13.1).[29] Again, the miraculous occurrence at the scene of execution finds an analogue in the *Martyrdom of Polycarp*, where the bishop of Smyrna, sentenced to be burnt alive, is untouched by the flames[30] – an event reminiscent of the story of Shadrach, Meshach, and Abednego in Daniel 3, which Jerome specifically adduces in *Letter* 1 (9.1) as a parallel to the situation of his heroine, the biblical context further assimilating the letter to martyr-literature.[31] Later martyrology provides more precise parallels; the martyrs Pantaleon and Thyrsus survive the blows of a sword because, in the case of the former, the weapon turns soft, like wax, while, in the case of the latter, it shatters like glass.[32]

At its more fantastical end, martyr-literature approaches in certain regards the kind of romantic hagiography represented by texts such as the *Acts of Paul and Thecla*.[33] In this second-century Christian fiction, the eponymous heroine, sentenced (like Polycarp) to be burned alive on the pyre, escapes, Croesus-like, through a divinely sent rainstorm; later, thrown to the beasts in the arena, she is saved by a friendly lioness and a series of further miracles.[34] In both these episodes she is depicted as naked,

---

[29] For further discussion of the representation of the governor in *Letter* 1, see pp. 319–22, 323–4 below; and on the stereotype of the 'persecuting judge', Harries 1999: 225–31.

[30] *Martyrdom of Polycarp* 15.2.

[31] The young men are condemned to the fiery furnace because they will not worship Nebuchadnezzar's golden image. Cf. also *Martyrdom of Montanus and Lucius* 3.4, Prudent. *Perist.* 6.109–11, for the story cited in similar (though less miraculous) contexts.

[32] See Delehaye 1921: 294.

[33] Greek text in Lipsius 1891; an English translation may be found in Schneemelcher 1991–2: II.239–46.

[34] *Acts of Paul and Thecla* 21–2, 33–5.

and in other ways too the story carries an erotic element seemingly at variance with a central 'message' of the text, which is renunciation, especially renunciation of sex.[35] Thecla's attraction to Paul's preaching on purity and virginity, which causes her to abandon her forthcoming marriage, is presented in terms of love and desire;[36] when she visits him in prison, she kisses his chains and (after his removal) rolls about on the spot where he had been sitting;[37] later, she has to beat off an attempted sexual assault by another man who falls in love with her at first sight.[38] Evident in all this are the traces of the tradition of the Greek ideal novel or romance, a genre intensely concerned with heterosexual love and the chastity (especially threats to the chastity) of the central female character (whose *telos* of course is not renunciation but legitimate marriage). The relevance of Greek romance to martyr-literature and early Christian hagiography more generally has indeed been well illustrated in recent scholarship,[39] and in this complex of texts we can identify key elements of the matrix which generated Jerome's *Letter* 1. To foreground for a moment the relationship of the letter with the Greek novel, the trial setting, the *Scheintod* motif, and the topos of male disguise are all easily paralleled,[40] while the torture-scene finds strong resonances in a passage in Achilles Tatius' *Leucippe and Clitophon* where the heroine, Leucippe, faces a similar prospect:[41] the texts closely resemble each other both in language and in the attitude of the victim, and in each case adultery forms part of the broader picture.[42]

---

[35] The *Acts of Paul and Thecla* thus presents a similar internal contradiction to the texts with which I am mainly concerned in this chapter. The recent studies of Andújar 2012 and Eyl 2012 are too ready to set aside the erotic content and dismiss this tension.

[36] See esp. chs. 8–10, where, along with the behavioural indications of Thecla's love-stricken condition, she is said to be 'overcome by a new desire and a terrible passion' (κρατεῖται ἐπιθυμίᾳ καινῇ καὶ πάθει δεινῷ), made captive (ἑάλωται) by Paul's words (9).

[37] *Acts of Paul and Thecla* 18, 20; at 19 she is found in the prison 'as it were bound with him in affection' (τρόπον τινὰ συνδεδεμένην τῇ στοργῇ).

[38] *Acts of Paul and Thecla* 26.

[39] See, e.g., Cooper 1996, esp. 45–67; Huber-Rebenich 1999 (who also (198–201) rightly associates Jerome's *Letter* 1 with his three hagiographic *Vitae*); Chew 2003a, 2003b (with emphasis on violence).

[40] For the trial setting see, e.g., Chariton, *Chaereas and Callirhoe* 1.5–6, 5.4–8; Longus, *Daphnis and Chloe* 2.14–17; Achilles Tatius, *Leucippe and Clitophon* 7.7–12, 8.8–11; Heliodorus, *Aethiopica* 8.9; for the *Scheintod* motif, Chariton 1.5.1 (Callirhoe appears to be dead), 1.8.1 (revives); Xenophon of Ephesus, *Ephesiaca* 3.6–8; Ach. Tat. 3.15–22; for male disguise, Xen. Eph. 5.1.7 (where the context is again escape from an undesirable situation).

[41] Ach. Tat. 6.21–2.

[42] Compare, for example, Jer. *Ep.* 1.6.1 *caede, ure, lacera* ('beat me, burn me, rip me apart') with Ach. Tat. 6.22.4 λάμβανε κατ' ἐμοῦ τὰς μάστιγας, τὸν τροχόν, τὸ πῦρ, τὸν σίδηρον ('take up the whips against me, the wheel, the fire, the sword'); *Ep.* 1.3.4 *praesto iugulum, micantem intrepida excipio mucronem, innocentiam tantum mecum feram* ('I offer my throat, I receive the gleaming blade without fear, as long as I take my innocence with me') with Ach. Tat. 6.22.4 ἓν ὅπλον ἔχω τὴν

But what I especially want to stress is the essential erotic character of the
ideal-novel genre, which, given the evident degree of connection between
the genre and *Letter* 1 in other respects, suggests a partial explanation for
the sexualization of Jerome's narrative which will be the focus of my
discussion: it is as if the novel tradition could provide Jerome with material
only in agglutinated form. In this way the gap between ideology and
narrative which I will argue the text discloses may be seen as the consequence of the tenacious grip exerted by classical literary traditions even on
a strident Christian dogmatist.

It is an immediately arresting feature of *Letter* 1 that the young man against
whom the adultery charge has been laid quickly gives way under torture,
while his female counterpart never yields. Jerome underlines this difference
early in the account first by describing the woman, stretched by the rack
(*eculeus*), as *sexu fortior suo*, 'stronger than her sex' (3.3), and then, in the next
chapter (4), by drawing a contrast between the 'weaker sex' (*sexus infirmior*)
and the 'male strength' (*robur virile*) which had capitulated to the tortures.
The woman's heroic endurance indeed renders her superior not just to her
supposed lover but to a whole series of male figures whom in different ways
she can be said to overcome: her husband, whose unsubstantiated charge
against her is shown by events to be false; two executioners, the first of whom
is driven off by the crowd after four failed attempts with the sword, while the
second has to deliver three blows to bring about a death that, as it turns out,
is only apparent; and the governor of the province, the embodiment of the
strength of the Roman state, who orders the tortures and execution.

These hints of female empowerment are realized in a remarkable way in
the passage where the woman first faces execution, immediately after the
death of the 'lover':

> postquam vero ad feminam ventum est et flexis in terram poplitibus super
> trementem cervicem micans elevatus est gladius et exercitatam carnifex
> dexteram totis viribus concitavit, ad primum corporis tactum stetit mucro
> letalis et leviter perstringens cutem rasurae modicae sanguinem aspersit.

ἐλευθερίαν, ἣ μήτε πληγαῖς κατακόπτεται μήτε σιδήρῳ κατατέμνεται μήτε πυρὶ κατακαίεται. οὐκ
ἀφήσω ποτὲ ταύτην ἐγώ ('my sole weapon is my freedom, which cannot be cut to pieces by the
lash, nor butchered by steel, nor burned up by fire. This I will never yield up'). The texts are
associated also by Shaw 1996: 269–74, who elsewhere (Shaw 1993: 9 = 2004: 291) notes the
relevance of the Achilles Tatius passage to texts depicting female martyrs; so too Cooper 1996: 30;
Chew 2003a: 205–6 and 2003b: 138; Morales 2004: 203–6. The torture-language also finds close
parallels in declamation, another formative influence on *Letter* 1 (adultery is another common
declamatory theme); cf., e.g., Sen. *Controv.* 2.5.6, 10.5.10 (quoted by Henderson, Chapter 6,
pp. 192–3, 208 above; the whole chapter is generally relevant), [Quint.] *Decl. mai.* 7.12.

inbellem manum percussor expavit et victam dexteram gladio marcescente miratus in secundos impetus torquet. languidus rursum in feminam mucro delabitur et, quasi ferrum ream timeret adtingere, circa cervicem torpet innoxium.

Then it was the woman's turn. As she knelt on the ground, the gleaming sword was raised above her trembling neck, and the executioner brought down his practised right arm with all his strength; but on touching her body the deadly blade stopped still, and lightly grazing the skin drew a few drops of blood from a little scratch. The striker gasped in fear at his powerless hand, and, astonished at his arm's failure as the sword turned limp, whirled it for a second blow. Again the blade flopped upon the woman, and as if the steel were afraid to touch the accused, lay feebly about her unharmed neck. (Jer. *Ep.* 1.7.2–3)

The language used here invests this scene with a layer of meaning which, I will argue, gathers force in association with other passages in the text.[43] It is well known that, in Latin, weapons provide a whole class of sexual metaphors; and the terms found in this passage for 'sword' – *gladius, mucro* – can be used to denote the penis.[44] In this case the executioner's *gladius* (and we might well think in this context of the renowned sexual appeal of gladiators[45]) is raised – *elevatus est* – over the woman's trembling *cervix*, 'neck', but also cervix, in a gynaecological sense.[46] The blow that follows fails to deliver more than a scratch, and the sword is described as turning limp (*gladio marcescente*); the second stroke, similarly, falls *languidus*, 'floppily', and the weapon *torpet*, lies sluggishly, feebly, on her neck.[47] The executioner is, in effect, rendered impotent, an idea underlined in the following chapter:

iam speculator exterritus et non credens ferro mucronem aptabat in iugulum, ut, qui secare non poterat, saltim premente manu corpori conderetur: – o omnibus inaudita res saeculis! – ad capulum gladius reflectitur et velut dominum suum victus aspiciens confessus est se ferire non posse.

Now the soldier, terrified and not trusting the sword, put the point of the blade to her throat, so that the weapon which could not cut might at least be plunged into her body under the force of his hand. Happening unheard of

---

[43] The sexual connotations in the letter are noted and elaborated also by Shaw 1996: 272–4, 304–5, and Burrus 2004: 54–6, in both cases in the context of a quite different kind of discussion and argument from my own.

[44] See in general Adams 1982: 19–21, citing (for *gladius*) Petron. *Sat.* 9.5, (in clear connotation) Plaut. *Cas.* 909; (for *mucro*) Auson. *Cent. nupt.* 121.

[45] Cf. Introduction, p. 12 with n. 45.   [46] So at Celsus, *Med.* 4.1.12.

[47] Both *languidus* and *torpere* occur with explicitly sexual meaning in Ovid's poem on the theme of impotence, *Amores* 3.7: see vv. 3, 66 (*languidus*; cf. *languere* at 27), 35 (*torpere*). Cf. also Adams 1982: 46. In the context, sexual overtones can also be heard in *impetus*; cf. Hor. *Sat.* 1.2.117, with Adams 1982: 159.

throughout all ages! The sword bent back to the hilt, and, as it were looking at its master in its defeat, admitted that it could not strike. (*Ep.* 1.8.2)

Instead of attempting to decapitate his victim, the executioner here seeks to plunge the blade into her body, only to find the blade bending back to face him: the woman is impenetrable.

I shall return to this eroticized scene of violence later, but first I want to make some observations about the presentation of torture and execution in this narrative more generally. Any reader is likely to be struck by the vividness of the descriptions, and the emphasis placed on the physicality of what the victims, especially the woman,[48] experience. With God's help, she is able to transcend the tortures: as the torturer burns and pierces her, she 'remains unmoved, and with her spirit freed from the pain her body feels and her conscience clear, she forbids the torments to rage around her'.[49] And yet it is precisely her body on which the text concentrates. Immediately prior to the passage just cited we read:

crines ligantur ad stipitem et toto corpore ad eculeum fortius alligato vicinus pedibus ignis adponitur, utrumque latus carnifex fodit nec papillis dantur induciae.

Her hair is tied to the stake, and with her whole body bound more tightly to the rack, fire is applied to her feet; the executioner stabs her on both sides, and not even her breasts are spared. (*Ep.* 1.5.1)

Specifically mentioned here are the woman's sides, breasts, feet, and hair, along with her body as a whole. The word *corpus* itself is in fact used in relation to her no fewer than eight times in a text that runs to no more than eight pages in both Hilberg's edition and the Loeb,[50] and in the course of the narrative this body is dismembered into numerous parts – the assault is directed at her hands (*manus*, 3.3), hair (*crines*, 5.1), feet (*pedes*, 5.1), sides (*latus*, 5.1), breasts (*papillae*, 5.1), limbs (*membra*, 5.2), neck (*cervix*, 7.2, 7.3), skin (*cutis*, 7.2), and throat (*iugulum*, 8.2; cf. 3.4); also

---

[48] Chew 2003b: 131–2 notes that in martyr-literature the torture of female martyrs tends similarly to receive greater prominence than that of male.

[49] Jer. *Ep.* 1.5.1 *inmota mulier manet et a dolore corporis spiritu separato, dum conscientiae bono fruitur, vetuit circa se saevire tormenta*; Schäublin 1973: 56 objected to the manuscripts' *vetuit* and proposed *patitur* or *perpetitur*, but see the rebuttal at Scourfield 1987: 488–9 (supported by Rebenich 2002: 178 n. 26). For the idea of the freedom of the spirit from the pain of the tortured body cf., e.g., *Acts of Gallonius* 50 (Chiesa 1996: 268); Greg. Naz. *Ep.* 32.10 (Epictetus on the rack 'philosophized as if in someone else's body' (ἐφιλοσόφει ὥσπερ ἐν ἀλλοτρίῳ τῷ σώματι), seemingly unaware of the violence being inflicted on him until his leg had been broken); Prudent. *Perist.* 3.91–5.

[50] Hilberg 1996; F. A. Wright 1933. The instances of *corpus* occur at *Ep.* 1.3.3; 1.3.4; 1.5.1 (twice); 1.6.2; 1.7.2; 1.8.2; 1.12.2.

mentioned are her back (*tergum*, 3.3), eyes (*oculi*, 3.3, 5.2, 8.1, 12.2), face (*ora*, 3.3), knees (*poplites*, 7.2), chest (*pectus*, 12.2), and naturally her blood (*cruor*, ch. 4; *sanguis*, 7.2, cf. ch. 4). Other body-parts feature in the torture-descriptions but do not belong to the woman herself – the governor gnashes his teeth (*dentes*, ch. 4), the imagined lover has his head (*caput*, 7.1) cut off – while after the woman's supposed burial, clerics call the bluff of the returning executioner, who cannot believe that she has actually died, by inviting him to dig up her bones (*ossa*, 13.2). By the end of the tortures the heroine's body is little more than a bleeding lump: *nec erat novo vulneri locus*, 'there was no room for a new wound' (6.2).[51]

At this sequence of violent acts – the stretching of the body on the rack, the limbs torn from their sockets, the burning of the feet, the stabbing of the breasts – and the scene of execution which follows, we are invited to look, and not only by the presence of the descriptions themselves[52] but by the inscription in the text of instances of viewing. When the innocent couple are taken to be executed, we are told that 'the entire city' – that is, everyone, including ourselves, had we been there – 'pours out to watch' (*totus ad spectaculum populus effunditur*, 7.1), with the people pressed together as they push through the city-gates. But more striking than this is a passage from the torture-episode. Formed in the tradition of the wicked tyrant,[53] Jerome's governor devours the scene:

> igitur consularis pastis cruore luminibus ut fera, quae gustatum semel sanguinem semper sitit, duplicari tormenta iubet et saevum dentibus frendens similem carnifici minitatus est poenam, nisi confiteretur sexus infirmior, quod non potuerat robur virile reticere.

> And so the governor, having feasted his eyes on the gore, like a wild beast which is always thirsting for blood once it has tasted it, ordered the tortures to be doubled, and, gnashing his teeth savagely, threatened similar punishment on the executioner if the weaker sex failed to confess what male strength had not been able to conceal. (*Ep.* 1.4)

---

[51] Cf. *Martyrs of Lyons and Vienne* 1.23 τὸ δὲ σωμάτιον μάρτυς ἦν τῶν συμβεβηκότων, ὅλον τραῦμα καὶ μώλωψ ('his poor body was witness to what had happened, a wound and a bruise in its entirety'; of the tortured martyr Sanctus); also Ov. *Met.* 6.388 (of the flayed Marsyas), quoted by Newlands, Chapter 5, p. 165 above.

[52] On the spectacularity of martyr-narrative cf., e.g., August. *Serm. Denis* 17.7 *quando leguntur passiones martyrum, specto* ('When the passions of the martyrs are read, I am spectating'), with Grig 2004: 42–5.

[53] Cf. p. 314 above, with n. 29, noting esp. the comment of Harries 1999: 228 on cruel governors in martyr-texts: 'The agent of the persecuting state displays all the tendencies of the standard bad ruler of the Graeco-Roman literary tradition, arbitrary tyranny, anger and lack of self-control.'

The idea of a judge or executioner feeding on blood finds parallels in the work on which I shall be placing the spotlight later, the *Liber peristephanon* ('Book of Crowned Martyrs') of Prudentius. In poem 3 of this collection, the emperor Maximian himself, closely assimilated to the governor before whom the twelve-year-old Eulalia actually stands, is described in these terms:

> dux bonus, arbiter egregius,
> sanguine pascitur innocuo,
> corporibusque piis inhians
> viscera sobria dilacerat,
> gaudet et excruciare fidem.[54]

The excellent commander, illustrious judge, feeds on innocent blood, and slavering at the bodies of the pious rips apart their continent flesh and rejoices to torment the faith.

(Prudent. *Perist.* 3.86–90)

Similarly, in poem 6, the executioner dragging the companions of Fructuosus to prison is represented as 'fed on blood' (*pastus sanguine*, 6.17).[55] Neither of these passages, however, makes explicit reference to viewing; in the present passage, it is the *eyes* that are fed, and this is very suggestive. The use of the metaphor in this kind of violent context goes back a long way: in the *Verrines*, for example, Cicero refers to Syracusan seafarers wishing to 'feed their eyes on and gratify their hearts with the torture and execution' of a pirate captain, while in the *Philippics* he refers to an incident in the province of Asia where Dolabella, after torturing and executing Trebonius, is described as having 'fed his eyes on the mutilation and abuse of [Trebonius'] body, since he could not satisfy his inner feelings'.[56] But the image of feeding the eyes is also frequently used in Latin literature in erotic contexts.[57] Early in the *De rerum natura*, Lucretius describes Mars, gazing at Venus, as 'feed[ing] his eager eyes with

---

[54] Citations of the Latin text of the *Peristephanon* are based, *faute de mieux*, on the edition of Cunningham 1966; I have made some changes (none substantive) to punctuation and orthography. For a balanced assessment of the available critical editions of Prudentius see Bastiaensen 1993: 101–3.

[55] On such metaphors of feeding in the *Peristephanon* see further Roberts 1993: 66–7.

[56] Cic. *Verr.* 2.5.65 *eius cruciatu atque supplicio pascere oculos animumque exsaturare vellent*; *Phil.* 11.8 *in eius corpore lacerando atque vexando, cum animum satiare non posset, oculos paverit suos*. Note too that the phrase *sanguinem ... sitit* at Jer. *Ep.* 1.4, though the usage is not strictly metaphorical, also finds a (metaphorical) parallel in the *Philippics* (5.20); cf., e.g., Sen. *Thy.* 103, Plin. *NH* 14.148.

[57] The employment of the figure in both types of context is noted also by Bartsch 2006: 151 n. 85, with further references there and at n. 84.

love' (*pascit amore avidos . . . visus*).[58] Still more interesting in the present connection is a passage in Ovid's *Metamorphoses*, where Tereus' desire for his sister-in-law Philomela is fed by watching her embrace her father:

> spectat eam Tereus praecontrectatque videndo,
> osculaque et collo circumdata bracchia cernens
> omnia pro stimulis facibusque ciboque furoris
> accipit.

Tereus gazes at her, and, in looking, fondles her body in anticipation; and seeing her kisses and her arms around her father's neck, he takes it all as spur and flame and food for his passion.

(Ov. *Met.* 6.478–81)

In this text, male desire comes to be associated directly with violence when Tereus first rapes Philomela, then cuts out her tongue to silence her;[59] but the viewing–desire–violence bond has already been established earlier in the episode, where Tereus' passion flares up at first sight of Philomela, and he is driven (*impetus est illi*, 461)[60] to possess her through deceit or seduction or rape (455–66). His gaze, emphasized by the use of three verbs of seeing in two lines at 478–9, not only stimulates his desire, it amounts to an anticipatory (and proleptic) enactment of that desire (strongly underwritten by *praecontrectat*, a *hapax*, at 478), which will be violently discharged.[61] In the case of Jerome's governor, the relationship

---

[58] Lucr. 1.36; cf. Ter. *Phorm.* 85, Ov. *Am.* 3.2.6. The ellipse conceals the phrase *inhians in te, dea* ('gaping at you, goddess'), the verb, as often, possessing strong connotations of desire. The desire need not be sexual, but the Lucretius passage may suggest an erotic element in the use of *inhiare* at Prudent. *Perist.* 3.88 (quoted above), especially given other such suggestions in the text of that poem (see, e.g., nn. 100, 114 below).

[59] Ov. *Met.* 6.519–62. Much in the description of Tereus preparing to cut out Philomela's tongue (549–53) is strongly reminiscent of Jerome's letter. Tereus is described as a *ferus tyrannus*, a 'wild tyrant' (549), suggesting kinship with Jerome's governor (cf. esp. ch. 4 *fera*); he is spurred to mutilate his victim by a combination of anger (*ira*) and fear (*metus*) (549–50), emotions similarly attributed to the governor (*ira excitus*, 'roused by anger', 6.2) or his surrogate, the first executioner (who grows pale, *pallet*, 8.1, and is *exterritus*, 'terrified', 8.2; he is also *furens*, 'raging', 7.3); he seizes Philomela by the hair and ties her hands behind her back (*[eam] flexis post terga lacertis | vincla pati cogit*, 552–3), just as the woman at Vercellae has her hair bound to a stake (5.1) and her hands likewise constrained as she is racked (*manus post tergum vincula cohiberent*, 'bonds held her hands behind her back', 3.3); and he is described as drawing his sword in language capable of being construed sexually (*vagina liberat ensem*, 'he frees his sword from its sheath', 551) in order to carry out an action easily understood as doubling the rape which has already taken place (cf. Richlin 1992c: 163). For discussion of the whole episode, see Newlands, Chapter 5, pp. 152–64 above.

[60] *impetus* may have sexual overtones; cf. n. 47 above.

[61] Cf. C. P. Segal 1994: 260: 'Tereus' "tyrannical" assertion of male domination over the female body . . . is enacted symbolically through the aggressive penetration of the male gaze.' Also important here is the simile at 515–18, where Tereus, taking Philomela from Athens to Thrace on his ship prior to raping her, is described as never turning his eye from her, like an eagle gazing at

between viewing and violence is constructed in a slightly different way, but the Ovid passage helps to direct our attention to the erotic implications of the phrase *pastis cruore luminibus* in chapter 4, which become fully evident in the light of the scene of (metaphorical) sexual assault in chapters 7–8.[62]

There begins to emerge, then, a high degree of latent erotic content in the presentation of violence in this letter. From this position we might consider further the dismembering of the heroine's body which the text sets before us. While this focus on dissociated body-parts might – in a more traditional interpretative mode – be regarded as underscoring the extent and cruelty of the tortures and the courageous resistance of the victim, another reading is available in which it is construed in sexual terms. Again Ovid is helpful here: another poem, *Amores* 1.5, depicts the female body similarly fragmented in an erotic context (and one in which violence is also present).[63] A more radical version of this reading might place the concentration on the dismembered body within an interpretative frame supplied by feminist critiques of pornography. This of course is a troublesome, loaded, and contested concept, but one historically prominent definition explicitly includes as one element of the pornographic the exhibition of female body-parts 'such that women are reduced to those parts'.[64] The notion of the 'reduction' of the female form to its constituent parts might itself be thought rhetorically reductive, but in a text and a context where the female body is patently objectified, violently subordinated to male control, lusted after in its tortured and bloodied state, and metaphorically (almost) raped, such atomization presents as an additional manifestation of a system of power-relations both central to the understanding of pornography which gave rise to the definition and

---

the prey which it has carried off to its eyrie, leaving it no escape. On figurations of the 'penetrating gaze' in Roman thought and culture, Bartsch 2006: 138–52 is fascinating.

[62] The figure of feeding in these contexts might also remind us of the association in ancient culture of women with food, for which see Henry 1992. Helpful remarks on the 'consumptive gaze', with particular reference to Achilles Tatius, where viewing, desire, and violence are again closely linked, may be found in Morales 2004: 32–3, 165–9.

[63] See esp. vv. 19–22 *quos umeros, quales vidi tetigique lacertos!* | *forma papillarum quam fuit apta premi!* | *quam castigato planus sub pectore venter!* | *quantum et quale latus! quam iuvenale femur!* ('What shoulders, what arms I saw and touched! The shape of her breasts – how perfect for squeezing! How flat her stomach beneath her tight bosom! How long and how fine her side! How youthful her thigh!'); for the violence, vv. 13–16. For this way of reading Ovid's poem cf. Greene 1998: 77–84, esp. 82–3; Greene is, however, too ready to dismiss alternative readings, especially that of Hinds 1988: 6–11 – texts, as this chapter seeks to demonstrate, are susceptible of multiple, and sometimes conflicting, interpretations.

[64] Model Antipornography Civil-Rights Ordinance, Section 2.1.f; cf. more generally Sections 2.1.d, 2.1.h. Full text in Dworkin and MacKinnon 1988: 138–42.

characteristic of classical Antiquity.[65] In saying this I do not mean to suggest that Jerome's letter is necessarily to be labelled 'pornographic', still less that such a label was available to ancient readers, but to emphasize further the close and (as will increasingly become clear) critically problematic connection between sex and violence in this text.

A related interpretative model, integrally connected to the idea of viewing, is offered by Laura Mulvey's classic article on the gaze in cinema.[66] Drawing on psychoanalytic theory, Mulvey distinguishes between two modes of (male) cinematic viewing pleasure, in one of which the woman is displayed as an erotic object for the stimulation of the viewer, while in the other the viewer identifies with an on-screen controlling male figure, whose power and gaze he therefore shares. The first of these modes, which Mulvey terms fetishistic scopophilia, 'builds up the physical beauty of the object' in a way which involves a focus on bodily fragments, while in the second, sadistic voyeurism, 'pleasure lies in ascertaining guilt ... asserting control and subjugating the guilty person through punishment or forgiveness'.[67] Incorporating Mulvey's analysis into his account of Ovid's Tereus episode, Charles Segal identifies both fetishistic and sadistic components in the representation of Tereus' gaze,[68] and it is possible to perceive a similar (though not identical) combination of these types of viewing pleasure in Jerome's letter. While one could not argue for the kind of scopophilic idealization of the object present in the Ovid passage and in the Hollywood movies which Mulvey discusses, the emphasis on the fragmentation of the heroine's body (an emphasis not shared by the description of Ovid's Philomela, though strongly evident, as we have seen, in *Amores* 1.5) points to a fetishism of a related kind, in which the beauty lies precisely in the broken body so (de)valued by ascetic Christianity, a body which the woman of Vercellae herself is said to hate and to wish to shed.[69] Much more closely aligned with Tereus is the sadistic voyeurism of the governor, who represents Mulvey's controlling authority figure and channels the reader's gaze.[70] That channelling, of

[65] Cf. H. N. Parker 1992: 99–100.

[66] Mulvey 1975, on which see further Introduction, pp. 29–30 with n. 105. Of a general relevance to the concerns of the present chapter is Caviness 2001, who engages closely with filmic gaze-theory in discussing depictions of female torture and mutilation in medieval religious art.

[67] Mulvey 1975: 14 (where 'subjugating' appears as 'subjecting') (= 2009: 22 (23 for fragmentation)).

[68] C. P. Segal 1994: 260–1.

[69] Jer. *Ep.* 1.3.4 *equidem et ipsa cupio mori, cupio invisum hoc corpus exuere* ('I too long to die, I long to cast off this hated body').

[70] Note also how the Mulveyan characterization of sadistic voyeurism in terms of guilt and punishment is closely echoed in the *mise en scène* of the trial.

course, is itself deeply complicating, because the governor is not the kind of character with whom many (ancient or modern) readers would choose to identify:[71] compared to a wild beast with an insatiable appetite for blood, his excess is indicated not only by the extent of the tortures but by the threat he makes to punish the torturer himself should the woman fail to admit the crime. Here too an observation of Segal's offers a route to understanding the process of identification: 'By stressing the contrast with his Athenian victims, Ovid establishes Tereus as the barbarian, the Other, the one whose desires and acts stand outside the limits of humanity. As the Other, Tereus also serves as the field upon which can be projected libidinal and aggressive wishes that the (male) Roman audience may be reluctant to accept consciously in themselves.'[72] Adopting the governor's position is transgressive; but that transgression may be just what we secretly (and without knowing it) long for.

The importance of viewing or (to put the emphasis differently) spectacle in Jerome's narrative is confirmed by a powerful contrast made in the text between the governor and the inhabitants of Vercellae on the one hand and the heroine herself on the other. While, as we have observed, they evince a desire to witness with their eyes the breaking of bodies and the deaths of those whose bodies they are, the accused woman turns *her* eyes to heaven:

> at vero mulier sexu fortior suo, cum eculeus corpus extenderet et sordidas paedore carceris manus post tergum vincula cohiberent, oculis, quos tantum tortor alligare non poterat, suspexit ad caelum . . .

> But the woman, stronger than her sex, while the rack was stretching her body, and her hands, filthy with the dirt of the prison, were bound behind her back, looked up to heaven with her eyes, which were all the torturer could not bind . . . (Jer. *Ep.* 1.3.3; cf. 1.5.2)

---

[71] Contrast Hitchcock's heroes, 'exemplary of the symbolic order and the law' (Mulvey 1975: 15 = 2009: 23).

[72] C. P. Segal 1994: 263. It is by a similar process of 'othering' that David Frankfurter sees the voyeurism of Christian readers of martyr-texts as legitimated: 'Spectacles we *should not* gaze at, that *should not* excite on their own terms, are sanctioned as legitimate, even pious, through their framing as the monstrous acts of Romans or heathens or savages' (Frankfurter 2009: 230; original emphasis); 'Repudiated as the judicial savagery of Roman governors, public spectacles, or the customs of the Other, graphic, often sexualized atrocities were safe to contemplate as fantasy' (238). I am not so sure, however, that I would describe this as 'a simple matter of impulse projection and fantasy as the audience identifies alternately with the brutalized martyr and the monstrous forces of brutality, cringes at the torture, and relishes the blood' (230–1), as if shifting from one position to the other were something that could be done in a straightforwardly binary way, without complication or dissonance; equally, Frankfurter's repeated emphasis on 'safety' and 'fantasy' in respect of the Other-identified/prurient position (see, e.g., 217, 237–8, 242) seems to me to raise significant questions (cf. pp. 332 n. 109, 336–7 below).

and she prays to Christ.[73] Later, between the second and third blows of the executioner's sword, she sees the man lose a gold clasp from his cloak, and draws his attention to it; Jerome continues:

> rogo, quae est ista securitas? inpendentem non timet mortem, laetatur percussa, carnifex pallet; oculi gladium non videntes tantum fibulam vident et, ne parum esset, quod non formidabat interitum, praestabat beneficium saevienti.

> What, I ask, is the source of this confidence? Though death hangs over her, she is unafraid; the sufferer of the blows rejoices, the executioner grows pale; her eyes, not seeing the sword, see only the clasp, and, in case it should be too little that she has no fear of death, she renders a kindness to the raging headsman. (*Ep.* 1.8.1)

There can be no doubt here what kinds of viewing are approved, and whom we are meant to emulate: the woman shows us what to do with our eyes, and in so doing countermands, one might say, the invitation to adopt the viewpoint (and attitude) of the governor or the crowd. Equally, the sexual act implicit in the scene with the first executioner in chapter 7 fails; the impotization this man experiences, which we might wish to regard, contrary to other suggestions in the text,[74] as symbolizing the defeat of patriarchal discourse, inverts the erotic content, with his failure both preserving and amounting to a proof of the alleged adulteress's chastity – her insistence on which underlies her refusal to capitulate to the suffering she is made to undergo, and which of course possessed a very high value in fourth-century Christianity.[75] And yet the very presence of the sexual suggestions, both here and in the governor's bestial response to the sight of the woman's body under torture in chapter 4, brings to the text an enhanced prurient appeal, feeding

---

[73] For the gesture cf., e.g., *Martyrdom of Polycarp* 14.1, Prudent. *Perist.* 2.410; what is especially arresting here is the emphasis on the eyes themselves and their physicality.

[74] Both story and text remain ultimately in male control: the narrative is Jerome's, his addressee is Innocentius; the woman overcomes her male assailants (see above, p. 316), but her rescue depends on certain clerics (12.1, 13.2), Evagrius, and the emperor (15.3); above all, her defence throughout her suffering is another male figure, Christ (see esp. ch. 11 *stat victima Christo tantum favente munita*, 'the victim stands protected only by the favour of Christ'). Her disguising as a man (ch. 14) can also be read as a patriarchal reflex (cf., e.g., Cameron 1989: 192). And yet a question this chapter very precisely poses is: What does it mean to say 'ultimately'?

[75] This should not, however, be overstressed; sexual fidelity within marriage (which is what is at issue here) was demanded of women, whether pagan or Christian, throughout Antiquity, and in the fourth century (as the letter itself implies) the legal penalties for adultery could be severe (see Evans Grubbs 1995: 216–21; Arjava 1996: 195–7, 201–2). But the woman's impenetrability assimilates her to those who dedicated themselves to a life of virginity, a characteristically Christian undertaking, greatly promoted and admired within the ascetic movement (cf. below, p. 328 with n. 84).

the kind of critique I described above in which the text is assimilated to pornography. To express the problem differently, on the one hand, the erotic and desiring content of the text may be said to be legitimated by the context in which it is presented, the clear identification of heroes and villains and the primary 'message'; on the other, if we are to read the text at all, we cannot but be (in a limited sense, to be sure) voyeurs, a role which the text itself suggests to us even as it withdraws it. And at the same time, the supposed adulteress of Vercellae is both a model to follow by reason of her subjective strength and an object of potential, if not of satisfied, desires. That is to say, the text itself, for all that its author has a specific ideologically based aim, opens up a space which offers us choices for the shaping of our own individual erotics of reading. Indeed, that ideology itself seems to come under threat in the continuation of the passage where the woman turns her eyes heavenwards:

> ... et volutis per ora lacrimis: 'tu,' inquit, 'testis, domine Iesu, cui occultum nihil est, qui es scrutator renum[76] et cordis, non ideo me negare velle, ne peream, sed ideo mentiri nolle, ne peccem.'

> ... and with tears rolling down her cheeks, she said: 'You are my witness, lord Jesus, from whom nothing is hidden, examiner of kidneys and heart, that it is not to prevent my death that I wish to deny this, but that it is to avoid sin that I am unwilling to tell a lie.' (*Ep.* 1.3.3)

The curious phrase *scrutator renum et cordis*, 'examiner of kidneys and heart', is derived from passages in the Old Testament;[77] 'kidneys and heart' represent a person's inmost thoughts and feelings, one's 'inner self'. But the suggestion in the context of this letter, where body-parts are strewn across the page and come under the desiring gaze, is that Jesus, 'from whom nothing is hidden', looks beneath the skin, deep into the woman's interior organs – rendering himself in the process the greatest voyeur of all.

## III

About a quarter of a century after Jerome wrote *Letter* 1, in the context of the development of martyr-cult,[78] the Spanish poet Prudentius turned his attention back to the martyrs in what has come down to us as a collection

---

[76] Hilberg, on the basis of the manuscripts, reads *renis*; see further n. 77 below.

[77] See esp. Vulg. Ps. 7: 10 *scrutans corda et renes deus* (Jerome's later translation from the Septuagint), Wisd. 1: 6 *renum illius testis est deus, et cordis eius scrutator est verus*. Here and in all similar passages *renes* appears in the plural (= Septuagint νεφροί); hence I have preferred *renum* (read by certain earlier editors) to Hilberg's *renis*.

[78] See in general Roberts 1993: 1–8, 189–97; the *Peristephanon* may be dated reasonably securely to the 390s or early 400s, but greater precision is impossible.

of fourteen lyric poems, the *Liber peristephanon*. Of these, two are specifically devoted to female martyrs: poem 3, on Eulalia of Mérida (Augusta Emerita, in Lusitania), and poem 14, on the Roman virgin Agnes. The latter poem in particular affords a further opportunity to explore the interplay of violence, desire, and the visual in a Christian text in which chastity is again a central theme.[79] As we shall see, the configuration of these elements is notably different from that in Jerome's account of the *septies percussa*, and evokes different questions; but the cultural problematics of the two texts are similar, and exposed all the more clearly when the texts are read side by side.[80]

The martyrdom of Agnes has commonly been dated to the Great Persecution of 303–4, but this is no more than conjecture,[81] and the nature of the evidence for her death is such that history and legend can hardly be disentangled. The first literary attestations appear in the second half of the fourth century: Agnes is celebrated in a verse inscription by Damasus (d. 384) and a chapter of Ambrose's treatise *De virginibus*, as well as an Ambrosian hymn of questionable authenticity; Prudentius may have been familiar with some of these texts.[82] His own account, in 133 Alcaic hendecasyllables, is selective. Rather than presenting a step-by-step narrative of the kind Jerome provides in *Letter* 1, Prudentius homes in on the key scenes, leaving the reader to fill in the gaps; he also includes a good deal of what might be called meditative material. The poem begins with a reference to Agnes' tomb, in Rome, and her protection of both Romans and strangers who come to supplicate her (1–6); and then goes on to state that 'a double crown of martyrdom was presented to her: her virginity untouched by any offence, and then the glory of a freely chosen death'.[83]

---

[79] Recent critical commentary on *Perist.* 14, with emphasis on its erotic aspects, includes Malamud 1989: 149–77 and 1990: 78–86 (70–8 is also relevant); Burrus 1995: 33–43; Ross 1995: 342–3, in the context of a fine discussion of *Perist.* 3 (338–44); Grig 2004: 79–85 and 2005 (whose concern is rather with the wider Agnes tradition than with the Prudentian account specifically).

[80] The texts are associated by G. Clark 1993: 57, Frankfurter 2009: 224 n. 22, and (implicitly) Burrus 2004: 54 with n. 4, but to the best of my knowledge detailed comparative analysis has not previously been undertaken.

[81] A Valerianic date has also been proposed; see generally Palmer 1989: 251.

[82] Damasus, *Epigram* 37 Ferrua/Trout = 40 Ihm; Ambros. *De virg.* 1.2, *Hymn* 8; helpful discussion in Palmer 1989: 240, 250–3. Also extant, in both Greek and Latin recensions, is a prose martyr-narrative, which is not, however, thought to predate the fifth century. The *De virginibus* chapter (datable to *c.* 377) may show the influence of Jer. *Ep.* 1: compare esp. *De virg.* 1.2.7 *fuitne in illo corpusculo vulneri locus?* ('Was there room for a wound in that small body?'; of the twelve-year-old Agnes) with *Ep.* 1.6.2 *nec erat novo vulneri locus* ('there was no room for a new wound'; of the woman of Vercellae, at the end of the torture sequence).

[83] Prudent. *Perist.* 14.7–9 *duplex corona est praestita martyri:* | *intactum ab omni crimine virginal,* | *mortis deinde gloria liberae;* cf. Ambros. *De virg.* 1.2.9.

The narrative proper elaborates in turn on these two aspects of Agnes' experience. When this young girl, as yet 'scarcely fit for the marriage-bed' (*iugali vix habilem toro*, 10), refuses to abandon her faith and sacrifice to the gods, despite both blandishments from the judge and threats of torture, the judge attacks her through her virginity, which had been dedicated (*dicata*, 24) to Christ, in a rejection of the traditional Roman values of marriage and family;[84] the challenge thus laid down to the norms of pagan society made the choice of a sexual target all the more obvious. Agnes is given the choice between laying her head on the altar of Minerva and asking the goddess for pardon and – in a punishment the judge thinks appropriate for a virgin who scorns a virgin goddess – being placed in a public brothel (25–30).[85] Convinced that Christ will not allow her chastity to be destroyed, Agnes takes the latter option. Exactly what happens is not entirely clear. The judge first orders that Agnes be exposed to view in the corner of a city square (38–9); subsequently, we are told, the girl 'went along in triumph, celebrating God the Father and Christ in holy song, because, after an unholy danger had fallen upon her, her virginity, victorious, had found the brothel pure and inviolable'.[86] This is all very obscure,[87] but in any event Agnes' virginity is preserved, and, as far as the judge is concerned, the only course is to have her executed.

Prudentius moves rapidly to the execution scene. The judge, earlier characterized as a *trux tyrannus* ('fierce tyrant', 21),[88] now as a *hostis cruentus* ('bloodthirsty enemy') worked up into an angry frenzy (63–4),[89] instructs the executioner to draw his sword and carry out the emperor's commands (65–6). There follows:

---

[84] For a helpful brief summary of the sexual/social 'paradigm shift' of Christian late Antiquity, in which the life of virginity was valorized, see Malamud 1990: 70–2 (contextualizing her discussion of *Perist.* 3 and 14). P. Brown 1989 remains fundamental for the entire subject of sexual renunciation in early Christianity.

[85] For this motif cf., e.g., Ambros. *De virg.* 2.4; Pallad. *Hist. Laus.* 65; in martyr-literature also *Martyrdom of Pionius* 7.6, *Martyrdom of Agape, Irene, and Chione* 5.8. It does not appear in any of the earlier texts on the martyrdom of Agnes; cf. Malamud 1989: 150 n. 3, 157. For broader literary contextualization, see Panayotakis 2002: 106–12, with further bibliography.

[86] Prudent. *Perist.* 14.52–6 *ibat triumphans virgo, deum patrem | Christumque sacro carmine concinens, | quod sub profani labe periculi | castum lupanar nec violabile | experta victrix virginitas foret.*

[87] That Agnes has somehow made the brothel pure is, however, confirmed at 128–9.

[88] For this phrase, cf. Damasus, *Epigram* 37.4 Ferrua/Trout = 40.4 Ihm.

[89] In this characterization the judge resembles Jerome's governor (see pp. 314, 319 above, with nn. 29, 53); and like the governor he has something of Ovid's Tereus about him: see above, p. 321 with n. 59, for Tereus as a *ferus tyrannus*, subject to *ira* (Ov. *Met.* 6.549) and *furor* (Ov. *Met.* 6.480). On Prudentius' representation of the presiding Roman officials and their torturers and executioners in the *Peristephanon* as a whole, Opelt 1967 remains useful, particularly for its collections of relevant data.

ut vidit Agnes stare trucem virum
mucrone nudo, laetior haec ait:
'exulto, talis quod potius venit
vesanus, atrox, turbidus armiger,                    70
quam si veniret languidus ac tener
mollisque ephebus tinctus aromate,
qui me pudoris funere perderet.
hic, hic amator iam, fateor, placet.
ibo inruentis gressibus obviam                       75
nec demorabor vota calentia;
ferrum in papillas omne recepero
pectusque ad imum vim gladii traham.
sic nupta Christo transiliam poli
omnes tenebras aethere celsior.'                     80

When Agnes saw the fierce man standing there with his naked sword, her delight grew and she said: 'I rejoice that there comes such a man as this, a raging, cruel, wild bearer of arms, rather than a listless, soft, delicate youth drenched in perfume, come to destroy me with the death of my virtue. This lover, this one, I confess, now pleases me. I shall go to meet him as he rushes upon me, and not delay his hot desires. I shall receive his whole blade into my bosom, and draw the force of his sword to the depths of my breast. Thus wed to Christ, I shall outleap all the darkness of the sky, rising higher than the aether.'

(Prudent. *Perist.* 14.67–80)

It is this passage of the poem which has particularly caught the eye of scholars in recent years.[90] Language and content are more overtly sexual than in the comparable execution scene in Jerome, *Letter* 1.7. Agnes' reaction to the sight of her executioner goes far beyond simple acceptance. Seeing him 'with his naked sword' (*mucrone nudo*, 68), she experiences a surge of pleasure (*laetior*, 68), and rejoices (*exulto*, 69) that the man she faces – already described, like the judge, as *trux* (67) – is 'a raging, cruel, wild bearer of arms' (*vesanus, atrox, turbidus armiger*, 70),[91] a macho he-man, rather than a listless (*languidus*; cf. Jer. *Ep.* 1.7.3, where, as we have seen,[92] the word connotes impotence), soft (*tener*), delicate, even woman-ish youth (*mollis ephebus*), steeped in perfume (71–2).[93] The executioner,

---

[90] It is a measure of how and how much Prudentian and early-Christian scholarship in general have changed in the last quarter-century that the first comprehensive, book-length study of the *Liber peristephanon* (Palmer 1989) does not even mention this passage.

[91] For *arma* in sexual metaphor see Adams 1982: 17, 21, 224.   [92] P. 317 above, with n. 47.

[93] Agnes' imaginary anti-lover is in fact stereotypically effeminate. The complex notion of *mollitia* is illuminatingly explored (with a late-Republican/early-Imperial focus) by C. Edwards 1993: 63–97; in the present context see esp. 68–70 on perfume as a marker of effeminacy and on the association of youth with sexual passivity – the only possible sexual role for a *languidus* male.

who has come to destroy, but also sexually corrupt (*perderet*, 73), her, is a lover (*amator*) whom she welcomes (*placet*, 74);[94] far from resisting, Agnes will throw herself at him (*ibo inruentis gressibus obviam*, 75), and not put off his 'hot desires' (*vota calentia*, 76). Taking his whole blade (*ferrum*, 77) into her bosom, and drawing 'the force of his sword' (*vim gladii*, 78)[95] to the depths of her breast, she will – by a neat twist – become the bride of Christ (79).[96]

There is a great deal that is of interest here, and another study might, for example, explore the passage as an unusually piquant instance of the common association of sex and death in classical literature, or in the context of the long tradition connecting death and marriage.[97] But what is most striking about the passage is that, whereas in Jerome's *Letter* 1 the desire that is evident belongs to the male figures, the governor and the executioner, and we are invited to share the visual perspective of those who gaze at the female victim, here it belongs to the victim herself. Her executioner may have his own desires – the *vota calentia* – but the scene is focalized through Agnes: it is her desires that are expressed in words, and through her eyes that we see the *turbidus armiger* with his *mucro nudus* (*ut vidit Agnes . . .*, 67). In fact, this emphasis may be even stronger than I have suggested. In assigning the *vota calentia* to the swordsman, I am aligning myself with the usual view, one that seems natural after the previous line (75), where the heroine refers to this man 'rushing upon [her]'; but we should observe that no possessive adjective accompanies the phrase, and the idea that these 'hot desires' might actually belong to Agnes[98] is supported by the phrase *Christo calentem* ('inflamed by Christ', 'hot for

---

[94] For *placere* implying sexual attraction (or more), see *OLD* s.v., sect. 1d, noting also Sen. *Phaed.* 684, quoted by Kennedy, Chapter 7 above, p. 224 n. 40.

[95] For *vis* used of a sexual act cf., e.g., Cic. *Verr.* 2.1.62; (with strong resonances in the present context) Ov. *Ars am.* 1.673 *vim licet appelles: grata est vis ista puellis* ('you may call it force, but that kind of force girls like').

[96] For this notion – a common trope for dedicated virgins in late-Antique Christianity, owing much to the Song of Songs as interpreted by Origen and later exegetes – see, e.g., P. Brown 1989: 274–6.

[97] Especially relevant here is D. Fowler 1987, a paper which brilliantly exposes and traces a powerful (and complex) association in Greek and Latin poetry between wounding/death and defloration/marriage. In this connection it should be observed that both poems in the *Peristephanon* devoted to female martyrs concern girls on the cusp of puberty or marriageable life. Eulalia in *Perist.* 3 is twelve years old (11–12), the same as Agnes in Ambrose's account in the *De virginibus* (1.2.7); Prudentius does not specify Agnes' age, but, as we have seen, she is described as being more or less ready for marriage (*Perist.* 14.10). The marriage theme is particularly prominent in Eulalia's case (see esp. *Perist.* 3.16–18, 104–13), but note the important observation of Palmer 1989: 203 on the possible epithalamial connotations of the metre of *Perist.* 14.

[98] So Corsaro 1997: 133, without comment; much more tentatively, Malamud 1989: 154, 170. Corsaro 1997: 128 also notes the presence of *calere* at v. 12, nodding towards its repetition at 76 and documenting at length the word's erotic force.

Christ'), used of the girl at line 12.[99] Making the same association also encourages us toward the notion that the executioner and Christ are somehow identified in Agnes' mind,[100] rather than that which regards the marriage to Christ foreseen in line 79 as the ironic (though desirable) consequence of her defloration at swordpoint.

As in Jerome's letter, vision is an important theme in this text. When Agnes, earlier in the narrative, is made to stand, clearly naked, in the public square, the crowd – in contradistinction to the people of Vercellae – averts its gaze, 'so that no one should look lasciviously upon her private parts' (*ne petulantius | quisquam verendum conspiceret locum*, 41–2).[101] But one man does look at her lustfully (*procaciter*, 43; *lumine lubrico*, 45),[102] and a flash of fiery light, like a thunderbolt, strikes his eyes (*oculos ferit*) and blinds him (46–9). Taken together with the later passage, this establishes for Prudentius' poem a quite different construction of the inscribed gaze from that evident in the story of the *septies percussa*, almost an inversion: the punishment dispensed to the peeping Tom strongly counters any invitation to look voyeuristically at Agnes (much more strongly than anything suggested in *Letter* 1), while the heroine's desire for her lover-executioner is itself stimulated by visual impulses (whereas the woman of Vercellae casts her eyes to heaven, Agnes looks straight at her killer, and is turned on by what she sees). Agnes' gaze is indeed intensely countercultural. In the *Passio Perpetuae et Felicitatis*, as Perpetua is led from the prison to the amphitheatre she is described as 'causing everyone to lower their gaze by the power of her eyes'[103] (18.2). Brent Shaw writes: '[Perpetua's] ability to stare directly back into the faces of her persecutors, not with the elusive demeanour of a proper *matrona*, broke with the normative body language in a way that signalled an aggressiveness that was not one of conventional femininity.'[104] Agnes shares something of Perpetua's look, but her breaking with 'normative body language' is yet more extreme because it is

---

[99] The inclusion at 106 of *vota* among the worldly things which Agnes as disembodied spirit laughs at (96) and tramples underfoot (112) might be thought to argue in the opposite direction; but we might equally see here a contrast between worldly and heavenly desires (with the *vota* of 76 understood as the desire to be with Christ).

[100] So Burrus 1995: 37. For the disconcerting ambivalence, cf. Ross 1995: 343–4 on the wounds suffered by Eulalia at the hands of torturers as the inscription of her body as martyr-text by Christ, perhaps with overtones of rape (*Perist*. 3.131–45).

[101] For the euphemism *verendus locus* ('fearful place', 'place inspiring awe') cf. Adams 1982: 53–4 (on *verenda*).

[102] On the phrase *lumine lubrico* see den Boeft and Bremmer 1991: 119.

[103] *vigore oculorum deiciens omnium conspectum.*

[104] Shaw 1993: 4 (= 2004: 287); cf. Perkins 1995: 112, C. Williams 2012: 66.

sexual.[105] This gaze evokes rather Propertius' Tarpeia – a Vestal Virgin – or Ovid's Scylla, both of whom conceive a passion for an enemy warrior through observing him from a teichoscopic vantage-point, and commit an act of treachery in an attempt to satisfy their passion; the transgressiveness of their viewing is marked by the punishment which follows.[106] In the case of Agnes, whose erotic desires are more explicitly expressed than either Tarpeia's or Scylla's, the punishment – death by the sword – is *also* the desired consummation;[107] but this does not make her gaze in itself any the less transgressive or shocking.[108]

As will already have started to become clear, interpretation of Prudentius' treatment of Agnes is challenging. One could, for example, firmly insist that the sexualization of the executioner and of Agnes' longing for death with her virginity and faith intact is, after all, metaphor; and, equally, one could say that her sexual desires are sublimated into a desire to be with God, a goal towards which an ideal route is afforded by the executioner's sword.[109] These are the kinds of view which readers are plainly 'supposed' to take: the premium set by late-Antique ascetic Christianity on female virginity outdid even the traditional patriarchal protectionism of pagan society,[110] and if the era of martyrdom had come to an end almost a century before, figures like Agnes could still provide models of faith and sexual purity to which women could aspire. Yet the celebration

---

[105] Perpetua's return gaze is properly read by Shaw 1993: 4 (= 2004: 287) as 'a sign of [her] rejection of the legitimacy of the onlookers' voyeurism'; but more than that, its effect is to drain the scene of its implicit sexual content.

[106] Prop. 4.4, esp. 19–22, 31–4; Ov. *Met.* 8.6–151, esp. 19–42. These texts provide a suggestive background for the Prudentius passage. It is not just a matter of the desiring female gaze, but of the oppositional status of the desired male figure, and his martial masculinity; further, like the Ovidian Scylla, Agnes is at the end metamorphosed (though in a manner that is, from the contemporary Christian perspective, unambiguously positive), her spirit leaping, bird-like, free into the air (91–2; cf. 79–80).

[107] Cf. n. 115 below.

[108] Contrast Tertullian's exhortation to Christian virgins, in his treatise on veiling, to 'build a wall for your sex, to prevent your looking out and others looking in' (*murum sexui tuo strue, qui nec tuos emittat oculos, nec admittat alienos; De virg. vel.* 16).

[109] Cf. Burrus 2004: 1. In a rich study concerning the development of a complex and multifaceted discourse of gender and desire in early Christianity, Averil Cameron explains how 'it became safe to describe religious experience, even the religious experience of young virgin girls, in explicitly erotic language'; the ascetic discourse of 'non-desire' 'neutralis[ed] and deflect[ed] real sexual desire into safer outlets' (Cameron 1994: 166 = 2011: 523–4). But quite how safe such description/deflection was in the case of any individual reader must remain wholly uncertain; and the figure of the Prudentian Agnes strongly destabilizes the notion of safety through the context in which her desire is expressed – if the executioner and Christ are in some way identified (see p. 331 above), the executioner also retains his own identity as an enemy purveyor of violence and cruelty.

[110] Cf. n. 84 above.

of these virtues which the poem represents[111] is confronted with a serious challenge, however 'metaphorical', on the part of the heroine;[112] far from having the male assailant lose his erection, de-eroticizing the erotic, as in Jerome, or even having Agnes passively accept the act forced upon her by male authority and strength, Prudentius makes of his (just) nubile star a woman who, if not exactly predatory, can be said to have her own desires, and to wish to satisfy them: *ibo inruentis gressibus obviam* (75). One might indeed go even further: the verb *inruere* found here also occurs earlier in the poem, where the judge declares his intention to thrust Agnes into the brothel. There, he says, *omnis iuventus inruet et novum | ludibriorum mancipium petet* ('all the young men will rush in and seek the new slave of their wantonness', 29–30); the echo hints at Agnes being not simply a desiring woman, but one eager to embrace the role of a whore.[113]

Throughout ancient literature the desiring woman is represented as a threat. By transforming this desire into a longing for death and divine union,[114] Prudentius may be said to contain it; on the other hand, the realization in sexual terms of longing for death arguably endows the desiring impulse with an energy that cannot be contained within the precise limits which legitimate it. From an intratextual point of view, Agnes' sexually conceived desire is ironic: in advancing upon the oncoming sword she participates in ensuring the eternal existence of her virgin status, and we should note that earlier (36–7) she tells the judge that while he may stain the sword with her blood, if he wishes, he will not defile her body with lust – in the event, both of these things can be seen to happen.[115] But

---

[111] The preservation of Agnes' virginity is re-emphasized at the end of the poem: freed from her body by death, Agnes tramples down the things of the world, and subdues the devil (in serpent guise) 'with virgin's foot' (*virginali … solo*, 116); God wreathes the brow of the 'unwedded martyr' (*martyris innubae*, 120) with the double crown already mentioned (with reference to the maintenance of her virgin status) at 7–8; at 124 she is apostrophized as *virgo felix*; her power to render the brothel pure (*castus*) is made explicit at 128–9.

[112] Cf. Burrus 1995: 42, for whom the text's 'message of virginal docility always carries with it the potential for its own subversion' through Agnes' complex representation as both 'docile *virgo*' and 'audacious *virago*'.

[113] Agnes' gaze may be held to reinforce this interpretation; cf. D. Cairns 2005: 134, who points out that in physiognomic writers a woman's failure to lower her eyes is taken to indicate that she is a prostitute. The echo is noted also by Malamud 1989: 153, without, however, the same conclusion being drawn.

[114] Cf. *Perist*. 3, where Eulalia is described as *anhela deo* (34, reasonably translated 'panting for God' by Thomson 1949–53: II.144; for the sexual overtones of *anhelus* cf., e.g., Ov. *Ars am.* 3.803, Petron. *Sat.* 87.8 (*anhelitus*), Tib. 1.8.37 (*anhelare*), with Adams 1982: 195), and as moved, at least potentially, 'by love of death' (*mortis amore*, 40).

[115] It might be thought to run counter to this view that Agnes is not in fact killed by sword-thrust but by decapitation (89). For Malamud 1989: 171 this amounts to a symbolic castration, an 'unsexing' of Agnes; elsewhere she describes the decapitation as 'function[ing] as a sort of curb on [Agnes']

if we move outside the boundaries of the text into its external world, we are forced, I think, to recognize the insidious quality of the poem, which admits in a permissive, even extreme, way the existence of female desire even as it tries to suppress it. The male voyeur, too, may in the end be permitted his gaze: as a coda to the episode where the peeping Tom is blinded, Prudentius reports a story (57–60) according to which Agnes prayed to Christ that the young man's sight be restored, and it was made whole.

# IV

Early Christian martyrdom was often figured as a contest or struggle, and the struggle centred on control. Roman authorities did not want martyrs; they wanted compliance, demonstrated principally through participation in traditional politico-religious rituals which asserted a collective and cohesive Romanness.[116] Christian resistance sought, for motivations that were complex, to escape such state regimentation in a way that was inevitably rich in paradox: Roman control could be avoided through maintaining control over one's own body – not making the required sacrifice or taking the prescribed oath – but this had to be sustained through violent physical assault, to the body's end. Death achieved victory; victory meant death.

threatening female sexuality', with the girl 'cheated of the death by phallic sword thrust she anticipates so eagerly' (Malamud 1990: 81–2). But we need not take this line. The sexual act envisaged in vv. 67–80 can be regarded as achieved even in the severing of Agnes' head. Thus, for Burrus 1995: 38–9, '[Prudentius] substitutes a submissively bent neck for the breast Agnes has defiantly offered, thereby compromising even Agnes' power to claim full complicity in her death-marriage, now still more clearly inscribed as rape'. This position, however, while attractive in itself, elides other details in the text. Agnes' speech at 69–80 is concluded (81–4) with a prayer to God and Christ, immediately after which she bows her head to receive the blow of the sword upon her neck; she is, then – as one would expect – fully aware of the kind of death she is actually facing. But more than that, the poet proceeds to write that the executioner *tantam spem peragit manu* ('fulfils with his hand her great hope', 88), where we should recall too that a basic meaning of *peragere* is 'to thrust through' (the word is also used of sexual accomplishment: see Adams 1982: 144). That is to say, it remains open to us to see Agnes' desire as fully consummated.

116  This is especially and most evidently true in the case of the systematic empire-wide persecutions that began under the emperor Decius, whose decree demanding universal sacrifice offers a particularly good illustration of the general point (on this decree see esp. Rives 1999, a masterly discussion). For attempts by Roman officials to persuade Christians to comply rather than be executed see, e.g., *Acts of the Scillitan Martyrs*, esp. 13, where the proconsul Saturninus offers those indicted thirty days' grace to reflect; *Martyrdom of Pionius* 19–20; *Martyrdom of Julius the Veteran*, where (2.4–5) the *praeses* Maximus goes so far as to offer the arraigned Julius financial incentives to sacrifice.

In the texts in which the Christians memorialized their martyrs the outcome of this struggle is always already known; like biography, the genre is intrinsically closural. This strong directionality – re-engineered in the case of Jerome's martyrial paranarrative into the heroine's achievement of freedom following a death that is merely apparent; the final word of the letter (15.3) presents her restored by the emperor to *libertas*, just as, in Prudentius' poem, Agnes' spirit, released from her body, leaps *liber* into the air (92)[117] – is accompanied in these particular texts by parallel drives. Though neither text is explicitly protreptic, they firmly guide the reader, especially the female reader, towards a particular kind of behaviour: the preservation of virginity, chastity within marriage, and undeviating faith even in extreme circumstances are the objects towards which s/he is urged. And yet, as I have endeavoured to show, both also afford quite different perspectives, at variance with the message which we might agree that they are 'meant' to deliver.[118]

The problem is that texts do not come hermetically sealed and with meaning locked in. In the context of a chapter that considers representations of violence in ancient narrative, it may be thought appropriate to illustrate this point and clarify some of the difficulties by touching briefly on a controversial instance of violence in modern cinema. Oliver Stone's *Natural Born Killers* of 1994 made a technically brilliant, satirizing assault on media culture, focusing specifically on the media's making celebrities of violent criminals. Some critics accused Stone simply of glorifying violence. But the essential problem for the film *qua* film is that, through its use (artistically superb in itself) of a style of montage that iconically reflects a media-saturated culture, its failure to discriminate morally between journalists, law enforcement officials, and mass murderers (in fact a moral centre is most closely approached in the characters of the serial killers Mickey and Mallory Knox themselves, who alone are uncaricatured), and its intense subjectivity, which work together to deny us an effective emotional and ethical distance, it comes to embody the very attitude

---

[117] For martyrdom troped as liberation cf. *Martyrdom of Felix the Bishop*, Appendix (Musurillo 1972: 270); *Martyrdom of Crispina* 4.2.

[118] Cf. P. C. Miller 1993: 23, discussing Jerome's *Letter* 22, to Eustochium, where powerful bridal and erotic imagery drawn from the Song of Songs is employed in the context of an argument urging perseverance in the virgin life: 'The explicit intentions of an author ... cannot always control or limit the meanings that arise from the associative movements and configurations of his or her text's tropes and metaphors. Texts can articulate perspectives and bear significations that are quite different from the announced goals of the author.' So too Frankfurter 2009: 241 can write: 'The spectacle of martyrdom clearly did not always convey what Christians wanted to declare to their audiences.'

which it seeks to criticize (we are 'supposed' to take one view, but are at the same time trapped into a kind of complicity with its opposite).[119] The self-unravelling of *Natural Born Killers* is not in fact replicated by Jerome's *Letter* 1 or Prudentius' poem on Agnes; but it sharply underlines the point that even texts with a committed ideology can contain within themselves a powerful voice of opposition. The struggle for control within the textualized martyrdom scenario thus finds its counterpart in the world outside the text; for what is a reader, authorially directed towards sexual self-restraint or self-denial, or at a minimum their approval, to do with the counter-invitation to slaver with the governor of Aemilia-Liguria over the tortured body of an alleged adulteress, or to share the erotic charge of a young virgin as she advances to meet her killer?

The short answer is: we do what we like. Once a text is put into the world, after all, the author loses ownership of it. Similarly, our critical readings are formulated on the basis of what we see or choose to privilege in the text, which is itself shaped by what we bring to the text from outside, mediated through ourselves. But our responses and judgements are not always without implication. Agnes offers an especially difficult case. How far is her erotic desire for the sword interpretable as liberation from one of the constraints imposed on women in Antiquity? How far, conversely, should it be held to reinforce standard gender-relations by expressing an acceptance of (and thereby further encouraging) male sexual violence against women? For us the issue is made yet more complicated by Agnes' age; whereas marriage at twelve was legal in the Roman world,[120] the attribution of powerful sexual desire, in a context of potential fulfilment (and with suggestions that she likes it rough), to a girl of that age is likely to evoke in the contemporary reader, in a climate of grave concern about child pornography, the memory of Lolita, and far worse. The vivid torture-descriptions in Jerome's *Letter* 1 are also troubling: Do these serve to glorify the sufferer by underlining her courage and endurance, or do they help to legitimate the breaking down of the female form into the sum of its parts? Can the brutality of the tortures be said to be distanced through the rhetorical stylization of the text (just as the violence in Tarantino's *Kill Bill* can claim to be distanced through

---

[119] Cf. J. Bailey 2000: 83: 'If [*Natural Born Killers*] is meant to be a de facto critique or satire of the American and media obsession with violence, I can only say that on this level it is ... a complete failure. The filmmaking tools which are wielded so artfully and with such panache distort the putative intent. The film eroticizes violence, wallows in it, and struggles to incite the viewer'; Prince 2000b: 33; Slocum 2001b: 21; Kinder 2001: 77–81.

[120] See Treggiari 1991a: 39–42; for Agnes' age, n. 97 above.

aestheticization and other techniques[121]), and if so, what are the interpretative effects of that?

In dealing with contentious, emotive topics such as violence and sex, the problems of interpretation are especially pronounced. Following the Dunblane massacre of 1996, the video of *Natural Born Killers* was withdrawn from the UK market by the distributor, in a move reflective of societal concern about the often uncomfortable relation between art and life.[122] A decade earlier, the feminist critic Susanne Kappeler, in a book on representation, had provocatively asserted, 'Art will have to go.'[123] These are useful reminders that the study of literary texts, like the study of the visual arts, does not take place in a vacuum; the act of criticism itself can be profoundly political. But it is a politics of pluralism that allows this debate to take place; the cultural space given to socially difficult topics such as the representation of violent acts in art and literature, and to the critical discussion of such representations, both derives from this political frame and helps to sustain it. If we accept pluralist principles, then far from demanding to be silenced, textual violence can be claimed as both an intellectual and a political good. Our responsibilities as readers and critics, of course, may not be evaded. The challenge for us, as we gaze with the governor at fire and rack, or walk with Agnes towards the executioner's unsheathed sword, is that of maintaining a clear sense of the partiality and the moral difficulties of those perspectives and of discriminating between the vicarious feelings we experience in the world of the mind and the enactment of those feelings in the world in which we live.

---

[121] See Introduction, p. 40 with n. 130.

[122] A relation problematized particularly acutely in the Roman context by Sen. *Controv.* 10.5: see Morales 1996, with much of relevance to my concerns here.

[123] Kappeler 1986: 221. Kappeler's book is the main theoretical reference-point for the essays in Richlin 1992b, where this phrase is twice quoted (xvii, 160), though its implications are in fact, and as needs to be recognized here also, less extreme than is there suggested: Kappeler is explicit (220–1) that she is not proposing a system of censorship, and her dismissal of 'Art', an expression here evidently used in a somewhat restricted sense in any case, is to be understood in terms of a radical shift in 'artistic' practice, arising from and promoting a changed cultural consciousness. Nevertheless, the phrase remains rhetorically potent, and sharply underscores Kappeler's essential point about the thoroughgoing cultural embeddedness of particular modes of representation and viewing.

# Works Cited

Abel, L. 1963. *Metatheatre: A New View of Dramatic Form.* New York.

Adams, J. N. 1982. *The Latin Sexual Vocabulary.* London.

Adelman, M. 2003. 'The Military, Militarism, and the Militarization of Domestic Violence', *Violence against Women* 9: 1118–52.

Africa, T. W. 1971. 'Urban Violence in Imperial Rome', *Journal of Interdisciplinary History* 2: 3–21.

Ahl, F. 1976. *Lucan: An Introduction.* Cornell Studies in Classical Philology 39. Ithaca, NY.

1985. *Metaformations: Soundplay and Wordplay in Ovid and Other Classical Poets.* Ithaca, NY.

Allen, D. S. 2000. *The World of Prometheus: The Politics of Punishing in Democratic Athens.* Princeton, NJ.

Alston, R. 1998. 'Arms and the Man: Soldiers, Masculinity and Power in Republican and Imperial Rome', in L. Foxhall and J. Salmon (eds.), *When Men Were Men: Masculinity, Power and Identity in Classical Antiquity.* Leicester–Nottingham Studies in Ancient Society 8. London: 205–23.

2011. 'Seeing Caesar in Ruins: Towards a Radical Aesthetic of Ruins', in A. Kahane (ed.), *Antiquity and the Ruin/L'Antiquité et les ruines* (= *European Review of History/Revue européenne d'histoire* 18.5–6). Abingdon: 697–716.

Alston, R. and Spentzou, E. 2011. *Reflections of Romanity: Discourses of Subjectivity in Imperial Rome.* Columbus, OH.

Alton, E. H., Wormell, D. E. W., and Courtney, E. (eds.). 1985. *P. Ovidi Nasonis Fastorum libri sex,* 2nd edn. Leipzig.

Anderson, W. S. 1960. 'Imagery in the Satires of Horace and Juvenal', *AJPh* 81: 225–60, reprinted in Anderson 1982a: 115–50.

1982a. *Essays on Roman Satire.* Princeton, NJ.

1982b. 'The Roman Socrates: Horace and his Satires', in Anderson 1982a: 13–49.

1993. *Barbarian Play: Plautus' Roman Comedy.* Toronto.

Andújar, R. M. 2012. 'Charicleia the Martyr: Heliodorus and Early Christian Narrative', in Futre Pinheiro, Perkins, and Pervo 2012: 139–52.

Arendt, H. 1970. *On Violence.* New York.

Arjava, A. 1996. *Women and Law in Late Antiquity.* Oxford.

1998. 'Paternal Power in Late Antiquity', *JRS* 88: 147–65.

Armstrong, N. and Tennenhouse, L. (eds.). 1989. *The Violence of Representation: Literature and the History of Violence*. London.

Arnott, W. G. 1988. 'New Evidence for the Opening of Menander's *Perikeiromene?'*, *ZPE* 71: 11–15.

Ash, R. 1998. 'Waving the White Flag: Surrender Scenes at Livy 9.5–6 and Tacitus, *Histories* 3.31 and 4.62', *G&R* 45: 27–44.

1999. *Ordering Anarchy: Armies and Leaders in Tacitus'* Histories. London.

2002. 'Epic Encounters? Ancient Historical Battle Narratives and the Epic Tradition', in D. S. Levene and D. P. Nelis (eds.), *Clio and the Poets: Augustan Poetry and the Traditions of Ancient Historiography*. Mnemosyne Supplementum 224. Leiden: 253–73.

2003. '"Aliud est enim epistulam, aliud historiam ... scribere" (*Epistles* 6.16.22): Pliny the Historian?', *Arethusa* 36: 211–25.

(ed.). 2007. *Tacitus: Histories, Book II*. Cambridge.

Ashworth, W. D. and Andrewes, M. 1957. 'Horace, *Sat*. i. 6. 104–5', *CR* 7: 107–8.

Aubert, J.-J. 2002. 'A Double Standard in Roman Criminal Law? The Death Penalty and Social Structure in Late Republican and Early Imperial Rome', in J.-J. Aubert and B. Sirks (eds.), *Speculum iuris: Roman Law as a Reflection of Social and Economic Life in Antiquity*. Ann Arbor, MI: 94–133.

Austin, R. G. (ed.). 1955. *P. Vergili Maronis Aeneidos liber quartus*. Oxford.

(ed.). 1977. *P. Vergili Maronis Aeneidos liber sextus*. Oxford.

Bailey, C. (ed.). 1922. *Lucreti De rerum natura libri sex*, 2nd edn. Oxford.

(ed.). 1947. *Titi Lucreti Cari De rerum natura libri sex*. 3 vols. Oxford.

Bailey, J. 2000. 'Bang Bang Bang Bang, *ad nauseum* [*sic*]', in Prince 2000a: 79–85.

Bakhtin, M. 1981. *The Dialogic Imagination: Four Essays*. Translated by C. Emerson and M. Holquist. University of Texas Press Slavic Series 1. Austin, TX.

Bal, M. 1991. *Reading 'Rembrandt': Beyond the Word-Image Opposition*. Cambridge.

Bannet, E. T. 1989. *Structuralism and the Logic of Dissent: Barthes, Derrida, Foucault, Lacan*. Urbana, IL.

Bannon, C. J. 1997. *The Brothers of Romulus: Fraternal Pietas in Roman Law, Literature, and Society*. Princeton, NJ.

Baraz, Y. Forthcoming. 'The Bitter Medicine of History: Seneca on the Genre of Declamation', in Dinter, Guérin, and Martinho forthcoming.

Barchiesi, A. 1997. *The Poet and the Prince: Ovid and Augustan Discourse*. Berkeley, CA.

(ed.). 2005. *Ovidio: Metamorfosi*, vol. I. Milan.

Barchiesi, A. and Cucchiarelli, A. 2005. 'Satire and the Poet: The Body as Self-Referential Symbol', in Freudenburg 2005a: 207–23.

Barigazzi, A. 1987. 'Lucrezio e la gioia per il male altrui', in S. Boldrini *et al.* (eds.), *Filologia e forme letterarie: studi offerti a Francesco della Corte*. 5 vols. Urbino: II.269–84.

Barkan, L. 1986. *The Gods Made Flesh: Metamorphosis and the Pursuit of Paganism.* New Haven, CT.

Barker, M. and Petley, J. (eds.). 2001a. *Ill Effects: The Media/Violence Debate*, 2nd edn. London.

2001b. 'Introduction: From Bad Research to Good – a Guide for the Perplexed', in Barker and Petley 2001a: 1–26.

Barnes, T. D. 2010. *Early Christian Hagiography and Roman History.* Tria corda: Jenaer Vorlesungen zu Judentum, Antike und Christentum 5. Tübingen.

Barrett, W. S. (ed.). 1964. *Euripides: Hippolytos.* Oxford.

Barsby, J. A. (ed.). 1973. *Ovid's* Amores, *Book 1.* Oxford.

Barthes, R. 1973. *Mythologies.* Translated by A. Lavers. St Albans.

1977. *Roland Barthes by Roland Barthes.* Translated by R. Howard. New York.

Barton, C. A. 1989. 'The Scandal of the Arena', *Representations* 27: 1–36.

1993. *The Sorrows of the Ancient Romans: The Gladiator and the Monster.* Princeton, NJ.

Bartsch, S. 1997. *Ideology in Cold Blood: A Reading of Lucan's* Civil War. Cambridge, MA.

2006. *The Mirror of the Self: Sexuality, Self-Knowledge, and the Gaze in the Early Roman Empire.* Chicago, IL.

Bastiaensen, A. A. R. 1993. 'Prudentius in Recent Literary Criticism', in J. den Boeft and A. Hilhorst (eds.), *Early Christian Poetry: A Collection of Essays.* Supplements to Vigiliae Christianae 22. Leiden: 101–34.

Bate, J. 1993. *Shakespeare and Ovid.* Oxford.

Beacham, R. C. 1991. 'Violence on the Street: Playing Rough in Plautus', in J. Redmond (ed.), *Violence in Drama.* Themes in Drama 13. Cambridge: 47–68.

Belfiore, E. S. 1992. *Tragic Pleasures: Aristotle on Plot and Emotion.* Princeton, NJ.

Bellido, J. A. 1989. 'El motivo literario de la *militia amoris* en Plauto y su influencia en Ovidio', *Estudios clásicos* 31: 21–32.

Benediktson, D. T. 1985. 'Propertius' "Elegiacization" of Homer', *Maia* 37: 17–26.

Benton, C. 2002. 'Split Vision: The Politics of the Gaze in Seneca's *Troades*', in Fredrick 2002a: 31–56.

Berger, J. 1972. *Ways of Seeing.* London.

Berkowitz, L. 2000. 'Some Effects of Thoughts on Anti- and Prosocial Influences of Media Events: A Cognitive-Neoassociation Analysis', in Prince 2000a: 205–36.

Bernstein, N. W. 2009. 'Adoptees and Exposed Children in Roman Declamation: Commodification, Luxury, and the Threat of Violence', *CPh* 104: 331–53.

2012. '"Torture Her Until She Lies": Torture, Testimony, and Social Status in Roman Rhetorical Education', *G&R* 59: 165–77.

Berthet, J. F. 1980. 'Properce et Homère', in A. Thill (ed.), *L'élégie romaine: enracinement, thèmes, diffusion.* Bulletin de la Faculté des lettres de Mulhouse 10. Paris: 141–55.

Beye, C. R. 1963. 'Lucretius and Progress', *CJ* 58: 160–9.

Bloomer, W. M. 1997a. *Latinity and Literary Society at Rome*. Philadelphia, PA.
1997b. 'Schooling in Persona: Imagination and Subordination in Roman Education', *ClAnt* 16: 57–78.
2011. *The School of Rome: Latin Studies and the Origins of Liberal Education*. Berkeley, CA.
Bömer, F. (ed.). 1958. *P. Ovidius Naso: Die Fasten*, vol. II. Heidelberg.
1969–86. *P. Ovidius Naso: Metamorphosen. Kommentar*. 7 vols. Heidelberg.
Bonner, S. F. 1977. *Education in Ancient Rome: From the Elder Cato to the Younger Pliny*. London.
Booth, J. 2001. 'Moonshine: Intertextual Illumination in Propertius 1.3.31–3 and Philodemus, *Anth. Pal*. 5.123', *CQ* 51: 537–44.
2009. 'The *Amores*: Ovid Making Love', in P. E. Knox (ed.), *A Companion to Ovid*. Chichester: 61–77.
Bosworth, C. E. 1976. *The Mediaeval Islamic Underworld: The Banū Sāsān in Arabic Society and Literature*. 2 vols. Leiden.
Bourdieu, P. 2004. 'Gender and Symbolic Violence', in Scheper-Hughes and Bourgois 2004: 339–42.
Bowditch, P. L. 2001. *Horace and the Gift Economy of Patronage*. Classics and Contemporary Thought 7. Berkeley, CA.
Bowersock, G. W. 1994. *Fiction as History: Nero to Julian*. Sather Classical Lectures 58. Berkeley, CA.
Boyd, B. W. 1997. *Ovid's Literary Loves: Influence and Innovation in the* Amores. Ann Arbor, MI.
Boyle, A. J. (ed.). 1987. *Seneca's* Phaedra. Latin and Greek Texts 5. Liverpool.
1997. *Tragic Seneca: An Essay in the Theatrical Tradition*. London.
(ed.). 2014. *Seneca: Medea*. Oxford.
Braden, G. 1985. *Renaissance Tragedy and the Senecan Tradition: Anger's Privilege*. New Haven, CT.
Bradley, K. R. 1987. *Slaves and Masters in the Roman Empire: A Study in Social Control*. New York.
1994. *Slavery and Society at Rome*. Cambridge.
Brandt, P. (ed.). 1902. *P. Ovidi Nasonis De arte amatoria libri tres*. Leipzig.
Braund, D. 1993. 'Piracy under the Principate and the Ideology of Imperial Eradication', in Rich and Shipley 1993: 195–212.
Braund, S. 1992. *Roman Verse Satire*. Greece and Rome New Surveys in the Classics 23. Oxford.
(ed.). 2009. *Seneca: De clementia*. Oxford.
Braund, S. and Gill, C. (eds.). 1997. *The Passions in Roman Thought and Literature*. Cambridge.
Bremmer, J. N. and Formisano, M. (eds.). 2012. *Perpetua's Passions: Multidisciplinary Approaches to the* Passio Perpetuae et Felicitatis. Oxford.
Bright, D. F. 1971. 'The Plague and the Structure of *De rerum natura*', *Latomus* 30: 607–32.
1978. *Haec mihi fingebam: Tibullus in His World*. Cincinnati Classical Studies 3. Leiden.

Brink, C. O. 1971. *Horace on Poetry*. II. *The 'Ars poetica'*. Cambridge.

Bronfen, E. 1992. *Over Her Dead Body: Death, Femininity and the Aesthetic*. Manchester.

Brooks, P. 1984. *Reading for the Plot: Design and Intention in Narrative*. New York.

Brougham, H. 1818. *A Letter to Sir Samuel Romilly, M.P. from Henry Brougham, Esq. M.P. F.R.S. upon the Abuse of Charities*. London.

Brown, P. 1989. *The Body and Society: Men, Women and Sexual Renunciation in Early Christianity*. London.

Brown, R. D. 1987. *Lucretius on Love and Sex: A Commentary on* De rerum natura *IV, 1030–1287, with Prolegomena, Text, and Translation*. Columbia Studies in the Classical Tradition 15. Leiden.

Brown, S. 1992. 'Death as Decoration: Scenes from the Arena on Roman Domestic Mosaics', in Richlin 1992b: 180–211.

Brownmiller, S. 1975. *Against Our Will: Men, Women and Rape*. London.

Brunt, P. A. 1971. *Italian Manpower, 225 B.C.–A.D. 14*. Oxford.

  1978. '*Laus imperii*', in P. D. A. Garnsey and C. R. Whitaker (eds.), *Imperialism in the Ancient World*. Cambridge: 159–91, reprinted in C. B. Champion (ed.), *Roman Imperialism: Readings and Sources* (Malden, MA, 2004), 163–85.

Brunt, P. A. and Moore, J. M. (eds.). 1967. *Res gestae divi Augusti: The Achievements of the Divine Augustus*. Oxford.

Bryen, A. Z. 2013. *Violence in Roman Egypt: A Study in Legal Interpretation*. Philadelphia, PA.

Buchheit, V. 1971. 'Epikurs Triumph des Geistes', *Hermes* 99: 303–23, published in English as 'Epicurus' Triumph of the Mind', in Gale 2007: 104–31.

Burkowski, J. M. C. 2013. 'The Symbolism and Rhetoric of Hair in Latin Elegy.' Unpublished D.Phil. thesis, University of Oxford.

Burrus, V. 1995. 'Reading Agnes: The Rhetoric of Gender in Ambrose and Prudentius', *JECS* 3: 25–46.

  2004. *The Sex Lives of Saints: An Erotics of Ancient Hagiography*. Philadelphia, PA.

Butler, H. E. 1909. *Post-Augustan Poetry: From Seneca to Juvenal*. Oxford.

Butler, H. E. and Barber, E. A. (eds.). 1933. *The Elegies of Propertius*. Oxford.

Butler, S. 2002. *The Hand of Cicero*. London.

Cahoon, L. 1988. 'The Bed as Battlefield: Erotic Conquest and Military Metaphor in Ovid's *Amores*', *TAPhA* 118: 293–307.

Cairns, D. 2005. 'Bullish Looks and Sidelong Glances: Social Interaction and the Eyes in Ancient Greek Culture', in Cairns (ed.), *Body Language in the Greek and Roman Worlds*. Swansea: 123–55.

Cairns, F. 1972. *Generic Composition in Greek and Roman Poetry*. Edinburgh.

  1979. *Tibullus: A Hellenistic Poet at Rome*. Cambridge.

  1984. 'The Etymology of *militia* in Roman Elegy', in L. Gil and R. M. Aguilar (eds.), *Apophoreta philologica Emmanueli Fernández-Galiano a sodalibus oblata*. 2 vols. Estudios clásicos 87–8. Madrid: 211–22, reprinted in

Cairns, *Papers on Roman Elegy: 1969–2003* (Eikasmos Studi 16; Bologna, 2007), 298–307.

2006. *Sextus Propertius: The Augustan Elegist.* Cambridge.

Calder, W. M., III. 1976. 'Seneca: Tragedian of Imperial Rome', *CJ* 72: 1–11.

Calderwood, J. L. 1971. *Shakespearean Metadrama.* Minneapolis, MN.

Cameron, A. 1989. 'Virginity as Metaphor: Women and the Rhetoric of Early Christianity', in Cameron (ed.), *History as Text: The Writing of Ancient History.* London: 181–205.

1994. 'Early Christianity and the Discourse of Female Desire', in L. J. Archer, S. Fischler, and M. Wyke (eds.), *Women in Ancient Societies: An Illusion of the Night.* Basingstoke: 152–68, reprinted (with an afterword) in J. A. North and S. R. F. Price (eds.), *The Religious History of the Roman Empire: Pagans, Jews, and Christians* (Oxford, 2011), 505–30.

Cantarella, E. 1991. *I supplizi capitali in Grecia e a Roma.* Milan.

Cappello, O. Forthcoming. 'Nomination and Systematisation in Seneca's *Controversiae*', in Dinter, Guérin, and Martinho forthcoming.

Carter, C. and Weaver, C. K. 2003. *Violence and the Media.* Buckingham.

Castelli, E. A. 2004. *Martyrdom and Memory: Early Christian Culture Making.* New York.

Caston, R. R. 2012. *The Elegiac Passion: Jealousy in Roman Love Elegy.* New York.

Cave, T. 1988. *Recognitions: A Study in Poetics.* Oxford.

Caviness, M. H. 2001. *Visualizing Women in the Middle Ages: Sight, Spectacle, and Scopic Economy.* Philadelphia, PA.

Chahoud, A. 2007. 'Antiquity and Authority in Nonius Marcellus', in J. H. D. Scourfield (ed.), *Texts and Culture in Late Antiquity: Inheritance, Authority, and Change.* Swansea: 69–96.

Chaniotis, A. 2005. 'Victory's Verdict: The Violent Occupation of Territory in Hellenistic Interstate Relations', in J.-M. Bertrand (ed.), *La violence dans les mondes grec et romain: actes du colloque international (Paris, 2–4 mai 2002).* Histoire ancienne et médiévale 80. Paris: 455–64.

Charney, L. 2001. 'The Violence of a Perfect Moment', in Slocum 2001a: 47–62.

Chew, K. 2003a. 'The Chaste and the Chased: σωφροσύνη, Female Martyrs, and Novelistic Heroines', *Syllecta Classica* 14: 205–22.

2003b. 'The Representation of Violence in the Greek Novels and Martyr Accounts', in S. Panayotakis, M. Zimmerman, and W. Keulen (eds.), *The Ancient Novel and Beyond.* Mnemosyne Supplementum 241. Leiden: 129–41.

Chiesa, P. 1996. 'Un testo agiografico africano ad Aquileia: gli *Acta* di Gallonio e dei martiri di Timida Regia', *AB* 114: 241–68.

Chomsky, N. 2000. *Rogue States: The Rule of Force in World Affairs.* London.

Chong, S. 2004. 'From "Blood Auteurism" to the Violence of Pornography: Sam Peckinpah and Oliver Stone', in S. J. Schneider 2004: 249–68.

Christenson, D. M. (ed.). 2000. *Plautus: Amphitruo.* Cambridge.

Citti, F. 2000. *Studi oraziani: tematica e intertestualità.* Testi e manuali per l'insegnamento universitario del latino 65. Bologna.

Cixous, H. 1988. *Manne: aux Mandelstams aux Mandelas.* Paris.

Clark, G. 1993. *Women in Late Antiquity: Pagan and Christian Life-Styles.* Oxford.

Clark, P. 1998. 'Women, Slaves, and the Hierarchies of Domestic Violence: The Family of St Augustine', in Joshel and Murnaghan 1998: 109–29.

Classen, C. J. 1993. 'Principi e concetti morali nelle satire di Orazio', in *Atti del convegno di Venosa, 8–15 novembre 1992.* Venosa: 111–28.

Clay, D. 1983. *Lucretius and Epicurus.* Ithaca, NY.

Clover, C. J. 1992. *Men, Women, and Chain Saws: Gender in the Modern Horror Film.* London.

Cobb, L. S. 2008. *Dying to Be Men: Gender and Language in Early Christian Martyr Texts.* New York.

Coffey, M. 1976. *Roman Satire.* London.

Coffey, M. and Mayer, R. (eds.). 1990. *Seneca: Phaedra.* Cambridge.

Cohn, C. 2004. 'Sex and Death in the Rational World of Defense Intellectuals', in Scheper-Hughes and Bourgois 2004: 354–61.

Cole, S. G. 2004. *Landscapes, Gender, and Ritual Space: The Ancient Greek Experience.* Berkeley, CA.

Coleman, K. M. 1990. 'Fatal Charades: Roman Executions Staged as Mythological Enactments', *JRS* 80: 44–73.

(ed.). 2006. *M. Valerii Martialis Liber spectaculorum.* Oxford.

Coleman, R. (ed.). 1977. *Vergil: Eclogues.* Cambridge.

Commager, H. S. 1957. 'Lucretius' Interpretation of the Plague', *HSCPh* 62: 105–18, reprinted in Gale 2007: 182–98.

Connolly, J. 2007. *The State of Speech: Rhetoric and Political Thought in Ancient Rome.* Princeton, NJ.

2009. 'The Strange Art of the Sententious Declaimer', in P. R. Hardie (ed.), *Paradox and the Marvellous in Augustan Literature and Culture.* Oxford: 330–49.

Connors, C. 1998. *Petronius the Poet.* Cambridge.

Conte, G. B. 1994. *Genres and Readers: Lucretius, Love Elegy, Pliny's Encyclopedia.* Translated by G. W. Most. Baltimore, MD.

Cooper, K. 1996. *The Virgin and the Bride: Idealized Womanhood in Late Antiquity.* Cambridge, MA.

Copley, F. O. 1947. '*Servitium amoris* in the Roman Elegists', *TAPhA* 78: 285–300.

Coppieters, S., Praet, D., Bossu, A., and Taveirne, M. 2014. 'Martyrdom, Literary Experiment and Church Politics in Jerome's *Epistula prima*, to Innocentius, on the *septies percussa*', *VChr* 68: 384–408.

Corbeill, A. 1996. *Controlling Laughter: Political Humor in the Late Roman Republic.* Princeton, NJ.

Corbier, M. 2001. 'Child Exposure and Abandonment', in S. Dixon (ed.), *Childhood, Class and Kin in the Roman World.* London: 52–73.

Cornell, D. 1992. *The Philosophy of the Limit.* New York.

Corsaro, F. 1997. 'Amore e morte nel *Peristephanon liber* di Prudenzio', *SicGymn* 50: 123–34.

Courtney, E. (ed.). 1993. *The Fragmentary Latin Poets*. Oxford.
2006. 'Lucretius and Others on Animals in Warfare', *MH* 63: 152–3.
Crook, J. 1967a. '*Patria potestas*', *CQ* 17: 113–22.
1967b. 'A Study in Decoction', *Latomus* 26: 363–76.
Crowther, N. B. 1979. 'Water and Wine as Symbols of Inspiration', *Mnemosyne* 32: 1–11.
Cunningham, M. P. (ed.). 1966. *Aurelii Prudentii Clementis Carmina*. Corpus Christianorum, series Latina 126. Turnhout.
Curran, L. C. 1978. 'Rape and Rape Victims in the *Metamorphoses*', *Arethusa* 11: 213–41, reprinted in J. Peradotto and J. P. Sullivan (eds.), *Women in the Ancient World: The Arethusa Papers* (Albany, NY, 1984), 263–86.
Curtis, L. 1998. *Ireland: The Propaganda War. The British Media and the 'Battle for Hearts and Minds'*, 2nd edn. Belfast.
Dalzell, A. 1980. 'Homeric Themes in Propertius', *Hermathena* 129: 29–36.
Damon, C. (ed.). 2003. *Tacitus: Histories, Book I*. Cambridge.
Dauge, Y. A. 1981. *Le barbare: recherches sur la conception romaine de la barbarie et de la civilisation*. Collection Latomus 176. Brussels.
David, J.-M. 1997. *The Roman Conquest of Italy*. Translated by A. Nevill. Oxford.
Day, H. J. M. 2013. *Lucan and the Sublime: Power, Representation and Aesthetic Experience*. Cambridge.
Deacy, S. and Pierce, K. F. (eds.). 1997. *Rape in Antiquity*. London.
de Jong, I. J. F. 1991. *Narrative in Drama: The Art of the Euripidean Messenger-Speech*. Mnemosyne Supplementum 116. Leiden.
De Lacy, P. H. 1964. 'Distant Views: The Imagery of Lucretius 2', *CJ* 60: 49–55, reprinted in Gale 2007: 146–57.
de Lauretis, T. 1987. 'The Violence of Rhetoric: Considerations on Representation and Gender', in de Lauretis, *Technologies of Gender: Essays on Theory, Film, and Fiction*. Bloomington, IN: 31–50.
Delehaye, H. 1921. *Les passions des martyrs et les genres littéraires*. Brussels.
den Boeft, J. and Bremmer, J. 1991. 'Notiunculae martyrologicae IV', *VChr* 45: 105–22.
Dench, E. 2005. *Romulus' Asylum: Roman Identities from the Age of Alexander to the Age of Hadrian*. Oxford.
Derrida, J. 1982. *Margins of Philosophy*. Translated by A. Bass. Brighton.
Desmond, M. 2006. *Ovid's Art and the Wife of Bath: The Ethics of Erotic Violence*. Ithaca, NY.
de Souza, P. 1999. *Piracy in the Graeco-Roman World*. Cambridge.
de Ste. Croix, G. E. M. 1981. *The Class Struggle in the Ancient Greek World: From the Archaic Age to the Arab Conquests*. Ithaca, NY.
de Wijze, S. 2008. 'Between Hero and Villain: Jack Bauer and the Problem of "Dirty Hands"', in Weed, Davis, and Weed 2008: 17–30.
Diggle, J. (ed.). 1994. *Euripidis Fabulae*, vol. III. Oxford.
Diken, B. and Laustsen, C. B. 2007. *Sociology through the Projector*. London.
Dimundo, R. 2003. *Ovidio: lezioni d'amore. Saggio di commento al I libro dell' Ars amatoria*. Scrinia 22. Bari.

Dinter, M., Guérin, C., and Martinho, M. (eds.). Forthcoming. *Seneca the Elder: Reading Roman Declamation*. Oxford.

Dixon, S. 1992. *The Roman Family*. Baltimore, MD.

Dodds, E. R. (ed.). 1960. *Euripides: Bacchae*, 2nd edn. Oxford.

Domínguez, M. J. and Martos Fernández, J. 2011. 'Violación', in Moreno Soldevila 2011: 453–8.

Dossey, L. 2008. 'Wife Beating and Manliness in Late Antiquity', *P&P* 199: 3–40.

Dowden, K. 1982. 'Apuleius and the Art of Narration', *CQ* 32: 419–35.

   1993. 'The Unity of Apuleius' Eighth Book and the Danger of Beasts', in H. Hofmann (ed.), *Groningen Colloquia on the Novel*, vol. V. Groningen: 91–109.

Drake, H. A. (ed.). 2006. *Violence in Late Antiquity: Perceptions and Practices*. Aldershot.

Dreyfus, H. L. and Rabinow, P. 1982. *Michel Foucault: Beyond Structuralism and Hermeneutics*. Chicago, IL.

Drinkwater, M. O. 2013. '*Militia amoris*: Fighting in Love's Army', in Thorsen 2013: 194–206.

Dryden, J. (tr.). 1709. *Ovid's Art of Love: Book I*, in J. Dryden *et al.*, *Ovid's Art of Love, in Three Books, together with his* Remedy of Love. *Translated into English Verse by Several Eminent Hands*. London.

duBois, P. 1991. *Torture and Truth*. New York.

Duff, J. D. (ed., tr.). 1928. *Lucan: The Civil War*. Loeb Classical Library 220. Cambridge, MA.

Duff, J. W. 1936. *Roman Satire: Its Outlook on Social Life*. Sather Classical Lectures 12. Berkeley, CA.

Dugan, J. 2001. 'How to Make (and Break) a Cicero: *Epideixis*, Textuality, and Self-Fashioning in the *Pro Archia* and *In Pisonem*', *ClAnt* 20: 23–77.

Dunkle, J. R. 1967. 'The Greek Tyrant and Roman Political Invective of the Late Republic', *TAPhA* 98: 151–71.

DuQuesnay, I. M. Le M. 1984. 'Horace and Maecenas: The Propaganda Value of *Sermones* 1', in T. Woodman and D. West (eds.), *Poetry and Politics in the Age of Augustus*. Cambridge: 19–58.

Dworkin, A. and MacKinnon, C. A. 1988. *Pornography and Civil Rights: A New Day for Women's Equality*. Minneapolis, MN.

Dyck, A. R. 1996. *A Commentary on Cicero*, De officiis. Ann Arbor, MI.

Eagleton, T. 2003. *Sweet Violence: The Idea of the Tragic*. Oxford.

   2005. *Holy Terror*. Oxford.

Ebel, H. 1970. 'Apuleius and the Present Time', *Arethusa* 3: 155–76.

Edmondson, J. C. 1996. 'Dynamic Arenas: Gladiatorial Presentations in the City of Rome and the Construction of Roman Society during the Early Empire', in W. J. Slater (ed.), *Roman Theater and Society: E. Togo Salmon Papers I*. Ann Arbor, MI: 69–112.

Edwards, C. 1993. *The Politics of Immorality in Ancient Rome*. Cambridge.

1997. 'Unspeakable Professions: Public Performance and Prostitution in Ancient Rome', in Hallett and Skinner 1997: 66–95.

2007. *Death in Ancient Rome*. New Haven, CT.

Edwards, M. W. 1987. *Homer: Poet of the* Iliad. Baltimore, MD.

Eidinow, J. S. C. 1993. 'A Note on Ovid's *Ars amatoria* 1.117–19', *AJPh* 114: 413–17.

Eisenhut, W. and Mayer-Maly, T. 1961. '*Vis*', *RE* IXA.1.310–47.

Eldred, K. O. 2002. 'This Ship of Fools: Epic Vision in Lucan's Vulteius Episode', in Fredrick 2002a: 57–85.

Eliot, T. S. 1951. *Selected Essays*. London.

Enterline, L. 2000. *The Rhetoric of the Body from Ovid to Shakespeare*. Cambridge Studies in Renaissance Literature and Culture 35. Cambridge.

Erdkamp, P. (ed.). 2007. *A Companion to the Roman Army*. Malden, MA.

Estévez Sola, J. A. 2011. 'Milicia de amor', in Moreno Soldevila 2011: 275–86.

Evans, S. 1971. 'Odyssean Echoes in Propertius IV.8', *G&R* 18: 51–3.

Evans Grubbs, J. 1995. *Law and Family in Late Antiquity: The Emperor Constantine's Marriage Legislation*. Oxford.

Eyl, J. 2012. 'Why Thekla Does Not See Paul: Visual Perception and the Displacement of *erōs* in the *Acts of Paul and Thekla*', in Futre Pinheiro, Perkins, and Pervo 2012: 3–19.

Fagan, G. G. 2011a. *The Lure of the Arena: Social Psychology and the Crowd at the Roman Games*. Cambridge.

2011b. 'Violence in Roman Social Relations', in M. Peachin (ed.), *The Oxford Handbook of Social Relations in the Roman World*. New York: 467–95.

Fairweather, J. 1981. *Seneca the Elder*. Cambridge.

Fantham, E. 1972. *Comparative Studies in Republican Latin Imagery*. Phoenix Supplementary Volume 10. Toronto.

(ed.). 1982. *Seneca's Troades*. Princeton, NJ.

1986. 'Ovid, Germanicus, and the Composition of the *Fasti*', in F. Cairns (ed.), *Papers of the Liverpool Latin Seminar: Fifth Volume, 1985*. ARCA Classical and Medieval Texts, Papers and Monographs 19. Liverpool: 243–81.

2004. *Ovid's* Metamorphoses. Oxford.

Farrar, L. 1998. *Ancient Roman Gardens*. Stroud.

Farrell, J. 1999. 'The Ovidian *corpus*: Poetic Body and Poetic Text', in Hardie, Barchiesi, and Hinds 1999: 127–41.

2007. 'Horace's Body, Horace's Books', in S. J. Heyworth (ed.), *Classical Constructions: Papers in Memory of Don Fowler, Classicist and Epicurean*. Oxford: 174–93.

Fear, T. 2000. 'The Poet as Pimp: Elegiac Seduction in the Time of Augustus', *Arethusa* 23: 217–40.

Fedeli, P. (ed.). 1980. *Sesto Properzio: Il primo libro delle elegie*. Accademia toscana di scienze e lettere 'La Colombaria', Studi 53. Florence.

Feeney, D. 1978. 'Wild Beasts in the *De rerum natura*', *Prudentia* 10: 15–22.

1991. *The Gods in Epic: Poets and Critics of the Classical Tradition*. Oxford.

1992. '*Si licet et fas est*: Ovid's *Fasti* and the Problem of Free Speech under the Principate', in A. Powell (ed.), *Roman Poetry and Propaganda in the Age of Augustus*. London: 1–25.

1999. 'Epic Violence, Epic Order: Killing, Catalogues, and the Role of the Reader in *Aeneid* 10', in C. Perkell (ed.), *Reading Vergil: An Interpretive Guide*. Oklahoma Series in Classical Culture 23. Norman, OK: 178–94.

Feldherr, A. 1997. 'Metamorphosis and Sacrifice in Ovid's Theban Narrative', *MD* 38: 25–55.

2010. *Playing Gods: Ovid's* Metamorphoses *and the Politics of Fiction*. Princeton, NJ.

Feldherr, A. and James, P. 2004. 'Making the Most of Marsyas', *Arethusa* 37: 75–103.

Felson, R. B. 2000. 'Mass Media Effects on Violent Behavior', in Prince 2000a: 237–66.

Ferrari, G. R. F. 1989. 'Plato and Poetry', in G. A. Kennedy (ed.), *The Cambridge History of Literary Criticism*. I. *Classical Criticism*. Cambridge: 92–148.

Finglass, P. J. (ed.). 2011. *Sophocles: Ajax*. Cambridge Classical Texts and Commentaries 48. Cambridge.

Fisher, C. D. (ed.). 1906. *Cornelii Taciti Annalium ab excessu divi Augusti libri*. Oxford.

(ed.). 1911. *Cornelii Taciti Historiarum libri*. Oxford.

Fiske, G. C. 1920. *Lucilius and Horace: A Study in the Classical Theory of Imitation*. Madison, WI.

Fitzgerald, W. 1988. 'Power and Impotence in Horace's *Epodes*', *Ramus* 17: 176–91, reprinted in M. Lowrie (ed.), *Horace: Odes and Epodes* (Oxford, 2009), 141–59.

2000. *Slavery and the Roman Literary Imagination*. Cambridge.

Forbes Irving, P. M. C. 1990. *Metamorphosis in Greek Myths*. Oxford.

Ford, A. 2002. *The Origins of Criticism: Literary Culture and Poetic Theory in Classical Greece*. Princeton, NJ.

Fordyce, C. J. 1938. 'The Whole Truth', *CR* 52: 59.

1952. '*Mittatur senex in scholas*', *PCA* 49: 28.

Foucault, M. 1966. *Les mots et les choses*. Paris.

1975. *Surveiller et punir*. Paris.

1976. *Histoire de la sexualité*. I. *La volonté de savoir*. Paris.

1984a. *Histoire de la sexualité*. II. *L'usage des plaisirs*. Paris.

1984b. *Histoire de la sexualité*. III. *Le souci de soi*. Paris.

2008. *Le gouvernement de soi et des autres: cours au Collège de France 1982–1983*. Edited by F. Gros. Paris.

Fowler, D. 1987. 'Vergil on Killing Virgins', in Michael Whitby, P. Hardie, and Mary Whitby (eds.), *Homo viator: Classical Essays for John Bramble*. Bristol: 185–98.

2002. *Lucretius on Atomic Motion: A Commentary on* De rerum natura *Book Two, Lines 1–332*. Oxford.

Fowler, P. G. 1997. 'Lucretian Conclusions', in D. H. Roberts, F. M. Dunn, and D. Fowler (eds.), *Classical Closure: Reading the End in Greek and Latin Literature*. Princeton, NJ: 112–38, reprinted in Gale 2007: 199–233.

Fraenkel, E. 1957. *Horace*. Oxford.

  1960. *Elementi plautini in Plauto*. Translated by F. Munari. Pensiero storico 41. Florence.

Fränkel, H. F. 1945. *Ovid: A Poet between Two Worlds*. Sather Classical Lectures 18. Berkeley, CA.

Frankfurter, D. 2009. 'Martyrology and the Prurient Gaze', *JECS* 17: 215–45.

Fredrick, D. 1997. 'Reading Broken Skin: Violence in Roman Elegy', in Hallett and Skinner 1997: 172–93.

  (ed.). 2002a. *The Roman Gaze: Vision, Power, and the Body*. Baltimore, MD.

  2002b. 'Introduction: Invisible Rome', in Fredrick 2002a: 1–30.

  2012. 'The Gaze and the Elegiac Imaginary', in Gold 2012: 426–39.

French, K. 1996. *Screen Violence*. London.

Freudenburg, K. 1993. *The Walking Muse: Horace on the Theory of Satire*. Princeton, NJ.

  2001. *Satires of Rome: Threatening Poses from Lucilius to Juvenal*. Cambridge.

  (ed.). 2005a. *The Cambridge Companion to Roman Satire*. Cambridge.

  2005b. 'Introduction: Roman Satire', in Freudenburg 2005a: 1–30.

Friedrich, W.-H. 2003. *Wounding and Death in the* Iliad*: Homeric Techniques of Description*. Translated by G. Wright and P. Jones. Appendix by K. B. Saunders. London.

Fuhrmann, C. J. 2012. *Policing the Roman Empire: Soldiers, Administration, and Public Order*. New York.

Fulkerson, L. 2013. '*Servitium amoris*: The Interplay of Dominance, Gender and Poetry', in Thorsen 2013: 180–93.

Furneaux, H. 1896–1907. *The* Annals *of Tacitus*, 2nd edn. 2 vols. Oxford.

Futrell, A. 1997. *Blood in the Arena: The Spectacle of Roman Power*. Austin, TX.

Futre Pinheiro, M. P., Perkins, J., and Pervo, R. (eds.). 2012. *The Ancient Novel and Early Christian and Jewish Narrative: Fictional Intersections*. Ancient Narrative Supplementum 16. Groningen.

Fyfe, W. H. and Levene, D. S. 1997. *Tacitus: The Histories*. Translated by W. H. Fyfe. Revised and edited by D. S. Levene. Oxford.

Gahan, J. J. 1987. '*Imitatio* and *aemulatio* in Seneca's *Phaedra*', *Latomus* 46: 380–7.

Gaisser, J. H. 1983. '*Amor, rura* and *militia* in Three Elegies of Tibullus: 1.1, 1.5, and 1.10', *Latomus* 42: 58–72.

Gale, M. R. 1994. *Myth and Poetry in Lucretius*. Cambridge.

  1997. 'Propertius 2.7: *Militia amoris* and the Ironies of Elegy', *JRS* 87: 77–91.

  2000. *Virgil on the Nature of Things: The* Georgics*, Lucretius and the Didactic Tradition*. Cambridge.

  (ed.). 2007. *Lucretius*. Oxford.

  (ed.). 2009. *Lucretius: De rerum natura V*. Oxford.

Galinsky, K. 1975. *Ovid's* Metamorphoses: *An Introduction to the Basic Aspects.* Oxford.

1988. 'The Anger of Aeneas', *AJPh* 109: 321–48.

1994. 'How to Be Philosophical about the End of the *Aeneid*', *ICS* 19: 191–201.

1996. *Augustan Culture: An Interpretive Introduction.* Princeton, NJ.

Gamel, M.-K. 1989. '*Non sine caede*: Abortion Politics and Poetics in Ovid's *Amores*', *Helios* 16: 183–206.

García-Moreno, C., Jansen, H. A. F. M., Ellsberg, M., Heise, L., and Watts, C. 2005. *WHO Multi-Country Study on Women's Health and Domestic Violence against Women: Initial Results on Prevalence, Health Outcomes and Women's Responses.* Geneva.

Gardner, J. F. 1986. *Women in Roman Law and Society.* London.

1993. *Being a Roman Citizen.* London.

Garnsey, P. 1970. *Social Status and Legal Privilege in the Roman Empire.* Oxford.

Garzya, A. 1967. *Note al* Rudens *di Plauto.* Quaderni di 'Le parole e le idee' 7. Naples.

Gershenson, D. E. 1992. 'Καὶ σὺ τέκνον: Caesar's Last Words', *Shakespeare Quarterly* 43: 218–19.

Gervais, K. 2013. 'Viewing Violence in Statius' *Thebaid* and the Films of Quentin Tarantino', in H. Lovatt and C. Vout (eds.), *Epic Visions: Visuality in Greek and Latin Epic and Its Reception.* Cambridge: 139–67.

Giardina, G. (ed.). 2010. *Properzio: Elegie.* Testi e commenti 25. Pisa.

Gibson, A. 1999. *Postmodernity, Ethics and the Novel: From Leavis to Levinas.* London.

Gibson, B. J. 2008. 'Battle Narrative in Statius, *Thebaid*', in J. J. L. Smolenaars, H.-J. van Dam, and R. R. Nauta (eds.), *The Poetry of Statius.* Mnemosyne Supplementum 306. Leiden: 85–109.

2014. 'The Representation of Greek Diplomacy in Tacitus', in J. M. Madsen and R. D. Rees (eds.), *Roman Rule in Greek and Latin Writing.* Impact of Empire 18. Leiden: 124–43.

Gibson, R. K. (ed.). 2003. *Ovid:* Ars amatoria, *Book 3.* Cambridge Classical Texts and Commentaries 40. Cambridge.

2007. *Excess and Restraint: Propertius, Horace, and Ovid's* Ars amatoria. BICS Supplement 89. London.

Gilliver, K. 2007. 'The Augustan Reform and the Structure of the Imperial Army', in Erdkamp 2007: 183–200.

Girard, R. 1977. *Violence and the Sacred.* Translated by P. Gregory. Baltimore, MD.

1996. 'Mimesis and Violence', in J. G. Williams (ed.), *The Girard Reader.* New York: 9–19.

Giroux, H. A. 2006. *America on the Edge: Henry Giroux on Politics, Culture, and Education.* New York.

Glancy, J. A. 2010. *Corporal Knowledge: Early Christian Bodies.* Oxford.

Gold, B. K. (ed.). 2012. *A Companion to Roman Love Elegy.* Malden, MA.

Goldberg, S. M. 1996. 'The Fall and Rise of Roman Tragedy', *TAPhA* 126: 265–86.

2000. 'Going for Baroque: Seneca and the English', in G. W. M. Harrison 2000: 209–31.

2005. *Constructing Literature in the Roman Republic*. Cambridge.

Goldstein, J. (ed.). 1998a. *Why We Watch: The Attractions of Violent Entertainment*. New York.

1998b. 'Why We Watch', in Goldstein 1998a: 212–26.

Gomme A. W. and Sandbach, F. H. (eds.). 1973. *Menander: A Commentary*. Oxford.

Goodyear, F. R. D. (ed.). 1972. *The* Annals *of Tacitus, Books 1–6. Volume I:* Annals *1.1–54*. Cambridge Classical Texts and Commentaries 15. Cambridge.

(ed.). 1981. *The* Annals *of Tacitus, Books 1–6. Volume II:* Annals *1.55–81 and* Annals *2*. Cambridge Classical Texts and Commentaries 23. Cambridge.

Gordon, P. 2002. 'Some Unseen Monster: Rereading Lucretius on Sex', in Fredrick 2002a: 86–109.

Gowers, E. 1993. *The Loaded Table: Representations of Food in Roman Satire*. Oxford.

Gowing, A. M. 2005. *Empire and Memory: The Representation of the Roman Republic in Imperial Culture*. Cambridge.

Gratwick, A. S. 1982. 'Drama', in Kenney and Clausen 1982: 77–134.

Green, P. (tr.). 1982. *Ovid: The Erotic Poems*. Harmondsworth.

Greene, E. 1998. *The Erotics of Domination: Male Desire and the Mistress in Latin Love Poetry*. Baltimore, MD.

1999. 'Travesties of Love: Violence and Voyeurism in Ovid *Amores* 1.7', *CW* 92: 409–18.

Griffin, J. 1977. 'Propertius and Antony', *JRS* 67: 87–105, reprinted in Griffin, *Latin Poets and Roman Life* (London, 1985), 32–47.

1980. *Homer on Life and Death*. Oxford.

Griffin, M. T. 1972. 'The Elder Seneca and Spain', *JRS* 62: 1–19.

Griffith, J. G. 1970. 'The Ending of Juvenal's First Satire and Lucilius, Book XXX', *Hermes* 98: 56–72.

Grig, L. 2004. *Making Martyrs in Late Antiquity*. London.

2005. 'The Paradoxical Body of Saint Agnes', in A. Hopkins and M. Wyke (eds.), *Roman Bodies: Antiquity to the Eighteenth Century*. London: 111–22.

Gros, F. 2003. 'Introduction', in F. Gros and C. Lévy (eds.), *Foucault et la philosophie antique*. Paris: 7–13.

Grünewald, T. 2004. *Bandits in the Roman Empire: Myth and Reality*. Translated by J. Drinkwater. London.

Grützmacher, G. 1901–8. *Hieronymus: eine biographische Studie zur alten Kirchengeschichte*. 3 vols. Studien zur Geschichte der Theologie und der Kirche 6.3, 10.1–2. Leipzig/Berlin.

Gunderson, E. 1996. 'The Ideology of the Arena', *ClAnt* 15: 113–51.

1997. 'Catullus, Pliny and Love-Letters', *TAPhA* 127: 201–29.

2003. *Declamation, Paternity, and Roman Identity: Authority and the Rhetorical Self.* Cambridge.

2005. 'The Libidinal Rhetoric of Satire', in Freudenburg 2005a: 224–40.

Gurval, R. A. 1995. *Actium and Augustus: The Politics and Emotions of Civil War.* Ann Arbor, MI.

Habinek, T. 1997. 'The Invention of Sexuality in the World-City of Rome', in Habinek and Schiesaro 1997: 23–43.

1998. *The Politics of Latin Literature: Writing, Identity, and Empire in Ancient Rome.* Princeton, NJ.

2005. *The World of Roman Song: From Ritualized Speech to Social Order.* Baltimore, MD.

Habinek, T. and Schiesaro, A. (eds.). 1997. *The Roman Cultural Revolution.* Cambridge.

Hadot, P. 1995. *Qu'est-ce que la philosophie antique?* Collection Folio/essais 280. Paris.

Hallett, J. P. 1973. 'The Role of Women in Roman Elegy: Counter-Cultural Feminism', *Arethusa* 6: 103–24.

1977. '*Perusinae glandes* and the Changing Image of Augustus', *AJAH* 2: 151–71.

2002. 'The Eleven Elegies of the Augustan Poet Sulpicia', in L. J. Churchill, P. R. Brown, and J. E. Jeffrey (eds.), *Women Writing Latin: From Roman Antiquity to Early Modern Europe. I. Women Writing Latin in Roman Antiquity, Late Antiquity, and the Early Christian Era.* New York: 45–65.

2009. 'Sulpicia and Her Resistant Intertextuality', in D. van Mal-Maeder, A. Burnier, and L. Núñez (eds.), *Jeux de voix: enonciation, intertextualité et intentionnalité dans la littérature antique.* Echo 8. Berne: 141–55.

Hallett, J. P. and Skinner, M. B. (eds.). 1997. *Roman Sexualities.* Princeton, NJ.

Hands, A. R. 1968. *Charities and Social Aid in Greece and Rome.* London.

Hanson, J. A. (ed., tr.). 1989. *Apuleius: Metamorphoses.* 2 vols. Loeb Classical Library 44, 453. Cambridge, MA.

Hardie, P. R. 1986. *Virgil's Aeneid: Cosmos and Imperium.* Oxford.

1990. 'Ovid's Theban History: The First "Anti-*Aeneid*"?', *CQ* 40: 224–35.

1993. *The Epic Successors of Virgil: A Study in the Dynamics of a Tradition.* Cambridge.

2002. *Ovid's Poetics of Illusion.* Cambridge.

Hardie, P. R., Barchiesi, A., and Hinds, S. (eds.). 1999. *Ovidian Transformations: Essays on the* Metamorphoses *and Its Reception.* Cambridge.

Harries, J. 1999. 'Constructing the Judge: Judicial Accountability and the Culture of Criticism in Late Antiquity', in R. Miles (ed.), *Constructing Identities in Late Antiquity.* London: 214–33.

2007. *Law and Crime in the Roman World.* Cambridge.

Harris, W. V. 1979. *War and Imperialism in Republican Rome, 327–70 B.C.* Oxford.

1994. 'Child-Exposure in the Roman Empire', *JRS* 84: 1–22.

2001. *Restraining Rage: The Ideology of Anger Control in Classical Antiquity.* Cambridge, MA.

Harrison, G. W. M. (ed.). 2000. *Seneca in Performance.* London.

Harrison, S. J. (ed.). 1991. *Vergil: Aeneid 10.* Oxford.

(ed.). 1995. *Homage to Horace: A Bimillenary Celebration.* Oxford.

Hattaway, M. 1982. *Elizabethan Popular Theatre: Plays in Performance.* London.

Hauthal, F. (ed.). 1864–6. *Acronis et Porphyrionis Commentarii in Q. Horatium Flaccum.* 2 vols. Berlin.

Heffernan, T. J. 2012. *The Passion of Perpetua and Felicity.* New York.

Helm, R. (ed.). 1931. *Apuleius: Metamorphoseon libri XI.* Leipzig.

Hemker, J. 1985. 'Rape and the Foundation of Rome', *Helios* 12: 41–7.

Henderson, J. G. W. 1987. 'Lucan: The Word at War', *Ramus* 16: 122–64.

1998. *Fighting for Rome: Poets and Caesars, History and Civil War.* Cambridge.

1999a. *Writing down Rome: Satire, Comedy, and Other Offences in Latin Poetry.* Oxford.

1999b. 'Suck It and See: Horace, *Epode* 8', in Henderson 1999a: 93–113.

1999c. 'Be Alert (Your Country Needs Lerts): Horace, *Satires* 1.9', in Henderson 1999a: 202–27.

2002. *Pliny's Statue: The Letters, Self-Portraiture and Classical Art.* Exeter.

2003. *Morals and Villas in Seneca's Letters: Places to Dwell.* Cambridge.

2004. *Hortus: The Roman Book of Gardening.* London.

2010. Review of Migliario 2007, *BMCRev* 2010.01.20.

2011. 'The Nature of Man: Pliny, *Historia naturalis* as Cosmogram', *MD* 66: 139–71.

Henderson Administration. 1994–6. *The Henderson Top 2000 Charities.* Continues *The Henderson Top 1000 Charities.* London.

Hengel, M. 1977. *Crucifixion in the Ancient World and the Folly of the Message of the Cross.* Translated by J. Bowden. Philadelphia, PA.

Henry, M. M. 1992. 'The Edible Woman: Athenaeus's Concept of the Pornographic', in Richlin 1992b: 250–68.

Herbert, Z. 1968. *Selected Poems.* Translated by C. Miłosz and P. D. Scott. Harmondsworth.

Herbert-Brown, G. 1994. *Ovid and the Fasti: An Historical Study.* Oxford.

Herington, C. J. 1966. 'Senecan Tragedy', *Arion* 5: 422–71.

1982. 'The Younger Seneca', in Kenney and Clausen 1982: 511–32.

Hershkowitz, D. 1998. *The Madness of Epic: Reading Insanity from Homer to Statius.* Oxford.

Herz, P. 2007. 'Finances and Costs of the Roman Army', in Erdkamp 2007: 306–22.

Heubner, H. 1963–82. *P. Cornelius Tacitus: Die Historien. Kommentar.* 5 vols. Heidelberg.

Heuzé, P. 1985. *L'image du corps dans l'oeuvre de Virgile.* Collection de l'École française de Rome 86. Rome.

Heyman, R. E. and Neidig, P. H. 1999. 'A Comparison of Spousal Aggression Prevalence Rates in U.S. Army and Civilian Representative Samples', *Journal of Consulting and Clinical Psychology* 67: 239–42.

Heyworth, S. J. 1992. 'Ars moratoria (Ovid, *A. A.* 1.681–704)', *LCM* 17: 59–61.
(ed.). 2007a. *Sexti Properti Elegi.* Oxford.
2007b. *Cynthia: A Companion to the Text of Propertius.* Oxford.
Hilberg, I. (ed.). 1996. *Sancti Eusebii Hieronymi Epistulae,* 2nd edn. 4 vols.
Corpus scriptorum ecclesiasticorum Latinorum 54–56/2. Vienna.
Hinds, S. 1985. *The Metamorphosis of Persephone: Ovid and the Self-Conscious Muse.* Cambridge.
1988. 'Generalising about Ovid', in A. J. Boyle (ed.), *The Imperial Muse: Ramus Essays on Roman Literature of the Empire.* Berwick, Victoria: 4–31.
1998. *Allusion and Intertext: Dynamics of Appropriation in Roman Poetry.* Cambridge.
2002. 'Landscape with Figures: Aesthetics of Place in the *Metamorphoses* and Its Tradition', in P. R. Hardie (ed.), *The Cambridge Companion to Ovid.* Cambridge: 122–49.
2005. 'Dislocations of Roman Time', in J. P. Schwindt (ed.), *La représentation du temps dans la poésie augustéenne.* Bibliothek der klassischen Altertumswissenschaften, neue Folge, 2. Reihe, 116. Heidelberg: 203–30.
Hite, S. 1981. *The Hite Report on Male Sexuality.* London.
Hollis, A. S. (ed.). 1977. *Ovid:* Ars amatoria, *Book I.* Oxford.
(ed.). 2007. *Fragments of Roman Poetry, c. 60 BC–AD 20.* Oxford.
Holzberg, N. 1997. *Ovid: Dichter und Werk.* Munich.
2002. *Ovid: The Poet and His Work.* Translated by G. M. Goshgarian. Ithaca, NY.
Hopkins, K. 1978. *Conquerors and Slaves.* Sociological Studies in Roman History 1. Cambridge.
1983. *Death and Renewal.* Sociological Studies in Roman History 2. Cambridge.
2002. 'Rome, Taxes, Rents and Trade', in W. Scheidel and S. von Reden (eds.), *The Ancient Economy.* Edinburgh: 190–230.
Horsfall, N. 1979. 'Epic and Burlesque in Ovid, *Met.* viii. 260ff.', *CJ* 74: 319–32.
Hubbard, M. 1974. *Propertius.* London.
Huber-Rebenich, G. 1999. 'Hagiographic Fiction as Entertainment', in H. Hofmann (ed.), *Latin Fiction: The Latin Novel in Context.* London: 187–212.
Hugh, G. R. 2004. 'The Professional Soldier in Menander and Plautus', *American Philological Association 135th Annual Meeting Abstracts* 320.
Hulse, S. C. 1979. 'Wresting the Alphabet: Oratory and Action in "Titus Andronicus"', *Criticism* 21: 106–18.
Hutchinson, G. O. 2001. 'The Date of De rerum natura', *CQ* 51: 150–62.
Jakobi, R. 1988. *Der Einfluss Ovids auf den Tragiker Seneca.* Untersuchungen zur antiken Literatur und Geschichte 28. Berlin.
Jal, P. 1963. *La guerre civile à Rome: étude littéraire et morale.* Publications de la Faculté des lettres et sciences humaines de Paris, série 'Recherches', 6. Paris.
James, S. L. 1997. 'Slave-Rape and Female Silence in Ovid's Love Poetry', *Helios* 24: 60–76.

2003a. *Learned Girls and Male Persuasion: Gender and Reading in Roman Love Elegy.* Berkeley, CA.

2003b. 'Her Turn to Cry: The Politics of Weeping in Roman Love Elegy', *TAPhA* 133: 99–122.

Janan, M. 2001. *The Politics of Desire: Propertius IV.* Berkeley, CA.

Jantzen, G. M. 2004. *Death and the Displacement of Beauty.* I. *Foundations of Violence.* London.

Jenisson, G. 1937. *Animals for Show and Pleasure in Ancient Rome.* Publications of the University of Manchester 258. Manchester.

Johnson, P. 1982. *Romano-British Mosaics.* Aylesbury.

Johnson, P. J. 2008. *Ovid before Exile: Art and Punishment in the* Metamorphoses. Madison, WI.

Johnson, W. R. 1987. *Momentary Monsters: Lucan and his Heroes.* Cornell Studies in Classical Philology 47. Ithaca, NY.

1996. 'The Rapes of Callisto', *CJ* 92: 9–24.

2000. *Lucretius and the Modern World.* London.

Jones, C. 1993. 'Women, Death, and the Law during the Christian Persecutions', in D. Wood (ed.), *Martyrs and Martyrologies: Papers Read at the 1992 Summer Meeting and the 1993 Winter Meeting of the Ecclesiastical History Society.* Studies in Church History 30. Oxford: 23–34.

Joplin, P. 1984. 'The Voice of the Shuttle Is Ours', *Stanford Literary Review* 1: 25–53.

Joshel, S. R. 1992. *Work, Identity, and Legal Status at Rome: A Study of the Occupational Inscriptions.* Oklahoma Series in Classical Culture 11. Norman, OK.

Joshel, S. R. and Murnaghan, S. (eds.). 1998. *Women and Slaves in Greco-Roman Culture: Differential Equations.* London.

Kajanto, I. 1981. 'Fortuna', *ANRW* II.17.1: 502–58.

Kant, I. 1913. *Kants gesammelte Schriften,* vol. V, 2nd edn. Berlin.

1987. *Critique of Judgment.* Translated by W. S. Pluhar. Indianapolis, IN.

Kany-Turpin, J. 1997. 'Cosmos ouvert et épidémies mortelles dans le *De rerum natura*', in K. A. Algra, M. H. Koenen, and P. H. Schrijvers (eds.), *Lucretius and His Intellectual Background.* Verhandelingen der Koninklijke Nederlandse Akademie van Wetenschappen, Afd. Letterkunde 172. Amsterdam: 179–85.

Kapparis, K. 2002. *Abortion in the Ancient World.* London.

Kappeler, S. 1986. *The Pornography of Representation.* Cambridge.

Kaster, R. A. 1998. 'Becoming "CICERO"', in P. E. Knox and C. Foss (eds.), *Style and Tradition: Studies in Honor of Wendell Clausen.* Beiträge zur Altertumskunde 92. Stuttgart: 248–63.

2005. *Emotion, Restraint, and Community in Ancient Rome.* New York.

Keane, C. 2006. *Figuring Genre in Roman Satire.* American Classical Studies 50. New York.

Keitel, E. 1984. 'Principate and Civil War in the *Annals* of Tacitus', *AJPh* 105: 306–25.

Keith, A. 1992. 'Amores 1.1: Propertius and the Ovidian Programme', in C. Deroux (ed.), *Studies in Latin Literature and Roman History VI*. Collection Latomus 217. Brussels: 327–44.

1994. '*Corpus eroticum*: Elegiac Poetics and Elegiac *puellae* in Ovid's *Amores*', *CW* 88: 27–40.

1997. '*Tandem venit amor*: A Roman Woman Speaks of Love', in Hallett and Skinner 1997: 285–310.

1999. 'Epic Masculinity in Ovid's *Metamorphoses*', in Hardie, Barchiesi, and Hinds 1999: 214–39.

2000. *Engendering Rome: Women in Latin Epic*. Cambridge.

2008. *Propertius: Poet of Love and Leisure*. London.

Kelly, A. 2012. 'The Cretan Slinger at War – a Weighty Exchange', *ABSA* 107: 273–311.

Kelly, J. N. D. 1975. *Jerome: His Life, Writings, and Controversies*. London.

Kennedy, D. F. 1993. *The Arts of Love: Five Studies in the Discourse of Roman Love Elegy*. Cambridge.

2002. *Rethinking Reality: Lucretius and the Textualization of Nature*. Ann Arbor, MI.

2008. 'Elegy and the Erotics of Narratology', in Liveley and Salzman-Mitchell 2008: 19–33.

2012. 'Love's Tropes and Figures', in Gold 2012: 189–203.

Kenney, E. J. (ed.). 1961. *P. Ovidi Nasonis Amores, Medicamina faciei femineae, Ars amatoria, Remedia amoris*. Oxford.

1972. 'The Historical Imagination of Lucretius', *G&R* 19: 12–24.

Kenney, E. J. and Clausen, W. V. (eds.). 1982. *The Cambridge History of Classical Literature*. II. *Latin Literature*. Cambridge.

Keppie, L. J. F. 1983. *Colonisation and Veteran Settlement in Italy, 47–14 B.C.* London.

1984. *The Making of the Roman Army: From Republic to Empire*. London.

Kermode, M. 2004. Review of *The Passion of the Christ, Sight & Sound* 14.4: 63.

Khan, H. A. 1966. '*Ovidius furens*: A Revaluation of *Amores* 1, 7', *Latomus* 25: 880–94.

Kiessling, A. and Heinze, R. (eds.). 1921. *Q. Horatius Flaccus: Satiren*, 5th edn. Berlin.

Kinder, M. 2001. 'Violence American Style: The Narrative Orchestration of Violent Attractions', in Slocum 2001a: 63–100.

Kirichenko, A. 2010. *A Comedy of Storytelling: Theatricality and Narrative in Apuleius' Golden Ass*. Bibliothek der klassischen Altertumswissenschaften, neue Folge, 2. Reihe, 127. Heidelberg.

Knoche, U. 1975. *Roman Satire*. Translated by E. S. Ramage. Bloomington, IN.

Koestermann, E. (ed.). 1963–8. *Cornelius Tacitus: Annalen*. 4 vols. Heidelberg.

Konstan, D. 1983. *Roman Comedy*. Ithaca, NY.

1994. 'Foreword: To the Reader', in Schiesaro, Mitsis, and Clay 1994: 11–22.

1995. *Greek Comedy and Ideology*. New York.

1997. *Friendship in the Classical World*. Cambridge.

2001. *Pity Transformed.* London.

2008. *A Life Worthy of the Gods: The Materialist Psychology of Epicurus.* Las Vegas, NV.

2013. 'Menander's Slaves: The Banality of Violence', in B. Akrigg and R. Tordoff (eds.), *Slaves and Slavery in Ancient Greek Comic Drama.* Cambridge: 144–58.

2014. 'Turns and Returns in Plautus' *Casina*', in I. N. Perysinakis and E. Karakasis (eds.), *Plautine Trends: Studies in Plautine Comedy and Its Reception.* Trends in Classics Supplementary Volume 29. Berlin: 3–12.

Kray, K. 2002. *The Twins: Men of Violence.* London.

Kremer-Marietti, A. 1985. *Michel Foucault: archéologie et généalogie*, revised edn. Paris.

Krenkel, W. (ed.). 1970. *Lucilius: Satiren.* 2 vols. Leiden.

Kristeva, J. 1982. *Powers of Horror: An Essay in Abjection.* Translated by L. S. Roudiez. New York.

Kroll, W. 1924. *Studien zum Verständnis der römischen Literatur.* Stuttgart.

Kyle, D. G. 1998. *Spectacles of Death in Ancient Rome.* London.

Labate, M. 2006. 'Erotic Aetiology: Romulus, Augustus, and the Rape of the Sabine Women', in R. K. Gibson, S. Green, and A. Sharrock (eds.), *The Art of Love: Bimillennial Essays on Ovid's* Ars amatoria *and* Remedia amoris. Oxford: 193–215.

Laigneau, S. 1999. *La femme et l'amour chez Catulle et les élégiaques augustéens.* Collection Latomus 249. Brussels.

Lambert, B. 1969–72. *Bibliotheca Hieronymiana manuscripta: la tradition manuscrite des oeuvres de saint Jérôme.* 4 vols. Instrumenta patristica 4. Steenbrugge.

Langlands, R. 2006. *Sexual Morality in Ancient Rome.* Cambridge.

Lape, S. 2004. *Reproducing Athens: Menander's Comedy, Democratic Culture, and the Hellenistic City.* Princeton, NJ.

Laqueur, T. 1990. *Making Sex: Body and Gender from the Greeks to Freud.* Cambridge, MA.

Larmour, D. H. J., Miller, P. A., and Platter, C. (eds.). 1998a. *Rethinking Sexuality: Foucault and Classical Antiquity.* Princeton, NJ.

1998b. 'Introduction: Situating the *History of Sexuality*', in Larmour, Miller, and Platter 1998a: 3–41.

Larosa, M. Forthcoming. 'The Mythical Exempla of Faithful Heroines in Seneca the Elder's Work: Literary Occurrences of a Declamatory Device', in Dinter, Guérin, and Martinho forthcoming.

Lausberg, H. 1998. *Handbook of Literary Rhetoric: A Foundation for Literary Study.* Translated by M. T. Bliss, A. Jansen, and D. E. Orton. Edited by D. E. Orton and R. D. Anderson. Leiden.

Leach, E. W. 1969. '*De exemplo meo ipse aedificato*: An Organizing Idea in the *Mostellaria*', *Hermes* 97: 318–32.

1971. 'Horace's *pater optimus* and Terence's Demea: Autobiographical Fiction and Comedy in *Sermo*, I, 4', *AJPh* 92: 616–32.

1974. 'Ekphrasis and the Theme of Artistic Failure in Ovid's *Metamorphoses*', *Ramus* 3: 102–42.

1980. 'The Soldier and Society: Plautus' *Miles gloriosus* as Popular Drama', *Rivista di studi classici* 28: 185–209.

Leatherman, J. L. 2011. *Sexual Violence and Armed Conflict*. Cambridge.

Lee-Stecum, P. 1998. *Powerplay in Tibullus: Reading Elegies Book One*. Cambridge.

Lefèvre, E. 1984. *Diphilos und Plautus: der* Rudens *und sein Original*. Mainz.

Leigh, M. 1995. 'Wounding and Popular Rhetoric at Rome', *BICS* 40: 195–212.

1997. *Lucan: Spectacle and Engagement*. Oxford.

2004. *Comedy and the Rise of Rome*. Oxford.

2007. 'Epic and Historiography at Rome', in J. Marincola (ed.), *A Companion to Greek and Roman Historiography*. 2 vols. Malden, MA: 483–92.

Leo, F. (ed.). 1878. *Seneca: Tragoediae*. I. *De Senecae tragoediis observationes criticae*. Berlin.

(ed.). 1895–6. *Plauti Comoediae*. 2 vols. Berlin.

Levin, D. N. 1983. 'Reflections of the Epic Tradition in the Elegies of Tibullus', *ANRW* II.30.3: 2000–127.

Lilja, S. 1965. *The Roman Elegists' Attitude to Women*. Annales Academiae Scientiarum Fennicae, Series B, 135. Helsinki.

Lindheim, S. H. 1998. 'Hercules Cross-Dressed, Hercules Undressed: Unmasking the Construction of the Propertian *amator* in Elegy 4.9', *AJPh* 119: 43–66.

Linklater, B. 2001. 'Philomela's Revenge: Challenges to Rape in Recent Writing in German', *German Life and Letters* 54: 253–71.

Lintott, A. 1993. *Imperium Romanum: Politics and Administration*. London.

1999. *Violence in Republican Rome*, 2nd edn. Oxford.

Lipsius, R. A. (ed.). 1891. *Acta apostolorum apocrypha*, vol. I. Leipzig.

Littlewood, C. A. J. 2004. *Self-Representation and Illusion in Senecan Tragedy*. Oxford.

Liveley, G. 1999. 'Reading Resistance in Ovid's *Metamorphoses*', in Hardie, Barchiesi, and Hinds 1999: 197–213.

Liveley, G. and Salzman-Mitchell, P. (eds.). 2008. *Latin Elegy and Narratology: Fragments of Story*. Columbus, OH.

Lloyd, T. 1993. *The Charity Business: The New Philanthropists*. London.

Logre, B. J. 1946. *L'anxiété de Lucrèce*. Paris.

Lorenz, S. 2002. *Erotik und Panegyrik: Martials epigrammatische Kaiser*. Classica Monacensia 23. Tübingen.

Louth, A. 2004. 'Eusebius and the Birth of Church History', in F. Young, L. Ayres, and A. Louth (eds.), *The Cambridge History of Early Christian Literature*. Cambridge: 266–74.

Lovatt, H. 2013. *The Epic Gaze: Vision, Gender and Narrative in Ancient Epic*. Cambridge.

Lucas, D. W. (ed.). 1968. *Aristotle: Poetics*. Oxford.

Luck, G. 1959. *The Latin Love Elegy*. London.

Lussky, E. A. 1953. 'Misapplications of the Term Zeugma', *CJ* 48: 285–90.

Lyne, R. O. A. M. 1979. '*Servitium amoris*', *CQ* 29: 117–30.

1980. *The Latin Love Poets: From Catullus to Horace*. Oxford.

1998. 'Propertius and Tibullus: Early Exchanges', *CQ* 48: 519–44.

Lyotard, J.-F. 1991. 'The Sublime and the Avant-Garde', in Lyotard, *The Inhuman: Reflections on Time*. Translated by G. Bennington and R. Bowlby. Stanford, CA: 89–107.

Macey, D. 1993. *The Lives of Michel Foucault*. New York.

MacManus, D., Dean, K., Al Bakir, M., Iversen, A. C., Hull, L., Fahy, T., Wessely, S., and Fear, N. T. 2012. 'Violent Behaviour in UK Military Personnel Returning Home after Deployment', *Psychological Medicine* 42: 1663–73.

MacMullen, R. 1986. 'Judicial Savagery in the Roman Empire', *Chiron* 16: 147–66.

Malamud, M. A. 1989. *A Poetics of Transformation: Prudentius and Classical Mythology*. Cornell Studies in Classical Philology 49. Ithaca, NY.

1990. 'Making a Virtue of Perversity: The Poetry of Prudentius', *Ramus* 19: 64–88.

Maltby, R. 1991. *A Lexicon of Ancient Latin Etymologies*. ARCA Classical and Medieval Texts, Papers and Monographs 25. Leeds.

(ed.). 2002. *Tibullus: Elegies*. Cambridge.

Mannering, J. Forthcoming. 'Objection! Contesting Taste and Space in Seneca's Declamatory Arena', in Dinter, Guérin, and Martinho forthcoming.

Marchesi, I. 2005. 'In Memory of Simonides: Poetry and Mnemotechnics *chez* Nasidienus', *TAPhA* 135: 393–402.

Marincola, J. 2013. 'Polybius, Phylarchus and "Tragic History": A Reconsideration', in B. J. Gibson and T. E. H. Harrison (eds.), *Polybius and His World: Essays in Memory of F. W. Walbank*. Oxford: 73–90.

Marshall, C. W. 2000. 'Location! Location! Location! Choral Absence and Theatrical Space in the *Troades*', in G. W. M. Harrison 2000: 27–51.

2006. *The Stagecraft and Performance of Roman Comedy*. Cambridge.

Martin, R. H. 1955. 'Tacitus and the Death of Augustus', *CQ* 5: 123–8.

Martin, R. H. and Woodman, A. J. (eds.). 1989. *Tacitus:* Annals, *Book IV*. Cambridge.

Marx, F. (ed.). 1904–5. *C. Lucilii Carminum reliquiae*. 2 vols. Leipzig.

Maslen, R. W. (ed.). 2002. *Sir Philip Sidney: An Apology for Poetry (or The Defence of Poesy)*, 3rd edn. Manchester.

Massaro, A. 2010. 'Ifigenia, la giovenca e le "guerre improbabili": aspetti del rapporto uomo-animale in Lucrezio', *Maia* 62: 261–82.

Masters, J. 1992. *Poetry and Civil War in Lucan's* Bellum civile. Cambridge.

Mattern, S. P. 1999. *Rome and the Enemy: Imperial Strategy in the Principate*. Berkeley, CA.

Matthews, J. 1975. *Western Aristocracies and Imperial Court A.D. 364–425*. Oxford.

Mayer, R. 2002. *Seneca: Phaedra*. London.

Mayne, J. 1993. *Cinema and Spectatorship.* London.

McCarroll, J. E., Ursano, R. J., Liu, X., Thayer, L. E., Newby, J. H., Norwood, A. E., and Fullerton, C. S. 2000. 'Deployment and the Probability of Spousal Violence by U.S. Army Soldiers', *Military Medicine* 165: 41–4.

McCarroll, J. E., Ursano, R. J., Newby, J. H., Liu, X., Fullerton, C. S., Norwood, A. E., and Osuch, E. A. 2003. 'Domestic Violence and Deployment in US Army Soldiers', *Journal of Nervous and Mental Disease* 191: 3–9.

McCarthy, K. 1998. '*Servitium amoris: amor servitii*', in Joshel and Murnaghan 1998: 174–92.

2000. *Slaves, Masters, and the Art of Authority in Plautine Comedy.* Princeton, NJ.

McCauley, C. 1998. 'When Screen Violence Is Not Attractive', in Goldstein 1998a: 144–62.

McGinn, T. A. J. 1998. *Prostitution, Sexuality, and the Law in Ancient Rome.* New York.

McKay, K. L. 1964. 'Animals in War and *isonomia*', *AJPh* 85: 124–35.

McKeown, J. C. (ed.). 1989. *Ovid: Amores. Text, Prolegomena and Commentary. II. A Commentary on Book One.* ARCA Classical and Medieval Texts, Papers and Monographs 22. Leeds.

1995. '*Militat omnis amans*', *CJ* 90: 295–304.

McKinney, D. 2000. 'Violence: The Strong and the Weak', in Prince 2000a: 99–109.

McLynn, N. B. 1994. *Ambrose of Milan: Church and Court in a Christian Capital.* The Transformation of the Classical Heritage 22. Berkeley, CA.

Melville, A. D. (tr.). 1990. *Ovid: The Love Poems.* Oxford.

Michie, J. (tr.). 1993. *Ovid: The Art of Love.* London.

Migliario, E. 2007. *Retorica e storia: una lettura delle* Suasoriae *di Seneca padre.* Quaderni di 'Invigilata lucernis' 32. Bari.

Miller, J. 1993. *The Passion of Michel Foucault.* New York.

Miller, J. F. 1983. 'Ovid's Divine Interlocutors in the *Fasti*', in C. Deroux (ed.), *Studies in Latin Literature and Roman History III.* Collection Latomus 180. Brussels: 156–92.

1991. *Ovid's Elegiac Festivals: Studies in the* Fasti. Studien zur klassischen Philologie 55. Frankfurt.

Miller, P. A. 1994. *Lyric Texts and Lyric Consciousness: The Birth of a Genre from Archaic Greece to Augustan Rome.* London.

1998a. 'The Bodily Grotesque in Roman Satire: Images of Sterility', *Arethusa* 31: 257–83, reprinted in M. Plaza (ed.), *Persius and Juvenal* (Oxford, 2009), 327–48.

1998b. 'Catullan Consciousness, the "Care of the Self", and the Force of the Negative in History', in Larmour, Miller, and Platter 1998a: 171–203.

2001. 'Why Propertius Is a Woman: French Feminism and Augustan Elegy', *CPh* 96: 127–46.

(ed.). 2002. *Latin Erotic Elegy: An Anthology and Reader.* London.

2004. *Subjecting Verses: Latin Love Elegy and the Emergence of the Real.* Princeton, NJ.

(ed.). 2005. *Latin Verse Satire: An Anthology and Critical Reader.* London.

2006. 'Truth-Telling in Foucault's "Le gouvernement de soi et des autres" and Persius 1: The Subject, Rhetoric, and Power', *Parrhesia* 1: 27–61.

2007. '"I Get Around": Sadism, Desire, and Metonymy on the Streets of Rome with Horace, Ovid, and Juvenal', in D. H. J. Larmour and D. Spencer (eds.), *The Sites of Rome: Time, Space, Memory.* Oxford: 138–67.

2009. 'Ethics and Irony', *Substance* 38: 51–71.

Miller, P. C. 1993. 'The Blazing Body: Ascetic Desire in Jerome's Letter to Eustochium', *JECS* 1: 21–45.

Mistry, R. 1997. *A Fine Balance.* London.

Mitsis, P. 1994. 'Committing Philosophy on the Reader: Didactic Coercion and Reader Autonomy in *De rerum natura*', in Schiesaro, Mitsis, and Clay 1994: 111–28.

Mommsen, T., Krueger, P., and Watson, A. (eds.). 1985. *The Digest of Justinian.* 4 vols. Philadelphia, PA.

Morales, H. 1996. 'The Torturer's Apprentice: Parrhasius and the Limits of Art', in J. Elsner (ed.), *Art and Text in Roman Culture.* Cambridge: 182–209.

2004. *Vision and Narrative in Achilles Tatius'* Leucippe and Clitophon. Cambridge.

Moreno Soldevila, R. (ed.). 2011. *Diccionario de motivos amatorios en la literatura latina (siglos III a. C.–II d. C.).* Exemplaria classica, Anejo 2. Huelva.

Morley, N. 2006. 'The Poor in the City of Rome', in M. Atkins and R. Osborne (eds.), *Poverty in the Roman World.* Cambridge: 21–39.

Morris, E. P. (ed.). 1968. *Horace: The Satires.* Norman, OK.

Moses, D. C. 1993. 'Livy's Lucretia and the Validity of Coerced Consent', in A. E. Laiou (ed.), *Consent and Coercion to Sex and Marriage in Ancient and Medieval Societies.* Washington, DC: 39–81.

Most, G. W. 1992. '*Disiecti membra poetae*: The Rhetoric of Dismemberment in Neronian Poetry', in R. Hexter and D. Selden (eds.), *Innovations of Antiquity.* New York: 391–419.

Mozley, J. H. (ed., tr.). 1979. *Ovid: The Art of Love and Other Poems.* Revised by G. P. Goold. Loeb Classical Library 232. Cambridge, MA.

Muecke, F. 2005. 'Rome's First "Satirists": Themes and Genre in Ennius and Lucilius', in Freudenburg 2005a: 33–47.

Mueller, M. 2009. *The Iliad*, 2nd edn. London.

Müller, H. 1998. 'Der älteste Brief des heiligen Hieronymus: zu einem aktuellen Datierungsvorschlag', *WS* 111: 191–210.

Mulvey, L. 1975. 'Visual Pleasure and Narrative Cinema', *Screen* 16: 6–18, reprinted in Mulvey 2009: 14–27.

1981. 'Afterthoughts on "Visual Pleasure and Narrative Cinema" Inspired by "Duel in the Sun" (King Vidor, 1946)', *Framework* 15–17: 12–15, reprinted in Mulvey 2009: 31–40.

2009. *Visual and Other Pleasures*, 2nd edn. Basingstoke.

Murgatroyd, P. 1975. '*Militia amoris* and the Roman Elegists', *Latomus* 34: 59–79.

1980. *Tibullus I: A Commentary on the First Book of the* Elegies *of Albius Tibullus*. Pietermaritzburg.

1981. '*Servitium amoris* and the Roman Elegists', *Latomus* 40: 589–606.

Musurillo, H. 1972. *The Acts of the Christian Martyrs*. Oxford.

Naiden, F. S. 2006. *Ancient Supplication*. Oxford.

Neumann, J. 1962. *Titian: The Flaying of Marsyas*. London.

Newby, Z. 2012. 'The Aesthetics of Violence: Myth and Danger in Roman Domestic Landscapes', *ClAnt* 31: 349–89.

Newlands, C. 1995. *Playing with Time: Ovid and the* Fasti. Ithaca, NY.

1998. 'The Role of the Book in *Tristia* 3.1', *Ramus* 26: 57–79.

2004. 'Ovid and Statius: Transforming the Landscape', *TAPhA* 134: 133–55.

Nippel, W. 1995. *Public Order in Ancient Rome*. Cambridge.

Nipperdey, K. and Andresen, G. (eds.). 1915. *P. Cornelius Tacitus, Erster Band: Ab excessu divi Augusti I–VI*, 11th edn. Berlin.

Nisbet, R. G. M. (ed.). 1961. *M. Tulli Ciceronis In L. Calpurnium Pisonem oratio*. Oxford.

Nisbet, R. G. M. and Hubbard, M. 1970. *A Commentary on Horace:* Odes, *Book I*. Oxford.

1978. *A Commentary on Horace:* Odes, *Book II*. Oxford.

Nisbet, R. G. M. and Rudd, N. 2004. *A Commentary on Horace:* Odes, *Book III*. Oxford.

Niżyńska, J. 2001. 'Marsyas' Howl: The Myth of Marsyas in Ovid's *Metamorphoses* and Zbigniew Herbert's "Apollo and Marsyas"', *Comparative Literature* 53: 151–69.

Nolder, M. J. 2001. 'The Domestic Violence Dilemma: Private Action in Ancient Rome and America', *Boston University Law Review* 81: 1119–47.

Nussbaum, M. C. 1986. 'Therapeutic Arguments: Epicurus and Aristotle', in M. Schofield and G. Striker (eds.), *The Norms of Nature: Studies in Hellenistic Ethics*. Cambridge: 31–74.

1994. *The Therapy of Desire: Theory and Practice in Hellenistic Ethics*. Princeton, NJ.

Ogden, D. 1996. *Greek Bastardy in the Classical and Hellenistic Periods*. Oxford.

1997. 'Rape, Adultery and Protection of Bloodlines in Classical Athens', in Deacy and Pierce 1997: 25–41.

O'Gorman, E. 2000. *Irony and Misreading in the* Annals *of Tacitus*. Cambridge.

O'Hara, J. J. 2007. *Inconsistency in Roman Epic: Studies in Catullus, Lucretius, Vergil, Ovid and Lucan*. Cambridge.

Oliensis, E. 1998. *Horace and the Rhetoric of Authority*. Cambridge.

2009. *Freud's Rome: Psychoanalysis and Latin Poetry*. Cambridge.

Olsen, M. 2003. 'Turning on a Dime', *Sight & Sound* 13.10: 12–15.

O'Mathúna, D. P. 2008. 'The Ethics of Torture in *24*: Shockingly Banal', in Weed, Davis, and Weed 2008: 91–104.

Omitowoju, R. 2002. *Rape and the Politics of Consent in Classical Athens*. Cambridge.

Opelt, I. 1967. 'Der Christenverfolger bei Prudentius', *Philologus* 111: 242–57.

Orr, C. 2006. 'Kiefer Madness', *The New Republic* 234.19 (22 May): 16–18.

Osborne, R. (ed.). 2004. *Studies in Ancient Greek and Roman Society*. Cambridge.

Otis, B. 1964. *Virgil: A Study in Civilized Poetry*. Oxford.

Otto, A. 1890. *Die Sprichwörter und sprichwörtlichen Redensarten der Römer*. Leipzig.

Pagán, V. E. 2007–8. 'Teaching Torture in Seneca *Controversiae* 2.5', *CJ* 103: 165–82.

Palmer, A.-M. 1989. *Prudentius on the Martyrs*. Oxford.

Panayotakis, S. 2002. 'The Temple and the Brothel: Mothers and Daughters in *Apollonius of Tyre*', in M. Paschalis and S. Frangoulidis (eds.), *Space in the Ancient Novel*. Ancient Narrative Supplementum 1. Groningen: 98–117.

Panofsky, E. 1969. *Problems in Titian, Mostly Iconographic*. The Wrightsman Lectures 2. London.

Pansiéri, C. 1997. *Plaute et Rome, ou les ambiguïtés d'un marginal*. Collection Latomus 236. Brussels.

Paoli, U. E. 1976. *Altri studi di diritto greco e romano*. Milan.

Paratore, E. (ed.). 1947. *Virgilio:* Eneide, *libro quarto*. Convivium: collana di autori greci e latini 4. Rome.

Parker, D. 1969. 'The Ovidian Coda', *Arion* 8: 80–97.

Parker, H. N. 1989. 'Crucially Funny or Tranio on the Couch: The *servus callidus* and Jokes about Torture', *TAPhA* 119: 233–46.

—— 1992. 'Love's Body Anatomized: The Ancient Erotic Handbooks and the Rhetoric of Sexuality', in Richlin 1992b: 90–111.

—— 1999. 'The Observed of All Observers: Spectacle, Applause, and Cultural Poetics in the Roman Audience', in B. Bergmann and C. Kondoleon (eds.), *The Art of Ancient Spectacle*. Studies in the History of Art, Symposium Papers 34. Washington, DC: 163–79.

Parry, H. 1964. 'Ovid's *Metamorphoses*: Violence in a Pastoral Setting', *TAPhA* 95: 268–82.

Patterson, O. 1982. *Slavery and Social Death: A Comparative Study*. Cambridge, MA.

Perelli, L. 1969. *Lucrezio, poeta dell'angoscia*. Biblioteca di cultura 85. Florence.

Perkins, J. 1995. *The Suffering Self: Pain and Narrative Representation in the Early Christian Era*. London.

Pianezzola, E. (ed.). 1991. *Ovidio: L'arte di amare*. Milan.

Pierce, K. F. 1997. 'The Portrayal of Rape in New Comedy', in Deacy and Pierce 1997: 163–84.

Plantinga, C. 1997. 'Notes on Spectator Emotion and Ideological Film Criticism', in R. Allen and M. Smith (eds.), *Film Theory and Philosophy*. Oxford: 372–93.

Plass, P. 1995. *The Game of Death in Ancient Rome: Arena Sport and Political Suicide*. Madison, WI.

Plaza, M. 2006. *The Function of Humour in Roman Verse Satire: Laughing and Lying*. Oxford.

Pociña, A. 1997. 'Épica y teatro', in C. Codoñer (ed.), *Historia de la literatura latina*. Madrid: 13–70.

Poe, E. A. 1846. 'The Philosophy of Composition', *Graham's Magazine* 28: 163–7, reprinted in Poe, *Essays and Reviews* (New York, 1984), 13–25.

Pomeroy, S. B. 2007. *The Murder of Regilla: A Case of Domestic Violence in Antiquity*. Cambridge, MA.

Prince, S. (ed.). 2000a. *Screening Violence*. London.

    2000b. 'Graphic Violence in the Cinema: Origins, Aesthetic Design, and Social Effects', in Prince 2000a: 1–44.

    2000c. 'The Aesthetic of Slow-Motion Violence in the Films of Sam Peckinpah', in Prince 2000a: 175–201.

Projansky, S. 2001. *Watching Rape: Film and Television in Postfeminist Culture*. New York.

Putnam, M. C. J. 1973. *Tibullus: A Commentary*. Norman, OK.

    1990. 'Anger, Blindness and Insight in Virgil's *Aeneid*', in M. C. Nussbaum (ed.), *The Poetics of Therapy: Hellenistic Ethics in its Rhetorical and Literary Context* (= *Apeiron* 23.4). Edmonton: 7–40, reprinted in Putnam, *Virgil's* Aeneid: *Interpretation and Influence* (Chapel Hill, NC, 1995), 172–200.

Puttfarken, T. 2005. *Titian and Tragic Painting: Aristotle's* Poetics *and the Rise of the Modern Artist*. New Haven, CT.

Quint, D. 1993. *Epic and Empire: Politics and Generic Form from Virgil to Milton*. Princeton, NJ.

Ramage, E. S. 1974a. 'Ennius and the Origins of Roman Satire', in Ramage, Sigsbee, and Fredericks 1974a: 8–26.

    1974b. 'Lucilius, the Discoverer of the Genre', in Ramage, Sigsbee, and Fredericks 1974a: 27–52.

Ramage, E. S., Sigsbee, D. L., and Fredericks, S. C. (eds.). 1974a. *Roman Satirists and Their Satire: The Fine Art of Criticism in Ancient Rome*. Park Ridge, NJ.

    1974b. 'Introduction', in Ramage, Sigsbee, and Fredericks 1974a: 1–7.

Ramelli, I. 2001. *I romanzi antichi e il Cristianesimo: contesto e contatti*. Graeco-Romanae religionis electa collectio 6. Madrid.

Rawson, B. (ed.). 1991. *Marriage, Divorce, and Children in Ancient Rome*. Oxford.

    2003. *Children and Childhood in Roman Italy*. Oxford.

Raymond, E. 2013. 'Caius Cornelius Gallus: "The Inventor of Latin Love Elegy"', in Thorsen 2013: 59–67.

Rebenich, S. 1992. *Hieronymus und sein Kreis: prosopographische und sozialgeschichtliche Untersuchungen*. Historia Einzelschriften 72. Stuttgart.

    2002. *Jerome*. London.

Redfield, J. M. 1994. *Nature and Culture in the* Iliad: *The Tragedy of Hector*, 2nd edn. Durham, NC.

Regenbogen, O. 1932. *Lukrez: seine Gestalt in seinem Gedicht*. Neue Wege zur Antike, 2. Reihe: Interpretationen, 1. Leipzig.

Reward Group. 1994–5. *Charity Rewards*. Continues *Charities Salary Survey*. Stone.

Rich, J. and Shipley, G. (eds.). 1993. *War and Society in the Roman World*. Leicester–Nottingham Studies in Ancient Society 5. London.

Richardson, L., Jr. (ed.). 1977. *Propertius: Elegies I–IV*. Norman, OK.

Richlin, A. 1981. 'Approaches to the Sources on Adultery at Rome', in H. P. Foley (ed.), *Reflections of Women in Antiquity*. New York: 379–404.

  1992a. *The Garden of Priapus: Sexuality and Aggression in Roman Humor*, revised edn. New York.

  (ed.). 1992b. *Pornography and Representation in Greece and Rome*. Oxford.

  1992c. 'Reading Ovid's Rapes', in Richlin 1992b: 158–79.

  1999. 'Cicero's Head', in J. I. Porter (ed.), *Constructions of the Classical Body*. Ann Arbor, MI: 190–211.

Rimell, V. 2002. *Petronius and the Anatomy of Fiction*. Cambridge.

  2006. *Ovid's Lovers: Desire, Difference, and the Poetic Imagination*. Cambridge.

Rives, J. B. 1999. 'The Decree of Decius and the Religion of Empire', *JRS* 89: 135–54.

Roberts, M. 1993. *Poetry and the Cult of the Martyrs: The* Liber peristephanon *of Prudentius*. Ann Arbor, MI.

Robinson, L. 1953. 'The Personal Abuse in Lucilius' *Satires*', *CJ* 49: 31–5, 47.

Roller, M. B. 1997. '*Color*-Blindness: Cicero's Death, Declamation, and the Production of History', *CPh* 92: 109–30.

  2004. 'Exemplarity in Roman Culture: The Cases of Horatius Cocles and Cloelia', *CPh* 99: 1–56.

Rosati, G. 1983. *Narciso e Pigmalione: illusione e spettacolo nelle* Metamorfosi *di Ovidio*. Florence.

  1999. 'Form in Motion: Weaving the Text in the *Metamorphoses*', in Hardie, Barchiesi, and Hinds 1999: 240–53.

  (ed.). 2009. *Ovidio: Metamorfosi*, vol. III. Milan.

Rosenstein, N. 2004. *Rome at War: Farms, Families, and Death in the Middle Republic*. Chapel Hill, NC.

Ross, J. 1995. 'Dynamic Writing and Martyrs' Bodies in Prudentius' *Peristephanon*', *JECS* 3: 325–55.

Rossi, A. 2000. 'The *Aeneid* Revisited: The Journey of Pompey in Lucan's *Pharsalia*', *AJPh* 121: 571–91.

  2004. *Contexts of War: Manipulation of Genre in Virgilian Battle Narrative*. Ann Arbor, MI.

Rouse, J. 1994. 'Power/Knowledge', in G. Gutting (ed.), *The Cambridge Companion to Foucault*. Cambridge: 92–114.

Rowe, K. 1999. *Dead Hands: Fictions of Agency, Renaissance to Modern*. Stanford, CA.

Rozelaar, M. 1941. *Lukrez: Versuch einer Deutung*. Amsterdam.

Rudd, N. 1982. *The Satires of Horace*. Berkeley, CA.

Salisbury, J. E. 1997. *Perpetua's Passion: The Death and Memory of a Young Roman Woman*. New York.

Saller, R. P. 1991. 'Corporal Punishment, Authority, and Obedience in the Roman Household', in Rawson 1991: 144–65.

1994. *Patriarchy, Property and Death in the Roman Family*. Cambridge Studies in Population, Economy and Society in Past Time 25. Cambridge.

1998. 'Symbols of Gender and Status Hierarchies in the Roman Household', in Joshel and Murnaghan 1998: 85–91.

Salzman-Mitchell, P. B. 2005. *A Web of Fantasies: Gaze, Image, and Gender in Ovid's* Metamorphoses. Columbus, OH.

2008. 'Snapshots of a Love Affair: *Amores* 1.5 and the Program of Elegiac Narrative', in Liveley and Salzman-Mitchell 2008: 34–47.

Sandbach, F. H. (ed.). 1990. *Menandri Reliquiae selectae*, revised edn. Oxford.

Sanders, P., Oyewole, A., and Mboup, A. 1998. 'Save Our Children', on P. Sanders, *Save Our Children*. Verve Records.

Sapolsky, B. S., Molitor, F., and Luque, S. 2003. 'Sex and Violence in Slasher Films: Reexamining the Assumptions', *Journalism and Mass Communication Quarterly* 80: 28–38.

Saunders, C. 1997. 'Classical Paradigms of Rape in the Middle Ages', in Deacy and Pierce 1997: 243–66.

Saylor, C. F. 1972. 'Man, Animal, and the Bestial in Lucretius', *CJ* 67: 306–16.

Scafuro, A. C. 1994. *The Forensic Stage: Settling Disputes in Graeco-Roman New Comedy*. Cambridge.

Scarry, E. 1985. *The Body in Pain: The Making and Unmaking of the World*. New York.

Schäublin, C. 1973. 'Textkritisches zu den Briefen des Hieronymus', *MH* 30: 55–62.

Scheid, J. and Svenbro, J. 1996. *The Craft of Zeus: Myths of Weaving and Fabric*. Translated by C. Volk. Revealing Antiquity 9. Cambridge, MA.

Scheidel, W. 1996. *Measuring Sex, Age and Death in the Roman Empire: Explorations in Ancient Demography*. JRA Supplement 21. Ann Arbor, MI.

Scheper-Hughes, N. and Bourgois, P. (eds.). 2004. *Violence in War and Peace: An Anthology*. Blackwell Readers in Anthropology 5. Malden, MA.

Schiesaro, A. 1990. *Simulacrum et imago: gli argomenti analogici nel De rerum natura*. Biblioteca di 'Materiali e discussioni per l'analisi dei testi classici' 8. Pisa.

2003. *The Passions in Play:* Thyestes *and the Dynamics of Senecan Drama*. Cambridge.

Schiesaro, A., Mitsis, P., and Clay, J. S. (eds.). 1994. *Mega nepios: il destinatario nell'epos didascalico* (= *MD* 31). Pisa.

Schlam, C. 1992. *The* Metamorphoses *of Apuleius: On Making an Ass of Oneself*. Chapel Hill, NC.

Schlegel, C. M. 2005. *Satire and the Threat of Speech: Horace's* Satires*, Book 1*. Madison, WI.

Schneemelcher, W. (ed.). 1991–2. *New Testament Apocrypha*, revised edn. English translation edited by R. M. Wilson. 2 vols. Cambridge.

Schneider, C. Forthcoming. 'Laughing Is No Laughing Matter: Laughs and Laughter in Seneca the Elder's *oeuvre*', in Dinter, Guérin, and Martinho forthcoming.

Schneider, S. J. (ed.). 2004. *New Hollywood Violence*. Manchester.

Schrijvers, P. H. 1970. *Horror ac divina voluptas: études sur la poétique et la poésie de Lucrèce*. Amsterdam.

1978. 'Le regard sur l'invisible: étude sur l'emploi de l'analogie dans l'oeuvre de Lucrèce', in O. Gigon (ed.), *Lucrèce: huit exposés suivis de discussions*. Entretiens sur l'Antiquité classique 24. Geneva: 77–114, published in English as 'Seeing the Invisible: A Study of Lucretius' Use of Analogy in *De rerum natura*', in Gale 2007: 255–88.

Schroeder, F. M. 2004. 'Philodemus: *avocatio* and the Pathos of Distance in Lucretius and Vergil', in D. Armstrong, J. Fish, P. A. Johnston, and M. B. Skinner (eds.), *Vergil, Philodemus, and the Augustans*. Austin, TX: 139–56.

Schroeder, J. A. 2004. 'John Chrysostom's Critique of Spousal Violence', *JECS* 12: 413–42.

Schwind, J. 1997. 'Hieronymus' *Epistula ad Innocentium* (*Epist.* 1) – ein Jugendwerk?', *WS* 110: 171–86.

Scourfield, J. H. D. 1986. 'Jerome, Antioch, and the Desert: A Note on Chronology', *JThS* 37: 117–21.

1987. 'Notes on the Text of Jerome, *Letters* 1 and 107', *CQ* 37: 487–97.

1993. *Consoling Heliodorus: A Commentary on Jerome*, Letter 60. Oxford.

Sedgwick, E. K. 1990. *Epistemology of the Closet*. Berkeley, CA.

Segal, C. P. 1969. *Landscape in Ovid's* Metamorphoses: *A Study in the Transformations of a Literary Symbol*. Hermes Einzelschriften 23. Wiesbaden.

1971. *The Theme of the Mutilation of the Corpse in the* Iliad. Mnemosyne Supplementum 17. Leiden.

1983. 'Boundary Violation and the Landscape of the Self in Senecan Tragedy', *A&A* 29: 172–87, reprinted in J. G. Fitch (ed.), *Seneca* (Oxford, 2008), 136–56.

1984. 'Senecan Baroque: The Death of Hippolytus in Seneca, Ovid, and Euripides', *TAPhA* 114: 311–25.

1986. *Language and Desire in Seneca's* Phaedra. Princeton, NJ.

1990. *Lucretius on Death and Anxiety: Poetry and Philosophy in* De rerum natura. Princeton, NJ.

1994. 'Philomela's Web and the Pleasures of the Text: Reader and Violence in the *Metamorphoses* of Ovid', in I. J. F. de Jong and J. P. Sullivan (eds.), *Modern Critical Theory and Classical Literature*. Mnemosyne Supplementum 130. Leiden: 257–80.

1997. *Dionysiac Poetics and Euripides'* Bacchae, expanded edn. Princeton, NJ.

1998. 'Ovid's Metamorphic Bodies: Art, Gender, and Violence in the *Metamorphoses*', *Arion* 5.3: 9–41.

2005. 'Il corpo e l'io nelle "Metamorfosi" di Ovidio', in Barchiesi 2005: xv–ci.

Segal, E. 1987. *Roman Laughter: The Comedy of Plautus*, 2nd edn. New York.

Seifert, A. 2011. 'Strafbar oder nicht? Sexualdelikte und häusliche Gewalt', in M. Reuter and R. Schiavone (eds.), *Gefährliches Pflaster: Kriminalität im römischen Reich*. Xantener Berichte 21. Mainz: 147–60.

Sharrock, A. 1994. 'Ovid and the Politics of Reading', *MD* 33: 97–122.

2002. 'Looking at Looking: Can You Resist a Reading?', in Fredrick 2002a: 265–95.

Shaw, B. D. 1984. 'Bandits in the Roman Empire', *P&P* 105: 3–52, reprinted (slightly revised, and with a postscript) in Osborne 2004: 326–74.

1987. 'The Family in Late Antiquity: The Experience of Augustine', *P&P* 115: 3–51.

1993. 'The Passion of Perpetua', *P&P* 139: 3–45, reprinted (slightly revised, and with a postscript) in Osborne 2004: 286–325.

1996. 'Body/Power/Identity: Passions of the Martyrs', *JECS* 4: 269–312.

2001. 'Raising and Killing Children: Two Roman Myths', *Mnemosyne* 54: 31–77.

2011. *Sacred Violence: African Christians and Sectarian Hatred in the Age of Augustine*. Cambridge.

Shelton, J. A. 1996. 'Lucretius on the Use and Abuse of Animals', *Eranos* 94: 48–64.

Sherman, M. D., Sautter, F., Hope Jackson, M., Lyons, J. A., and Han, X. 2006. 'Domestic Violence in Veterans with Posttraumatic Stress Disorder Who Seek Couples Therapy', *Journal of Marital and Family Therapy* 32: 479–90.

Sigismund-Nielsen, H. 2012. 'Vibia Perpetua – an Indecent Woman', in Bremmer and Formisano 2012: 103–17.

Sigsbee, D. L. 1974. 'The Disciplined Satire of Horace', in Ramage, Sigsbee, and Fredericks 1974a: 64–88.

Silk, M. 1987. *Homer: The Iliad*. Cambridge.

Sivan, H. 1998. 'Le corps d'une pécheresse, le prix de la piété: la politique de l'adultère dans l'Antiquité tardive', *Annales (HSS)* 53: 231–53.

Six-Hohenbalken, M. and Weiss, N. (eds.). 2011. *Violence Expressed: An Anthropological Approach*. Farnham.

Skinner, M. B. 1997. '*Ego mulier*: The Construction of Male Sexuality in Catullus', in Hallett and Skinner 1997: 129–50.

Skjelsbæk, I. 2001. 'Sexual Violence and War: Mapping Out a Complex Relationship', *European Journal of International Relations* 7: 211–37.

Sklenář, R. J. 2003. *The Taste for Nothingness: A Study of Virtus and Related Themes in Lucan's Bellum civile*. Ann Arbor, MI.

Skoie, M. 2002. *Reading Sulpicia: Commentaries 1475–1990*. Oxford.

Skutsch, O. (ed.). 1985. *The Annals of Q. Ennius*. Oxford.

Slocum, J. D. (ed.). 2001a. *Violence and American Cinema*. New York.

2001b. 'Introduction: Violence and American Cinema: Notes for an Investigation', in Slocum 2001a: 1–34.

Small, J. P. 1982. *Cacus and Marsyas in Etrusco-Roman Legend*. Princeton, NJ.

Smith, R. A. 1997. *Poetic Allusion and Poetic Embrace in Ovid and Virgil*. Ann Arbor, MI.

Solmsen, F. 1961. 'Propertius in His Literary Relations with Tibullus and Vergil', *Philologus* 105: 273–89.

Solodow, J. B. 1988. *The World of Ovid's* Metamorphoses. Chapel Hill, NC.

Sontag, S. 2003. *Regarding the Pain of Others*. London.

Spies, A. 1930. *Militat omnis amans: ein Beitrag zur Bildersprache der antiken Erotik*. Tübingen.

Stacey, J. 1994. *Star Gazing: Hollywood Cinema and Female Spectatorship*. London.

Stahl, H.-P. 1985. *Propertius: 'Love' and 'War'. Individual and State under Augustus*. Berkeley, CA.

    1990. 'The Death of Turnus: Augustan Vergil and the Political Rival', in K. A. Raaflaub and M. Toher (eds.), *Between Republic and Empire: Interpretations of Augustus and his Principate*. Berkeley, CA: 174–211.

Stålenheim, P., Kelly, N., Perdomo, C., Perlo-Freema, S., and Sköns, E. 2009. 'Appendix 5A: Military Expenditure Data 1999–2008', in Stockholm International Peace Research Institute, *SIPRI Yearbook 2009: Armaments, Disarmaments and International Security*. Oxford: 212–46.

Staley, G. A. 2010. *Seneca and the Idea of Tragedy*. Oxford.

Stampacchia, G. 1982. 'Schiavitù e libertà nelle "Satire" di Orazio', *Index* 11: 193–219.

Stevenson, J. 2005. *Women Latin Poets: Language, Gender, and Authority, from Antiquity to the Eighteenth Century*. Oxford.

Stewart, R. 2012. *Plautus and Roman Slavery*. Malden, MA.

Stirrup, B. E. 1973. 'Irony in Ovid *Amores* I, 7', *Latomus* 32: 824–31.

Stroh, W. 2003. '*Declamatio*', in B.-J. Schröder and J.-P. Schröder (eds.), *Studium declamatorium: Untersuchungen zu Schulübungen und Prunkreden von der Antike bis zur Neuzeit*. Beiträge zur Altertumskunde 176. Munich: 5–34.

Studlar, G. 1988. *In the Realm of Pleasure: Von Sternberg, Dietrich, and the Masochistic Aesthetic*. New York.

Sturken, M. and Cartwright, L. 2009. *Practices of Looking: An Introduction to Visual Culture*, 2nd edn. New York.

Sussman, L. A. 1977. 'Arellius Fuscus and the Unity of the Elder Seneca's *Suasoriae*', *RhM* 120: 303–23.

    1978. *The Elder Seneca*. Mnemosyne Supplementum 51. Leiden.

Sutherland, S. and Swan, S. 2007. '"Tell Me Where the Bomb Is, or I Will Kill Your Son": Situational Morality on *24*', in S. Peacock (ed.), *Reading 24: TV against the Clock*. London: 119–32.

Sutton, D. F. 1986. *Seneca on the Stage*. Mnemosyne Supplementum 96. Leiden.

Sykes Davies, H. 1932. 'Notes on Lucretius', *The Criterion* 11: 25–42, reprinted in C. J. Classen (ed.), *Probleme der Lukrezforschung* (Hildesheim, 1986), 273–90.

Syme, R. 1939. *The Roman Revolution*. Oxford.

    1958. *Tacitus*. 2 vols. Oxford.

    1978. *History in Ovid*. Oxford.

Tabacco, R. 1978. 'Povertà e ricchezza: l'unità tematica della declamazione XIII dello pseudo-Quintiliano', *Materiali e contributi per la storia della narrativa greco-latina* 2: 37–70.

1985. 'Il tiranno nelle declamazioni di scuola in lingua latina', *MAT* 9: 1–141.

Tarrant, R. J. 1978. 'Senecan Drama and Its Antecedents', *HSCPh* 82: 23–63.

(ed.). 2004. *P. Ovidi Nasonis Metamorphoses.* Oxford.

(ed.). 2012. *Virgil: Aeneid Book XII.* Cambridge.

Theodorakopoulos, E. 1999. 'Closure and Transformation in Ovid's *Metamorphoses*', in Hardie, Barchiesi, and Hinds 1999: 142–61.

Thomas, E. 1964. 'Variations on a Military Theme in Ovid's *Amores*', *G&R* 11: 151–65.

Thomas, R. F. (ed.). 1988. *Virgil: Georgics.* 2 vols. Cambridge.

Thomson, H. J. (tr.). 1949–53. *Prudentius.* 2 vols. Loeb Classical Library 387, 398. London.

Thorsen, T. S. (ed.). 2013. *The Cambridge Companion to Latin Love Elegy.* Cambridge.

Tissol, G. 1997. *The Face of Nature: Wit, Narrative, and Cosmic Origins in Ovid's Metamorphoses.* Princeton, NJ.

Tovey, D. F. 1935. *Essays in Musical Analysis: Symphonies (II), Variations and Orchestral Polyphony.* London.

Treggiari, S. 1991a. *Roman Marriage: Iusti coniuges from the Time of Cicero to the Time of Ulpian.* Oxford.

1991b. 'Divorce Roman Style: How Easy and How Frequent Was It?', in Rawson 1991: 31–46.

Tsouna, V. 2003. '"Portare davanti agli occhi": una tecnica retorica nelle opere "morali" di Filodemo', *CErc* 33: 243–7.

2007. *The Ethics of Philodemus.* Oxford.

van den Berg, C. Forthcoming. 'The Rhetoric of Decline and the Rhetoric for *declamatio*', in Dinter, Guérin, and Martinho forthcoming.

van Wees, H. 1992. *Status Warriors: War, Violence and Society in Homer and History.* Dutch Monographs on Ancient History and Archaeology 9. Amsterdam.

Vernant, J.-P. 1991. 'A "Beautiful Death" and the Disfigured Corpse in Homeric Epic', translated by A. Szegedy-Maszak, in Vernant, *Mortals and Immortals: Collected Essays.* Edited by F. I. Zeitlin. Princeton, NJ: 50–74.

Viljamaa, T., Timonen, A., and Krötzl, C. (eds.). 1992. *Crudelitas: The Politics of Cruelty in the Ancient and Medieval World. Proceedings of the International Conference, Turku (Finland), May 1991.* Medium aevum quotidianum Sonderband 2. Krems.

Ville, G. 1981. *La gladiature en occident des origines à la mort de Domitien.* Bibliothèque des Écoles françaises d'Athènes et de Rome 245. Rome.

Vizier, A. 1998. '*Incipit philosophia*', in Larmour, Miller, and Platter 1998a: 61–84.

Volk, K. 2010. 'Lucretius' Prayer for Peace and the Date of *De rerum natura*', *CQ* 60: 127–31.

von Albrecht, M. 1997. *A History of Roman Literature from Livius Andronicus to Boethius with Special Regard to Its Influence on World Literature.* 2 vols. Revised by G. Schmeling and M. von Albrecht. Translated by M. von Albrecht and G. Schmeling with the assistance of R. R. Caston, F. and K. Newman, and F. Schwartz. Leiden.

von Schlegel, A. W. 1972. 'Senecas Tragödien', in E. Lefèvre (ed.), *Senecas Tragödien.* Wege der Forschung 310. Darmstadt: 13–14.

Walbank, F. W. 1960. 'History and Tragedy', *Historia* 9: 216–34, reprinted in Walbank, *Selected Papers: Studies in Greek and Roman History and Historiography* (Cambridge, 1985), 224–41.

Walker, B. 1969. Review of Zwierlein 1966, *CPh* 64: 183–7.

Walker, L. E. 2009. *The Battered Woman Syndrome,* 3rd edn. New York.

Wallace-Hadrill, A. 1997. '*Mutatio morum*: The Idea of a Cultural Revolution', in Habinek and Schiesaro 1997: 3–22.

Walters, J. 1997. 'Invading the Roman Body: Manliness and Impenetrability in Roman Thought', in Hallett and Skinner 1997: 29–43.

　1998. 'Making a Spectacle: Deviant Men, Invective, and Pleasure', *Arethusa* 31: 355–67.

Wardman, A. E. 1965. 'The Rape of the Sabines (Ovid, *Ars amatoria* 1. 89 ff.)', *CQ* 15: 101–3.

Wardy, R. 1988. 'Lucretius on What Atoms Are Not', *CPh* 83: 112–28.

Warmington, E. H. (ed., tr.). 1979. *Remains of Old Latin,* vol. III, revised. Loeb Classical Library 329. Cambridge, MA.

Warren, J. 2004. *Facing Death: Epicurus and His Critics.* Oxford.

Watson, L. C. 1995. 'Horace's *Epodes*: The Impotence of *iambos*?', in S. J. Harrison 1995: 188–202.

　2003. *A Commentary on Horace's* Epodes. Oxford.

Webb, R. 1997. 'Imagination and the Arousal of the Emotions in Greco-Roman Rhetoric', in Braund and Gill 1997: 112–27.

　2009. *Ekphrasis, Imagination and Persuasion in Ancient Rhetorical Theory and Practice.* Farnham.

Weed, J. H., Davis, R., and Weed, R. (eds.). 2008. *24 and Philosophy: The World according to Jack.* Malden, MA.

West, D. A. 1969. *The Imagery and Poetry of Lucretius.* Edinburgh.

　2002. *Horace,* Odes *III: Dulce periculum.* Oxford.

Wiedemann, T. 1992. *Emperors and Gladiators.* London.

Wilamowitz-Moellendorff, U. von (tr.). 1919. *Griechische Tragödien.* 4 vols. Berlin.

Wilkinson, L. P. 1955. *Ovid Recalled.* Cambridge.

Williams, C. 2012. 'Perpetua's Gender: A Latinist Reads the *Passio Perpetuae et Felicitatis*', in Bremmer and Formisano 2012: 54–77.

Williams, G. 1995. '*Libertino patre natus*: True or False?', in S. J. Harrison 1995: 296–313.

Williams, G. D. 1996. *The Curse of Exile: A Study of Ovid's Ibis.* Proceedings of the Cambridge Philological Society Supplementary Volume 19. Cambridge.

Williams, R. 1973. *The Country and the City*. London.

Williams, R. D. (ed.). 1962. *P. Vergili Maronis Aeneidos liber tertius*. Oxford.

1967. 'The Purpose of the *Aeneid*', *Antichthon* 1: 29–41, reprinted in S. J. Harrison (ed.), *Oxford Readings in Vergil's* Aeneid (Oxford, 1990), 21–36.

Williamson, E. 2012. 'Domestic Abuse and Military Families: The Problem of Reintegration and Control', *British Journal of Social Work* 42: 1371–87.

Willink, C. W. 1966. 'Some Problems of Text and Interpretation in the *Bacchae*: I', *CQ* 16: 27–50.

Wilson, M. 2008. 'Your Writings or Your Life: Cicero's *Philippics* and Declamation', in T. Stevenson and M. Wilson (eds.), *Cicero's* Philippics: *History, Rhetoric, Ideology* (= *Prudentia* 37–8 (2005–6)). Auckland: 305–34.

Windrum, K. 2004. '*Fight Club* and the Political (Im)potence of Consumer Era Revolt', in S. J. Schneider 2004: 304–17.

Winkler, J. J. 1985. *Auctor & Actor: A Narratological Reading of Apuleius's* Golden Ass. Berkeley, CA.

Winkler, M. M. 1991. 'Satire and the Grotesque in Juvenal, Arcimboldo, and Goya', *A&A* 37: 22–42.

Winterbottom, M. (ed., tr.). 1974. *Seneca the Elder: Declamations*. 2 vols. Loeb Classical Library 463, 464. Cambridge, MA.

(ed.). 1984. *The Minor Declamations Ascribed to Quintilian*. Texte und Kommentare 13. Berlin.

Wirszubski, C. 1950. Libertas *as a Political Idea at Rome during the Late Republic and Early Principate*. Cambridge.

Wiseman, T. P. 1979. *Clio's Cosmetics: Three Studies in Greco-Roman Literature*. Leicester.

1994. *Historiography and Imagination: Eight Essays on Roman Culture*. Exeter Studies in History 33. Exeter.

1995. *Remus: A Roman Myth*. Cambridge.

2000. 'Liber: Myth, Drama and Ideology in Republican Rome', in C. Bruun (ed.), *The Roman Middle Republic: Politics, Religion, and Historiography c. 400–133 B.C.* Acta Instituti Romani Finlandiae 23. Rome: 265–99.

Wistrand, M. 1992. *Entertainment and Violence in Ancient Rome: The Attitudes of Roman Writers of the First Century A.D.* Studia Graeca et Latina Gothoburgensia 56. Göteborg.

Woodman, A. J. 1985. *Tacitus and Tiberius: The Alternative Annals*. Durham.

1988. *Rhetoric in Classical Historiography: Four Studies*. London.

1993. 'Amateur Dramatics at the Court of Nero: *Annals* 15.48–74', in T. J. Luce and A. J. Woodman (eds.), *Tacitus and the Tacitean Tradition*. Princeton, NJ: 104–28.

1995. 'A Death in the First Act: Tacitus, *Annals* 1.6', in R. Brock and A. J. Woodman (eds.), *Papers of the Leeds Latin Seminar: Eighth Volume, 1995*. ARCA Classical and Medieval Texts, Papers and Monographs 33. Leeds: 257–73, reprinted in Woodman, *Tacitus Reviewed* (Oxford, 1998), 23–39.

(tr.). 2004. *Tacitus: The Annals*. Indianapolis, IN.

2005. 'Textual Notes on Tacitus' *Annals*', in F. Cairns (ed.), *Papers of the Langford Latin Seminar: Twelfth Volume, 2005*. ARCA Classical and Medieval Texts, Papers and Monographs 44. Cambridge: 321–9.

2006. 'Mutiny and Madness: Tacitus *Annals* 1.16–49', *Arethusa* 39: 303–29.

Woodman, A. J. and Martin, R. H. (eds.). 1996. *The* Annals *of Tacitus, Book 3*. Cambridge Classical Texts and Commentaries 32. Cambridge.

Woolf, G. 1993. 'Roman Peace', in Rich and Shipley 1993: 171–94.

Wright, F. A. (tr.). 1933. *Select Letters of St Jerome*. Loeb Classical Library 262. Cambridge, MA.

Wright, J. 1974. *Dancing in Chains: The Stylistic Unity of the* Comoedia palliata. Papers and Monographs of the American Academy in Rome 25. Rome.

Wright, M. R. 1997. '*Ferox virtus*: Anger in Virgil's *Aeneid*', in Braund and Gill 1997: 169–84.

Wyke, M. 1989. 'Mistress and Metaphor in Augustan Elegy', *Helios* 16: 25–47.

2002. *The Roman Mistress: Ancient and Modern Representations*. New York.

Wyss, E. 1996. *The Myth of Apollo and Marsyas in the Art of the Italian Renaissance: An Inquiry into the Meaning of Images*. Newark, DE.

Zillmann, D. 1998. 'The Psychology of the Appeal of Portrayals of Violence', in Goldstein 1998a: 179–211.

Žižek, S. 2006. 'The Depraved Heroes of *24* Are the Himmlers of Hollywood', *The Guardian*, 10 January, online at www.theguardian.com/media/2006/jan/10/usnews.comment.

Zwierlein, O. 1966. *Die Rezitationsdramen Senecas*. Beiträge zur klassischen Philologie 20. Meisenheim am Glan.

(ed.). 1986. *L. Annaei Senecae Tragoediae*. Oxford.

# Index